A Kind of Compulsion 1903–1936

Eric Arthur Blair – better known as George Orwell – was born on 25 June 1903 in Bengal. He was educated at Eton and then served with the Indian Imperial Police in Burma. He lived in Paris for two years, and then returned to England where he worked as a private tutor, schoolteacher and bookshop assistant. He fought on the Republican side in the Spanish Civil War and was wounded in the throat. During the Second World War he served as Talks Producer for the Indian Service of the BBC and then joined *Tribune* as its literary editor. He died in London in January 1950.

Dr. Peter Davison is Professor of English and Media at De Montfort University, Leicester. He has written and edited fifteen books as well as the Facsimile Edition of the Manuscript of *Nineteen Eighty-Four* and the twenty volumes of Orwell's *Complete Works*. From 1992 to 1994 he was President of the Bibliographical Society, whose journal he edited for twelve years. From 1961 Ian Angus was Deputy Librarian and Keeper of the Orwell Archive at University College, London, and from 1975 Librarian of King's College, London. With Sonia Orwell he co-edited the *Collected Essays, Journalism and Letters of George Orwell* (4 vols., 1986). Since early retirement in 1982 he has divided his time equally between assisting in the editing of the complete edition and growing olives in Italy.

Sheila Davison was a teacher until she retired, for some time teaching the deaf. She checked and proofread all twenty volumes of the complete edition and assisted with the research and indexing.

Down and Out in Paris and London

Burmese Days

A Clergyman's Daughter

Keep the Aspidistra Flying

The Road to Wigan Pier

Homage to Catalonia

Coming Up for Air

Animal Farm

Nineteen Eighty-Four

A Kind of Compulsion (1903–36)

Facing Unpleasant Facts (1937–39)

A Patriot After All (1940–41)

All Propaganda is Lies (1941–42)

Keeping Our Little Corner Clean (1942–43)

Two Wasted Years (1943)

I Have Tried to Tell the Truth (1943–44)

I Belong to the Left (1945)

Smothered Under Journalism (1946)

It is What I Think (1947–48)

Our Job is to Make Life Worth Living (1949–50)

Also by Peter Davison

Books: *Songs of the British Music Hall: A Critical Study; Popular Appeal in English Drama to 1850; Contemporary Drama and the Popular Dramatic Tradition; Hamlet: Text and Performance; Henry V: Masterguide; Othello: The Critical Debate; Orwell: A Literary Life*

Editions: Anonymous: *The Fair Maid of the Exchange* (with Arthur Brown); Shakespeare: *Richard II*; Shakespeare: *The Merchant of Venice*; Shakespeare: *1 Henry IV*; Shakespeare: *2 Henry IV*; Shakespeare: *The First Quarto of King Richard III*; Marston: *The Dutch Courtesan; Facsimile of the Manuscript of Nineteen Eighty-Four*; Sheridan: *A Casebook; The Book Encompassed: Studies in*

Series: Theatrum Redivivum 17 Volumes; Literature, Culture, and Mass Communication 14 Volumes (with Meyersohn)

Academic Journals: ALTA: *University of Birmingham Review*, 1966–70; The Library: *Transactions of the Bibliographical Society*, 1971–82

Publication of *The Complete Works of George Orwell* is a unique
bibliographic event as well as a major step in Orwell
scholarship. Meticulous textual research by
Dr Peter Davison has revealed that all the current editions
of Orwell have been mutilated to a greater or lesser extent.
This authoritative edition incorporates in Volumes 10–20
all Orwell's known essays, poems, plays, letters, journalism,
broadcasts, and diaries, and also letters by his wife, Eileen,
and members of his family. In addition there are very many of
the letters in newspapers and magazines of readers' reactions
to Orwell's articles and reviews. Where the hands of others
have intervened, Orwell's original intentions have been restored.

A Kind
of Compulsion
1903-1936

GEORGE ORWELL

Edited by Peter Davison
Assisted by Ian Angus and Sheila Davison

SECKER & WARBURG

LONDON

Revised and updated edition published by Secker & Warburg 2000

2 4 6 8 10 9 7 5 3 1

First published in Great Britain in 1998 by
Secker & Warburg
Random House, 20 Vauxhall Bridge Road,
London SW1V 2SA

Random House Australia (Pty) Limited
20 Alfred Street, Milsons Point, Sydney,
New South Wales 2061, Australia

Random House New Zealand Limited
18 Poland Road, Glenfield,
Auckland 10, New Zealand

Random House South Africa (Pty) Limited
Endulini, 5A Jubilee Road, Parktown 2193, South Africa

The Random House Group Limited Reg. No. 954009

A CIP catalogue record for this book
is available from the British Library

ISBN 0 436 20542 4

MIX
Paper | Supporting
responsible forestry
FSC® C018179

Typeset in Monophoto Bembo
by Deltatype Ltd, Birkenhead, Merseyside

The Random House Group Limited supports The Forest Stewardship
Council® (FSC®), the leading international forest-certification organisation.
Our books carrying the FSC label are printed on FSC®-certified paper.
FSC is the only forest-certification scheme supported by the leading
environmental organisations, including Greenpeace. Our
paper procurement policy can be found at
www.randomhouse.co.uk/environment

Printed and bound in Great Britain by Clays Ltd, St Ives plc

CONTENTS

Titles may be modified and shortened

Contents

Contents

Contents

Contents

Contents

George Orwell: The Complete Works
With Eileen Blair's Letters and those of his Sisters
Edited by Peter Davison
Assisted by Ian Angus and Sheila Davison

GENERAL INTRODUCTION

'ANYTHING ABOUT ORWELL IS INTERESTING. He was a man, like Lawrence, whose personality shines out in everything he said or wrote.' So Cyril Connolly in 1962.[1] This is doubtless sufficient encouragement to publish anything about and by Orwell—a *Complete Orwell*. But an editor of Orwell must be conscious of his author peering over his shoulder, self-deprecating and wryly amused. Orwell views the business of editing with suspicion. When in *Nineteen Eighty-Four* he describes Ampleforth as being engaged 'in producing garbled versions—definitive texts, they were called'[2] there is a lurking suspicion that this is Orwell himself speaking: 'garbled' was his word to describe a text that had been corrupted. His attitude is even clearer in a sardonic introduction to a review written forty years ago:

> The chief difficulty of writing a book nowadays is that pots of paste are usually sold without brushes. But if you can get hold of a brush . . . and a pair of scissors and a good-sized blank book, you have everything you need. It is not necessary to do any actual writing. Any collection of scraps—reprinted newspaper articles, private letters, fragments of diaries, even "radio discussions" ground out by wretched hacks to be broadcast by celebrities—can be sold to the amusement-starved public.[3]

Today's public is hardly amusement-starved and there are improvements on stiff-brushed pots of Gloy, but to bring together all that Orwell wrote that has survived requires more than glue, scissors and even several good-sized blank books. It also demands a great deal of writing and explication. No editor would approach this task without believing as did Connolly, yet aware simultaneously of Orwell's doubts. Why try to reconcile this conflict?

One of the most interesting and percipient articles about Orwell, and one little known, is that by Nicolas Walter in *Anarchy: A Journal of Anarchist Ideas* published some thirty-six years ago. He writes of Orwell's 'sense of compassion and guilt, and a determination to be tested and not to be found wanting'; a man who wore down 'his health and his talent, fighting the evils of the world and the weakness of his body to the day of his death, always striving, striving to tell the truth about what he saw and what he felt.' Walter is good on Orwell's faults: 'He often spoke out without verifying his facts . . . often he was grossly unfair' especially about sandal-wearers, pacifists, feminists, and bearded fruit-juice drinkers. 'Hardly any literary or political

xvii

group escaped his bitter criticism. But,' he continues, 'he should not be seen just as an angry middle-aged man but as an extreme example of the English middle-class dissenter against any group, even a group of conscious rebels; . . . He was a man full of logical contradictions and emotional ambivalences, but the point is that this made him better, not worse. He was always able . . . to realise the imperfections of every position including his own, and his honesty about the difficulties this raised was one of his most valuable characteristics.'⁴ These virtues and contradictions are even more valuable now than when Orwell lived and, in everything he wrote, as Connolly says, the man's personality shines out. Bringing together all his writing, even the trivia that sprang from his organisation of BBC broadcasts to India and the Far East during the War, may bring home those characteristics even more forcefully to contemporary readers. And the contexts of what he wrote—the twilight of Imperialism, the Depression, the Thirties, the Spanish Civil War, the Second World War, and the post-war Labour Government – illuminate his writing and his writing gives those events a renewed significance and force.

George Orwell was born Eric Arthur Blair on 25 June 1903 at Motihari, Bengal. His father, Richard Walmesley Blair, was a sub-deputy agent in the Opium Department of the Indian Civil Service; his mother, Ida Mabel Blair, though born in England, was the daughter of Frank Limouzin, a teak merchant of French extraction in Moulmein, Burma. Richard Blair was born in 1857, the son of the vicar of Milborne St Andrew, Dorset. His wife, Ida, was born in 1875. When Orwell was born they already had one daughter, Marjorie Frances, born at Gaya, Bengal on 21 April 1898. A second daughter, Avril Nora, was born at Henley-on-Thames on 6 April 1908. Ida returned to England with the two children in 1904. Orwell's father came home for three months in the summer of 1907 and then returned to India when his leave was over. Orwell did not see his father again until he retired from the Opium Department in January 1912. The children were educated first at an Anglican convent school. In September 1911, Orwell went to St Cyprian's private preparatory school at Eastbourne, and, after a term at Wellington in 1917, he took up a King's Scholarship at Eton in May of that year. A Chronology will be found in the preliminaries to each volume, but the letters, articles, diaries, reviews, broadcasts (and, indeed, the annotations) take up the story of Orwell's life very fully from this time at his prep school until his death on 21 January 1950 at the age of forty-six.

Apart from his books, most of what Orwell wrote might fairly accurately be called journalism—articles, reviews, a personal column, war despatches—and several of his books walk a delicate line between reportage and fiction. Although the events and conditions they describe are, superficially, of the past, we seriously mistake their significance if we imagine that, say, Down and Out in Paris and London and The Road to Wigan Pier, and even a novel Orwell later rejected, A Clergyman's Daughter, are no longer directly relevant to us today. In the decade after Homage to Catalonia was published it failed to sell even the fifteen hundred copies Secker & Warburg had printed: its sales did not recoup the modest advance Fredric Warburg had paid Orwell. With the death of Franco in 1975, the Spanish Civil War, already overtaken by an even more awful war, seemed destined to be thrust even further into the past's unconscious. Yet *Homage to Catalonia* now sells far more copies *a year* than it did in the whole decade after it was published sixty years ago. In 1984 we were assured that we had safely surmounted that hurdle and that *Nineteen Eighty-Four* need no longer trouble our waking nightmares. Wrong, of course; that is seriously to misunderstand what Orwell was about and what that novel still has to say to us. On the fiftieth anniversary of the first publication of *Animal Farm*, a new edition once again topped the best-seller list as it had done in 1945. Hardly a day passes without Orwell's words or his ghost being invoked. It is not merely the obvious inheritance that is still pertinent—all animals are equal (only some more so), thoughtcrime, Big Brother, doublethink and the like—but the complex responses prompted by the word 'Orwellian' which still carry force: fear, integrity, directness, concern for language, plain prose, individual humanity, a striving to see things as they really are, a willingness to admit error, and, above all, the concept of a sense of decency in human relations. Orwell, what he said, what he wrote, and what he stood for remain astonishingly alive. The man and his writing are a vital point of reference in uncertain times, a touchstone.

Our understanding of Orwell is based on only a portion of what has been reprinted and what is available is sometimes inaccurate and can be downright misleading. The nine books have been available in authoritative editions complete with textual notes for a decade and it is possible to study drafts of *Nineteen Eighty-Four* in facsimile.[5] Thirty years ago, Sonia Orwell and Ian Angus produced their invaluable four-volume selection of Orwell's essays, journalism and letters.[6] It draws generously on the essays, reprints many reviews, gives extracts from diaries, some fairly fully, some not at all, and a good selection of letters. Some articles and letters are cut and, inevitably, the editors could only draw on what was then available. Its annotations and biographical notes were appropriate for its day but experience shows that these can no longer adequately satisfy either the general reader, the student, or, sometimes, the scholar. Whole areas of Orwell's work were omitted. Not one of more than eighty films and theatrical performances that Orwell reviewed was included, nor were any of the articles he had published in French journals in 1928–29. What Orwell called his 'two wasted years' at the BBC had to be taken at his own dismissive estimate for, owing to the difficulty of gaining access to the BBC Written Archive in the days before trained archivists (especially Jacqueline Kavanagh) opened up this resource, its holdings were inevitably virtually unknown. Thirty years ago what was selected by Sonia Orwell and Ian Angus offered an adventurously large choice. As Orwell's reputation has grown, in part because of that edition, something much fuller is required to do him justice and satisfy scholarly and general interest.

This edition—the nine books and these eleven volumes, to which can be added the *Facsimile of the Extant Manuscript of Nineteen Eighty-Four*, published in that year—attempts to print all that it has been possible to recover that Orwell wrote.[7] Inevitably an editor can only print what has survived and a reader must always bear in mind the different kinds of omissions: lost and untraced letters, excisions on grounds of libel (none from letters, scarcely any from articles, all of which are noted), and articles reported but probably never written such as 'An American Reverie' (see 3 January 1946, *2839*) and on Hong Kong (see 10 January 1946, *2853*).

The edition has been produced with difficulty, in part because of the size of the task, in part owing to the shifts and changes that have afflicted publishing in England and the United States during the past fifteen years. After the editing of the new editions of Orwell's nine books had been completed in 1982 (though they would not appear in the United Kingdom until 1986 and 1987, and have still not been published in the United States), a complete edition of all that Orwell wrote was commissioned. As the wealth of 'new' material became almost embarrassingly apparent, a five- or six-volume edition was proposed, but eventually the virtue of completeness, despite the size of an edition of eleven volumes, proved convincing. It had been decided that these volumes would be printed in the United States though published jointly in that country and England. The project was suspended by the publishers in November 1985 for two years but despite the uncertainty as to whether the edition would ever appear, editorial work continued. Proofs of the first volume, set in New York, were delivered in June 1990 and the final batch of copy was delivered on 3 February 1993. By December 1993 2,125 of 7,840 pages of text-copy had been set and proofread. The American publishers then gave up and the edition looked as if it might be abandoned. However, the determination of Secker & Warburg, and in particular of Max Eilenberg, ensured that the work would be carried forward and setting started again in England in July 1995. The final page-proof revises (of the re-set American setting) were received in January 1997. Publication was then scheduled for 11 August 1997 and the text up-dated accordingly. In spring 1997 Secker & Warburg became part of Random House and publication had to be postponed until summer 1998. I am grateful to Geoffrey Mulligan and Rowena Skelton-Wallace for overseeing the final stages of publication with such consideration.

What does this *Complete Edition* offer? So far as the books are concerned, it provides authoritative texts with textual explanations. Obviously the eleven volumes of essays, letters, broadcasts, reviews, diaries, and notebooks offer far more in sheer bulk than does the four-volume edition. Obviously, the annotations, the textual and historical explanations, and the biographical details are very much fuller. Readers' letters responding to Orwell's articles and reviews have in nearly all instances been reproduced in full or summarised. Such responses are of particular interest in the case of *Tribune*, for with *Tribune* one has a real sense of Orwell and his audience, and, what is more, an audience only too willing not to let Orwell get away with anything it thought wrong or inappropriate. This gives a valuable sense of how that constituency thought at an important time in left-wing political life—the post-war Labour administration—but also suggests how Orwell's own thought and learning developed on matters as insignificant as the name of 'the bomb-site plant' (*2537* and *2547*) and as important a subject as revenge

(*2547* and see also *2631*), helping shape his thinking for 'Revenge is Sour' (*2786*) a year or so later. It is easy to recapture how Orwell always had a 'contemporary corrective' to his thinking.

Orwell's first review was published in 1930 and his last in 1949. In those twenty years he reviewed some seven hundred books, films and plays in 379 reviews; of these, *CEJL* printed 68 reviews. All Orwell's reviews are printed here. There is, too, a pamphlet, 'British Cookery', commissioned by the British Council but not published at the time (and not since) because it was thought tactless to print a book praising British cooking at a time of severe rationing.

Among them are those which have never appeared, for example, of Harold Laski's *Faith, Reason, and Civilisation*, and C. S. Lewis's *Beyond Personality*, both rejected in their day. The 1968 edition printed 169 articles (though of these the 73 (of eighty) 'As I Please' columns were often cut). All Orwell's 263 articles are now published and one could summarise by saying that the lengthy list of desiderata noted by Nicolas Walter thirty-six years ago,[8] and the annotations and explanations he called for (e.g. the provenance of 'Anti-Semitism in Britain' and the fate of 'Benefit of Clergy') are satisfied. Among the essays now reprinted are the five written and printed in Paris on unemployment, tramps, the beggars of London, imperialist exploitation in Burma, and John Galsworthy; 'Can Socialists Be Happy?' (written under a second pseudonym); four articles on 'The Intellectual Revolt' together with an 'Afterword' written for the German translation; 'Britain's Struggle for Survival: The Labour Government After Three Years'; 'Marx and Russia', and 'Grandeur et décadance du roman policier anglais' ('The Detective Story'). Articles published in French or German are in every case printed in those languages and in English versions, 'back translated' because the original English texts have not survived. Similarly, French and English versions are given of letters Orwell wrote or had written to him in French. Almost all the articles and reviews can only be reproduced in the form in which they have survived in print but it should be borne in mind that Orwell's copy was often cut or changed by sub-editors. Articles in *The Observer* were 'habitually' cut to fit the space available and in newspapers such as the *Evening Standard* Orwell told his agent, Leonard Moore, on 2 November 1946, 'I have had things not merely cut but altered' (*3105*). What has been remarkable to the editors in the course of assembling, editing and proofreading these articles and reviews is how freshly they read after all these years, how wide the range of topics, how vigorous their style, and how independent is Orwell's mind. Although it will be some years before he can make political writing an art as in the brief but perfect essay, 'Some Thoughts on the Common Toad' (12 April 1946, *2970*), the tyro articles on censorship (*79*), unemployment (*82*), beggars (*84*), and imperialism in practice (*86*) are 'Orwell' long before he took that name. His insight and his gift for a striking opening is beautifully shown in a review of Peter Fleming's *News from Tartary* of 15 August 1936 (*322A*), reprinted here for the first time:

A journey by train or car or aeroplane is not an event but an interregnum between events, and the swifter the vehicle the more boring the journey becomes. The nomad of the steppe or the desert may have to put up with every kind of discomfort, but at any rate he is living while he is travelling, and not, like the passenger in a luxury liner, merely suffering a temporary death.

A very large number of additional letters are included. When *CEJL* was prepared, 692 letters were available and of these 226 were published. Since then, *apart from letters written by Orwell in his work for the BBC*, 383½ letters (one is incomplete) have been found with seven more in extracted or sale-catalogue form. The edition also publishes the letters of Orwell's wife, Eileen, and some written by his sisters, Marjorie and Avril, and other relatives. Eileen's letters are particularly engaging. There are 587 BBC letters, telegrams, and memoranda by Orwell or written on his behalf, and, associated with them in the organisation of Orwell's programmes, sum-maries of 395 Talks Booking Forms. All these are published here. Some letters reveal new aspects of Orwell's life and work, for example, his relationship with Lydia Jackson; the sequence of letters he wrote to Yvonne Davet (whom he never met) before and after the war in connexion with her translations of his books; and correspondence with Ihor Szewczenko regarding the Ukrainian translation of *Animal Farm*, which offers touching testimony of the circumstances and reactions of Displaced Persons facing an uncertain fate in Germany at the end of the war. Orwell's experiences in Spain led indirectly to *Animal Farm* and the deposition charging him and Eileen with espionage and high treason (charges unknown to him) is subjected to a detailed analysis which fully explains Orwell's response to violent revolution and hence his last two books and much else he wrote. There are letters in support of Victor Serge and Joseph Czapski, the latter in an attempt to get published an account which squarely laid the blame on the Russians for the slaughter of so many Poles (the Katyn Massacres) but which English publishers refused to print for fear of upsetting the Soviets (an attitude fostered by British Governments for several decades after the event); the 'Kronstadt letter' to Dwight Macdonald makes clear just what Orwell was saying in *Animal Farm*, a message many left-wing intellectuals (but not Displaced Persons) found difficult to grasp. Some letters reveal deep personal relationships and others, to people whom he never met, and from whom he had nothing to gain, but who wrote to him out of the blue seeking information and advice drew patient replies. Of many letters that could be given as examples, one last that came to Orwell from Nancy Parratt, a former BBC secretary, just before he died, implies much about his character. She wrote simply and cheerfully to tell Orwell that she had married and was living in the United States; and she describes her life there and tells, simply and directly, how things were with her. Though she and Orwell had not met for several years, and she did not know he was dying, she wrote in the expectation that he would be pleased to hear from her about simple events far removed from the political and social battles he fought to the last.

Much of the new material is that associated with Orwell's time as a Talks Producer at the BBC. Selections of this material have been published but they are often inaccurate, incomplete, and sometimes not by Orwell.[9] Difficult textual problems are ignored (e.g., of the imaginary interview with Jonathan Swift), the effect of censorship has been exaggerated, and, most important, it has been claimed that after 13 March 1943 Orwell no longer played a part in the BBC's direct propaganda. Further, although it is suggested he wrote forty-nine news commentaries, he actually wrote at least 220, many of which he himself broadcast to Occupied Malaya and Indonesia *after* 13 March. Only a few fragments of those commentaries survive. Sadly, Orwell thought those to whom he broadcast had never heard him—that he was speaking into a void—but evidence is given to show he *was* heard. Thus, to one nun listening secretly to him in Occupied Malaya, he was 'that good man, George Orwell', whose voice kept hope alive. The newsletters for Malaya and Indonesia, and those he wrote for translation into several vernacular Indian languages, add little to the bulk of the edition because the scripts have not survived, but the evidence for these broadcasts (from letters and Talks Booking Forms) shows how incredibly hard Orwell worked at the BBC. Of news commentaries alone he produced four a week, designed for audiences of different cultures and for audiences in free and occupied countries.

Yet such direct propaganda was only a small part of what Orwell did at the BBC. He claimed, with justification, that he had kept his 'little corner' of the BBC clean. He did so by concentrating on culture rather than propaganda. A fuller analysis of Orwell's work at the BBC is given in the Introduction to Volume XIII; suffice here to say that what Orwell dismissed as 'two wasted years' can, in contrast, be seen as a demonstration of how far ahead of his time he was. First, the continuity of his struggle against imperialism, begun in his article on Burma published in Paris in 1929 (*86*), obvious in *Burmese Days*, continued at the BBC and was, in effect, a precursor to post-colonialism in literature and in broader cultural matters. Secondly he started what we would now call an Open University. And thirdly, he developed, especially in his advocacy and practice of broadcasting poetry (when possible, spoken by its authors), what would lead to the BBC's Third Programme (now Radio Three) three years after he left the Corporation's service. The importance of the BBC material is as much for what it tells us of Orwell's vision, imagination, and integrity, as for the picture it gives of a great Corporation which, despite its good intentions, was wrong-headed and unimaginative. This is plainly shown in the advice given Sir Stafford Cripps about the BBC's Indian Section before he went to India to treat with Nehru, Gandhi and Jinnah over Indian independence (see XIII, 20–21). In the BBC volumes, we are offered, in epitome, a picture of the United Kingdom, that does much to illumine the misdirected efforts of the past fifty years and from which there is still much to be learned.

Orwell kept diaries throughout his life and a number have survived. In 1968, the Hop-Picking and Wigan Pier diaries, and selections from two Wartime diaries and some notebooks were published. His diaries and notebooks are now reproduced in full, in the main in chronological order so that what he published and what he entered in his diaries are juxtaposed. He often illustrated his diaries (as he had his letters to his mother from St. Cyprian's) and all his illustrations are reproduced. What Orwell chose to set

down often tells as much of him as of what he recorded. As one reads through
the sorry catalogue of events leading up to the outbreak of war in 1939, it is
impossible, with the benefit of hindsight, not to be amazed at the
misconceptions and miscalculations of that time, none more remarkable than
Parliament's decision, without a division, to adjourn for a week just two days
before Germany invaded Poland. Because Orwell's diaries and notebooks are
many and confusing, it might be helpful to list them here with their starting
reference numbers and with item numbers for selected entries from
notebooks printed in the edition where they are chronologically relevant.
The numbering of the diaries is Orwell's unless numbers are within square
brackets.

Hop-Picking Diary, *111*, 25 August to 8 October 1931
Wigan Pier Diary, *270*, 31 January to 25 March 1936
[Spanish War Diary; seized by police, Barcelona, 1937
This diary may be in the NKVD files in Moscow; an attempt to find it has so far
proved unsuccessful]
Morocco Diary, *478*, 7 September 1938 to 28 March 1939
Domestic Diary [I], *518*, 9 August 1938 to 31 December 1938
Domestic Diary [I], ctd., *582*, 1 January to 26 May 1938
Domestic Diary II, *582* ctd., 27 May 1939 to 31 December 1939
Domestic Diary II, ctd., *729A*, 1 January to 29 April 1940
Diary of Events Leading Up to the War, *553*, 2 July to 3 September 1939
War-Time Diary I, *628*, 28 May 1940 to 28 August 1941
War-Time Diary [II, unnumbered by Orwell], *1025*, in Manuscript and
Typescript:
Manuscript: no title; 14 March to 15 October 1942.
Ms ends: '(continued in Vol IV)'
Typescript: headed 'WAR DIARY (continued)', 14 March to 15 November 1942
Typescript also has entries for 17 October and 15 November 1942
No reference to Vol IV
No 'IV' has been traced and 'III' is actually 'II' (see *1573*, *n. 3*)
Literary Notebook, *2375*, late September 1943?
(includes notes for 'The Quick and the Dead' and 'Last Man in Europe')
Domestic Diary III, *2996*, 7 May to 8 October 1946,
plus 4 and 5 January 1947, *3147*
This diary has the notes for 'Politics and the English Language'
Domestic Diary IV, *3213*, 12 April to 11 September 1947
Domestic Diary V, *3430*, 31 July 1947 to 24 December 1948
(*3319* and *3514*, 27 December 1947 to 10 May 1948: kept by Avril whilst Orwell
was in hospital)
Second Literary Notebook, *3515*, 1948; and see *3347, 3352, 3365, 3367, 3374,
3381, 3384, 3396, 3402, 3407, 3463*
Last Literary Notebook, *3721-2* and *3725*; and see *892, 3578-9, 3586, 3602, 3687*
Notebook with manuscript draft for 'A Smoking-room Story, *3723* (and see
3721-2 and *3724*)

Also included in this edition are a selection of Orwell's research materials
used in preparing *The Road to Wigan Pier* and *Homage to Catalonia*; his lectures
on weapons and tactics to his Home Guard platoon; and the one surviving
notebook listing what he earned (apart from his salary as Literary Editor of

Tribune) for his journalism from 12 July 1943 to 31 December 1945, a record he kept so that he could make an accurate income tax return.

In the final volume, his unfinished writings are printed; also his lists of those he believed might undermine Britain to benefit the Soviets together with a detailed analysis of documents released in July 1996 by the Information Research Department (*3590A* and *B*); the books he owned and the 144 books he read in the last year of his life; his will and details of his estate; there is an unpublished memoir by Miranda Wood, who lodged in his Canonbury flat whilst he was at Barnhill, Jura, and who typed drafts of *Nineteen Eighty-Four* and 'Such, Such Were the Joys'; and a detailed listing of the pamphlets he collected, now in the British Library.

The titles of volumes are drawn from Orwell's writing:

X: *A Kind of Compulsion*: 'Why I Write,' Summer 1946, *3007*, XVIII, 317
XI: *Facing Unpleasant Facts*: 'Why I Write,' Summer 1946, *3007*, XVIII, 316
XII: *A Patriot After All*: *New English Weekly*, 25 April 1940, *615*, XII, 151
XIII: *All Propaganda is Lies*: War-time Diary, 14 March 1942, *1025*, XIII, 229
XIV: *Keeping Our Little Corner Clean*: letter to George Woodcock, 2 December 1942, *1711* XIV, 214 (text has 'I have kept our little corner of it fairly clean)
XV: *Two Wasted Years*: letter to Philip Rahv, 9 December 1943, *2390*, XVI, 22
XVI: *I Have Tried to Tell the Truth*: London Letter, Winter 1944–45, *2553*, XVI, 411
XVII: *I Belong to the Left*: letter to Duchess of Atholl, 15 November 1945, *2795*, XVII, 385
XVIII: *Smothered under Journalism*: letter to Dorothy Plowman, 19 February 1946, *2903*, XVIII, 115
XIX: *It is What I Think*: letter to Philip Rahv, 9 April 1946, *2966*, XVIII, 232
XX: *Our Job is to Make Life Worth Living*: 'Reflections on Gandhi,' January 1949, *3516*, XX, 7

I should like to say a word about those described as assisting the editor. From what has been said above, Ian Angus's importance will be apparent. But he has played a more significant role than that. He, too, kept going when things looked black, especially when, on more than one occasion, it seemed the whole project would be abandoned, in particular trailing off to Caversham day after day from Central London to dig out material at the BBC Archive, and to the British Library at Colindale to search its newspaper collection. He has throughout kept a scrupulous eye on all that has been printed and annotated. His knowledge of those in the Orwell Circle (or Circles) and beyond proved of the greatest importance. Then, when the volumes had reached page-proof stage, he spent exhausting hours tracking down provenances and copyright owners, a task of wearying difficulty in so large a project. My wife's role has *not* been that of typist as might easily be supposed. Almost all the typing fell to me. She has read and commented on everything, as has Ian Angus, and demonstrated the sharpest eye of the four proof-readers; she has spotted inconsistencies, proved adept reading manuscript that foxed Ian and me, searched at Caversham and University College, and regularly shamed me by pointing to what I, as a professional editor, had missed. To both of them, for their work and their support, I am immensely grateful.

We all three have been responsible for these volumes and in all parts of them. In the main the editing and annotation is mine but I must, and am glad to take responsibility for all the flaws that inevitably exist in so vast a work, compiled under difficult circumstances, interrupted time and again by other teaching and writing demands, and protracted beyond need by unnecessary abandonments.

These volumes are far more than a rich quarry for Orwell scholars; they offer a wonderful insight into the social, literary, and political events of the thirties and forties from the point of view of one of the most socially and politically conscious writers of this century; as such they have much to say to us over half-a-century on. Perhaps I might repeat something I published elsewhere:

> It is too easy to claim that Orwell's novels do not accord with what are taken to be the canons of high literature; Orwell is central to the developments that have challenged such notions, and especially through his essays, he has been instrumental in broadening and redefining concepts of culture. His influence in so doing is still felt and will continue. . . . The fact that he is accessible to younger people is of the greatest importance, prompting, infuriating, enlightening, nagging and warning his readers in so many areas of thought and action. The one characteristic of Orwell's writing that, it seems to me, is too often overlooked is his wit and his wry humour. The impression of a grim prophet, a forbidding Old Testament figure, is too easily conjured up. He had a marvellous gift of humour and I suspect that, in the last analysis, he will have the laugh over those who would belittle him.[10]

It has been my good fortune in my academic life to work, in the main, on Shakespeare and Orwell. I wish to make no trite comparisons, but what I can say, wholeheartedly, is that I have never tired of their company and my delight in their work has grown day by day.   D. G.

Peter Davison
De Montfort University

1. Cyril Connolly commenting on letters to him printed in *Encounter*, January 1962, p. 56. His comment begins, 'These letters seem to me interesting because anything about Orwell is interesting. . . .'
2. Winston Smith, *Nineteen Eighty-Four*, CW IX, 44–5.
3. Review of H. G. Wells, *'42 to '44. A Contemporary Memoir upon Human Behaviour During the Crisis of the World Revolution*, *The Observer*, 21 May 1944, 2474.
4. Nicolas Walter, 'George Orwell: An Accident of History'. a review of *Collected Essays* by George Orwell (Secker & Warburg 1961), *Anarchy: A Journal of Anarchist Ideas*, 8 (October 1961), 246–55, especially 253–54. This ill-considered selection of essays was published without reference to Sonia Orwell. It omitted 'Rudyard Kipling' and 'Reflections on Gandhi'. Fredric Warburg was forced to withdraw the book (a hardback). He used the remaining unbound sheets for a paperback edition and published a new hardback edition, which included these two essays, also in 1961.
5. The nine books were published in corrected editions by Secker & Warburg in 1986–87 and reprinted in Penguin Twentieth-Century Classics (with a Note on the Text but no lists of variants) in 1989; *The Penguin Complete Novels of George Orwell* reprints the old, uncorrected texts. For the facsimile, see *George Orwell, Nineteen Eighty-Four: The Facsimile of the Extant Manuscript*, edited by Peter Davison, London, New York, and Weston Mass., 1984.
6. *The Collected Essays, Journalism and Letters of George Orwell*, edited by Sonia Orwell and Ian Angus, 4 volumes, London, 1968; published by Penguin Books, 1970.

7. A very few letters and some proofs (thought to be uncorrected) are known to exist in the United States and Germany. Repeated pleas to those who might know of their whereabouts have remained unanswered. Their absence makes the ready and generous response of so many libraries great and small, and so many individuals, even more appreciated by the editors. Inevitably, once this edition appears such items will pop up. As the 'ʌ' letters following item numbers indicate, more has come to light during the long-drawn-out process of printing.
8. Nicolas Walter, pp. 250–51.
9. *Orwell: The War Broadcasts*, edited by W. J. West, London, 1985; and *Orwell: The War Commentaries*, edited by W. J. West, London, 1985 (see especially note 385 on p. 219).
10. Peter Davison, *Orwell: A Literary Life*, Basingstoke, 1996, p. 147.

EDITORIAL NOTE TO THE SECOND EDITION

Publication of a reprint of this edition enables me to include twelve letters which came to light after the edition was published. Three are from Orwell to Daniel George (Bunting) and two from Lord David Cecil to W. J. Turner in connection with Orwell's *The English People* in the series *Britain in Pictures*. I am grateful to T. E. D. Klein (through the agency of Peter Cannon) for permission to publish the letters to Daniel George of 17 February and 28 December 1944; and to Messrs Maggs Bros. Ltd. for permission to publish the letter to him of 10 April 1944. I am grateful to Denis Roy Bentham for supplying the two letters from Lord David Cecil and for permission to publish these; they throw an interesting light on the publication of *The English People*. I am grateful to the Hon. David Astor for finding six letters that illuminate Orwell's relationship with the *Observer*, especially as a reviewer, and also a letter from Avril Dunn to David Astor and for making me photocopies of these. Seven letters are included in Appendix 15; that from Avril Dunn apears on XX/187; the others are incorporated in notes in the body of the text. There is also a supposed recommendation by Orwell for a book published in 1952.

The edition includes a corrected Spanish text of item *374A*, the report to the Tribunal for Espionage and High Treason in Valencia, and an improved translation. I am very grateful to Robert A. McNeil, Head of Hispanic Collections, Bodleian Library, Oxford, for providing these and for checking documents in Barcelona.

I have been enabled to correct typographical errors, amend mistakes, and provide some additional notes and dates of the deaths of those who have died since the edition was published. The extent and manner of additions has been restricted by the necessity of retaining the existing pagination to avoid re-indexing but some additional allusions are listed at the very end of Volume XX. I am deeply grateful to all those who wrote, and especially to Jeffrey Meyers and Nicolas Walter, both of whom went to considerable trouble to help me. I am also grateful to the publishers, Secker & Warburg, for allowing these additions and corrections.

P. D.

INTRODUCTION to VOLUME X

1903–1936: *A Kind of Compulsion*

In 'Why I Write' (1946), George Orwell traces his earliest attempts at writing, at home, at his preparatory school, and at Eton. He is quick to reject all he then wrote and describes how, between the ages of seventeen and twenty-four, he tried 'to abandon this idea.' But 'almost against my will, under a kind of compulsion from outside', he found himself searching for the right words to describe what he did and what he saw. This volume begins with Orwell's letters home from St. Cyprian's from the age of eight (his illustrations to which are reproduced), all that has survived of his tyro work, and the trial sketches that led on to *Burmese Days*. Orwell explained that he did not write to produce a work of art but 'because there is some lie I want to expose' and, for the first time since their publication in Paris in 1928–29, this volume prints (in their original French and in English translations) the articles he wrote to expose the sufferings of the unemployed, tramps, and beggars, and the imperialist exploitation of other people—by the British of the Burmese. These articles, with one on John Galsworthy, and others on censorship in England, and on a popular French farthing newspaper, epitomise what would be centres of concern for Orwell's writing throughout his life: literature, social and political issues, freedom of the individual, and popular culture. In 1930 Orwell had published the first of the 379 reviews he would write over the next twenty years (only a small proportion of which have ever been reprinted) and in 1931, 'A Hanging', the first of his most important essays. The volume includes the correspondence leading up to the publication of *Down and Out in Paris and London*, that dealing with censorship of *Burmese Days*, *A Clergyman's Daughter*, and *Keep the Aspidistra Flying*, and includes the text of his school play, *King Charles II*, which underlies the play Dorothy struggled to produce in *A Clergyman's Daughter*. The volume concludes with Orwell's research materials for *The Road to Wigan Pier* and an analysis of what Orwell was paid for writing this book, which indicates that suggestions that he received an advance of £500 cannot be correct. Throughout the edition, there is very full annotation and biographical details are given for virtually everyone mentioned. There is a personal, place, and title index.

ACKNOWLEDGEMENTS

applicable to the edition as a whole

A small army of people has helped in the compilation of these volumes. My first thanks are due to Sonia Orwell and Ian Angus for the pioneer work they did in editing *The Collected Essays, Journalism and Letters of George Orwell* (1968). This was more than a mere starting point. Ian Angus continued to collect documents and search out information between the publication of those volumes and the time when this edition was first mooted by Tom Rosenthal (then with Secker & Warburg). I am greatly indebted to him for that and for his constant concern that justice should be done to Orwell and his work.

The Orwell Estate, especially in the person of Mark Hamilton, the Orwell Archive, University College London, particularly Gill Furlong and her assistants and Janet Percival, has provided information and materials with unfailing patience and courtesy. Ian Willison's 1953 Librarianship Diploma thesis, 'George Orwell: Some Materials for a Bibliography,' has been a constant source of reference and he has given generous personal support. Bernard Crick was warmly encouraging from the start and his *George Orwell: A Life* (1980, 1982 and 1990) has, as the notes indicate, proved an essential guide. The staff of the BBC Written Archive, especially Jacqueline Kavanagh, were indefatigable in assisting the search through archives indexed in a fashion they had inherited and which can only be described as arcane. Dr Clive Fleay helped by advising on the history of the period and by digging out facts and documents. I have been privately encouraged in moments of despondency by Barry Bloomfield who seemed confident when I did not that the edition would appear, even in my lifetime. That it has got into print is due in large part to Max Eilenberg of Secker & Warburg, who rescued the project when the American publishers gave up and the project was left in disarray. I should like to express my thanks to Anica Alvarez of Secker & Warburg who then steered the volumes through the press with skill and patience. Following the acquisition of Secker & Warburg by Random House UK Ltd early in 1997, the final stages of the production of these volumes were supervised by Rowena Skelton-Wallace. I am most grateful to her for assuming this formidable task. To Roberta Leighton I am greatly indebted. She not only prepared the text for the press in New York but went beyond the call of duty in digging out information on United States references on my behalf and, most important of all, when Harcourt Brace gave up, kept on working even when no prospect of publication looked likely (just as Yvonne Davet had done for Orwell before World War II in the hope of getting *Homage to Catalonia* published in French, something that did not happen until sixteen years later, five years after Orwell's death, taking, by

Acknowledgements

coincidence, as long as it has taken to get this edition into print). I am enormously grateful to Roberta, not simply for her work, but for her confidence that all would be well in the end.

The layout and typography for the edition was designed by Meyer Miller. Alas, he died some years before the edition on which he worked hard saw the light of day, but in thanking him for his work I should like to record the memory of a man of great skill and friendliness. He is much missed.

The copy for this edition ran to 7,840 pages, many of them paste-ups. Three copies were required and, because of their nature, had to be hand-fed, with variable densities, into a xerox machine. This enormous task was undertaken, without payment, by Gill Brownlee, who gave up many Saturday mornings to complete the task. I am very grateful to her and, in Marlborough, to Barbara Fernley and Amanda Hughes, who have continued to produce what has seemed to be a never-ending stream of xeroxes. My daughter-in-law, Mara, gave up two days of Christmas holiday in 1996 to prepare the map of Jura that serves as a frontispiece to Volumes XVIII and XIX and I should like to thank her for the very attractive result. Too often we hear the excuse, 'It must have been lost in the post.' Something like £4,000 has been spent on posting copy, proofs, page-proofs, revises, etc., from England to New York and back, within England, and between England and Italy. Not a single item has been lost and only one packet was delayed for a while (and that, ironically, by a private courier: Orwell would smile). I commend and thank the postal services involved.

A very large number of libraries, institutions, and people have enabled this edition to be compiled because they have allowed documents owned by them or in their care to be reproduced. Many have made searches on behalf of the editors, or provided them with information, or given help of other kinds. We have very rarely met with refusals or had letters unanswered. To all those who have helped, libraries, institutions, and people, we express our gratitude.

Specific acknowledgement to those who have allowed documents to be reproduced (and who have often furnished copies) and a list of provenances (compiled by Ian Angus) are given in each volume. Willing help was given by newspapers and journals who had, many years ago, published essays, articles and reviews by Orwell, not only in giving permission for items to be reproduced but often in searching for those it was thought might exist. Particular thanks are due to *Tribune* for allowing the many letters from respondents to Orwell's articles, in their copyright, to be printed.

I am grateful to Orwell's Literary Executors, especially Mark Hamilton, for entrusting me with this task and for continual support and to Secker & Warburg for its encouragement and support, and also for allowing items from its archive to be reproduced. Gratitude is expressed to Victor Gollancz Ltd (in particular Livia Gollancz), Faber & Faber Ltd, George Allen & Unwin Ltd, and Harcourt Brace, for searching their archives and for making their Orwell materials available.

The following libraries bore the burden of requests for materials and their help is especially acknowledged: Henry W. and Albert A. Berg Collection of the New York Public Library. Astor, Lenox, and Tilden Foundations;

Bristol University Library (Penguin Books and Hamish Hamilton Archives); British Library Reading Room and Department of Manuscripts (for Orwell Papers, Add. Mss 49384 and 78083); British Library Newspaper Library, Colindale; Brotherton Library, Leeds Russian Archive, Leeds University; University Research Library, University of California, Los Angeles; Eton College, School Library; Harry Ransom Humanities Research Center, University of Texas at Austin; Helsinki University Library (*Parhaat-Echo: International Review*); Imperial War Museum Library (S. E. A. C. and C. O. I. literary digests); India Office Library and Records; Internationaal Instituut voor Sociale Geschiedenis, Amsterdam (*S.I.A. Bulletin*); Lilly Library, Indiana University, Bloomington; McFarlin Library, University of Tulsa; Nuffield College, Oxford (Cripps Papers); William R. Perkins Library, Duke University (*S. I. A. Bulletin*); Library of Political and Economic Science, L. S. E. (I. L. P. Papers); Reading University Library (Secker & Warburg and George Routledge Archives); Working Class Movement Library, Salford (*Socialist Correspondence*). To these libraries, their librarians and their staffs, our warm thanks are extended. Specific acknowledgement is made in each volume to these libraries which provided materials reproduced in this edition. Two other libraries, which, though they did not provide items for publication, gave much help must be mentioned: The London Library, in whose recesses all kinds of valuable information were tracked down; and Marlborough Public Library, which always managed to find books for me on inter-library loan.

The following (some of whom are now, alas, dead) helped in the production of this edition and sincere thanks are offered to them (and the institutions of which they are sometimes a part).

Alvar Alsterdal
Robin Alston
Mulk Raj Anand
Ann Stokes Angus
Keith Arbour
Hon David Astor
Tony Atienza (Marx Memorial
 Library)
Fernand Auberjonois
I. Aver
Bill Baker
Honor Balfour
Frank D. Barber
Peter Beal (Sotheby's)
John Bernard (for searching
 Australian newspapers)
Sam Bornstein
Jim Binns
Stephen Bird (National Museum of
 Labour History)
Karen Bishop (now Sadler)

Bill Blair
Alcuin Blamires
George and Rita Blocke
Barry Bloomfield
Guido Bonsaver
Laurence Brander
Brendan Brown (*Commentary*)
Clare Brown
Gill Brownlee (for hours of devoted
 zeroxing)
Mark Bryant
Jacintha Buddicom
Janet Carleton
S. T. Chapman
Sir William Coldstream
Robert Colodny
Alex Comfort
Lettice Cooper
Diana Coppleman
R. Cornwall (Ministry of Defence,
 Naval Records)

Acknowledgements

David Cotterill
Stafford Cottman
Bernard Crick
Andy Croft
Ian and David Dannreuther
Yvonne Davet
Rosemary Davidson
John Davies
Richard D. Davies
Hugh Davison (for information on
    BBC radio practice)
John Davison (for searching
    Customs & Excise records)
Mara Davison (for the map
    reproduced in volumes XVIII and
    XIX)
Michael Davison (for the translation
    from Spanish)
Margaret Dyas (Library and
    Research Dept., Foreign and
    Commonwealth Office)
Bertha Doran
Geoffrey Dowling
Anne Dunn
Avril and Bill Dunn
Mary Elliott
Sir Roger Falk
Gillian Fenwick (for locating 322A)
Barbara Fernley
Allan Ferris
Howard Fink (for Orwell's
    recommended 'Best Books' 166)
Clive Fleay
Rt. Hon. Michael Foot
Michael R. D. Foot
Mirjam Foot
Nick Forbes (Public Record Office)
Elvina Foster
Peter Frank
Gill Furlong
Guy and Reg Gadney
Donald Gallup
R. A. Gekoski
Livia Gollancz
Celia Paget Goodman (Celia Kirwan)
Bert Govaerts
Sir Lawrence Gowing

Ronald Gray (Hammersmith Books)
Andrew Grima
Charles Hadfield
Mark and Bill Hamilton
Karen Hatherley
Desmond Hawkins
Michael P. Hawkins
Cathy Henderson
Patricia Herbert
William Hetherington (Peace Pledge
    Union)
Richard Hewlett
A. R. A. Hobson
Stephen Holland
Alan Hollinghurst (*TLS*)
Amanda Hughes
Monica Humphries
Denzil Jacobs
James Joll
Gwyniver Jones
Shirley E. Jones (for help with
    translations)
John Jordan
Alain Kahan (Working Class
    Movement Library, Salford)
Jacqueline Kavanagh
Michael Kennard
Jon Kimche
David King
B. J. Kirkpatrick
Michel Kopp
Miklos Kun
John Laidlar
Robert Lamb
K. A. G. S. Lane (Christy & Moore)
Dan Leab
John Lehmann
Peter Lübbe
Sally McEwan
David McKitterick (for tracking
    down watermarks)
W. M. McCrea
Amanda Mares
Peter Marshall
Michael Meredith
Patricia Methven (Liddell Hart
    Centre for Military Archives)

Michael Meyer
Peter Miles
Douglas Moyle
Alan Munton
National Army Museum
Elizabeth Oliver (for help with
  translations)
Vanessa Parker
Noel Parker-Jervis
Janetta Woolley Parladé
Patrick Parrinder
Janet Percival
Dennis Perry
Lady Antonia Pinter
RAF Museum
Cyril and Jonathan Ray
Challice B. Reed
Kenneth W. Rendall
Vernon Richards
Peggy and Eric Robertson
Abha Sharma Rodrigues
Hinda Rose (Maggs Bros)
Sir Steven Runciman
Brenda Salkeld
Trevor Sergeant
John Screen
Ihor Ševčenko
Michael Shelden
Daniel G. Siegel
Murray Simpson
Neil Sinyard
Ralph B. Sipper
Anthony Smith
John Smith (Christy & Moore)
J. Alan B. Somerset

Neil Sommerville
Maria Sorge
Sir Stephen and Lady Spender
Hilary and John Spurling
John Sterling
Helen and Telfer Stokes
Norman Swallow
David Sylvester
Julian Symons
Christine Thomas
David Thomas
Peter Thwaites
Peter Tucker
A. Tyabji (OUP, Bombay)
Sarah Tyacke (PRO)
UK Passport Agency, Record Office
Corydon Unwin
Peter Vansittart
Mary Varcoe
Stephen Wadhams
Jeff Walden
Michael J. Ward
Marina Warner
Cedric Watts
Lord Weidenfeld
W. J. West (for providing an
  invaluable Orwell typescript)
William Wheeler (for reprocessing
  Wigan Pier illustrations)
Judith Williams
Keith Williams
Ian Willison
Diana Witherby (Lady Cooke)
Miranda Wood
George Woodcock
Francis Wyndham

There are in addition many individual acknowledgements in footnotes, especially when reference has been made to books quoted or information that has been given orally.

The editor and publishers have made great efforts to trace copyright holders of the material published in this volume but in some cases this has not proved possible. The publishers therefore wish to apologise to the authors or copyright holders of any material which has been reproduced without permission and due acknowledgement.

P.D.

ACKNOWLEDGEMENTS and PROVENANCES

specific to Volume X

The editor wishes to express his gratitude to the following institutions and libraries, their trustees, curators, and staffs for their co-operation and valuable help, for making copies of Orwell material available, and for allowing it to be reproduced: Henry W. and Albert A. Berg Collection, New York Public Library, Astor, Lenox, and Tilden Foundations; BBC Written Archives Centre, Caversham; The British Library, Department of Manuscripts (for the Orwell papers, Add. Mss 49384 and 73083); Eton College Library; Lilly Library, Indiana University, Bloomington, Indiana; Harry Ransom Humanities Research Center, University of Texas at Austin; University Research Library, University of California, Los Angeles; and the Library of University College London for material in the Orwell Archive.

Gratitude is expressed to Faber and Faber Ltd and Victor Gollancz Ltd for making their Orwell material available, with particular thanks to Livia Gollancz for her help and valuable information.

Thanks are due to Bill Blair for making available Orwell's play, *King Charles II*, and to Henry Dakin for a letter Orwell wrote to Mabel Ida Blair. I am deeply indebted to those whose Orwell letters are available because they donated, deposited, or gave copies of them to the Orwell Archive: Jacintha Buddicom, Dennis Collings, Geoffrey Gorer, Dorothy Plowman, Anthony Powell, Sir Richard Rees, Sir Steven Runciman, and Brenda Salkeld.

I would like to thank *The Listener* (by courtesy of the BBC and the Independent Television Association Ltd) and *The New Statesman* for permission to reproduce material which first appeared in their pages.

I would also like to thank the following for allowing me to use material whose copyright they own: the Estate of Cyril Connolly, c/o Rogers, Coleridge & White, 20 Powis Mews, London, W11 1JN, to quote from two letters by Cyril Connolly; Guinever Buddicom and Dione Venables for quotations from Jacintha Buddicom's *Eric and Us*; and the University of Sussex Library to quote from a letter by Geoffrey Gorer.

A number of individual acknowledgements are made in foot and headnotes to those who have provided information in books or verbally that I have quoted or referred to.

The editor and publishers have made every effort to trace copyright holders of the material published in this volume, but in some cases this has not proved possible. The publishers therefore wish to apologise to the authors or copyright holders of any material which has been reproduced without permission and due acknowledgement.

PROVENANCES

The locations of letters and documents printed in this volume are indicated against their item numbers in the list given below. Where there are letters or documents at an item which come from more than one source, this is indicated, e.g. 329 Lilly, VG.

However, letters and documents which are not listed below should be taken as being available for consultation in the Orwell Archive, University College London, either as originals or in the form of copies. Sonia Orwell gave all the Orwell papers then in her possession to the Orwell Archive at its foundation in 1960. Many friends, relations and associates of Orwell have given their Orwell letters or copies of them to the Orwell Archive. There were in Orwell's pamphlet collection that Sonia Orwell gave to the British Museum in 1950 some Orwell papers (now in the British Library. Department of Manuscripts, Add. Mss. 49384 and 73083) and copies of these, at her request, were given by the Director and Principal Librarian of the British Museum to the Orwell Archive in 1965. For simplicity's sake, the British Library Orwell papers are not indicated as such in the location list, but are regarded as being available for consultation in the form of copies in the Orwell Archive.

KEY TO LOCATIONS

BBC	BBC Written Archives Centre, Caversham
Berg	Henry W. and Albert A. Berg Collection, The New York Public Library, Astor, Lenox and Tilden Foundations
Dakin	Henry Dakin
Eton	Eton College Library
Faber	Faber and Faber Ltd
Lilly	Lilly Library, Indiana University, Bloomington, Indiana
Texas	Harry Ransom Humanities Research Center, University of Texas at Austin
UCLA	Department of Special Collections, University Research Library, University of California, Los Angeles
VG	Victor Gollancz Ltd

26 Dakin	136 Berg	169 Berg
46A Eton	137 Berg	170 Berg
117 Faber	146 Berg	172 Berg
119 Faber	148 Berg	177 Berg
120 Berg	149 Berg	181 Berg
121 Berg	155 Berg	183 Berg
122 Faber	156 Berg	184 Berg
124 Berg	158 Berg	187 Berg
128 Berg	159 Berg	188 Berg
132 Berg	162 Berg	189 Berg
133 Berg	167 Berg	190 Berg

191 Berg
192 Berg
193 Berg
195 Berg
198 Berg
199 Berg
200 Berg
206 Berg
208 Berg
209 Berg
210 Berg
212 Eton
213 Berg
215 Berg
216 Berg
218 Berg
219 VG
220 Berg
221 Berg
222 Berg
223 VG
225 Berg
226 Berg
227 VG
228 VG
229 VG
230 Berg

231 VG
232 VG
233 VG
234 Lilly
236 VG
238 Lilly
239 VG
241 Lilly
243 Lilly
244 Lilly
246 Lilly
247 Berg
250 Lilly
251 Lilly
252 Lilly
253 Texas
255 Lilly
257 Texas
259 Texas
260 Lilly
262 Lilly
264 Lilly
267 VG
268 VG
269 VG
273 Lilly
275 Lilly
279 VG

281 VG
283 VG
284 Lilly
286 Lilly
292 VG
293 Lilly
295 Berg
297 Lilly
298 Berg
299 Lilly
300 Berg
302 Lilly
306 Lilly
309 Lilly
312 Texas
313 Lilly
317 Texas
323 UCLA
327 Berg
329 Lilly, VG
337 Lilly
338 Berg
339 Berg
340 Lilly
341 VG
343 BBC

A Note on the Editing

THE CONTENTS are, in the main, arranged in chronological order of Orwell's writing. Letters arising from his articles or reviews are usually grouped immediately after that item and Orwell's replies to those letters follow thereon; see, for example correspondence with F. Tennyson Jesse arising from his review of her *The Story of Burma* (*2909–11*). If there is a long delay between when it is known an article or essay was completed and its publication, it is printed at the date of completion. For items Orwell entered into his Payments Book, which he kept from 12 July 1943 to 31 December 1945 (*2831*), the date he completed a review or article is known precisely. If items are printed much earlier in the chronological sequence than their date of publication, a cross-reference is given at the date of publication. All entries, whether written by Orwell or anyone else, including lengthy notes and cross-references, are given an item number. Because the printing of the edition has taken place over seven years, some letters came to light after the initial editing and the numbering of items had been completed. These items (or those that had in consequence to be repositioned) are given a letter after the number: e.g., *335A*. Some items included after printing and page-proofing had been completed are given in a final appendix to Volume XX and two (received by the editor in mid January 1997) in the Introduction to Volume XV. Numbers preceding item titles are in roman; when referred to in notes they are italicised.

The provenance of items is given in the preliminaries to each volume. Every item that requires explanation about its source or date, or about textual problems it may pose, is provided with such an explanation. Some articles and broadcasts exist in more than one version. The basis upon which they have been edited is explained and lists of variant readings provided. No Procrustean bed has been devised into which such items must be constrained; individual circumstances have been taken into account and editorial practice explained. See, for example, the complex problems posed by Orwell's 'Imaginary Interview' with Jonathan Swift, recorded 2 November 1942, broadcast 6 November 1942, and published in *The Listener*, 26 November 1942 as 'Too Hard on Humanity', *1637*. It is hoped that what has been done, and the alternatives open to readers, will be plain.

Although this is not what is called a 'diplomatic edition'—that is, one that represents the original precisely even in all its deformities to the point of reproducing a letter set upside down—the fundamental approach in presenting these texts has been to interfere with them as little as possible consistent with the removal of deformities and typographic errors. Orwell took great pains over the writing of his books: the facsimile edition of *Nineteen Eighty-*

Four[1] shows that, but in order to meet the demands of broadcasting and publication schedules he often wrote fast and under great pressure. He has, justifiably, a reputation for good, clear prose. The speed with which he sometimes wrote meant that what he produced was not always what he would have wished to have published had he had time to revise. And, of course, as with any printing, errors can be introduced by those setting the type (though the accuracy of the compositors was remarkably good despite the wartime conditions). It would be easy in places to surmise what Orwell would have done—a comma here, a semi-colon there. I have only made even such changes where there would otherwise have been confusion. Obvious spelling mistakes, which could well be the compositor's or typist's (and the typist might be Orwell), have been corrected silently, but if there is any doubt, a footnote has drawn attention to the problem. Examples from one broadcast will illustrate what has been done. The typescript of Weekly News Review, 53, 16 January 1943 (*1825*), has 'failling,' 'Chin's,' 'existance,' 'Incidentlly,' and 'agression.' The first four are corrected silently ('failling' to 'falling'); the fifth is corrected but a footnote points out that from childhood to the writing of *Nineteen Eighty-Four* Orwell spelt 'aggression' with a single 'g.' It is likely that Orwell typed this script, which he himself read to India.

In brief, therefore, I have tried to present what Orwell wrote in his manuscripts and typescripts, not what I thought he should have written; and what he was represented as having written and not what I think should have been typed or printed on his behalf. This is not a 'warts and all' approach because gross errors are amended, significant changes noted, and textual complexities are discussed in preliminary notes. The aim is to bring Orwell, not the editor's version of Orwell, to the fore. Although textual issues are given due weight, an attempt has been made to produce an attractive, readable text.

The setting of this edition has been directly from xeroxes of original letters (if typed), typed copies of manuscript (prepared by one or other of the editors), surviving scripts for broadcasts, and xeroxes of essays, articles, and reviews as originally published (unless a headnote states otherwise). For *The Collected Essays, Journalism and Letters of George Orwell* a 1968 house style was adopted but for this edition, no attempt has been made to impose a late twentieth-century house style on the very different styles used by journals and editors of fifty to eighty years ago. I must confess that I blanched at the thought of marking up this large body of texts in an attempt to conform to a single style, and I was only too well aware of the errors I should be liable to introduce. Texts are therefore reproduced in the style given them in the journals from which they are reprinted. I did, however, have more scholarly reasons. To 'correct' might well cause even more confusion as to what was and was not Orwell's: see below regarding paragraphing. Nevertheless, although it is not possible *to know*, one may sometimes hazard a guess at what underlies a printed text. Thus, I believe that most often when 'address' and 'aggression' are printed, Orwell typed or wrote 'adress' (especially until about the outbreak of World War II) and 'agression.' Some scholars might wish to pursue this further. Although American spellings (such as 'Labor') have been retained in articles published in the United States, on very rare occasions, if I could be certain that a form of a word had been printed that Orwell would not have used—such as the American 'accommodations' in London Letter, *Partisan Review*, 15 January 1944 (*2405*)—I have changed it to the form he would have used: 'accommodation' (in the first paragraph of the section headed PARLIAMENT). Some variations, especially of proper names, have been accepted even if they look incongruous; so, 'Chiang Kai-Shek' as part of a book title but 'Chiang Kai-shek' throughout the text that follows.

Hyphenation presents tricky problems, especially when the first part of a word appears at the end of a line. Examples can be found in the originals of, for example, 'the middle-class,' 'the middle class', and 'the middleclass.' What should one do when a line ends with 'middle-'? Is it 'fore-deck' or 'foredeck'? If 'fore-' appears at the end of a line of the copy being reproduced, should the word be hyphenated or not? *OED* 1991 still hyphenates; Chambers in 1972 spelt it as one word. Where it would help (and it does not include every problem word), the ninth edition of F. Howard Collins, *Authors' & Printers' Dictionary*, Oxford University Press, 1946 (an edition appropriate to the mature Orwell) has been drawn upon. But Collins does not include fore-deck/foredeck. On a number of occasions Orwell's letters, or the text itself, is either obscure or wrong. In order to avoid the irritating repetition of *sic*, a small degree sign has been placed above the line at the doubtful point (°). It is hoped that this will be clear but inconspicuous. It is not usually repeated to mark a repetition of that characteristic in the same item. Orwell was sparing in his use of the question-mark in his letters; his practice has in the main been followed.

Paragraphing presents intractable problems. Orwell tended to write in long paragraphs. Indeed, it is possible to show from the use of many short paragraphs that News Review scripts so written are not by Orwell. The key example is News Review, 30, 11 July 1942 (*1267*), for which there is also external evidence that this is not by Orwell. This has twenty-one paragraphs as compared to eight in the script for the following week. It so happens that we know that Orwell was not at the BBC for two weeks before the 11 July nor on that day: he was on holiday, fishing at Callow End, Worcestershire (and on that day caught a single dace). But though paragraph length is helpful in such instances in identifying Orwell's work, that is not always so. It is of no use when considering his articles published in Paris in 1928–29 nor those he wrote for the *Manchester Evening News*. These tend to have extremely short paragraphs—sometimes paragraphs of only a line or two, splitting the sense illogically. A good example is the series of reviews published on 2 November 1944 (*2572*) where a two-line paragraph about Trollope's *The Small House at Allington* should clearly be part of the preceding four-line paragraph, both relating the books discussed to Barchester; see also *2463*, n. 2 and *2608*, n. 4. There is no question but that this is the work of sub-editors. It would often be possible to make a reasonable stab at paragraphing more intelligently, but, as with verbal clarification, the result might be the more confusing as to what really was Orwell's work and what this editor's. It has been thought better to leave the house-styles as they are, even if it is plain that it is not Orwell's style, rather than pass off changes as if the edited concoction represented Orwell's work.

Usually it is fairly certain that titles of essays are Orwell's but it is not always possible to know whether titles of articles are his. Reviews were also frequently given titles. Orwell's own typescript for his review of Harold Laski's *Faith, Reason and Civilisation* (*2309*), which survived because rejected by the *Manchester Evening News*, has neither heading (other than the name of the author and title of the book being reviewed), nor sub-headings. That would seem to be his style. In nearly every case titles of reviews and groups of letters, and cross-heads inserted by sub-editors, have been cut out. Occasionally such a title is kept if it is an aid to clarity but it is never placed within quotation marks. Other than for his BBC broadcasts (where Orwell's authorship is clear unless stated otherwise), titles are placed within single quotation marks if it is fairly certain that they are Orwell's.

Telegrams and cables are printed in small capitals. Quite often articles and reviews have passages in capitals. These look unsightly and, in the main, they have been reduced to small capitals. The exceptions are where the typography makes a point, as in the sound of an explosion: BOOM! Orwell sometimes abbreviated words. He always wrote an ampersand for 'and' and there are various abbreviated forms for such words as 'about'. It is not always plain just what letters make up abbreviations (and this sometimes applies to his signatures) and these have regularly been spelt out with the exception of the ampersand for 'and'. Because the usual ampersand has the size of a capital letter, and these stand out from pages of text in an unsightly manner, a small ampersand has been designed. This serves as a reminder that the original is handwritten. Orwell often shortened some words and abbreviations in his own way, e.g., Gov.t, Sup.ts (Superintendents), NB. and N.W (each with a single stop), and ie.; these forms have been retained. In order that the diaries should readily be apparent for what they are, they have been set in sloped roman (rather than italic, long passages of which can be tiring to the eye), with roman for textual variations. Square and half square brackets are used to differentiate sources for the diaries (see, for example, the headnote to War-Time Diary II, *1025*) and for what was written and actually broadcast (see, for example, Orwell's adaptation of Ignazio Silone's *The Fox*, *2270*). Particular usages are explained in headnotes to broadcasts etc., and before the first entries of diaries and notebooks.

Orwell usually dated his letters but there are exceptions and sometimes he (and Eileen) give only the day of the week. Where a date has to be guessed it is placed within square brackets and a justification for the dating is given. Letters sent to Orwell's literary agent, Leonard Moore, were often date-stamped on receipt and these can give an approximate date of sending. This cannot be quite exact because then, even in wartime, letters might arrive on the same day as they were posted. If Orwell simply signs a letter, the name he used is given without comment. If he signs over a typed version of his name, or initials a copy of a letter, what he signed or initialled is given over the typed version. There has been some slight regularisation of his initialling of letters.

If he omitted the final stop after 'E. A. B', no stop is added (and, as here, editorial punctuation *follows* the final quotation mark instead of being inside it). Sometimes Orwell placed the stops midway up the letters: 'E·A·B'; this has been regularised to 'E. A. B'.

Wherever changes are made in a text that can be deemed to be even slightly significant the alteration is either placed within square brackets (for example, an obviously missing word) or the alteration is footnoted. Attention should be drawn to one particular category of change. Orwell had a remarkably good memory. He quoted not only poetry but prose from memory. Mulk Raj Anand has said that, at the BBC, Orwell could, and would, quote lengthy passages from the Book of Common Prayer.[2] As so often with people with this gift, the quotation is not always exact. If what Orwell argues depends precisely upon what he is quoting, the quotation is not corrected if it is inaccurate but a footnote gives the correct reading. If his argument does not depend upon the words actually quoted, the quotation is corrected and a footnote records that.

So far as possible, I have endeavoured to footnote everything that might puzzle a reader at the risk of annoying some readers by seeming to annotate too readily and too frequently what is known to them. I have found in recent years that not too much knowledge of even recent history can be assumed, even if it is rare to come across someone who has not heard of the Second World War, as was my lot with a graduate student some fifteen years ago. I have, therefore, tried to identify all references to people, events, books, and institutions. However, I have not been so presumptuous as to attempt to rewrite the history of this century and, in the main, have relied upon a small number of easily accessible histories. Thus, for the Spanish Civil War I have referred in the main to *The Spanish Civil War* by Hugh Thomas; and for the Second World War, to Winston Churchill's and Liddell Hart's histories. The former has useful and conveniently available documents, and the latter was by a historian with whom Orwell corresponded. They were both his contemporaries and he reviewed the work of both men. These have been checked for factual information from more recent sources, one by Continental historians deliberately chosen as an aid to objectivity in an edition that will have world-wide circulation. It is assumed that readers with a particular interest in World War II will draw on their own knowledge and sources and the annotation is relatively light in providing such background information. Similarly, biographical details are, paradoxically, relatively modest for people as well known as T. S. Eliot and E. M. Forster, but far fuller for those who are significant to Orwell but less well known and about whom information is harder to track down, for example, George(s) Kopp, Joseph Czapski, and Victor Serge. It is tricky judging how often biographical and explicatory information should be reproduced. I have assumed most people will not want more than one volume at a time before them and so, have repeated myself (often in shortened form with cross-references to fuller notes) more, perhaps, than is strictly necessary. Whilst I would claim that I have made every attempt not to mislead, it is important that historical and biographical information be checked if a detail is significant to a scholar's argument. History, as Orwell was quick to show, is not a matter of simple, indisputable fact. In annotating I have tried not to be contentious nor to direct the reader unfairly, but annotation cannot be wholly impartial.[3]

Each opening is dated. These dates, though drawn from the printed matter, are not necessarily those of the text reproduced on the page on which a date appears. The dates, known or calculated of letters, articles, broadcasts, diaries, etc., will correspond with the running-head date, but, for example, when correspondence (which may have run on for several weeks) springs from an article and follows directly on that article, the date of the article is continued *within square brackets*. Sometimes an item is printed out of chronological order (the reason for which is always given) and the running-head date will again be set within square brackets. Wherever practicable, the running-head date is that of the first item of the opening; if an opening has no date, the last date of a preceding opening is carried forward. Articles published in journals dated by month are considered for the purpose to be published on the first of the month. Inevitably some dates are more specific than is wholly justified, e.g., that for 'British Cookery' (*2954*). However, it is hoped that if readers always treat dates within square brackets with circumspection, the dates will give a clear indication of 'where they are' in Orwell's life.

A year or two ago, Jim McCue wrote an article, 'An error-free book? Surely some mistake', and it had the subtitle, 'Inaccuracies and misprints between hard covers used to be the exception, now they are the rule.'[4] He gave many examples and was honest enough to point out that his *Selected Poems of Arthur Hugh Clough* (1991) was 'not innocent of mistakes.' Great efforts have been made to ensure the accuracy of these volumes. The three editors and Roberta Leighton (in New York) have read and re-read them a total of six times but it is obvious that errors will arise. At a late stage it was realised that none of us had noticed that a complete item had appeared twice. (It does not now.) If such a gross error could get through even one reading, what typos and mistakes that spring less readily to the eye must (as it used to be put so charmingly in the sixteenth century) have 'escaped in the printing.' One excuse, or rather plea for understanding, I would advance. Much of the copy-preparation and proof-reading has been of type set during and after the war when newsprint was in short supply and mere literary articles would be set in microscopic-sized type. Many of the BBC scripts were blown up from microfilm and extremely difficult to puzzle out. It is often difficult to tell whether a colon or a semi-colon is intended, or 'these' or 'those', and some words are barely decipherable. When one proof-reads against xeroxes of dim printing on creased paper, the possibilities for error are increased and the eyes so run with tears that vision is impaired. We hope we have corrected most errors, but we know we shall have not have caught them all.

P. D.

1. *George Orwell, Nineteen Eighty-Four: The Facsimile of the Extant Manuscript*, edited by Peter Davison, London, New York, and Weston Mass., 1984.
2. Information from W. J. West, 22 July 1994.
3. The problems of presenting acceptable history even for the professional historian are well

outlined by Norman Davies in *Europe: A History*, Oxford University Press, Oxford and New York, 1996, 2–7. I am obviously attempting nothing so grand, yet even 'simple' historical explication is not always quite so simple.

4. *Daily Telegraph*, 18 July 1993.

BIBLIOGRAPHY and LIST of REFERENCES

This bibliography does not list all that has been written on Orwell and his work. It is chiefly confined to the reference works, books, memoirs, and essays that have been found helpful in preparing Volumes X to XX of *The Complete Works of George Orwell*. Place of publication is London unless specified otherwise.

References to Orwell's books are to the editions in Vols I to IX of the *Complete Works* (edited P. Davison, published by Secker & Warburg, 1986–87). The pagination is almost always identical with that in the Penguin Twentieth-Century Classics edition, 1989–90. The volumes are numbered in chronological order and references are by volume number (in roman), page, and, if necessary (after a diagonal) line, so: II.37/5 means line five of page 37 of *Burmese Days*. Secker editions have Textual Notes and apparatus. Penguin editions have A Note on the Text; these are not identical with the Secker Textual Notes and Penguin editions do not list variants. There is a 32-page introduction to the Secker *Down and Out in Paris and London*. Items in Volumes X to XX are numbered individually; they (and their notes) are referred to by italicised numerals, e.g. *2736* and *2736 n. 3*.

REFERENCE WORKS: These are the principal reference works frequently consulted:

The Oxford English Dictionary, second edition (Compact Version, Oxford 1991): (*OED*).
The Dictionary of National Biography (Oxford 1885–1900, with supplements and *The Twentieth-Century*, 1901–): (*DNB*).
Dictionary of American Biography (New York, 1946, with supplements).
Dictionnaire biographique du mouvement ouvrier français, publié sous la direction de Jean Maitron, 4ᵉ ptie 1914–1939: De la Première à la Seconde Guerre mondiale (t. 16–43, Paris, Les Éditions Ouvrières, 1981–93).
Who's Who; Who Was Who; Who's Who in the Theatre; Who Was Who in Literature 1906–1934 (2 vols., Detroit, 1979); *Who Was Who Among English and European Authors 1931–1949* (3 vols., Detroit 1978); *Contemporary Authors* and its *Cumulative Index* (Detroit, 1993); *Who's Who In Filmland*, edited and compiled by Langford Reed and Hetty Spiers (1928); Roy Busby, *British Music Hall: An Illustrated Who's Who from 1850 to the Present Day* (London and New Hampshire, USA, 1976).
The Feminist Companion to Literature in English, edited by Virginia Blain, Patricia Clements, and Isobel Grundy, Batsford 1990.
The New Cambridge Bibliography of English Literature, edited by George Watson and Ian Willison, 4 vols., Cambridge, 1974–79.

Martin Seymour-Smith, *Guide to Modern World Literature*, 3rd revised edition, Macmillan 1985.

The War Papers, co-ordinating editor, Richard Widdows, 75 Parts, Marshall Cavendish, 1976–78.

The following are referred to by abbreviations:

CEJL: The Collected Essays, Journalism and Letters of George Orwell, ed. Sonia Orwell and Ian Angus, 4 volumes, Secker & Warburg 1968; Penguin Books, 1970; references are by volume and page number of the more conveniently available Penguin edition.

Crick: Bernard Crick, *George Orwell: A Life*, 1980; 3rd edition, Penguin Books, Harmondsworth, 1992 edition. References are to the 1992 edition.

Eric & Us: Jacintha Buddicom, *Eric and Us: A Remembrance of George Orwell*, Leslie Frewin, 1974.

Lewis: Peter Lewis, *George Orwell: The Road to 1984*, Heinemann, 1981.

Liddell Hart: B. H. Liddell Hart, *History of the Second World War*, Cassell, 1970; 8th Printing, Pan, 1983.

Orwell Remembered: Audrey Coppard and Bernard Crick, eds., *Orwell Remembered*, Ariel Books, BBC, 1984.

Remembering Orwell: Stephen Wadhams, *Remembering Orwell*, Penguin Books Canada, Markham, Ontario; Penguin Books, Harmondsworth, 1984.

Shelden: Michael Shelden, *Orwell: The Authorised Biography*, Heinemann, London; Harper Collins, New York; 1991. The American pagination differs from that of the English edition; both are given in references, the English first.

Stansky and Abrahams I: Peter Stansky and William Abrahams, *The Unknown Orwell*, Constable 1972; edition referred to here, Granada, St Albans, 1981.

Stansky and Abrahams II: Peter Stansky and William Abrahams, *The Transformation*, Constable 1979; edition referred to here, Granada, St Albans, 1981.

Thomas: Hugh Thomas, *The Spanish Civil War*, 3rd edition; Hamish Hamilton and Penguin Books, Harmondsworth, 1977.

Thompson: John Thompson, *Orwell's London*, Fourth Estate 1984.

West: *Broadcasts*: W. J. West, *Orwell: The War Broadcasts*, Duckworth/BBC 1985.

West: *Commentaries*: W. J. West, *Orwell: The War Commentaries*, Duckworth/BBC, 1985.

Willison: I. R. Willison, 'George Orwell: Some Materials for a Bibliography,' Librarianship Diploma Thesis, University College London, 1953. A copy is held by the Orwell Archive, UCL.

2194 Days of War: 2194 Days of War, compiled by Cesare Salmaggi and Alfredo Pallavisini, translated by Hugh Young, Arnoldo Mondadori, Milan 1977; rev. edn Galley Press, Leicester 1988.

The following have been consulted; many other works are referred to in annotations and full details are given of those at the point of reference.

Bill Alexander, *British Volunteers for Liberty: Spain, 1936–1939*, Lawrence & Wishart, 1982.

Keith Alldritt, *The Making of George Orwell: An Essay in Literary History*, Edward Arnold, 1969.

John Atkins, *George Orwell: A Literary Study*, John Calder, 1954.

Maung Htin Aung, 'George Orwell and Burma,' *Asian Affairs*, 57 (ns 1), Pt 1, (1970), 19–28.

l

'Orwell and the Burma Police,' *Asian Affairs*, 60 (ns 4), Pt II, (1973), 181–6.

Deirde Beddoe, 'Hindrances and Help-Meets: Women in the Writings of George Orwell,' in Norris (below), pp. 139–54.

Burnett Bolloten, *The Spanish Civil War: Revolution and Counterrevolution*, Harvester, Wheatsheaf, New York and London, 1991.

Laurence Brander, *George Orwell*, Longmans, Green & Co., 1954.

Beatrix Campbell, *Wigan Pier Revisited: Poverty and Politics in the 1980s*, Virago, 1983.

'Orwell – Paterfamilias or Big Brother?,' in Norris (below), pp. 126–39.

Christy Campbell, *The World War II Fact Book*, Macdonald 1985.

Winston Churchill, *The Second World War*, 6 vols, Cassell 1949–54. The edition published in the United States has different volume titles and pagination. Reference is by both English and U.S. titles and pagination.

Cyril Connolly, *Enemies of Promise*, Routledge & Kegan Paul, 1938; Penguin Books, Harmondsworth, 1961.

Murray Constantine (= Katherine Burdekin), *Swastika Night*, Gollancz, 1940.

David Corkhill and Stewart Rawnsley, eds., *The Road to Spain*, Borderline, Dunfermline, 1981.

Bernard Crick, *Nineteen Eighty-Four*, With a Criticial Introduction and Annotations, Clarendon Press, Oxford, 1984.

Valentine Cunningham, *The Penguin Book of Spanish Civil War Verse*, Penguin Books, Harmondsworth, 1980.

Peter Davison, *Nineteen Eighty-Four: The Facsimile of the Extant Manuscript*, (ed.), Preface by Daniel G. Siegel, Secker & Warburg, London; M&S Press, Weston, Mass.; Harcourt Brace Jovanovich, New York, 1984.

'Editing Orwell: Eight Problems,' *The Library*, VI, 6, (1984), 217–28.

'What Orwell Really Wrote,' *George Orwell & 'Nineteen Eighty-Four': The Man and the Book*, Library of Congress, Washington, DC., 1985, pp. 5–21.

'Bangkok Days: Orwell and the Prisoner's Diary,' *Manuscripts*, 41, (1989), 303–10.

'George Orwell: Dates and Origins', *The Library*, VI, 13, (1991), 137–50.

'Orwell: Balancing the Books,' *The Library*, VI, 16, (1994), 77–100.

George Orwell: A Literary Life, Macmillan 1996.

'Of Sugar-loaves and Horsemeat: The Value of Archives and the Limitations of their Printed Forms,' *The Founders' Library, University of Wales, Lampeter: Bibliographical and Contextual Studies*, edited by C. W. Marx (Lampeter 1997).

Ruth Dudley Edwards, *Victor Gollancz: A Biography*, Gollancz, 1987.

Elisaveta Fen, 'Orwell's First Wife,' *The Twentieth Century*, 168, (1960), 114–26.

Tosco Fyvel, *George Orwell: A Personal Memoir*, Weidenfeld and Nicolson, 1982.

Martin Gilbert, *The Second World War*, Weidenfeld and Nicolson, 1989.

Miriam Gross, *The World of George Orwell*, Weidenfeld and Nicolson, 1971; includes a shortened version of Maung Htin Aung's, 'George Orwell and Burma' (though the origin and abbreviation are not noted).

J. R. Hammond, *A George Orwell Companion*, Macmillan, 1982.

Rayner Heppenstall, *Four Absentees*, Barrie and Rockliff, 1960.

Robert Hewison, *Under Siege: Literary Life in London 1939–45*, Weidenfeld and Nicolson, 1977.

Tribune 40: The first forty years of a socialist newspaper, edited by Douglas Hill, Quartet Books, 1977.

Sheila Hodges, *Gollancz: The Story of a Publishing House, 1928–1978*, Gollancz, 1978.

Christopher Hollis, *A Study of George Orwell: The Man and his Works*, Hollis & Carter, 1956.

Lynette Hunter, *George Orwell, The Search for a Voice*, Open University Press, Milton Keynes, 1984.

'Stories and Voices in Orwell's Early Narratives,' in 'Norris (below), pp. 163–82.

James Joll, *The Anarchists*, 2nd edn, Harvard University Press, Cambridge, Mass., 1980.

Robert Kee, *The World We Left Behind: A Chronicle of the Year 1939*, Weidenfeld and Nicolson, 1984.

Jeffrey Meyers, ed., *George Orwell: The Critical Heritage*, Routledge & Kegan Paul, 1975.

Gordon Barrick Neavill, 'Victor Gollancz and the Left Book Club,' *The Library Quarterly*, 41 (1971), 197–215.

Christopher Norris, ed., *Inside the Myth; Orwell: Views from the Left*, Lawrence & Wishart, 1984.

Daphne Patai, *The Orwell Mystique: A Study in Male Ideology*, University of Massachussetts, Amherst, 1984.

Robert Pearce, 'Truth and Falsehood: George Orwell's Prep School Woes,' *RES*, ns. 43, No 171 (1992), 367–86;
'The Prep School and Imperialism: The Example of Orwell's St. Cyprian's,' *Journal of Educational Administration and History*, (1991), 41–53;
'Orwell and the Harrow History Prize,' *N&Q*, ns 37, Vol 235, (1990), 442–3.

Paul Preston, *The Spanish Civil War, 1936–39*, Weidenfeld and Nicolson, 1986.

Alok Rai, *Orwell and the Politics of Despair: A Critical Study of the Writings of George Orwell*, Cambridge University Press, Cambridge, 1988.

Sir Richard Rees, *George Orwell: Fugitive from the Camp of Victory*, Secker & Warburg, 1961.
For Love or Money, Southern Illinois University Press, Carbondale, 1960.

Patrick Reilly, *George Orwell: The Age's Adversary*, Macmillan, 1986.

John Rodden, *The Politics of Literary Reputation: The Making and Claiming of 'St. George Orwell'*, Oxford University Press, New York, 1989.

Abha Sharma Rodrigues, 'George Orwell, the BBC and India: A Criticial Study' (Edinburgh University, PhD thesis, 1994); see especially chapter 5, 'Child of the Raj?' and chapter 6, 'Unusual Contemporaries—Orwell and Mulk Raj Anand: A Comparative Study.'
Orwell's War, 1939–1945, Cassell Archive, 1997.

William Rust, *Britons in Spain: The History of the British Battalion of the XVth International Brigade*, Lawrence & Wishart, 1939.

D. S. Savage, 'The Fatalism of George Orwell,' *The New Pelican Guide to English Literature*, 8: *The Present*, edited by Boris Ford, Harmondsworth, 1983, 129–46.

Ian Slater, *Orwell: The Road to Airstrip One*, W. W. Norton & Co., New York, 1985.

David Smith and Michael Mosher, *Orwell for Beginners*, Writers and Readers Publishing Cooperative Ltd., 1984.

Christopher Small, *The Road to Miniluv*, Gollancz, 1975.

Louis L. Snyder, *Guide to World War II*, Greenwood Press, Westport, Conn., 1982.

Iain Sproat, *Wodehouse at War*, Milner and Co., 1981.

Peter Stansky, ed., *On Nineteen Eighty-Four*, W. H. Freeman & Co., New York, 1983.

William Steinhoff, *George Orwell and the Origins of 1984*, University of Michigan Press, Ann Arbor, 1975.

William B. Todd and Ann Bowden, *Tauchnitz International Editions in English 1841–1955*, Bibliographical Society of America, New York, 1988.

Richard J. Voorhees, *The Paradox of George Orwell*, Purdue University Press, West Lafayette, Indiana, 1961.

Nicolas Walter, 'George Orwell: An Accident in Society,' *Anarchy: A Journal of Anarchist Ideas*, 8 (1961), 246–55.

'Orwell and the Anarchists,' *Freedom: Anarchist Review*, 42 (30 January 1981), 9–12.

Fredric Warburg, *An Occupation for Gentleman*, London, Hutchinson, 1959; Houghton Miflin, Boston, Mass., 1959.

Eugen Weber, *The Hollow Years: France in the 1930s*, Sinclair-Stevenson, 1995.

George Orwell, edited by Courtney T. Wemyss and Alexej Ugrinsky, Greenwood Press, Westport, Conn., 1987 (under the auspices of Hofstra University).

Gary Werskey, *The Visible College*, Allen Lane, 1978.

W. J. West, *The Larger Evils: 'Nineteen Eighty-Four' – The Truth Behind the Satire*, Cannongate Press, Edinburgh, 1992.

Keith B. Williams, 'The Will to Objectivity: Egon Kisch's *Der Rasende Reporter*', *MLR*, 85 (1990), 92–106.

Raymond Williams, *Orwell*, Fontana (Wm. Collins & Co.), 1971.

George Woodcock, *The Crystal Spirit: A Study of George Orwell*, Jonathan Cape, 1967.

The Writer and Politics, Freedom Press, 1948.

Orwell's Message: 1984 and the Present, Harbour Publishing, Madeira Park, BC, 1984.

David Wyckes, *A Preface to Orwell*, Longman, 1987.

Alex Zwerdling, *Orwell and the Left*, Yale University Press, New Haven, 1974.

CHRONOLOGY

In the main, Orwell's publications except books are not listed

25 June 1903 Eric Arthur Blair born to Richard Walmesley Blair and his wife, Ida (*née* Limouzin) in Motihari, Bengal. They already had a daughter, Marjorie Frances, born in Gaya, Bengal, in 1898. Richard Blair was a sub-deputy agent in the Opium Department of the Indian Civil Service. Motihari and Gaya are now in Bihar State.

1904 Ida Blair returns with Marjorie and Eric to England and settles at Henley-on-Thames, Oxfordshire.

Summer 1907 Richard Blair on three months' leave in England.

6 April 1908 Eric's younger sister, Avril Nora, born.

1908–1911 Attends a day-school at Henley run by Anglican nuns (as did his sisters).

Sept 1911–Dec 1916 Boards at St Cyprian's, a private preparatory school at Eastbourne, Sussex.

1912 Richard Blair retires from the Opium Dept., and returns to England. The family moves to Shiplake, Oxfordshire (probably early in December).

2 Oct 1914 First appearance in print: Poem, 'Awake! Young Men of England', *Henley and South Oxfordshire Standard*.

1915 The Blairs move back to Henley-on-Thames (to autumn 1917)

Lent Term 1917 At Wellington College as a scholar.

May 1917–Dec 1921 At Eton as a King's Scholar. Contributes to *The Election Times* and *College Days*.

13 Sept 1917 Orwell's father commissioned as 2nd Lieut.; posted to 51st (Ranchi) Indian Pioneer Company, Marseilles. His mother soon after let the Henley house and moved to Earl's Court, London, to work in the Ministry of Pensions.

Dec 1921 The Blairs move to Southwold on the Suffolk coast.

Oct 1922–Dec 1927 Orwell serves in Indian Imperial Police in Burma; resigns whilst on leave in England, Autumn 1927.

Autumn 1927 First expeditions to East End of London to examine the conditions of the poor and exploited.

Aut/Wint 1927 Lives in Portobello Road, Notting Hill, London.

Spring 1928 About this time lives for a while as a tramp.

Spring 1928–late 1929 Lives in working-class district of Paris; writes a 'ballade' (after Villon?), several articles and short stories, and either one or two novels. Five articles are published in French translations in Paris and one in English in London. His other writing from this period has not survived. In autumn 1929 works as a dishwater and kitchen porter in a luxury hotel, probably the Crillon but there is circumstantial evidence suggesting the Lotti.

6 Oct 1928 'La Censure en Angleterre' appears in Henri Barbusse's paper, *Monde*—his first professional publication.

29 Dec 1928 'A Farthing Newspaper', *G.K.'s Weekly*—first professional publication to appear in England.

7 Mar 1929 Admitted to Hôpital Cochin, Paris, with 'une grippe'. Discharged 22 March.

1930–31 Uses his parents' home in Southwold as his base, writing there but going off to tramp and live with down-and-outs in London.

1930 Begins writing for *The Adelphi*; by October has completed 'Days in London and Paris', a 35,000-word version of *Down and Out in Paris and London*.

Autumn 1931 Picks hops in Kent. Writes four short stories which have not survived. Starts to write *Burmese Days*.

17 Oct 1931 'Hop-Picking', *New Statesman & Nation*.

Spring 1932 Jonathan Cape and Faber & Faber reject versions of *Down and Out in Paris and London*. Leonard Moore becomes his literary agent.

April 1932–July 1933 Teaches at The Hawthorns, a private school for boys aged 10–16, Hayes, Middlesex. Writes and directs a school play, *Charles II*, Christmas 1932.

19 Nov 1932 Puts forward several names, including 'George Orwell,' as his pen-name.

9 January 1933 *Down and Out in Paris and London*, by George Orwell (the first use of that name), published by Victor Gollancz. Published on 30 June 1933 in New York; as *La vache enragée*, Paris, May 1935; and as *Trosečníken v Paříži a Londýně*, Prague, 1935.

Autumn 1933 Teaches at Frays College, Uxbridge, Middlesex. Finishes *Burmese Days*. In December, ill with pneumonia in hospital; gives up teaching.

January–October 1934 Lives with his parents in Southwold. Writes *A Clergyman's Daughter*.

25 Oct 1934 *Burmese Days* published by Harper & Brothers, New York. Published 24 June 1935 by Gollancz, London, with alterations required by the publisher; as *Tragédie Birmane*, Paris, August 1946; *Giorni in Birmania*, Milan, November 1948; *Tragédia Burmában*, Budapest, 1948.

Oct 1934–Mar 1935 Takes a room at 3 Warwick Mansions, Pond Street, Hampstead, London.

Oct 1934–Jan 1936 Part-time assistant (with Jon Kimche), at Booklovers' Corner, 1 South End Road, Hampstead.

11 March 1935 *A Clergyman's Daughter* published by Gollancz. Published by Harper & Brothers, New York, 17 August 1936.

August 1935 Begins writing for *The New English Weekly*. Moves to Kentish Town, London.

End Jan 1936 Completes *Keep the Aspidistra Flying*.

31 January–30 March 1936 In North of England to collect material for a book commissioned by Gollancz, on the depressed areas.

2 April 1936 Moves to The Stores, Wallington, Hertfordshire.

20 April 1936 *Keep the Aspidistra Flying* published by Gollancz. Published by Harcourt, Brace, New York, December 1955.

May 1936 Starts *The Road to Wigan Pier* and begins reviewing for *Time and Tide*.

9 June 1936 Marries Eileen O'Shaughnessy.

15 Dec 1936 Delivers ms of *The Road to Wigan Pier*.

Christmas 1936 Leaves to fight for the Republicans in Spanish Civil War.

————————

21 January 1950 Orwell dies of pulmonary tuberculosis, aged 46.

THE COMPLETE WORKS OF
GEORGE ORWELL   TEN

A KIND OF COMPULSION

1911–1916

1. St Cyprian's

In September 1911, when Orwell was a little over eight years of age, and after he had attended a small Anglican convent school for three years, he was sent to St Cyprian's School, a private preparatory school at Eastbourne, Sussex. One of his contemporaries was Cyril Connolly.[1] He boarded at St Cyprian's until he left, in December 1916, going home only for the school holidays. Twenty-six of the letters he wrote home from St Cyprian's have survived. These are all addressed to his mother, Ida Blair, initially because his father, Richard Walmesley Blair, was abroad, serving as a sub-deputy agent in the Opium Department of the Indian Civil Service. He continued to address his letters to his mother only, perhaps from habit, after his father returned home when he retired in January 1912. Between 1938 and 1948, Orwell was to write an account of his time at St Cyprian's: *Such, Such Were the Joys, 3409* not published in his lifetime. See Crick, 58–99; *Orwell Remembered*, 19–20, 25–32 (for Mrs. Blair's diary for 1905 and for "My Brother, George Orwell," by his sister Avril); Shelden, 12–35, 47–49, 73–74; U.S.: 12–33, 42–45, 68–69.

It was common practice in schools such as St Cyprian's for a teacher to inspect, and often amend, letters for home; emendation sometimes went well beyond the eradication of spelling mistakes. Except for the first of Orwell's letters, for which all corrections and errors are noted, the letters have been reproduced as he completed them, without remarking on errors, false starts, and corrections by him or in someone else's hand unless these are of interest. Some of the references in the letters (e.g., Togo, Gussy, Vivy, and the uncle) were identified by Avril Dunn, Orwell's younger sister, in a letter of 9 March 1964. The letters were in the possession of Avril Dunn, except for the last, which was Henry Dakin's. They were bought for the Orwell Archive, University College London, in 1993. This purchase included three letters and the last part of a letter which were not available when this part of the edition was prepared and set in type. They are included here as 2A, 3A, 11A, and 14A.

Items 2 to 22 are letters written from St Cyprian's, but Orwell only began giving the place from where he wrote with his letter of 2 December 1911. His first letter was written to his mother at 'Nutshell,' Western Road, Henley-on-Thames, Oxfordshire. After his father retired, the family moved to 'Roselawn,' Shiplake, in the same county, probably in December 1912 (see *22*). Throughout this edition, dates of letters have been incorporated into headings; conjectural details are enclosed within square brackets. Italic numbers refer to item numbers. Reproductions of Orwell's drawings are approximately same size unless stated otherwise.

1. Cyril Connolly (1903–1974) was with Orwell at St Cyprian's and Eton, where he was also a Colleger, in the Election after Orwell's. They met again in 1935, after Connolly had reviewed *Burmese Days*, and were associated in a number of literary activities, particularly *Horizon*, which Connolly edited. See his *Enemies of Promise* (1938); extracts in *Orwell Remembered*, 32–

34. His novel, *The Rock Pool*, was published in 1936 and reviewed by Orwell in *New English Weekly*, 23 July 1936; see *321*. Orwell also reviewed Connolly's collection of essays, *The Condemned Playground*, in *The Observer*, 2 December 1945; see *2811*. Orwell's second wife, Sonia Brownell, worked for *Horizon*; Connolly introduced them. See Michael Shelden, *Friends of Promise: Cyril Connolly and the World of Horizon* (1989).

2. To his mother

14 September 1911   Handwritten

Dear Mother

I hope you are quite well, thanks for that letter[1] you sent me[2] I havent° read it yet. I supose[3] you[4] want to know what schools° like, its°? alright we have fun in the morning. When[5] we are in bed.

from[6]
E. Blair

° Means *sic*. Used throughout.
1. 1 *crossed out between* that *and* letter.
2. m *crossed out between* sent *and* me.
3. *Corrected to* suppose *in pencil in another hand.*
4. u *rewritten; in the early letters,* you *frequently looks like* yow.
5. Whe *crossed out.*
6. m *is a correction.*

2A. To his mother

1 October [1911]   Handwritten

My dear Mother,

I hope you are quite well. Its ben[1] quite as hot as it was at Looe,[2] every day exept° one. And[3] that was Frieday,[4] and its jolly hot today, we[5] went to the Devonshires bathes[6] they are simpely[7] loovely,° its sea water pumped in.
I am top in History, and Kirkpatrick and I are top in French, I am third in Latin[8] and 2ond[9] in Arithmatick.[10]
Bits[11] very nearly time for Chapel so godbye.[12]

With lots of love from,
E A Blair.

1. *Corrected in another hand (as elsewhere) by the addition of a superior* e
2. The Blairs spent much of their summer holidays at Looe in Cornwall.
3. *Preceded by* and, *crossed out.*
4. *The corrector has crossed out the* e.
5. *Followed by a second* we, *which has been crossed out.*
6. *The final* s *of* Devonshires *and the* e *of* bathes *crossed out.* Although the building survives it is no longer used as a swimming bath.
7. e *crossed out.*
8. t *not crossed, and a correction made above* Latin.
9. *The corrector has crossed out* 2 *and written* sec *above it.*

10. *Orwell omitted the second* t *and wrote it above the word;* a *and* k *crossed out and* e *written over* a *by corrector.*
11. *In his haste, Orwell ran* But *and its* together; *corrector added* ut *above* i.
12. *The corrector added* o *above the one Orwell wrote.*

3. To his mother

Sunday, 8 October 1911   Handwritten

My dear Mother,
I hope you are quite well, I am top in arithmetic, and I have been moved up in Latin. I cannot quite read your letters yet, but I can read Margies.[1] How is Togo,[2] we had a magick lantern the other day.
   It is Kirkpatricks[3] birthday today he is eight years old, Last time we played football I shot seven goals.

from
E A Blair.

P.S. I forgot to tell you I had a letter from Margie and I will write to her soon. Love to Avril.[4]

1. His older sister, Marjorie Frances, born 21 April 1898.
2. A wire-haired terrier, eventually run over when the family lived at Roselawn, Shiplake, between late 1912 and the latter part of 1915. See *22* regarding 'the house in Shiplake.' (Italic numbers in notes refer to item numbers.)
3. Colin Kirkpatrick, later a banker and businessman who settled in Rhodesia. See Crick, 595, n. 18 for additional information.
4. His younger sister, Avril Nora, born 6 April 1908.

3A. To his mother

15 October 1911   Handwritten

My dear mother,
I hope you are quite well, we had thee° mtches[1] yesterday and beat them easily, the first eleven won seven[2] one, and the second game won by seven one while the third won by six duck. That school was called the Grange.
I am sending you a card to tell when the matches are[3] and who have got the first eleven coulers.[4]

From E A Blair

1. *Missing* a *written above* mtches, *probably by corrector.*
2. *Orwell originally wrote* six; *the* seven *looks like his handwriting.*
3. are *is preceded by another* are, *which has been crossed out.*
4. *Orwell forgot the* r *and added it in above the word afterwards.*

4. To his mother

5 November 1911   Handwritten

My dear Mother
Thank you very much for that shilling you sent me and my album. We had thee° Matches yesteday° we won two and lost one, while the Matches went on we went for a lovely walk on the Downs, and[1] called Smallman picked up ten shillings on the road.
On Sunday it is halfterm. Will you please send me Marjerys° adress.[2] Next time you write to Auntie Hay[3] and ask her to send me stamps.

lots of love from
E. Blair

Thank you for the 1/– you sent me.

1. a boy *appears to have been omitted.*
2. The spelling 'adress' was to persist throughout much of Orwell's life.
3. Probably a sister of his mother, Ida Blair; the request for foreign stamps may indicate that she usually lived abroad.

5. To his mother

12 November [1911]   Handwritten

My dear Mother
What kind of weather are you having? We are having lots of rain, but it is not raining this morning, but it is very dull. Will yoou° please send me one of one° or two of the new penny stamps for I have not got one yet.
The swimg[1] races were on Monday, and a boy called Murray started last in a race and won by a good deal. I was third in the race, I had a rathe° tight bathing dress on and could not swim a bit fast.
I am second, in Arithmetic, and this week I am first[2] in Latin. And I am 8th in French.
We are breaking up on the 20th Dec: that is on a Wensday° Give my love to Avril, and to Father.

Much love from
E. Blair.

1. min *inserted in adult hand.*
2. first *crossed out*; 2nd *written above in adult hand.*

6. To his mother

[November 1911?]   Handwritten

My dear mother
I hope you are quite well, please send my stamp album as soon as you can. We played 3 Matches yesterday, and lost all.
It is a lovely day quite warm.
Give my love to Avril.

Much love from your son
Eric Blair x++++[1]

1. The x and +'s are as added by Orwell.

7. To his mother

[November 1911?]   Handwritten

My dear Mother,
I hope you are quite well. I am second in Latin and first in arithmatick° and third in history.
Its° raining like mad this moring° and at about five aclock° this morning and the house rattled like paper with the wind.
There is an aufly° naughty boy hear° called Lesly° Cohen he has only just had

9

his seventh birthday. We have had severl° nice games of footbal° this week.
+++++++++++++++++++++

from your loving son
E. Blair

8. To his mother

2 December [1911]   Handwritten

St: Cypriann's°   Eastbourne

My dear Mother, I hope you are alright,
It was Mrs: Wilkes[1] birthday yesterday, we had aufel° fun after tea and played games all over the house. We all went for a walk to Beachy-Head.
I am third in Arithmatick.°
'Its'° very dull today, and dosent° look as if its° going to be very warm.
Thank you for your letter.
It is getting very near the end of the term, there are only eighteen days more. On Saturday evening we have dncing,° and I am going to say a piece of poetry, some of the boys sing.
Give my love to Father and Avril. Is Togo alright,° We had the Oxford and Cambridge Matches yesterday. Cambridge won in the first and third, and the second did not have a Match. I am very glad Colonel Hall[2] has given me some stamps, he said he wold° last year but I thought he had forgoten.° Its° a beastly wet day today all rain and cold.
I am very sorry to hear we had those beastly freaks of smelly white mice back. I hope these arnt° smelly one. if° they arnt° I shall like them.

From your loveing° son,
E. A. Blair.

1. Mrs. Vaughan Wilkes, wife of the Headmaster and owner of St Cyprian's. See Crick, 71–74.
2. Colonel Hall, a neighbour of the Blairs in Shiplake.

9. To his mother

4 February 1912   Handwritten

St: Cyprians   Eastbourn°

My dear Mother.
I hope you are quite well.
Thank you for your letter, "its"[1] snoing° like anything this morning, and its'
snowed in the night and yeterday.°
I have been in the sickroom again because I have got an aufel° cold. Yesterday
of course everything iced and the boys went and skated, but I was stuffed up
in the sickroom and I couldent° get a bit of peace to read for Leslie Cohen kept
on worrying and in the end I had to go and read to *him*.
We have not begun footer yet because theres° so much frost and stuf° that if
you fell down you'd simply break your neck.
Has Marery° begun school yet, and how is she and Avril and every body in
the house, have you given away the white mice yet, and does Vivy[2] still sleep
on their cage?
I am first of my division in Arithmatick,° and first of the form in Latin, and
second in French, and fifth in English and Geography. But "its"° about time I
learnt my Scripure° now, so gooby.°

From your loving son
Eric Blair.

1. Omission or erroneous placement of apostrophe for 'its'/'it's' is not hereafter noted.
2. Vivy was a pale-grey cat which produced forty-five kittens in three years, much to Mr. Blair's
   annoyance.

10. To his mother

11 February 1912   Handwritten

St Cyprian's   Eastbourne

My darling Mother,
I hope you and everybody are alright, thank you for your letter. We played
footer twice but I wasent° aloud° to play, are the mice alright.
If we have got any draughts will you please send them and will you send me
some of those peas that were left over frome° the bags because theres° a boy
here who's got a kink[1] of cannon that has to have those peas to shoot, are° you
having nice weather at home, we are having an aufly° nice lot of sun here, I am
second in everything in lessons.

With lots of love frome°
Eric Blair.

1. kink *for* kind

11. To his mother

18 February 1912   Handwritten

St: Cyprians   Eestbourne°

My darling Mother,
I hope you and everybody are alright, has Vivy run away or is she still staying, and have the mice had any babys,° if they have *dont*[1] let the cat get them, the boys went to see an aeroplane on Thursday but I and a lot of other chaps played footer amd° we won easily nine three.
If there are any tadpoles in the rain tub please dont let any leeches in, because I certainly dont want to come home and find that all the tadpoles are eaten up by the beasts of leeches.
The boy who got such a rotten cut on his knee is Much° better, and is sitting up in a big armchir° but he cannot get up and come down and work and and° run about and everything because he has to be carried about and silly things like that.
Its alright and dry today but its rather dull it lookes° rather as if its going to be sort of still like this for today and tomorrow and perhaps more, just nice weather for footer as long as it keeps dry.

With much love from
Eric Blair.

1. Omission of apostrophe from 'don't' and similar words is not noted hereafter.

11A. To his mother

25 February 1912   Handwritten

St: Cyprians   Eastbourne

My darling Mother,
Thank you for that letter you sent me, but I couldent° read it somewon[1] tore it up before I red[2] it, so if you had anything you specialy[3] wanted me to know you had better put it in your next letter and I hope that wont get torn up on Wensday° we had a loveley° lecture all about the moon, it was aufly° interesting and mr:° Sillar[4] showed us what an exclipse° of the moon was, with a football with shuger[5] on the top.
If I have got some fairly comen° stampes° at home you might send them to me because there a° boy here called Morens III who isent° English and hes° got absolutely go[6] no English stamps and he wants some badly.
And by the way I forgot to tell you that we also had a ripping lecture how different things were made we saw how steel was manafactured° and penknives and things like that, and also how soap is made and different° things you see when they were made, and so much that I haven't[7] time to tell you.

I am fifth in French and English and first in Latin and Second in Aritmatic.°
With lots of love from
E. A. Blair

[Drawing in pencil]

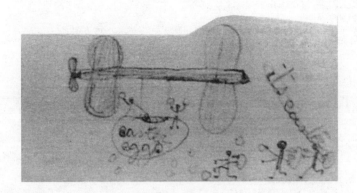

1. What is intended as an 'e' (as a correction ?) seems to follow the 'n'.
2. a *written in pencil over the word* by corrector.
3. *A second* 1 *(inserted by corrector?) seems to be added after the first* 1.
4. Robert L. Sillar ('Mr Brown' in 'Such, Such Were the Joys') taught geography and drawing, illustrating what he said with magic-lantern slides. He took the boys on nature walks on the Downs and he gave dramatic readings from Dickens at Christmas and on his birthday. He also had great skill in teaching rifle shooting. He was an enthusiastic and much-loved teacher. See Shelden, 47–48; U.S.: 43–44.
5. *Orwell originally spelt the word* sugar *and then added* h *over the word.*
6. *It looks as if Orwell started to repeat* got *but forgot to cross it out.*
7. *The apostrophe is uncertain.*

12. To his mother

3 March 1912   Handwritten

St: Cyprians   Eastbourne

My darling Mother,
Thank you for your letter, if you are going to have a small black kitten and Marjerey° is going[1] a baby guinea-pig.
Our sixes have begun and I was going to play but Hanning II is coming back, and he is twelve years old and of course he is much better than me and a place is being kept for him.
We played ordinary fooball° at least on Thursday everybody did, I was in the third game ur° side won easily 5 to 1° I was goalkeeper all the second halh,° and they only got past the half-line twise° while I was in goal but both of those times it[2] nearly a goal and I had to be jolly quick to pick them up and kick

13

them, because most of the chaps[3] the other side were in aufel° rats and they were runing° at me like angry dogs

From your loving son
E. A. Blair. + + + + + + + + +
+ + +x+x+x+x+x+xxx+ + +x+ P.S.[4]

1. to have *omitted (at turn of page).*
2. was *omitted.*
3. on *omitted. The several omissions possibly suggest Eric's excitement in telling his story.*
4. The line of +'s and x's is the postcript.

13. To his mother

10 March 1912   Handwritten

St: Cyprians   Eastbourne

My darling Mother,
I wrote you a letter last week and I dont know why it wasent° forwarded on to you.
we° have been having ripping weather just now and have been playing much more footer.
I am second in Arith: and French, and firs-t° in Latin and fourth in English. Are you having decent weather where yo° are.
The boys are having an aearoplane° compertition° and some of them go jolly weel,° but I think the one called Dotto will win.

From your loving son
E. Blair.

14. To his mother

17 March 1912   Handwritten

St: Cyprians   Eastbourne

My darling Mother,
Thank you for your letter, please tell me what couler° the giune-pig° is. W° are coming back on the third of April, and going back to school on the first of May.
When are you going to have your black kitten soon.°
We have been having a lot of footer again, and there were sixes on Thursday, and one of the sixes was the best we had ever had, neither sides° got any goals.
Hav° you seen any practis-ing° for the boat-racing on the Thames.
I hope everybody is alright, and are the animals alright.
I am first in Latin and Arithmatic° and third in English and French.

give° my love to every[1] at home. The° was[2] fairly big ship wrecked some way out, and you can see the masts sticking[3] up.

With lots of love to everybody
from E. A. Blair.

1. one *inserted (by a teacher?)*.
2. a *inserted (by a teacher?)*.
3. *Reads as* slicking *but the second letter is an uncrossed* t.

14A. To his mother

[24 March 1912?]

Only the final page of this letter has survived. Orwell wrote home each week on Sundays. In his letter of 17 March 1912 he said he would be coming home on 3 April and returning to school on 1 May. The handwriting and especially the capital letters A, E, F, and L are as identical as handwritten letters can be with those of the spring term's letters. There is a complete run of letters home from 4 February to 17 March, so this one seems likely to be that for either 24 or 31 March, the former date marginally preferable because Orwell might be expected to conclude his last letter home with an indication that he would be seeing his mother in a day or two.

I am first in Arithmatic° and second in English and French and forth[1] in Latin its a loveley° day today rippingly sunny and warm is everybody at home alright

With lots of love from Eric Blair.

[Drawing in pencil]

1. *A u has been written, in what looks like a corrector's hand, over* or; it is strange, however, that so many obvious errors have not been marked.

15. To his mother

12 May 1912   Handwritten

St: Cyprians   Eastbourn[1]

My darling Mother,
Is evreybody° all-right, thank you° for the letter you sent me.
I am fourth in Latin and fifth in Arith and I cant remember all the others, I am in such a hurry It is a lovley° day today and I expect we shall go for[2] long walk to–day but it is time for meto° get ready for Chapel so good by.°
With lots of love frome°
E. Blair

1. *Changed from* Eastbourian.   2. a *omitted.*

16. To his mother

2 June 1912   Handwritten

St: Cyprians   Eastbourne

My darling Mother,
I hope you are alright, thank[1] for your letter, I think I should like a gunmettle° watch for my birthday. Thank you for the card you sent me, will you send my coat and my bathing dress I want my coat now and then and shall soon be wanting my bathing dress soon if you send me one of my old pairs dont send those beastsley° things that come all over my body.
Did you know Uncle's name[2] is in the papper° if you did can you tell me if he won.
I am first in Latin 8th in English and[3] French, 2nd in Arith.

With lots of love from
Eric Blair.

1. you are *crossed out—you erroneously.*
2. Mrs. Blair's brother, Charles Limouzin, a golfer of some ability.
3. Histo *crossed out.*

17. To his mother

23 June 1912   Handwritten

St Cyprians   Eastbourne

My darling Mother,
I hope you are alright, thank you very much for your postcard.
We are having fairley° decent weather. just° now and then a little shower of rain. We had two matches against Kent House and in the first XI we made 91 and they made 53 and in the 2<u>nd</u> we made 159 and they made 37.

With lots of love from
Eric. A. Blair

18. To his mother

30 June 1912   Handwritten

Orwell was born on 25 June 1903. This is clearly a thank-you letter for his ninth-birthday gifts.

S^t: Cyprians   Eastbourne

My darling Mother
I hope you are alright.
Thank you very much for the ripping little watch you sent me and the Little

Paper,[1] thank Father for the book for me and someone sent me a knife and someone else a box of toffy° and someone else a cake that looks as if it is a seed one.

I am 2nd in Latin and 4th in English and 6th in History and Geography and 5th in French and 11th in Arith.

With lots of love from
Eric Blair

1. Inverted commas, or quotation marks, were placed round Little Paper, perhaps by an adult. Avril Dunn could not identify this but agreed it might be a comic.

19. To his mother
21 July 1912   Handwritten

St Cyprians   Eastbourne

My darling Mother,
I hope you are alright. Will you please ask to° the tobaconest° to sell you some cigarette cards he will give you a good many for about four-pence.

We had two matches yesterday in the 1st we lost, in the II we won they made 52 and we mad° 246, one of our boys mad° 90.

With lots of love from
Eric Blair. P.S. I send my

love to everybody at home and give Guissy[1] my love.

1. 'Guissy,' or Gussy, was a piebald guinea pig, nominally Marjorie Blair's pet; see 12.

20. To his mother
17 November 1912   Handwritten

St Cyprians

My darling Mother,
I hope you are quite well.
Aunt Nora[1] sent me two shillings a few days ago. We played four matches on Wednsday° we won in all of them but I do not remember the scores. I am 1st this week in Latin and[2] English and 4th in French and 10th in Arithmatic.° But I forgot to tell you we played two matches yesterday against St Christofers° we won in them both in the 1st the score was 3 to 1 in the 2nd it was 4 0. But I must say my Collect now so good-bye.

With lots of love from
E. Blair.

1. Aunt Nora [Limouzin] was one of the sisters of Orwell's mother. She became Mrs. Ward and in the 1940s lived in a second flat in the house at Ealing where Orwell's favourite aunt, Nellie Limouzin, lived.
2. Readin° crossed out.

21. To his mother

1 December [1912]   Handwritten

St Cyprians

My darling Mother,
thank° you for your letter, I am glad you thought my writing is better. On Friday we are going to have a Magic Lantern Lecture and a fancy dress dance but I am not shure° what day it is. This week I am 1st in the same forms and 9th in French 8th in Arith: and third in my other English form.

With lots of love from
E. Blair

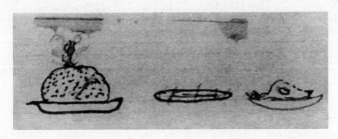

22. To his mother

8 December [1912]   Handwritten

St. Cyprians

My darling Mother,
I hope you are quite well. We have had a Magic Lantern Lecture on Thersday[1] and a Fancy Dress Dance on Friday, I went to the dance as a footman with a red velvet coat, and a white silk flowered waist-coat, and red silk trousers, and black stockings, and a lace frill, and a wig. One of the boys went as a pirate, three as revelutionests,° one went as a sun flower, and one as Puss in Boots, another as a frog, and one as the White Rabbit in Alice in Wonderland, and a lot of other things. I am 2nd in Latin this week, and 2nd in one of my English forms, and 3rd in Arithmetic, 7th in French and my other English form. We played four matches yesterday and won in them all. I hope Marjorie is quite well now and that everybody likes the house in Shiplake. please° give Avril my love and Guissy as well, and pleas° write to me when you are not too busy and tell me all about the new house.

With lots of love from
Eric Blair.

1. Thersday *written above* Friday, *which has been crossed out.*

23. 'Awake! Young Men of England'

The Henley and South Oxfordshire Standard, 2 October 1914[1]

The following verses were composed and written by Master Eric Blair, the eleven-year-old son of Mr. R. W. Blair, of Rose Lawn, Shiplake:—

> Oh! give me the strength of the lion,
>   The wisdom of Reynard the fox,
> And then I'll hurl troops at the Germans,
>   And give them the hardest of knocks.
>
> Oh! think of the War lord's mailed fist,
>   That is striking at England to-day;
> And think of the lives that our soldiers
>   Are fearlessly throwing away.
>
> Awake! oh you young men of England,
>   For if, when your Country's in need
> You do not enlist by the thousand,
>   You truly are cowards indeed.
>
> Eric Blair

1. See Crick, 85.

24. 'Kitchener'[1]

The Henley and South Oxfordshire Standard, 21 July 1916,

> No stone is set to mark his nation's loss,
> No stately tomb enshrines his noble breast,
> Not e'en the tribute of a wooden cross
>   Can mark this hero's rest.
>
> He needs them not; his name ungarnished stands
> Remindful of the mighty deeds he worked,
> Footprints of one, upon time's changeful sands,
>   Who n'er his duty shirked.
>
> Who follows in his steps no danger shuns,
> Nor stoops to conquer by a shameful deed,
> As honest and unselfish race he runs,
>   From fear and malice freed.
>
> E. A. Blair[1]

1. Earl Kitchener (1850–1916) was drowned when HMS *Hampshire*, which was taking him to visit the Russian war fronts at the invitation of the Tsar, struck a mine. The loss of the 'hero of Khartoum' was regarded as a national tragedy, but he had been a difficult colleague in the administration of the war, and his death proved something of a relief to the government. St Cyprian's shared the national idolatry of Kitchener and its pupils were set a task of commemorating his loss. Eric Blair and Cyril Connolly wrote poems, and in a letter to his

mother dated 16 July, Connolly states, Blair 'did a very good poem, which he sent to his local paper where they took it.'

25. Criticism of Cyril Connolly's Poem "Kitchener"

[c. 10–16 July 1916]   Handwritten

Cyril Connolly asked Orwell (as the school's 'best poet'—the accolade he gave his friend in a letter to his mother) to criticise his poem on Kitchener's death.

Dashed good.[1] Slight repetition. Scansion excellent. Meaning a little ambiguous in places. Epithets for the most part well selected. The whole thing is neat, elegant, and polished.

E. A. Blair.

1. Beside '*Dashed* good,' Connolly wrote: 'My dear Blair!! I am both surprised and shocked.'

26. To his mother

[Mid–July 1916?]   Handwritten

This letter is undated, and there is no indication of the place it was written. The reference to the offer of publication of one of Orwell's two poems suggests either the end of September 1914 or mid-July 1916. It has been proposed that the poem referred to is 'Awake! Young Men of England' (e.g., Crick, 85–86), but the reference to receiving his remaining pocket money at the end of term and to a whole-day holiday and picnic imply July. The reference to Savonarola, though not impossible for an eleven-year-old, is more likely for a thirteen-year-old, also suggesting July of 1916. Though there might have been an outbreak of mumps in 1914, it is known from one of Cyril Connolly's letters that there was mumps at St Cyprian's in 1916. When writing on 16 July 1916, Connolly said that he had not yet got mumps, that he had written his poem on Kitchener 'a few nights ago,' and that he had asked Orwell to criticise it. Connolly also indicated that term was to end in thirteen days' time—eight days after Orwell's 'Kitchener' appeared in print.

Darling Mums,
Thanks for your letter. Today there was a whole holiday, and we took our dinner out to East Dean, and went to have tea at Jevington. The tea was unspeakably horrible, though it did cost 1/6. Thanks most frightfully for the two bob you sent me: it will be especially useful in one way; because you see, when I'm given my money at the end of the term, I shall probably be given a crisp, crackling, and dirty ten-shilling note, so that I can put it and your postal order into a letter and send them straight off to Gamages.[1] Then I'll get the things in about a week, I hope. If I do go and get mumps, which is quite probable, it will muck up things considerably. However, lets° hope I won't. Do you think they'll have these things in stock at Gamages? Because I found

them in the Christmas catalogue. I do hope poor little Roy will live through all right: I've a sort of presentiment that he will. By the way, do you think you could send 2 copies of the paper they've offered to take my poem in? It doesn't matter much if you don't, but still I should like it. It was ripping on the picnic we went [on] today,—I've never drunk water from a bucket drawn straight up from a well before. We did this at a farm where six of us went with a master to buy milk. By the way, I have 3 catterpillars° now, as my partner made over his stock to me. They're called, Savonarola, Paul, and Barnabas. Please give my love to Father and Avril and everyone.

Your loving son
Eric.

1. A large department store in High Holborn, London. Among a wide range of items, it stocked school uniforms and paraphernalia for those at boarding schools, and it had an excellent toy department. Its catalogues were eagerly studied by many schoolboys.

1916–1921

27. 'The Vernon Murders'

[1916–1918?]

In 1960 Avril Dunn (formerly Avril Blair) described how, when her brother 'was about fourteen or fifteen he used to be continually scribbling short stories in notebooks. He never offered to read them to us or made any suggestion that we should read them, but I know that at that time he was actually writing them.'[1] This appears to be one such story. It may be later than 'The Man and the Maid' (which is marked 'Master piece ii') and date from the end of Orwell's time at St Cyprian's rather than Eton. The text is written in a lined petty-cash book about 4 by 6 inches; it covers all thirty-two pages. There are a considerable number of minor errors and idiosyncratic spellings (e.g. 'débonair,' 'into to,' 'granfather,' 'ommitting'). Use of apostrophes is wayward. A few errors are marked with a° (for *sic*), but it should be assumed that errors in this text are to be found in the manuscript.

It was a stiflingly hot evening. Leonard Vernon paced slowly backwards & forwards beneath the great oak-trees that fringed the smooth green lawn in front of the Vernon Manor House. The sky was overcast, & everything was silent in the darkening twilight save for the whispering in the boughs & for Vernons° breath as he pulled at his cigar. But the air was full of evil suggestions, of[2] thoughts of *murder*.

A little explanation is here needed. The Vernon estates were not entailed. There were therefore probably two people to either of whom old Bellingham Vernon, Leonard's grandfather, might leave them. The choice was generally believed to lie between Leonard & his cousin Derek Sudley. The latter he had never liked. There seemed something sinister in his deep-set black eyes, & something catlike in his quick noiseless tread. Yet old Bellingham gave signs of liking him well enough. And lately he had been particularly ingratiating. Then, only lately, while Leonard & his friend Cyril Tipley had been strolling on this very lawn, Mr Crump, the family lawyer, had driven up, & remained for 2 hours closeted with old Bellingham Vernon. A new will, without doubt. And in favour of whom? So Leonard mused on that hot evening, with the thought ever & again occurring to him that suppose Sudley thought it was in his favour, suppose he had designs on old Bellingham x x x Suddenly a figure pushed its way through the bushes; Leonard started sharply, then peered through the darkness at the strange squat figure which seemed to huddle itself against the gnarled trunk of a mighty oak. "Old Mary Denver" he exclaimed in astonishment. "Yes" said the old creature in a strange cracked voice, "Old Mary Denver, the White Witch of Vernon Hamlet, come to bring warning to the heir of the Manor House. There is *murder* in the

25

air." Leonard started, & turned deadly pale. "My grandfather?" he gasped. "Even now." She began, but Vernon was speeding with long strides towards the tall mullioned windows that looked out on the lawn. With a bound he was up the steps, & through the iron-studded oaken door into the hall.

"Grandfather!" he shouted, "Grandfather!" No reply. Evil faces seemed to peer at him from every corner. He fancied he saw something stir beneath the tapestry. Fear clutched at his heart. He tiptoed into the drawing room almost afraid of his own footsteps. Groups of shadows seemed to form themselves into dim, suggestive shapes.

He blundered against a sofa, he put out his hand to support himself, Heavens! What was this? It was a *body*. Suddenly it turned over with a faint groan. He almost screamed in terror, then, to his relief, his grandfather's voice broke on the silence of the room. "My boy," he said, "What are you doing? I was asleep, & you woke me." "It's nothing" said Leonard, "its so dark in here, I —— o look! *What's that?*" Something seemed to flit across the room like a large dark moth, getting out by the window the other end. Bellingham Vernon clasped Leonard's wrist sharply. "The *warning!*" he hissed. "When the head of the family is to die, they are said to see, —— that!" "Let's have a light" said Leonard with a shudder. "Of course that's all nonsense about the warning, you know," he continued more cheerfully as he lit the lamp. "You'll be frightening yourself to death soon." But he could not shake off the sense of foreboding that had pursued him the whole evening.

Chapter II.

Leonard awoke from an unpleasant dream to lie a few moments sleepless in the overpowering heat. Then suddenly every sense was galvanised to wakefulness & terror, by the terrible persuasion that *there was someone else in the room*. He could hear nothing, & it was too dark to see, but he *felt* it. The cold perspiration stood out on his brow. He moved his hand towards the place where he knew the matches lay, then brought it back in terror. Suppose some skinny fingers should grasp his wrist & draw him slowly down, the other hand groping on his throat. Suppose —— but at last he cast off his fears, & with a quick spasm of resolution struck a match; as he lit his candle, he fancied something glided under the bed: he looked beneath; it was not there, but he seemed to see a dark shape hovering just behind him. He turned sharply round, but again it was behind him. So it went on; there was always something intangible & elusive following him with the persistence of a shadow. At last he could stand it no longer. He opened the door, & walked carrying his candle towards his grandfather's room. He wondered if all was well. He knocked at the door, opened it; Old Bellinghams bed was empty! With fear at his heart Leonard ran down the creaking stairs, & rushed from room to room. There was no sign of his grandfather. At last he had searched everywhere but in the cellars. He quailed at the thought, but, — it must be done. Slowly he began his descent down the worn stone steps, & at the second started back with a gasp. His bare foot was in a pool of something warm & wet. He looked down but knew before he looked, — blood! Two steps further down lay old Bellingham, a great claret-coloured stain on his nightshirt, his head lying carelessly against the wall, dead beyond all doubt. Leonard recoiled in horror, then stooped to pick his grandfather up, then saw that he must leave him where he was. He turned round, & walked again up the stairs, ever looking fearfully over his shoulder. Before six o'clock had struck he had telephoned for Cyril Tipley, & for Henry Grant, the famous London detective.

Chapter III.

Morning brought them both. Cyril was, as ever, cheerful & débonair, as he walked into to° the room where Leonard sat at breakfast. "What's up, old chap?" he asked, "why did you telephone in the middle of the night?" "Cyril" said Leonard in a low voice, "my granfather° has been murdered." Cyril started in horror, "What!" he cried, "when did it happen?" "You shall hear about it all when Grant arrives," said Leonard. In ten minutes Grant had come, & Leonard had told his story, ommitting° only his experiences in his bedroom, & merely saying that he had felt uneasy, & had looked about his room for a few minutes before[3] leaving it. "And now," concluded Leonard, "perhaps you would like to see the body." They went down together. "You see, of course" said Grant, "that the body has been moved downwards; that pool of blood is above it. It must have taken a good two[4] minutes to flow, & it couldn't have flowed uphill. That means they moved him down. Now if they[5] were going up they would hardly have had to move him away." "But they might have tripped over him & kicked him into that position coming down, eh?" Put in Cyril. "Well," said Grant reflectively, "it's more likely that he was *pulled* into that position by dragging out the knife. And that more or less certainly means that they stabbed him from downhill, which of course means that they came out of the cellar to do it. On the other hand, with a knife in the wound, that pool would have taken a couple of minutes to accumulate. So that they may have stabbed him from above & gone afterwards down into the cellar. At any rate they came *in* or *out* by the cellar, & possibly both. "Do you know of any opening?" "There is a small barred window," said Leonard, "They could hardly have got through that: its about six inches wide, no more really than a grating where the cellar is a little wider than the room above." "No holes." °None" "Well, let us go down." Their steps rang loudly on the old worn stones of the cellar, but there was no sound of hollowness beneath, though Grant kicked every foot of the place. At last he shook his head, & the three wended their way slowly up the stairs. Arrived at the top, Cyril Tipley took his leave, & Leonard led Grant into the library to talk things over. "Is there anyone" asked the detective, "who might benefit by your Grandfather's death?" "Well" said Leonard, "we don't know whom he was leaving the money to, but he made few friends, the only people at all likely to benefit by his will were myself, my cousin Derek Sudley, & my other cousin, little Molly Stanhope," —— "Who?" cried Grant, "Is miss° Stanhope your cousin?"[6] "Why, yes" gasped Leonard, "What's wrong?" "Haven't you seen the paper?" "No, I never looked at it, I was so distracted," —— Grant silently

27

pulled a paper from his pocket & handed it to Leonard. The first words that caught his eye were "Melancholy tragedy in Berkshire" . . . .he read no more. He let the paper drop from his fingers in horror. "Two places at once!" he said, "Two in one night!"

Chapter IV.

The circumstances of Molly Stanhope's death were similar to those of old Bellingham Vernon's. She had simply been stabbed, this time in the passage outside her room. The window on the landing was wide open, & a rope ladder hung from the window-sill; both doors of the house were locked inside. "A good touch, that" said Grant; "even the newspapers could see all that was a blind. Everyone knows you can lock & unlock doors from either side; he or they probably got down by the rope-ladder. They even overdid the obviousness a little." The two men smoked in silence for a few minutes. "Is there anyone you suspect?" said Grant suddenly. " Well" replied Leonard in a low voice, "I can't help suspecting my cousin Derek Sudley. You see, the chances were fairly even between me & him. But he may have thought that if he polished off everyone in the way the money would descend to the next relative". Grant shook his head. "A clumsy plan" he said, "And why should he have left his principal rival untouched while killing Miss Stanhope?" Some minutes later Grant left the room, & stayed away perhaps ten minutes. "I thought so," he said as he reentered, "You have lost a hogshead of beer." "Eh?" Said Leonard, puzzled. "I didn't like to say anything in front of your friend" continued Grant[7] as he shut the door, "but it was obvious at once how they got in or out of the cellar. They bored a hole down from the bottom of the barrel, — from which the beer was removed, — & connected it up with a[8] well. A good week it must have taken. It was lucky that there happened to be that disused well so near the house. They chose a barrel well at the back, too." "Who is being employed on Molly Stanhope's case?" asked Leonard. "I don't know" said Grant, "but the footmarks won't be the same, though it's almost certainly the same gang. There must be at least two on the job." At 6 o'clock in the evening Cyril Tipley returned, & the three men sat & talked, there being, as Grant pointed out nothing to do until the inquest. When Cyril had gone, Leonard, rather shamefacedly, told Grant of the affair in the drawing-room, & in his bedroom. "Why didn't you tell me this before?" asked Grant, "it may be most important." "I was half ashamed to," said Leonard.

"If I may" said Grant, "I think I'll go & have a look at your bedroom." In a few minutes he returned with a half-satisfied air, but he would tell Leonard nothing.

Chapter V.

The inquest of course adjourned with the usual verdict, though certain small particulars came out, such as the extreme length of the knife used, & the substitution of a home-made handle for its own, together with the removal of the maker's name from the hilt; these last devices were to prevent its owner

28

being traced by means of the maker. However, Grant, who said that knives of that length were seldom made, found out the maker, & the shop to whom most knives of this description were sold. More he could not discover, but the fact of the knife being left beside the body after it had been drawn from the wound was significant, particularly in a careful murder such as this. In Molly Stanhope's case no knife had been found, but a shorter one seemed to have been used.

The day after the inquest Grant came to warn Leonard that an attempt might be made at any moment on his, Leonard's, life. "For" he said, "your grandfather left instructions with his lawyer that the will should not be opened till 1 month after his death. The murderer can hardly have seen it, & he must know that you would be better out of the way." He also advised Leonard to look out particularly for *poison*. "The fellow must see" he said, "that it is no⁹ use dressing these murders up as accidents. He must also see that you would be on the look out for knives."

Accordingly Leonard ceased to use his pipes, his silver & cutlery, even his usual glasses & crockery, while he arranged privately for other food to be brought than what was served by his own kitchen. This last he gave to Grant to have anylised,° but for some days no signs of poison were discovered. One day, However,° Grant came to Leonard, looking rather excited. "I think I've got it," he said, "we never thought of accidental slips which might bring the poison into your blood. I've examined your razors & everything that might have a pin in it, but what about a nail sticking up in your boot?" Leonard changed colour. "Good Heavens!" he said. Together they examined all his boots & shoes, but nothing came to light. "Have we tried everything?" asked Leonard, "no, I remember, pumps of course." But he could find no pumps. "This is a nuisance" he said, "but I've got some old ones. I wonder if they've taken the others to get them ready." A few moments' search rewarded him with an old pair of pumps. "Of course, it's no use" he said, "but I might as well look in these, . . . " his hand was half in when Grant siezed° his arm. Leonard dropped the shoe in astonishment, & Grant picked it up, spread a newspaper, & probed inside it with a pencil, finally shaking it over the paper. Sure enough out dropped a tiny but sharp splinter of flint. With the aid of another pencil Grant managed to transfer it to a pill-box, which he carried gingerly away. "I must hurry," he said. At about 5 o'clock he returned. "I thought so" he said, "this is a powerful alkali which only spreads very slowly; it takes about 36 hours to kill you. Are you doing anything this evening?" "Yes, Sudley & Tipley are both coming. You were going to see if you could get anything out of Derek, & Cyril we thought might assist if there was any trouble." "Ah, yes" said Grant, "I had forgotten. Well, you must give it out that you aren't well. Let your valet actually see you into bed, & just before dinner I will conceal you somewhere in the dining-room. Then you can hear everything."

At the appointed time Leonard stationed himself behind the curtain which covered an alcove in the dining room, & presently the guests arrived. Both asked for Leonard. "He isn't well," said Grant, "he began to feel ill last night just after dinner. He may have started just before, though; he was late, but

29

possibly he only lost something." "Poor old chap" said Cyril, "can't we see him?" "I'm afraid not; the doctor said he was to see no one." The conversation turned to more insignificant topics, but last[10] it came round to the inevitable topic,—the murders. Both guest° agreed that the murders were obviously the work of one man. Sudley suggested that someone had a grudge against the family, but admitted that it was not a likely Solution.

At last Grant dropped a thunderbolt between them. "As a matter of fact" he said casually, "I think I know the man." Both started in surprise. "You can't tell us, of course?" Said Cyril when they had recovered. "I think I can." said Grant. Leonard, crouching amazed behind his curtain heard a spring, two cries of surprise & a scuffle. He burst out, shouting as he did so, "It's no good, Sudley you're" —— the words died away in his mouth. He saw Cyril standing beside an overturned chair, with Sudley & Grant each holding a wrist.[11] "Grant," he cried, "what are you doing?" "Holding onto your grandfather's murderer" said Grant. "But how could it be Cyril?" cried Leonard, "He's no more than a boy!" "Oh is[12] he?" said Grant, & with the° words he plucked at Cyril's head, the close-fitting yellow curls came away in his hand, leaving a smooth & shining bald head.

Chapter VI.

"You see" said Grant to the two others when the police had removed the prisoner, "I recognized your friend immediately. Colonel Begby is his favourite name. I don't know his real one. He fixed on you about a year ago, didn't he?, & he hasn't done altogether so badly out of you. And almost instinctively he was making himself pleasant to your grandfather all the time. Then I suppose he realized that he might be down for something in his will. So, by the easy method of fixing a mirror onto the top part of one of the library windows, — which open diagonally he managed to read off the will, which was made that morning you & he saw Mr. Crump arrive on another mirror, probably in his handkerchief. There being two mirrors put the print right. Possibly rather to his surprise, he saw some thing to this effect; that Miss Stanhope was to receive a portion of the money, Mr Sudley here another, & you the principal quantity. Well, your grandfather knew few people, & had taken a fancy to Tipley. So he put in a clause that if the money left you & your family by your dying childless it was to go to him & his family; I am fairly certain that he intended to fix the guilt on you, Mr Sudley, & make it believed that you had simply killed everyone else under the belief that you would thus receive the money automatically. In this way he would have got the money & none of the suspicion. So that Miss Stanhope's murder was simply to fill in the picture. The picture would have been very convincing if that bit of flint had pricked your foot. One more word; as to the super-natural happenings, you can see that Tipley, or Begby, was an ingenious man from his method of reading the will. Well, any instructive magazine will tell you how to make a spectre appear *in midair* with a contrivance of a magic lantern & various mirrors. Well, a portable form of that was given to one of his mates, — there are three in the gang, one of whom was employed at Miss Stanhope's murder. It was designed simply to keep you in your room while your grandfather was murdered. In this it succeeded. The "warning," which had, as far as I can see, no reason, was accomplished in much the same way."

1. BBC Third Programme; printed in 'My Brother, George Orwell,' *Twentieth Century*, March 1961; reprinted in *Orwell Remembered*, 25–32.
2. of] with. Here, and in similar notes throughout, Orwell's substituted word or wording is given first; what he originally wrote is given after the square bracket.
3. before] without going
4. two] three
5. they] he was
6. cousin] sister
7. Grant] Leon
8. a] the
9. no] too no
10. last] at last
11. Originally, 'Chapter VI' followed here on a separate line.
12. is] isn't

28. 'The Man and the Maid'

[1916–1918?]

It is not possible to date this play precisely. It has in the top left corner of the first page, in Orwell's hand, 'Master piece ii.' There is no means of knowing whether 'The Vernon Murders' is the first 'masterpiece' or whether that is a work now lost, but because the play is 'ii' it here follows the story. From the handwriting, they look to have been written about the same time.

There are two indications that the play was written while Orwell was still at St Cyprian's, or shortly after he left at Christmas 1916. When the principal character, Lucius, after a thirty-year search, discovers the whereabouts of his damsel in distress, it is in Sussex, the county in which St Cyprian's was located. The second clue is the book in which the play is written. Whereas 'The Vernon Murders' is written in a small petty-cash book (a size inconvenient for writing a play), this one is written in a book measuring 8 by 6½ inches of the kind young children use to write out exercises. The lines are half an inch apart. Such a book is far more likely to have been used by Orwell at St Cyprian's than at Eton; or it could have been a book intended for a younger child in his or a neighbour's family. Given the 'magic' characteristics of the story, it was possibly intended as a family Christmas play for 1916.

Two spelling errors, 'agressive' and 'adress,' that Orwell repeated throughout his life are to be found in the text. Act and scene designations, in the style of running heads are sometimes repeated in the manuscript; to avoid confusion, those have not been included here.

Each fold was numbered by Orwell. Number 5 (four pages) is missing. This would have contained the end of I.3 and all II.1; see *n. 10*. Although the end of the play is ruled off and marked 'FINIS,' it comes abruptly. Lucius, having at last discovered the whereabouts of his lost damsel, does not actually meet her.

Act I. Scene I.

Scene. An enchanter's cave, evening, very warm & comfortable. MIRALDO the sorcerer & his son LUCIUS seated before the fire.

———————

Miraldo.   And yet, my dear son, I cannot see what cause there is for thee to be discontented. Art thou not well fed? Clothed? Educated in all the arts of nature?

Lucius.   Nevertheless, father, it is with these very things that I am in disagreement. I feel the desire for adventure & romance.

Mir.   But what could be more romantic than an enchanter's cell? Or more adventurous than our mode of live,° with, (I may say,) the devil on one side & the gallows on the other? What more couldst thou[1] wish?

Luc.   Nay, father, my mind is made up. I can feel God calling me.

Mir.   Heaven forbid, my son! For what is god but nature? And what is the Call of Nature but another name for debauchery? Assuredly thou shalt not go.

Luc.   I wish for no debaucheries, father. I am only anxious to be quit of this island.

Mir.   And that thou shalt not be,[2] my son; rest assured of that. For is not this island a full mile from the shore? And did I not omit to teach thee[3] to swim when I taught thee the secrets of the beasts & plants?

Luc.   Nevertheless I will escape, father.

Mir.   And will some seagull carry thee on its back, or wilt thou float ashore upon a limpet shell?

Luc.   Jest no more, father. Thou wilt not jest when I am gone, & there is noone to grow thy herbs, or keep account of thy customers.

Mir.   I will take my risk of that, son. For the present we will get to work for tomorrow. Hast thou thy book? (Himself produces a large account book.)

Luc.   I have it. Who is first tomorrow?

Mir.   Old Mother Gaffins wishes advice about her cow, whose milk always turns sour in the churn, due, she believes, to witchcraft. Write opposite her name, "one packet of salt for the cow, & advice to wash[4] the churn." Salt is cheap on an island, & advice is cheap anywhere. Nevertheless she shall give me a young sucking-pig for my help.

Luc.   I have written it father; and the next?

Mir.   There is little else of importance. Chiefly love charms. But stay! Here is a matter of more importance. Dick Bunse, the butcher, declares himself insulted by Robin Tripp, the greengrocer. The latter has sworn that until a post-mortem examination on a joint bought of Dick Bunse shall have discovered of what disease the animal died, he will in no wise allow the joint to be buried, though it has been kept these eighteen days, & the neighbours are suffering great distress. A very nice dilemma, indeed! Offend Robin Tripp, & my green food is no more. Offend Dick Bunse, & where is my beef & mutton? Canst see any way out of the difficulty?

Luc. A compromise, father. Thou must say that some magical malady has struck the meat.

Mir. Assuredly. Write "Aspidopterix Sanguineosa" opposite their names.

Luc. It is done.

Mir. Then that is all. We must arise betimes tomorrow, my son. Mother Gaffins will be here before seven.

x   x   x   x   x

LATER. Miraldo is lying asleep upon the hearthrug, & Lucius sitting looking sleepily at the remains of the fire. The moon shines in obliquely, so that it illuminates the other side of the cave. Presently Lucius rises, takes a mandolin[5] from the wall & walks over to the patch of light.

Song.

Come up, Come up, ye kindly waves,
And wash the cold sea sand.
Come kiss the shore that I live on
For ye are come from land.

Oh happy waves that ride so free
And know nor rein nor fear!
While I must stay & watch ye[6] break,
For the strong Fates hold me here.

Oh send me help from out your deeps,
And I will weep no more.
For fish-tailed maid or wingèd horse
Would bear me safe to shore.

Oh look on me again, hard Fates,
And stay my father's hand:
And the gay sea that tumbles here
Shall bear me yet to land.

Scene II.

Seven o'clock. *Miraldo* in full sorcerer's dress, high headgear, long black gown covered with signs, etc; various opaque bottles of curious shape are on the table. *Lucius* is very much in the background, & evidently something in the nature of a servant. They are awaiting their visitors.

Lucius. Mother Gaffins is a long while a coming.

Miraldo. I doubt not she is a trifle rheumatic. Perchance I might sell her a cure for it.

Lucius. Nay, she is a thrifty old woman. She knows it is but for a few years.

[Enter ROBIN TRIPP and DICK BUNSE, the former a little thin agressive[7] looking man, & the latter solid & rather stupid.]

Dick Bunse. Good morrow, Master Miraldo. Thou knowest our business with thee ——

[Enter *Mother Gaffins*, a pugnacious old woman. She throws unfriendly
glances at both the other clients.]

Miraldo.   I fear, Master Bunse, that this good woman hath the seven o'clock
appointment. Nevertheless do not depart. I doubt not Mother Gaffins
will not mind if thou stay. And now, good mother, what of thy cow?
Doth he° show signs of internal maladies?

Mother Gaffins.   Nay, but his milk turns sour when I put it into the churn.

Mir.   Good mother, I fear thy cow is bewitched. I will hie to my crystal.
(Bends over the crystal.) I seem to see an old woman sitting & gnashing
her teeth. She is infirm & ugly. (Mother Gaffins starts angrily.) What is it
she is thinking? Ah! She is jealous of thy beauty.

M.G. (surprised & pleased.)   That same misfortune hath[8] ever pursued me.

Mir. (seeming not to hear.)   She is moving her hands in curious wise. Ha!
She is casting a spell! Mother Gaffins, some woman hath[9] bewitched thy
cow. But no matter; bake this packet, & give it to him; he will devour it
readily. Then take thy churn, & wash it nine times with boiling water,
reciting the while "Discedite o diaboli," & do this same on the first of
every month, & thou shalt find it keep perpetually sweet.

M.G. (impressed.)   I will do it, o most unsurpassable of sorcerers. And
what is thy charge?

Mir.   A fat sucking pig is all I ask, good mother.

M.G.   Thou shalt have it, good Master Miraldo. (Exit.)

[Dick Bunse & Bob Tripp come forward, somewhat overawed by this
exhibition. The latter drags forth a large & dirty sack, from which the
other three draw back.]

Bob Tripp.   The meat, Master Miraldo, that yon lying knave sold me. See if
one sniff is not enough to convince thee of its condition.

D.B.   And is not all meat subject to time? Wilt not thou, Bob Tripp, be
putrid eighteen days after I have killed thee for a lying hound?

B.T.   If I am dead in eighteen days, friend Bunse, I shall have been hanged
for thy murder.

Mir.   Nay, friends, what avail these quarrels? Justice shall be done. Lay the
meat upon the table, Master Tripp.

[Bob Tripp does so.]

Mir.   Now cut a piece from it, Master Bunse: *thy* hand is skilled in such
tasks. [Dick Bunse cuts off a piece callously, & Miraldo, taking it in a pair
of forceps, drops it into a bowl.] Behold, neighbours; I now pour upon it
water collected from the seven mouths of the Nile, & add to it mud
collected from the lip of Etna. [He stares profoundly into the bowl.]
Yea, it is true; some malady has attacked the meat.

B.T.   What did I tell thee, Good Bunse?

Mir.   But this is no fault of the butcher. The meat hath been bitten by the
venomous & dreaded fly Aspidopterix Sanguineosa.

B.T. (still suspicious.)   I have not observed any such fly in my house, master
sorcerer.

Mir.   Nay, for it enters no houses. It lives nestling on the wing of the owl, &

drinks the dew that forms on the dog fennel. It must have bitten thy meat while the boy conveyed it to thy house.

B.T. Dick Bunse, I have done thee grievous injustice.

D.B. Nay, but I was unneighbourly not to give thee new meat. Master sorcerer, I thank thee, from this day hence I will put gauze upon my meat. And what is thy charge?

Mir. Perhaps a little lambkin, friend Dick; & from thee, friend Tripp, perhaps a sack of new peas?

Both. Assuredly thou shalt have it.

D.B. And now to shore, Bob Tripp, to drink upon our reconciliation. And we will bury the meat before all the neighbours. (Exeunt.)

Scene III.

In front of a public house on shore. Enter Dick Bunse & Bob Tripp, the latter carrying the bag, on the best of terms.

D.B. Well, brother Bob, assuredly we shall find no better liquor than at the Blue Boar here.

B.T. That we will not. But first let me put down this carrion. [Drops the bag. They go in.]

Enter a beggar, very ragged & filthy, with a stick.

The Beggar. Now what's in yon bag? Assuredly it hath an appetising smell! I will inspect the bag.

[Lucius comes out of the bag, & stands up.]

Ah, a conjuror, art thou? Hast a small audience then. What is thy name, that walkest out of bags?

Luc. Friend beggar, I escaped from my father in that bag.

Beggar. Escaped from thy father? That is strange. Why, my father threw me out of the house.

Luc. Those in there think there is meat in that bag, but I threw it all into the sea.

Beggar. Then they will make meat of thee, my friend, if thou dost not depart.

[Dick Bunse & Bob Tripp are heard shouting within.]

[The rest of Scene III and Act II, Scene I are missing.[10]]

Act II. Scene II.

About 2 o'clock. *Peter & Lucius* are standing undecidedly before a little thatched cottage, standing on grassy downland. A castle shows somewhere in the distance. About a month later than Scene I.

Luc. But this is ill weather for walking on these slopes, Peter. It is past two now, & we have no sign of dinner.

Pet. This is a bad country for beggars, my freind.[11] Nevertheless we can but try this shepherd's cottage.

Luc.   Assuredly; for may they not have heard of my damsel in distress?

Pet.   That same damsel will be thy undoing, Lucius. Have we not been turned out of two inns already because of thy questions? Hast thou not been attested mad by thirteen different sheriffs? Have I not assured thee a thousand times that there is no such damsel?

Luc.   I know it; never the less I must ask, wherever I go [Knocks loudly on the door.]

Pet.   Put on thy most doleful expression, Lucius. These country people are thrifty.

[An old man suddenly appears at the door, holding a decrepit longbow in his left[12] hand, & a half feathered arrow in his right.[13]]

The Old Man.   How now, sirs? Are ye robbers? Speak, ere I pierce one of you with my arrow!

Pet.   Put down thy bow, old man, or thou'lt break the string. 'Twere pity to break such an antique relic; I'll warrant thy grandfather shot with that bow.

The Old Man.   Ay, & his grandson is not afraid to shoot with it either. Never the less I would not kill an innocent man. Who are ye, sirs?

Luc.   Two honest men who stopped at thy door to make a simple request.

[The Old Man's wife, an ugly old creature, suddenly thrusts her head out of the window above.]

Wife.   Now, Abel, send them about their business, or they will be stealing thy sheep like the last thieves who came here for alms.

Pet.   We steal no sheep, good mother; we wish but a cup of cold water on this hot day.

Wife.   (Calmer).   Water is it thou wantest? Ay, thou shalt have water, poor man. Assuredly thou needest it. Behold, here is thy water.

[A pailful of filthy water crashes to the ground, narrowly missing *Peter's* head.]

Peter. (moving away.)   Old man, thy wife loves me not. We had best be gone.

Abel.   Then go to the castle yonder. They will give thee food.

Luc.   I thank thee. And, Abel; hast heard aught of a maiden in distress upon a desert island hereabouts?

Abel.   Nay, that I have not.

Luc.   No matter; then we must go[14] the castle.

Pet.   Ay, assuredly they'll give us food there.

Scene III.

[About 3 months later, early evening. *Lucius & Peter* have evidently just been rebuffed at another cottage, this one of a much more prosperous aspect. A child sits on the doorstep sucking its thumb at them.]

Lucius. (shouting up.)   Mistress Burnett, Mistress Burnett!

[Mistress Burnett, a pretty widow of thirty, puts her head out of the window.]

M.B. Not gone yet, thou idle vagabond? Have I not told you both that I give no food to tramps & beggars?

Luc. Nay, this is no demand; only a civil question.

M.B. Ask on, then: I will answer questions.

Luc. Hast heard, then, of aught in the way of a maiden left on a desert island hereabouts?

M.B. Maiden on a desert island! The man talks fairy tales!

Luc. Not a passing fair maiden, imprisoned by a jealous fairy?

M.B. There is none about here of that sort, unless I might suit thy requirements myself; for I live alone, though[15] not on an island; & then I have a jealous sister in law, though I am a widow & not a maid.

Pet. And passing fair, Mistress Burnett, remember that.

M.B. Peace, thou saucy man. Thinkest thou I will have every beggar in the neighbourhood a making love to me?

Pet. I see thou art accustomed to it. And small wonder; for all lovers are beggars in a manner of speaking.

M.B. Peace, thou! A fine position hast thou to make love to a respectable widow woman with a house of her own.

Pet. Thou art right, Mistress Burnett; lovers never prosper. Lucius here had to run from home because he loved freedom, & is a beggar because he loves a maiden who never existed. My father turned me out of the house because I loved idleness, & now thou wilt drive me away for loving thee.

M.B. Art a philosophic pauper, I perceive.

Pet. 'Twere more civil to say an impoverished philosopher, Mistress Burnett.

M.B. I think thou shalt have a little food after all, thou beggar. (Disappears from window.)

Luc. Peter, there is no beggar to equal thee. Thou couldst get water out of a rock.

Pet. Nay, I hope to get something better than water out of this rock; & a very stony heart she surely has.

[*Mistress Burnett* reappears at the front door with a small table & two chairs, which she sets down between *Lucius* & *Peter*.]

M.B. Sit yourselves down, hungry men.

[*Lucius* & *Peter* sit down a little diffidently. *Mistress Burnett* disappears into the house.]

Luc. Peter, somehow I like not to be fed by a woman.

[*Mistress Burnett* comes from the house with a large round of beef, & several loaves of bread, & dragging a heavy leather bottle.

[*Peter* & *Lucius* lose their shamefacedness at once.]

M.B. Now, good beggar, see if thou canst eat as well as thou canst philosophise.

Pet. Ay, assuredly I can eat. 'Tis but one of my accomplishments.

M.B. And what canst thou do besides talk & eat, good man?

Pet. (with his mouth full.) Why, I can sing a song, & play a flute in some fashion, wire rabbits, dig roots, keep chickens, & pick a pretty woman.

M.B. Nay, now; I did not ask if thou couldst be impudent as well.

37

Pet. Surely it were not impudence to call thee pretty?

M.B. Why, thou wilt be calling me by my Christian name next!

Pet. Ay, that I will; what is thy Christian name?

M.B. Nay, bold man; thou must earn that. We will try over thy accomplishments. I have seen thee talk & eat. Now sing me a song.

Pet. (draining his cup.) Ay, & gladly; Lucius, put off that long face; thou'lt crack my voice.

Song.

Three beggars begged by noon & night,
They begged to left & they begged to right,
But nought had got for their trouble:
So two sat them down & wept full sore,
But the third one said they should weep no more
And vowed they should yet feed double.

They parted ways at the rise of sun,[16]
And swore to meet when the day was done,
And each should tell his findings.
So one went east, & one went west,
But the third went on, for he thought it best,
And followed the path way's windings.

They met on the road as the sun went down,
Back from the field & back from the town,
And two came slow & sadly.
But the third was filled with wine & meat,
His face was calm, & his voice was sweet,
And he tripped his way right gladly.

'O what hast thou?' said the last to the first,
'Alack' said he, 'my fate was the worst,
'Twas naught but blows & kicking.
A few little scraps of cold pork fat,
And a handful of bones I stole from a cat
Were all I had for my picking.'

'Alas' said the second, 'the same had I;
Nor bread nor meat, nor pudding nor pie,
No food what e'er I did — o.'
'But I' said the third, 'sat me down to dine,
And I have had meat, & I have had wine,
For I went to the house of the widow.'

M.B. Enough, man. Thy impudence passes belief.

Pet. O, Mistress, 'twere pity to interrupt. There were forty seven more verses to come. Nevertheless, is it not a good song?

M.B. Nay, 'tis a foolish song.

Pet. Yet has it not earned me thy Christian name? Assuredly it must be a most delightful Christian name?

M.B. Since thou art so persistent, know bold man, that they call me Polly.

Pet. Then, o most enchanting Polly, will I speak what is in my mind. Wilt thou marry me, o Polly?

Pol. I marry thee, thou beggar from the road! I, a respectable widow, marry thee!

Pet. Nay, Polly, call me not 'beggar' so readily. Have I not told thee of my accomplishments?

Pol. Accomplishments, forsooth! Tricks of any tramp or vagabond.

Pet. Nevertheless, wilt thou not give me a trial?

Pol. Have I not tried thee, foolish man? Have I not listened to thy impudent song?

Pet. Yea, but I can do other things. I can play the flute, wire rabbits, dig roots, keep chickens —

Pol. Yea, I know it. Think'st thou then that I wish to hear thee piping, or see thee digging up my most precious herbs, or find myself° in gaol for poaching?

Pet. Then thou canst but try my chicken keeping. My father kept chickens, & they in some degree kept him. Wilt thou not ask me a question?

Pol. Yea, if it please thee. Answer then these three questions: First, if ten hens eat ten handfuls of corn, how many does one hen eat?

Pet. Why, ten, or for that matter, ten thousand.

Pol. Right; thou hast passed the first test. And the second: in a brood of thirteen chicks, how shall I tell the cocks from the hens?

Pet. That is simpler still; let thy cat into their coop for five minutes, & those alive at the end will be cocks.

Pol. Right again; this shall be a harder one. If one of my hens is eating eggs, & I must needs kill it, how shall I know which it is?

Pet. Oh Polly, thy questions are but fit for children; need I say that it will be thy best layer?

Pol. Man, thou art a chicken-farmer! Thou, knowest the trade from end to end.

Pet. Then, dear Polly, I doubt not thou wilt marry me. [Takes her hand.]

Pol. And why should I marry thee, bold man? [Pretends to try to retreive° hand.]

Pet. Nay, Polly, thou must. Thou canst not escape me now.

Pol. What can I say to the man? He will not listen to what I say. Have I not told thee, 'no'?

Pet. Nay, Polly, that is not thy answer.

Pol. Then I must marry thee,[17] since thou wilt take no refusal.

Luc. (starting up.) Peter, wilt thou desert the friend thou wast to have followed across the world? Mistress Burnett, wilt thou marry a beggar from the road, who has deceived thee by his jests?

Pet. Nay, Lucius, every beggar ceases to beg when he finds a home; thou wouldst have deserted me for thy damsel, shall I not desert thee for my widow?

Luc. Ay, thou art right; so I must go on alone. Mistress Burnett one

question; art thou sure thou hast not heard aught of a maiden upon a
desert island?

Pol. Ay, sure enough; have I not told thee so once? Thou must look further
a field, but any time thou art passing thou wilt be welcome here.

Luc. Nay, I shall not come this way again.

Act III.   Scene I.

[About 15 years later. *Lucius* is sitting, a good deal travel-worn, on a rock
upon a lonely & desolate beach. A little boat with a lug-sail lies dragged up on
the sand.]

Lucius. What magic land is this? No human hand has touched these red
rocks or that green sea. Methinks this should be Africa, seeing that I
came south from Spain. Ah, that boat! How glad I am to be on dry land
again, even if my skin should turn black, as travellers' do in Africa.
Nevertheless, I doubt I shall not find my lady in this land of celapods &
negroes. I must cross it quickly & begone. [Enter from the land side an
elderly man in skins, with a long beard. *Lucius* starts up on hearing him.]

Lucius. His skin is not black! Who art thou, stranger? [The other is silent.]
He answers not; how shall I adress[18] him? Latin? Surely all foreign
peoples understand Latin. [Scratches his head, trying to remember a
little Latin.] Ah, I have it. Discedite o diaboli!

The Old Man. Young man, thou art not over civil.

Luc. English! Dost speak English, stranger? And why is thy skin not black?

O.M. [Producing some tablets, & preparing to take a note.] Ha! A new
school of philosophy. Didst thou say, young man, that it was an
attribute of righteousness to be black?

Luc. I said naught of righteousness, nor am I a young man: indeed I am close
on thirty three.

O.M. When thou hast reached my age, boy, thou wilt count thirty three as
childhood. And as to the other part of thy reply, do not all men seek after
righteousness?

Luc. Ay, assuredly.

O.M. Then, young man, if thou didst count blackness righteousness, &
wert surprised that I was not black, how is it that thou art not thyself
black?

Luc. [Looking at his own sunburnt hand.]   And have I not approached it
somewhat, o stranger?

O.M. [Becoming deferential.]   Then it is a gradual process, o most learned
young man?

Luc. Ay, true perfection is but slowly attained.

O.M. Wilt thou permit me, o youth, to present thee to my nine hundred &
ninety eight brethren?

Luc. Thine was a large family, friend! But who are these brethren of thine?

O.M. Young man, we are the school of Purely Primitive Philosophers. We live here a simple life on roots & herbs, & enquire into the mysteries of life & the causes of true righteousness.

Luc.   Then, stranger, I will readily come with thee & enquire into the mysteries of thy roots & herbs. For I have eaten nought but fish for ten days.

O.M.   Follow, then, o friend.   [Exeunt.]

———————

Scene II.

[The assembling place of the Purely Primitive Philosophers. *Lucius* is seated & is about to be fed by his friend & the Chief Philosopher. Vast trees throw their shade all round.]

Lucius [remembering something.]   Stay! I must not touch food yet; 'tis an oath I took long ago. (Shouting.) All ye around! Has any here heard at any time aught of a maiden left upon a desert island by a jealous sorceress?

Chief Philosopher.   Ha! Is this another part of thy philosophy, o learned stranger?

Luc.   Ay, that is my philosophy: a romantic quest to spent° my life on. Has no such thought occurred to thee, good philosopher?

C.P.   Nay, but I will make a note of it.

[Meanwhile another Philosopher has made his way to the front.]

Luc.   What! hast thou heard aught of my damsel?

Philosopher.   That, o young man, I cannot say.

Luc.   Then why didst thou seek me out?

Ph.   Because, o youth, I have heard some talk of a maiden upon an island. But whether she be thine or no I cannot say.

Luc.   Plague on thee! Talk faster. How long hath she been there?

P.L.   It may be twenty years or thereabouts.

Luc. [Beginning to buckle his belt.]   It fits!

C.P.   Young man, dost thou not consider it possible that thy damsel may have lost her charms in twenty years?

Luc.   And thou a philosopher! O sordid soul! [To the other.] And have all the noblest knights in Christendom given their lives to rescue her?

Ph.   I would not say all; still there have been several. But they have all come away of a sudden as though struck by magic. Young man, attempt not this mad adventure, for this is a strange land, full of cannibals who file their dog teeth, & pygmies who blow poisoned darts from long pipes. Assuredly thou wilt perish.

Luc.   A fig for thy savages! Give me a sword, Master Philosopher, & I am gone.

C.P.   What avails thee a sword, young man, against the will of God? If thou must perish, perish thou wilt. The true philosopher takes no weapons & fears not death. We here have seen no weapon since we came, & we fear nought. Oh Death, where is thy sting? —

Luc.   There is a wasp upon thy neck!

C.P. [Jumping in terror & slapping his neck.] What! Off, damned insect!
Luc. That wasp is non-existent, o philosopher; an abstract wasp. In fact, I might say "O wasp, where is thy sting?" I think that were the act of a true philosopher. But so much for thy creed; I'll be gone now. Since thou hast not a sword to give me, I'll make me a bow upon my way, & feather my arrows where the kestrel has killed a sparrow. So fares the true knight. Fare[19] well, good philosophers.

Act III. Scene III.

[About 6.a.m. next morning. *Lucius* has found the place where the water is narrowest round the maiden's island. The gap is only about 12 feet wide, & looks as if it might well be waded. The maiden's cave stands exactly opposite.]

Luc. Awake, o most beauteous maiden, & behold thy deliverer!
[The maiden, a fat passé woman of forty, comes from the cave.]
Lucius. [alarmed.] Good morrow, fair damsel.
Maiden. Good morrow, o most noble knight. Hast come to deliver me from the dragons that ingirt me round?
Luc. [relieved at having something definite to do.] Ay, surely. On ye dragons! Come forth to your death! (Silence.)
M. I will call one forth for thee. [She gives a curious whistle, & a harmless looking water-lizard waddles out of the river to Lucius' feet. He promptly kills it with an arrow.] Well done! o noble knight. Now am I free to come to land, & thou canst marry me as reward.
Luc. Nay, fair maiden, I am married. I came only to deliver thee from bondage. But 'twas nought; he is scarce four feet long.
M. [Suddenly bursting into tears.] And so it is fruitless again! Twenty long years have I been upon this island in hopes that some noble knight would carry me off & marry me. And I have kept seven lizards as my dragons, & they knew me & fed from my hand. And then six men came as thou didst to deliver me, & each time I saw one of the creatures that came to my call slain, & each time his slayer declared himself married & departed.
Luc O maiden, thou & I have been fools, it seems. Thou hast waited on this island for thy knight, & I have roamed the world seeking my maiden because of a message in a bottle —
M. Message? I sent no messages in bottles.
Luc. Thou didst not! Then my maiden lives! I knew it. Go thou home to thy relations, o damsel, & I must on again to seek my true lady. [Exit.]

Act IV. Scene I.

[In England again, about fifteen years later, *Lucius*, a vigorous old man of nearly fifty, is sitting before a public house talking to a yokel.]

Lucius. Well, good yokel, this is not a bad country of thine.
Yokel. Nay, I never heard any complaint of it.

Luc. A not insufficient eulogy, good yokel.

Y. I am no scholar, good master; I cannot understand thy long words.

Luc. No matter, friend; thou'lt hear no harm of thyself.

Y. Nay, I never heard any complaint, good master.

Luc. (Looking at him reflectively.) Dost believe in magic, good fellow?

Y. Ay, surely.

Luc. Then hast heard aught of a maiden upon a desert island hereabouts?

Y. Nay, that is out of date.

Luc. Thou liest, but no matter. Thou hast islands round this coast; dost ever visit any?

Y. Nay, I cannot. There are but two islands here, & one is haunted, & the other hath some kind of religious person who lives[20] on it.

Luc. Haunted, thou sayest? And by whom?

Y. Why, 'tis by the ghosts of a sorcerer & his son.

Luc. (Springing up in excitement.) A sorcerer man? His name?

Y. Why his name was Miraldo. He was hung for a murdering his son when I was a little boy.

Luc. (Curbing himself.) Murdered his son, sayest thou? How did he it?

Y. Why, we know not. His son disappeared, it might be thirty years since. And so they hanged him.

Luc. The like fate to all sorcerers, good yokel. So this county is Sussex?

Y. Ay, didst not know that?

Luc. I have been here long since; yet I thought I knew the country. But no matter; why canst thou not visit the other island, didst thou say?

Y. Why, I told thee; 'tis because of the lady who lives thereon.

Luc. (Springing up again.) A lady! I thought thou saidst a religious person!

Y. Ay, I think she be religious; at least she hath lived there as long as I remember.

Luc.[21] Where is her island, good yokel?

Y. Why, 'tis perhaps ten miles east of the sorcerer's island.

Luc. That next island, on which I looked each morning! Assuredly I have found my real maiden this time!

Y. Thy pardon, master; thou speakest thy long words again; at least I cannot understand thee.

Luc. No matter; dost know of a boat that will carry me to the island?

Y. Ay, thou'lt find one in the harbour.

Luc. Is it a good quick boat, fellow?

Y. Ay, I never heard any complaint of it. [Exit Lucius.]

FINIS.

1. thou] you
2. be] do
3. thee] me
4. wash] watch
5. mandolin] banjo
6. ye] *started as* you
7. Orwell spelt 'aggressive' with one g throughout his life. See *Nineteen Eighty-Four*, Facsimile Edition, 180 verso, line 11; see also *CW*, IX, 185, line 22.
8. hath] is; *then* has
9. hath] has

10. Fold 5, four pages, is lost. The story requires Lucius to seek a damsel in distress on an island; his quest is initiated by a message found in a bottle; see III.3. II.1 presumably included the finding of this bottle with its message.
11. The animals in *Animal Farm* also reverse the i and e of friend; see *CW*, VIII, 16.

12. left] right
13. right] right; *then* left
14. to *omitted*

15. though] but
16. sun] son
17. thee] me

18. Orwell spelt 'address' with one d throughout much of his life.
19. Fare] Fare thee; thee *crossed out*
20. lives] liveth

21. *Luc.*] *Y. crossed out*

29. Three Stories in *The Election Times*, June 1918

Orwell left St Cyprian's Preparatory School in December 1916. He then spent one term at Wellington, but in March 1917 he learned he had belatedly been admitted to Eton as a King's Scholar in the Election (the scholarship winners) of 1916. Not quite fourteen, he entered Eton in May 1917; he left in December 1921, at eighteen and a half.[1]

Orwell participated in the production of at least three publications at Eton: *The Election Times*, *College Days* (see 37) and *Bubble and Squeak* (see 47, n. 1). *The Election Times* was 'a handwritten set of pages to be lent for reading at a cost of one penny' (Crick, 112); at sixpence according to Denys King-Farlow.[2] Five issues were produced by members of the 1916 Election. Only one, Number 4, 3 June 1918, seems to have survived entire, though contributions to it, possibly in enlarged form, or to one or more other issues, many probably by Orwell, are extant. The editor was Roger Mynors (1903–1989; Kt. 1963), later Professor of Latin at the universities of Cambridge, 1944–53, and Oxford, 1953–70; Denys King-Farlow was the art editor, and Orwell the business manager.

Contributions to Number 4, were anonymous, and the precise makeup of the issue is unclear. Attributions of authorship are complicated because those who produced the journal sometimes wrote out each other's contributions. Nine items seem certainly to have made up this issue, at least as first conceived: the Editorial (Mynors), 'The She Devil' (Steven Runciman; see 56, *n. 2*), Correspondence (Mynors), 'The Bully of the Fifth' (King-Farlow), 'The Adventure of the Lost Meat-card' (Orwell), from 'A Peep into the Future' (probably Orwell), 'Extracts from the Diaries of Famous Persons' (Bobbie Longden[3]), 'The Slack-bob' (Orwell), and 'The New Night Watches' (either Mynors or Brent Grotrian, more probably the former). Five other items, all of which can be attributed to Orwell with some certainty, may have formed part of this issue, or may have been intended for another issue; all were eventually printed in *College Days*, Number 5. These are: 'Free Will,' 'The Wounded Cricketer,' 'The Photographer,' some or all of 'The Millionaire's Pearl,' and two stanzas of 'The Youthful Mariner.' The last might have been no more than a trial on a spare side of a page intended for a later issue of *The Election Times*.

To endeavour to ascertain authorship, Denys King-Farlow, Cyril Connolly, Sir Steven Runciman, Sir Roger Mynors, and Jacintha Buddicom were consulted. The handwriting of all contributions was examined.

'The Slack-bob,' which follows, is in the form it was later printed in *College Days*, Number 5, with notes giving the earlier readings.

King-Farlow attributed the extract from 'A Peep into the Future,' in Orwell's hand, to Freddie Burgess and George Wansbrough (later Director of the Bank of England); Connolly and Runciman attributed it to Orwell. One or two clues do point to him. Towards the end of the story, the 'mighty woman' sticks out her chin 'agressively,' Orwell's usual spelling of this word—though if he had merely copied it, he could have rendered incorrectly what was correct in the original. More revealing is Piggy Hill's first name, Pigling, a name almost certainly derived from Beatrix Potter's story *Pigling Bland*. Although anyone else connected with *The Election Times* could have read this story, or known its title, it had a peculiarly close association for Orwell and was coupled with H. G. Wells's *Modern Utopia* by Jacintha Buddicom. In *Eric and Us* she recalls: "We had in our house a copy of Wells' *Modern Utopia*. . . . Eric . . . said he might write that kind of book himself. Broadly *Nineteen Eighty-Four* is classifiable as 'that kind of book.' And the genealogical tree of *Animal Farm* has its roots in *Pigling Bland*, by Beatrix Potter. *Pigling Bland* was Guiny's book: Eric and I were far too old for it, but we adored it all the same. I remember his reading it to me twice over from beginning to end, to cheer me up one time when I had a cold. And we used to call each other Pigling Bland and Pigwig in moments of frivolity" (39). She had in mind here only connections with Orwell's last two novels, but there seems to be an association with 'A Peep into the Future' too.

There are two last, tenuous, pointers to Orwell's authorship. 'The Adventure of the Lost Meat-card' and 'A Peep into the Future' both conclude with 'The End.' Orwell regularly concluded his novels this way, so far as one can gather through the veil of print, and did so on the typescripts of *Animal Farm* and *Nineteen Eighty-Four*. He had strong feelings about finishing a story. 'I hate a novel,' he wrote to Leonard Moore in 1934 (see *192*), in response to Eugene Saxton's proposal that the conclusion of *Burmese Days* be cut, 'in which the principal characters are not disposed of at the end'; see *CW*, II, 322, final note. And later he was to argue for spelling 'onto' as one word in certain circumstances; see General Introduction, *CW*, I, xxi.

The glossary of Eton terminology in *Eton Microcosm*, edited by Anthony Cheeth and Derek Parfit (1964), 195–97, has been drawn on in preparing explanatory notes, and the assistance of Jonathan Ray is also acknowledged.

1. For Orwell's time at Eton, see Crick, 100–38. Wellington, Orwell told Jacintha Buddicom, was 'beastly,' but at Eton he said he was 'interested and happy' (*Eric and Us*, 58). Jacintha Laura Buddicom (1901–1993) was the eldest child of Laura and Robert Buddicom. Her father had been curator of Plymouth Museum, but had moved to Shiplake-on-Thames to take up market gardening. Jacintha, Prosper (1904–1968), and Guinever ('Guiny'; 1907–) were Orwell's childhood companions when he was at home. Her vivid memoir, *Eric and Us* (1974), tells how they first met in the summer of 1914 and how 'Eric, often accompanied by [his sister] Avril, played in our garden practically every day' (15).
2. Denys King-Farlow (1903–1982) was a Colleger in the same Election as Orwell at Eton. They produced *The Election Times* and co-edited *College Days*, Numbers 4 and 5. He won scholarships to Cambridge and Princeton, and then worked for Royal Dutch Shell in Canada, the United States, and Europe. He and Orwell renewed their acquaintance in 1936. For his reminiscences of Orwell, see *Orwell Remembered*, 54–60.
3. Robert P. ('Bobbie') Longden was to become headmaster of Wellington, where, according to Orwell, he greatly liberalised the school's regime. He was killed in 1940, the single fatal casualty when a German bomber released its load on the way home from a raid over England; see David Pryce-Jones, *Cyril Connolly: Journal and Memoir* (1983), 78.

30. 'The Slack-bob'

The Election Times, No.4, 3 June 1918

There was once a boy who was a Slack-bob.[1] He used to walk about and say to his friends, "What fools you are to go worrying about[2] rowing and playing cricket! Look at me." And they used to look at him[3] and go on their way. Then he went to the other Slack-bobs and said to them, "We are the only sensible people, aren't we?" But they used to pretend that they were not Slack-bobs, so they laughed and went on their way. So then he decided that he was the only sensible boy in the School. But that year he went to Lord's,[4] being unable to avoid it, and there his mother introduced him to his cousins. He had never seen them before, and they were all big, fat, noisy girls with red hair, seven in number. "Why aren't you in the Eleven?" asked Agatha, who was the eldest. "I expect he's in the Second Eleven," said Tabitha, the next. "Are you?" said the third, who was called Grace (she turned her toes in and squinted). "Er, no. I'm afraid I'm not very fond of cricket," said the boy. "Perhaps he's a Wet-bob," squeaked Beryl, the fourth. "Yes," said the boy, glad of the chance, "I'm a Wet-bob." "I don't like rowing," said Mary, the youngest, who was considered the family beauty. "You're in the Eight, of course?" said all the other six together, "No, not quite," said he, "but," he went on desperately, "I'm not far off it; I've got my Lower Boats, and I'll get my Upper Boats[5] next 1st of March." "That's not bad," said Eliza, the fifth sister. "I bet I'd be in the Eight if I was a boy," said Maudie, the sixth.

By the end of the day he had told them that he was going to win Junior Sculling, and probably be in the Eight next year. But this made them so fond of him that he wished he had told them the truth. At last, however, he escaped, and thought that all was well.[6]

A few weeks afterwards a postcard came saying, "We are all coming to watch you. I hope you win," and signed by Agatha. "What's happening today?" he asked a friend. "Junior Sculling," said the friend. The boy turned pale, but he went and met them. "If you win I'm going to give you a nice kiss," said Grace. "We all will," said Agatha. "I'm sorry, I can't row," said he, "I've hurt my arm." "Never mind," said Tabitha. "I'm not allowed to, though," said he. "Don't mind that," said Grace. "But I can't," said he. "Coward!" said Mary. "You're letting us all down," said Eliza. "Never mind," said Agatha, "we'll all come and have tea in your room now, and next year we'll come and watch you in the Procession of Boats."

Moral: Honesty is the best policy.

1. Wet-bob was a rower; dry bob, a cricketer; slack bob, someone too lazy to engage in either sport.
2. In *The Election Times*, the story originally began in the first person: 'I used to be a slack bob° once. I used to walk about and say to my friends "what° fools you are to go round worrying about . . ." '
3. *The Election Times* had 'me' for 'him.' Thereafter the third person was used.
4. Lord's Cricket Ground, St John's Wood, London, is named after its originator, Thomas Lord (though not on the present site). It is the headquarters of English cricket and the setting for the annual Eton versus Harrow cricket match.

5. Upper Boats is a rowing colour, as is Lower Boats (Glossary, *Eton Microcosm*, 197).
6. *The Election Times* originally ran on here: '. . . all was well. But a few . . .'; it was marked to be set as here.

31. 'The Adventure of the Lost Meat-card'

The Election Times, No. 4, 3 June 1918

Next morning I awoke early, to find Holmes shaking me by the shoulder; "I am sorry to wake you up at this hour, Watson," he remarked, "but we have got to continue with this case." I sprang out of bed, and in half an hour I had had breakfast, and was prepared to start. "Today I shall visit the inn in my usual capacity" said Holmes, "Lestrade will arrive at about eleven". In spite of the fact that he had been considering the case all night, Holmes was as active as ever. As he crept round the room, sometimes on all fours, and sometimes standing on his head, he looked like some terrible, remorseless machine for tracking down criminals. As he moved[1] about the floor he occasionally gave vent to small ejaculations of triumph or annoyance. He also took a careful survey of the[2] whole room with his lense:° he took a handful of cigarette-ash from the waste-paper basket, a handful of ashes from the fireplace, and a little spilled beer from the bar, and put them into an envelope. Lestrade arrived at eleven, and stood looking on with a sardonic smile: "Mr Holmes is at his theories as usual," he said. At last my friend stood up: "The criminal," he said, "was an American, of short stature, with red hair and a long moustache." "My dear Holmes," I cried. "How on earth—" "Elementary," he replied, "the landlord told me those facts himself yesterday." He walked across to the sofa and siezed° one of the legs: "Here Lestrade" he said, "help me with this sofa." Lestrade knelt down; next moment there was a sharp click, and a muffled exclamation: both men sprang to their feet, and I saw that there were handcuffs on Lestrade's wrists. "Gentlemen," cried Holmes, "Let me introduce you to inspector Lestrade, of Scotland yard.° alias "Darkey Ted", the perpetrator of five audacious burglaries and three forgeries. And now, Watson, come along, for Charlie Chaplin acts in half an hour at "The Vulgarity"." He stamped his foot, and two burly policemen appeared from the chimney, and took Lestrade away."

x x x x x x x x x x x x

"A simple case, Watson, but not without its interest. I suspected Lestrade from the first. The red hair and the moustache suggested a disguise, and I saw that his trowsers° were marked with the dust from beneath the sofa. I knew too that he was no American." "Why?" I ejaculated. "What American," said Holmes, "would spit on the floor-boards when he could spit on the carpet?"

(The End.)

1. moved] crept   2. the] his

32. 'A Peep into the Future'

The Election Times, No.4, 3 June 1918

Although purporting to be two parts or chapters of a longer work, what was included in *The Election Times* and is given here was probably all that Orwell intended to write.

(Part II.)

"Where's Longden?"[1] "Oh: Piggy Hill[2] had him taken away,—that was when he had been made Head-master,—because he encouraged too much exercise by making people play in juniors. He tried to get off by saying that at any rate he never did any work in juniors himself, but it was no good." There was a silence of a few moments. "Hallo" said Whittome,[3] it's half-time." "Here" I said, "where's my gown? I can't find it." "O, here it is," said Whittome, handing me a narrow strip of black cloth, perhaps three inches wide. "The old gowns have been stopped, unhygienic and extravagant. This hooks onto[4] your shoulders." "I suppose you eat pills and things now, don't you?" I said, prepared for the worst. "No, but we get a reasonable amount, not too much or not too rich." The "not too much" filled my soul with a chill that was not relieved by seeing, as we entered hall, a sprawling legend above the door, bearing the words,

> "Full stomach, full coffin."
> Sir Pigling Hill, 1919.

Mr Hills° touch was indeed apparent everywhere: the pictures which once adorned the walls were super eded° by notices, such as "Thirty bites," (in 5 languages). And in the most prominent place I saw the words,

"Blessings on Science! When the bread seems old,
"The water tasteless, or[5] the meat is cold
" 'Tis she that shows us that those things are right
"And teaches us the unwelcome food to bite."

I had, naturally, concluded that no form of grace was now existant,° and was about to start on the food before me, when one of the sixth form pronounced the words "Stand up", and, as we obeyed, "Science bless us." The meal consisted of meat, vegetables, water (distilled) and bread spread with brown sugar. The time of hall had been increased, and, for the first time since[6] my arrival, I had time to look about me and reflect on the changes. I observed that everyone had a graver air than of old, and seemed more preoccupied. Each boy munched his food with a slow steady motion, and made no attempt at conversation till his food was finished. I learnt that on the following day there was to be a school lecture. Professor Hill was to lecture in the one time° chapel. Gibson[7] was coming down to hear it, and was[8] bringing his son. I was aroused from my reflections by the words "Stand up" again: these were followed by "Blessings of Science" "Bless her" we responded, and trooped out. I have not yet mentioned the impression made on me, namely, that

48

Science had had a hardening effect on my schoolfellows. This impression was strengthened by one incident which took place shortly after hall. We had assembled in King-Farlow's[9] room, and soon Gibson appeared, now heavily bearded, and carrying his son in a string bag. Having come in he set the child on the floor to amuse itself as best it could, and entered into the conversation. This was not of an amusing nature, and I fell to watching the baby. It was with some interest I watched it upset a[10] bottle of ink upon Gibson's hat, which lay upon the floor. Suddenly someone, following my eyes, observed the child, and directed Gibson's attention to it. I was horrified to see him shoot out a huge foot, and give the poor child a savage kick, which sent it rolling on the floor. "You beast!" I said; "Do the little brute good," he said, callously, "he's always getting into mischief."

Chapter III.

I had lost all interest, and had become aware of the lecturer's voice only as the last barrier between myself and sleep. Suddenly, however, a familiar word roused me; it was "irritability". "I will show you" said Professor Hill, "an instance of irritability, or response to a stimulus." He turned and shouted to the attendant, who presently brought in Mr Brinton,[11] whom I had last seen at the Collection of Curiosities. It was now that I first observed a peculiar wooden structure, erected somewhere near the pulpit. I can only describe it as being like the ceiling, back wall and floor of a room. Inside was a chair, and a few desks. Mr Brinton was seated in the chair, and a few youths in the desks, while two more boys were surreptitiously led up the wooden staircase leading from the floor to the ceiling. "How do you do? Brinton," said Mr Hill, "You see, I've got you a few pupils." Mr Brinton began to teach the boys in the desk, and while he was engaged in this pursuit a slender chain was attached from his ankle to a ring in the floor. This being done the two boys on top began a lively dance, shouting the while. At first Mr Brinton only shifted in his chair. Then he made a sudden rush, and attained the top of the staircase, but the chain pulled him down. At the third attempt he broke his bonds, and, siezing° his tormentors by the ears, he beat their heads together till he was forced to stop from very weariness. When he had been removed, Mr Hill continued. "You observe" he said, "the great muscular energy generated by anger. The subject could never have broken the chain ordinarily. It is well known that a woman when fighting for her children displays immense muscular activity; yet in the ordinary way females are[12] greatly inferior to males both in strength and physical courage:—" "Ho!" said a deep voice from the end of the chapel suddenly, "har they, indeed?" We turned, amazed, to see a mighty woman standing in the arch above which the organ once had stood, massive hands on her hips,[13] a heavy chin stuck out agressively.° A dead silence prevailed: at last it was broken by the woman's footsteps as she strode towards the pulpit.[14] "A good smackin's what *you* want," she said, seizing the lecturer, who seemed frozen with horror, by the collar. A sharp slap rang out, Mr Hill's face was entirely covered for one second, then he collapsed upon the stone floor, and lay still. Scarcely had he done so when the

captain of the school leaped[15] to his feet, and shouted, "let's go back to the good old fashions and drop all this scientific stuff." There was a roar of acclamation, and we left chapel, bearing Professor Hill, gagged and bound with us.
The reign of Science was at an end.

The End.[16]

1. Bobbie Longden, a contributor to *The Election Times*; see *29, n. 3*.
2. Hill is unidentified.
3. W. G. Whittome, later Sir Maurice Whittome, was a member of the 1916 Election.
4. Orwell later made a particular issue of spelling 'onto' as one word in certain circumstances; see General Introduction, *CW*, I, xxi.
5. or] and
6. since] of
7. There was a J. A. W. Gibson in the 1916s Election. According to Denys King-Farlow, he had a weak heart. What the joke about the baby was has not been recovered.
8. was] was given; given *crossed out*
9. King-Farlow's] Longden's. King-Farlow was another contributor to *The Election Times*. See *29, n. 2*.
10. a] the
11. Unidentified.
12. are] are not to°; not to *crossed out*
13. 'a mighty woman . . . massive hands on her hips': compare the 'monstrous woman, solid as a Norman pillar, with brawny red forearms' who sings in the courtyard below the room in which Winston and Julia meet in *Nineteen Eighty-Four, CW*, IX, 144, 228.
14. pulpit] lecturer
15. leaped] leapt
16. The only other item in *The Election Times* to conclude with 'The End' is 'The Adventure of the Lost Meat–card.' Orwell nearly always concluded his books, even the collections of essays, *Inside the Whale* (1940) and *The Lion and the Unicorn* (1941), with 'The End.' The rare exceptions may be printers' or publishers' omissions. The typescripts of *Animal Farm* and *Nineteen Eighty-Four* conclude with 'The End.' This does not prove Orwell's authorship of this story, but it is consistent with his later practice.

33. 'The Pagan'

[Autumn 1918]

Three of the poems that Orwell wrote to Jacintha Buddicom have survived. These were included in her *Eric and Us* (71, 87, 117). See also Crick, 113–14, 119, 134. A draft of 'The Pagan' is in the Orwell Archive; its variant readings are given in the notes.

> So here are you, and here am I,
> Where we may thank our gods to be;
> Above the earth, beneath the sky,
> Naked souls alive and free.
> The autumn wind goes rustling by
> And stirs the stubble at[1] our feet;
> Out of the west it whispering blows,
> Stops to caress and onward goes,[2]

Bringing its earthy odours sweet.
See with what pride the setting sun
Kinglike in gold and purple dies,[3]
And like a robe of rainbow spun
Tinges the earth with shades divine.
That mystic light is in your eyes
And ever in your heart will[4] shine.[5]

1. at] around *in draft*
2. In the draft, this line follows the next one.
3. Originally, after this line there followed 'Softly he shines before our eyes' but this is crossed out.
4. will] shall
5. Although Jacintha Buddicom prints the version given here, she also explains that she suggested it should have been 'unarmoured,' not 'naked' souls as they were confiding one with another 'freely and guilelessly . . . not cavorting around in the altogether.' She preferred 'veil' to 'robe,' which was 'too man-made for a natural phenomenon.' Orwell later wrote those amendments into her copy of the poem, making it, he said, 'more authentic' than writing out the poem again; however, she comments that that was more 'trouble-saving' than a desire for authenticity (71).

34. 'Our minds are married, but we are too young'

[Christmas 1918][1]   For Jacintha Buddicom

Our minds are married, but we are too young
For wedlock by the customs of this age
When parent homes pen each in separate cage
And only supper-earning songs are sung.

Times past, when medieval woods were green,
Babes were betrothed, and that betrothal brief.
Remember Romeo in love and grief—
Those star-crossed lovers—Juliet was fourteen.

Times past, the caveman by his new-found fire
Rested beside his mate in woodsmoke's scent.
By our own fireside we shall rest content
Fifty years hence keep troth with hearts° desire.

We shall remember, when our hair is white,
These clouded days revealed in radiant light.

1. Shortly before Orwell returned to Eton in September 1917, and after his father had joined the army, his mother left Henley and, with his older sister, Marjorie, took rooms at 23 Cromwell Crescent, Earls Court, London (now demolished). She worked at the Ministry of Pensions; Marjorie became a motorcycle despatch rider for the Women's Legion; Avril went to a boarding school at Ealing. In 1917 and 1918, Mrs. Blair arranged for Orwell and Avril to spend Christmas with the Buddicom family, as paying guests. She saw little or nothing of them. In the spring of 1918, she had moved to 23 Mall Chambers, near Notting Hill Gate, London, a flat she kept until 1921. Orwell stayed there when in London. Mall Chambers is illustrated in Thompson, 8, commentary, 5–6; see Crick, 107, 118–19, and also *139, n. l.*

35. 'Then up waddled Wog'[1]

[c. 1919]

Then up waddled Wog[2] and he squeaked in Greek:
'I've grown another hair on my cheek.'
Crace[3] replied in Latin with his toadlike smile:
'And I hope you've grown a lovely new pile.
With a loud deep fart from the bottom of my heart!
How d'you like Venetian art?'

1. From Denys King-Farlow, 'College Days with George Orwell,' MS., c. 1967, five pages, Orwell Archive.
2. 'Wog' was Andrew S. F. Gow (1886–1978), Orwell's Tutor. He was later appointed to a fellowship of Trinity College, Cambridge. He and Orwell corresponded occasionally in the 1930s and 1940s. See Crick, 105.
3. John Crace (1878–1960) was the Master in College; he lived there, but, not being a tutor or a housemaster, he lacked their authority. He prepared Orwell for confirmation in November 1918. See Crick, 115–16. For Crace, see also *43, n. 1.*

36. Inscription, 'E. A. Blair K.S.'

[c. 1919][1]

E.A. Blair K.S.
Bought this Book
Much against his will
For the study
of Milton
a poet
for whom
he had
no
love;
but
he was
compelled
to study
him or abandon
English Extra Studies
which not being
Commendable to him
He was compelled to
Squander three & sixpence
On this nasty little book.

1. Jacintha Buddicom records in *Eric and Us* that, in August 1921, Orwell gave her sister, Guinever, his copy of *Milton's Poems* in the Everyman edition. Written on the decorative endpaper was this inscription. Orwell, a K.S. or King's Scholar, had taken English Extra

Studies in 1919. See Plate 31 in *Eric and Us* (discussed on 122–23). For lines from *Paradise Lost* that sent shivers down Orwell's spine when he was about sixteen, see 'Why I Write,' *3007*.

37. Contributions to *College Days*, 1919–1920

There were five issues of *College Days* while Orwell was at Eton. These were dated 24 March 1919, 27 June 1919, 29 November 1919, 1 April 1920, and 9 July 1920. There were no issues in 1921.

College Days was initiated by George Binney. On a card dated 10 May 1967, Sir George said that he was co-editor with Clive Burt of the first issue, which he dates November 1918, and sole editor of the second, which he dates 4 June 1919. In a letter of 28 April 1967, he stated that Orwell had not contributed to any of the issues he had edited in 1917–18 and, as far as he was aware, Orwell had not contributed anything by the time he, Binney, left Eton in the summer of 1919. It is possible that Orwell did make one contribution to the second issue; Denys King-Farlow attributed 'To A. R. H. B.' to himself and Orwell. It is therefore included here, but Binney's doubts are important.

When Binney left, King-Farlow and Orwell inherited *College Days*. They are said to have made a handsome profit of £86, in 1920, and £128, in 1921, from the periodical; see Stansky and Abrahams, I, 109. Crick is less specific about dates but gives both amounts on 125 and 131. King-Farlow, in a manuscript in the Orwell Archive, 'College Days with George Orwell' (partly published in *Orwell Remembered*), relates the £128 to 1920 and to issue Number 4, intended for the Eton versus Harrow cricket match at Lord's Cricket Ground. However, that issue is dated 1 April, and the cricket season had not yet begun; he must have meant Number 5, which bears on its title page the subhead 'Lord's, 1920.' He suggested to Stansky and Abrahams that the periodical was 'of interest to its editors as a money-making rather than a literary enterprise' (109) and said the Lord's issue was 'heavy with snob-appeal advertisements.' Unlike *The Election Times*, it was commercially printed.

It is difficult to be sure who wrote what, especially because so many of the contributions are pastiche. However, Orwell gave a copy of issue Number 5, marked with what he had contributed, to Jacintha Buddicom; the eight items included here as by Orwell are those that he marked as his. King-Farlow, Cyril Connolly, and Steven Runciman independently agreed (see *29*) with these assignments, although Runciman doubted whether 'The Cricket Enthusiast' and 'The Millionaire's Pearl' were Orwell's, and Connolly had doubts about the second of these. It will be noted that several of the items in Number 5 originated in *The Election Times*.

Four items included here as possibly Orwell's are from issue Number 3 and four are from issue Number 4. Runciman thought that nothing in Number 3 was by Orwell but that 'Ode to Field Days' in Number 4 was Orwell's; he assigned 'Spring Time' to Anthony Richards, as stated in the text. Connolly thought 'Spring Time' was unlikely to be Orwell's but assigned him 'Ode to Field Days.' 'Spring Time' has therefore not been included, though it is marginally a candidate for Orwell's authorship. King-Farlow said that he and Orwell did the mock advertisement and that Orwell wrote 'After Twelve' and 'Ode to Field Days.' He did not think Orwell contributed to Number 3; Connolly thought 'Wall Game' was his. Jacintha Buddicom, stressing that she was recalling events long past, thought 'Things we do not want to know' might be Orwell's, 'Eton Masters' Strike' was 'vaguely familiar,' and 'The White Man's Burden' was possibly Orwell's. She credited him with 'Ode to Field Days' and 'A Summer Idyll,' and thought 'After Twelve' seemed 'slightly familiar.' Connolly and Buddicom thought Orwell was probably the author of 'Stalky at Beton.'° It appeared in *It* in July 1919. No copy of this issue has been traced.

Each of the items included here from Numbers 3 and 4 has been annotated to indicate the degree of uncertainty as to authorship.

38. 'To A. R. H. B.'

College Days, No. 2, 27 June 1919
Attributed to Orwell with considerable uncertainty

IMPORTANT NOTICE.

Any Parents, Guardians or Friends (male or female) of Wykehamists or Etonians whom *I* see not bowing or curtseying to *me*, when *I* am in sight or whom *I* see in possession of a copy of *College Days* will be severely dealt with by *ME*.

A. R. HANBURY BATEMAN.

To A. R. H. B.[1]
Who is the mighty Captain? Who is he
That every Upper Boat doth wish to be?
'Tis he who sets the Ark a stroke sublime
To which they vainly try to keep in time.
'Tis he who puts up notices galore,
Then changes his great mind and puts up more;
Who fines us heavily for damaging
Our boats, or oars, or sculls, or anything;
Who scorns the rules so slavishly obeyed
By lesser lights than he; who's not afraid
To put a dry-bob in the Boats, if so
It pleases him, and even make him row;
Who's great enough to scorn such petty rules,
Only laid down for novices and fools.
This is the mighty Captain, this is he
That every Upper Boat doth wish to be.

1. A. Roland Hanbury Bateman was an Oppidan (a boy who was not a King's Scholar) and Captain of the Eton Eight. Rowing colours were awarded to Upper Boats; a dry-bob was a cricketer, as opposed to a wet-bob, or oarsman. The verse parodies Wordsworth's 'Character of the Happy Warrior,' which begins: 'Who is the happy Warrior? Who is he / That every man in arms should wish to be?'

39. 'Things We Do Not Want to Know'

College Days, No. 3, 29 November 1919
Attributed to Orwell with considerable uncertainty

What happened to Gundry's hat on the way to Bagshot?

What would happen if Lea, K.S., forgot to wind himself up at night?

What would happen if the 'Back Bench' gave way?

Whether his late Majesty King Henry VI, must not be getting a bit tired of his position in the middle of School Yard?

If not, why not?

What is a mouse when it spins?

Whether Akroyd, in the Army Exam, lost marks equal to one-fifth of the value, for writing in the wrong coloured note-book?

Whether the late Captain of the Eleven enjoys his company at Cambridge?

Whether there is a game of football to-day?

Whether our Division master remembered to set any Sunday questions?

Whether this is not the obvious place to stop?[1]

---

1. It has not proved possible to recover the meanings of many of the allusions. Still relevant is that to the statue of Henry VI, founder of Eton College (1440), which stands in the School Yard. A division (or 'div') is a form; thus a division master is a form master.

40. 'Wall Game'[1]

College Days, No. 3, 29 November 1919   Probably by Orwell

If you can keep your face, when all about you
      Are doing their level best to push it in.
If you can swear (though, swearing, all men doubt you)
      It wasn't you who slicked the keeper's shin,
If you can furk and not get killed while furking,
      Or being fisted, fist 'em back again,
Or can invent convenient aunts, thus shirking
      An afternoon of mud, and blood, and rain.
If you can play without too great disaster,
      Or even try to think you like the game,
If you can meet with Mixed Wall and with Master,
      And treat those two impostors just the same,
If you can bear to have the shy you're claiming,
      Not given, the Lord — and referee — know why,
Or miss the blasted goal at which you're aiming,
      Because the ball went half-an-inch too high,
If you can gently moderate your linguo
      So as to turn the common bargee pink,
And, when rebuked, reply, "I said, 'By Jingo'
      Four times, no more, and 'Bother' twice, I think."
If you can force your wall and fly and second
      To do your job long after they are done,
And still hold on, when hours since they had reckoned
      The time for holding would be past and gone.
If you can play at third and keep your shirt new,
      Or flying-man, nor lose the common clutch,
If neither fists nor fearsome feet can hurt you,
      But you can hurt all men, though none too much,
If you can fill the unforgiving minute
      With sixty second's worth of slaughter done,
Yours is the game and everything that's in it,
      And you may wear your College Wall, my son.

1. The poem, obviously a parody of Kipling's 'If,' concerns a game that is peculiar to Eton. It is a form of football, more often than not indecisive in its outcome, played 'at the wall' rather than 'in the field.' Orwell played both games; see Hollis, 23; Crick, 117. An account of the complexities of the wall game is in *The Oxford Companion to Sports and Games*, edited by John Arlott (1975). A brief summary may help explain some of the references in the poem.
    The game is played in an area 4 to 5 yards wide and 118 yards long against a red brick wall that separates Eton playing fields from Slough Road. At one end, an old elm tree (now a cemented stump) served as a goal in Orwell's day and, at the other, a doorway in a wall at right angles to that against which the game is played serves the same purpose. In Orwell's day there were eleven players to a side (ten after World War II). Seven form a 'bully' (equivalent to the pack in rugby). There are three 'walls,' one behind the other against the wall; two 'seconds' (line 21), also one behind the other; a 'third' (line 25), a 'fourth,' and 'lines,' who is nearest the

touchline, four to five yards from the wall. The front line initially has five players, four of these with the second line of two, and the third line – the third 'wall' – forming the bully. Behind the bully is 'fly' (line 21) or 'flying-man' (line 26), who is crucially important, especially if it is muddy, in directing his side and identifying where the ball is as the scrimmage intensifies. At the rear is a tenth player, 'long,' and, in Orwell's day, the eleventh man, 'goals.' The captain is known as 'keeper.'

Progress is mainly made by each bully, in tight formation, attempting to 'force the wall' (line 21). Open fighting is not allowed – note 'fisting' (line 6) – but players can 'knuckle' opponents with their outside hand (with respect to the wall). Progress may also be made by a loose ruck (the bully in loose formation) or by kicking the ball forward, though that can be tactically dangerous. Passing is allowed sideways only, and the ball may not be heeled backward until the opponent's scoring area (akin to the circle in hockey) is reached. It is known as 'Calx,' from the Latin for chalk, used to indicate the area on the wall. Once in Calx, the ball may be 'furked' (line 5), or heeled; in the opponent's Calx, the ball can be touched when it is off the ground and against the wall. A shy (line 13) can then be demanded, and, if granted by the referee (line 14; there are also two umpires), scores one point and entitles the team to a throw (ten points if it hits) or kick (five points) at goal. A goal is rarely hit, only about once every two years. The game is much played by the seventy Collegers (the King's Scholars), and on St Andrew's Day they play a team drawn from the Oppidans (the fee-paying boys). Between 1845 and 1973, only three goals were scored in these matches. Wall colours (last line) date from 1852: College Wall is narrow purple and white stripes; Oppidan Wall is broad purple and orange. There are also games between teams made up of both College and Oppidan players, 'Mixed Wall' (line 11), and scratch sides of old boys. Mixed Wall (or School Wall) colours are red and blue stripes.

The Annals of Lower College Foot-Ball, Vol. 13, 1916–1921 (for 1920) show that Orwell played 'at the wall' on eighteen occasions and 'in field' sixty times, and in three unspecified games, between September 1918 and December 1920; he missed thirteen games. He began badly. On 28 September 1918, he was described as 'conspicuously bad' and 'owing to a gross mistake by our goals (Blair), the ball was kicked just behind our calxline.' On 5 October 1918, 'Blair was v. slack,' and ten days later 'was not at all energetic.' The following year he 'only sneaked and cornered' on 4 October, but reports on his playing began to improve (though on 22 October 1919 'we lost Blair temporarily'). In 1920, he seems to have come into his own. On 6 October, the 'feature of the first half was a superb goal neatly shot by Blair from the halfway line; in fact all through the game he was not so slack as usual and kicked well into the bully.' He and Turner were 'best' on 27 October, and on 3 November the Keeper scored off 'a good penalty kick by Blair.' His prowess culminated in the St Andrew's Day game, 4 December: 'Blair kept and kicked very competently under considerable difficulties.'

41. 'Eton Masters' Strike'

College Days, No. 3, 29 November 1919   Possibly by Orwell

Mr. Baker received this morning, a telegram from headquarters (unavoidably delayed owing to the fact that the telegraph girl's hair slipped under receiver). The Ushers and Teachers Union had come out on strike in sympathy with the washerwomen, bootmakers, and bottlewashers who are demanding nationalization.

The news spread like wild fire round the school, the masters received it with varying degrees of enthusiasm. There were those who openly rejoiced, even before the boys, there were those who took it indifferently, and those who openly cursed bottlewasher and bootmaker; these were no longer allowed to sit in their nicely heated schoolrooms engaged in the arduous tasks of declining 'Mensa,'[1] or looking up the answer to a rule of three sum, but were turned out into their houses to sit before cheerless grates, where from afar they could hear the cheering of the demonstration meeting held in the School Hall.

This was an immense affair. The School met to hold an indignation meeting and decide what should be done. James K.S. presided at the meeting and Royds took the chair. Nothing was decided, but everybody agreed that it was most impressive. Little groups gathered round the 'burning bush' to gossip and watch some of the better pleased masters, attired in sporting checks, bicycling to Burnham Beeches.[2]

Later on in the day a most regrettable scene occurred, a master disguised as an ordinary man was seen creeping up Common Lane and approaching the New Schools where he let himself into his schoolroom and proceeded to warm himself by sitting on the hot pipes, he was about to produce his copy of "The Young Visiters"[3] and make himself comfortable when suddenly a tumult arose without. Masters seemed to collect from all directions, there was a scuffle and shouts of 'Blackleg! Blackleg!' The door was burst in and unfortunately the master still lies in a critical condition.

This scene considerably amused the idle crowds of boys who collected to watch the spectacle.

Two youths, who had gone out early for a walk and who were complacently sitting by arches discussing the respective merits of Lenin, Trotsky and Boguslavsky,[4] were the only two in the school who did not realize what had come to pass. Just before "lunch time" ("boys' dinner" was given up during the strike as a protest against the peaceful picketing of some of the masters), they[5] strolled back to their 'tutors' and one of them remembered he, unfortunately, had an interview with his tutor that morning as he had been caught cribbing. He strode nervously into his tutor's study. His tutor began. "I am in a very awkward position to-day and I am not sure yet what I am to do about this."

The boy quailed and saw visions of his parents' wrath when they heard from his tutor.

His tutor added in a kind voice. "You see, my boy, it is like this." The boy cheered up. "I must confess we are on strike." After this, of course, the interview fell rather flat!

The masters this evening held a mass meeting in Schoolyard and sought inspiration from the kindly countenance of Henry Founder.[6]

The Government are determined to fight to the finish and it is difficult to see where this terrible state of affairs will lead us.

1. The first, and simplest, task given those learning Latin is to memorise the inflexions of *mensa*.
2. A favourite picnic spot, the setting for Gordon and Rosemary's excursion in *Keep the Aspidistra Flying*.
3. *The Young Visiters, or, Mr. Salteenas Plan* was an utterly naïve yet precocious story by a nine-year-old girl, Daisy Ashford, published on 22 May 1919, with an introduction by J. M. Barrie. By November, when this issue of *College Days* was published, it had been issued sixteen times, totalling 111,000 copies. It was published in New York in 1919. The following year, three earlier stories by Margaret Mary (Daisy) Ashford (1881–1972), dictated by her to

her father, and a story by her sister Amanda, were published in *Daisy Ashford: Her Book*. She published nothing else. *The Young Visiters* was, and has remained, a cult book, still captivating by its remarkable charm. Orwell's affection for such stories as *Pigling Bland* (see *29*) and his interest in fairy stories to the end of his life suggest that this reference to *The Young Visiters* points to his authorship of 'Eton Masters' Strike.'

4. Mikhail Solomonovich Boguslavskiy (1888–1937), Russian composer and revolutionary, was arrested by tsarist police in 1904 for his part in organising the Printers' Trade Union, of which he became chairman after the 1917 revolution. In 1905, he joined the Jewish Socialist Party. From 1917 to 1927, he served as a state official in the Ukraine and Moscow. After siding with the Trotskyist opposition, he was expelled from the Communist Party in 1927. Tried for treason in the second of Stalin's show trials of former colleagues, he was found guilty on 29 January 1937 and executed the following morning.

5. masters), they] masters. They

6. Henry VI, founder of Eton College.

42. 'The White Man's Burden'

College Days, No. 3, 29 November 1919   Probably by Orwell;
illustrations probably by Bobbie Longden[1]

The meaning of that mysterious phrase, "The White Man's Burden,"[2] has at last been revealed.

Have you ever had the whole of your family thrust upon you at once? If not, pray to Heaven that you may yet be spared.

Young and innocent, black haired and of a ruddy countenance, young David went to meet the fateful train. A third class smoker gushed forth its mighty cargo of parents, aunts, uncles and, of course, their dear, dear little ones, who did so want to come. David grinned sheepishly, kissed his mother, and passed on to Aunt Bertha, big, bulgy and boisterous, whose boys,

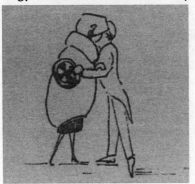

Bobbie and Bill, had both been 'bloods,' in their day at Winchester.

Then there was Aunt Celia, thin, scraggy, spectacled and horribly supercilious. Her son Simon, stood smiling at her side. Scholar obviously (shape and colour of his collar clearly stamped him as such). David hated him, nasty snivelling little beast! Uncle George, grousing and grumbling as usual, grunted an inaudible greeting. Uncle Henry, whose harsh voice and horribly hairy face had always repelled young David, came next. He was one of those people with whom one hesitates to shake hands; scrunch, scrunch go the bones, and the blood seems to go tearing through one's head, down one's legs, and ooze out of the soles of one's shoes.

David's hand fell limply to his side as he led the way out of the station with his mother. "Cousin Bill," she said, "Rufus, Arabella and Ermyntrude are going to join us for lunch at the 'White Hart.' What's the time now? I expect your uncles would like to go and see the match."

David, however, was mercifully spared this, and the animals went in to feed.

"Which is our table, dear," said Aunt Bertha, bustling up in a hurry from somewhere. "The waiters in this place are always so damned slow," grumbled Uncle George.

"Oh dear, oh dear, I've left my glasses in the train," added Aunt Celia.

At this point, Bill burst in, and slapping David on the back, broke into a torrent of enthusiasm. "Well, old bean, your dear old college ai'nt doin' as well as it might. Our fellers are fairly pushin' along. Old Thomas, our skipper, has already knocked up about 30." (Bill's heartiness was almost overpowering.)

The meal was a prolonged agony for David. Aunt Celia started by saying she didn't think he had grown much lately. Now David had put on his 'tails' that morning for the first time and was proud of his 5ft. and 4½ ins. Uncle George mumbled and cursed, Simon snivelled, Arabella and Ermyntrude giggled at Bill and Aunt Bertha, who bellowed loud and unceasing torrent° of nonsense. Aunt Celia inadvertently upset her soup on Uncle Henry, which did

nothing to improve the situation, and only increased Arabella's giggles and Aunt Bertha's boisterosity.

David took care to walk ahead with his mother to the match, where he deposited his 'burden' on the various seats he had wisely secured beforehand. He then joined a friend. "That's all Wykehamists," he grunted dejectedly. "Poor devil," said his companion. "What are you doing about tea. You ought not to feed the walruses with the pelicans, you know."

David returned in due course to find his family in ecstasies over the now almost inevitable defeat of Eton College.

Tea (the next and final nightmare) came at last. David packed and stacked the crowd into his small

room, put the teapot in front of his mother, and was suddenly inspired. "I must get my tutor's leave for tonight," he said, and stepped out. He ran into Peter in the passage. "Hello, David," he said, "Is that arkful yours? You're looking awfully bored. Come and have some tea; my sister's here."

David's face lit up, and off they went together. "I've just rescued David from a crowd of old men," said Peter, as they sat down. David forgot his family for at least ten minutes. He was not free yet though—"Where the devil has that fellow got to? there's no water for the tea-pot." Uncle George had got loose in the passage. "Peter, you might show him the kettle, I can't go out and meet the old brute." David forgot his family again for a minute or two.

Peter came back again. "I think the crowd is moving on. One or two have dropped out, and they are look-ing for you, David, bad luck, old chap!" David had to go.

"I wish you hadn't finished so soon. I've had hardly any tea, and my tutor says I can't come and see you off. I'm so sorry."

"Do tell me, David, what are all those pieces of paper pinned on your wall," said Aunt Bertha, in a final burst. "Why don't you get a lot more and make some sort of pattern? I wish we had had time to see the dormitories, but I suppose we must be going." "It's getting beastly cold and dark," said Uncle George. "Let's go."

David hustled the crowd out into the street, and kissed his mother again, and said "Good Night," in a general way to the rest, waving the remains of his right hand to Uncle Henry as he strode away.[3]

"Thank God I shan't be here next summer," said David, as he turned back into the house.

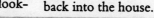

1. Denys King-Farlow contributed illustrations to *The Election Times*, of which he was art editor, and *College Days*, but these are probably not his. For Longden, see *29, n. 3*.
2. A seven-stanza poem by Kipling with this title was published in New York, in February 1899, addressed to the Americans after their victories in Cuba and the Philippines. It was included in his *Five Nations* (1903). Kipling's call to take on imperial responsibilities, not now fashionable, attracted much criticism then. If one gets beyond the title, it can be seen that it demands taking on responsibilities for others, the only reward for which is blame and hate.
3. 'as he strode away' was on a separate line and erroneously placed after, instead of before, David's final remark.

43. Mock Advertisement

College Days, No. 4, 1 April 1920   By Orwell and Denys King-Farlow[1]

A.R.D. —— After rooms. —— JANNEY.

1. In an interview with Sonia Orwell and Ian Angus, 20 April 1967, Denys King-Farlow explained that Janney was the Master in College, John Crace, and he 'had a tendency to be overfond of some boys.' One such was A. R. D. Watkins, later a master at Harrow. After seeing the 'advertisement,' 'Crace was furious and had Blair on the mat straightaway, without really being able to do anything effective about it because he was compromised.' King-Farlow, co-editor with Orwell of this issue of *College Days*, escaped, since he had already left for Italy on vacation, so Orwell, not greatly pleased, faced Crace's wrath alone. All material in Eton's ephemeral journals had to be approved; this 'advertisement' got through because King-Farlow had persuaded a new master, fresh from naval service, to vet it. On Crace, see *35, n. 3*.

44. 'After Twelve'[1]

College Days, No. 4, 1 April 1920   Possibly by Orwell

> "Oh, what can ail thee, loafer lorn,
> Alone, thy visag° overcast?
> The crowd has ebbed from Cannon Yard,
> And third School's past.
>
> "Oh, what can ail thee, loafer lorn,
> So haggard and so woebegone?
> The Bar in Tap is nearly full,
> And the Bill's near done."
>
> "I saw a cake in Fuller's shop,
> Full, beautiful, of pinkish hue,
> And set with green angelica,
> And violets too.
>
> "I bought it from the shopman straight,
> To take it home, a joy to eat,
> I looked on it with eyes of love,
> And smiled full sweet.

"I set it in a paper bag,
And nothing else in rapture saw.
When lo! there stood a master stern
    Without the door.

"And there he took my name and House,
And there I dreamed—ah woe betide!—
The saddest dream I ever dreamed
    On the High Street's side.

"I saw young boys, and older too,
Pale prisoners, death-pale were they all,
Who cried, 'The rules of Sunday bounds
    Have thee in thrall.'

"And that is why I sojourn here,
Alone and pale by school-yard gates,
The last boy's coming off the Bill,[2]
    And the fusee[3] waits."

1. After 'La Belle Dame Sans Merci' by Keats.
2. Bill is the prosecution list for the Headmaster.
3. Possibly a watchman (after a soldier, armed with a fusee).

45. 'Ode to Field Days'

College Days, No. 4, 1 April 1920   Probably by Orwell[1]

Hills we have climbed and bogs that we have sat in,
    Pools where we drenched our feet in mid-December,
Trains we have packed, woods we have lost our hat in,
    When you are past and gone, we will remember.

Oh open fields and dinner halting places,
    In the hot summer how we shall regret you!
Oh nice bleak heaths and open windy spaces,
    Though you are lost to us, could we forget you?

Stumbling on stones and falling over boulders,
    What pangs of grief the memory will bring us!
Marching to trains with greatcoats on our shoulders,
    With what despair the loss of these will wring us.

Oh summer haste to press thy footsteps past us,
    Speed the hot months we have to suffer yearly,
Bring back at last to thankful boys and masters
    Those blessèd field-days that we love so dearly.

1. Orwell is remembered by Christopher Eastwood as 'a most unwilling member' of the Eton Officers' Training Corps, a compulsory activity then in most public schools. Eastwood followed Orwell's example 'in getting in the Signal Section, which was the refuge of the lazy and the inefficient' (Crick, 109). A field day was a war-game exercise; 'blessèd' in the last line implies its converse.

46. 'A Summer Idyll'

College Days, No. 4, 1 April 1920   Possibly by Orwell

I was up for my Saturday afternooner at the "Tar and Tartar."

"Say, stranger," the lantern-jawed individual who sat on the other side of the table, squash-hatted, bow-tied and belted, removed the four-inch cigar from the corner of his mouth. "I guess you College students on this side of the duckpond know what's what in the liquor department. I'm not much on to many things in this little island, but after they cut out the alcohol in God's own country I thought I'd best beat it here. But as you were just saying, stranger ———"

"Was I?" I murmured meekly.

"As you were saying, it ain't partic'lar North Pole weather right here. Gee, I guess you ain't gone far of° the mark just there. I don't mind if I do imbibe just one. Hi, you, Mose, or whatever name you go by with your godparents, bring me a stiff—a big stiff, and put it down to this guy. Yep," he resumed, turning to me, "this is a verry curious little island of yours, and of all the verry curious places in it I reckon this young hamlet of Windsor annexes it, sure. I've experienced several exceeding queer goings on in more than one part of the globe, stranger, but what yours truly went through here four years gone just beat the whole jazz-band."

"Do tell me about it," said I.

"Waal, stranger," answered he, "I'm usually most taciturn, but I guess I'll just break the regulation for once. It was four years back. The climate was much similar to that of the present era. I was perambulating some purty bully fields in the neighbourhood of your Thames one evening—bully fields I say, but, of course, if you stuck them downside of any bit of prairie land near the River Mississip° they'd look purty dam silly. Waal, it was my first day here, and I guessed I'd just like to cast an eyeball over this River Thames, on which you Britishers consider there ain't no flies. I was trekking along purty slow when suddenly what should I hear but a shooter do the bang trick? 'Gee whizz,' said I to a hedge, 'maybe there's someone being croaked. At any rate there's a mix up in progress somewhereabouts. I guess this is where I hit the trail.' So I padded the hoof on a bit further towards the bank. I was still a few fields in distance from the river when suddenly I heard the bang-bang start again, and a great yell seemed to come right straight from the river side. I pulled my six-shooter from its hip-case, stranger, and broke Applegarth's 100 yards record in a Marathon scamper for that bank. I jumped three hedges, and crashed over a stout female in a striped shirt-waist. She called several improper names, student, and shouted something about cops after me. Of course, I was streaking through the next field before she'd completed her paragraph, and in a few rapid strides I'd reached the bank. A bunch of ugly-looking muts in grey bean-covers were moving along the side-path, shouting like Mexicans with their back teeth under. They were kicking up an ear-splitting shindy, pointing meanwhile at rough-looking galoots who were rowing away down stream in a long thin coracle as if the Old Man himself was after them. 'Come on, boys,' I cried, 'we don't want any cops in this derned show. Why hasn't somebody put a bead on those boobs already? We don't let croaksters vamoose like that in Arizona. Come on, we'll round up the guys ourselves and lynch 'em on the nearest telegraph wires.' With these words, stranger, I waved my shooter and emptied two rounds of dope into the galley-pullers, who were already looking like doing a clear vamoose. There were five junks in the bateau, four with the oars and one squatting in the stern with the tiller ropes. I queered the rudder with six cents' worth of lead and blew a cranny through the steering galoot's arm.

"Immediately all the shouting on the bank stopped. A queue of other vessels, which were presumably doing a chase after the first bunch, stopped too, and next thing I knew was that a bum-guy in a Panama cranium lid with white knickerbocker pants and about eight foot of hairy shin caught me a clip over the head-piece. I went down like a felled prairie ox. When I came to I'd been clapped into a cell, a prison cell, mister, in a British prison, and me a free Yank from Milwaukee, Wisconsin! And that was not all, either. Next day they had me up in court, surrounded by a whole crush of blue-coated cops with great black jacks in their mits. The judge, a crustaceous creature in a wig too small for him and with a face like a Boston saloon-keeper, told me I'd broken the British peace, was an undesirable alien, had assaulted a British woman (the beldam in the shirt waist, you know), had fired into an open boat without provocation, and altogether was quite worthy of the eight months I was to undergo breaking stones and perambulating tread-mills. Then as I was being frog-marched out, one of the cops asked why I fired into the boat. 'Why?' I roared, 'those muts had croaked some boob. I heard them firing myself, and saw the guys on the bank trying to stop them, and shouting like mad.'

" 'Say, bo,' replied the cop, grinning and showing his ugly yellow teeth, 'didn't you grip they were only having a boat race?—one of those blessed Eton four-oar turns, you know.'

"You could have knocked me down with a match end."

The lean stranger rose slowly to his feet, finished my glass as well as his own, spat ruminatingly through the open window, and then turned on his heel. "So long, pard," he said, and turning passed through the door.

46A. Inscription in Copy of Shaw's *Misalliance*
Eton College Reading Room   June 1920

Presented by E. A. Blair   June 1920

47. 'Mr. Simpson and the Supernatural'

Bubble and Squeak, No. 2, 4 June 1920   Probably by Orwell[1]

Mr. Simpson braced himself up in his chair. His pet subject had been touched upon, and he prepared to launch into it with his usual pithy and irrefutable arguments. Now Mr. Simpson was essentially a practical man. He had achieved his present comfortable position in life (his expectant relatives said he must be worth quite £50,000) by sheer hard business. Sentiment played no part in his existence, and the subtler influences of life left him unmoved; he believed what he could see or feel for himself, and nothing more. Consequently, when the quiet man opposite him let fall the word "ghosts," Mr. Simpson pricked up his ears. "Ghosts!" he snorted, "Ridiculous! Puerile! The childish creation of a distorted brain. 'They that make them are like unto them'—worth nothing. Don't you talk to me of ghosts!" "Very well," said the man opposite—his chief characteristic seemed to be an unruffled quietness—"I'll try not to annoy you any more. But since you appear to place no faith in the supernatural, I am willing to bet you a hundred pounds that you don't sleep a whole night in the haunted room in this very inn; I give you fair warning, it's got a bad reputation." This statement was confirmed by the landlord with a gloomy nod. "A hundred pounds!" echoed Mr. Simpson. "It doesn't seem fair to take your money. Still, I'll make the bet, if only to disprove your extravagant theory." "Very well," said the quiet man. "Mine host here will, I am sure, oblige us by holding the stakes"; and he placed a bank-note in the landlord's hand: Mr. Simpson did the same: he turned to leave the room. "No. 7, on the first floor," said the quiet man as he reached the door. "Good-night, and pleasant dreams!"

Mr. Simpson walked up to the first floor. When he reached No. 7, the door opened itself, the electric light turned itself on, the window shut with a bang, and the curtains drew themselves together. Mr. Simpson could not help feeling a little surprised. "Dear me," he said, "I am beginning to get nervy." His words were echoed loudly from all sides of the room, the echoes continuing for several minutes after he had spoken. When he went over to wash, the taps turned themselves on. "Upon my word," said Mr. Simpson to himself, "these ghosts are extremely obliging," and he laughed softly at his own little joke. Immediately there were unmistakable sounds of laughter from all round the room. As he crossed over to [the] bed the curtains (or something in them) gave him a violent slap on the face. "Damn!" he said. No sooner had he spoken than something tripped him up and he fell headlong on the ground, hurting his knee and bumping his head hard against the bedpost. After this little incident he got into bed in a thoroughly bad temper. As soon as he did so, the bed began to sway and rock about in the most unaccountable manner. "Really," murmured Mr. Simpson, "I didn't *think* I had drunk too much at dinner to-night." Just as he was getting off to sleep he felt something tickling his feet: now Mr. Simpson objected extremely to being tickled, in fact there was only one thing he objected to more, and that was having his hair pulled. So that by now he was really annoyed: but when, a few minutes later, he felt his hair violently pulled, this was the last straw. Mr. Simpson leaped wildly out of bed and over to the door; it refused to open, despite his furious struggles. With the last remnant of his strength he rushed to the window, broke the pane, and jumped madly out and through a glass-house below. Two minutes later might have been seen the diverting spectacle of a staid and respectable City man, half-fainting, entering the inn parlour in his pyjamas, covered with earth and fragments of glass, and red as a lobster with terror. He sank into a chair and beckoned to the landlord for a drink. "Well," he gasped, "you may take my hundred pounds, but all the money in the Mint wouldn't make me spend another minute in *that* room!" "Don't say I didn't warn you," said the quiet man, taking his own and Mr. Simpson's note from the landlord. "But perhaps you would like my card." Mr. Simpson took it: on it was written:

SLITHIO,
Society Conjuror and Illusionist.

He jumped up, cursing loudly. But the quiet man was not there to hear.

1. Cyril Connolly singled out this story as probably by Orwell; Jacintha Buddicom thought it a reasonable attribution. *Bubble and Squeak* described itself as 'The Super Ephemeral' and was sold for one shilling.

48. To Mrs. Laura Buddicom

27 June 1920   Handwritten

Eton College, Windsor.

My dear Mrs Buddicome,°
You said very kindly last holidays that I might come & watch the race at Henley on the 30th from your punt. Do you still intend going there, & may I come? I should be very glad if you could let me know before Wednesday. I am sorry I have given you such short notice; if you are not going I shall of course spend the day with my Father. I should be very glad if you could tell me your arrangements, & where & when to meet you. I might pick you up at Shiplake, as my train would pass there about 11.35 or so. I am going to meet Father in Henley. I hope the weather will be a little better than it is today on Wednesday.

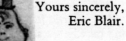

Yours sincerely,
Eric Blair.

49. 'Free Will'

College Days, No. 5, 9 July 1920

Orwell and Denys King-Farlow continued to collaborate in producing *College Days* Number 5. Orwell was also a major contributor. Several of his items had appeared earlier in *The Election Times*, Number 4, or had been associated in some uncertain way with it; see *29*. 'The Slack-bob,' first published in *The Election Times*, Number 4 (see *30*) reappeared in *College Days*, Number 5. The items included here are in the order in which they occurred in *College Days*, though 'Free Will' and 'The Wounded Cricketer,' and probably 'The Millionaire's Pearl' and 'The Youthful Mariner' were written before 1920. Because Orwell ticked all these contributions as his in the copy of *College Days* he gave Jacintha Buddicom, they can fairly securely be credited to him. Conolly and Runciman expressed reservations about his authorship of 'The Cricket Enthusiast' and 'The Millionaire's Pearl.'

(A One-act Drama.)

Scene. Husband and Wife, with daughter of thirteen, seated at breakfast.

Husband (casually). Are we going to take Tommie to Lord's this year, darling?

Wife. Well, someone must take him, I suppose.

Husband (biting thumb-nail). Yes.

Wife. I thought you said *you* were taking him, though.

Husband. I? No. I made sure you'd like to go.

Wife. But women don't understand cricket.

Husband. Lots of men don't either. I don't see that it matters. Anyway, who's going to take him?

Wife. I don't know, I'm sure.

Daughter. Oh, Mummie, aren't we going then? I did want to go.

Husband. Nonsense, child, you don't want to watch cricket. You don't understand it, do you?

Wife. Of course not; she's really getting much too tomboyish lately. Write and tell Tommie that we won't go, Herbert.

Husband (relieved). Very well, dear.

Daughter. Oh, Mummie, I did want to go.

Wife. Nonsense. (*Picking up a letter*.) Oh, here's a letter from Tommie. I hadn't noticed it. (*Opens it*.) Why, he says he doesn't want to go to Lord's, and may he go and stay somewhere else?

Husband. Oh, does he?

Wife. But where else is he to go without us,[1] I should like to know?

Husband. Besides, I'm not sure that's the right spirit for a boy of his age. When I was fifteen I'd have been only too glad to go. I don't approve of these blasé modern boys.

Wife. Yes, Tommie's much too blasé nowadays. Write and tell him of course he's to go.

Husband. And then who's to take him?

Wife. Oh, I think we might all go after all.
Husband. Yes, perhaps we may as well.

1. without us] *after* to know *in* The Election Times, *but marked for transposition*

50. 'The Photographer'

College Days, No. 5, 9 July 1920

Not a breath is heard, not a moving of lip,
    As his hand stays poised o'er the shutter,
And only the gnat on the neck gives a nip,
    And we think of the words we mayn't utter.

He develops them darkly by dead of night
    In a little black hole of an attic;
He pulls all the curtains to shut out the light,
    And stays there for ages, ecstatic.

He takes bits of paper and puts them in frames,
    And leaves them to print all the morning,
And thinks they'll be printed (and signed with our names),
    The chemist or jeweller scorning.

But many and loud are the words he speaks,
    And much more in anger than sorrow,
And he looks at the things he has worked at for weeks,
    But he starts them again on the morrow.

We thought as we saw him undoing a clip,
    As he walked unobserving toward us,
It were wiser no longer to stay, but to skip
    For what refuge the gods might afford us.

Quickly and gaily we made our way,
    And showed no traces of sadness,
For we felt we were free from his grasp for the day,
    And we left him alone to his madness.

1. Pastiche of 'The Burial of Sir John Moore after Corunna' by Charles Wolfe (1791–1823), a poem most secondary-school (and probably all public-school) boys were required to learn before World War II. Orwell quotes a line in his August letter to Runciman; see *56*.

51. 'The Wounded Cricketer (*Not by Walt Whitman*)'[1]

College Days, No. 5, 9 July 1920

I am a Wet-bob[2] who was trying to play cricket
(Not because I wanted to, but because I had to).
Then I got hit in the eye by a ball;
So I lie on the grass here under a lime tree.
The grass looks nice, and so does the sky too.
The leaves look green, and there are such lots of them.
One, two, three, four . . . seven, eight, nine, ten,
. . . Eighteen, nineteen . . . I can't count them.
The sky looks all blue and white and grey.

I can hear someone walking on the road over there.
His feet go up and down, up and down;
He treads in the puddles and kicks the little pebbles, so that
     they rattle all over the place.
The ground underneath me is all rough and humpy.[3]
I can feel a little beetle running down my backbone,
And there's an ant on my ear.
I can see a rook up there; he's black all over.
I don't think I shall move: I feel nice and comfortable.

1. A modern typed copy of this poem, signed 'Eric Blair,' is in the University of Tulsa library. The signature is not in Orwell's hand; but, according to Michael Shelden, Connolly's biographer, it is perhaps in Connolly's hand 'when he was younger.'
2. A wet-bob was an oarsman, as opposed to a dry-bob, a cricketer.
3. Typescript at the University of Tulsa has 'lumpy.'

52. 'Is There Any Truth in Spiritualism?'

College Days, No. 5, 9 July 1920

BY THE BISHOP OF BORSTALL.°

As long as the modern world concerns itself so much with spiritualism, we of the more intellectual professions must not omit our attention. No doubt there is a great deal to be said on both sides. The spiritualists may be right, and they may be wrong. Those are my views on the subject. "You never know till you've found out" goes the old country proverb, and admirably it expresses the case in point. No one could ever call me narrow-minded, nevertheless I think there is another aspect from which we ought to consider the matter: are we right in interfering with these things? Were they meant for us? Moreover, do they have an altogether good effect upon us? To illustrate this point I will give the story of a young man whom I know, whom I shall call X. He had always been, to the best of my knowledge, an orderly and well-doing young man, but I sometimes observed that he seemed to be in a rather debilitated and depressed condition. One evening, a few months ago, I met him with several friends, all walking along together, and seemingly on the best of terms. I greeted him, and asked his destination. "We're going for a little gathering in ——'s rooms," said he, "just a little friendly séance, don't you know!" "A séance!" said I in surprise. "Are you a spiritualist, then?" "Oh, I'm rather fond of spirits," he said rather flippantly, as it seemed, and went on. Next morning he was in the deplorable state I have mentioned, his cheeks pale, his eyes dull, and every movement languid and listless. Can it be possible that spiritualism saps the life from us? I cannot help feeling that it must do us no good. But far be it from me to state the case too strongly. Seeing is believing with me, and I accept nothing unproved. Nevertheless, I should like to put forward for consideration the curious experience recently undergone by a lady of my acquaintance. She had been invited to lunch with a friend, and did not feel inclined to depart at once. To her surprise, after about an hour, her hostess began, my friend assures me, to give a strong impression that she wished her to depart. My friend, however, dismissed it as imagination, but as the afternoon wore on towards tea-time the feeling grew stronger than ever. At last, at about 4 o'clock, her hostess actually asked her if she did not think that perhaps her grandchildren (of whom three were staying with her) might be missing her. My friend, however, replied that she did not think she need go yet, and proceeded to stay to tea. As the evening passed, however, her hostess seemed more than ever uneasy and disturbed, and several times repeated her former question. At last my friend began to think that perhaps there might be more significance than she had believed in her hostess' behaviour, and, close on 7 o'clock, she left for home. Arrived there, her first question was the whereabouts of the children, and the maid whom she had asked replied that ever since their tea, at about 4 o'clock, they had been alone in the nursery and very quiet. She at once hastened thither, to see her three small grandchildren seated on the floor and playing with burning pieces of paper which they tore from books and lighted at the fire.

Now I do not ask you to believe there is anything curious in all this; still, the remarkable behaviour of my friend's hostess, and the very unusual occupation of the children, might seem to point to something. Is it possible that some exterior influence conveyed to the hostess' mind that feeling, which my friend herself at last began to experience, of the necessity of departure? Perhaps, and perhaps not. As usual, Shakespeare has a ready word to fit the occasion: "There are more things in heaven and earth, Horatio . . ."

53. 'The Cricket Enthusiast'

College Days, No. 5, 9 July 1920[1]

There goes Jones. Jones is our cricket enthusiast. He will sit for hours over pictures of fat old men, who ought to know better, throwing a ball about, and tell you any bowler's average to two places of decimals. Once he has got hold of you there is no escaping. He comes up to you and asks you whether

Dashford are going to beat Blankshire: if you say yes or no you have to explain your reasons, and Jones proves them all wrong: if you say you don't know, you get all Jones' reasons, and all that there is to be said on each side. Finally, he shews you pictures of all the principal players.

And yet Jones wouldn't watch a cricket match if he was paid to, much less play. I used to think cricket enthusiasts were people who liked cricket: not a bit of it. They are people who like talking about cricket. The nearest Jones ever got to playing cricket is shewing you somebody or other's favourite late cut with a paper-knife. I asked him to come and watch a match with me the other day, but he said he hadn't time. And next day, when I met him, he started telling me all about it all the same. "Hullo," said I, "I thought you weren't there." "I wasn't," said Jones, "but I read the account." "Sniffins did well, didn't he?" said I. "Not bad," said Jones. "I thought it was better than not bad," I said, "forty-eight." "Forty-seven," says Jones carelessly. "It was forty-eight," I said; "I watch[ed] the whole thing." "Look here," says Jones, producing a newspaper, "forty-seven, you see." And sure enough it was forty-seven. Now is that fair when I watched the whole match?

I thought I'd play him a trick once, for, of course, Jones will never own up to not having heard of any cricketer. So one day I let him capture me particularly easily, and after he had talked a bit I said casually, "Boffington's coming on well this season, isn't he?" "Very," said Jones. "Likely to do a lot of damage, the papers say." "Sure to," says Jones. "By the way," said I, feeling I had got him now, "what's his average?" "Nine point seven two," snapped Jones, quite in his usual voice. "Jones," I said, laughing, "I've caught you at last. There's no such person as Boffington; I made him up." "What!" gasped Jones, with his eyes starting out of his head, "no such person as Boffington!—E. M. Boffington! Are you mad? Look here," and he lugged out one of those fat green books full of photographs.

·   ·   ·   ·   ·

And he still can't believe I hadn't heard of E. M. Boffington.

1. This story was preceded by 'The Slack-bob' (see *30*) in issue Number 5.

54. 'The Millionaire's Pearl'

College Days, No. 5, 9 July 1920

Craig Kennedy had been working the whole morning at a chemical analysis, evidently of some delicacy, and I was surprised to see him look up and say with a sigh, "Nearly finished now, Jameson." "What are you working at?" I enquired. "Oh, merely a murder case," drawled Craig. "Poisoning, of course. It is a curious thing," he went on reflectively, filling his large briar pipe, "that a woman cannot commit murder without giving herself away by carelessness. Here is a woman who used to put arsenic on her husband's toothbrush every morning. Of course she threw it away as soon as he was dead. But did she throw away the bristles that had come out? No. I found one of them; here it is." Craig pointed to a tiny test-tube in which a single bristle was swimming in some thick yellow liquid. "It has been immersed for 24 hours in a 3 per cent. solution of Borium oxide; I now add just a drop of Barium topside, and"—the solution turned a vivid blue, and finally changed to purple. "The well-known test," said Craig, "that test has done for more men than the public executioner." Just then the telephone bell rang, and I got up to answer it. "Hullo," said I, "who is that?" "Is that Mr. Kennedy?" cried a distracted female voice. "Come at once! I am Sadie Van Slapp, Twenty-ninth Avenue," and without further ado I was cut off. "Come on, Craig," I said, "it's Mrs. Van Slapp, the Society beauty." "What!" cried Craig, springing from his chair, "the wife of Xerxes P. Van Slapp, who owns the famous Samoan pearl?" It was the work of a few minutes for Craig to button his big blue automatic pistol under his jacket and slip a detectagraph into his pocket. In a moment we were walking briskly down the street, and soon we were at the door of the Van Slapps' house. Within everything was in confusion. Mr. Van Slapp, a large man with a bald head, met us in the hall. "My dear sir," he cried, "the most terrible things are happening! My pearl gone! My wife locking herself up! Elaine arrested!—" "Elaine?" snapped Kennedy. "My niece—" began Mr. Van Slapp, but Kennedy cut him short. "Show me where the pearl was last seen," he shot out. Van Slapp led us to a small ante-room full of cupboards and chests of drawers. "In here," he said, "we used to keep most of our valuables." Kennedy had hardly begun his usual systematic search when a tramping of heavy boots announced the arrival of the regular police. One of them held a bandbox in his hand. "What's that?" rapped out Craig. "This is strictly confidential, sir," replied the officer, laying the box down. "There's more in this than meets the eye," whispered Craig to me. Then aloud, "I wonder if you would care to examine the back of the house?" he said. The officers withdrew, and Craig whipped out the detectagraph from his pocket and thrust it behind a curtain, none too soon, for we heard Van Slapp's heavy step outside almost at once. "My wife is still locked up, sir," said he as he entered; "she will see no one except Molly O'Brien, her maid." "Ha!" said Kennedy. "Well, I think that will do for today. Kindly see that nothing is touched. I shall return at this hour tomorrow."

.   .   .   .   .

Next day found us once more alone in the little room. Craig extracted the detectagraph from its place, and we went out almost at once. Scarcely were we on the pavement, however, when a disreputable loafer, with his coat collar turned up, sidled up to us. "Say, mister," he said hoarsely, "are you Craig Kennedy, the private detective?" "Yes," returned Craig. "Are you Deadlock Denver of Pinkerton's?" "Right, mister," said the other. "Well, I hear you're on this job. We aren't. Well, there was a suspicious looking tough hanging about the back of Van Slapp's house night before last. Bite on that." And he was gone. "Wait for me," said Craig, and dived at once into the little alley behind the house. In a moment he returned, and we went home without further incident. Scarcely had we arrived, however, when the telephone bell

73

rang. It was Van Slapp. "My wife has come out," he said in a relieved voice. "Tell him to bring her round, and Molly O'Brien," said Craig to me. I did so, and in half an hour a ring at the bell announced their arrival. "Kindly sit down," said Craig, arranging chairs round the table, "and hold these little handles." So saying, he distributed little copper rods connected by thin wires to a clocklike instrument, opposite which he himself sat. For a few moments all was silence. "Ladies and gentlemen," he shot out suddenly, "a pearl has been stolen!" All the levers on the instruments jumped, and Craig paused to take a few notes. "It was stolen with the object of making money." One of the levers jumped again, "and was hidden in some peculiar place. Jewels," he said, grinding the words out slowly, "can be hidden in very curious places. In a cupboard, for instance," the lever jumped again, "or *behind* a cupboard. They have even been hidden in women's hair, or wigs. This jewel has left the house." Here he paused as abruptly as he had begun, and our guests departed.

"Jameson," said Craig to me as they went, "there was something funny about that bandbox. Here is that detectagraph. Here is the line which the instrument was drawing. It continues straight until the place marked on the scale 1 a.m. Then it begins to shake, denoting the entry of someone into the room. It remains still for a moment—they were standing still—and grows shaky again. Jameson," he said tensely, "we are going to burgle the Van Slapps' house to-night. It's for Elaine's sake."

It was very dark that night, and we had little difficulty, with soundproof rubber climbing boots on our feet, in scaling the wall up to the third floor of the Van Slapps' luxurious mansion, and into the little room. Craig picked up the bandbox, and spent a few moments in brushing the walls and tables with his own patent fingerprint eraser, and we returned at once. I awoke at half-past nine to find Kennedy fully dressed and chuckling over some suppressed joke. "Come along," said he, "we must go to the Van Slapps' at once." Once more on our arrival we found the master of the house extremely disturbed. "My wife has shut herself up again," he cried. "In the little room?" shot out Craig. "Yes," said Van Slapp. "Since when?" "The servants heard her enter it about 6 o'clock." "Ah," said Craig, "then we will act at once." He blew a whistle sharply, and two sturdy policemen stepped into the room. "Xerxes Van Slapp," ground out Kennedy, "you are arrested for fraud. You pretended that the pearl was stolen, so as to get the insurance money. You hid it carelessly, and it was found by——" "Oh, sir," cried little Molly O'Brien, "I didn't think it was real. I promise I didn't——"; but here a new interruption stopped her. Two more policemen entered, bringing between them a young man, evidently much frightened. "This is him, sir," said one of the officers; "we caught him skulking about your back-yard again." "Oh, Freddie," sobbed Molly O'Brien, "I oughtn't to have given it to you! I oughtn't to have given it to you!" "Molly O'Brien's fiancé," said Craig, "in the grocery trade. She picked up the pearl, thought it was imitation, and gave it to him. I recognised him, Jameson, by his feet," he interjected. "I went round that day to the back of the house with the footstep-photometer. I suppose," he continued, turning to the policemen, "Miss Dodge has been released?" "Miss Dodge?" said the man blankly. "Elaine," said Kennedy, with a note of surprise in his voice. "Oh, Miss Elaine Van Slapp, this gentleman's niece? Yes, sir, here she is now." And a stout young woman with glasses walked beaming into the room. It was not Elaine Dodge after all . . .

"And now, sir," said Kennedy grimly to the handcuffed Van Slapp, "I will solve the mystery about your wife." He picked up the bandbox and led the way to the little room. "Stand back!" he snapped, and a few well directed shots from his automatic blew the lock from the door. A curious sight met our eyes. A bald-headed man in woman's clothes stood cowering against the far wall. Kennedy handed him the bandbox. "Your property, I believe," said he. "I borrowed it, as the police did previously." The curious figure snatched the lid from the box, and out of it came a splendid blonde wig, which it thrust upon its head. It was Sadie Van Slapp, the Society beauty!

"You will please keep the case out of court, Mr. Kennedy," she said. "It is true that Xerxes had given me the pearl, but I don't want to prosecute."

55. 'The Youthful Mariner (Extract)'[1]

College Days, No. 5, 9 July 1920

The Mariner blesseth the wind that helpeth him upon his way.

> The sun shone out, the clouds went down,
>   The wind sprang up behind;
> I blest the wind that blew me on,
>   And was so soft and kind.
>
> The boat clove through the rippling stream,
>   And merrily splashed the oar;
> I blest the wind*, so soft and kind,
>   And the boat that ran before.

He inadvertently runneth upon a sand bank.

> Then struck mine ear a jarring scrape
>   Like wood that grinds on sand,
> And looking round, I lay aground
>   And close beside the land.

And, when he hath righted himself, findeth that the good weather is changing.

> I pushed her out with left-hand scull,
>   And backed her down with right:
> But when I reached the middle stream
>   The sun was out of sight.

The weather rapidly changeth for the worse.

> The wind sprang up and blurred the stream,
>   And ever colder grew;
> The rising swell was rough as hell:
>   Ye gods, but how it blew!

Until he is in danger of ship-wreck.

> The clouds were black, they whirled along,
>   And madly ran the wave.
> Alas, thought I, that such a sky
>   Should see me in my grave!

He turneth for home.	I turned for home; but still the flood
	    Rose high and ever higher;
	It splashed my back and, cold as ice,
	    It burnt my skin like fire.

But maketh	The rain came down by pints and quarts,
	    And soaked me to the bone;
	The waves rose free and wild as the sea,
	    And I was all alone.

Small progress.	My boat began to rock and sway,
	    The water trickled in.
	Alas for home, in the leaping foam
	    That drowned me with its din!

	Then on and on and down the stream
	    That never seemed to end.
	(Suppose the boat had overturned!—
	    But heav'n such thoughts forfend.)

He heareth the voice of a fellow sufferer.	Then in by bank, and down and down;
	    The trees scarce let me pass.
	Then struck mine ear a human voice,
	    Cried, "Look ahead, you ass!"

	Oh joyful sound that met mine ear!
	    As sweet as wedding bell,
	That saved my mind in wave and wind,
	    And very mouth of hell.

And, the weather abating, reacheth home safely.	Then fell the wind and shone the sun
	    At the kindly voice of man;
	And I was home from flood and foam
	    Before Fourth School began.

*See Schoeffenheimer's Etymological Dictionary:
"I cannot find it in my mind to call it wind,
But I can find it in my mind to call it wind."

1. '(Extract)' is part of the original: all that was printed is given here. The model is Coleridge's
'The Rime of the Ancient Mariner.' The last two stanzas formed part of the material for *The
Election Times*, Number 4; see *29*.

56. To Steven Runciman

August 1920   Handwritten

                             Grove Terrace   Polperro RSO[1]   Cornwall.

My dear Runciman,[2]
I have a little spare time, and I feel I *must* tell you about my first adventure as
an amateur tramp. Like most tramps I was driven to it. When I got to a

wretched little place in Devonshire, — Seaton Junction, Mynors,[3] who had to change there, came to my carriage & said that a beastly Oppidan who had been perpetually plaguing me to travel in the same compartment as him was asking for me. As I was among strangers, I got out to go to him whereupon the train started off. You need two hands to enter a moving train, & I, what with kit-bag, belt etc had only one. To be brief, I was left behind. I despatched a telegram to say I would be late (it arrived next day), & about 2 ½ hours later got a train: at Plymouth, North Rd, I found there were no more trains to Looe that night. It was too late to telephone, as the post offices were shut. I then made a consultation of my financial position. I had enough for my remaining fare & 7 ½d over. I could therefore either sleep at the Y.M.C.A. place, price 6d, & starve, or have something to eat but nowhere to sleep. I chose the latter, I put my kit-bag in the cloak-room & got 12 buns for 6d: half-past-nine found me sneaking into some farmer's field, — there were a few fields wedged in among rows of slummy houses. In that light I of course looked like a soldier strolling round, — on my way I had been asked whether I was demobilized yet, & I finally came to anchor in the corner of a field near some allotments. I then began to remember that people frequently got fourteen days for sleeping in somebody else's field & "having no visible means of support", particularly as every dog in the neighbourhood barked if I ever so much as moved. The corner had a large tree for shelter, & bushes for concealment, but it was unendurably cold; I had no covering, my cap was my pillow, I lay "with my martial cloak (rolled cape) around me".[4] I only dozed & shivered till about 1 oc, when I readjusted my puttees, & managed to sleep long enough to miss the first train, at 4.20. by about an hour, & to have to wait till 7.45 for another. My teeth were still chattering when I awoke. When I got to Looe I was forced to walk 4 miles in the hot sun; I am very proud of this adventure, but I would not repeat it.

Yours sincerely,
E. A. Blair.

1. Railway Sorting Office, which acted as poste restante. Polperro has, and had, no station. The nearest is at Looe, three miles to the east. The Blair family spent most of its summer holidays in Cornwall at either Looe or Polperro. On this particular journey Orwell was returning from an Eton Officers' Training Corps exercise and was therefore in uniform.
2. Steven Runciman (1903–; Kt., 1958) was a King's Scholar in the same Election as Orwell, and later a distinguished historian whose works include *A History of the Crusades*, *The Sicilian Vespers*, and *The Fall of Constantinople*.
3. Roger Mynors was a member of Orwell's Election; see *29*.
4. From stanza 3 of 'The Burial of Sir John Moore after Corunna,' the poem parodied in *College Days*, Number 5; see *50*: 'But he lay like a warrior taking his rest / With his martial cloak around him.'

57. To Prosper Buddicom

28 [December 1920]   Handwritten; dated from postmark

usual [address]

My dear Prosper,[1]
Thanks awfully for your invitation. I shall be very pleased to come & stay at
Quarry House[2] from the 17th to the end of the holidays. I expect this will find
you at Ticklerton.[3] My address will be

Walnut tree House
Bursball[4]
nr Ipswich.

I go on Thursday. We are going to the Blue Lagoon[5] this afternoon & the
Beggars' Opera[6] tomorrow. I hope you will have a good time in Shropshire.
I must write & congratulate your mother on her marriage.

Yours
Eric.

1. Prosper Buddicom was one year younger than Orwell; see Crick, 130.
2. Quarry House was built for the Buddicoms on the Bolney Estate, Shiplake-on-Thames, about 1903. See *Eric and Us*, 3–4.
3. Ticklerton Court, near Church Stretton, Shropshire, was the home of Grandfather Buddicom and Aunt Lilian Buddicom. Orwell spent Easter and most of the summer holiday of 1917 there. A chapter (58–69) of *Eric and Us* is devoted to this time.
4. Cousins of Orwell's father lived at Bursball. Prosper fell ill, so the visit to Quarry House was cancelled; see Crick, 130.
5. *The Blue Lagoon* was originally a novel (1908), by the popular Henry de Vere Stacpoole (1863–1951). It was adapted for the stage by Norman MacOwan and Charlton Mann in 1920, and later became a film. The play was regarded as rather risqué, because it dramatised the adventures of a girl and boy shipwrecked on a deserted island and their growing to maturity. It was produced at the Prince of Wales Theatre, London, by Basil Dean, and had 263 performances. An excellent illustration appears in Thompson, 11. It was presented in New York in 1921.
6. This was Sir Nigel Playfair's production. Less acidic than Brecht's adaptation later in the decade, it proved enormously popular, running for 1,469 performances, even though it was given at the Lyric Theatre in Hammersmith. The conductor was Eugene Goosens. An impression of what Orwell heard can be gained from the recording of eighteen numbers by the original cast, conducted by the arranger, Frederic Austin, who also sang Peachum, made in the month Orwell went to the Lyric, and reissued in 1980.

58. To Prosper Buddicom

Monday [10 January 1921]   Handwritten; dated from postmark

Walnut tree house   Bursball

My dear Prosper,
Thanks for your letter. It was most awfully good your shooting the two snipe
& the woodcock. You ought to get at least one of them stuffed, I think.

I have bought one of those big cage-rat traps. This place is over-run with
rats. It is rather good sport to catch a rat, & then let it out & shoot at it as it
runs. If it gets away I think one ought to let it go & not chase it. If they are

threshing the corn while you are there, I should advise you to go,—it is well worth it. The rats come out in dozens. It is also rather sport to go at night to a corn-stack with an acetylene bycicle° lamp, & you can dazzle the rats that are running along the side & whack at them,—or shoot them with a rifle. I rather wish I had my rifle here, as there are no rabbits.

Au revoir, please give my regards (or whatever it is,) to your aunt & uncle & everyone.

Yours
Eric.

59. To Prosper Buddicom

Wednesday, 19 January 1921   Handwritten; dated from postmark

23 Mall Chambers   Nottinghill gate   W8.

My dear Prosper,
So sorry to hear you aren't well; it is rather a dismal way to end the holidays, but I suppose you wont mind much if you have to go back to school late. Mummie was going to have written to your mother, only she has been awfully busy lately. I didn't shoot anything much in Suffolk. All the rabbits had been wired; There were three covies of partridges there, but they were so wild that I could[1] get a shot inside seventy yards. I trapped & shot a few rats. I hope you had a nice time in Shropshire,—the shooting must have been just about at its best. I suppose Guinever was allowed to shoot this time.

I have got an idea of buying Turkish tobacco, & making cigarettes of it, but it's awfully hard to get.

Well, au revoir; we are just going out. I hope you'll get better soon. Please remember me to everyone.

Yours
Eric.

1. He probably meant 'couldn't.'

60. Extract from letter to Cyril Connolly

Easter 1921

The original and the complete text of this letter are lost. What survives does so because Cyril Connolly quoted part of Orwell's letter when writing to Terence Beddard at Easter 1921; Connolly copied out this section for the Orwell Archive in June 1967. Another version, with interspersed ironic comments by Connolly, exists at Tulsa University, and that is given in Michael Shelden's biography of Orwell. In a note added to the copy made for the Archive, Connolly explained that this extract was part of a letter to Beddard which Connolly printed in *Enemies of Promise* (1938), 256–59. Beddard was dead by the time Connolly made this copy. He was a King's Scholar in the Election before Orwell's; he left Eton exactly a year before Orwell and was no longer there when Connolly wrote to him. Christopher Eastwood[1] is described by Connolly in his notes as 'an attractive boy with a good voice & rather a prig.' He went on: 'The point of the letter is that Eastwood, being in my election, was bound to see much more of me than of Blair, in the election above us.' E. A. Caröe[2] was in Blair's Election, and Redcliffe-Maud[3] two Elections below Connolly's. For something of the background to this letter, see chapters 20 and 21 of *Enemies of Promise*. Michael Shelden remarks that it would be unwise to assume that Orwell's 'adolescent affections for other boys ever reached an advanced stage of sexual contact. He may well have been as chaste in his relationships with boys as he was in his relationship with Jacintha. As his letter to Connolly reveals, he was awkward in romantic matters and was slow to assert himself.'[4]

I am afraid I am gone on Eastwood. This may surprise you but it is not imagination I assure you. The point is that I think you are too, at any rate you were at the end of last half. I am not jealous of you. But you though you aren't jealous are apt to be what I might call 'proprietary'. In the case of Maud & Caroe° you were quite right but what I want you to do is not regard me as another Caroe whatever points of resemblance there may be. Don't suspect me of any ill intentions either. If I had not written to you, about 3[5] weeks into next half you would notice how things stood, your proprietary instincts would have been aroused & having a lot of influence over Eastwood you would probably have put him against me somehow, perhaps even warned him off me. Please dont° do this I implore you. Of course I dont ask you to resign your share in him only dont say spiteful things.

Connolly's copy in the Orwell Archive concludes: 'Rather a revelation . . . Anyhow Eastwood has noticed it and is full of suspicion as he hates Blair.'

1. Christopher Eastwood (1905–1983) became a senior civil servant. He was Assistant Under-Secretary of State, Colonial Office, 1947–52 and 1954–66, and Commissioner for Crown Lands, 1952–54. See *Remembering Orwell*, 16–18, for his reminiscences of Orwell at Eton.
2. Einar Athelstan Caröe (1903–1988) became a grain merchant and broker, associated particularly with Liverpool. According to Connolly's notes, he was unpopular at Eton.
3. Baron Redcliffe-Maud (1906–1982) became a particularly distinguished civil servant. Among his important appointments were, Permanent Secretary, Ministry of Education, 1945–52, and at Ministry of Fuel and Power, 1952–59; High Commissioner, then Ambassador, to South Africa, 1959–63; Master of University College, Oxford, 1963–76.
4. See Shelden, 75–76; U.S.: 70–71.
5. Connolly's manuscript originally has '6' but this has been crossed out. This may indicate fidelity to Orwell's original, but because there are a considerable number of differences between the version Connolly gave the Orwell Archive and that at Tulsa (in addition to Connolly's ironic comments), it is impossible to be sure how reliable Connolly's text is.

61. 'Mr Puffin and the Missing Matches'
[c. 1919–22][1]   Handwritten

"And now, dear," said Mrs. Puffin, "here is the taxi. Are you sure you've got everything?" Mr Puffin was going to stay for a week with some friends in the country: he looked over his belongings. "Yes my dear, I think so," "And, Walter," added his wife, "don't forget to think of your poor little wife sometimes." "No, my love," said Mr Puffin dutifully, "I'll tie a knot in my handkerchief." Mrs Puffin reflected on this remark as they walked to the taxi, but finally put it down to the confusion of departure. "And now, Walter" she said again, "you're quite certain there's nothing you've forgotten?" "No, dear, I've got everything."

. . . .

But he hadn't. It was four o'clock when he stepped out at the little station of Ditchby-in-the-Mud, junction for Brambleton. Already it was almost dark. "When's the next train for Brambleton?" he asked the solitary porter. "Five forty five" said the porter shortly, & walked out of the station, whistling. Heavens! nearly two hours, & he'd read all his magazines. He looked sourly at the unlighted, fireless waiting room. "Go & have a smoke," he thought. Then a chill seemed to fall upon him. Smoke? He thrust his hands into his overcoat-pockets: no matches. His coat-pockets & trouser pockets were as empty. A hasty search through his waistcoat-pockets proved useless. There was no hope. There wasn't a match about him. He tried the penny-in-the-slot machine, but after wasting fourpence & a great deal of bad language, he noticed that it was empty. Then he thought of the porter: but the porter was out of sight, & there didn't seem to be a house within miles. In dumb despair he sat down at last in the chilly waiting room, his head between his hands, to wait for his train. At last he looked at[2] his watch: the hands pointed to twenty minutes past four; it seemed as though centuries had passed. With a sigh he rose,—thinking perhaps someone might have dropped a match in the room,[3]—& began to grope[4] about the floor. An age of searching (five minutes by his watch) produced eleven used matches & four toothpicks, after which he again took his seat in despair. But even as he did so a glad sound struck his ear: another man was coming to the waiting room. Radiant[5] with hope Mr Puffin leapt towards him. "Have you got a match?" he cried. The stranger collapsed limply into a chair. "I was going to have asked you the same" he said feebly. "An hour & a quarter in this frozen mortuary, & no matches: My God!" "Surely there is some way of getting a light" exclaimed Mr Puffin. "What[6] is it they always do in adventure stories?" "We might try flint & steel," said the stranger hopefully. They tried it: they also broke Mr Puffin's knife, & the stranger's knife, & gashed Mr Puffin's finger, but they got no light. "If I ever meet a writer of adventure stories in this life or the next—" began the stranger between clenched teeth, but he broke off suddenly as another pair of feet could be heard coming towards the waiting room. A little man, looking in the gloom like a solicitor, or perhaps an undertaker, came into the room. "Have you got a match?" cried both men together. "I am a

81

non–smoker," replied the new–comer, "but it is possible . . . ah, yes. I have just one match." The two erstwhile friends now glared at each other with the hatred of rivalry. "Of course," continued the newcomer suavely, "I may need this match. I think it should be bought from me at the price of a box." "Righto!" cried Mr Puffin's rival, "here's three-hapence." "Nonsense!" cried Mr Puffin, elbowing him aside, "I've as much right as him." "Then I shall be compelled to sell it by, er—auction." The auction began briskly, & continued by penny bids up to two shillings, but two & fourpence saw Mr Puffin the victor. "Here's half a crown," he cried; "I've no change. Give me the match." With trembling hands he carried it to the window. Then he turned round, convulsed with rage. "Damn you!" he screamed, "this is a safety!" "That, sir, was not mentioned in the contract." But Mr Puffin's rival sidled up to him with longing in his face. "I say" he said, "if I tell you something, will you give me a light after you've lit yours?" "Give you a light—well what is it?" "Safety matches strike on glass." "Do they?" With renewed hope Mr Puffin turned to the window. The match struck at the second attempt: and then, before it was well alight, some adverse draught put it irrevocably out. "Our troubles," said the man who had sold the match, "are better faced in a philosophical spirit"—but something in the two men's faces caused him to leave the waiting-room in haste.

The rest of their vigil will not bear description.

. . . .

The Brambleton train entered another station, & the ticket collector entered the carriage where Puffin & the stranger, his friend again now, sat icy & dejected. "Tickets please!" he said briskly. Mr Puffin began his usual search. Oh, yes, it was in his ticket-pocket. He put a hand[7] into his ticket-pocket, & his fingers closed on something hard. He drew it out.

It was his match box.

1. Date is very uncertain. The story is not dissimilar to those Avril Dunn reported her brother as scribbling in notebooks when he was fourteen or fifteen (see 27), but the handwriting is more mature, so it might have been written as much as a decade later.
2. at] for
3. room] roomed
4. grope] groped
5. Radiant] Mr Radiant
6. Single quotation mark before 'What'
7. hand] finger

62. 'Friendship and love'

Summer 1921

Orwell's last poem to Jacintha Buddicom:[1]

> Friendship and love are closely intertwined,
> My heart belongs to your befriending mind:
> But chilling sunlit fields, cloud-shadows fall—
> My love can't reach your heedless heart at all.

Jacintha Buddicom responded with:

> By light
> Too bright
> Are dazzled eyes betrayed:
> It's best
> To rest
> Content in tranquil shade

1. Reproduced from *Eric and Us*, 117. Jacintha Buddicom commented, 'Typical of both of us, Eric with his straightforward, ten-syllable couplets, and me chopping up the same metre into shorter lines with extra rhymes to them, which I thought more fun to do and more singable' (118). See Crick, 134.

1922–1927

63. Burma, 1922–1927

It is not possible to date precisely the material Orwell wrote (or, rather, drafted) in Burma or, based on his experiences in Burma, soon after his return to England. Some, especially the poems, is written on the backs of official memorandum paper; some on large sheets measuring 13½ by 8½ inches. The use of official stationery is consistent with, though not proof of, composition in Burma or soon after Orwell's return home. Orwell began writing *Burmese Days* in the autumn of 1931 and completed it two years later; in 'Why I Write' he says he wrote the novel when he was thirty (1933) but had 'projected' it much earlier.

Orwell left Eton in December 1921. His application to join the Indian Imperial Police and to compete at the 1922 examination was received by the India Office on 7 April 1922, and a copy of the second edition of the current regulations was sent to him four days later. References were provided by P. Hope, formerly a sixth-form master at Dulwich College, at whose tutorial establishment in Southwold Orwell enrolled in January 1922 to prepare for the examination, and by John Crace, Master in College, Eton, see *35, n. 3*. These were dated 4 and 24 April 1922 respectively. In the 23 November 1922 printed report on the competitive examination, Eric Arthur Blair was seventh of twenty-nine successful candidates. He obtained 8,464 marks out of a possible 12,400, the pass mark being 6,000. His marks (each out of 2,000) were: English, 1,372; English History and Geography, 1,019; Elementary Mathematics, 1,158; French, 1,256; Latin, 1,782; Greek, 1,703; in addition, he scored 174 out of 400 for Freehand Drawing. Of the twenty-three candidates who passed the Indian Imperial Police riding test in September 1922, Orwell was twenty-first, with 104 marks out of 200 (100 being the pass mark). In completing his preference form, he opted for Burma.

Orwell arrived in Burma on 27 November 1922 and joined the Mandalay Training School two days later. One of his colleagues, Roger Beadon, in a Telediphone recording made for the BBC on 5 December 1969, recalled that whereas he found it very difficult to switch rapidly from instruction in the Burmese language to Hindustani, Orwell did this with ease. Before he left Burma, Orwell was able to speak fluently with Burmese priests in 'very high-flown Burmese.' His movements from Mandalay are officially recorded as: to Maymyo 30 November 1923; Mandalay 17 December 1923; Mayaungmya 26 January 1924; Twante 31 May 1924; Syriam 16 December 1924; Insein 26 September 1925; Moulmein 19 April 1926; and Katha 23 December 1926. He left Burma on 12 July 1927 on five months' and twenty days' leave. Katha provided a basis for Kayauktada in *Burmese Days*.

Orwell arrived back in England in August 1927, and while on holiday with his family in Cornwall in September decided not to return to Burma. During the rest of his leave he lived in a cheap room next door to Ruth Pitter (see *139, n. 1*) in Portobello Road, Notting Hill, London W 11. He made his first expedition into the East End that autumn, and was permitted to resign from the Indian Imperial Police as from 1 January 1928. In the spring he went to Paris.

Another colleague of Orwell's in Burma, possibly, was George Stuart, a recording of whose reminiscences is in the Orwell Archive. A G. R. T. Stuart is recorded in Thacker's Directory in the India Office Library as being assistant engineer, Burma Railways, Katha, in 1929, though that would not preclude his being there earlier. The recorded interview was by Jane Langdon-Davies and John Wall; they gave their address as 50 Lawford Road, N 1 (presumably an error for NW5) Orwell's address in 1935–36. Michael Shelden was unable to trace the recordists but Crick did and believed them to be 'thoroughly reliable witnesses' (Crick, 3rd edition, 586–89). These reminiscences show a detailed knowledge of Burma at the time. Stuart states that Orwell was easygoing and keen about his job; he was the life and soul of parties, and very fond of animals, rescuing waifs and strays. He spoke slowly and softly, was not anti-establishment, was very popular and an excellent linguist. He learned not only Burmese quickly, but also 'the most difficult languages' (Shaw-Karen?), particularly for the thousand-rupee bonus given for each examination passed. Even at that time, he had a weak chest and failed to look after himself, so he suffered badly now and then. Mrs Stuart kept Orwell's clothes in repair. Stuart states that Orwell was sent to Katha as punishment for shooting an elephant in Lower Burma, which, if correct, throws an interesting light on the essay 'Shooting an Elephant.'

See Crick, 139–75, 586–89; Stansky and Abrahams, I, 151–85; Hollis, 27; Shelden, 101–05, 506, n. 2; U.S.: 93–97, 460, n. 2; also *Orwell Remembered*, 62–66, for reminiscences of Roger Beadon and L. W. Marrison, who knew Orwell in Burma, and 68–75 for Ruth Pitter's reminiscences; 'George Orwell and Burma' by Maung Htin Aung, and 'Imperial Attitudes' by John Gross, in *The World of George Orwell*. Orwell describes his Burma experiences in chapters 8 and 9 of *The Road to Wigan Pier*. He is mentioned in *Land of Chindits and Rubies* by May Hearsey (published by Mrs J. Leverston-Allen, London, 1982), 94–95.

The paper Orwell used offers evidence of two kinds. Some of the government paper bears production dates; some of the typing and writing paper has watermarks. The section beginning 'I said at the end of the last chapter' (see 72) is written on two sheets of paper. The first measures 13½ by 8½ inches (foolscap) and has on the verso the stock date 15 September 1916. Since 150,000 of this form were produced, it may have been one of the last. Flory's autobiography (73) is written on the reverse of quarto-sized paper (8½ by 6½ inches). This form, an Office Memorandum, has the same wording as the larger one, except that the date line is '192– ' instead of '19 '; its production date is 1 February 1925. Clearly what it contains must have been written after that date, perhaps a short time after, allowing time for distribution and the possibility that old stocks were not exhausted. The survival of two or three sheets of still unused paper suggests that Orwell could have taken a supply with him for use on the ship going home, though it is so unpleasant that it is hardly a kind one would bother to carry, bearing in mind that he was not too badly paid. See Stansky and Abrahams, I, 168, where his pay as Assistant District Superintendent is described as 'an adequate sum in the early 1920s to live a comfortable life' and Davison, *A Literary Life*, 15. The likelihood (it can be no more) is that the first three sections (71, 72, 73) on government paper were written in Burma or on the way home.

The fourth section (74) has paper with no marks by which it might be identified. The final two pages, section 5 (75) are on two sizes and two qualities of paper bearing the word Aviemore, with an illustration of a buckled belt surrounding a gauntleted hand holding a dagger. This paper was made at least as early as 1922 by John Muir of Manchester and subsequently by Jacobsen, Welch and Co Ltd of Cheshire.

The paper used for section 3 (73) has a watermark that probably appeared first in 1928, or possibly a year earlier. This has the words BRITISH EMBLEM and carries the design of a rose. It was made by Thomas and Green Ltd of Buckinghamshire. (That the copy starts 'I was born in Buckinghamshire' is presumably coincidental.) It is probable, therefore, that 'The Autobiography of John Flory' was typed, and perhaps written, shortly after Orwell's return to England.

On this evidence, a precise chronological order of the sections cannot be given. See 70 for the reminiscences of George Stuart regarding the stories Orwell wrote in Burma; 64, 66, and 67 are in manuscript.

64. 'Dear Friend: allow me for a little while'

[1922–1927?]   Written in Burma?   Handwritten

> Dear Friend: allow me for a little while
> To speak without those high & starry lies
> Wherein we use to drown our thoughts until
> Even ourselves believe them. Hear then, first,
> Not all the screams of twenty thousand victims
> Broken on the wheel or plunged in boiling oil
> Could pain me like one tooth in my own head;
> And secondly, I do not care what comes
> When I am gone, though kings or peoples rot,
> Though life itself grow old; I do not care
> Though all the streams & all the seas ran blood;
> I care not if ten myriad blazing stars
> Rain on the earth & burn it dead as stone;
> I care not if God dies.// And all because
> Frankly, & look at it which way you will,
> This life, this earth, this time will see me out,
> And that is about all I care about.

65. 'Romance'

[1922–1927?]   Written in Burma? Only a typewritten version survives

> When I was young and had no sense,
> In far off Mandalay
> I lost my heart to a Burmese girl
> As lovely as the day.

Her skin was gold, her hair was jet,
Her teeth were ivory;
I said "For twenty silver pieces,
Maiden, sleep with me."

She looked at me, so pure, so sad,
The loveliest thing alive,
And in her lisping,[1] virgin voice,
Stood out for twenty five.

1. lisping] gentl *crossed out*

66. Draft of Poem, 'When the Franks have lost their sway'

[1922–1927?]   Written in Burma?   Handwritten

When the Franks have lost their sway
And their soldiers are slain or fled,
When the ravisher has his way
And the slayer's sword is red;
When the last lone Englishman dies
In the painted Hindu towers,
Beneath ten thousand burning eyes
In a rain of bloody flowers, or again[1]
Moving more westward to the lands we know,[2]

When the people have won their dreams,
And the tyrant's flag is down,
When the blood is running in streams
Through the gutters of London town;
When the air is burst with the thunder
And crash of the falling thrones,
And the crack[3] of the empires[4] torn asunder
And the dying tyrant's groans, when, as I said[5]
These things all happen, which, one fears, they may.
Or moving onward through the mist of time
To[6] watch the last wild[7] ending of the world,—
When the birds fall out of the sky,
And leaf is black on the tree,
When the creatures of earth all die,
And the ice grows over the sea;
When the suns & moons in their flight
Stand still at an icy breath,
And the wheel of the day & the night
Is locked in the freedom of death;
When the toil of a thousand years[8]
Is lost in a second of time,

When the hopes are gone with the fears
And the prayer is vain as the rhyme;
When the gods have had their day
And[9] Death with the others dies,
When the stars are empty for ever & aye
As they hang in the jet black skies,—oh my dear brethren
Is it not dreadful thus to contemplate
These mighty ills that[10] will beset the world
When we are dead & won't be bothered with them?
Do not these future woes transcend our own?

1. or again] *originally only a dash*
2. Moving . . . we know] Or, again, look a little nearer home, *off-set in left margin*
3. crack] shrieks
4. empires] virgins
5. when, as I said] or yet again; *the w of* when *may be intended to be a capital* W; *comma after groans may have been altered to a period*
6. *An asterisk appears to precede this line.*
7. wild] cold
8. *This and the next three lines are written at the bottom of the page and marked for insertion at this point.*
9. *An asterisk appears to precede 'And.'*
10. that] they

67. 'My love & I walked in the dark'

[1922–1927?]   Written in Burma?   Handwritten

My love & I walked in the dark
Of many a scented night in June;
My love & I did oft remark
How yellow was the waning moon,
How yellow was the moon.

My love & I walked in the sun
Of many a golden summer day;
My love & I were quite at one
To say how sweetly smelt the hay,
How sweetly smelt the hay.

And all throughout that pleasant while,
When life & earth appeared so fair,
My love & I did often smile
To think what happy folks we were,
What happy folks we were.

But now, with one thing & another,
When we are old & wise, it seems
My love & I do never bother
To talk upon those ancient themes,
Those idle, ancient themes.

The suns & moons are much the same,
But all their golden charms are fled,
And she & I look back with shame
To think of all the things we said,
The foolish things we said.

68. 'Suggested by a Toothpaste Advertisement'

[1922–1927]   Written in Burma? Only a typewritten version survives

(Long ago, I used to chant this sometimes as I washed my teeth, but that is a practice I have abandoned for two years or more. My self respect and my last tooth brush both wore out soon after I got here.)

Brush your teeth up and down, brother,
Oh, brush them up and down!
All the folks in London Town
Brush their teeth right up and down,
Oh! How they shine!
Aren't they bloody fine?
Night and morning, my brother,
Oh brush them up and down!

69. 'The Lesser Evil'

[1922–1927?]   Written in Burma? Typescript with handwritten revisions

Empty as death and slow as pain
The days went by on leaden feet;
And parson's week[1] had come again
As I walked down the little street.

Without, the weary doves were calling,
The sun burned on the banks of mud;
Within, old maids were caterwauling
A dismal tale of thorns and blood.

I thought of all the church bells ringing
In towns that Christian folks were in;
I heard the godly maidens singing;
I turned into the house of sin.

The house of sin was dark & mean,
With dying flowers round the door;
They spat their betel juice between
The rotten bamboos of the floor.

Why did I come, the woman cried,
So seldom to her beds of ease?
When I was not, her spirit died,
And would I give her ten rupees.

The weeks went by, and many a day
That black-haired woman did implore
Me as I hurried on my way
To come more often than before.

The days[2] went by like dead leaves falling.
And parson's week came round again.
Once more devout old maids were bawling
Their ugly rhymes of death and pain.

The woman waited for me there
As down the little street I trod;
And musing upon her oily hair,[3]
I turned into the house of God.

Stanzas four and five are handwritten replacements for what was originally typed:

The woman oiled her hair of coal,
She had no other occupation.
She swore she loved me as her soul,
She had no other conversation.

The only thing that woman knew
Was getting money out of men.
Each time she swore she loved me true
She struck me for another ten.

1. From Monday to Saturday in the next week (thirteen days inclusive), when a parson takes the intervening Sunday as a holiday. The persona of a parson adopted here might be compared with Orwell's poem 'A happy vicar I might have been,' written at the end of 1935 and published in 'Why I Write'; see 3007.
2. days] weeks
3. And musing . . . hair,] I mused upon her oily hair, The metre requires upon to be changed to on but Orwell did not do this.

70. Preliminaries to Burmese Days

There are nineteen pages of manuscript[1] that, though not drafts of Burmese Days, would seem to be sketches for the novel. Whether they were written in Burma or shortly after Orwell's return from there, either in England or in France, is impossible to ascertain. Stansky and Abrahams speak of this material as 'early drafts of Burmese Days,' though it is doubtful if it has quite that status. They argue that Flory's 'Epitaph' may have been written in 1927–28, and add, 'there has even been a suggestion that it was written when Blair was still in Burma,' but

93

they are of the opinion that it is slightly later, 'early in 1930 perhaps—after Blair's return from Paris, where his literary apprenticeship had really got under way' (I, 203). Crick thinks that, from handwriting and paper, this material was written either in the winter of 1927–28 in London or during 1928–29 in Paris.

Crick suggests that the pages 'are either part of a longer, missing manuscript or a trial run for sections of "The Tale of John Flory". It is in the first person and "the author," John Flory, seems to be writing his autobiography in prison, awaiting execution indeed, as a cautionary tale or final confession. It begins, in fine black humour, with "My Epitaph" . . . ' (195). It is not certain that Flory is in prison, awaiting execution. He might be in some remote part of the jungle where there is no one who could form the letters of his epitaph. In prison, he might be denied an epitaph on a nearby peepul tree, but there would be plenty who could form letters. His end is, perhaps, more akin to what Lackersteen's might have been were he to spend his days in the jungle without a wife to minister to him, limit his drink, and ward off women. Some support for this interpretation might come from the place name 'Nyaunglebin' (not 'Nyauglebiu,' as in Crick, 196). This is a common village name in Burma and means 'Four Banyan Trees.' There is no prison connection.

The surviving material, apart from the poems on Burmese subjects or with Burmese references, is in five sections: 1. My Epitaph (1 page); 2. 'I said at the end of the last chapter . . .' (1½ pages), which promises 'ten thousand words about my childhood'; 3. Autobiography (4 pages), 600 words only and ending in mid-sentence; 4. Incident in Rangoon, beginning 'Here for awhile I abandon autobiography . . .' (10 pages), which seems complete and could almost be a short story; it mentions Kyauktada (of *Burmese Days*); 5. Rebuke by a superior officer for consorting with Eurasians (2 pages, numbered 19 and 20) which begins and ends in mid-sentence.

It is extremely unlikely that these pages form 'one draft.' The handwriting, though recognisably Orwell's, differs, and the order given above has no authority or certainty. Crick places 4 after the Epitaph and quotes its opening as being the 'first paragraph of the rest of the manuscript' (196). Orwell may have sketched an outline for 'The Tale of John Flory,' and these sections could represent the order for it, though written at different times. It is at least as probable that they are disjunct sketches. The handwriting of the Epitaph is not unlike that of the two poems written on official stationary ('Dear Friend' and 'When the Franks have lost their sway') and that of the rebuke not dissimilar to that of 'My love & I.' It is dangerous to hazard such guesses, but it is possible that at least 'My Epitaph' was written before Orwell left Burma, and not unlikely that 4 was written in Paris rather than in London. See *63* for details on the paper used.

A colleague of Orwell's in Burma, George Stuart (see *63*), in an interview, in the Orwell Archive, states that Orwell started to be interested in writing stories of Burma when they and Stuart's wife were in Katha (or Quatar). Indeed, he says, 'his original manuscript of *Burmese Days* was written up in Quatar . . . most of the people referred to were local government officers like the deputy commissioner and the superintendent of police.'

1. Crick gives a figure of twenty-one (195), but he has counted separately the manuscript and typed versions of 'The Autobiography of John Flory'; see *73*.

71. 1. 'John Flory: My Epitaph'

[1926–1930?]   Handwritten in ink on reverse of Government of Burma paper

Goodness knows where they will bury me,—in their own grave yard I suppose, two feet deep in a painted coffin. There will be no mourners, and no rejoicers either, which seems sadder still,[1] for the Burmese celebration of[2] a funeral with music & gambling is[3] nicer than our beastly mummeries. But if there were anyone here[4] whose hand could form the letters, I would [like][5] him to carve this on the bark of some great peepul tree above my head.[6]

JOHN FLORY

B o r n   1 8 9 0

Died of Drink 1927.

"Here lies the bones of poor John Flory;
His story was the old, old story.
Money, women, cards & gin
Were the four things that did him in.

He has spent sweat enough to swim in
Making love to stupid[7] women;
He has known misery past thinking
In the dismal art of drinking.

O stranger, as you voyage here
And read this welcome, shed no tear;
But take the single gift I give,
And learn from me how not to live."

1. which seems sadder still] *interlinear addition*
2. celebration of] custom of celebrating
3. is] seems
4. here] *interlinear addition*
5. like] *editorial addition*

6. head] bed
7. stupid] married

72. 2. Extract, Preliminary to Autobiography

[1926–1930?]   Handwritten in ink on reverse of Government of Burma paper

I said at the end of the last chapter that I was trying to make love to Mrs. Lackersteen, although Lackersteen was my best friend, & although I liked him much better than I liked his wife. He was much the more attractive of the two; more alive, more intelligent, less selfish, & even perhaps better looking. My feeling for him was affection, & for his wife a sort of hostility. Nevertheless I made love to her, & so acted treacherously towards him. This often happens.

To explain why I should do anything so curious, it is necessary to go back & say something about my early life. I am reluctant to do this, & I would not do it if I could help[1] it. To begin with, I hate[2] novels which go in for[3] everlasting[4] parentheses of the hero's past history; & also I hold that in telling a story you should tell as little as you possibly can of what happened before the story began, & after it ended. I think you should show people as they are, without[5] explaining how they became like that; & altogether use the least number of words possible.[6] But here[7] as everywhere you have to compromise, or else your novel must logically be reduced to a short story, thence to a paragraph, to a phrase, & perhaps even to a word. Adultery! There is a novel for you. But it lacks something. Very few people would buy it.

I therefore make my compromise, & ask myself, "What is it that I am writing?" Answer "The tale of John Flory." What is this tale? It is the tale of the degeneration & ruin, through his native faults, of a gifted man?[8] How was he ruined? That is the story; my degeneration began when I came to Burma, aged eighteen. But a boy of eighteen is not a blank sheet to be written on; his character is half formed already, & so, dear reader, you are in for perhaps ten thousand words about my childhood. It is not enough to say "John Flory was a man who got drunk at least once a week, & made love to any woman who would let him."[9] There are many men like that, but they are not all the same. You have to go° little deeper.

To understand any act which a man performs, even the lighting of a cigarette, it is necessary[10] to know his entire history from the moment of his birth, & beyond that the entire history of the universe. Fortunately no novel has yet gone to this extreme. I myself am trying[11] to err in the other direction. Also I shall do[12] my best to avoid weeping over the lost beauty[13] of my youth, & I shall try not to make myself out a more poetic young[14] creature than I was. If, in spite of these promises, the reader feels that he cannot face this chapter, there is an easy[15] remedy. Skip it.

1. help] avoid	8. gifted man] man
2. hate] have always disliked	9. *This and next sentence inserted*
3. which go in for] beg *crossed out*; introduce you to the hero	10. it is necessary] you have
4. everlasting] eternal	11. am trying] have tried
5. without] and try to avoid	12. Also I shall do] I should also like to say that I have done
6. & altogether . . . possible] *interlinear insertion*	13. beauty] poetry
7. But here] Here	14. young] *inserted*
	15. an easy] a ready

73. 3. Extract, The Autobiography of John Flory[1]

[1926–1930?]

I was born in Buckinghamshire in 1890. My father was an Indian civil servant, & met & married[2] my mother in 1882 in India, where she had gone to stay with an aunt for the cold weather. In '83 my father was sent to Burma on some job or other, & there in '84 my brother was born, & died, aged seven months. My eldest sister was born in '85, & my second in '88. In that year my mother went home, bringing her two daughters, aged two & a half, & four months. In '89 my father came home on leave, & I was born early the next year. I saw my father twice in the next ten years, for about six months at a time. In 1903 he retired, & died very suddenly at the end of 1908.

Before 1900[3] I do not remember much except odd incidents & patches of existence, some of which remain in my mind more clearly than what happened yesterday. After 1900 my reccollections° become pretty continuous.

My father was rather like myself, only taller, thinner & with more colour in his face. He always had a rather harassed look, except when he was sitting in his library, where my mother seldom penetrated. The atmosphere of this room was quite unlike the° that of any other room in the house. There were perhaps a thousand books in it, many of them books about Hindu mythology, or about fishing, shooting or travelling in India. I cannot say that I ever read any of these books, but I remember oftening° turning over their pages & looking at strange pictures of people hanging upon hooks, or elephants composed of maidens in extraordinary postures, & wondering vaguely about them in my own mind. I never troubled to enquire their real significance, for the curiosity of children is not very intelligent.

My father used to sit reading these books, with his white shirt open at the neck, smoking cigars from Dindigul. The chairs in the room were of wicker work, such as one finds in India, & there were two faded[4] tiger skins upon the floor. On the walls were old yellow photographs, & a few eastern weapons, among them one or two beautiful[5] dahs captured in the Burma war. I used to look at the handles & scabbards[6] of these dahs, bound with plaited fibres,[7] & speculate dully about the men who used them. The windows[8] were always open, & there was generally a fire in the grate, so that a current of air flowed through the room. And this wind, mingled with cigar smoke, seemed to me like a wind from another land, bearing with it the names of far off dusty places. When I came into the room, & stayed quiet for awhile, my father would talk to me sometimes, & tell me the simple stories of the rubbish that lay about here & there; empty cartridge cases, bad rupees, or dried up peacock feathers. My mother often threatened to "do out" this room, but refrained, probably from mere laziness.

My father & I might have been called friends. The reticence that lies between all blood relatives held us apart, & then I had scarcely seen him till I was thirteen years old. Still, in the family

1. This exists in two forms: handwritten in ink on the verso of Government of Burma paper, stock date 1 February 1925; and typed (not by Orwell?) on thin foolscap typing paper (13 by 8 inches) with the watermark BRITISH EMBLEM, a rose, and MADE IN ENGLAND. This watermark was first recorded in 1928. The handwritten version is printed here; the notes refer to this manuscript. The changes made in typing are slight.
2. & married] *inserted*
3. 1900] 1900 I find
4. faded] faded mouldy
5. beautiful] very beautiful
6. scabbards] sheaths
7. fibres] strands of fibres
8. windows] windows of this room

74. 4. An Incident in Rangoon

[1926–1930?]   Handwritten in pencil on unidentifiable paper

Here for awhile I abandon autobiography & commence fiction writer.° That is, the main facts of the story here told[1] are known to me, & I have supplied the rest out of my imagination. I take so much[2] trouble because this chain of events led to my downfall; not however by any real poetic justice, but simply through coincidence. Nevertheless I am, after all, here in Nyaunglebin through my own fault, for if this mischance had not come my way, there was bound to have been some other. My own temperament & way of living had made sure that I would fall into any trap of this kind that fortune laid me.

One night, then, soon after I went to Kyauktada, I called for poker dice in the club. Lackersteen & I were arguing about who should call for drinks, each maintaining that it was his own turn.

"Very well," said I, "We'll toss for it. The winner calls. Boy, bringing poker dice."

"No poker dice, sir."

"What! No poker dice!"[3]

"No sir, Last secretary sahib stopping, sir. Secretary sahib telling me throwing away poker dice, sir."

"A damned high handed action," said I, & the next day I ordered a set from Rangoon. The evening of the day they arrived was an[4] evening of torrential rain, which hammered onto the rooves with deafening & dreary persistence. It was the last onslaught of the wet weather. As I got into my car to go to [the] club I remembered the poker dice, & took them along with me.

I[5] found the club empty & spent a dismal hour smoking cigarettes & reading the shiny papers, while the stupid rain still poured down out of the skies. At eight[6] o'clock[7] it cleared up suddenly, & at a quarter past, when I was about to shout for my car, Thein Shwe came in, & we had a drink together. Thein Shwe began fingering the leather dice box;

"What is this for, please, Mr Flory?"

"It is a game," I said, "designed for men whose minds are unequal to the strain of thought."

"How do you play it, yes?"

I explained the game, & Thein Shwe began to tell me of how much he had wanted to go[8] to the Races in Rangoon on Saturday, & how much he feared that his father would never give him the money. Besides, his father was going to Rangoon himself tomorrow, (this was Wednesday,) & life altogether was difficult for the gay sons of pious fathers. Then he produced all the money he had in the world, which was five rupees, & we began to throw the dice at a rupee a throw. I had no money on me, but played with matches, & at the end sent Ko S'Hla[9] home in the car for money. Shwe Thein's° luck was astounding, & he threw five aces more than a dozen times in the evening. When he had won thirty five rupees off me, I threw him double or quits, & he won again. After this we both went home.

How much I wish that I could tell this as the tale of a Young Man's Ruin, & how I, the Tempter, sowed the Fatal Passion in his breast, & thereby reaped the bitter crop of my own undoing! It is so much more satisfying to trace one's fate to a single[10] Sin, rather than to weakness & native idiocy. But a man's acts are not thus significant & separable; & though in outward seeming they make up the history of his life, they are in truth only the by-products of the greater life which goes on[11] in his mind & spirit. The fact which matters is[12] not that I supplied Shwe Thein° with money to gamble, & that his gambling led by chance to the detection of my misdeeds, but that I was a fool & scoundrel who must have destroyed himself, if not in one way, then in another. Besides, I never taught Shwe Thein to gamble; like most Mongolians, he did not need teaching. It[13] is a native taste of these people, as drunkenness is with us.

Next morning Ba Sein came to [the] office with a sad face & a grimy sheet of ruled note paper, which said that his little brother was dying, & he must come to Rangoon at once. So I asked him about the little brother, & Ba Sein told me he was a boy of rare promise, but a few years back he had shown the signs of consumption, & they had sent him to the Shan States in hopes of curing him. This, & the doctor's bills, were a great strain on the family, & Ba Sein himself had had to leave the shop where he was learning engineering, & take up a clerkship. The little brother grew no better, & they sent him from place to place, never abandoning hope. At one time he stayed with Ba Sein himself, & Ba Sein, though he worked all day, often had to stay half the night at the sick boy's bedside. So he was tired at his work, & was dismissed from that office for idleness,[14] & there was a long period of months when the brother grew rapidly worse for lack of comforts & medicine. And now as a last hope[15] they had brought him to the Rangoon Hospital; but it was no use,[16] & Ba Sein wished only to see his brother alive for the last time, & to close his eyes when they could see no more.

I knew all this was a lie from start to finish. But I thought how sad it would have been if true, & how painful it must be to[17] confine one's sorrows between a Friday & a Monday, & then come back to the brisk & banal tasks of an office. I was touched by the quiet stoicism with which Ba Sein faced his quite imaginary misfortunes, & I gave him two[18] days' leave & thirty rupees advance from his pay. So when Ba Sein & Thein Shwe set out for Rangoon on Friday[19] they had about a hundred rupees between them; & as they travelled as deck passengers, nearly[20] all this was left them to bet[21] with.

They got to Rangoon on Saturday morning, & at once went along to the house of Ba Sein's uncle, where they were going to stay. The uncle was a head clerk in a government office, drawing about two hundred rupees a month. He had a nice house in Kemmendine, & a daughter at school who talked English & wore[22] European clothes. Morning after morning he ate his breakfast at half past eight, twisted up his long hair under a pink silk gaungbaung, & ran for the tram with a black cheroot[23] in his mouth. On Sundays he took his wife & daughter to the Zoo or the Park, & sometimes to a football match on Saturdays. On public holidays he went to the Pagoda to pray & watch the pwes.[24] He was a man of exemplary character, but like many elderly Burmans he liked to believe that he had been a lu hmike (a bold blade)[25] in his youth, & had led a terrible life with gambling & women. When the two young men arrived & said they were going to the races, he told them of how he had once won two thousand rupees, & spent it all in a fortnight. Then he hurried away to [the] office as usual.

Thein Shwe & Ba Sein went to the races, & by some astounding chance won five thousand rupees. About two thirds of this belonged to Thein Shwe. They were rendered almost delirious by their good fortune, & were ready to listen to any scheme for burning money. They fell in with a Burman who wanted to sell a motor bicycle & side car, & demanded a trial run along the Prome Road. Six miles out the back tyre was ripped off & the inner tube split in half. The owner of the bicycle had no spare tube. Thein Shwe & Ba Sein had never meant to buy the machine, & they hailed a taxi that was passing & went back to Rangoon. The owner of the bicycle was left on the road, almost weeping at his loss & disappointment. But the two millionaires had no pity for him.

They struck up a friendship with the driver of the taxi, & he took them to a Chinese eating shop, where they all had dinner. Then, to begin the evening, Thein Shwe led the way to a restauraunt° patronized mostly by Europeans, & going in, called for beer. The proprietor, the European guests, & the barboys all looked askance at the two Burmans, but they could do nothing. Thein Shwe was defiant in manner, but Ba Sein was rather timid until after his second beer. After their second beer, Thein Shwe called for brandy cocktails, & they drank two each. Ba Sein then bought a tin of cigarettes, & began to offer them to all the men in the bar. The white men all refused rather offensively, except for a young boy just out from home, who was too bashful not to accept. Thein Shwe clapped him on the shoulder, & said he was "a jolly good fellow." Then he suddenly began to sing "For he's a jolly good fellow;" the boy[26] blushed & looked acutely miserable, & a young man with fair hair walked across to Thein Shwe & said "You'd better clear out of here, or I'll put you out myself."

"Who the hell are you?" cried Thein Shwe.

The man with fair hair caught him by the shoulder & began to push him to the door. Thein Shwe broke loose & would have struck him, but the other white men intervened, & the two Burmans were ejected. They then got into their taxi again, & went off to a low dive where they drank Beehive Brandy. After an hour of this they asked the taxi driver to show them the way to some women, & he replied that it was late at night but he would do his best. // The car moved eastwards through the now quiet streets, & finally halted in a little evil-smelling alley full of shuttered houses dimly lighted within. The taxi driver went[27] up to one of the houses, knocked on the door, & began to call out.

"Ko Pa! Ko Pa! Hey, Ko Pa!" After two or three minutes, as there was no response, he knocked with all his might, at which a dog began an angry yelping, & a woman's voice from within suddenly screamed out as though in terror.

"Who's that?"

The taxi driver said something in a reassuring tone, & after[28] somebody had looked out of an upper window, the door opened & an enormously fat man came out, carrying a lantern in his hand. The lantern[29] showed a bedraggled dead rat lying on the doorstep, & shone dimly upon the man's huge belly, for he was half naked,[30] & his great pockmarked face. He was scratching his side with his free hand, & though apparently half asleep, was chewing betel. His front teeth were mostly gold, & this with the betel juice gleamed an unearthly red in the lamplight. After a few words with the taxi driver, he called to someone within, & then sat on[31] his heels, giving many noisy yawns. Presently an old woman appeared, & then a thin boy, blind in one eye but with a sweet childlike face. The boy was sent off somewhere on a bicycle, & the others sat down to wait: the stench of the dead rat seemed to grow stronger each minute, & the cur never ceased to yelp & snarl. Thein Shwe, Ba Sein, the driver & the bawds[32] were all half dead with sleep.

In about twenty minutes a young woman in a blue longyi came down the road, rubbing the sleep out of her eyes & grumbling at the lateness of the hour. The one eyed boy explained that this was the only girl he could get. The others, he said, had all gone out somewhere. Thein Shwe now became a little more alert, & began to ask who lived in all the houses round about. It appeared they were mostly prostitutes.

"Who lives in that house?" he asked, pointing at a house a little way down the road, which, though shuttered up, appeared to be brightly lighted within.

"Ah, there is nothing doing there. That's the second wife of a diamond merchant from Moulmein. He's a very rich man."

"Well, so am I. I'm going into that house."

"There is nothing doing, I tell you."

But Thein Shwe was in a perverse & drunken mood.

"Drive the car down opposite the house," he said. "I'm going to have a look inside."

"Ah ma lay! he is mad!" protested the driver.

"Go on. Drive it down. What are you afraid of?"

The driver obeyed, though he was now growing a little sulky, for his fare had run up to more than sixty rupees, & he was not quite certain of getting it. When they were opposite the house, Thein Shwe climbed onto the top of the car, & leaned against the window shutters, at the top of which was a broad crack of light. Here for a moment he swayed drunkenly, & his head rolled heavily upon his breast, but he recovered himself, & stared into the room.

It was much like many other Burmese rooms in Rangoon. The floor was covered with mats, but there was a little European furniture; namely two or three straight backed chairs & a round table, all covered with cloths of Burmese lace work. There was a bowl of roses on the table, a grandfather clock, not going, & a shrine, also covered with lace, with three candles burning in it.[33] Framed advertisements for Japanese beer hung on the walls, & a petrol lamp from the ceiling. What Thein Shwe looked at, however, was a girl sitting on the mats, smoking a cigarette. She was wearing a longyi of pale blue flowered Chinese satin, & had many gold ornaments on her wrists & about her neck. She was possibly nineteen years old, had an oval[34] face of fair complexion, very elegant & calm, but with a hard mercenary expression. She looked rather like an evil-minded doll. // But Thein Shwe was in a strange mood between[35] drunkenness & sleep, so that lust moved him with a peculiar heavy power. At this moment the girl seemed to him the most desirable in the world, & her cold face & rich clothes seemed to double her value. He determined that by hook or by crook the girl must be his, & that for him to lose her would be simply an absurd injustice. He felt that he had a first call upon all living women, & that any woman must submit to him if he would only exert his power. So he began to scheme how he should enter the house; for when that was done, he felt, the battle was over.

But[36] at this moment a door in the room opened, & Thein Shwe saw his rival face to face; an old man with a sad & noble face, & grey hair gallantly knotted. He took the cigarette from the girl's mouth, & sat down beside her.

> By gis, & by St Charity,
> Alack & fie for shame,
> Old men will do it—[37]

Thein Shwe swayed on the car & almost fell, for the diamond merchant from Moulmein was his venerable father!

1. told] known to
2. so much] this
3. *Not indented in manuscript, and no end quote*
4. an] dreary
5. I] At the club I
6. eight] a quarter past eight
7. o'clock] o'clock when I wo° the
8. go] go to Rangoon
9. *Compare with Ko S'la of* Burmese Days
10. a single] *inserted*
11. on] in on
12. fact which matters is] facts which matter are
13. It] It was bred in him
14. idleness] slack idleness
15. as a last hope] *inserted*
16. it was no use] all hope was given up
17. to] to be given three days' leave
18. two] three
19. on Friday] *inserted*
20. nearly] they had nearly
21. bet] gamble *started but not completed*
22. wore] *inserted*
23. cheroot] cigar
24. *Flory, in* Burmese Days, *explains to Elizabeth*, 'They're having a *pwe*—that's a kind of Burmese play; a cross between a historical drama and a revue' (*CW*, II, 104).
25. *Orwell's translation of* lu hmike *is a little doubtful. Until recently the meaning was 'a stupid man,' possibly with the implication of 'hooligan' or 'tearaway.' In recent slang it has come to mean 'clever' or 'neat.'*
26. boy] young boy
27. went] went to
28. after] after an upper window
29. lantern] lantern betrayed
30. for he was half naked] *inserted*
31. on] *inserted*
32. bawds] brothel-keepers
33. in it] *inserted*
34. oval] *inserted*
35. between] of
36. But] But that
37. *See* Hamlet, *4.5.58–60*

75. 5. Extract, A Rebuke to the Author, John Flory[1]

[1926–1930?]

19.[2]

yourself up with all these yellow-bellies (Eurasians.) See what happens,—get into a fight immediately. Don't want to hear this about you again. Now what about this tart you were running round with, eh?"

Here I determined to show some resistance; but my breath came uncomfortably fast, & I was unable to look the old man in the face.

"She was nothing of the kind," I said. "I did certainly meet a girl at the dance, a Eurasian, but she was an absolutely respectable girl in every way. I don't think it's fair to call her such names,[3] knowing nothing about her."

I expected an outburst of rage: but while I was speaking he had lighted a cheroot, & this perhaps soothed him a little. At any rate he began to lecture me in a mild & even fatherly way, his gruff voice considerably softened.

"You see, my boy," he said, "we white men in this country have to think of something besides ourselves. We are a garrison, so to speak . . . Empire, & all that, white man's burden . . . you see the sort of thing I mean, eh? We've got to *keep the flag flying*, you see. Now as soon as you go mixing yourself up with these natives & Eurasians—

"Yes, sir," I broke in, "I know all that, but—

At this interruption[4] he turned his liverish eyes, which had been gazing at the window, towards my face with a less friendly expression. But he continued speaking in the same strain.

"A white man," he said, "is always on his best behaviour before the native. Esprit de corps! Prestige! Once lower that, & it's all up with you. We white men have to hang together . . . Now this girl you've made friends with, — perfectly respectable girl, I don't doubt, perfectly respectable, —but you've got to realize, my boy, that *it won't do*. Get entangled with a woman like that, —& where are you? Ruined. Ruined!"

Here he paused & relighted his cheroot, continuing his discourse between puffs of smoke.

"I've known fellows who married 'em, plenty of fellows; & where are they now? Every one of them repented it. You've got to have some sort of pride, my boy, in being a white man. Don't lower yourself. I don't say, of course, treat the native badly; nothing sillier. Treat 'em properly, kind & firm at the same time, you understand. Treat 'em properly, & there's no one more charming. Always polite to them, make allowances & all that, strictly impartial, but—*you are the sahib*. Never forget that, my boy . . . Just the same with these Eurasians; politeness, of course, take off your hat to the ladies if you like, encourage the youngsters, —very good subordinates sometimes,— but *no nonsense*. Intermarry with 'em, treat 'em as equals, & you're done. You see[5] that, my boy?"

"Yes, sir," I said weakly. What, indeed could I have replied? "Of course", he went on not unsympathetically, "women, out here, are a big problem. It's hard, I know. You understand, of course, that the firm wouldn't let you marry for some years yet?"

"Yes, sir."

"Well,[6] of course, young fellows will be young fellows; & some of these women, native & half-caste, are very charming. When I was your age, — well, no nonsense, that's all. No marrying. You understand that."

"Yes, sir."

"Very well, my boy, that's all, I think." I stood up to go, he also rose & put one hand upon my shoulder.

"Always remember, my boy, that we must think of others before ourselves. Esprit de corps! Never forget it. Esprit de Corps! All white men hang together. That's all. Run along, now. Be a good boy, eh?" These[7] last words were

1. Only two pages of this manuscript, 19 and 20, survive. It is written in ink, 19 on fairly thick unlined quarto (9 by 6¾ inches), 20 on thinner lined foolscap (13 by 8¼ inches). Both carry the watermark Aviemore with an illustration of a buckled belt within which is a gauntleted hand, raised, holding a dagger. This watermark was used from 1922.
2. 19] *the page number*
3. such names] a tart
4. At this interruption] *begins page 20*
5. You see] See
6. *This paragraph and the next not indented in manuscript*
7. These] At these

76. Scenario and Dialogues from an Untitled Play, [Francis Stone]

c. 1927–1928   Handwritten in ink and pencil

The manuscript for this scenario and dialogues from a draft play is written on Government of Burma paper. It is in three sections, each individually numbered, the first on unlined foolscap, the second on lined foolscap, and the third on unlined quarto. The sections are: 1. Scenario of Scenes I and II (4 pages); 2. Dialogue from Scene I (4 pages); 3. Dialogue from Scene II (3 pages). An association with Burma and with *Burmese Days* is indicated by the use of the name Pereira's Surefire Lung Balm in section 2. Molly Pereira is a 'smelly little bitch' in *Burmese Days*; the name had to be changed to Walters for the 1935 Gollancz edition; see *CW*, II, 23, line 1 and n.

The more important changes Orwell made in writing out this manuscript are listed in the notes; slight alterations and false starts have been ignored. Full square brackets in this manuscript are Orwell's; editorial additions are in half brackets.

⌈1. Scenario of Scenes I and II⌉

Scenario.

Scene I. A mean & poverty stricken room which is painted on a curtain half way down the stage. In the middle is a small bed with a pale child lying in it flat on its back & apparently asleep. There[1] is a low table beside the bed on which are half a loaf of bread, a medicine bottle & a ragged picture paper.— To the right of the stage is a double bed with ragged sheets, & a chair beside it. (see plan.)[2] Facing up to the table is a delapidated° arm chair, in which FRANCIS STONE sits opening letters. His wife, LUCY STONE, leans over the head of the bed. Stone announces that the letters are all bills, amounting to nearly £40, while all the money he has is –/7/4d. The[3] conversation shows that, the child, aged about 4 years, is suffering from a disease of the spine which will kill her in a year or two, but which could be cured by a very expensive operation, which only a certain specialist can perform. His usual price is a hundred guineas, & Stone & his wife despair utterly of raising this.

Stone is a man of about 33, good looking, but with a weak & rather cynical expression. His voice is dreary. He is obviously much his wife's intellectual superior, & this makes ⌈for⌉ misunderstanding between them. Mrs Stone is about 28, pretty but worn. The clothes of both are good, but battered. Their shoes are very old.

There remains one letter unopened, & Stone is about to throw it away, saying it looks like a bill, but his wife makes him open it. It then appears that this letter is an offer from an advertising agency to write advertisements, offering good terms, & fifty pounds down in advance. Stone & his wife are in ecstasies, & Mrs Stone wakes the child up to tell her that she is going to be made well again & soon. Stone, however, has read the letter to the end, & announces that the advertisements he is required[4] to write are for Pereira's Salvation Balm, a quack panacea for all diseases which he personally knows to be made of plain water flavoured with aniseed & coloured with cochineal. He says it is a swindle & he will have nothing to do with it. His wife is totally unable to understand his idea of honour, & after her first surprise becomes angry with him, & finally begins to beseech him,[5] with her arms round his neck. The child, seeming to understand what it is about, keeps up a dismal howling. Stone suggests that his wife buy a bottle of the Salvation Balm & give it to the child; at this his wife is horrified. Then he suggests that his wife might raise the money by prostituting herself on the streets. She treats this as an insult, & Stone begins to talk about the different ideas of honour in his wife & himself.[6] His wife will not hear him, & tells him she will leave him to think it over, & go out to get milk for the child's dinner. Stone gives her the money. — As she goes, the heel breaks off her shoe — She begins to cry at having to go into the street like this, but goes all the same. Stone sinks down into the arm chair & shuts his eyes.

Immediately everything goes dark, & there is ⌈a⌉ sound like the roaring of waters. What actually happens is that the furniture is removed & the curtain drawn up, exposing the background of scene II. The darkness should not continue for more than a few seconds.

Scene II. The interior of an extemporised prison. There are doors at left, right, & another rather towards the right. Immediately beside this is an empty fireplace, over which hangs a placard with RULES printed at the top. The text printed is too small to be legible—near door C (see plan) is a small barred window, high up in the wall, through which a dreary grey sky can be seen. Near this window is a stool. There is a bench up against the wall at the left, & 2 chairs, one at the right, & one in the middle of the stage. (See plan.) Present are Stone, who is standing on the stool, & looking out of the window; THE CHRISTIAN, a fine looking bearded old man in rags, who sits in the chair at the right, reading a large book. He has a placard inscribed DEAF round his neck. THE POET & THE POET'S WIFE are standing looking up at Stone. This scene is mostly in blank verse.

Almost immediately there is a roar of guns, & it appears from the conversation that some kind of revolution has occurred, & all present are awaiting trial as enemies of the State. The roar of guns is the execution of the prisoners in the next cell but one, & Stone & the others will be tried in an hour or less.

Those present begin to explain their position. The Poet & his wife, who are dark, beautiful & romantic looking people dressed in XVIIth century clothes, have been arrested as aristocrats. The Poet admits that he never cared what the state of the People was so long as he was left in peace to write his poems. His wife similarly was engaged chiefly with her house, her estates, her husband, & the arts, & in living what seemed to her a comely life. Stone declares himself merely a man of pleasure, & declares that the revolution is solely due to the lower classes' jealously° of the upper classes' elegant manners—The Christian is induced by signs also to explain himself, & coming over & standing in front of door B, he begins a speech about Christianity, explaining that he was sent deaf by the noise of guns in the fighting[7] at the beginning of the revolution, & afterwards arrested as a Christian, Christianity having been abolished by the State. During his speech enter THE JAILOR by door B, which opens into his office. The Christian, being deaf, does not hear him coming. He gives the Christian a kick on the bottom, which knocks him down. The Jailor is a short, tremendously powerful man, with a jeering[8] & coarse face, & very swift movements. He looks rather like a pugilist. He never loses his temper, but always remains derisive & hostile. He is frankly enjoying himself in getting his own back on some of his former tyrants. After knocking down the Christian, he begins to bully the others, particularly the Poet, who is made to cut a rather ridiculous figure. The jailor talks a little about his physical superiority to these effeminate aristocrats, & returns to his room.

The others continue their conversation. The Poet's wife makes a speech saying they cannot grumble, as they are only getting what they have been asking for. Stone agrees, but points out that it has always been so, & deplores his bad luck in not living in some time between revolutions, when he could have lived a quiet life grinding the faces of the poor.

The Poet's wife lights a cigarette. The Jailor promptly emerges & tells her to throw it away. She points to rules, & reads out that prisoners are allowed the use of tobacco. The Jailor says this only applies to men, as smoking by women has been put down as an aristocratic habit.

⌈2. Dialogue from Scene I⌉

Scene.° A curtain is drawn down about half way back[9] on the stage, & on this is painted a mean & dreary room. The only actual furniture is an arm chair covered with dingy chintz on which Francis Stone is sitting. He has a few letters on the floor beside him,[10] & is reading one of them. He is a very handsome man, but not looking either strong or determined. He has a rather absent, & at the same time sceptical expression. His clothes are old, but good.

Francis Stone. (reading in a dismal voice)° Dear Sir, Kindly allow us to draw
your attention to the little account for four pounds fifteen shillings,
which has been outstanding for a year. You will[11] kindly inform us
immediately when you intend payment. Failing a satisfactory reply
from you, we shall be compelled [He throws the letter away & opens
another & reads it.] Dear Sir, Your account with us for nine pounds
eleven & ten pence is now long over due [He throws it away & begins
another.] Dear Sir, We beg to point out. [He sighs & throws it away.
Then he draws a tin cigarette case from his pocket, opens it, finds it
empty, & sighs again. There is a loud knock on the door. Stone springs
to his feet with a guilty look, & begins to creep on tiptoe towards the exit
at the other end of the stage. There is another loud bang as he goes. Then
a female voice cries out]
Open the door, can't you, Frank.
⌈Stone loses his guilty look, and runs to the door, which he opens. A
pretty but peevish[12] looking woman comes in, trailing a thin lethargic
child by the arm. The woman's clothes are like Stone's, good but
battered.⌉

Stone. Oh, it's you. I thought it was a dun.

Mrs Stone. [Seeing the letters.] Any letters?

Stone. Only bills.
⌈The child coughs.⌉

Mrs Stone. [Patting her gently on the back.] Now don't cough, dear. Go &
lie down for a little. You'll have your dinner in half an hour. [The child
trails out.]

Stone. Did you weigh her.°

Mrs Stone. Yes,° The same machine as last time.[13] She's dropped another
pound.
⌈Stone sits down in the arm chair.⌉

Mrs Stone. Well, why don't you say something.° What do you intend
doing? We've *got* to do something. The child's dying, & that's all there is
about it. We've got to send her away somewhere, six months at least,
somewhere out of this beastly air. And I'll have to go with her. Where's
the money coming from?
⌈Stone puts his hand over his eyes.⌉
Oh, don't sit there like a stuck pig! Say something [Her voice rises.]
Oh Lord! What sort of man do you call yourself? If I was you, I'd rob a
bank before I'd see my child dying.

Stone. So would I, my dear, if I only could. But I couldn't. I don't know
how. And don't shout, dear; you'll disturb the child.

Mrs Stone. Oh, well. [Looking at the letters again.] Why didn't you open all
the letters.°

Stone. What's the point? They're all bills.

Mrs Stone. [Picking up an envelope.] No they aren't. What's this one?
⌈Stone opens it & reads a few lines. His face brightens at once.⌉

Stone. I say, here's good luck! Hurray! You & Sally can go tomorrow. What a piece of luck! [While saying this he again draws out his cigarette case & finds it empty.] Damn. Got a cigarette?

Mrs Stone. No. Never mind, we'll get some in a minute. What is it, dear?

Stone. It's an offer of a job. Writing some advertisements. A fee for each advertisement, & fifty pounds advance to start with. How's that, eh?

Mrs Stone. Oh, how lovely! [She looks over his shoulder at the letter, & flings her arm round his neck. Then she kisses him hurriedly, & runs towards the room where the girl is lying down].

Mrs Stone. [As she runs.] Sally! Sally! come out here a minute. I've got such a surprise for you°

Sally. Yes, mummie. [She appears.]

Mrs Stone. [Falling on her knees & kissing the child.] What do you think, Sally! You're going away to the seaside tomorrow, & mummie's coming with you. And we're going to stay at a beautiful farm by the sea, & you'll play with the ducklings & the little pigs all day. [She gazes far away, & goes on more slowly.] Do you remember, Frank, where we stayed when we were married first? How we used to lie about in the grass & pick flowers half the day?
⌈Stone is silent.⌉

Mrs S. What is it, dear?

Stone. I say, do you know who these advertisements are for?

Mrs S. No, who? What's wrong?

Stone. Why, it's for Pereira's Surefire Lung Balm!

Mrs S. Who are they?

Stone. *You* know. That advertisement of a mother holding up a child, & saying "Little Elsie was wasting away to a skeleton," & then a lot of lying testimonials. You know the thing. It's a most infernal swindle. It's on a line with the electric belts. I can't have anything to do with it.

Mrs S. But, Frank! You must! We've *got* to have that money.
⌈Stone looks away, distressed. Mrs Stone rises to her feet.⌉

Mrs S. (Cajolingly)° Now, Frank, don't be silly; please don't. Never you mind whether it's a swindle. All business is a swindle. You're always saying so. [She catches hold of his coat lapels.]

Stone. [Freeing himself.] All business is a swindle, but not in this sense. I haven't time to explain to you. I tell you I won't touch this thing. It's a beastly, low-down fraud on desperate people dying of tuberculosis. I won't touch the thing.

Mrs S. Oh, how *do* you know? It may be the best medicine in the world for all you know.

Stone. I haven't time to argue the general principles. But I may tell you that analyses of these patent[14] medicines are published sometimes, & I looked this Pereira's stuff up once. Well, it's made of pure water, coloured with cochineal & flavoured with aniseed. And it's sold at half a crown a bottle. If it was a hair restorer or some such rubbish, I wouldn't mind. But not a consumption cure.

Mrs S. Oh Lord! What's it matter to *you*? *You* don't have to drink the stuff. *Let* people buy it, if they're such fools![15] I cannot understand you.

⌈All this while the child stands by, dully looking up into one face or the other.⌉

Stone.   Don't you understand, dear, that if I write those advertisements I shall be doing my best to betray the hopes & wheedle out the pennies of people situated very much as we are? And the more people I take in, the more money I shall earn.

Mrs. S.   Oh, I've no patience with you! You make me sick! Here's one God sent chance to do you° duty by your own child, & you throw it away out of shere° namby pamby nonsense! I could hit you, really I could. [Kneeling again, & caressing the child.] Look, Sally; look at your father there. He won't send you to the seaside after all. [The child howls, & then begins coughing.]

Stone.   Look out, dear, don't start her coughing. Go & lie down a little longer, Sally dear. I'll see if we can't manage that seaside after all. [The child goes out snivelling.] Now look here, we must have this out properly.

⌈3. Dialogue from Scene II⌉

Well, brother Christian, only a half hour more
To find a way between the claws of death.
The tightest corner I ever yet was in.
[He pauses for a moment in meditation.]
Yes, it's a hole, the devil of a hole.
[Speaking in a more conversational manner.]
You see, dear Christian, ever since I was born.° I have been exercised by two problems; to keep a whole skin, & to call my soul my own. For what shall it profit a man if he gain the whole world & lose his own soul? & again, what shall it profit a man if he save his own soul & lose his own life? That is the problem, Christian; to serve God & Mammon, & cheat them both. So far, I have been not unsuccessful. I dodge the bludgeonings of fate, my head is bloodless but unbowed. I have cheated everyone except myself, for remember, Christian, to thine own self be true, & it must follow as the night the day, that thou canst then be false to any man. Long ago, when I was a boy at school, we gave another boy a bath in ink for reading poetry, & I poured in my bottle with the best of them. But I read poetry myself in private. Since then I have never flinched; the passage of the years, I said to myself, finds & shall find me still alive. I never despair; even now those poetical friends of ours may give me my opportunity. I shall know in half a minute. It is good to have a confidant like you, dear Christian, to whom I can tell all my secrets. I never met a man I could talk to so freely. Hope on! I have never been quite the slave of another, either in mind or body. No man conquers me; I am the bosun of my fate, I am the sergeant of my soul—

P.W° (Interrupting to call across the room.)°
Are you true friend to us?

Stone.   Ay, to the death. (Whispering to Chr.)° Whose death I did not say. What[16] would you, sister.°

[P.W° shakes her head towards J's door, & beckons to Stone. He walks across. Chr. resumes his reading.]

P.W° [Whispering.]   Now listen, friend; within this bottle here
[Holds up a tiny bottle which she has extracted from the heel of her shoe.]

Is poison enough to kill a hundred men.
The death is swift; 'tis better so to die
Than at these creatures° hands. So let it be;
Mingling the poison in this brandy here;
We'll drink & die together.

Stone.   Oh, brave plan!
So at last they'll have not their revenge.

P.W.   Wait, there is more. That jailor too shall drink.
Before we go to trial, we'll say to him

⌐Manuscript ends⌐

1. There] Besides this there
2. *No plan has been traced.*
3. The] It emerges from the convers°
   with became *written above* emerges; *all
   crossed out*
4. required] wanted
5. beseech him] beg him
6. his wife & himself] a man & a
   woman
7. fighting] first fight
8. jeering] brutish
9. back] acro°
10. on the floor beside him] in his lap
11. will] *followed by* oblige us by
12. peevish] *followed by* Stone: [as he
    opens the door] *on a new line*
13. The same machine as last time.] *marked
    to be transposed here from after* pound
14. that analyses of these patent] that lists
    of analyses of these sacred patent
15. fools!] *followed by* [All this while
16. What] *followed by* is it

1928–1929

77. Paris, 1928–1929

In spring 1928, Orwell went to Paris and took a room at 6 rue du Pot de Fer in the Fifth Arrondissement, a working-class district. His aunt Nellie Limouzin was living in Paris throughout the time he was there.

On 6 October 1928, 'La Censure en Angleterre,' Orwell's first article as a professional writer, appeared in Henri Barbusse's paper, *Monde*,[1] as did another, 'John Galsworthy,' on 23 March 1929. Four other articles, also in French translation, on unemployment in England, a day in the life of a tramp, the beggars of London, and Burma, appeared between December 1928 and May 1929 in the paper *Le Progrès Civique: Journal de Perfectionnement Social*. His first article to appear in England, 'A Farthing Newspaper,' was printed on 29 December 1928 in *G. K.'s Weekly*.

In February 1929, he fell ill with pneumonia and spent 7 to 22 March in the Hôpital Cochin, in the Fifteenth Arrondissement. Shortly after his discharge, he met L. I. Bailey, of the McClure Newspaper Syndicate. Bailey was based in London, but the syndicate had offices in New York and Sydney. He was later (23 April) to comment on three stories Orwell had written: 'The Sea God' was 'immature . . . you deal with sex too much in your writings'; 'The Petition Crown' showed 'very good powers of description, but this power becomes tedious when a whole page of description could be much more effective in [a] few brief sentences . . . Sex here *ad lib!*' The third story, 'The Man in Kid Gloves,' impressed him very much: 'I consider it an extremely clever story. It holds the attention of the reader and strikes a crisp note.' On 20 June, Bailey wrote to say that he had not managed to place 'The Man in Kid Gloves' but had not abandoned hope of doing so. It is plain from his letters that he had met Nellie Limouzin with Orwell when he was in Paris, so evidently Orwell was seeing his aunt. None of these stories was printed; no manuscripts survive. From Bailey's comments, however, Orwell's technique was apparently improving.

In addition to letters from *Le Progrès Civique*, correspondence survives from two other French journals, which tell of Orwell's attempts to place his work. Pierre Yrondy, Directeur of le *MonT-Parnasse*,° *Hebdomadaire International*, wrote to Orwell, probably in January 1929, to express his willingness to publish Orwell's poetry, though written in English – because of the 'International' in the name, presumably. He said he had found a 'ballade' by Orwell 'extrêmement amusante' and thought that some humorous articles entitled 'Ayant toujours trait au Quartier Montparnasse' could readily find a place in his journal. On 27 January, he wrote to say that he would publish Orwell's work when the resources of the journal permitted. There seem never to have been adequate resources, however. Perhaps the poem 'When the Franks have lost their sway' (*66*) was one of the items submitted. No issues of le *MonT-Parnasse* for 1928–30 have been traced, so it is not possible to tell whether that journal published anything of Orwell's.

On 30 May, one of the editors of *l'européen*° ('économique – artistique – littéraire'), André Lamandé, discussed the possibility of publishing an essay by Orwell on 'les tendances du roman Anglais contemporain.' That came to nothing, but Orwell was to contribute an article on John Galsworthy to *Monde* (*85*), which might indicate what he had in mind. These letters and all but one from *Le Progrès Civique* were addressed to Orwell at 6 rue du Pot de Fer; the exception, dated 22 March 1929, was sent to him at the Hôpital Cochin. Orwell completed two novels in Paris,[2] but these have not survived. All that has been traced is reproduced here. 'This never happened to me . . .' (*78*) cannot be dated and may not have been written in Paris. English translations are given here; the French originals are at the end of 1929; see *89–94*.

For about ten weeks in the late autumn of 1929, Orwell worked as a dishwasher and kitchen porter in a luxury hotel and a restaurant in Paris. Sam White, the London *Evening Standard*'s Paris correspondent, stated in his column, 16 June 1967, that Sonia Orwell identified this as the Crillon. Stansky and Abrahams offer evidence in support of the Hôtel Lotti: I, 225–26. He returned to England at the end of 1929.

Orwell was paid 225 francs for each of his four articles for *Le Progrès Civique* (900 francs was then about £7.25; approximately $35 at the rate of $4.85 to the pound). As a *plongeur* he was paid about £6.00 ($29) a month; as an assistant district superintendent of police in Burma, his pay was £65.00 ($315) per month. See Crick, 200; Stansky and Abrahams, I, 168. For his second and third articles for *Le Progrès Civique*, payment was made in a single cheque, for 450 francs, on 8 February 1929. Orwell then paid a month's rent of 200 francs; most of the rest was stolen. In chapter 3 of *Down and Out in Paris and London*, he describes how, 'one day, in summer, I found that I had just four hundred and fifty francs left'; see *CW*, I, 12. The amount may be coincidental.

See Crick, 172–74, 191–99; Stansky and Abrahams, I, 213–16; Richard Mayne, 'A Note on Orwell's Paris,' *The World of George Orwell*, 40–45. Peter Lewis, *George Orwell: The Road to 1984* illustrates rue du Pot de Fer and the Hôpital Cochin, with commentary, 18–25.

1. This journal has no connection with the well-known daily *Le Monde*, which was first published 18 December 1944.
2. In the introduction to the first French translation of *Down and Out in Paris and London*, *La Vache Enragée* (1935), Orwell says, 'In the spring of 1928 I set off for Paris so as to live cheaply while writing two novels'; see *211*. Writing to Michael Meyer, 12 March 1949, he said, 'I simply destroyed my first novel after unsuccessfully submitting it to one publisher, for which I'm rather sorry now'; see *3570*.

78. 'A Short Story'

[c. 1928–1929?]

Inexpertly typed, probably by Orwell, this has a few emendations in his hand. Obvious typing mistakes (such as 'whxt' for 'what') and words run together are corrected silently. The more important changes are listed in the notes. The story is headed precisely as above in the original typescript.

(This never happened to me, but it would have if I had had the chance.)

Once in the wild romantic days of my youth I contrived to win the affection of a lady whose fortune was so large as to compensate for the astounding ugliness[1] of her face. In a darkened room, which makes all women sisters, I took her hand and informed her with perfect truth that I worshipped the very ground she walked on and the very jewels she wore; and she informed me, what I had no difficulty in believing, that I was the first man who had so spoken to her. We were duly betrothed, and my beloved's family, who seemed well pleased with the arrangement, gave no opposition. Nevertheless, I found it expedient to represent myself as a young man of good birth, but without kith or kin, for I felt that my relatives did not quite accord with the state to which I was about to become accustomed. There now remained only one difficulty, an unfortunate entanglement with a young person of inferior rank and fortune to whom I had been so foolish as to promise marriage two years before. To an unscrupulous man this would have given no uneasiness, but to a man of honour like myself it was extremely embarrassing, particularly because the girl had sometime since lent me a considerable sum of money, her savings, which I was not yet in a position to repay. It was therefore with some diffidence, though with a sense of rectitude, that I went to acquaint her with the change in my feelings.

As I walked down the mean street, where white and ruined faces flitted about beneath the lamps, and entered my late mistress° squalid room, I saw how wise I had been to remove myself to a sphere more suited to my delicate nature. The young person with whom I had compromised myself was frying potatoes over a gas fire, which besides a bed, a table and two chairs, was almost all the room contained. As I entered she threw her arms about my neck with an ardour[2] naturally embarrassing to a man of honour who had come on such an errand as mine; so that I postponed saying what I had to say until later. After expressing her joy at my visit, she asked me whether I would not eat something, as she had half a crown in hand, and could easily get a bottle of beer and some bread and cheese at the public house opposite. But I refused, after thanking her for her hospitality, which I considered very proper for one in her position, but not such as I could enjoy with much pleasure to myself. She then seemed to detect a coldness in my manner, and again flinging her arms about my neck, declared that she trusted me in all thing° and that she wished to hear from my own lips a denial of something that had been said against me, so that she could answer my accusers with authority. It appeared that her brother had told her that I intended deserting her for a richer woman, and had actually named the lady to whom I was then affianced. I perceived at once that what I had come to say could not now be said without great pain, and that I must communicate it by letter and so avoid the embarrassment of a personal interview. I accordingly swore to her upon my honour as a gentleman that my feelings for her had never changed, at the same time kissing her passionately to prove my words. Then, as a man of true gallantry neglects no opportunity, I asked her to attest her love[3] by giving herself to me, which she had not hesitated to do in the past; for she had[4] said that even if her perfect trust in me had not made my promise of marriage as something already accomplished, she would nevertheless do whatever I asked of her. She at once agreed, saying as before that my wishes[5] were her law and her happiness.

Two hours later I left the house, and would have hurried away at once, for I did not wish to be seen in this low neighbourhood. But even as I came down the steps, I was horrified to see approaching a few paces distant my future brother in law and another wealthy friend of his. In my acute dismay I could think of no explanation of my presence, and I could only reflect how much it would prejudice me in their eyes if I were found to have any friend or relation in so mean a locality. They greeted me without much warmness, and I could see doubt and uncertainty in their faces. My heart sank within me, for it seemed to me in my agitation that the whole story of my promise of marriage to this girl would come to light, and all my hopes be destroyed. To[6] their greeting I answered nothing, for I was in truth hardly capable of speech.[7] I stood there silent and smiling nervously° But at this moment luck came to my aid. My late mistress, possibly hearing voices on the doorstep, pulled aside the curtain and looked from the window. My brother in law saw her, and at once a great difference[8] appeared in his expression, which seemed to change from suspicion to relief and amusement. I immediately understood his thought, and looking back at him with a suitably roguish air winked my eye, and we all walked on together. My brother in law thought that the girl I had been visiting[9] was a prostitute, and her house a brothel. So his good opinion of me was restored, and I was married, and (my wife dying early) lived happily ever afterwards.

1. astounding ugliness] complete absence of charm
2. an ardour] a fervour which
3. love] love for me
4. had] *inserted in ink in Orwell's hand*
5. my wishes] whatever I asked
6. To] At
7. speech] *preceded by* truth, *which is crossed out*
8. difference] change
9. been visiting] *typed in capital letters*

79. 'Censorship in England'

Monde, 6 October 1928[1]

Orwell's English original has not been traced. It was translated into French by H.-J. Salemson (see *89*); the version below was translated from the French by Janet Percival and Ian Willison.

The present state of affairs regarding censorship in English is as follows. In the theatre, each play, before it is staged, must be submitted for inspection by a censor nominated by the government, who can ban its performance or request alterations if he thinks it a danger to public morality. This censor is just like any other civil servant and is not selected for his literary talents. He has either forbidden or held up the production of half the significant modern plays which have been produced in England in the last fifty years. Ibsen's *Ghosts*, Brieux's *Damaged Goods*, George Bernard Shaw's *Mrs Warren's Profession*—all strictly, even painfully moral plays—were kept off the English stage for many years. By contrast ordinary, and frankly pornographic, reviews and musical comedies have only suffered the minimum of alterations. As far as novels are concerned, there is no censorship before publication. However, any novel can be suppressed after publication, as were Mr James Joyce's *Ulysses*, or *The Well of Loneliness*.[2] This is usually the result of public outcry; there is no body of civil servants employed to do this. A clergyman preaches a sermon, someone writes to the newspapers, a Sunday journalist produces an article, petitions are sent to the Home Secretary—and the book is suppressed, with clandestine copies selling at five guineas. However—and this is the strangest part of the whole affair—there is *no censorship* on any but contemporary books or plays. All Shakespeare is produced on the English stage; Chaucer, Swift, Smollett and Sterne are published and sold in unabridged editions without hindrance. Even Sir Thomas Urquhart's translation of Rabelais (probably the coarsest book in the world) can be purchased without trouble. Yet if one of these writers were living in England today and writing in his usual way, he would be certain to find his books suppressed and he himself would be prosecuted.

It is easy to imagine the disputes which arise in this connection. They are proof that no one wants any sort of censorship. But to understand how we have reached this extraordinary state of affairs, we must note something very strange that seems to have happened to the English mind in general in the last hundred and fifty years. Smollett and Sterne were, as we have said, decidedly coarse writers. In Sir Walter Scott and Jane Austen, who only wrote some sixty or seventy years later, coarseness has completely disappeared. Traces remain in Surtees and Marryat, writing between 1820 and 1850. In Thackeray, Dickens, Charles Reade and Anthony Trollope there is no trace of coarseness, and almost none of sexuality.

What happened so suddenly and so strangely to the English mind? What explains the surprising difference between Smollett and his disciple, Dickens, who was writing less than a century later?

To answer these questions, we must remember that there was hardly any literary censorship in England until the eighteenth century, except for the short puritan regime in the seventeenth century; and when we consider this it seems reasonable to conclude that the industrial revolution, which brought the puritan merchants and factory-owners back into power, was the reason for this sudden growth in prudery. The puritan middle class was certainly just as prudish in 1750 as it was in 1850 or as it is today, but with less political power it was unable to impose its opinions on the public. It is impossible to prove the truth of this explanation, but it does fit the facts better than any other.

This gives rise to another very curious question. Why is the sense of decency so different at different times and with different people? English intellectuals have returned spiritually to the eighteenth century; neither Smollett nor Rabelais shocks them any longer. On the other hand, the great British public, still very like that of Dickens's day, have booed at Ibsen in the eighties and would boo him again if he reappeared tomorrow. Why is there such a different spirit between these two classes of people? Because—and this is a point to remember—if Rabelais shocked the public in Dickens's day, Dickens shocks the cultivated Englishman today. Not only Dickens, but almost all the English-language writers of the mid-nineteenth century (including the Americans) are profoundly distasteful to a sensitive modern reader because of their taste for the macabre and the lugubrious. These writers had a fondness for deathbed scenes, corpses and funerals. Dickens wrote an account of a case of spontaneous combustion which is nauseating to read today. Mark Twain, the American humorist, used frequently to make jokes about unburied corpses. Edgar Allan Poe wrote stories which were so horrific that some of them (notably *The Case of M. Valdemar*) were considered unfit for publication *in extenso* in France. Yet these writers never caused public outcry in England, quite the contrary.

What conclusion can we draw? We can only say that the extraordinary and illogical censorship in England today is the result of a prudery which would suppress Chaucer and Shakespeare as well as James Joyce, but for the snobbish regard for an established reputation. And this prudery stems from that strange English puritanism, which has no objection to dirt, but which fears sexuality and detests beauty.

Today it is illegal to print a swearword, and even to swear, yet no race is more given to swearing than the English. In the same way, any play on prostitution is likely to be banned from the English stage, just as any prostitute is likely to be prosecuted, yet we know that prostitution is just as widespread in England as it is elsewhere. There are signs that this state of affairs will not last for ever—we can already see a little more freedom for the written word than there was fifty years ago.

If a government dared to abolish all moral literary censorship we should find that we have been ill-used for decades by a smallish minority. And a century after its abolition we can be sure that the strange institution of moral censorship in literature would seem as distant and as fantastic as marriage customs in Central Africa.

E.-A. BLAIR[3]

1. This was Orwell's first professionally published writing; see Crick, 191; Stansky and Abrahams, I, 214–15. The directeur of *Monde* was Henri Barbusse (1873–1935), author of what is perhaps the finest account in French of life in the trenches in World War I: *Le Feu* (Under Fire) (1916); see *787, n. 2*.
2. (1928), by Radclyffe Hall (1880–1943); see *3172, n. 1*.
3. The pen-name 'George Orwell' was first used in January 1933 for *Down and Out in Paris and London*, but it was not regularly used for reviews and articles and so on until December 1936. Unless the pen-name is used, the form used for individual publications is given at the end of each item—E. A. Blair, Eric Blair, E. A. B., E. B., and typographic variants.

80. 'A Farthing Newspaper'

G. K.'s Weekly, 29 December 1928[1]

The *Ami du Peuple* is a Paris newspaper. It was established about six months ago, and it has achieved something really strange and remarkable in the world where everything is a "sensation," by being sold at ten centimes, or rather less than a farthing the copy. It is a healthy, full-size sheet, with news, articles, and cartoons quite up to the usual standard, and with a turn for sport, murders, nationalist sentiment and anti-German propaganda. Nothing is abnormal about it except its price.

Nor is there any need to be surprised at this last phenomenon, because the proprietors of the *Ami du Peuple* have just explained all about it, in a huge manifesto which is pasted on the walls of Paris wherever billsticking is not *defendu*. On reading this manifesto one learns with pleased surprise that the *Ami du Peuple* is not like other newspapers, it was the purest public spirit, uncontaminated by any base thoughts of gain, which brought it to birth. The proprietors, who hide their blushes in anonymity, are emptying their pockets for the mere pleasure of doing good by stealth. Their objects, we learn, are to make war on the great trusts, to fight for a lower cost of living, and above all to combat the powerful newspapers which are strangling free speech in France. In spite of the sinister attempts of these other newspapers to put the *Ami du Peuple* out of action, it will fight on to the last. In short, it is all that its name implies.

One would cheer this last stand for democracy a great deal louder, of course, if one did not happen to know that the proprietor of the *Ami du Peuple* is M. Coty, a great industrial capitalist,[2] and also proprietor of the *Figaro* and the *Gaulois*. One would also regard the *Ami du Peuple* with less suspicion if its politics were not anti-radical and anti-socialist, of the goodwill-in-industry, shake-hands-and-make-it-up species. But all that is beside the point at this moment. The important questions, obviously, are these: Does the *Ami du Peuple* pay its way? And if so, how?

The second question is the one that really matters. Since the march of progress is going in the direction of always bigger and nastier trusts, any departure is worth noticing which brings us nearer to that day when the newspaper will be simply a sheet of advertisement and propaganda, with a little well-censored news to sugar the pill. It is quite possible that the *Ami du Peuple* exists on its advertisements, but it is equally possible that it makes only an indirect profit, by putting across the sort of propaganda wanted by M. Coty and his associates. In the above mentioned manifesto, it was declared that the proprietors might rise to an even dizzier height of philanthropy by giving away the *Ami du Peuple* free of charge. This is not so impossible as it may sound. I have seen a daily paper (in India) which was given away free for some time with apparent profit to its backers, a ring of advertisers who found a free newspaper to be a cheap and satisfactory means of blowing their own trumpet. Their paper was rather above the average Indian level, and it supplied, of course, just such news as they themselves approved, and no other. That obscure Indian paper forecast the logical goal of modern journalism; and the *Ami du Peuple* should be noticed, as a new step in the same direction.

But whether its profits are direct or indirect, the *Ami du Peuple* is certainly prospering. Its circulation is already very large, and though it started out as a mere morning paper it has now produced an afternoon and late evening edition. Its proprietors speak with perfect truth when they declare that some of the other papers have done their best to crush this new champion of free speech. These others (they, too, of course, acting from the highest altruistic motives) have made a gallant attempt to [have] it excluded from the news-agents' shops, and have even succeeded as far as the street-corner kiosks are concerned. In some small shops, too, whose owners are socialists, one will even see the sign "Ici on ne vend pas *l'Ami du Peuple*" exhibited in the windows. But the *Ami du Peuple* is not worrying. It is sold in the streets and the cafés with great vigour, and it is sold by barbers and tobacconists and all kinds of people who have never done any newsagency before. Sometimes it is simply left out on the boulevard in great piles, together with a tin for the two-sou pieces, and with no attendant whatever. One can see that the proprietors are determined, by hook or by crook, to make it the most widely-read paper in Paris.

And supposing they succeed—what then? Obviously the *Ami du Peuple* is going to crowd out of existence one or more of the less prosperous papers— already several are feeling the pinch. In the end, they will presumably either be destroyed, or they will survive by imitating the tactics of the *Ami du Peuple*. Hence every paper of this kind, whatever its intentions, is the enemy of free speech. At present France is the home of free speech, in the Press if not elsewhere. Paris alone has daily papers by the dozen, nationalist, socialist, and communist, clerical and anti-clerical, militarist and anti-militarist, pro-semitic and anti-semitic. It has the *Action Française*, a Royalist paper and still one of the leading dailies, and it had *Humanité*, the reddest daily paper outside Soviet Russia. It has *La Liberta*, which is written in Italian and yet may not even be sold in Italy, much less published there. Papers are printed in Paris in

French, English, Italian, Yiddish, German, Russian, Polish, and languages whose very alphabets are unrecognizable by a western European. The kiosks are stuffed with papers, all different. The Press combine, about which French journalists are already grumbling, does not really exist yet in France. But the *Ami du Peuple*, at least, is doing its gallant best to make it a reality.

And supposing that this kind of thing is found to pay in France, why should it not be tried elsewhere? Why should we not have our farthing, or at least our half-penny newspaper in London? While the journalist exists merely as the publicity agent of big business, a large circulation, got by fair means or foul, is a newspaper's one and only aim. Till recently various of our newspapers achieved the desired level of "net sales" by the simple method of giving away a few thousand pounds now and again in football competition prizes. Now the football competitions have been stopped by law, and doubtless some of the circulations have come down with an ugly bump. Here, then, is a worthy example for our English Press magnates. Let them imitate the *Ami du Peuple* and sell their papers at a farthing. Even if it does no other good whatever, at any rate the poor devils of the public will at last feel that they are getting the correct value for their money.

E. A. BLAIR

1. This was Orwell's first writing to be published professionally in England. 'G. K.' was G. K. Chesterton (1874–1936), essayist, biographer, novelist, and poet, remembered particularly for his comic verse, the Father Brown detective stories (1911–35), and *The Man Who Was Thursday* (1908). He was converted to Roman Catholicism in 1922. He founded his weekly in 1925 and edited it until his death, when it was taken over by Hilaire Belloc; see *214, n. 1*. See Crick, 192; Stansky and Abrahams, I, 215. For the journal, see *G. K.'s Weekly: an Appraisal* by Brocard Sewell [1995?].
2. François Coty (1874–1934) built a famous perfumery business, the name of which long outlasted its founder, and became one of France's wealthiest men. He subsidised *L'Ami du Peuple* and *Gaulois*, both of which pursued nationalist and anti-left policies. The title *L'Ami du Peuple* was, ironically, that of the inflamatory radical newspaper edited by Jean-Paul Marat (1743– 1793), so influential in the cause of the French Revolution.

81. 'An Inquiry into "Civic Progress" in England: The Plight of the British Workers'

Le Progrès Civique, 1928–1929

In a letter dated 29 December 1928, Raoul Nicole explained to Orwell that the usual fee paid by *Le Progrès Civique* for an article was 75 francs per page (about 60 pence in today's coinage; $2.90 in 1928, although the value then would obviously have been considerably more). For each of these articles, and for that on Burma, Orwell was paid 225 francs (about £1.81 or $8.75). Payment for the first was made on 4 February 1929, for the others on 8 February. The articles were: 'Le chômage' (Unemployment), 'La journée d'un "tramp"' (A Day in the Life of a Tramp) – see 'The Spike,' (*104*), and 'Les mendiants de Londres' (Beggars in London).

Raoul Nicole translated Orwell's English into French for publication in *Le*

Progrès Civique. The English originals have not survived; for this edition, they have been translated into English by Janet Percival and Ian Willison. The French text often gives monetary and other values in French and English, although not in every instance. Where it does, these are reproduced here. The paragraphing of the articles is almost certainly not Orwell's. It is possible that the asterisks indicate his original paragraphing. Since reparagraphing could not recover his style, and would be more misleading than helpful, no attempt has been made to do so. For the French texts see *90, 91, 92.*

Orwell's articles were referred to in issues of *Le Progrès Civique* of 30 March and 7 September 1929. In the first, Pierre Vignes discussed the Liberal Party's plan to end unemployment; in the second, Maurice Nibart wrote about the way 'les vagabonds' (tramps) were treated in Germany.

82. 1. 'Unemployment'

Le Progrès Civique, 29 December 1928
Translated into English by Janet Percival and Ian Willison

The prices and measurements given in French in the original have been retained, despite a certain incongruity (with old-style English equivalents where helpful), so that where the original French uses English denominations, such as shillings, this will be clear. The same practice has been adopted for all three articles.

England! Unemployment! You cannot speak of one without raising the ghost of the other.

Unemployment is one of the realities of postwar English life; it is also the reward given to the British worker for his war service.

Before the war, unemployment was certainly not unknown, but the relatively small number of the unemployed was of negligible significance. They constituted what could be termed 'the reserve army of labour', and acted as a brake on the over-rapid rise in wages; they were also sometimes used as stopgaps when there was a labour shortage.

At that time the economic mechanism ran, or at least seemed to run, fairly smoothly.

Public opinion viewed things calmly, assuming that the machinery could never go far wrong.

But war came and suddenly everything did go wrong. Competition, the very foundation of modern trade, which forces the industrialists from one country into cut-throat rivalry with those of another, was to blame. In all competition there must be a winner and a loser. Before the war England was the winner; today she is the loser. That, in a nutshell, was the cause of all the trouble.

The war put an end to England's industrial supremacy. The countries which did not fight, notably America, gained possession of most of her export markets for their own profit. But, even worse, the rest of the world was becoming industrialised more quickly than she was.

The very fact that she had led the way in the race to industrialise told against her.

Her capital was tied up in obsolete machinery, which was unsuited to new methods, but which had cost too much to allow it to be scrapped.

Other countries, which had started later in the race, were better equipped for modern needs. England's main industries, coal and steel, are among those which have suffered most.

At the present time, the coal mines are the hardest hit. They are in such a deplorable state that many of them can only be run at a loss under the present system.

In England, the system of dual property rights in the mining regions gives rise to an enormous waste of fuel, labour and machinery.

Exorbitant rates are paid to the owners of the ground under which the coal seams lie. In addition, each mine is devoured by its own collection of hangers-on: the shareholders, whose demands for dividends push up the price of coal accordingly.

Given all these disadvantages, can we be surprised that English coal no longer finds a market?

To remedy this state of affairs, the capitalists have attempted to force the miners to work for inadequate wages. Their efforts here have failed, but in the meantime Polish coal is selling at a price some 10 or 15 francs [1s 8d or 2s 6d] below the lowest price which England can offer under the present system.

It is the same in steelworks and cotton mills. Today England is paying dearly for her former industrial supremacy.

Result: one and a quarter million, one and a half million, sometimes nearly two million unemployed in England.

With one or two million people starving in a country, there is a threat of imminent revolution, so it was realised from the outset that the state had a duty to come to the aid of the unemployed.

With the end of the war there came an end to the misleading and short-lived prosperity of wartime. The soldiers returning home had been told that they had been fighting for civilisation and for a country 'fit for heroes to live in', as Lloyd George put it; in short, that postwar England would be an Eldorado where riches would go hand in hand with a higher standard of living.

Alas! As Eldorado did not materialise, it was necessary to think up something at once, before the ex-servicemen had time to find out that they had been deceived and realised that, in the end, they had fought for nothing after all.

And that is why the Government rushed through the Unemployment Insurance Act in 1920; under this act any worker in regular employment could choose to pay a sum of money which would indemnify him should he lose his job. These payments would give him the right to claim benefit in the case of forced unemployment—a wise precaution against the starvation and revolution which would inevitably result.

Here is a brief summary of the clauses of this act:

Each week the workers pay a premium of 3 francs for men and 2 francs 50 for women. In return, if they have made at least thirty payments, they can, if necessary, draw the special unemployment benefit.

This benefit amounts to an allowance of 18 shillings (110 francs) a week for a total of twenty-six weeks of unemployment. This period can be extended in certain exceptional circumstances.

Besides this, if the unemployed man is married, he receives a weekly allowance of 5 shillings (30 francs) for his wife, and of 1 shilling (6 francs) for each of his children. For unemployed women and young persons under twenty-one the allowances are even smaller.

It should be pointed out straightaway that this has nothing at all to do with charity. It is, in fact, a kind of insurance, and the majority of workers receive nothing in return for their payments.

It must be added that these subsidies for the unemployed have become an absolute necessity as a result of a decline in the English economy for which the workers are by no means responsible.

It is also worth noting that the unemployment benefits do not err on the side of generosity.

One shilling per week is not much to keep a child on. Even with 18 shillings a week a grown man has difficulty in making ends meet.

This needs to be stressed, because there is a ridiculous story in the Conservative press which states that unemployment is due only to the laziness and the greed of the workers.

According to this story, the sole aim of the British worker is to avoid all tiring labour in order to live in idleness on his 18 shillings a week.

And the inventors of this story have coined the word 'dole' for unemployment benefits.[1]

'Dole' is a wicked word, an expression full of disdain evoking the idea of money paid out by charity to unworthy scroungers.

The belief that the unemployed represent a veritable army of sybarites enjoying themselves on money begged from the charity of the taxpayers is widely held by the comfortably-off in England.

In fact, the lot of the unemployed is in reality far from enviable. How, after all, can one live on 18 shillings a week? The reply is simple: one does not live, one just avoids dying.

Take, for example, the case of an unemployed married man with a wife and two young children. His total weekly income amounts to 25 shillings (150 francs).

Could anyone believe for a minute that he could buy many luxuries with this sum, and that the poor devil would not prefer any job, however arduous, which would bring in more?

A poor family, in the situation I have just described, lives herded together in one room in some stinking slum in London, Manchester, or perhaps some Welsh mining town.

They probably pay 7 shillings, (42 francs) a week in rent alone. The remainder must suffice to feed and keep four people.

Given this sort of income, what can their meals consist of? Bread and tea, tea and bread, week in, week out.

This is wretched sustenance: bad bread, white and lacking nutriment, and very strong tea is the staple diet for very poor people in England.

In winter, it is almost impossible to heat the one shabby room properly. The man cannot afford to buy tobacco. Beer is out of the question.

Even the children's milk is rationed. Spare clothes and the less essential pieces of furniture make their way one by one to the pawnbroker's. Dismal day follows dismal day without bringing an end to unemployment.

So 'idleness in luxury', as the Conservative newspapers say in righteous indignation, turns out to mean, on closer inspection 'a state of near starvation'.

It may be that the unemployed man is single. Then he will take up residence in one of the enormous barracks known as 'lodging houses' reserved for very poor people. By doing this he will be able to save a shilling or two on his weekly rent.

These lodging houses are run by large companies, which make a significant income for them.

The lodgers sleep in enormous dormitories where thirty or forty campbeds—like those of soldiers—are lined up about three feet apart (90 centimetres).

They spend their days in underground kitchens, built under the street, where they can cook their food, if they have any, in a frying pan on a coke fire.

Most of the unmarried down-and-outs in England—the unemployed, beggars, newspaper-sellers and the like—live in these lodging houses; overcrowded, insanitary, comfortless places. The beds, usually revoltingly filthy, are crawling with vermin.

And it is here that the unemployed man takes his meals, consisting of bread and tea. He sits in a blank stupor in front of the fire for those long hours when he is not searching for some kind of work.

Apart from this constantly frustrating search for work, he has nothing at all to do. One can understand that in his situation he desperately hopes to work, to accomplish any task at all, however disgusting and poorly paid, for this completely empty existence, with no entertainment or distraction of any kind—and where hunger is never far away—is one of monotony and crushing boredom.

The unemployed man has just about enough money to meet the essential necessities of life, and the idleness which is forced upon him is a hundred times worse than the worst possible task.

Moreover his unemployment benefit will not be paid to him for ever, and even collecting it is not exactly easy.

He has to go to the Labour Exchange every day to see if there is any work and must often wait there for several hours before anyone has time to attend to him.

To draw his weekly allowance, he has to appear in person and again wait around. Thus one can see at any hour of the day long queues of shabbily dressed, haggard men crowding round the doors of the Labour Exchange. Passers-by look at them with pity or contempt. The officials whose job it is to pay them are at pains to make them aware of the inferiority of their situation. They will not let the unemployed forget for a minute that they are outcasts, living at public expense, who must therefore behave humbly and submissively in all circumstances. The officials are within their rights in refusing payment if the unemployed present themselves drunk or even smelling of drink.

Then comes the dreaded day when the 'dole' runs out. The twenty-six weeks have passed and the unemployed man, still with no work, finds himself with no money either.

What can he do now? Perhaps he has saved a few shillings which will carry him on for a day or two longer. He could give up his four-franc bed and spend his nights in the open, reduce his meals to the bare minimum which will just allow him to stay alive. What is the use? If the longed-for job does not materialise, he must make the choice between begging, stealing, or dying of poverty.

He will probably decide to beg. He will ask for money in the street or else he will seek the assistance reserved for paupers from the local rates under the terms of the Poor Law. Perhaps he will have himself admitted to the workhouse where the poor, treated more or less like prisoners, are kept at public expense.

If he is lucky he will obtain, under that same law, a weekly payment of 10 shillings (62 francs), on which he will have to exist as best he can.

He could also become a 'tramp', and wander up and down the country looking for work on the way and seeking bed and board in a different workhouse[2] every night.

But there are so many of these unfortunate creatures that the whole edifice of the Poor Law is in danger of crumbling. It was conceived to cope with normal conditions, and cannot bear the additional weight of the thousands of jobless who, since they no longer receive unemployment pay, are often obliged to go on being supported by the community.

In South Wales, where the failure of the pits has thrown half a million men onto the streets, the relief funds for the needy paid from the local rates have now gone bankrupt.

*
* *

These are the conditions of unemployment in England. To remedy this state of affairs, the present Conservative government has done nothing except make optimistic pronouncements.

At the beginning of this year, when Mr Baldwin was asked to make subsidies from the public purse on behalf of South Wales, the Prime Minister replied that he was 'counting on private charity' to help the miners deep in destitution.

Tentative projects were proposed aimed at creating an artificial demand for labour by undertaking wide-scale public works, such as the building of roads or canals, but as it would have needed new taxes to set up the project, nothing very much has been achieved.

The mass emigration of the unemployed has also been encouraged, but the conditions offered were not very attractive. What is more, Canada and Australia have their own industrial problems to solve, just like their mother country.

They have no use at the moment for surplus English miners, and have made this quite clear to the miners themselves.

Thus it seems unlikely that emigration will smooth over the difficulty.

The government has striven to hide its mistakes by varnishing the truth. The official unemployment statistics have been drawn up quite deliberately to give an erroneous impression. They only count the *insured* unemployed, omitting the tens of thousands of people who have never had a regular job since the war. Wives and children supported by the jobless do not appear in these lists either.

The real number of those in need is thus grossly underestimated. The Conservative press avoids mentioning unemployment as much as possible: when it is mentioned, it is with dismissive allusions to the 'dole' and to the laziness of the working classes.

So the comfortably-off middle-class Englishman, who knows nothing—and prefers to know nothing—of the life of the poor, learns nothing which might shake him out of his complacent indifference.

And how, we ask, will all this end? What solution can be envisaged?

One thing alone seems certain. Efforts will be made to prevent most of these poor creatures from actually dying of hunger. For example, no government would dare to make a stand against half-a-million starving miners. Whatever happens, to avoid revolution they will make sure that the unemployed can receive subsidies from somewhere.

But apart from that, any great improvement seems impossible. Unemployment is a by-product of capitalism and large-scale industrial competition. As long as this state of affairs persists, poverty will hold the workers in thrall, now in one country, now in another.

For the moment, the English worker is the scapegoat. He will no doubt continue to suffer until there is a radical change in the present economic system.

Meanwhile his only real hope is that one day a government will be elected which has sufficient strength and intelligence to bring about the change.

E.-A. BLAIR

1. 'Dole' as a gift of food or money goes back at least to the fourteenth century. It is used by Langland (anything but a 'Conservative' writer) in *Piers Plowman*. Its pejorative use, especially in the twentieth century, is ironic, because employees as well as employers contribute to unemployment insurance, which is the source of unemployment benefits. The idea was first put forward in England by Lloyd George, a Liberal, in his budget for 1909, which the House of Lords rejected.
2. The French text renders 'workhouse' as *l'asile* and adds the English word, in italics in parentheses, immediately after. Several words are given in both English and the closest

French equivalent, or simply in English in italics. Thus, 'tramp' appears in italics and also translated as *vagabond*.

83. 2. 'A Day in the Life of a Tramp'

Le Progrès Civique, 5 January 1929
Translated into English by Janet Percival and Ian Willison

First, what is a *tramp*?

A tramp is a native English species. These are his distinguishing characteristics: he has no money, he is dressed in rags, he walks about twenty kilometres a day and never sleeps two nights together in the same place.

In short, he is a wanderer, living on charity, roaming around on foot day after day for years, crossing England from end to end many times in his wanderings.

He has no job, home or family, no possessions in the world apart from the rags covering his poor body; he lives at the expense of the community.

No-one knows how many individuals make up the tramp population. Thirty thousand? Fifty thousand? Perhaps a hundred thousand in England and Wales when unemployment is particularly bad.

The tramp does not wander for his own amusement, or because he has inherited the nomadic instincts of his ancestors; he is trying first and foremost to avoid starving to death.

It is not difficult to see why; the tramp is unemployed as a result of the state of the English economy. So, to exist, he must have recourse to public or private charity. To assist him, the authorities have created *asiles* (work-houses)[1] where the destitute can find food and shelter.

These places are about twenty kilometres apart, and no-one can stay in any one spike more than once a month. Hence the endless pilgrimages of tramps who, if they want to eat and sleep with a roof over their heads, must seek a new resting-place every night.

That is the explanation for the existence of tramps. Now let us see what sort of life they lead. It will be sufficient to look at just one day, for the days are all the same for these unfortunate inhabitants of one of the richest countries in the world.

Let us take one of them as he comes out of the spike at about ten in the morning.

He is about twenty kilometres from the next workhouse. He will probably take five hours to walk that distance, and will arrive at his destination at about three in the afternoon.

He will not rest much on the way, because the police, who look on tramps with a suspicious eye, will make quick work of sending him packing from any town or village where he might try to stop. That is why our man will not tarry on the way.

It is, as we have said, around three o'clock in the afternoon when he turns up at the spike. But the spike does not open until six in the evening. Three weary hours to kill in the company of the other tramps who are already waiting. The herd of human beings, haggard, unshaven, filthy and tattered, grows from minute to minute. Soon there are a hundred unemployed men representing nearly every trade.

Miners and cotton-spinners, victims of the unemployment which is raging in the North of England, form the majority but all trades are represented, skilled or not.

Their age? From sixteen to seventy.

Their sex? There are around two women for every fifty tramps.

Here and there, an imbecile jabbers meaningless words. Some men are so weak and decrepit that one wonders how they could possibly walk twenty kilometres.

Their clothes strike you as grotesque, tattered and revoltingly filthy.

Their faces make you think of the face of some wild animal, not perhaps a dangerous one, but one which has become at once savage and timorous through lack of rest and care.

There they wait, lying on the grass or squatting in the dust. The bravest prowl around the butcher's or the baker's, hoping to glean some scrap of food. But this is dangerous, because begging is against the law in England, so for the most part they are content to remain idle, exchanging vague words in a strange slang, the tramps' special language, full of bizarre and picturesque words and phrases which cannot be found in any dictionary.

They have come from all four corners of England and Wales, and tell each other their adventures, discussing without much hope the likelihood of finding work on the way.

Many have met before in some spike at the other end of the country for their tracks cross again and again in their ceaseless wanderings.

These workhouses are miserable and sordid caravanserais where the miserable English pilgrims assemble for a few hours before scattering again in all directions.

All the tramps smoke. As smoking is forbidden inside the spike, they make the most of their waiting hours. Their tobacco consists mainly of cigarette-ends which they pick up in the street. They roll it in paper or stuff it into old pipes.

When a tramp does come by some money, which he has worked for or begged on the way, his first thought is to buy tobacco, but mostly he has to make do with cigarette-ends picked up from the pavement or road. The spike only gives him his board: for the rest, clothes, tobacco etc. he has to shift for himself.

But it is nearly time for the gates of the spike to open. The tramps have got up, and are queuing by the wall of the huge building, a vile yellow cube of brick, built in some distant suburb, and which might be mistaken for a prison.

A few more minutes and the heavy gates swing open and the herd of human beings enters.

The resemblance between one of these spikes and a prison is even more striking once you are through the gates. In the middle of an empty yard, surrounded by high brick walls stands the main building containing bare-walled cells, a bathroom, the administrative offices, and a tiny room furnished with plain deal benches which serves as a dining-room. Everything is as ugly and as sinister as you care to imagine.

The prison atmosphere can be found everywhere. Uniformed officials bully the tramps and push them about, never neglecting to remind them that in coming into the workhouse they have given up all their rights and all their freedom.

The tramp's name and trade are written in a register. Then he is made to have a bath, and his clothes and personal possessions are taken away. Then he is given a coarse cotton workhouse shirt for the night.

If he should happen to have any money, it is confiscated, but if he admits to more than two francs [fourpence] he will not be allowed into the spike and will have to find a bed somewhere else.

As a result those tramps—there are not many of them—who have more than two francs have taken pains to hide their money in the toes of their boots, making sure they are not observed, for this fraud could be punished with imprisonment.

After his bath, the tramp, whose clothes have now been taken away, receives his supper: half a pound of bread with a little margarine and a half-litre of tea.

The bread made specially for tramps is terrible. It is grey, always stale, and has a disagreeable taste which makes one think that the flour it is made from comes from tainted grain.

Even the tea is as bad as it can be, but the tramps drink it gladly, as it warms and comforts them after the exhaustion of the day.

This unappetising meal is gulped down in five minutes. After that, the tramps are ordered into the cells where they will spend the night.

These cells, real prison cells of brick or stone, are about twelve feet by six. There is no artificial light—the only source of light is a narrow barred window very high up in the wall and a spyhole in the door which allows the guards to keep an eye on the inmates.

Sometimes the cell contains a bed, but normally the tramps have to sleep on the floor with only three blankets for bedding.

There are often no pillows, and for this reason the unfortunate inmates are allowed to keep their coats to roll into a sort of cushion for their heads.

Usually the room is terribly cold, and as a result of long use the blankets have become so thin that they offer no protection at all against the severity of the cold.

As soon as the tramps have entered their cells, the doors are firmly bolted on the outside: they will not open until seven o'clock next morning.

Usually there are two inmates in each cell. Walled up in their little prison for twelve weary hours with nothing to keep out the cold but a cotton shirt and three thin blankets, the poor wretches suffer cruelly from the cold and the lack of the most elementary comfort.

The places are nearly always bug-infested, and the tramp, a prey to vermin, his limbs worn out, spends hours and hours tossing and turning in a vain wait for sleep.

If he does manage to fall asleep for a few minutes, the discomfort of sleeping on a hard floor soon wakes him up again.

The wily old tramps who have been living like this for fifteen or twenty years, and have become philosophical as a result, spend their nights talking. They will rest for an hour or two next day in a field, under some hedge which they find more welcoming than the spike. But the younger ones, not yet hardened by familiarity with the routine, struggle and groan in the darkness, waiting impatiently for the morning to bring their release.

And yet, when the sunlight finally shines into their prison, they consider with gloom and desperation the prospect of another day exactly like the one before.

Finally, the cells are unlocked. It is time for the doctor's visit—indeed, the tramps will not be released until this formality is completed.

The doctor is usually late, and the tramps have to wait for his inspection, lined up half-naked in a passage. Then one can get an idea of their physical condition.

What bodies and what faces!

Many of them have congenital malformations. Several suffer from hernias, and wear trusses. Almost everyone has deformed feet covered in sores as a result of lengthy tramping in ill-fitting boots. The old men are nothing but skin and bone. All have sagging muscles, and the wretched look of men who do not get a square meal from one end of the year to the other.

Their emaciated features, premature wrinkles, unshaven beards, everything about them tells of insufficient food and lack of sleep.

But here comes the doctor. His inspection is as rapid as it is cursory. It is designed, after all, merely to detect whether any of the tramps are showing the symptoms of smallpox.

The doctor glances at each of the tramps in turn rapidly up and down, front and back.

Now most of them are suffering from some disease or other. Some of them, almost complete imbeciles, are hardly capable of taking care of themselves. Nevertheless they will be released as long as they are free from the dreaded marks of smallpox.

The authorities do not care whether they are in good or bad health, as long as they are not suffering from an infectious disease.

After the doctor's inspection, the tramps get dressed again. Then, in the cold light of day, you can really get a good look at the clothes the poor devils wear to protect themselves against the ravages of the English climate.

These disparate articles of clothing—mostly begged from door to door— are hardly fit for the dustbin. Grotesque, ill-fitting, too long, too short, too big or too small, their quaintness would make you laugh in any other circumstances. Here, you feel enormous pity at the sight of them.

They have been repaired as far as possible, with all kinds of patches. String does duty for missing buttons. Underclothes are nothing but filthy tatters, holes held together by dirt.

Some of them have no underclothes. Many do not even have socks; after binding their toes in rags, they slide their bare feet into boots whose leather, hardened by sun and rain, has lost all suppleness.

It is a fearful sight watching tramps getting ready.

Once they are dressed, the tramps receive their breakfast, identical to the previous night's supper.

Then they are lined up like soldiers in the yard of the spike, where the guards set them to work.

Some will wash the floor, others will chop wood, break coal, do a variety of jobs until ten o'clock, when the signal to leave is given.

They are given back any personal property confiscated the previous evening. To this is added half a pound of bread and a piece of cheese for their midday meal, or sometimes, but less often, a ticket which can be exchanged at specified cafés along the way for bread and tea to the value of three francs [sixpence].

A little after ten o'clock, the gates of the spike swing open to let loose a crowd of wretched and filthy destitute men who scatter over the countryside.

Each one is making for a fresh spike where he will be treated in exactly the same way.

And for months, years, decades perhaps the tramp will know no other existence.

In conclusion, we should note that the food for each tramp consists, all in all, of around 750 grammes [2 pounds] of bread with a little margarine and cheese, and a pint of tea a day; this is clearly an insufficient diet for a man who must cover twenty kilometres a day on foot.

To supplement his diet, to obtain clothing, tobacco and the thousand other things he might need, the tramp must beg when he cannot find work (and he hardly ever finds work)—beg or steal.

Now begging is against the law in England, and many a tramp has become acquainted with His Majesty's prisons because of it.

It is a vicious circle; if he does not beg, he dies of starvation; if he begs, he is breaking the law.

The life of these tramps is degrading and demoralising. In a very short time it can make an active man unemployable and a sponger.

Moreover it is desperately monotonous. The only pleasure for tramps is coming by a few shillings unexpectedly; this gives them the chance to eat their fill for once or to go on a drinking spree.

The tramp is cut off from women. Few women become tramps. For their more fortunate sisters the tramp is an object of contempt. So homosexuality is a vice which is not unknown to these eternal wanderers.

Finally the tramp, who has not committed any crime, and who is, when all is said and done, simply a victim of unemployment, is condemned to live more wretchedly than the worst criminal. He is a slave with a semblance of liberty which is worse than the most cruel slavery.

When we reflect upon his miserable destiny, which is shared by thousands of men in England, the obvious conclusion is that society would be treating him more kindly by shutting him up for the remainder of his days in prison, where he would at least enjoy relative comfort.

E.-A. BLAIR

1. The original French has *asiles* or the English 'workhouses' in italics; on this first occasion, both words are used, as here. Thereafter, where the French has *asile*, it is rendered as 'spike'; where it has 'workhouse' in italic, it is given in roman. See the note on 'casual ward' in *Down and Out in Paris and London*; n. 140/4, *CW*, I, 226.

84. 'Beggars in London'

Le Progrès Civique, 12 January 1929
Translated into English by Janet Percival and Ian Willison

Any visitor to London must have noticed the large number of beggars one comes across in the streets.

These unfortunates, often crippled or blind, can be seen all over the capital. You might say they are part of the scenery.

In some areas one can see every three or four yards a sickly, ragged, tattered character standing at the kerb carrying a tray of matches which he is pretending to sell.

Others sing some popular song in a weary voice.

Others, again, make discordant sounds with any old musical instrument.

They are all without exception beggars who have lost their livelihood because of unemployment and are now reduced to seeking the charity of passers-by in a more or less open fashion.

How many are there in London? No-one knows exactly, probably several thousand. Perhaps ten thousand in the worst part of the year. Anyway, it is likely that among every four hundred Londoners there is one beggar who is living at the expense of the other three hundred and ninety-nine.

Among these down and outs, some have suffered industrial injuries, others suffer from hereditary diseases. Many are old soldiers who devoted the best years of their lives to the war that was supposed 'to end wars' instead of learning a well-paid trade, and found, when they returned home, that their grateful country had rewarded their services by offering them nothing except the choice between a slow death through starvation and begging.

They have no unemployment insurance; or, if they did have, the period of twenty-six weeks laid down by law for which they could draw unemployment benefit has elapsed before they could find work.

In this confraternity, where old men rub shoulders with young men who are little more than adolescents, there are relatively few women.

The beggars, like the tramps I described in my last article, vary tremendously in their origins, in their character, and in the trades they followed in more prosperous times, but they are all alike in their filth, their rags, their invariable air of wretchedness.

Before we go any further with the examination of the way the London beggars live off the public, we should be clear of the strange anomaly of their position with respect to the authorities.

London is full of people whose sole support is private charity. There are thousands of people asking for money, and yet begging is strictly forbidden in the metropolis of the British Empire on pain of imprisonment. How can it be that every day thousands of citizens break the law of the land and get away with it without being punished?

The answer is that it is in fact the easiest thing in the world to evade the law.

To ask outright for money, food or clothing is a crime, yet on the other hand it is perfectly legal to sell or pretend to sell any objects, or to annoy one's fellow citizens by pretending to entertain them.

These are peculiarities of the English law which defy the most elementary common sense.

Let us now see how the law can be evaded.

First, music.

Singers and devotees of the flute or the trombone are legion. Those who cannot play any instrument wheel a gramophone through the streets on a barrow, but the largest number of these street musicians are organ grinders.

The 'piano organ' is a musical instrument about the same size as an ordinary upright piano, mounted on a hand-cart. To play it, you turn a handle.

There are an enormous number of organ-grinders in London, indeed there are so many that in some areas it is well-nigh impossible to escape from their din.

You can find a poor devil grinding out a tune at every street corner. This plaintive music, which belongs specifically to London, is mournful in the extreme.

We must note in passing that organ grinders should not be confused with genuine artists trying their best to amuse and entertain their fellows. They are simply beggars in every sense of the word. Their dreadful music is the result of a purely mechanical gesture, and is only intended to keep them on the right side of the law.

Their—very real—misfortune is the subject of downright exploitation. For there are in London around a dozen firms specialising in the manufacture of piano organs, which they hire out for 15 shillings (90 francs) a week. As an instrument lasts for around ten years on average, the organ-builder makes a handsome profit; more than can be said for the wretched street 'musician'.

The poor devil drags his instrument around from ten in the morning till eight or nine at night.

Once he has paid for the hire of his piano organ, he will be left with about a pound sterling (about 124 francs) all in all at the end of the week.

He would earn more if he could work alone, but that is impossible, for he needs an assistant to 'pass the hat round' while he is turning the handle.

For the public only tolerates them grudgingly. If they did not insist on passing around the hat (which is their begging bowl), no one would give them anything. So all street musicians, without exceptions, are obliged to team up with a mate with whom they share their earnings.

They prefer to play in cafés and popular restaurants, setting up outside the door at mealtimes.

One of them plays an instrument or sings in the street, while the other collects the money.

Of course, this is only possible in working-class districts, for in the richer districts the police will not allow begging at all, even when it is disguised.

As a result, the beggars of London live mainly on the poor.

Let us now return to our organ grinder.

He works, as we have seen, some nine or ten hours a day, dragging his instrument, which weighs 600 kilos, round from café to café, stopping in front of each one just long enough to grind out a tune.

It is difficult to imagine a more desperately monotonous existence just to earn, after six days of exhausting effort in all weathers, one miserable pound.

And there are a thousand in London just like them.

The beggar must, as we have said, pretend to be a tradesman or artist in order to avoid falling foul of the law . . . a poor sham which, in reality, deceives no-one.

We have just looked at the work of the street musician; let us now turn to the 'pavement artist'.

London's pavements are usually made of broad flagstones, where our man, with his sticks of colour, draws portraits, still life and violently coloured landscapes.

I think that 'artists' like this do not exist anywhere else in Europe. Like the musicians, they are supposed to be working to entertain the public, so by following their 'profession' they are not technically breaking the law.

The pavement artist is at his pitch from nine o'clock in the morning until nightfall.

He begins by drawing three or four pictures very quickly, showing the King, the Prime Minister, a snow scene, or perhaps fruit, flowers etc. Then he sits on the ground and asks for money.

Sometimes, like the organ grinder, he relies on the help of a friend to pass the hat round as soon as a sufficiently large crowd has stopped to watch.

It goes without saying that the more wretched he looks, the more pity he will arouse.

So he spends his days squatting on the hard, cold stone. A stool or folding chair would make him look too 'rich', and would prejudice his success.

Clearly, a beggar must be something of a psychologist.

As you can well imagine the pictures are anything but masterpieces. Some of them would shame a ten-year-old child.

One has even seen some of these pavement artists who have never learnt to draw more than one subject, which they go on reproducing for years.

The life of these poor devils is as bare and empty as that of the street musicians.

This calling can sometimes bring in up to three or even four pounds a week, but one must bear in mind the problems. It is impossible, for example, to draw on the pavement when the paving-stones are wet, with the result that, taking one year with another, weekly earnings do not exceed a pound.

Poorly dressed, ill fed, the pavement artists, who spend whole days exposed to the cold and wind, fall prey sooner or later to the rheumatism or pulmonary tuberculosis which will finally carry them off.

Let us now turn to those who sell, or rather pretend to sell, matches, bootlaces, lavender etc. in the streets.

The match-seller must buy his matches 23 centimes [a halfpenny] a box, and the retail price must not exceed 50 centimes [one penny].

A useful margin, one might think. Perhaps so at first glance, but we must remember that in order to earn 15 francs [half a crown] a day, the bare minimum needed to live in London, he will have to sell sixty boxes. This is clearly impossible, and our 'sellers', like the street musicians and the pavement artists, are only beggars in disguise; their lot is even less enviable than that of the others.

In good or bad weather, they have to stand still for six whole days on the kerb, peddling their wares in a plaintive voice.

There is no more stupid or more degrading trade.

No-one buys their matches, their laces or their lavender, but from time to time a passer-by takes pity on them, and throws a coin onto the little tray they wear round their necks to display their wares.

Sixty hours a week of this stupefying drudgery will bring in just over a hundred francs [16 shillings]—just enough to avoid starvation.

Then there are those who beg openly. They are fairly rare, for sooner or later they will get caught, and will make the acquaintance of His Majesty's prisons.

However an exception is made for the blind, who, by a sort of tacit agreement enjoy total immunity.

Now that we have cast an eye over the diverse forms of begging in London, let us look at the private lives of those who are obliged to live on charity.

Many beggars are married, and are at least sometimes responsible for children.

By what miracle do they meet their needs? One hardly dares ask this question.

Firstly, what about lodging?

The single man has the advantage here, because he can pay 4 francs [eightpence] a night for a bed in one of those common lodging houses which proliferate in the populous districts.

The married man, on the other hand, must rent his own room if he wishes to live with his wife, which will cost him a lot more.

Indeed, it is against lodging-house rules for both sexes to sleep under the same roof, even in separate dormitories.

As we can see, the London authorities take no chances with morals.

The beggars feed themselves almost entirely on bread and margarine washed down with tea.

They rarely drink beer or any other alcoholic drink, for beer costs 6 francs a litre [sixpence a pint] in London.

So tea is their only stimulant. They drink it at all hours of the day and night, whenever they can afford it.

Like the tramps, the London beggars talk together in a special language, a kind of slang full of strange expressions mostly referring to their dealings with the police.

They observe a certain etiquette among themselves. Each one has a pitch reserved on the pavement, which no-one else will try to steal.

No organ grinder or pavement artist will take up his pitch less than thirty meters from another.

These established rules are rarely broken.

Their great enemy is the police, who have quasi-discretionary power over them. A policeman can order them to move on when he feels like it, and can even arrest them if he wants to.

If he thinks a pavement artist's picture indecent, if an organ grinder ventures into the road in a 'smart' district where music is forbidden, the representative of law and order will quickly send him packing.

Woe betide the beggar who does not move on; prison awaits him 'for obstructing a policeman in the course of his duty'.

Sometimes one of these poor devils sinks even lower.

Perhaps he was ill, and could not go out to earn the 4 francs needed to pay for a bed for the night.

Now, the proprietors of lodging houses never give credit.

So every night he has to pay 4 francs or resign himself to sleeping in the open.

Spending the night out of doors has nothing attractive about it in London, especially for a poor, ragged, undernourished wretch.

Moreover sleeping in the open is only allowed in one thoroughfare in London.

You can, if you so desire, wander up and down all the streets you like during the night, sit down on a flight of steps, on the kerb or anywhere else, but you are not allowed to sleep there.

If the policeman on his beat finds you asleep, it is his duty to wake you up.

That is because it has been found that a sleeping man succumbs to the cold more easily than a man who is awake, and England could not let one of her sons die in the street.

So you are at liberty to spend the night in the street, providing it is a sleepless night.

But, as I have said, there is one road where the homeless are allowed to sleep. Strangely, it is the Thames Embankment, not far from the Houses of Parliament.

Here there are a few iron benches where every night some sixty or seventy people come to sleep, representatives of the most abject poverty to be found in the capital.

It is bitterly cold beside the river, and their worn and tattered clothes are no protection against the severity of the cold. So, as they have no blankets, they wrap themselves in old newspapers.

The uncomfortable seats and the freezing night air are no inducement to sleep, and yet these poor devils are so exhausted that in spite of everything they manage to sleep for an hour or two, huddled up one against the other.

Some of them have for decades known hardly any other bed but these Embankment benches.

We advise all those visitors to England who would like to see the reverse side of our apparent prosperity to go and look at those who habitually sleep on the Embankment, with their filthy tattered clothes, their bodies wasted by disease, their unshaven faces, a living reprimand to the Parliament in whose shadow they lie.

E.-A. BLAIR

85. 'John Galsworthy'

Monde, 23 March 1929[1]
Translated into English by Janet Percival and Ian Willison

'Born in 1867. Educated at Harrow and Oxford. Destined for the Bar, but never practised, preferring literature to the law'. That could be the story of many a polished and cultivated English writer. The usual products of such a career are epigrammatical short stories, and essays on Spanish painters, or on Italian baroque architecture.

But John Galsworthy is a completely different kind of writer. There is nothing about him of the elegant gentleman-littérateur. It is at once his strength and his weakness that he concerned himself less with art than with the cruelty, injustice and folly of his time and his country. Author of some twenty-five plays and twenty-five novels and collections of short stories,[2] he is primarily a moralist and social philosopher. Born into the *upper middle class*[3] (the class of the rich bourgeois which gives England most of her legislators, lawyers, army and naval officers, as well as her dilettantes and *minor poets*[4]), he made this class the particular butt of his attacks. Here indeed lies the theme of everything he wrote—the conflict between the comfortably-off English philistines and something indefinably softer in texture, more sensitive and less virile. Only rarely was he content with mere storytelling.

Let us look first at his novels. They were the least successful of all his works, but it is so much easier to assess their relative strengths and weaknesses. The most noteworthy is undoubtedly *The Man of Property*, and to this we can add *The White Monkey, Chancery* etc. which continue it. *The Man of Property* is a finely conceived portrait of an upper-middle-class English family, the Forsytes. The Forsytes are lawyers, bankers or businessmen, all tremendously rich, watching their fortune grow steadily. The distinguishing characteristic of these people is that the whole family has reached the point where they can neither acknowledge nor concern themselves with anything except as a matter of property. Not only land, houses, railways or animals, but even human beings appear to these people to be possessions. Their only concern in life is acquiring and defending their property.

A woman from another world, from the enemy camp, comes into this family—a woman lacking a sense of property. One of the Forsytes marries her. For him, his wife is a chattel, like everything else. He keeps her, well treated, but captive, like a dog or horse, and when she falls in love with another man, her husband exercises his 'rights',[5] with violence. He thinks this act justifiable (because it is legal), and until the end of his days, he will never understand why she holds it against him and finally leaves him. This woman has a strange and disturbing effect on the Forsyte family; her beauty arouses the men's possessive instinct, yet they cannot understand her, and can only think of her as an immoral woman. She epitomises the collapse of all the laws of their world.

His other novels, on different subjects, are moved by the same spirit. In all of them we see the insensitive, brave, domineering, grasping side of the English character struggling with something weaker and more sensitive. We can see these middle-class Englishmen—men of property, judges, policemen and soldiers—with their strong, powerful characters; opposed to them are artists, thinkers, 'fallen' women, criminals, weak men. Everywhere there is the oppression of the weak by the strong.

The Country House and *The Freelands* contain studies of landed property and of the agricultural question in England. A harsher satire on the same question can be seen in *The Island Pharisees*. In *Beyond*, the story tells of a young Englishwoman, idealistic and generous but stupid, the wife of a foreign artist. This artist is a man with a fine and sensitive, but temperamental disposition. Husband and wife suffer terribly because of their mutual incomprehension. In *Fraternity* we can see a group of upper-middle-class people who are at pains to appear cultured and civilised, and beside them, the ill-treated sons of the working class who are necessary to keep up their level of refinement. Everywhere is the division between the haves and the have-nots, between the oppressors and the oppressed.

John Galsworthy does not make the mistake of attacking the oppressors as individuals. His target is the system and habits of mind which make oppression possible. He is impartial and avoids cheap satire. But his attacks have a certain bitterness, a disgust at the cruelty of men, which he does not trouble to hide. One has the impression in his writings of an admirable and tireless fanaticism.

When that has been said, one has probably given John Galsworthy's novels the greatest praise one can. One can admire them as moral and sociological treatises, yet they are second-rate novels. There is no comparison with the best English novels of yesterday and today. The plot is slight, nothing but 'situations' which are usually built up artificially, without any thought for verisimilitude. The characters, always types rather than individuals, are sketchy and unconvincing. No character is properly developed; each of the characters is the same from beginning to end. The dialogue, which should be the most important thing, is almost always weak. Humour is unfortunately lacking.

We should nevertheless note that the didactic novel—the novel which aims to be a picture and a criticism of contemporary life rather than a straight-forward story—has only had a short, and, as we shall admit, an inglorious reign in England. Among younger English writers the tradition which demands that an artist should be exclusively or primarily a moralist is quite dead. It existed for a few years and gave England Bernard Shaw, H. G. Wells, Galsworthy himself, and a few others, but it never resulted in a first-rate work. Galsworthy's novels, which seemed admirable some twenty years ago, have not lasted, and seem tiresomely 'dated'. Our verdict on them must be that they have not realised the promise of *The Man of Property*, once compared to *Anna Karenina*. Could one imagine anyone in Europe making that comparison today?

And then, even if we restrict ourselves to considering Galsworthy's novels as history and social criticism, they will not pass the test. The lack of humour, the invariably gloomy outlook, a seemingly absurd and out-of-date attitude to women—in short, sentimentalism—stifle them. All in all, they do not paint an authentic and convincing picture of life. They are indeed sincere, and have never offended against good taste or humanitarian sentiments, but they do not have in them the stuff which could guarantee them a long life.

But if we move on from Galsworthy's novels to his plays and short stories, it becomes easier to praise him. On the stage his main faults—ever-present propaganda and improbability—are less disturbing. Propaganda is not out of place in the theatre and improbability is hardly noticed because of the acting. Galsworthy's plays are admirably constructed, and he is a master of theatrical technique. The dialogue, so weak in the novels, here becomes fluent and convincing. The moral significance is never disguised, but it has the advantage of being free from those tiresome speeches after the manner of Shaw. The conflict between the weak and the strong, the sensitive and the insensitive, the very foundation of all Galsworthy's writings, tends to drama, and results in lively and powerful plays.

The most famous and undoubtedly the best is *Justice*. Here we see a weak and sensitive young clerk who embezzles some money to run away with the woman he loves. He is caught, and sentenced to four years in prison. The author shows us his sufferings under the atrocious English penal system. No-one wants to hurt him—the judge, the prison governor, even his victim— they all take pity on him; but he has committed a crime against society, and, as they say, he must face the consequences. When he comes out of prison, he is marked for life. He has paid the penalty for his error, but that is of little benefit to him. In the end, he takes his own life. In this play the prison scenes are well conceived and show an undisguised hatred of the loathsome torture of solitary confinement. One scene without dialogue is particularly striking; here the prisoner beats like a madman on his cell door to break the horrible silence of the gaol.

Nearly all his plays have social themes. In *The Pigeon* we see a young woman with refined ideas refusing to perform the degrading work society offers her, seeing in prostitution the only escape from her drudgery. But confronted with reality she throws herself into the Thames; when rescued by the police she is arrested for attempted suicide. In *The Silver Box* and *The Eldest Son* we are shown, in the most forceful manner, the difference in the treatment of rich and poor in similar circumstances. In *The Silver Box*, a 'young man of good family' steals a prostitute's purse. He is drunk at the time, and commits the theft in a moment of unawareness. At the same time a poor devil, also drunk and also unaware of his actions, steals a silver cigarette case from the rich man's father's house. Both are arrested. The 'young man of good family' explains that he had drunk too much champagne, and is let off with a smile and a caution. The poor man also claims he was drunk and says that this was the reason for his theft. He is told that this, far from being an excuse, only makes his crime worse, and he is sent to prison. In *The Eldest Son* we see a rich landowner imbued with the principles of the most rigid morality, suddenly forced to contemplate the idea of his son's marriage to a chambermaid who is the mother of his child. His respect for morality suddenly evaporates at the idea of a misalliance. *Strife*, another well-known play by Galsworthy, is the account of a major strike in a factory. The development of a bitter but finally ineffectual struggle has parallels with some of Zola's descriptions in *Germinal*.

We should note—and this is a tribute to the technical skill of John Galsworthy the dramatist—that his plays were usually well received. At a time when most plays in England are full of vulgar triviality, we must give full credit to a writer whose plays can be at once popular and serious. There is no doubt that *Justice* and *Escape* (a recent play by Galsworthy likewise dealing with prison life) have had a significant effect on the best of public opinion in England.[6]

Like his plays, Galsworthy's short stories are distinctly above the English average. In this genre, in which his countrymen have never excelled, he has produced some remarkable works. *A Stoic*, the story of a dishonest but likeable man who meets with a death comparable to that of Petronius the Arbiter, or *The Apple Tree*, a love story, must certainly be considered among his best. They are more likely to survive than any of his novels.

How long, we ask, will Galsworthy's works endure? In a hundred years, will they be remembered or forgotten?

He will perhaps be forgotten, but, after all, does this matter? Our admiration for him is based on many things. It is true that he is sentimental, that he is also probably lacking in true creative genius, and has been too much a didactic writer, especially preoccupied with the problems of the day. But he is a sincere and disinterested man, whose protests against cruelty and ineptitude have been so forceful. His influence could only have been favourable. Let us be grateful for his sincerity, because, after all, it is not as easy as all that to be sincere. Many writers with a greater talent than his have used it to less good purpose.

1. This, Orwell's second article in *Monde*, appeared in the section 'Les Lettres: Notre Galerie,' the day after Orwell was discharged from the Hôpital Cochin. It may suggest the sort of thing he had in mind for *l'européen°*; see 77. No records have been traced giving details of who translated the article into French or what Orwell was paid. The translation given here is from the French text (see *93*) as printed in *Monde*. Stansky and Abrahams mistakenly state that *Monde* did not publish this article in the issue for 23 March 1929, though it was prominently listed, and that Orwell's essay was not printed in any future number. This, they comment, was 'a disconcerting, experience,' and 'the episode began to take on the quality of an omen' (I, 219–20).
2. The French has 'romans et nouvelles.' The total of twenty-five was about right for 1929; by the time Galsworthy died in 1933, it was approximately three dozen.
3. The French has '*upper middle class*' in English.
4. The French has '*minor poets.*'
5. The French has '*droits.*'
6. The dramatisation of solitary confinement in *Justice* caused the Home Secretary, Winston Churchill, then a Liberal, to draft the reform of this practice in 1911.

86. 'How a Nation Is Exploited: The British Empire in Burma'

Le Progrès Civique, 4 May 1929
Translated into English by Janet Percival and Ian Willison

Following the recent troubles in India, we have asked our contributor, Mr E. A. Blair, whose investigations on 'The Plight of the British Worker' have already appeared in these pages, to tell us something of the unrest which has been fermenting in the sub-continent for some years, and which is threatening to spread to English Indo-China.

Mr E. A. Blair, who lived in Burma for some years, has written the following interesting article for us,[1] which shows the methods the British Empire uses to milk dry her Asian colonies.

Burma lies between India and China. Ethnologically it belongs to Indo-China.

It is three times the size of England and Wales, with a population of about fourteen million, of whom roughly nine million are Burmese.

The rest is made up of countless Mongol tribes who have emigrated at various periods from the steppes of Central Asia, and Indians who have arrived since the English occupation.

The Burmese are Buddhists; the tribesmen worship various pagan gods.

To be able to talk in their own language to the people of such diverse origins living in Burma, you would need to know a hundred and twenty different languages and dialects.

This country, the population of which is one-tenth as dense as that of England, is one of the richest in the world. It abounds in natural resources which are only just beginning to be exploited.

Its forests are full of timber trees, an ideal source of first-class building materials.

There are tin, tungsten, jade and rubies, and these are the least of its mineral resources.

At this moment it produces five per cent of the world's petroleum, and its reserves are far from exhausted.

But the greatest source of wealth—and that which feeds between eighty and ninety per cent of the population—is the paddy-fields.

Rice is grown everywhere in the basin of the Irawaddy, which flows through Burma from north to south.

In the south, in the huge delta where the Irawaddy brings down tons of alluvial mud every year, the soil is immensely fertile.

The harvests, which are remarkable in both quality and quantity, enable Burma to export rice to India, Europe, even to America.

Moreover, variations in temperature are less frequent and sharp than in India.

Thanks to abundant rainfull, especially in the south, drought is unknown, and the heat is never excessive. The climate as a whole can thus be considered one of the healthiest to be found in the tropics.

If we add that the Burmese countryside is exceptionally beautiful, with broad rivers, high mountains, eternally green forests, brightly coloured flowers, exotic fruits, the phrase 'earthly paradise' naturally springs to mind.

So it is hardly surprising that the English tried for a long time to gain possession of it.

In 1820 they seized a vast expanse of territory. This operation was repeated in 1852, and finally in 1882 the Union Jack flew over almost all the country.

Certain mountainous districts in the north, inhabited by small savage tribes, had until recently escaped the clutches of the British, but it is more and more likely that they will meet the same fate as the rest of the country, thanks to the process euphemistically known as 'peaceful penetration', which means, in plain English, 'peaceful annexation'.

In this article I do not seek to praise or blame this manifestation of British imperialism; let us simply note it is a logical result of any imperialist policy.

It will be much more profitable to examine the good and bad sides of British administration in Burma from an economic and a political standpoint.

*
* *

Let us turn first to politics.

The government of all the Indian provinces under the control of the British Empire is of necessity despotic, because only the threat of force can subdue a population of several million subjects.

But this despotism is latent. It hides behind a mask of democracy.

The great maxim of the English in governing an oriental race is 'never get something done by a European when an Oriental can do it'. In other words, supreme power remains with the British authorities, but the minor civil sevants who have to carry out day-to-day administration and who must come into contact with the people in the course of their duties are recruited locally.

In Burma, for example, the lower grade magistrates, all policemen up to the rank of inspector, members of the postal service, government employees, village elders etc. are Burmese.

Recently, to appease public opinion and put a stop to nationalist agitation which was beginning to cause concern, it was even decided to accept the candidature of educated natives for several important posts.

The system of employing natives as civil servants has three advantages.

First, natives will accept lower salaries than Europeans.

Secondly, they have a better idea of the workings of their fellow contrymen's minds, and this helps them to settle legal disputes more easily.

Thirdly, it is to their own advantage to show their loyalty to a government which provides their livelihood.

And so peace is maintained by ensuring the close collaboration of the educated or semi-educated classes, where discontent might otherwise produce rebel leaders.

Nevertheless the British control the country. Of course, Burma, like each of the Indian provinces, has a parliament—always the show of democracy—but in reality its parliament has very little power.

Nothing of any consequence lies within its jurisdiction. Most of the members are puppets of the government, which is not above using them to nip in the bud any Bill which seems untimely.

In addition, each province has a Governor, appointed by the English, who has at his disposal a veto just as absolute as that of the President of the United States to oppose any proposal which displeases him.

Yet although the British government is, as we have shown, essentially despotic, it is by no means unpopular.

The English are building roads and canals—in their own interest, of course, but the Burmese benefit from them—they set up hospitals, open schools, and see to the maintenance of law and order.

And after all, the Burmese are mere peasants, occupied in cultivating the land. They have not yet reached that stage of intellectual development which makes for nationalists.

Their village is their universe, and as long as they are left in peace to cultivate their fields, they do not care whether their masters are black or white.

A proof of this political apathy on the part of the people of Burma is the fact that the only British military forces in the country are two English infantry battalions and around ten battalions of Indian infantry and mounted police.

Thus twelve thousand armed men, mostly Indians, are enough to subdue a population of fourteen million.

The most dangerous enemies of the government are the young men of the educated classes. If these classes were more numerous and were *really* educated, they could perhaps raise the revolutionary banner. But they are not.

The reason is firstly that, as we have seen, the majority of the Burmese are peasants.

Secondly, the British government is at pains to give the people only summary instruction, which is almost useless, merely sufficient to produce messengers, low-grade civil servants, petty lawyers' clerks and other white-collar workers.

Care is taken to avoid technical and industrial training. This rule, observed throughout India, aims to stop India from becoming an industrial country capable of competing with England.

It is true to say that in general, any really educated Burmese was educated in England, and belongs as a result to the small class of the well-to-do.

So, because there are no educated classes, public opinion, which could press for rebellion against England, is non-existent.

*
* *

Let us now consider the economic question. Here again we find the Burmese in general too ignorant to have a clear understanding of the way in which they are being treated and, as a result, too ignorant to show the least resentment.

Besides, for the moment they have not suffered much economic damage.

It is true that the British seized the mines and the oil wells. It is true that they control timber production. It is true that all sorts of middlemen, brokers, millers, exporters, have made colossal fortunes from rice without the producer—that is the peasant—getting a thing out of it.

It is also true that the get-rich-quick businessmen who made their pile from rice, petrol etc. are not contributing as they should be to the well-being of the country, and that their money, instead of swelling local revenues in the form of taxes, is sent abroad to be spent in England.

If we are honest, it is true that the British are robbing and pilfering Burma quite shamelessly.

But we must stress that the Burmese hardly notice it *for the moment*. Their country is so rich, their population so scattered, their needs, like those of all Orientals, so slight that they are not conscious of being exploited.

The peasant cultivating his patch of ground lives more or less as his ancestors did in Marco Polo's day. If he wishes, he can buy virgin land for a reasonable price.

He certainly leads an arduous existence, but he is on the whole free from care.

Hunger and unemployment are for him meaningless words. There is work and food for everyone. Why worry needlessly?

But, and this is the important point, the Burmese will begin to suffer when a large part of the richness of their country has declined.

Although Burma has developed to a certain extent since the war, already the peasant there is poorer than he was twenty years ago.

He is beginning to feel the weight of land taxation, for which he is not compensated by the increased yield of his harvests.

The worker's wages have not kept up with the cost of living.

The reason is that the British government has allowed free entry into Burma for veritable hordes of Indians, who, coming from a land where they were literally dying of hunger, work for next to nothing and are, as a result, fearsome rivals for the Burmese.

Add to this a rapid rise in population growth—at the last census the population registered an increase of ten million in ten years—it is easy to see that sooner or later, as happens in all overpopulated countries, the Burmese will be dispossessed of their lands, reduced to a state of semislavery in the service of capitalism, and will have to endure unemployment into the bargain.

They will then discover what they hardly suspect today, that the oil wells, the mines, the milling industry, the sale and cultivation of rice are all controlled by the British.

They will also realise their own industrial incompetence in a world where industry dominates.

*
★ ★

British politics in Burma is the same as in India.

Industrially speaking, India was deliberately kept in ignorance.

She only produces basic necessities, made by hand. The Indians would be incapable, for example, of making a motor-car, a rifle, a clock, an electric-light bulb etc. They would be incapable of building or sailing an ocean-going vessel.

At the same time they have learnt in their dealings with Westerners to depend on certain machine-made articles. So the products of English factories find an important outlet in a country incapable of manufacturing them herself.

Foreign competition is prevented by an insuperable barrier of prohibitive customs tariffs. And so the English factory-owners, with nothing to fear, control the markets absolutely and reap exorbitant profits.

We said that the Burmese have not yet suffered too much, but this is because they have remained, on the whole, an agricultural nation.

Yet for them as for all Orientals, contact with Europeans has created the demand, unknown to their fathers, for the products of modern industry. As a result, the British are stealing from Burma in two ways:

In the first place, they pillage her natural resources; secondly, they grant themselves the exclusive right to sell her the manufactured products she now needs.

And the Burmese are thus drawn into the system of industrial capitalism, without any hope of becoming capitalist industrialists themselves.

Moreover the Burmese, like all the other peoples of India, remain under the rule of the British Empire for purely military considerations. For they are in effect incapable of building ships, manufacturing guns or any other arms necessary for modern warfare, and, as things now stand, if the English were to give up India, it would only result in a change of master. The country would simply be invaded and exploited by some other Power.

British domination in India rests essentially on exchanging military protection for a commercial monopoly, but, as we have tried to show, the bargain is to the advantage of the English whose control reaches into every domain.

To sum up, if Burma derives some incidental benefit from the English, she must pay dearly for it.

Up till now the English have refrained from oppressing the native people too much because there has been no need. The Burmese are still at the beginning of a period of transition which will transform them from agricultural peasants to workers in the service of the manufacturing industries.

Their situation could be compared with that of any people of eighteenth-century Europe, apart from the fact that the capital, construction materials, knowledge and power necessary for their commerce and industry belong exclusively to foreigners.

So they are under the protection of a despotism which defends them for its own ends, but which would abandon them without hesitation if they ceased to be of use.

Their relationship with the British Empire is that of slave and master.

Is the master good or bad? That is not the question; let us simply say that his control is despotic and, to put it plainly, self-interested.

Even though the Burmese have not had much cause for complaint up till now, the day will come when the riches of their country will be insufficient for a population which is constantly growing.

Then they will be able to appreciate how capitalism shows its gratitude to those to whom it owes its existence.

E.-A. BLAIR

1. Raoul Nicole wrote on 22 March 1929, while Orwell was still in the Hôpital Cochin, to say he was sorry Orwell was ill and thanking him for his article on Burma. This would, he said, be included in an early issue of *Le Progrès Civique*, and, indeed, would have appeared already were it not that the journal had been embarrassed by a large number of articles on foreign affairs. Orwell was paid 225 francs for the article on 11 June. This was the last article he is known to have had published in Paris.

87. To the Editor, *The New Adelphi*[1]

22 September   Handwritten

6 Rue du Pot de Fer, Paris 5

Dear Sir,

During August I sent you an article describing a day in a casual ward.[2] As a month has now gone by, I should be glad to hear from you about it. I have no other copy of the article, & I want to submit it elsewhere if it is no use to you—

Yours faithfully
E. A. Blair

1. *The Adelphi* changed its name to *The New Adelphi* for a time when edited by Sir Richard Rees; John Middleton Murry remained its owner. See *95* for biographical details and Crick, 203.
2. Presumably 'The Spike,' published in a shortened form in *The Adelphi*, April 1931. See letters to Max Plowman, *99*, *100*; for the article, see *104*.

88. To the Editor, *The New Adelphi*

[12 December 1929][1]   Handwritten postcard; dated from postmark

6 Rue du Pot de Fer   Paris 5.

Dear Sir

Please excuse the delay in answering your letter. You may have the article on the terms mentioned by you. If there are any further communications, will you adress°   to

3 Queen St
Southwold
Suffolk.

which is my permanent adress.°

Yours faithfully
E A Blair

1. Orwell was evidently about to return to his parents' home in Southwold; see Crick, 200–02.

French-Language Originals of Orwell's Paris Articles

89. 'La Censure en Angleterre'

Monde, 6 October 1928

La situation, en ce qui concerne la censure en Angleterre est en ce moment la suivante: pour la scène, chaque piéce doit être soumise, avant présentation, à l'insection d'un censeur nommé par le Gouvernement, qui peut en défendre la représentation, ou la faire changer, s'il la considère comme dangereuse pour la moralité publique. Ce censeur est un fonctionnaire comme n'importe quel autre, non choisi à cause de ses capacités littéraires. Il a ou interdit ou entravé la représentation de la moitié des pièces modernes de valeur qui ont été représentées en Angleterre au cours de ces cinquante dernières années. *Les Revenants* d'Ibsen, *Les Avariés* de Brieux, et *La Profession de Mrs Warren*, de George Bernard Shaw — toutes des pièces strictement, et même douloureusement, morales — ont été exclues de la scène anglaise pendant de longues années. Par contre les revues et comédies musicales habituelles, franchement pornographiques, n'ont subi que le minimum de changements. Pour ce qui est des romans, il n'y a pas de censure avant la publication; mais n'importe quel roman peut-être supprimée après la publication, comme, par exemple, l'ont été l'*Ulysse* de M. James Joyce ou *le Puits de la solitude*. Cette suppression est amenée surtout par la clameur publique, il n'y a aucun corps de fonctionnaires employés dans ce but. Un clergyman fait un sermon, quelqu'un écrit une lettre aux quotidiens, un des journalistes du dimanche pond un article, on fait des pétitions auprès du Home Secretary, et — le livre est supprimé, et les exemplaires se vendent en secret à cinq guinées. Mais — et là est l'élément le plus étrange de toute l'affaire — il n'y a *pas de censure* des livres ou pièces non d'origine moderne. On joue sur la scène anglais tout Shakespeare; Chaucer, Swift, Smollett et Sterne sont publiés et vendus non abrégés sans aucun empêchement. Même la traduction de Rabelais par Sir Thomas Urquhart (probablement le livre le plus grossier au monde) s'achète sans grande difficulté. Cependant si l'un de ces écrivains vivait en Angleterre aujourd'hui et écrivait dans sa manière habituelle, il serait certain, non seulement de la suppression de ses livres mais d'être poursuivi en justice.

Les controverses qui s'élèvent à ce sujet peuvent facilement s'imaginer. Elles démontrent que personne ne désire aucune censure. Mais pour comprendre comment on en est arrivé à cette situation extraordinaire, il est nécessaire de remarquer quelque chose de très curieux qui semble s'être produit dans l'esprit anglais en général pendant les cent cinquante dernières années. Smollett et Sterne, on l'a dit, étaient des écrivains décidément grossiers; chez Sir Walter Scott et Jane Austen, qui n'écrivirent que 60 ou 70 ans plus tard, la grossièreté a entièrement disparu. Une légère trace en reste chez Surtees et Marryatt, écrivant entre 1820 et 1850. Chez Thackeray, Dickens, Charles Reade et Antony Trollope, aucune trace non seulement de grossièreté, mais presque de sexualité.

Que s'était-il produit si soudainement et si étrangement dans l'esprit anglais? Qu'est-ce qui explique la différence étonnante entre Smollett et Dickens son disciple, qui écrivait moins d'un siècle plus tard?

En répondant à ces questions, l'on doit se souvenir qu'il n'y eut en Angleterre presque aucune censure littéraire avant le dix-huitième siècle, sauf pendant le court ascendant politique puritain au dix-septième, et lorsqu'on se souvient de cela, il semble raisonnable de conclure que la révolution industrielle, qui amena de nouveau au pouvoir les marchands et les fabricants puritains, fut la cause de cette croissance subite de la pruderie. Sans doute la classe moyenne puritaine était aussi prude en 1750 qu'elle l'était en 1850, ou qu'elle l'est aujourd'hui: mais ayant moins de puissance politique, elle ne pouvait imposer ses opinions au public. Cette explication ne peut se vérifier, mais elle s'accommode aux faits mieux qu'aucune autre.

Il ressort de ceci une autre question très curieuse. Pourquoi le sens de la décence diffère-t-il tant en d'autres temps et chez d'autres gens? Les intellectuels anglais sont revenus, spirituellement, au dix-huitième siècle: ni Smollet° ni Rabelais ne les choquent plus. Le grand public anglais, par contre, encore très semblable au public de Dickens, a conspué Ibsen dans les années quatre-vingt, et le conspuerait de nouveau s'il réapparaissait demain. Pourquoi y a-t-il une telle différence spirituelle entre ces deux classes de gens? Car — ceci est un point à remarquer — si Rabelais choquait le public de Dickens. Dickens choque l'Anglais cultivé d'aujourd'hui. Non seulement Dickens, mais presque tous les écrivains de langue anglais du milieu du dix-neuvième siècle (y compris les Américains) dégoûtent profondément un homme moderne sensible, par leur goût du macabre et du lugubre. Ces écrivains avaient un penchant pour les chambres mortuaires, les cadavres, les funérailles. Dickens écrivit une description d'un cas de combustion spontanée qu'il est maintenant nauséabond de lire. Mark Twain, l'humoriste américain, plaisantait fréquemment à propos de charognes non-enterrées. Edgar Allan Poe écrivit des histoires si épouvantables que certaines d'entre-elles (notamment Le cas de M. Valdemar) furent considérées comme impropres à être publiées inextenso en France. Pourtant ces écrivains ne causèrent jamais de manifestations parmi le grand public anglais — bien au contraire.

Que conclure? Nous pouvons seulement dire que cette censure extra-ordinaire et inconséquente que connaît aujourd'hui l'Angleterre est le résultat d'une pruderi qui supprimerait (sauf la crainte d'une grande réputation) Chaucer et Shakespeare aussi bien que James Joyce. Et la cause de cette pruderi se trouve dans l'étrange puritanisme anglais, que ne répugne pas à la saleté, mais qui craint la sexualité et déteste la beauté.

Aujourd'hui, il est illégal d'imprimer un juron, et même de jurer, et pourtant aucune race n'est plus portée à jurer que l'anglaise. De même, toute pièce sérieuse sur la prostitution est susceptible d'être interdite à la scène anglaise, comme toute prostituée est susceptible d'être poursuivie, et pourtant on sait bien que la prostitution est aussi répandue en Angleterre qu'ailleurs. Il y a des signes que cet état de choses ne durera pas toujours — déjà on constate un peu plus de liberté d'écriture qu'il y a cinquante ans.

Si quelque gouvernement osait abolir toute censure morale littéraire, nous trouverions que nous avons été malmenés pendant quelques dizaines d'années par une assez petite minorité. Et un siècle après son abandon, nous pouvons être sûrs que cette étrange institution d'une censure morale en littérature semblerait aussi éloignée de nous et aussi fantastique que les coutumes maritales de l'Afrique centrale.

E.-A. BLAIR.

Traduit de l'anglais par H.-J. Salemson.

90. 'Une enquête du "Progrès Civique" en Angleterre: La grande misère de l'ouvrier britannique'

1. 'Le chômage'

Le Progrès Civique, 29 December 1928

Angleterre! chômage! On ne peut parler de l'une sans évoquer le spectre de l'autre.

Le chômage est une des caractéristiques de la vie anglaise d'après guerre; c'est aussi la récompense offerte au travailleur britannique en échange de ses services comme soldat.

Avant la guerre le chômage n'était certes pas inconnu, mais les sans-travail, relativement peu nombreux, représentaient une quantité négligeable.

Ils constituaient, pour ainsi dire, «la réserve de l'armée du travail» et servaient de régulateur pour empêcher une ascension trop rapide des salaires; on les utilisait aussi, de temps en temps, pour buocher les trous quand la main-d'œuvre venait à manquer.

A cette époque la mécanique économique fonctionnait, ou tout au moins semblait fonctionner sans trop d'à-coups.

L'opinion publique envisageait la situation avec sérénité, en se distant que jamais la machine pourrait beaucoup se détraquer.

Mais vint la guerre et soudain tout se détraqua. La concurrence, essence même du commerce moderne, que pousse les industriels d'un pays à rivaliser à outrance avec ceux d'un autre, en fut la cause. Dans toute compétition, il y a forcément un gagnant et un perdant. Avant la guerre l'Angleterre était le gagnant; aujourd'hui elle est le perdant. Voilà, en deux mots, la source de tout le mal.

*
* *

La guerre mit fin à la suprématie industrielle de l'Angleterre. Les pays non combattants, et notamment l'Amérique, détournèrent à leur profit la majeure partie de son commerce d'exportation. Mais, pis encore, le reste du monde s'industrialisait plus vite qu'elle même.

Le fait même de s'être lancée la première dans la voie de l'industrialisation militait contre elle.

Ses capitaux étaient engagés dans un outillage désormais désuet, qui ne s'adaptait plus aux méthodes nouvelles, mais qui avait coûté trop cher pour qu'on pût se résoudre à le mettre à la ferraille.

Les autres pays, plus tard partis dans la course, possédaient un équipement plus en rapport avec les besoins modernes. Parmi les industries qui ont davantage souffert les principales de l'Angleterre: le charbon et le fer.

A l'heure actuelle, les mines de houille sont les plus éprouvées. Leur état est lamentable au point que nombre d'entre elles ne peuvent, avec le système actuellement en vigueur, être exploitées sans perte.

En Angleterre, la dualité de la propriété dans les régions minières occasionne une formidable déperdition de combustible, de labeur et d'outillage.

Des droits exorbitants sont payés aux propriétaires du sol sous lequel passent les veines de charbon. En outre, chaque mine est dévorée par son groupe organisé de parasites: les actionnaires, que veulent des dividendes et, par suite, font hausser le prix du charbon.

Etant donnés tuos ces désavantages, peut-on s'étonner de ce que le charbon anglais ne trouve plus d'acheteurs?

Pour remédier à cet état de choses, les capitalistes ont essayé de contraindre les mineurs à travailler pour un salaire insuffisant. Leurs efforts dans ce sens ont échoué mais, en attendant, le charbon polonais se vend à un prix de dix ou quinze francs inférieur au plus bas que puisse offrir l'Angleterre dans les conditions actuelles.

Il en va de même dans les aciéries et les filatures de colon. L'Angleterre paie cher aujourd'hui sa suprématie industrielle autrefois.

Résultat: un million et quart, un million et demi, parfois presque deux millions de chômeurs en Angleterre.

Avec un million ou deux millions d'individus affamés dans un pays, la révolution menace à bref délai, aussi comprit-on, dès le début, que l'Etat devait venir en aide aux sans-travail.

Finie la guerre, finie également la prospérité trompeuse et éphémère du temps de guerre. Aux soldats qui regagnaient leurs foyers, ou avait dit qu'ils se battaient pour la civilisation pour un pays «où des héros pussent vivre dignement», selon l'expression de M. Lloyd George; en bref que l'Angleterre d'après guerre serait un Eldorado où la richesse irait de pair avec le confort.

Hélas! comme l'Eldorado ne se matérialisait pas, il fallut improviser quelque chose, et cela sans perdre un instant, avant que les anciens soldats eussent le temps, de s'apercevoir qu'on les avait trompés et se rendissent compte qu'ils s'étaient, en somme, battus pour rien du tout.

Et c'est pourquoi le Gouvernement passa hâtivement, en 1920, la loi d'assurances contre le chômage, aux termes de laquelle tout ouvrier régulièrement employé avait la faculté de verser une somme qui l'assurât contre la perte de son emploi. Ces versements lui conféraient le droit de réclamer des secours en cas de chômage forcé. Sage précaution contre la famine et la révolution qui, fatalement, en résulteraient.

Voici succinctement résumés les articles de cette loi:

Les travailleurs versent par semaine une prime de: trois francs pour les hommes, de deux francs cinquante pour les femmes. En retour, s'ils ont effectué au moins trente versements, ils peuvent, le cas échéant, bénéficier des secours spéciaux accordés aux sans-travail.

Ces secours sont représentés par une allocation hebdomadaire de 18 shillings (110 francs) pour une durée de vingt-six semaines de chômage. Cette période peut être prolongée dans certains cas exceptionnels.

En outre, le chômeur, s'il est marié, reçoit une allocation hebdomadaire de 5 shillings (30 francs) pour sa femme, et d'un shilling (6 francs) pour chacun de ses enfants. Pour les femmes sans travail et les jeunes gens de moins de vingt et un ans, les sommes alouées sont plus minimes encore.

Remarquons d'abord qu'il ne saurait être ici question de charité. Il ne s'agit en l'espèce que d'une assurance, et le plus grand nombre des travailleurs ne recoivent rien en échange de leurs versements.

Ajoutons que ces subsides aux chômeurs sont devenus une nécessité absolue, par suite de la déchéance économique de l'Angleterre dont les ouvriers ne sont en rien responsables.

Notons aussi que les secours aux chômeurs ne pêchent pas par excès de libéralité.

Un shilling par semaine, ce n'est pas beaucoup pour un jeune enfant. Même avec 18 shillings par semaine, un homme adulte joint péniblement les deux bouts.

Il faut le dire, car une légende absurde circule dans la presse conservatrice d'après laquelle le chômmage est uniquement dû à la paresse et à la rapacité des travailleurs.

Cette légende veut que l'ouvrier anglais n'ait d'autre but dans la vie que d'éviter tout labeur fatigant pour vivre, sans rien faire, de ses 18 shillings par semaine.

Et ce sont les inventeurs de cette légende qui ont inventé le terme «aumône» pour désigner les indemnités de chômage.

«Aumône» est un vilain mot, une expression pleine de mépris qui évoque l'idée d'argent versé par charité à des parasites indignes.

Cette croyance, que les sans-travail représentent une véritable armée de sybarites faisant bonne chère avec de l'argent mendié à la charité des contribuables, est assez répandue parmi les classes aisées d'Angleterre.

Or, le sort des sans-travail est en réalité loin d'être enviable. Comment, à tout prendre, peut-on vivre avec 18 shillings par semaine? La réponse est simple: on ne vit pas, on arrive tout juste à ne pas mourir.

Prenons par exemple le cas d'un chômeur marié, avec une femme et deux enfants en bas âge. Ses ressources se chiffrent, au total, par 25 shillings (150 francs par semaine).

Croit-on, pour un seul instant, qu'il puisse s'offrir beaucoup de lux avec celle somme, et que le pauvre diable ne préférerait pas un labeur, si ardu soitil, qui lui rapportât davantage?

Une famille pauvre, dans les conditions que nous venons de décrire, habite, pêle-mêle, une seuele pièce de quelque taudis infect à Londres, à Manchester ou bien encore dans une ville minière du pays de Galles.

Elle pai probablement 7 shillings (42 francs) par semaine, de loyer seulement. Le reste devra suffire à la nourriture et à l'entretien de quatre personnes.

Avec de semblabes revenus, en quoi peuvent consister leurs repas? Du pain et du thé, du thé et du pain d'un bout de la semaine à l'autre.

Ce misérable régime: du pain, très mauvais, blanc et peu nutritif et du thé très fort, telle est la base de l'alimentation des gens très pauvres en Angleterre.

En hiver, il est presque impossible de chauffer convenablement la pièce unique et délabrée. L'homme n'a pas les moyens d'acheter du tabac. Quant à la bière, il n'y faut point songer.

Le lait même des enfants est rationné. Les vétements de recehange, les meubles les moins indispensables prennent, l'un après l'autre, le chemin du

153

Mont-de-Piété, et les jours mornes se succèdent sans amener la fin du chômage.

Ainsi «l'oisivelé sans le luxe», comme disent avec une indignation vertueuse les journaux conservatuers, se traduit, vue de près, par un «état voisin de la famine».

Il se peut que le chômeur soit célibataire. Dans ce cas il élira domicile dans une de ces vastes casernes (lodging houses) à l'usage des gens très pauvres. Il pourra, de cette façon, arriver a économiser un shilling ou deux sur son loyer hebdomadaire.

Ces logis sont exploités par d'importantes sociétés qui en retirent d'appréciables bénéfices.

Les locataires couchent dans d'immenses dortoris où sont alignés de trente à quarante lits de sangle, comme ceux des soldats, séparés par un intervalle de trois pieds (environs 90 centimètres).

Ils passent leurs journées dans des cuinines souterraines, creusées sous la rue, où ils peuvent préparer leurs aliments, quand ils en ont, dans des poêles à frire sur un feu de déchets de charbon.

La plupart des miséreux non mariés en Angleterre: chômeurs, mendiants, crieurs de journaux et autres de même acabit, vivent dans ces logis; locaux surpeuplés, insalubres, dépourvus de toute espèce de confort. Les lits, le plus souvent d'une saleté repoussante, grouillent de vermine.

Et c'est là que le chômeur prend ses repas, consistant en pain et en thé. Il passe, hébété, le cerveau vide, devant le feu, les longues heures qu'il ne consacrera pas à la recherche d'un travail quelconque.

Sauf cette quête de l'emploi, toujours décevante, il n'a absolument rien à faire. On comprend que, dans ces conditions, il aspire à travailler, à accomplire n'importe quelle besogne, même la plus répugnante et la moins rémunérée, car cette existence absolument vide, sans amusements ni distractions d'aucune sorte — et d'où la faim n'est jamais entièrement exclue — est d'une monotonie et d'une tristesse insupportables.

Le chômeur a tout juste assez d'argent pour subvenir aux besoins essentiels de la vie, et l'oisiveté qui lui est imposée est cent fois plus pénible que le plus pénible labeur.

D'ailleurs son indemnité de chômage ne lui sera pas éternellement versée, et même la toucher n'est pas précisément une sinécure.

Il lui faut se rendre chaque jour aux bureaux de placement pour demander s'il n'y a pas de travail, et attendre là très souvent plusieurs heures avant qu'on ait le tempes de s'occuper de lui.

Pour se faire verser son allocation hebdomadaire, il doit se présenter en personne et attendre encore. On voit ainsi, à toute heure du jour, se presser aux portes des bureaux de placement de longues queues de loqueteux aux traits émaciés. Les passants leur jettent un regard de pitié ou de mépris. Les foncionnaires chargés de les payer ne laissent pas de leur faire entendre toute l'infériorité de leur situation. Ils veillent à ce qu'ils n'oublient pas un seul instant qu'ils ne sont que des parias, vivant aux dépens du public, et qu'ils doivent par conséquent, en toute circonstance, se montrer humbles et soumis. S'ils se présentent en état d'ivresse ou simplement sentant la boisson, on est endroit de leur refuser leur allocation.

Vient un jur l'échéance fatale. Les vingt-six semaines sont écoulées et le chômeur, toujours sans travail, se trouve par surcroît sans ressources.

Que lui reste-t-il à faire? Peut-être a-t-il économisé quelques shilings qui lui permettront de patienter un jour ou deux de plus. Il pourra abandonner son lit à quatre francs et passer ses nuits à la belle étoile, réduire ses repas à l'extrème limite qui lui permettra tout juste de ne pas mourir de faim. A quoi bon? Si l'emploi rêvé ne se trouve pas, il n'a plus que le choix entre mendier, voler, ou crever de misère.

Il se décidera probablement à mendier. Il tendra la main dans la rue ou bien encore il sollicitera les secours prélevés pour les pauvres sur les taxes locales, aux termes de la Lois sur la Pauvreté. Peut-être aussi se fera-t-il admetrre à l'asile (workhouse) où les miséreux, traités à peu près comme des prisonniers, sont entretenus aux frais du public.

S'il a de la chance il obtiendra, toujours d'après la même loi, une allocation hebdomadaire de dix shilligs (62 francs) de laquelle il lui faudra subsister tant bien que mal.

Il pourra aussi se faire «*tramp*» (vagabond) et arpenter le pays dans tous les sens, cherchant du travail en route et demandant chaque soir à un différent «workhouse» son gîte et sa nourriture.

Mais ils sont en si grand nombre, ces malheureux, que tout l'édifice de la «*Loi sur la Pauvreté*» menace de s'effondrer. Prévu pour faire face à des conditions normales, il ne peut supporter le poids additionnel de ces milliers de sans-travail qui, ne recevant plus d'allocation de chômage, doivent parfois continuer à vivre sur la communauté.

Dans le Sud du Pays de Galles, où la défaillance des mines de charbon a jeté sur le pavé un demi-million d'hommes, les caisses de secours aux pauvres, prélevés sur les taxes locales, ont aujourd'hui fait faillite.

Telles sont les conditions du chômage en Angleterre. Pour remédier à cet état de choses, le gouvernement conservateur actuel n'a su que prononcer des discours optimistes.

Au début de cette année, comme on demandait à M. Baldwin de prélever sur les deniers publics des subsides pour le Sud du Pays de Galles, le Premier ministre répondit qu'il «comptait sur la charité privée» pour aider les mineurs plongés dans le dénûment.

On a timidement proposé de vagues projets dans le but de créer une demande artificielle de main-d'œuvre, en entreprenant des travaux publics sur une grande échelle: construction de routes ou de canaux, mais comme il aurait fallu, pour les organiser, avoir recours à de nouveaux impôts, rien d'important n'a été fait.

On a aussi essayé de faire émigrer en masse des chômeurs. Mais les conditions offertes n'avaient rien de bien séduisant, et de plus le Canada et l'Australie ont, comme la métropole, leurs problèmes industriels à résoudre.

Ils n'ont que faire pour le moment du surplus des mineurs anglais, et ils l'ont nettement fait savoir.

Il ne semble donc pas probable que l'émigration doive aplanir la difficulté.

Le gouvernement s'est efforcé de dissimuler ses folies en maquillant la vérité. Les statistiques officielles se rapportant au chômage sont à dessein rédigées de façon à induire en erreur. Elles n'énumèrent que les chômeurs *assurés*, et omettent les dizaines de milliers d'individus qui n'ont jamais tenu un emploi régulier depuis la guerre. Ne figurent pas non plus sur ces listes les femmes et les enfants à la charge des sans-travail.

Le chiffre réel des miséreux est donc immensément sous-estimé. La presse conservatrice évite le plus possible de mentionner le chômage; quand elle en parle, c'est pour faire des allusions méprisantes à l'*aumône* et à la paresse des classes ouvrières.

Ainsi, le bourgeois aisé d'Angleterre qui ne connaît rien—et préfère ne rien connaître—dela vie des pauvres, n'apprend-il rien qui puisse l'arracher à l'indifférence où il se complaît.

Et comment, demandera-t-on, tout cela finira-t-il? Quelle solution est-il permis d'envisager?

Une seule chose paraît certaine. On fera tout pour empêcher que le plus grand nombre de ces misérables meure vraiment de faim. Aucun gouvernement n'oserait, par exemple, se trouver en face d'un demi-million de mineurs affamés. Quoi qu'il arrive, on veillera, pour éviter la révolution, à ce que les chômeurs reçoivent n'importe comment des subsides.

Mais, à part cela, toute grande amélioration semble impossible. Le chômage est un sous-produit du capitalisme et de la concurrence industrielle sur une grande échelle. Tant que se perpétuera cet état de choses, la misère sévira chez les ouvriers, tantôt dans un pays, tantôt dans un autre.

Pour le moment c'est l'ouvrier anglais le bouc émissaire. Sans doute continuera-t-il à souffrir jusqu'à ce que se produise un changement radical dans le système économique actuel.

En attendant, son seul espoir réel est qu'un jour sera élu un gouvernement assez fort et assez intelligent pour amener ce changement.

E.-A. BLAIR.

(*A suivre.*)
Traduit de l'anglais par Raoul Nicole.

91. 2. 'La journée d'un tramp'

Le Progrès Civique, 5 January 1929

D'abord, qu'est-ce qu'un *tramp*?

Un *tramp* appartient à la faune de la Grande-Bretagne. On le reconnaît aux caractéristiques suivantes. Il n'a pas d'argent, il est vêtu de haillons, il se déplace à raison d'une vingtaine de kilomètres par jour et ne dort jamais deux nuits de suite au même endroit.

Somme toute, c'est un vagabond qui vit de la charité, erre à pied jour après jour, pendant des années entières et, au cours de ses pérégrinations, traverse plusieurs fois l'Angleterre de bout en bout.

Il n'a ni emploi, ni domicile, ni famille, ne possède rien au monde sauf les loques qui recouvrent sa pauvre carcasse; il vit aux dépens de la communauté.

Nul ne sait combien d'individus comprend la gent *tramp*. Trent mille? Cinquante mille? Cent mille peut-être en Angleterre et dans le Pays de Galles aux époques où sévit plus particulièrement le chômage.

Le *tramp* ne vagabonde pas pour son plaisir, ni parce qu'il a hérité les instincts d'ancêtres nomades; il cherche avent tout à ne pas mourir de faim.

La chose s'explique aisément: le *tramp* est sans travail par suite des conditions économiques de l'Angleterre. Donc, pour vivre, il lui faut compter sur la charité publique ou privée. Pour lui venir en aide, les autorités ont créé des asiles (*workhouses*) où les indigents trouvent nourriture et abri.

Ces asiles sont éloignés les uns de autres d'environ vingt kilomètres et il est interdit à quiconque de s'y faire hospitaliser plus d'une fois par mois.

D'où les pèlerinages sans fin des vagabonds qui, s'ils veulent manger et dormir sous un toit, sont obligés de gagner chaque soir un nouvel abri où passer la nuit.

Voilà donc expliquée la raison d'être des *tramps*. Voyons maintenant quelle peut être leur existence. L'examen d'une seule de leurs journées suffira, car elles se ressemblent toutes, pour ces habitants infortués d'un des pays les plus riches du monde.

Prenons l'un d'eux à sa sortie de l'asile, vers 10 heures de matin.

Une distance de vingt kilomètres, plus ou moins, le sépare du prochain *workhouse*. Il la parcourra probablement en cinqu heurs, arrivant à sa destination vers 3 heures de l'après-midi.

Il ne se reposera guère en ruote, car la police, qui regarde les *tramps* d'un œil soupçonneux, aura tôt fait de le forcer à déguerpir de toute ville ou village où il tenterait de s'arrêter. Et c'est pourquoi notre homme ne s'attarde géneralement pas en route.

Il est, nous l'avons dit, environs 3 heures de l'après-midi quand il se présente à l'asile. Mais celui-ci n'ouvrira ses portes qu'à 6 heures du soir. Trois mortelles heures à tuer en compagnie d'autres vagabonds qui attendent déjà. Le troupeau d'êtres humains, hâves, hirsuites, crasseux et déguenillés , grossit d'instant en instant. Ils se trouvent bientôt une centaine de sans-travail appartenant à presque tous les corps de métier.

Les mineurs et les filateurs de coton, victimes du chômage qui se fait cruellement sentir dans le Nord de l'Angleterre, sont les plus nombreux, mais toute la main-d'œuvre spécialisée ou non est représentée.

Leur âge? De seize à soixante-dix ans.

Leur sexe? On compte environ deux femmes sur une cinquantaine de vagabonds.

Par-ci, par-là, un idiot marmonne des mots sans suite. D'autres sont dans un état de faiblesse et de décrépitude tels qu'on se demande comment ils ont pu jamais parcourir vingt kilomètres à pied.

Leurs vêtements sont, dans leur ensemble, grotesques, en lambeaux et d'une saleté repoussante.

Leur visage fait songer au mufle de quelque animal sauvage; peu dangereux peut-être, mais devenu à la fois farouche et timide par suite du manque de repos et de confort.

Ils sont là, qui attendent, allongés sur l'herbe ou accroupis dans la poussière. Les plus hardis vont rôder autour de la boutique du boulanger ou du boucher, ans l'espoir de glaner quelque nourriture. Mais cette pratique est dangereuse, car la mendicité est interdite en Angleterre, aussi, pour la plupart, se contentent-ils de demeurer oisifs en échangeant de vagues paroles dans un étrange argot, langage spécial des *tramps*, fourmillant de mots et d'expressions bizzares et pittoresques qu'on ne trouve dans aucun dictionnaire.

Arrivés de tus les coins de l'Angleterre et du Pays de Galles, ils se racontent leurs aventures, et envisagent sans trop d'espoir la possibilité de trouver du travail en route.

Beaucoup se sont déjà rencontrés dans quelque asile à l'autre bout du pays, car ils traversent et retraversent maintes fois les mêmes pistes dans leurs incessantes pérégrinations.

Lugubres et sordides caravansérails, ces *workhouses*, où ces tristes pélerins d'Angleterre s'assemblent pour quelques heures avant de s'égailer de nouveau dans toutes les directions.

Tous les *tramps* fument. Comme il est interdit de fumer à l'intérieur de l'asile, ils mettent à profit les heures d'attente. Leur tabac consiste principalement en bouts de cigarettes ramassés dans les rues. Ils le roulent dans un papier ou s'en servent pour bourrer de vieux brûle-gueules.

Quand par hasard un vagabond possède quelque argent, gagné par son travail ou mendié sur la route, son premier soin est d'acheter du tabac, mais le plus souvent il doit se contenter des mégots qu'il trouve sur les trottoirs ou la chaussée. L'asile ne lui fournit que le couvert et la nourriture; pour le reste, vêtements, tabac, etc., il lui faut se débrouiller de son mieux.

Mais l'heure approche où les portes de l'asile vont s'ouvrir. Les *tramps* se sont levés et forment la queue appuyés au mur de l'immense édifice, cube hideux de briques jaunâtres, situé dans un lointain faubourg, et qui ressemble à s'y méprendre à une prison.

Encore quelques minutes, les lourds battants s'écartetet le bétail humain pénètre à l'intérieur.

La ressemblance entre un de ces asiles et une prison frappe davantage encore quand on a franchi le seuil. Au milieu d'une cour sans verdure, close de hauts murs en briques, s'élève le bâtiment principal comprenant des cellules aux parois nues, une salle de bain, les bureaux de l'administration, et une pièce exiguë, meublée de bancs grossiers en bois, qui sert de réfectoire. Le tout laid et sinistre à plaisir.

Cette atmosphère de prison se retrouve partout. Des fonctionnaires en uniforme molestent les vagabonds, les mènent à la baguette, et ne manquent aucune occasion de leur rappeler qu'en pénétrant dans le *workhouse* ils ont fait abandon de tous leurs droits, de toutes leurs libertés.

Le nom et al profession du *tramp* sont inscrits sur un registre. Puis, on lui fait prendre un bain, on lui enlève ses vêtements et tous les objects en sa possession. On lui prête ensuite une grossière chemise de coton pour la nuit.

Si par hasard il a de l'argent, on le lui confisque, mais s'il avoue posséder plus de deux francs, il ne sera pas admis à passer la nuit à l'asile et devra se procurer un lit où il pourra.

En conséquence, les vagabonds—ils ne sont pas très nombreux—qui possèdent plus de deux francs ont eu soin de dissimuler leur argent dans le bout de leurs souliers, en prenant bien garde den'être pas vus, car cette fraude peut être punie de prison.

Après son bain, le vagabond, dont les vêtements ont été confisqués, reçoit son souper: une demi-livre de pain avec un peu de margarine et un demi-litre de thé.

Le pain fabriqué à l'usage exclusif des *tramps* est abominable. De couleur grise, invariablement rassis, il an un goût désagréable qui laisserait croire que la farine dont il est fait provient de grains avariés.

Le thé lui-même est mauvais au possible, mais les vagabonds le boivent avec plaisir, car il les réchauffe et les réconforte après les fatigues de la journée.

Ce repas peu appétissant est englouti en cinq minutes. Après quoi, les *tramps* reçoivent l'ordre de gagner les cellules où ils passeront la nuit.

Ces cellules, véritables cachots de brique ou de pierre, mesurent environ quatre mètres de long sur deux de large. Pas d'éclairage artificiel; la lumière n'y pénètre que par une étroite fenêtre grillagée percée très haut dans le mur et par un guichet pratique dans la porte, pour permettre aux gardiens de surveiller leurs hôtes.

Quelquefois la cellule continent un lit, mais le plus souvent les vagabonds doivent dormir à même le plancher sans autre literie que trois couvertures.

Il arrive aussi fréquemment que les oreillers manquent, auqel cas les malheureux sont autorisés à conserver leur veste pour s'en faire tant bien que mal une sorte de coussin où reposer leur tête.

Généralement, la pièce est terriblement froide et les couvertures sont devenues, par suite d'un long usage, si minces qu'elles n'offrent pour ainsi dire aucune protection contre les rigueurs de la température.

Dès que les vagabonds ont pris possession de leurs cellules, les portes sont solidement verrouillées à l'extérieur; elles ne s'ouvriront que le lendemain matin à 7 heures.

D'habitude, chaque cellule est occupée par deux personnes. Emmurés dans leur petit cachot pendant douze longues heures, le corps uniquement protégé par une chemise de coton et des couvertures trop minces, les infortunés souffrent cruellement du froid et du manque de confront le plus élémentaire.

Presque toujours les locaux sont infestés de punaises et le vagabond, dévoré par la vermine, les membres brisés de fatigue, passe des heures et des heures à se retourner en attendant en vain le sommeil.

Peut-être arrivera-t-il à s'assoupir pendant quelques instants, mais les souffrances cruelles que lui fait éprouver la dureté de sa couche ont tôt fait de le réveiller.

Les vieux chemineaux expérimentés aui supportent cette existence depuis quinze ou vingt ans, et sont par suite devenus philosophes, passent leur nuit à bavarder. Ils se reposeront le lendemain pendant une heure ou deux dans un champ, à l'abri de quelque haie plus hospitalière pour eux que l'asile. Mais les jeunes gens, que l'accoutumance n'a pas encore endurcis, se débattent et gémissent, dans l'obscurité, attendant avec impatience que le matin leur apporte la délivrance.

Et pourtant, quand la lumiére du soleil pénètre enfin dans la prison, c'est avec un morne désespoir qu'ils envisagent la perspective d'une journée toute semblable à celle de la veille.

Enfin les cellules s'ouvrent. C'est l'heure de la visite du docteur; les vagabonds ne seront en effet relâchés qu'après cette formalité.

Le practicien est généralement en retard et les vagabonds doivent attendre sa venue, parqués, à demi nus, dans un corridor. On peut alors avoir un aperçu de leur physique.

Quels corps et quels visages!

Un grand nombre sont atteints de tares congénitales. Plusieurs souffrent de hernies et portent des bandages. Presque tous ont les pieds déformés et couverts de plaies par suite de leurs longues marches avec des chaussures mal ajustées. Les vieillards n'ont plus que la peau et les os. Tous ont les chairs flasques, l'aspect minable de gens qui, d'un bout de l'année à l'autre, ne font jamais un vrai repas.

Leures traits émaciés, leurs rides prématurées, leur barbe inculte, tout en eux dénote l'insuffisance de nourriture et le manque de sommeil.

Mas voici le docteur. Son examen est aussi rapide que superficiel. Il n'a d'ailleurs d'autre but que de découvrir si parmi les chemineaux, il n'en est pas qui présentent des symptômes de petite vérole.

Le médecin enveloppe d'un coup d'œil rapide, par devant et par derrière, chacun des miséreux, á tour de rôle.

Or la plupart d'entre eux souffrent d'une maladie quelconque. Quelques-suns, presque totalement idiots, sont à peine capables de se conduire. Peu importe, ils seront relâchés tant qu'ils ne porteront pas sur leur personne les stigmates redoutés dela petite vérole.

Qu'ils soient en bonne ou mauvaise santé, les autorités n'en ont cure, du moment que leur mal n'est pas contagieux.

La visite médicale terminée, les *tramps* se rhabillent. C'est là, sous la lumière crue du jour, qu'on peut vraiment voir les vêtements dont se couvrent les pauvres hères pour se protéger contre les intempéries du climat anglais.

Ces vêtements disparates—en majeure partie mendiés aux portes des maisons—sont à peine bons à mettre à la poubelle.

Grotesques, mal ajustés, trop longs, trop courts, trop larges ou trop étroits, leur étrangeté prêterait à rire dans toute autre circonstance. En l'espèce, on se sent à les voir envahir par une immense pitié.

On les a rapiécés tant bien que mal avec des bouts d'étoffe de toutes les couleurs. Des ficelles remplacent les boutons absents. Les sous-vêtements ne sont que des haillons malpropres que seule la crasse semble empêcher de tomber en lambeaux.

D'aucuns n'ont pas de sous-vêtements; beaucoup ne possèdent même pas de chaussettes et, après s'être enveloppés les orteils de chiffons, glissent leurs pieds nus dans des souliers dont le cuir, durci par la pluie et le soleil, a perdu toute souplesse.

La toilette des *tramps* est un affreux spectacle.

'Sitôt vêtus, les chemineaux reçoivent leur déjeuner dont le menu est en tous points semblable à celui de leur souper.

On les aligne ensuite, comme des soldats, dans la cour de l'asile où les gardiens répartissent les corvées.

Les uns laveront les planchers, les autres fendront du bois, casseront du charbon, accompliront diverses besognes jusqu'à dix heures, où sera donné le signal du départ.

On leur rend tous les objets personnels confisqués le soir précédent. On y ajoute une demi-livre de pain et un morceau de fromage pour leur repas de midi, ou bien encore, mais plus rarement, un coupon en échange duquel ils pourront se procurer en route, chez certains commerçants spécifiquement désignés, du pain et du thé jusqu'à concurrence de trois francs.

Un peu après dix heures, les portes de l'asile livreront passage à un flot de miséreux hâlves et sales qui se répandront aussitôt à travers le pays.

Chacun d'eux se dirige vers un nouvel asile où il sera fait usage exactement des mêmes procédés à son égard.

Et pendant des mois, des années, des dizaines d'années peut-être, le vagabond ne connaîtra pas d'autre existence.

Pour conclure, remarquons que le régime appliqué à chaque *tramp* comprend, en tout et pour tout, environ 750 grammes de pain avec un peu de margarine et de fromage, et un demi-litre de thé par jour; alimentation manifestement insuffisante pour un homme qui doit parcourir quotidiennement vingt kilomètres à pied.

Pour suppléer au manque de nourriture, pour se procurer des vêtements, du tabac et mille autres chose dont il peut avoir besoin, le chemineau, quand il ne trouve pas de travail—et il en trouve rarement—doit mendier . . . mendier ou voler.

Or la mendicité est interdite en Angleterre, et plus d'un chemineau a pour avoir tendu la main, fait connaissance avec les prisons de son pays.

Cercle vicieux: s'il ne mendie pas, il meurt d'inanition, s'il mendie, il enfreint la loi.

L'existence de ces vagabonds est avilissante et démoralisatrice. Elle fait, au bout de très peu de temps, d'un homme actif un incapable et un parasite.

Elle est en outre d'une monotonie désespérante. Les seuls plaisirs que connaissent les vagabonds sont représentés par le gain inattendu de quelques shillings, grâce auxquels ils pourront, pur une fois, manger à leur faim ou se livrer à une orgie de boisson.

Le *tramp* est privé de femmes. Peu de femmes deviennent *tramps*. Quant aux autres, plus fortunées, le *tramp* n'est pour elles qu'un objet de mépris. Aussi l'homosexualité n'est-elle pas un vice inconnu parmi ces éternels errants.

Enfin, le *tramp* qui ne s'est rendu coupable d'aucun crime, qui n'est somme toute qu'une victime du chômage, est condamné à vivre plus misérablement que le pire des criminels. C'est un escalve avec un semblant de liberté, plus cruel encore que le plus cruel des esclavages.

Quand on réfléchit à son triste sort, qui est celui de milliers d'individus en Angleterre, la conclusion s'impose que la sociéte montrerait plus de bienveillance à son égard en l'enfermant, pour le reste de ses jours, dans une prison où il jouirait tout au moins d'un bien-être relatif.

E.-A. BLAIR.

(*A suivre.*)
Traduit de l'anglais par Raoul Nicole.

92. 3. 'Les mendiants de Londres'

Le Progrès Civique, 12 January 1929

Quiconque a visité Londres n'a pu manquer d'être frappé par le grand nombre de mendiants qu'on rencontre dans les rues.

Ces infortunés, souvent estropiés ou aveugles, apparaissent dans tous les coins de la capitale. Ils sont, pour ainsi dire, partie intégrante du décor.

Dans quelques quartiers, on peut voir, tous les trois ou quatre mètres, debout sur le bord du trottoir, un être malingre, malpropre, en haillons, muni d'un plateau garni de boîtes d'allumettes qu'il fait semblant de vendre.

D'autres chantent d'une voix lasse une chanson populaire.

D'autres encore tirent d'un quelconque instrument demusique des sons discordants.

Tous sont sans contredit des mendiants qui, privés de leur gagne-pain par suite du chômage, se voient réduits à solliciter d'une façon plus ou moins déguisée la charité des passants.

Combien sont-ils à Londres? Nul ne le sait au juste, pluseurs milliers probablement. Dix mille peut-être aux pires époques de l'année. En tout cas, il est à peu près certain que, sur quatre cents londoniens, on compte un mendiant qui vit aux dépens des trois cent quatre-vingt-dix-neuf autres.

Parmi ces miséreux, les uns sont des mutilés du travail, les autres souffent de maladies héréditaires. Un grand nombre aussi sont d'anciens soldats qui, après avoir passé les plus belles années de leur jeunesse à la guerre qui devait «mettre fin aux guerres», au lieu d'apprendre un métier lucratif, ont trouvé, à leur retour dans leurs foyers, que la patrie reconnaissante avait, en récompense de leurs services, à leur offrir pour tout potage le choix entre la mort lente par inanition ou la mendicité.

Ils ne sont pas assurés contre le chômage ou bien, s'ils l'ont été, la période de vingt-six semaines pendant lesquelles, aux termes de la loi, ils avaient droit à l'allocation spéciale prévue pour les sans-travail est arrivée à expiration sans qu'ils aient pu trouver le moindre emploi.

Dans cette confraternité où se coudoient des vieillards et des jeunes hommes à peine sortis de l'adolescence, on trouve relativement peu de femmes.

Les mendiants, comme les chemineaux dont j'ai parlé dans mon dernier article, peuvent varier à l'infini quant à leurs origines, leur caractère, les métiers qu'ils ont exercés en des temps plus prospères, mais ils s'apparentent tous par leur crasse, leurs haillons, leur aspect invariablement minable.

Avant de pousser plus avant l'examen des moyens mis en œuvre par les mendiant londoniens pour vivre aux crochets du public, constatons la curieuse anomalie de leur situation vis-à-vis des autorités?

Londres fourmille d'individus qui ne vivent que de la charité privée. Ils sontdes milliers à tendre la main, et pourtant la mendicité dans la métropole de l'Empire britannique est rigoureusement interdite sous peine de prison. Comment donc se fait-il que, chaque jour, des milliers de citoyens enfreignent la loi de leur pays et vivent impunément dans l'illégalité?

C'est qu'à vrai dire la loi se tourne le plus aisément du monde.

Demander franchement de l'argent, des aliments, des vêtements est un délit, mais il est par contre parfaitement licite de vendre ou faire semblant de vender des objects quelconques, ou de casser le tête à ses concitoyens sous prétexte de les amuser.

Ce sont là singularités de la loi anglaise que le bon sens le plus élémentaire se refuse à comprendre.

Voyons maintenant par quels moyens on tourne la loi.

D'abord, la musique.

Les chanteurs, les amateurs de flûte ou de cornet à piston sont légion. Ceux qui ne savent jouer d'aucun instrument promènenet à travers les rues un gramophone sur une prouette, mais l'element le plus important des musiciens ambulants est constitué par les joueurs de «piano-orgue».

Le piano-orgue est un instrument de musique de la granduer à peu près d'un piano droit ordinaire et monté sur une charrette à bras. Pour en jouer, on turne une manivelle.

Le nombre des joueurs de piano-orgue est énorme à Londres. A tel point que, *dans certains quartiers, il est presque impossible d'échapper à leur tintamarre.*

On trouve à chaque coin de rue des miséreux occupés à moudre des airs.

Cette «musique» plaintive, spécifiquement londonienne, est lugubre à l'extrême.

Remarquons en passant que les joueurs d'orgue ne sauraient en aucun cas être assimilés à des artistes de bonne foi s'efforçant de distraire ou d'amuser leurs semblables. Ce sont bel et bien des mendiants dans toute l'acception du mot. Leur abominable musique est le résultat d'un geste purement mécanique et n'a d'autre but que de les mettre d'accord avec la loi.

Leur infortune, très réelle, fait l'object d'une véritable exploitation. Il existe en effet à Londres environ une douzaine de firmes spécialisées dans la fabrication de pianos-orgues qu'elles louent à raison de 15 shillings (90 francs) par semaine. Comme un instrument dure en moyenne une dizaine d'années, le constructeur y trouve son compte; on ne peut en dire autant du malheureux «musicien» ambulant.

Le pauvre diable remorque son instrument de 10 heures du matin à 8 on 9 heures du soir.

Déduction faite du montant de la location de son piano-orgue, il lui restera en tout et pour tout environ une livre sterling (environ 124 francs) à la fin de la semaine.

Il gagnerait davantage s'il pouvait travailler seul, mais cela lui est interdit, car il a besoin d'un compagnon pour «faire le tour de l'honorable société» tandis que lui-même tuorne sa manivelle.

Le public, en effet, ne les tolère qu'à son corps défendant. S'ils ne faisaient avec insistance circuler le chapeau qui leur lient lieu d'aumônière, on ne leur donnerait rien. Aussi tous les musiciens des rues, sans exception, sont-ils obligés de s'adjoindre un associé avec lequel ils partagent leurs gains.

Ils fréquentent de préférence les cafés et les restaurants populaires devant la porte desquels ils s'installent aux heures des repas.

L'un d'eux joue d'un instrument quelconque ou chante dans la rue, tandis que l'autre fait la quête.

Ceci, bien entendu, n'est possible que dans les quartiers ouvriers, car dans les quartiers riches, la police ne tolère généralement aucune mendicité, même déguisée.

D'où il résulte que les mendiants de Londres vivent surtout des pauvres.

Revenons au joueur de piano-orgue.

Il travaille, avons-nous dit, de neuf à dix heures par jour, trainant son instrument qui pèse de cinq à six cents kilos de restaurant en restaurant, s'arrêtant devant chaque établissement juste le temps de moudre un air.

Il est difficile de s'imaginer existence plus désespérément monotone, pour, après six jours d'un labeur épuisant, par tous les temps, arriver à gagner péniblement une livre sterling.

Et ils sont environ un millier comme cela à Londres.

Le mendiant, nous l'avons démontré, doit, pour éviter de tomber sous le coup de la loi, faire figure de commerçant ou d'artiste . . . Piètre figure en vérité et que ne trompe personne!

Nous venons de voir à l'œuvre le musicien ambulant; passons maintenant au «dessinateur de trottoir».

Les trottoirs de Londres sont pour la plupart formés de larges dalles en pierre sur lesquelles notre homme, à l'aide de crayons de couleur trace des potraits, des natures mortes, des paysages violemment teintés.

Ce genre «d'artistes» n'existe, croyons-nous, nulle part ailleurs en Europe. Comme les musiciens, ils sont censés travailler pour amuser le public. Aussi l'exercice de leur «profession» ne constitue-t-il pas, techniquement parlant, une infraction à la loi.

Le «dessinateur de trottoir» est à son poste depuis 9 heures du matin jusqu'à la nuit.

Il commence par exécuter raidement trois ou quatre tableaux représentant le Roi, le Premier ministre, un coucher de soleil, un effet de neige, ou bien encore des fruits, des fleurs, etc., puis il s'assied à même le sol et tend la main.

Quelquefois, comme le joueur de piano-orgue, il a recours aux bons offices d'un ami pour faire circuler le chapeau dès qu'un nombre suffisant de badauds s'est assemblé.

Il va sans dire que plus il aura l'air misérable, plus il incitera la pitié.

Aussi passe-t-il ses journées accroupi sur la pierre dure et froide. Un tabouret ou un pliant feraient trop «riche» et nuiraient à son succès.

Les mendiants, on le voit, doivent être quelque peu psychologues.

Comme bien on pense, les tableaux sont loin d'être des chefs-d'œuvre. Certains d'entre eux feraient honte à un enfant de dix ans.

On a vu aussi de ces «artistes de trottoir» incapables d'apprendre à dessiner plus d'un seul sujet qu'ils reproduiront indéfiniment pendant des années.

L'existence de ces pauvres hères est aussi vide et aussi dénuée d'intérêt que celle des musiciens ambulants.

Ce métier peut rapporter parfois jusqu'à trois ou même quatre livres par semaine, mais il faut tenir compte des aléas. Il est impossible, par example, de dessiner sur le trottoir quand les dalles sont humides, si bien que, bon an mal an, le gain hebdomadaire ne dépasse pas une livre.

Mal vêtus, mal nourris, les «artistes de trottoir», exposés pendant des journées entières au vent et au froid, sont guettés par les rhumatismes ou la tuberculose pulmonaire qui, tôt ou tard, finiront par les terrasser.

Examinons à présent le cas de ceux qui vendent, ou plutôt font semblant de vendre dans les rues des allumetes, des lacets de souliers, de la lavande, etc.

Le marchand d'allumettes doit acheter ses allumettes à raison de 25 centimes la boîte dont le prix de détail ne devra pas dépasser 50 centimes.

Marge intéressante, dira-t-on. A première vue peut-être, mais songeons que, pour gagner quinze francs par jour, minimum indispensable pour vivre à Londres, il faudrait vendre soixante boîtes. La chose est évidemment impossible et nos «commerçants», comme les musiciens des rues et les artistes de trottoir, ne sont que des mendiants déguisés, dont le sort est moins enviable encore que celui de ces derniers.

Par beau ou mauvais temps, il leur faut demeurer six jours par semaine immobiles, pendant huit ou dix heures sur le bord deu trottoir, à offrir leur marchandise d'une voix dolente.

Il n'est pas de métier moins intelligent ou plus avilissant.

Nul n'achète leurs allumettes, leurs lacets our leur lavande, mais de temps en temps un passant apitoyé depose une pièce de monnaie dans le petit plateau, suspendu à leur cou, qui leur sert d'étalage.

Soixante heures par semaine de cette corvée abrutissante leur rapporteront un peu plus de cent francs . . . juste de quoi ne pas mourir.

Restent ceux qui mendient ouvertement. Ils sont assez rares, car tôt ou tard ils se font prendre et font connaissance avec les prisons de Sa Majesté.

Exception est faite cependant pour les aveugles lesquels, par une sorte d'entente tacite, jouissent d'une immunité totale.

Après avoir succinctement passé en revue les diverses formes qu'épouse la mendicité à Londres, jetons un coup d'œil sur la vie privée de ceux qui sont obligés, pour vivre, de faire appel à la charité.

Nombre de mendiants sont mariés et ont des enfants, sinon en totalité, du moins en partie à leur charge.

Par quel miracle subviennent-ils à leurs besoins? On ose à peine se le demander.

D'abord, le logement.

Le célibataire, sur ce point, est avantagé en ce sens qu'il a la ressource de louer, pour quatre francs par nuit, un lit dans le dortoir d'un de ces logis pour pauvres qui pullulent dans les quartiers populeux.

L'homme marié, par contre, s'il veut vivre avec sa femme, devra se procurer une pièce à part qu'il paiera beaucoup plus cher.

Les règlements, en effet, qui régissent les *lodging houses* (logis pour pauvres), s'opposent à ce que des individus de sexe différent couchent, même dans des dortoirs séparés, sous le même toit.

Les autorités londoniennes, on le voit, ne plaisantent pas avec la morale.

Les mendiants se nourrissent presque exclusivement de pain et de margarine arrosés de thé.

Il est rare qu'ils boivent de la bière ou toute autre boisson fermentée. La bière, en effet, coûte environ six francs le litre à Londres.

Le thé donc est leur unique stimulant. Ils en absorbent à toute heure du jour ou de la nuit, quand ils ont les moyens de s'en procurer.

Comme les chemineaux, les mendiants de Londres conversent entre eux dans une langue spéciale, sorte d'argot qui fourmille d'expressions étranges ayant trait surtout à leurs rapports avec la police.

Ils observant entre eux une certaine étiquette. Chacum a sur le trottoir son emplacement réservé que nul autre n'essaiera jamais d'usurper.

Aucun joueur d'orgue, aucun «artiste de trottoir», ne s'installera à moins de trente mètres d'un confrère.

Ce sont là règles reconnues rarement violées.

Leur grand ennemi est la police qui exerce sur eux un pouvoir quasi discrétionnaire. L'argent peut, quand il le veut, leur ordonner de circuler, ou même les arrêter si bon lui semble.

Que le tableau d'un «artiste de trottoir» lui paraisse indécent, que le joueur d'orgue s'aventure dans la rue d'un quartier «chic» où la musique est interdite, le représentant de la force publique a tôt fait de l'obliger à déguerpir.

Malheur au mendiant's s'il résiste: la prison l'attend pour avoir «fait obstacle à un policeman dans l'accomplissement de son devoir».

Il arrive parfois qu'un de ces malheureux tombe encore plus bas.

Malade, il n'a peut-être pas pu sortir et, par suite, gagner les quatre francs nécessaires à la location de son lit.

Or, les propriétaires de *lodging houses* n'accordent jamais de crédit.

Il faut donc, chaque soir, verser quatre francs ou se résigner à passer la nuit à labelle étoile.

Passer la nuit dehors n'a rien d'attrayant à Londres, surtout pour un pauvre diable mal nourri et en haillons.

Ajoutons qu'il est permis de dormir en plein air dans une seule artère de Londres.

Vous pouvez, si le cœur vous en dit, arpenter toutes les rues qu'il vous plaira pendant la nuit, vous asseoir même sur les marches d'un perron, au bord du trottoir ou partout ailleurs, mais il vous est interdit d'y dormir.

Si le policeman, au cours de sa ronde, vous truve endormi, son devoir est de vous réveiller.

On a constaté, en effet, qu'un homme endormi succombe plus facilement au froid qu'un homme éveillé, et l'Angleterre ne saurait tolérer qu'un de ses fils mourût dans la rue.

Donc, libre à vous de passer la nuit dans la rue, à condition toutefois que ce soit une nuit d'insomnie.

Mais, nous l'avons déjà dit, il existe une artère où les sans-logis ont le droit de dormir. Chose étrange, c'est le quai de la Tamise, a proximité du Parlement.

On trouve en cet endroit quelques bancs en fer où, chaque nuit, viennent s'installer de cinquante à soixante individus qui représentent la misère la plus atroce de la capitale.

Il fait cruellement froid au bord du fleuve, et leurs vêtements usés jusqu'à la corde et en lambeaux ne suffisent pas à les protèger contre les rigueurs de la température. Aussi, à défaut de couvertures, s'enveloppent-ils dans de vieux journaux.

Le sièges peu confortables, l'air glacé de la nuit n'invitent guère au sommeil, et cependant l'épuisement de ces malheureux est tel qu'ils arrivent quand même à dormir pendant peut-être une heure ou deux, serrés les unes contre les autres.

Il en est qui, depuis des dizaines d'années, n'ont connu qu'à de rares intervalles d'autres couches que les bancs du quai.

A tous ceux qui, visitant l'Angleterre, veulent connaître les dessous de notre apparente prospérité, nous conseillons d'aller vois ces habitués du quai de la Tamise, avec leurs haillons crasseux, leurs corps rongés de maladies, leurs visages hirsutes, vivantes critiques de ce Parlement à l'ombre duquel ils reposent.

E.-A. BLAIR.

FIN

Traduit de l'anglais par Raoul Nicole.

93. 'John Galsworthy'

Monde, 23 March 1929

«Né en 1867. Elevé à Harrow et à Oxford. Destiné au barreau mais n'ayant jamais plaidé, préférant la littérature aux lois.» Voilà qui pourrait être l'histoire de tout écrivain anglais poli et cultivé. Des nouvelles à forme d'épigrammes, des essais sur les peintres espagnols ou sur l'architecture baroque de l'Italie, ce sont là les produits habituels de ce genre de carrière.

Mais John Galsworthy est un écrivain d'une espèce entièrement *opposée*. Il n'y a rien chez lui de l'élégant gentleman-littérateur. C'est à la fois sa force et sa faiblesse de s'être moins intéressé à l'art qu'aux cruautés, aux injustices et aux folies de son temps et de son pays. Auteur d'environ 25 pièces de théâtre et de 25 romans et nouvelles, il est en tout premier lieu un moraliste et un philosophe social, Né lui-même dans l'*upper middle class*—la classe de riches bourgeois qui fournit à l'Angleterre la plupart de ses législateurs, de ses avocats, de ses officers de terre et de mer, ainsi que ses dilettantes et ses *minor poets* (ses petits poètes)—il a fait de cette classe la cible particulière de ses attaques. C'est là, en effet, que réside le thème de tout ce qu'il a écrit: le conflit entre les confortables philistins anglais et je ne sais quoi d'un grain plus fin, plus sensible, et moins viril qu'eux-mêmes. Rarement il n'a été que le conteur d'histoires.

Examinons d'abord ses romans. De toutes ses œuvres ce sont eux qui ont eu le moins de succès et la part des qualités ainsi que des défauts s'y fait le plus facilement. Le plus remarquable est sans conteste *Le propriétaire* (The man of Property) et nous pouvons lui en adjoindre plusieurs autres *Le singe blanc* (The white monkey), *Chancery*, etc., qui font suite. *Le propriétaire* est un portrait, admirablement conçu, d'une famille de grands bourgeois anglais, les Forsyte. Les Forsyte sont avocats, banquiers ou hommes d'affaires; tous formidablement riches et voyant leur fortune's s'accroître avec constance. La caractéristique de ces gens est que toute la famille en est arrivée au stade où elle ne peut ni admettre ni s'inquiéter d'une chose, si ce n'est en tant que propriéte. Non seulement la terre, les maisons, les chemins de fer ou les animaux, mais même les êtres humains apparaissent à ces gens comme une propriéte. Leur unique souci dans la vie est d'acquérir et de défendre leur bien.

Une femme d'un autre monde, du camp adverse, entre dans cette famille,—une femme dépourvue du sens de la propriété. Un des Forsyte l'a épousée. Pour lui, son épouse, comme toute autre chose, est une portion de propriété. Il la garde, bien traitée, mais captive, comme un chien ou un cheval; et lorsqu'elle tombe amoureuse d'un autre homme, son mari exerce sur elle ses «droits» par la violence. Il estime que son geste est justifiable (puisque légal) et jusqu'à la fin de ses jours il n'arrivera pas à comprendre pourquoi elle lui en veut, et finalement le quitte. Cette femme passe par la famille des Forsyte comme une influence étrangère et troublante; sa beauté excite l'instinct de possession des hommes, et cependant ils sont incapables de la comprendre, et ne peuvent que la considérer comme une femme immorale. Elle est la faillite de toutes les lois de leur monde.

Ses autres romans aux sujets différents procèdent du même esprit. Dans tous nous voyons le caractère dur, courageux, dominateur et âpres au gain des Anglasi, en lutte avec quelque chose de plus faible et de plus sensible qu'eux-mêmes. Nous les voyons, ces bourgeois britanniques,—propriétaires, juges, policiers et soldats,—avec leur caractère fort et puissant; et on leur oppose des artistes, des penseurs, des femmes «déchues», des criminels, des faibles. Partuot c'est l'oppression du faible par le fort.

La maison de campagne (The country-house) et *Les Freelands*, contiennent des études sur les propriétés foncières et la question agraire en Angleterre. Une satire bien plus amère encore de la même question se dégage de l'*Ille des Pharisiens* (The Island pharisees). Dans *Beyond* (De l'autre côté), il est question d'une jeune Anglaise, idéaliste, généreuse mais bête, femme d'un artiste étranger. Ce tartiste est un homme doué d'une âme fine et sensible, mais fantasque. Le mari et la femme souffrent atrocement du fait de leur incompréhension mutuelle. Dans *Fraternité* nous voyons une collection de grands bourgeois cultivés et civilisés à grand'peine, et, à côte d'eux, les fils maltraités de la classe ouvrière qui sont nécessaires pour entretenir élevé le niveau de leur culture. Partout c'est la division entre ceux qui possèdent et ceux qui no possèdent pas, entre les oppresseurs et les opprimés.

John Galsworthy ne commet pas l'erreur d'attaquer les oppresseurs en tant qu'individus. Il vise le système et les habitudes d'esprit qui rendent l'oppression possible. Il est impartial et évite la satire à bon marché. Mais ses attaques ont une certaine amertume, un dégoût de la cruauté des hommes, dégoût qu'il ne prend pas la peine de déguiser. On sent chez lui un admirable et infatigable fanatisme.

Lorsqu'on a dit cela, on a peut-être fait des romans de John Galsworthy le plus grand éloge qu'on en puisse faire. On peut les admirer en tant que traités de morale et de sociologie; mais ce sont de médiocres romans. On ne saurait les comparer avec les meilleurs romans anglais d'hier et d'aujourd'hui. Ils ont peu d'intrigue, rien que des «situations» et ordinairement celles-ci sont échafaudées artificiellement, sans que l'auteur songe à la vraisemblance. Les personnages, qui sont toujours des types plutôt que des individus, sont flous et peu convaincants. Il n'y a pas de caractère réellement développé et chacun des personnages est le même du commencement à la fin. Le dialogue, qui devrait constituer la partie la plus significative est presque toujours faible. Et l'humour est malheureusement absent.

Il faut noter toutefois que le roman «à thèse»—le roman qui vise à être le portrait et la critique de la vie contemporaine plutôt qu'une simple histoire— n'a eu en Angleterre qu'un règne court et, comme nous le constatons ici, peu glorieux. Parmi les jeunes écrivains anglais la tradition que veut qu'un artiste soit exclusivement ou avant tout un moraliste est définitivement morte. Elle exista pendant quelques lustres et donna à l'Angleterre Bernard Shaw, H. G. Wells, Galsworthy lui-même, et quelques autres, mais elle ne fit jamais naître une œuvre de première grandeur. Les romans de Galsworthy, qui paraissaient admirables il y a quelque vingt ans, n'ont pas tenu et ils «datent» fâcheusement. Notre jugement sur eux doit être qu'ils n'ont pas réalisé les promesses du *Propriétaire*, comparé jadis avec *Anna Karénine*. Imagine-t-on quelqu'un en Europe distant cela ajourd'hui?

Et puis, si même nous nous bornons à considérer les romans de Galsworthy comme de l'histoire et de la critique sociale, ils ne sortiront pas victorieux de l'épreuve. Le manque d'humour, la perspective invariablement douloureuse, une sorte d'attitude absurde et surannée envers les femmes,—en un mot le sentimentalisme,—les étouffent. Ils ne sont pas, en fin de compte, un tableau authentique et convaincant de la vie. Sincères, oui, et ils n'ont jamais péché contre le bon goût ou les sentiments d'humanité, mais ils n'ont pas en eux l'étoffe qui saurait leur assurer une longue vie.

Mais si de ses romans, nous passons à son théâtre et à ses nouvelles, l'éloge de Galsworthy devient bien plus aisé. A la scène ses défauts principaux,— propagande toujours présente et invraisemeblance,—dérangement moins. La propagande n'est pas déplacée au théâtre et l'invraisemblance n'est guère remarquée grâce au jeu des acteurs. Les pièces de Galsworthy sont admirablement construites, et sa maîtrise de la technique théâtrale est grande. Le dialogue, si faible dans les romans, se fait ici facile et convaincant. Le sens moral n'est jamais déguisé, mais il a l'avantage d'être dépourvu de ces fatigants discours à la manière de Shaw. Le conflit entre les faibles et les forts, les sensibles et ceux qui ne le sont pas, en un mot le fond même de tous les écrits de Galsworthy tend au drame, et donne naissance à des pièces vivantes et puissantes.

La plus connue, et sans doute la meilleure, est *Justice*. Nous y voyons un jeune clerc, mou et sensible, escroquer de l'argent pour fuir avec la femme qu'il aime. Il est pris et conadamné à quatre ans de prisoni. L'auteur nous montre ses tourments dans l'atroce système pénitentiaire anglais. Nul ne lui veut de mal—le juge, le gouverneur de la prison et jusqu'à sa victime,—tous ont pitié de lui: mais il a commis un crime contre la société et, comme ils disent, il doit en porter les conséquences. Sorti de prison, il est stigmatisé pour la vie. Il a expié sa faute, mais cela ne l'aide guère. Finalement, il se tue. Dans cette pièce les scènes de prison sont finement conçues et portent la marque d'une haine non déguisée de l'abominable torture qu'est la détention solitaire. Une scène muette, notamment, est très impressionnante, où le prisonnier frappe comme un fou sur la porte d'airain pour rompre l'horrible silence de la geôle.

Presque toutes ses pièces ont des thèmes sociaux. Dans *Le Pigeon*, nous voyons une jeune fille aux idées élevées refusant d'exécuter les travaux avilissants que lui offre la société, et qui voit dans la prostitution la seule échappatoire à ses corvées. Mais en présence de la réalité elle se jette dans la Tamise; sauvée par la police elle est poursuivie pour tentative de suicide. Dans *Silver Box* (la boîte d'argent) et *le Fils ainé* (The eldest son) on nous démontre, de la manière la plus forte, les différences de traitement du riche et du pauvre dans des circonstances analogues. Dans *Silver Box*, un jeune «fils de famille» vole le porte-monnaie d'une prostituée. Il est ivre au moment donné, et commet son vol dans un instant d'inconscience. Simultanément un pauvre diable, ivre également, et pareillement inconscient, vole un porte-cigarette en argent dans la maison du père du riche jeune homme. Tous les deux sont poursuivis. Le «fils de famille» explique qu'il avait bu trop de champagne; on le relâche avec un sourire et une admonestation. Le pauvre allègue aussi l'état d'ivresse dans lequel il se trouvait et déclare que c'est là la cause de son vol. On lui dit que, loin d'être une excuse, cela constitue une aggravation de sa faute et on le met en prison. Dans *le Fils ainé*, nous voyons un riche propriétaire foncier, tout imbu des principes de la plus rigide morale, brusquement forcé d'envisager le mariage de son fils avec une femme de chambre que celui-ci a rendue mère. Son respect de la morale fond soudain, à l'idée d'une mésalliance. *Strife* (lutte), autre pièce bien connue de Galsworthy, est la description d'une grande grève dans une usine. Le développement d'une lutte ardue mais en fin de compte inefficiente a des rapports avec certains descriptions de Zola dans *Germinal*.

Il faut noter,—et c'est un tribut dû à l'habileté technique de John Galsworthy dramaturge,—qu'en général ses pièces ont eu du succès. Tandis qu'en Angleterre la plupart des drames sont de la trivialité la plus vulgaire, il nous faut rendre hommage au mérite d'un écrivain de que les pièces peuvent être à la fois populaires et sérieuses. Il n'est pas douteux que *Justice* et *Evasion* (Escape) (une récente pièce de Galsworthy traitant également de la vie de prison) on teu, sur le meilleur de l'opinion anglaise, un effet appréciable.

De même que ses pièces, les nouvelles de Galsworthy s'élèvent sensiblement au-dessus du niveau anglais habituel. Dans ce dernier genre, où ses compatriotes n'excellèrent jamais, il a donné quelques kœuvres remarquables. *Un Stoicien*, l'histoire d'un homme malhonnête mais sympathique et qui trouve une mort comparable à celle de Pétrone l'Arbitre, ou *le Pommier* (The Apple tree) une histoire d'amour, comptent certainement parmi les meilleurs d'entre elles. Elles survivront plus probablement qu'aucun de ses romans.

Combien de temps, demande-t-on, l'œuvre de Galsworthy pourra-t-elle durer? Dans cent ans, se le rappellera-t-on ou l'aura-t-on oublié?

Il sera peut-être oublié, mais, somme toute, qu'importe? De nombreuses raisons fondent notre admiration pour lui. Sans doute est-il un sentimental, il est probable aussi que le véritable génie créateur lui fasse défaut et qu'il a trop été un auteur à thèse, préoccupé surtout de problèmes de son temps. Mais c'est un homme sincère et désintéressé dont la protestation contre la cruauté et l'ineptie a été des plus fortes. Son influence n'a donc pu être qu'heureuse. Soyons-lui reconnaissants de sa sincérité, parceque après tout, il n'est même pas si facile que cela d'être sincère. Bien des écrivains d'un talent plus grand que le sien, l'ont employé à de bien moins bonnes fins.

E.-A. BLAIR

94. 'Comment on exploite un peuple: L'Empire britannique en Birmanie'

Le Progrès Civique, 4 May 1929

A propos des troubles récents qui se sont produits l'Inde, nous avons demandé à notre collaboratdeur, M. E. A. Blair, dont nos lecteurs ont pu apprécier les enquêtes sur la «Grande misère de l'ouvrier britannique», de bien vouloir nous dire quelques mots sur les causes de l'effervescence qui, depuis plusieurs années déjà, règne dans la péninsule et menace de s'étendre à l'Indochine anglaise.

M. E. A. Blair, qui a longtemps habité la Birmanie, a écrit pour nous l'intéressant article qu'on va lire, où l'on verra les méthodes employées par l'Empire britannique pour s'assurer la part du lion dans ses colonies asiatiques.

La Birmanie est située entre l'Inde et la Chine. Ethnologiquement, elle appartient au groupe indochinois.

Trois fois plus étendue que l'Angleterre et le Pays de Galles, elle possède une population d'environs 14.000.000 d'habitants, dont 9.000.000 à peu près sont des Birmans.

Le reste est représenté par d'innombrables tribus mongoles qui ont, à diverses époques, émigré des plateaux de l'Asie centrale, et aussi par des Hindous venus depuis l'occupation anglaise.

Les Birmans sont bouddhistes; les tribus sauvages pratiquent diverses sortes de paganisme.

Pour pouvoir converser dans leur langue avec les peuples d'origines diverses qui habitent la Birmanie, il faudrait connaître cent vingt idiomes ou dialectes différents.

Ce pays, dont la population n'atteint pas en densité un dixième de celle de l'Angleterre, est un des plus riches qui soient. Il regorge de richesses naturelles qu'on commence seulement à exploiter.

Ses forêts abondent en arbres dehaute futaie, propres à fournir d'excellents matériaux de construction.

On y trouve de l'étain, du wolfram, du jade, des rubis. Et ce sont là les moindres de ses ressources.

Il produit, d'ores et déjà, 5% du pétrole mondial, et ses réserves sont loin d'être épuisées.

Mais sa plus grande source de richesse, celle qui nourrit de 80 à 90% de la population, est représentée par ses rizières.

Dans tout le bassin de l'Irouaddi qui traverse la Birmanie du Nord au Sud, on cultive le riz.

Au Sud, sur l'immense delta où l'Irouaddi dépose chaque année des tonnes de vase alluviale, le sol est d'une fertilité incroyable.

Les récoltes, remarquables par leur quantité et leur qualité, permettent à la Birmanie d'exporter du riz dans l'Inde, au Japon, en Europe et jusqu'en Amérique.

En outre, les sautes de température sont moins fréquentes et moins brusques que dans l'Inde.

Grâce à d'abondantes pluies, surtout dans le Sud, la sécheresse est inconnue, la chaleur n'est jamais excessive. Aussi le climat dans son ensemble peut-il être considéré comme un des plus salubres qui soient sous les tropiques. Si l'on ajoute que les paysages birmans sont d'une beauté exceptionnelle, avec leurs larges fleuves, leurs hautes montagnes, leurs forêts éternellement verdoyantes, leurs fleurs aux couleurs chatoyantes, leurs fruits merveilleux, l'expression «Paradis terrestre» monte tout naturellement aux lèvres.

Dans ces conditions, peut-on s'étonner de ce que les Anglais aient depuis longtemps cherché à se l'annexer?

En 1820, ils s'emparèrent d'une vaste étendue de territoire. Ils répétèrent l'opéraration en 1825 et, finalement, en 1882, le drapeu de l'Union flottait sur la presque totalité du pays.

Certains districts montagneux, dans le Nord, habités par des peuplades sauvages, avaient jusqu'à ces temps derniers échappé aux convoitises britanniques, mais ils tendent de plus en plus à subir le même sort que le reste du pays, grâce au procédé désigné par euphémisme: «pénétration pacifique» ce qui, en langage clair, se traduit par: «annexion pacifique».

Le but de cet article n'est pas de critiquer ou d'approuver cette manifestation de l'impérialisme britannique; bornons-nous à constater qu'elle est la conséquence logique de toute politique impérialiste.

Il sera beaucoup plus intéressant d'examiner les bons et les mauvais côtés de l'administration brittanique en Birmanie aux points de vue économique et politique.

*
* *

Voyons d'abord la politique.

Le gouvernement de toutes les provinces de l'Inde soumises à l'Empire britannique est nécessairement despotique, parce que seule la menace du sabre peut tenir en respect une population comprenant plusieurs millions de sujets.

Mais ce despotisme est latent. Il se dérobe aux regards sous un masque démocratique.

Le grande maxime des Anglais, quand il s'agit de gouverner un peuple oriental, est de «ne jamais faire faire à un Européen ce que peut faire un Oriental».

En d'autres termes: le pouvoir suprême demeure entre les mains des autorités brittaniques, mais les petits fonctionnaires, ceux qui exécutent les besognes administratives et doivent, de par leurs fonctions, se trouver en contact direct avec le peuple, se recrutent parmi les indigènes.

En Birmanie, par exemple, les magistrats de second plan, les policiers jusqu'au grade d'inspecteur exclusivement, les postiers, les employés du gouvernement, les édiles villageois, etc., sont des Birmans.

Au cours de ces dernières années, pour clamer les esprits et mettre un fein à une agitation nationalste qui commençait à devenir inquiétante, on décida même d'accepter la candidature d'indigènes instruits à divers postes importants.

Ce système, qui consiste à employer des indigènes comme fonctionnaires, présente un triple avantage.

En premier lieu, les indigènes sont moins exigeants en ce qui concerne leur rémunération que les Européens.

En second lieu, ils connaissent mieux que ceux-ci la mentalité de leurs compatriotes, ce qui leur permet de régler beaucoup plus facilement les questions litigieuses.

En troisième lieu, ils ont intérêt à se montrer loyaux envers un gouvernement qui les emploie et les nourrit.

Et de cette façon on maintient la paix en s'assurant la collaboratio étroite des classes instruites ou semi-instruites, dont le mécontentement risquerait de faire des leaders de rebelles.

Il n'en demeure pas moins que les Britanniques sont les maîtres du pays La Birmanie, comme chacune des provinces de l'Inde, bien un parlement— toujours la parade de la démocratie—mais ce parlement n'exerce en réalité presque aucun pouvoir.

Aucune mesure de quelque importance n'est de son ressort. Les députés sont pour la plupart des créatures du gouvernment, lequel ne manque pas de s'en servir pour étouffer dans l'œuf tout project de loi qui lui semble inopportun.

De plus, chaque province est dotée d'un gouverneur, nommé par l'Angleterre, et qui peut opposer à toute proposition qui lui déplait un veto aussi absolu que celui du président des Etats-Unis.

Cependant, bien que le gouvernement britannique soit, comme nous venons de le démontrer, essentiellement despotique, il n'est pas impopulaire.

Les Anglais construisent des routes et des canaux—dans leur propre intérêt bien entendu, mais les Birmans en profitent—ils créent des hôpitaux, ouvrent des écoles et veillent au maintien de l'order et de la sécurité publics.

Et puis les Birmans sont de simples paysans, occupés aux travaux de la terre. Ils n'ont pas encore atteint ce degré de développement intellectuel qui fait les nationalistes.

Leur village est leur Univers, et tant qu'on les laisse en paix cultiver leurs champs, ils se préoccupent fort peu de savoir si leurs maîtres sont de race blanche ou noire.

Comme preuve de cette apathie politique de la part des habitants de la Birmanie, il suffit de citer le fait que les forces militaires britanniques sont représentées en tout et pour tout par deux bataillons d'infanterie anglaise et environ dix bataillons hindous d'infanterie et de police montée.

Ainsi, 12,000 hommes armés, en majorité des Hindous, suffisent à tenir en respect une population de 14,000,000 d'âmes.

Les plus dangereux ennemis du gouvernement sont les jeunes gens des classes instruites. Si ces classes étaient plus nombreuses et *vraiment* instruites, peut-être pourraient-elles lever l'étendard de la révolte. Mais tel n'est pas le cas.

D'abord, parce que la grande majorité des Birmans se compose, nous l'avons vu, de paysans.

Ensuite, parce que le gouvernement britannique prend grand soin de ne donner au peuple qu'une instruction sommaire, presque inutile, tout juste suffisante pour des employés, des fonctionnaires en sous-ordre, des petits clercs d'hommes de loi et autres travailleurs non manuels.

On se garde bien d'enseigner des métiers ou des industries. Cette règle observée dans l'Inde entière a pour but d'empêcher l'Inde de devenir un pays industriel susceptible de concurrencer l'Angleterre.

On peut donc avancer qu'en règle générale, tout Birman vraiment érudit a fait ses études en Angleterre et que, par suite, il appartient à la catégorie fort peu nombreuse des gens aisés.

Donc, faute de classes instruites, l'opinion publique, qui pourrait pousser à la rébellion contre l'Angleterre, est inexistante.

Envisageons à présent la question économique. Là encore nous trouvons les Birmans en général trop ignorants pour bien comprendre la manière dont on les traite et, par suite, témoigner du moindre ressentiment.

Pour le moment, d'ailleurs, ils n'ont pas, économiquement, trop souffert.

Il est vrai que les Britanniques se sont emparés des mines et des puits à pétrole. Il est vrai qu'ils contrôlent l'exploitation forestière. Il est vrai que des intermédiaires de tout acabit: courtiers, meuniers, exportateurs, ont réalisé, grâce au riz, des fortunes colossales, dont n'a profité en aucun cas le producteur, c'est-à-dire le paysan.

Il est vrai aussi que les affairistes, qui se sont enrichis dans le négoce du riz, du pétrole, etc., ne contribuent pas comme ils le devraient au bien-être du pays, que leur argent, au lieu d'aller grossir, sous forme de taxes, les revenus locaux, s'évade vers l'Angleterre et se dépense là-bas.

Il est vrai, pour appeler les choses par leur nom, que les Britanniques volent la Birmanie et la pillent sans vergogne.

Mais, répétons-le, les Birmans s'en aperçoivent à peine, *quant à présent*. Leur pays est si riche, leur population si disséminée, leurs besoins, comme ceux de tous les Orientaux, se réduits, qu'ils n'ont pas conscience d'être exploités.

Le paysan qui cultive son lopin de terre vit à peu près comme ses ancêtres au temps de Marco Polo. Il peut, s'il le désire, acheter des terrains vierges dans des conditions raisonnables.

Certes, il mène une existence laborieuse, mais à tout prendre, exemple de soucis.

La faim, le chômage sont pour lui des mots vides de sens. Il y a du travail, de la nourriture pour tout le monde. Pourquoi se tracasser inutilement?

Mais, et c'est là le point important, le Birman commencera à souffrir quand se sera évanouie une grande partie des richesses de son pays.

Déjà, quoique la Birmanie se soit, dans une certaine mesure, développée depuis la guerre, le paysan y est plus pauvre qu'il y a vingt ans.

Il commence à sentir le poids d'impôts fonciers, dont ne le compense pas le produit accru de ses récoltes.

les salaires de l'ouvrier n'ont pas suivi la progression ascendante du coût de la vie.

Il faut en attribuer la cause à ce que le gouvernement britannique a laissé entrer librement en Birmanie de véritables hordes d'Hindous qui, venant d'un pays où ils mouraient littéralement de faim, travaillent pour presque rien et sont par suite, pour les Birmans, de redoutables concurrents.

Si l'on ajoute que la population s'accroit rapidement—au dernier recensement elle accusait dix millions de plus qu'il y a dix ans—il est facile de prévoir que, tôt ou tard, les Birmans, comme il arrive dans tous les pays surpeuplés, se verront dépossédés de leurs terres, réduits à l'état de semi-esclaves au service du capitalisme et auront par surcroît à souffrir du chômage.

Ils découvriront alors ce dont ils se doutent à peine à l'heure actuelle, à savoir: que tout ce qui constitue la richesse de leur pays: les puits, à pétrole, les mines, la mouture, la vente et l'exportation du riz, sont entre des mains britanniques.

Ils découvriront aussi leur incompétence en matière industrielle dans un monde dominé par l'industrie.

★
★ ★

La politique britannique en Birmanie est la même que dans l'Inde.

Industriellement, l'Inde a été volontairement maintenue dans l'ignorance.

Elle ne produit pour ainsi dire que des objets de première nécessité, façonnés à la main. Les Hindous seraient bien incapables, par exemple, de fabriquer une automobile, un fusil, une pendule, une ampoule électrique, etc. Ils ne sauraient ni construire, ni gouverner un navire de haute mer.

En même temps, dans leurs rapports avec les Occidentaux, ils ont appris à ne plus pouvoir se passer de certains articles faits à la machine. Aussi les produits des usines anglaises trouvent-ils dans l'Inde, incapable de les fabriquer elle-même, un important débouché.

La concurrence étranger s'arrête devant une barrière infranchissable de tarifs douaniers prohibitifs. Dès lors, les usiniers anglais, n'ayant rien à redouter de ce chef, demeurent les maîtres absolus du marché et réalisent des bénéfices exorbitants.

Les Birmans n'ont pas encore trop souffert, avons-nous dit, mais parce qu'ils sont demeurés, dans leur ensemble, un peuple agricole avant tout.

Cependant, chez eux comme chez tous les Orientaux, le contact avec les Européens a créé le besoin, que ne connaissent pas leurs pères, des produits de l'industrie moderne. Il en résulte que les Anglais volent la Birmanie de deux façons:

En premier lieu, ils font main basse sur ses richesses naturelles; en second lieu, ils s'octroient le droit exclusif de lui vendre les produits manufacturés dont elle ne saurait plus se passer.

Et les Birmans sont ainsi, peu à peu, entraînés dans l'engrenage du capitalisme industriel, sans pouvoir jamais espérer devenir eux-mêmes des industriels capitalistes.

En outre, les Birmans, de même que tous les autres peuples de l'Inde, demeurent sous la tutelle de l'Empire britannique pour des considérations d'ordre militaire. Ils sont, en effet, incapables des construire des navires, de fabriquer des canons ou aucune des armes nécessaires à la guerre moderne, et, dans l'état actuel des choses, si les Anglais abandonnaient l'Inde, celle-ci ne ferait sans doute que changer de maîtres. Elle serait simplement envahie et exploitée par quelqu'autre puissance.

La domination britannique, dans l'Inde, repose essentiellement sur l'échange d'une protection militaire contre un monopole commercial, mais, comme je me suis efforcé de le démontrer, le marché est tout à l'avantage des Anglais dont le contrôle s'étend à tous les domaines.

En résumé, si les Anglais rendent incidemment quelques services à la Birmanie, ils les lui font payer très cher.

Jusqu'à présent, ils n'ont pas trop brimé les indigènes, parce que le besoin ne s'en est pas encore fait sentir. Les Birmans sont encore au début d'une période de transition que, de paysans agriculteurs, fera d'eux des employés au service de la grande industrie.

Leur situation peut se comparer à celle de n'importe quel peuple d'Europe au XVIIIᵉ siècle, avec cette différence toutefois que les capitaux, le matériel d'exploitation, le savoir, la puissance nécessaires à leur commerce et à leurs industries, appartiennent exclusivement à des étrangers.

Ils se trouvent aussi placés sous la protection d'un despotisme qui les défend pour s'en servir, mais qui les abandonnerait sans scrupules s'ils cessaient de lui être utiles.

Leurs rapports avec l'Empire britannique sont ceux d'un esclave avec son maître.

Le maître est-il bon, est-il mauvais? Là n'est pas la question; constatons seulement que son autorité est despotique et, disons le mot: intéressée.

Si jusqu'ici les Birmans n'ont pas eu trop à se plaindre, un jour viendra où les richesses de leur pays ne subviendront plus que difficilement aux besoins d'une population sans cesse croissant.

C'est alors qu'ils pourront apprécier la reconnaissance du capitalisme envers ceux dont il a besoin pour subsister.

E.-A. BLAIR.

Traduit de l'anglais par Raoul Nicole.

1930

95. The (New) Adelphi

In August 1929 Orwell sent *The Adelphi* an article from Paris (see *87, 88*), presumably with an eye to his return to England at the end of the year. He was to become indebted to the journal and to those who directed it for encouragement in the early stages of his career as a writer. He remained friends with its owner, John Middleton Murry (despite quite sharp differences of opinion), and Sir Richard Rees throughout his life, and with Max Plowman, who predeceased him, all of whom edited the journal at one time or another.

It was founded by Murry in June 1923 and was published as *The New Adelphi* from September 1927 to June–August 1930 (Vols. 1–3, No. 4); as *The Adelphi* (new series), October 1930 to 1955. Lewis (48) shows an issue featuring Orwell's name on its cover. *The Adelphi* published about fifty contributions from Orwell, mainly reviews but including 'The Spike,' 'A Hanging,' and half a dozen poems.

John Middleton Murry (1889–1957) was nominally editor for some fourteen years but was intimately associated with the journal throughout its life. In the main, it reflected his interests, which were, in 1923, independent of the then dominant Bloomsbury group. He was successively a fervent disciple of D. H. Lawrence, an unorthodox Marxist, a pacifist, and a back-to-the-land farmer, all of which were proclaimed in editorials and articles. He also edited *Peace News* from July 1940 to April 1946. Despite his deeply entrenched pacifism (over which he and Orwell disagreed), they remained on good terms. On 7 March 1948, Orwell wrote to Dwight Macdonald that, to his surprise, 'Middleton Murry has just renounced his pacifism & written a book (practically) demanding a preventive war against the USSR! This after writing less than 10 years ago that "Russia is the only inherently peaceful country".' The book was *The Free Society* (1948).

Sir Richard Rees (1900–1970) became Orwell's joint literary executor, with Sonia Orwell. He had been an attaché at the British Embassy in Berlin, 1922–23, and Honorary Treasurer and Lecturer, London District of the Workers' Educational Association, 1925–27. From October 1930 to 1937, he was editor of *The Adelphi* (1930–32 with Max Plowman) and introduced a more political and less self-consciously literary tone to its pages. He gave much encouragement to Orwell. Ravelston of *Keep the Aspidistra Flying* owes something to his generous nature. He was to partner Orwell in his farm on Jura, and he showed him much kindness to the end of his life. His *George Orwell: Fugitive from the Camp of Victory* (1961) gives some account of Orwell's work published in *The Adelphi* (141–47); much of this is reprinted in *Orwell Remembered* (115–26), with part of a BBC interview. Among other books by Rees are *For Love of Money: Studies in Personality and Essence* (1960) and *A Theory of My Time: An Essay in Didactic Reminiscences* (1963). Orwell told Rees that when he was in Burma he had thought *The Adelphi* a 'scurrilous rag' and had used it for target practice; see

Stansky and Abrahams, I, 186–87; Jack Common in *Orwell Remembered*, 139–40. See also Crick, 202–05, 212; Stansky and Abrahams, I, 229–31, 236–37; Shelden, 223–24; U.S., 203–04.

Max Plowman (1883–1941) worked on *The Adelphi* from 1929 until his death. He was Warden of the Adelphi Centre, 1938–41, an ardent supporter of the Peace Pledge Union from its foundation in 1934 and its General Secretary, 1937–38. His publications include *Introduction to the Study of Blake*, *A Subaltern on the Somme*, and *The Faith Called Pacifism*. He and his wife, Dorothy, remained friends of Orwell.

One of the writers introduced in *The Adelphi* by Rees was Jack Common (1903–1968), a worker from Tyneside, who also worked for the journal, first as a circulation pusher (from June 1930), then as assistant editor (from 1932) and co-editor (in 1935–36). He and Orwell became friends, and he stayed in Orwell's Hertfordshire cottage when Orwell and his wife were in Marrakech. See Stansky and Abrahams, I, 247–48, and *Orwell Remembered*, 139–43.

96. Review of *Herman Melville* by Lewis Mumford

The New Adelphi, March–May 1930

This admirable book is rightly termed a biography, but its chief concern is to analyze Melville's intellect—in Mr. Mumford's words, "his ideas, his feelings, his urges, his vision of life." Just enough detail is given to show the dismal quotidian round which enslaved Melville when his voyages were over. We see him as an overworked man of genius, living among people to whom he was hardly more than a tiresome, incomprehensible failure. We are shown how poverty, which threatened even when he was writing *Moby Dick*, infected him through nearly forty years with such loneliness and bitterness as to cripple his talents almost completely. Mr. Mumford does not allow this background of poverty to be forgotten; but his declared aim is to expound, criticize, and—unpleasant but necessary word—interpret.

It is just this aim which is responsible for the only large fault of the book. The criticism which sets out to interpret—to be at the deepest meaning and cause of every act—is very well when applied to a man, but it is a dangerous method of approaching a work of art. Done with absolute thoroughness, it would cause art itself to vanish. And therefore when Mr. Mumford is interpreting Melville himself—analyzing his philosophy and psychology, his religion and sexual life—he is excellent; but he goes on to interpret Melville's poetry, and therein he is not so successful. For one can only 'interpret' a poem by reducing it to an allegory—which is like eating an apple for the pips. As in the old legend of Cupid and Psyche, there are times when it is wise to accept without seeking knowledge.

It follows that Mr. Mumford is least happy when he is dealing with *Moby Dick*. He is justly appreciative and nobly enthusiastic, but he has altogether too keen an eye for the inner meaning. He asks us, in effect, to take *Moby Dick* as an allegory first and a poem afterwards:—

Moby Dick . . . is, fundamentally, a parable on the mystery of evil and the accidental malice of the universe. The white whale stands for the brute energies of existence . . . while Ahab is the spirit of man, small and feeble, but purposive, that pits its puniness against this might, and its purpose against the blank senselessness of power . . .

That much no one will deny, but it was a pity that Mr. Mumford should pursue the allegory to the bitter end. Whaling, he continues, is the symbol of existence and livelihood, the common whales (as opposed to *Moby Dick*) are tractable nature, the crew of the Pequod are the races of mankind—and so forth. It is the old mistake of wanting to read too much between the lines. Here is an example of interpretation altogether too acute:—

In . . . Hamlet, an unconscious incest-wish incapacitates the hero for marriage with the girl he has wooed . . .

Very ingenious, one feels, but how much better not to have said it! One is reminded of the ghosts in Fielding's underworld, who plagued Shakespeare for the meaning of "Put out the light, and then put out the light." Shakespeare himself had forgotten—and in any case who cares what it meant? It is a fine line, let it go at that. And so with *Moby Dick*. It were much better to have discoursed simply on the form, which is the stuff of poetry, and left the "meaning" alone.

It has been necessary to mention this fault at some length, but it does not seriously spoil the book, because Mr. Mumford is concerned with Melville's mind as a whole rather than his mere artistry. And for that purpose the analytical, interpretative method is the best. For the first time Melville's strange and conflicting qualities are disentangled. He was, it is clear, a man as proud as Lucifer, raging against the gods like his own Ahab, and yet full of a native joy that made him embrace life even while he saw its cruelty. He was a kind of ascetic voluptuary, disciplined and (so far as one can discover) superhumanly chaste, and yet amorous of delightful things wherever he found them. More important than his strength, he had—what is implied in real strength—passionate sensitiveness; to him seas were deeper and skies vaster than to other men, and similarly beauty was more actual and pain and humiliation more agonizing. Who but Melville would have seen the beauty and terror of a ridiculous beast like a whale? And who else could have written scenes like the bullying of Harry in *Redburn*, or that shocking and ludicrous account of an amputation in *White Jacket*? Such things were done by a man who felt more vividly than common men, just as a kestrel sees more vividly than a mole.

The best chapters of Mr. Mumford's book are those in which he relates Melville to his times, and shows how the changing spirit of the century made and marred him. It is evident that Melville owed much to American liberty— or, it may be, the tradition of liberty; the American wildness of spirit that showed itself, though so diversely, in *Life on the Mississippi* and *Leaves of Grass*. Melville lived a wretched life, and was generally poor and harassed, but at least he had an improvident youth behind him. He had not been bred, like so many Europeans, in respectability and despair. America before the

Civil War may have been a rough place for a man of culture, but it was at any rate a hard country to starve in. Young men were not always tethered to safe jobs, and they could wander—how many American artists of the nineteenth century spent their youth, like Melville, in adventurous, irresponsible, ungenteel ways. Later, when industrialism was tightening its grip, something in Melville's spirit wilted with the times. The country was being debauched by "progress," scoundrels were prospering, leisure and free thought were declining—necessarily his joy and therefore his creative power waned in such years. But the older, freer America played a part in *Moby Dick*, and still more in the inimitable freshness of *Typee* and *Redburn*.

Such a book as this should do whatever criticism can for Melville's reputation. Whoever is not queasy in the presence of strength will always love Melville, and the same kind of reader will salute Mr. Mumford's book for its enthusiastic praise as well as for its discernment. It will not convert the doubtful (and what book ever does that?), but it can teach a great deal to Melville's admirers, and will certainly persuade them to go further afield among his works than the two or three successes by which he is known.

E. A. BLAIR

97. Review of *Alexander Pope* by Edith Sitwell, *The Course of English Classicism* by Sherard Vines

The New Adelphi, June–August 1930

It is possible, and perhaps necessary, to divide all art into classical and romantic; to see as two separate things the trim formal garden of classicism, and the wild romantic jungle, full of stupendous beauty, and also of morasses and sickly weeds. And yet the two encroach, and claim neutral ground, so that sometimes it is hard to say which is jungle and which is garden. Something of the sort occurs in the two books under review. Both touch the same subject, and both are agreed on one point, namely, that Pope was a supreme poet—in some ways *the* supreme English poet; and yet they praise him for qualities which are not only different but mutually exclusive. Mr. Sherard Vines, as an upholder of the classical tradition, presents Pope as the high-water mark of classicism; Miss Sitwell, essentially a romantic, discovers romantic qualities in Pope, and praises him for those. They do agree, in a manner, about Pope, but they contradict one another on the fundamental principles of poetry.

Mr. Sherard Vines gives an admirable account of the main drift of classicism. He presents the classical mind as something at once strong and elegant, noble and moderate, simple and sophisticated. It will have as much beauty as you like, but no noise, no violent novelty, no exuberance, no mystification. All the assaults on eye, ear and fancy which from the romantic point of view *are* art, it regards simply as a kind of hitting below the emotional belt:

" 'Spell' and 'incantation,' words that have crept into modern poetic, have nothing to do with the polite, they are merely Gothic. In Cato, a model of polite tragedy, there is no disturbing magic, but instead that rarer thing equilibrium, dearer to the mind of a Chinese sage than to superstitious England . . . It is indeed a perverse age that extols Hamlet and ignores Cato. . . ."

And again:

"Music has its own way of being efficient, and poetry quite another way. When they approach, it is not along the path imagined by quasi-mystical theorists, but on the broad trysting ground, the Hyde Park, may we say, of opera and oratorio. . . ."

This is the reply churlish to all romantic poetry. Mr. Sherard Vines is perforce hard on Shakespeare, and very rude indeed to Shelley, Coleridge and Wordsworth; he could not be otherwise, for from the classical point of view these writers broke all the rules, and their gift was largely of music, which is the foe of elegance. Poetry therefore, as Mr. Sherard Vines sees it, is a thing of wit, grandeur and good sense, not of "magic" and seductive sounds; and Pope, the "unfailingly efficient" poet, who made no high flights and no lapses, is its supreme exponent.

But turn to Miss Sitwell, and we are back immediately to the spells and incantations. This is how Miss Sitwell approaches the subject of technique:

"The poet feels the poem in the palm of his sensitive hands, understanding its exact weight . . . letting the poem grow in his veins . . . the poet knows, through his sensitive hands, the difference between the sea-cold marble of the Ode, with all its divine variation of ivy-dark veins (cold as the satyrine forests)—veins, with the shape of the Aegean waves within them, veins full of the light—the difference between this and the hot velvet petals of that rose the lyric. . . ."

This is not, so to say, classical talk. So far from frowning upon "magic," Miss Sitwell comes to Pope for the same enchantment as one finds in people like Francis Thompson or Gerard Manley Hopkins. She classes Pope with Shakespeare, Shelley and Coleridge—she even likens *The Dunciad* to *The Ancient Mariner*, whereas all Mr. Sherard Vines says about *The Ancient Mariner* is that it "recounted improbable things of an albatross." And poetry, she says, is not to be valued primarily for its subject matter, nor even for metrical form, but for "texture"; that is for the music, with its vast inexplicable power of pleasing or disgusting, contained in the mere impact of one syllable on another.

As a general proposition most people will agree with this, but it is disconcerting to see a writer like Pope praised chiefly for his music. Miss Sitwell is almost a fanatic in prosody; she is so minute in her examination, so sensitive to "the thick, muffled dull thud of the alliterating M's," and the "appalling deafening blows caused by the alliterative B's," and so forth, that she forgets sometimes that even melodious verse must not be hackneyed in sentiment. She will tell you for instance that such a passage as

> 'Twas now the time when Phoebus yields to Night,
> And rising Cynthia casts her silver light,

> Wide o'er the world in solemn pomp she drew
> Her airy chariot, hung with pearly dew.

has "an exquisite lightness," not noticing, apparently, that it has also an insufferable staleness and obviousness. And she finds a kind of hell-born inspiration in the very ordinary couplet,

> So watchful Bruin forms, with plastic care
> Each growing lump, and brings it to a bear

One is not accusing Miss Sitwell of exaggeration; discovering vast musical profundities in Pope, naturally she proclaims them. But when one sees such phrases as "terrible trumpet scream of rage," "smoky and appalling beauty," and the like, applied to Pope's urbane lines, one begins to wonder whether there is not something in the classical, non-musical view of poetry.

Thus, between the classicist who admires Pope because he was not like Shakespeare, and the romantic who thinks he *was* like Shakespeare you are left in doubt. And yet, however sound are the classical arguments, what man of spirit will relinquish his Shakespeare? One remembers too that even the classical rules are only provisional. There is a passage in Mr. Sherard Vines' book in which he declares that Shakespeare's use of "lads" in "golden lads and lasses" stamps him for a romantic—the proper classical word being "youths"; and it seems that other authorities say, on the contrary, that "lads" is classical and "youths" romantic; which shows how much hair-splitting is sometimes needed to define what is classical and what is not. And then it appears that Ossian, who is manifestly *not* classical, was accepted as such by some of his contemporary critics. And Mr. Sherard Vines says that Fuseli was classical, if not of the purest breed; but Fuseli, one remembers, was the only man Blake ever knew who did not almost make him spew—that is, was admired by the high priest of romanticism. So, even in the formal garden, the jungle encroaches.

It remains to be added that Mr. Sherard Vines has performed a difficult feat in treating such a large and crowded subject adequately in small space. Miss Sitwell's life of Pope is distinguished by her warm-hearted defence of the poet against all his detractors. Her English is queer and, one must add, precious, but there is a charm in her love of sonorous words for their own sake. Her book is finely printed, with some interesting illustrations.

E. A. BLAIR

98. Review of *Angel Pavement* by J. B. Priestley

The Adelphi, October 1930

Abandoning provincial life, Mr. Priestley has turned his attention to London, in a novel about one Mr. Golspie, an able rogue who descends upon a struggling city firm, quietly ruins it, and vanishes. The intention, more or less explicit, is to set forth the romance of London, to make a pattern of beauty from the eventless, dismal lives which interlace in a city office. Abandon, says Mr. Priestley in effect, all your sneering about industrial civilisation. Remember that these clerks and typists who look so unpleasantly like ants as they stream over London Bridge at the rush hour, these clerks whom you in your superiority despise—they too are human—they too are romantic. And thus far, who will contradict him? Clerks are men and brothers, and fit material for art—applause, therefore, to the writer who can use them.

But unfortunately, a novelist is not required to have good intentions but to convey beauty. And when one has finished applauding Mr. Priestley's effort to make clerks and typists interesting, one must add that the effort does not, even for a single page, come off. It is not that he writes ineptly, or is lumpishly dull, or consciously plays for cheap effects; it is simply that his writing does not touch the level at which memorable fiction begins. One compares these six hundred competent pages (and one must make the comparison, after all that has been said of Mr. Priestley) with other novels of London; with Mr. Arnold Bennett in *Riceyman Steps*, with Conrad in *The Secret Agent*, with Dickens in *Bleak House*; and one wonders incredulously whether anyone has really mistaken Mr. Priestley for a master. His work has no damning faults, but neither has it a single gleam of beauty, nor any profundity of thought, nor even memorable humour; the book is simply a middle article spun out to six hundred pages, with all the middle article's high spirits and conscientious wit, and the same utter lack of anything intensely felt or profitably conveyed.

"Warwick's restaurant . . . might have been French or Italian or even Spanish or Hungarian; there was no telling; but it was determinedly foreign in a de-nationalised fashion, rather as if the League of Nations had invented it."

". . . the bus stopped by the dark desolation of Lord's cricket ground, swallowed two women who were all parcels, comic hats, and fuss (a sure sign this that Christmas was near, for you never saw these parcel-and-comic-hat women at any other time) and rolled on . . ."

The point about these two extracts is that they are as good as anything in *Angel Pavement*; there are thousands of sentences like them, seldom worse, never better, never going deeper than this beneath the skin of things. And yet consider what themes Mr. Priestley is handling in this shallow and sprightly way! A cunning business swindle, dinner parties in an Earl's Court maisonette, squabbles in a Stoke Newington villa, a hospital deathbed, an attempted murder, a projected suicide! One imagines what these things might have become in other hands. One imagines, for example, Conrad brooding in his own sombre way over Turgis, the pimply and lovesick clerk; or Hardy describing the scene in which Turgis, intending suicide, has not a shilling for the gas meter; or Mr. H. G. Wells, in his earlier manner, reporting the conversations of Mr. Pelumpton, the boozy second-hand broker; or Mr. Bennett upon the women's hostel where incipient old maids starved for adventure. But one does not get what these writers would have given, nor anything resembling it more closely than London draught beer resembles beer made with hops. What one does get is six hundred pages of middle article, quite readable and quite forgettable, with—when the plot calls for intense feeling—something like this:

"He sat there in a dream ecstasy of devotion, in which remembered kisses glittered like stars."

When a novel lacks the indefinable, unmistakable thing we call beauty, one looks in it for sound delineation of character, or humour of situation, or verbal wit. But one looks in vain in *Angel Pavement*—Mr. Priestley can be clever, but he cannot be in any way memorable. All his characters—Mr. Dersingham the incompetent business man, Mr. Golspie the adventurous rogue, Miss Matfield the bored typist, Mr. Smeeth the desiccated accountant—are alike in their unreality, mere attenuated ghosts from the pages of Mr. Hugh Walpole and Mr. Arnold Bennett. All the dialogue is the same in this, that being neither incredible nor unreadable, it is not funny and has not the compelling semblance of life. All the analysis, the reflections, are alike in the ease with which they are understood, and, having been understood, are forgotten. Even the observation is suspect. Towards the end of the book there is an account of a game of bridge, and the account contains two errors which would never have been made by a careful observer. It is a small point, but it confirms the general impression that Mr. Priestley's work is written altogether too easily, is not laboured upon as good fiction must be—not, in the good sense of the phrase, *worked out*.

One would not thus assail a competent and agreeable novel, if Mr. Priestley had not been so extravagantly praised. He has been likened, absurdly, to Dickens, and when a novelist is likened to Dickens one must stop and ask the reason. Is it not a safe guess that Mr. Priestley owes his popularity to his frank optimism? In *Angel Pavement*, it is true, he deals with gloomy subjects, but by implication—by his manner of writing—he is as cheerful as ever. He is not a professional backslapper, but he can be quoted by such, and to some of them, probably, he appears as a champion against those gloomy and obscene highbrows who are supposed to be forever corrupting English literature. It is for this reason that such a blatantly second-rate novelist has been likened to Dickens, the great master of prose, psychology and wit. Once this absurd praise is discounted, we can salute Mr. Priestley for the qualities which he really possesses, and take *Angel Pavement* for what it is; an excellent holiday novel, genuinely gay and pleasant, which supplies a good bulk of reading matter for ten and sixpence.

E. A. BLAIR

99. To Max Plowman

24 October 1930   Handwritten

3 Queen St   Southwold   Suffolk

Dear Mr Plowman,

Thanks very much for your postcard. I should like very much to review something for the December Adelphi, but I don't know of any especial book I should prefer, as I can't, in this place, get hold of lists of forthcoming books. Please send me whatever you think suitable. The one mentioned by you (Storm Jameson's "The Decline of Merry England") sounds interesting, but if it is *too* historical it might be above my head. However, I leave that to you.

When we met in London you said something about wanting that other article[1] which you have of mine made shorter. If you want that done, perhaps you will send it to me, & I will attend to it. But if you find after all that you cannot use the article, I should like it back, as I might be able to send it elsewhere.

Yours sincerely
Eric A. Blair

1. 'The Spike'; see *100*. The article in its revised form was published in *The Adelphi*, April 1931; see *104*.

100. To Max Plowman

1 November 1930   Handwritten

3 Queen St   Southwold   Suffolk

Dear Mr Plowman

Thank you very much for the copy of the Adelphi, which I found an interesting one. I see that Mr Murry says in his article, "Because orthodox Christianity is exceedingly elaborate, it presents a greater appearance of unity than (childish superstition)". I know this is so, but the *why* is beyond me. It is clear that the thicker the fairy tales are piled, the more easily one can swallow them, but this seems so paradoxical that I have never been able to understand the reason for it. I don't think Roger Clarke in his article on Sex & Sin gets to [the] very bottom of the question. He says rightly that the "spiritual love" stuff fixes the desires on something unattainable, & that this leads to trouble. The point he doesn't bring out is that the "sinful lust" stuff also fixes it on something unattainable, & that attempts to realise the impossible *physical* desire are even more destructive than attempts on the spiritual side. Of course it is important to teach boys that women like Esther Summerson[1] don't exist, but it is just as important, & far harder, to teach them that women like the Vie Parisienne illustrations[2] don't exist. Perhaps the writer had not the space to bring this out thoroughly. You will, I know, forgive my troubling you with my reflections, as I was interested by the questions raised.

Thanks very much for the books. I find the novel[3] well enough, the Cayenne book[4] interesting, though it is almost certainly exaggerated. The book on Bodley[5] is more solid stuff, but I don't know that it is the kind of thing you would care to use much space on. What I suggest is doing about 1000 words altogether on the three, either in one article or separately as you prefer. I think they are worth mentioning, but not worth more than 1000 words between them. Would this do? If so, I can let you have the review in about 10 days. If you don't think it worthwhile, I will send the books back.

I enclose the other article, reduced to 3500 words.[6] Thank you for giving my M.S° to Mr Murry. I hope he understands that there is no hurry & I don't want to be a nuisance to him.

Yours sincerely
Eric A. Blair

1. The heroine and pseudo part-author of *Bleak House* by Charles Dickens. Her sensitive, docile demeanour, combined with a maturity greater than her years and her willingness to serve, even accepting an offer of marriage out of duty and gratitude (though all ends happily for her: she marries a young doctor, whom she loves), mark her off as one of Dickens's saints.
2. Highly glamourised pictures of showgirls.
3. In the April 1931 issue, Orwell reviewed *Hunger and Love* by Lionel Britton and *Albert Grope* by F. O. Mann; see *105*. Neither may be referred to here, though Britton's book is a possibility. That would mean that Plowman wished to give it more attention than Orwell proposed.
4. Reviewed; see *101*.
5. Not reviewed.
6. From its length and timing, this is probably 'The Spike,' published in *The Adelphi* in April 1931; see *104*.

101. Review of *The Horrors of Cayenne* by Karl Bartz; translated by Beatrice Marshall

The Adelphi Supplement, December 1930

This is an account of his experiences by a German who spent fourteen years as a convict in the French penal settlement of Cayenne. Some of the incidents are almost certainly exaggerated, but one can accept the book as a genuine document in the main, because any fabricator would have written it with more art. It is a naive catalogue of horrors. The prisoners of Cayenne, it seems, pass their lives in beast-like toil on the plantations, under the command of warders whose mere word can send them to sixty days' solitary confinement, and whose favour they have to buy with gifts of stolen property. The food and quarters are not fit for cattle, and fighting and homosexual vice are the only consolations of the prisoners. Many of them try to escape into Dutch Guiana, but they rarely succeed, because the jungles are thronged by negroes who receive ten francs for any fugitive's head. Only a few men manage to live out their sentences, save money, and set up small plantations of their own; the majority die of tropical diseases, hastened by the vile condition of the prisons. The author was transported because, being a

German soldier in the Foreign Legion, he mutinied at the outbreak of war. It is a pity he does not mention a fact which should be better known than it is, namely that the French sent not only mutineers but also many conscientious objectors to Cayenne. At the end of the war the government refused to pay their passage home, with the result that some were there as late as 1929. This book, crudely set down and probably improved by the translation, cannot be called an able piece of work; but as a first-hand account of one of the by-products of civilisation, it is well worth reading.

E. A. B.

1931

102. To Max Plowman

Monday, [12 January 1931]   Handwritten lettercard; dated from postmark

[Postmark, Golders Green. N.W.11.[1]]

Dear Mr Plowman,

Thanks very much for your letter. I am in & about London at present, but when I get home I will send that article & you can have a look at it.[2] I didn't in any case suppose that you could use it yet awhile, but I thought if you liked it you might like to keep it by you. As to the review, I cannot of course let you pay for it. It was a poor piece of work, & that should be an end of it.

As to those books, I should like very much to have a try at the Carlyle book.[3] You ask what kind of thing I like reviewing. If you ever get any book (fiction or travel stuff) on India, or on low life in London, or on Villon, Swift, Smollett, Poe, Mark Twain, Zola, Anatole France or Conrad, or anything *by* M. P. Shiel or W. Somerset Maugham, I should enjoy reviewing it. Please excuse a post office pen.[4]

Yours sincerely
Eric A. Blair

1. Orwell was presumably staying at the home of Mabel Sinclair and Francis Ernest Fierz, at 1B Oakwood Road, Golders Green, London, N.W.11. (illustrated in Thompson, 25). Born in Brazil, they had made their home in England since 1908, and had met Orwell when on holiday in Southwold in 1930. They shared literary interests. Mrs. Fierz reviewed for *The Adelphi* from time to time, and her husband was a Dickens enthusiast. They often gave Orwell shelter in the early 1930s, and Mrs. Fierz was instrumental in introducing him to Leonard Moore, who became his literary agent. Orwell sometimes referred to her as Mrs Sinclair Fierz; see Crick, 211; Shelden, 160; U.S.: 146. She died in 1990, aged 100.
2. Probably 'A Hanging,' published in *The Adelphi*, August 1931; see *108*.
3. *The Two Carlyles* by Osbert Burdett, reviewed by Orwell in *The Adelphi*, March 1931; see *103*.
4. Before the advent of the ballpoint pen, post offices provided pens with steel nibs and liquid ink. The nibs were often worn or had crossed points.

103. Review of *The Two Carlyles* by Osbert Burdett

The Adelphi, March 1931

This discerning, quietly able book deals chiefly with Carlyle's married life, but it is also an acute study of his intellect. It should greatly help the general reader to get Carlyle's large vague renown into focus.

Mr. Burdett sums up Carlyle, finally, as an egoist, and on the literary side it is perhaps just to call him that fairly subtilised form of egoist, an orator. Only a historian, of course, can judge his historical work; but if we test him by *Heroes and Hero-Worship*—and that is fair, for it was his creed, and done in his best period—we find nothing better than oratory. There are fine panegyrics in it, fine adjectives—adjectives which, living a strange life of their own, give an air of profundity—but no real depth of thought. It is only a splendid vestment of words, draped about a few worn, rather mean ideas. Language apart, the whole purport of the book is this: that there exists some vast world-purpose, unquestionably good, and that great men (meaning *successful* men) are its instruments. The true Hero is the man who fights on the side of fate; a sort of Achilles in god-given armour, licensed to trample on mere mortals. Sincerity is the virtue we are bidden to admire in him; but we are also bidden to test his sincerity by his success. Nothing but the good prevails—and so, in the name of virtue *væ victis!*

> "I will allow a thing to struggle for itself in the world, with any sword or tongue or implement it has . . . very sure that it will, in the long run, conquer nothing which does not deserve to be conquered. What is better than itself, it cannot put away, but only what is worse."

This means no more than *væ victis*—woe to the creed that is not backed by machine guns! But the oratory arising from this text, those fine vague sermons on Mahommed and Luther and Cromwell, are another matter.

Clearly this Great Man cult of Carlyle's was the symptom of egoism, of buried ambition. Mr. Burdett points out how Carlyle's heroes grew more dominant, more grandiose, as he himself grew richer; he passed from Burns to Cromwell, from Cromwell to Frederick—from successful rebels to successful scoundrels. Briefly, his love of a conqueror, his gusto in battle scenes, was a sort of vicarious bullying. And yet one must not forget that it was *unconscious* egoism; there was a mysticism in his ugly creed. With his sense of a world-purpose ("the great deep law of the world"), he did feel that his conquering heroes served something noble, some scheme greater than their own. He had a feeling, half poetic, for the flowing of time and history; it is always at least latent in his work, and it produces his finest sentences. "The Merovingian kings, slowly wending on their bullock carts through the streets of Paris, with their long hair flowing, have all wended slowly on into Eternity." It is a simple enough idea behind the words; and yet, what splendid words! A few passages such as this are the best justification of Carlyle's opinions.

The other symptom of Carlyle's egoism was his personal unhappiness. Even if one knew nothing of his life, one could not read ten of his pages without being struck by the ill-humour, the queer, wounding adjectives ("O seagreen Prophet", and so forth), the instinctive sneer. At its worst (in his spiteful remarks about Lamb and Hazlitt, for instance, or that ugly whoop of triumph after the French defeats of 1870), his rancour suggests a man permanently soured by ill-luck. And yet Carlyle was not inevitably unhappy. His ill-health was not serious—at least, the "baleful Nessus shirt of perpetual pain" did not prevent him from living to eighty-six. His marriage was not unhappy in itself; it was merely the marriage of two unhappy people. And he was successful, even strikingly so, from early middle life onwards. The unhappiness of Mrs. Carlyle, sickly and childless, is much more understandable. Nevertheless, Carlyle was nearly always desperately unhappy, and to some extent the bitter tone of his work is a reflection of this.

"Clay in his blood, Calvinism in his head, dyspepsia in his stomach", is Mr. Burdett's diagnosis. He suggests that even Carlyle's occasional championship of the poor came more from a desire to thump society than from benevolence. Spleen, of course, is the exact word for Carlyle's peculiar temper; the spleen of the *unconscious* egoist, the denouncer of this and that, the discoverer of new sins. Consider the base, prying spite of this description of Marat, at the moment of Charlotte Corday's entrance:

> "Stewing in slipper bath; sore afflicted; ill of Revolution Fever,—of what other malady this History had rather not name. Excessively sick and worn, poor man; with precisely eleven-pence-halfpenny of ready money, in paper; with slipper bath; strong three-footed stool for writing on, the while; and a squalid—Washerwoman, one may call her. . . ."

It is really an occasion for pity rather than sneers. But some obscure spite moves Carlyle to damn Marat, and so he damns him, when the facts give out, by tricks of repetition, even by punctuation; every semi-colon is an insult. It will do, also, as an example of the strange impressiveness of Carlyle's abuse. No one, surely, was ever such a master of belittlement. Even at his emptiest sneer (as when he said that Whitman "thought he was a big man because he lived in a big country") the victim does seem to shrink a little. That again is the power of the orator, the man of phrases and adjectives, turned to a base use.

It should be added that almost half of Mr. Burdett's book deals with the life of Carlyle and Jane Welsh before their marriage. Their love story, he says, was not an abnormal one, but it was unusual in being so well documented. As a revelation, therefore, of the frame of mind in which people get married, and of the astonishing selfishness that exists in the sincerest love, it is interesting. This book should appeal to many readers besides those specially interested in Carlyle.

ERIC BLAIR

104. 'The Spike'[1]

The Adelphi, April 1931

It was late afternoon. Forty-nine of us, forty-eight men and one woman, lay on the green waiting for the spike to open. We were too tired to talk much. We just sprawled about exhaustedly, with home-made cigarettes sticking out of our scrubby faces. Overhead the chestnut branches were covered with blossom, and beyond that great woolly clouds floated almost motionless in a clear sky. Littered on the grass, we seemed dingy, urban riff-raff. We defiled the scene, like sardine-tins and paper bags on the seashore.

What talk there was ran on the Tramp Major of this spike. He was a devil, everyone agreed, a tartar, a tyrant, a bawling, blasphemous, uncharitable dog. You couldn't call your soul your own when he was about, and many a tramp had he kicked out in the middle of the night for giving a back answer. When you came to be searched he fair held you upside down and shook you. If you were caught with tobacco there was hell to pay, and if you went in with money (which is against the law) God help you.

I had eightpence on me. "For the love of Christ, mate", the old hands advised me, "don't you take it in. You'd get seven days for going into the spike with eightpence!"

So I buried my money in a hole under the hedge, marking the spot with a lump of flint. Then we set about smuggling our matches and tobacco, for it is forbidden to take these into nearly all spikes, and one is supposed to surrender them at the gate. We hid them in our socks, except for the twenty or so per cent. who had no socks, and had to carry the tobacco in their boots, even under their very toes. We stuffed our ankles with contraband until anyone seeing us might have imagined an outbreak of elephantiasis. But it is an unwritten law that even the sternest tramp majors do not search below the knee, and in the end only one man was caught. This was Scotty, a little hairy tramp with a bastard accent sired by cockney out of Glasgow. His tin of cigarette ends fell out of his sock at the wrong moment, and was impounded.

At six the gates swung open and we shuffled in. An official at the gate entered our names and other particulars in the register and took our bundles away from us. The woman was sent off to the workhouse, and we others into the spike. It was a gloomy, chilly, limewashed place, consisting only of a bathroom and dining room and about a hundred narrow stone cells. The terrible Tramp Major met us at the door and herded us into the bathroom to be stripped and searched. He was a gruff, soldierly man of forty, who gave the tramps no more ceremony than sheep at the dipping pond, shoving them this way and that and shouting oaths in their faces. But when he came to myself, he looked hard at me, and said:

"You are a gentleman?"

"I suppose so," I said.

He gave me another long look. "Well, that's bloody bad luck, guv'nor," he said, "that's bloody bad luck, that is." And thereafter he took it into his head to treat me with compassion, even with a kind of respect.

It was a disgusting sight, that bathroom. All the indecent secrets of our underwear were exposed; the grime, the rents and patches, the bits of string doing duty for buttons, the layers upon layers of fragmentary garments, some of them mere collections of holes held together by dirt. The room became a press of steaming nudity, the sweaty odours of the tramps competing with the sickly, sub-fæcal stench native to the spike. Some of the men refused the bath, and washed only their "toe rags", the horrid, greasy little clouts which tramps bind round their feet. Each of us had three minutes in which to bathe himself. Six greasy, slippery roller towels had to serve for the lot of us.

When we had bathed our own clothes were taken away from us, and we were dressed in the workhouse shirts, grey cotton things like nightshirts, reaching to the middle of the thigh. Then we were sent into the dining room, where supper was set out on the deal tables. It was the invariable spike meal, always the same, whether breakfast, dinner or supper—half a pound of bread, a bit of margarine, and a pint of so-called tea. It took us five minutes to gulp down the cheap, noxious food. Then the Tramp Major served us with three cotton blankets each, and drove us off to our cells for the night. The doors were locked on the outside a little before seven in the evening, and would stay locked for the next twelve hours.

The cells measured eight feet by five, and had no lighting apparatus except a tiny, barred window high up in the wall, and a spyhole in the door. There were no bugs, and we had bedsteads and staw palliasses, rare luxuries both. In many spikes one sleeps on a wooden shelf, and in some on the bare floor, with a rolled up coat for pillow. With a cell to myself, and a bed, I was hoping for a sound night's rest. But I did not get it, for there is always something wrong in the spike, and the peculiar shortcoming here, as I discovered immediately, was the cold. May had begun, and in honour of the season—a little sacrifice to the gods of spring, perhaps—the authorities had cut off the steam from the hot pipes. The cotton blankets were almost useless. One spent the night in turning from side to side, falling asleep for ten minutes and waking half frozen, and watching for dawn.

As always happens in the spike, I had at last managed to fall comfortably asleep when it was time to get up. The Tramp Major came marching down the passage with his heavy tread, unlocking the doors and yelling to us to show a leg. Promptly the passage was full of squalid shirt-clad figures rushing for the bathroom, for there was only one tub full of water between us all in the morning, and it was first come first served. When I arrived twenty tramps had already washed their faces. I gave one glance at the black scum on top of the water, and decided to go dirty for the day.

We hurried into our clothes, and then went to the dining room to bolt our breakfast. The bread was much worse than usual, because the military-minded idiot of a Tramp Major had cut it into slices overnight, so that it was as hard as ship's biscuit. But we were glad of our tea after the cold, restless night. I do not know what tramps would do without tea, or rather the stuff they miscall tea. It is their food, their medicine, their panacea for all evils. Without the half gallon or so of it that they suck down a day, I truly believe they could not face their existence.

After breakfast we had to undress again for the medical inspection, which is a precaution against smallpox. It was three-quarters of an hour before the doctor arrived, and one had time now to look about him and see what manner of men we were. It was an instructive sight. We stood shivering naked to the waist in two long ranks in the passage. The filtered light, bluish and cold, lighted us up with unmerciful clarity. No one can imagine, unless he has seen such a thing, what pot-bellied, degenerate curs we looked. Shock heads, hairy, crumpled faces, hollow chests, flat feet, sagging muscles—every kind of malformation and physical rottenness were there. All were flabby and discoloured, as all tramps are under their deceptive sunburn. Two or three figures seen there stay ineradicably in my mind. Old "Daddy", aged seventy-four, with his truss, and his red, watering eyes: a herring-gutted starveling, with sparse beard and sunken cheeks, looking like the corpse of Lazarus in some primitive picture: an imbecile, wandering hither and thither with vague giggles, coyly pleased because his trousers constantly slipped down and left him nude. But few of us were greatly better than these; there were not ten decently-built men among us, and half, I believe, should have been in hospital.

This being Sunday, we were to be kept in the spike over the week-end. As soon as the doctor had gone we were herded back to the dining room, and its door shut upon us. It was a lime-washed, stone-floored room unspeakably dreary with its furniture of deal boards and benches, and its prison smell. The windows were so high up that one could not look outside, and the sole ornament was a set of Rules threatening dire penalties to any casual who misconducted himself. We packed the room so tight that one could not move an elbow without jostling somebody. Already, at eight o'clock in the morning, we were bored with our captivity. There was nothing to talk about except the petty gossip of the road, the good and bad spikes, the charitable and uncharitable counties, the iniquities of the police and the Salvation Army. Tramps hardly ever get away from these subjects; they talk, as it were, nothing but shop. They have nothing worthy to be called conversation, because emptiness of belly leaves no speculation in their souls. The world is too much with them. Their next meal is never quite secure, and so they cannot think of anything except the next meal.

Two hours dragged by. Old Daddy, witless with age, sat silent, his back bent like a bow and his inflamed eyes dripping slowly on to the floor. George, a dirty old tramp notorious for the queer habit of sleeping in his hat, grumbled about a parcel of tommy that he had lost on the road. Bill the moocher, the best built man of us all, a Herculean sturdy beggar who smelt of beer even after twelve hours in the spike, told tales of mooching, of pints stood him in the boozers, and of a parson who had peached to the police and got him seven days. William and Fred, two young ex-fishermen from Norfolk, sang a sad song about Unhappy Bella, who was betrayed and died in the snow. The imbecile drivelled about an imaginary toff who had once given him two hundred and fifty-seven golden sovereigns. So the time passed, with dull talk and dull obscenities. Everyone was smoking, except Scotty, whose tobacco had been seized, and he was so miserable in his smokeless state that I stood him the makings of a cigarette. We smoked furtively, hiding our cigarettes like schoolboys when we heard the Tramp Major's step, for smoking, though connived at, was officially forbidden.

Most of the tramps spent ten consecutive hours in this dreary room. It is hard to imagine how they put up with it. I have come to think that boredom is the worst of all a tramp's evils, worse than hunger and discomfort, worse even than the constant feeling of being socially disgraced. It is a silly piece of cruelty to confine an ignorant man all day with nothing to do; it is like chaining a dog in a barrel. Only an educated man, who has consolations within himself, can endure confinement. Tramps, unlettered types as nearly all of them are, face their poverty with blank, resourceless minds. Fixed for ten hours on a comfortless bench, they know no way of occupying themselves, and if they think at all it is to whimper about hard luck and pine for work. They have not the stuff in them to endure the horrors of idleness. And so, since so much of their lives is spent in doing nothing, they suffer agonies from boredom.

I was much luckier than the others, because at ten o'clock the Tramp Major picked me out for the most coveted of all jobs in the spike, the job of helping in the workhouse kitchen. There was not really any work to be done there, and I was able to make off and hide in a shed used for storing potatoes, together with some workhouse paupers who were skulking to avoid the Sunday morning service. There was a stove burning there, and comfortable packing cases to sit on, and back numbers of the *Family Herald,* and even a copy of *Raffles* from the workhouse library. It was paradise after the spike.

Also, I had my dinner from the workhouse table, and it was one of the biggest meals I have ever eaten. A tramp does not see such a meal twice in the year, in the spike or out of it. The paupers told me that they always gorged to the bursting point on Sundays, and went hungry six days of the week. When the meal was over the cook set me to do the washing up, and told me to throw away the food that remained. The wastage was astonishing; great dishes of beef, and bucketfuls of bread and vegetables, were pitched away like rubbish, and then defiled with tea leaves. I filled five dustbins to overflowing with good food. And while I did so my fellow tramps were sitting two hundred yards away in the spike, their bellies half filled with the spike dinner of the everlasting bread and tea, and perhaps two cold boiled potatoes each in honour of Sunday. It appeared that the food was thrown away from deliberate policy, rather than that it should be given to the tramps.

At three I left the workhouse kitchen and went back to the spike. The boredom in that crowded, comfortless room was now unbearable. Even smoking had ceased, for a tramp's only tobacco is picked-up cigarette ends, and, like a browsing beast, he starves if he is long away from the pavement-pasture. To occupy the time I talked with a rather superior tramp, a young carpenter who wore a collar and tie, and was on the road, he said, for lack of a set of tools. He kept a little aloof from the other tramps, and held himself more like a free man than a casual. He had literary tastes, too, and carried one of Scott's novels on all his wanderings. He told me he never entered a spike unless driven there by hunger, sleeping under hedges and behind ricks in preference. Along the south coast he had begged by day and slept in bathing machines for weeks at a time.

We talked of life on the road. He criticised the system which makes a tramp spend fourteen hours a day in the spike, and the other ten in walking and dodging the police. He spoke of his own case—six months at the public charge for want of three pounds' worth of tools. It was idiotic, he said.

Then I told him about the wastage of food in the workhouse kitchen, and what I thought of it. And at that he changed his tune immediately. I saw that I had awakened the pew-renter who sleeps in every English workman. Though he had been famished along with the rest, he at once saw reasons why the food should have been thrown away rather than given to the tramps. He admonished me quite severely.

"They have to do it," he said; "if they made these places too pleasant you'd have all the scum of the country flocking into them. It's only the bad food as keeps all that scum away. These tramps are too lazy to work, that's all that's wrong with them. You don't want to go encouraging of them. They're scum."

I produced arguments to prove him wrong, but he would not listen. He kept repeating:

"You don't want to have any pity on these tramps—scum, they are. You don't want to judge them by the same standards as men like you and me. They're scum, just scum."

It was interesting to see how subtly he disassociated himself from his fellow tramps. He had been on the road six months, but in the sight of God, he seemed to imply, he was not a tramp. His body might be in the spike, but his spirit soared far away, in the pure æther of the middle classes.

The clock's hands crept round with excruciating slowness. We were too bored even to talk now, the only sound was of oaths and reverberating yawns. One would force his eyes away from the clock for what seemed an age, and then look back again to see that the hands had advanced three minutes. Ennui clogged our souls like cold mutton fat. Our bones ached because of it. The clock's hands stood at four, and supper was not till six, and there was nothing left remarkable beneath the visiting moon.[2]

At last six o'clock did come, and the Tramp Major and his assistant arrived with supper. The yawning tramps brisked up like lions at feeding time. But the meal was a dismal disappointment. The bread, bad enough in the morning, was now positively uneatable; it was so hard that even the strongest jaws could make little impression on it. The older men went almost supperless, and not a man could finish his portion, hungry though most of us were. When we had finished, the blankets were served out immediately, and we were hustled off once more to the bare, chilly cells.

Thirteen hours went by. At seven we were awakened, and rushed forth to squabble over the water in the bathroom, and bolt our ration of bread and tea. Our time in the spike was up, but we could not go until the doctor had examined us again, for the authorities have a terror of smallpox and its distribution by tramps. The doctor kept us waiting two hours this time, and it was ten o'clock before we finally escaped.

At last it was time to go, and we were let out into the yard. How bright everything looked, and how sweet the winds did blow, after the gloomy, reeking spike! The Tramp Major handed each man his bundle of confiscated possessions, and a hunk of bread and cheese for midday dinner, and then we took the road, hastening to get out of sight of the spike and its discipline. This was our interim of freedom. After a day and two nights of wasted time we had eight hours or so to take our recreation, to scour the roads for cigarette ends, to beg, and to look for work. Also, we had to make our ten, fifteen, or it might be twenty miles to the next spike, where the game would begin anew.

I disinterred my eightpence and took the road with Nobby, a respectable, downhearted tramp who carried a spare pair of boots and visited all the Labour Exchanges. Our late companions were scattering north, south, east and west, like bugs into a mattress. Only the imbecile loitered at the spike gates, until the Tramp Major had to chase him away.

Nobby and I set out for Croydon. It was a quiet road, there were no cars passing, the blossom covered the chestnut trees like great wax candles. Everything was so quiet and smelt so clean, it was hard to realise that only a few minutes ago we had been packed with that band of prisoners in a stench of drains and soft soap. The others had all disappeared; we two seemed to be the only tramps on the road.

Then I heard a hurried step behind me, and felt a tap on my arm. It was little Scotty, who had run panting after us. He pulled a rusty tin box from his pocket. He wore a friendly smile, like a man who is repaying an obligation.

"Here y'are, mate," he said cordially, "I owe you some fag ends. You stood me a smoke yesterday. The Tramp Major give me back my box of fag ends when we come out this morning. One good turn deserves another— here y'are."

And he put four sodden, debauched, loathely cigarette ends into my hand.

ERIC BLAIR

1. 'The Spike' is closely related to chapters 27 and 35 of *Down and Out in Paris and London*, the first version of which Orwell had completed in October 1930. Compare it also with 'A Day in the Life of a Tramp,' *83*. In 1996 the government ordered the closure of the last of some 750 spikes, that at Bishopbriggs, near Glasgow.
2. 'And there is nothing left remarkable / Beneath the visiting moon'; Cleopatra's response to Antony's death, *Antony and Cleopatra*, 4.15.67–68.

105. Review of *Hunger and Love* by Lionel Britton; *Albert Grope* by F. O. Mann

The Adelphi, April 1931

Hunger and Love is not so much a novel as a kind of monologue upon poverty. Its central character, Arthur Phelps, is a youth of promise, born in the slums. He begins life as an errand boy on twelve shillings a week, then works his way up to be an assistant in a bookshop; when he has partially educated himself and attained an income of twenty-seven shillings a week, the war intervenes and finishes him. He is not a very nice youth, but he is as nice as you could expect him to be on twenty-seven shillings a week; and the peculiar merit of the book is that it does approach life from the twenty-seven-shilling-a-week angle. Most fiction is written by the well-fed, about the well-fed, for the well-fed. This is the ill-fed man's version; the world as it appears to an unskilled workman—a workman, necessarily, with enough brains to grasp what is happening to him. There are plenty of these men about nowadays, and they are thinking night and day of the world they live in. This (it will also do to illustrate Mr. Britton's curious style) is the way in which they think:

"The little meannesses they subject you to, the incessant degradation, foulness—collar on jugular, little toe twisted ankylosed° through pressure of shoe, get up in morning no bath, wear clothes till rot with body sweat, drain stink sink stink w.c. stink live in sleep in work in, mean little jobs consume life activity: can you go through life and be unaware of this great foul disease of humanity?"

Such thoughts recur and recur—a sort of mental eczema, a perpetual restless irritation over mean things. To the well-fed it seems cowardly to complain of tight boots, because the well-fed live in a different world—a world where, if your boots are tight, you can change them; their minds are not warped by petty discomfort. But below a certain income the petty crowds the large out of existence; one's preoccupation is not with art or religion, but with bad food, hard beds, drudgery and the sack. "Culture and love and beauty are so *damned* silly when you're out of work." Serenity is impossible to a poor man in a cold country, and even his active thoughts will go in more or less sterile complaint.

This is a thing that wants remembering, and the virtue of *Hunger and Love* is that it rubs in the irritating, time-wasting nature of poverty; the nasty, squalid little things which by their cumulative effect make life on less than two pounds a week radically different from life on even three or four pounds. Arthur Phelps can hardly live an hour without being reminded that the world means to starve him. He wants comfort and cleanliness; he gets a stuffy slum bedroom, and fat men coughing into his plate in cheap eating houses. He wants leisure; he gets sixty or seventy hours a week at dull, unnecessary work. He wants knowledge; he gets a board school "education", and thereafter peeps into textbooks when the boss is not looking. He wants love, but love costs money; he gets moments with half-witted shop-girls, or prostitutes. However much he struggles he flounders back into his poverty, like a sheep floundering into mud. As a social document, with its insistence on mean, recurrent troubles, this book is entirely sound.

Having said this, however, one must add that as a novel *Hunger and Love* is almost worthless. Obviously the thing to do with such important material— the world of an intelligent poor man—was to make it into a memorable story. Instead of this we have a book that is one long digression, telling, certainly, the truth about life, but making no attempt to be readable. The tricks of style, and particularly the repetitions, become very tiresome after a few chapters. (It must be several hundred times that Mr. Britton reminds us that the earth moves round the sun at 18.5 miles a second—this apropos of man's tininess amid the universe; it is worth knowing, but one does not want to read it every two pages.) No doubt Mr. Britton would say that his object was to tell the truth, not to compose an elegant novel; but even so, truth is not served by leaving out commas. A writer with any sense of selection would have cut this book down from 700 pages to 200, and lost nothing. If Mr. Britton had done this, while keeping a firm hold on the realities of his subject, *Hunger and Love* might have been a first-rate book instead of merely an unusual one. Still, it *is* unusual.

It is a far cry from *Hunger and Love* to *Albert Grope*. *Albert Grope* is also the story of a man born and bred in the slums, but these are picturesque slums, not the smelly variety. *Hunger and Love* is compounded of discontent and astronomy, with perhaps a touch of James Joyce; *Albert Grope* is Dickens—rather diluted. The hero begins life as a shop-boy, sets up as a bookseller, then as an advertising agent, and ends moderately rich and happily married. He is very like a faded portrait of David Copperfield, which is perhaps what the author intended. The pleasant and simple nature of the hero, and the eccentric characters whom he meets, are described with a competence worthy of something more original.

ERIC BLAIR

106. Review of *The Good Earth* by Pearl S. Buck

The Adelphi, June 1931

This is a very exceptional book. It starts uncertainly, and it is handicapped by a bad style, rather like the style of Lang's crib to the Odyssey. But one scarcely worries about this, the story goes so straight to the very heart of truth. There is no plot, and yet not a single redundant incident; no words spent in pity, but a fidelity to life which simply withers optimism. The account of the life of rickshaw coolies in an eastern city is particularly moving. Anyone who has seen that vile sight of men running between shafts like horses, will welcome this description. The author evidently knows China as her native land, but has been away from it just long enough to notice the things which a Chinaman would miss. *The Good Earth* can be added at once to the very small list of first-rate books about the East.

It is the story of Wang Lung, a Chinese peasant. Born into crushing poverty, he digs his field with a wooden hoe, drinks hot water, because tea is too expensive, eats meat only on feast days. He is the very type of the oriental, narrowly dutiful, abysmally ignorant, brutishly industrious. He has the hunger for land which outlives all other passions and turns everything else—every vice and every altruism—into nonsense. He loves land as some men love beauty. All his wisdom is summed up in this, that to own land is good, to sell land the ultimate folly. He is a peasant.

Perhaps the best-done thing in the book is the story of Wang Lung's relations with his wife, O Lan. O Lan is a slave girl, chosen for her ugliness, because pretty women (women with small feet, that is) are no use on the land. She bears child after child to Wang Lung, works at his side till the very hour of her confinements, obeys him like a dog. Wang Lung's feeling for her has nothing of love as we know it, only duty. Certain things are due to her, as certain things are due to an ox, and in these he never fails. But she is only a convenience; to love her would be slightly shameful, a kind of infatuation, like loving an ox. How could one love a woman with large feet? Love is for concubines. When O Lan lies dying, worn out with work and childbirths, Wang Lung looks at her and thinks how ugly she is. He knows that she has been a good wife, even dimly feels that he might be sorry for her. But he is not sorry; her big feet repel him too much. Still, he knows his duty. He buys her an expensive coffin.

E. A. B.

107. To Brenda Salkeld

Sunday night, [July 1931][1]   Handwritten

3 Queen St   [Southwold]

Dearest Brenda,[2]

I assume that your friends *did* turn up today? This morning I went to the Bell, & they told me, 'Some of your St Felix friends have been here having high jinks'. I suppose that was you? I hope you were quite sober. Way showed me a piece of his bergamot, which is now flowering. It is very deep red, & not unlike a thistle head—not at all coming up to its beautiful name, I thought. How important names are. If I have the choice of going through two streets, other things being equal I always go by the one with the nicer name. Yesterday evening there were ten or fifteen swans flying over the sea. I saw them in the distance & thought they were swans, & today I was told they were so—I can't think where they came from; certainly they weren't the local ones.

What day are you going away? Surely not till the end of the week? Try & see me some evening if you can. As soon as possible I will give you an adress° in town, & when you are coming up let me know *well* in advance, so that I can keep the day free. I don't know what condition I shall be in. I suppose you won't object to a 3-day beard? I will promise to have no lice, anyway. What fun if we could both go hopping together. But I suppose your exaggerated fear of dirt would deter you. It is a great mistake to be too afraid of dirt.

I have been reading the ballad of Robin Hood & George of Gisbone.[3] When we were children we had a story that after Robin Hood was done to death in the Priory, his men raped & murdered the nuns, & burned the priory to the ground. It seems this has no foundation in the ballads—we must have made it up. An instance of the human instinct for a happy ending.

This is the last stanza of the ballad of R. H. & G. of G.:

'But he cold° neither runne so fast,
   Nor away so fast cold ryde,
But Little John with an arrowe so broad,
   He shott him in the backe-syde.'[4]

Rather sweet, what?

You might ask somebody whether 'melons' in 17th century poems means vegetable marrows. cf. Marvell

'Stumbling on Melons as I pass,
   Ensnared by[5] flowers, I fall on grass,'

This is from his 'Thoughts in a garden', implying that the 'melons' grew in the open. I think also Milton mentions them somewhere. It is also common for poets of that period to speak of grapes growing in the open. I wonder whether the climate has changed at all?

Best love
Eric

1. Bergamot flowers in late June and July; school vacations begin in July. So Orwell would be more likely to be writing to Brenda Salkeld in that month.
2. Brenda Salkeld (1900–1999) met Orwell in 1928, when she was working as a gym mistress at St Felix Girls' School, Southwold. She returned home to Bedford for vacations. They remained good friends until Orwell died. See *Orwell Remembered*, 67–68, for her reminiscences; Stansky and Abrahams, I, 244–46; Shelden, 157; U. S.: 143. St Felix's was still open in 1996. She left £1,400,042 (net before tax).
3. First published by Thomas Percy, Bishop of Dromore, in his *Reliques* (1765) but, as he wrote, it 'carries marks of much greater antiquity than any of the common popular songs on this subject.'
4. The old-style spelling is not that of the Everyman edition, a copy of which, in two volumes, was among Orwell's books at his death.
5. by *should be* with.

108. 'A Hanging'

The Adelphi, August 1931; reprinted in *The New Savoy*, 1946

It was in Burma, a sodden morning of the rains. A sickly light, like yellow tinfoil, was slanting over the high walls into the jail yard. We were waiting outside the condemned cells, a row of sheds fronted with double bars, like small animal cages. Each cell measured about ten feet by ten and was quite bare within except for a plank bed and a pot for drinking water. In some of them brown silent men were squatting at the inner bars, with their blankets draped round them. These were the condemned men, due to be hanged within the next week or two.

One prisoner had been brought out of his cell. He was a Hindu, a puny wisp of a man, with a shaven head and vague liquid eyes. He had a thick, sprouting moustache, absurdly too big for his body, rather like the moustache of a comic man on the films. Six tall Indian warders were guarding him and getting him ready for the gallows. Two of them stood by with rifles and fixed bayonets, while the others handcuffed him, passed a chain through his handcuffs and fixed it to their belts, and lashed his arms tight to his sides. They crowded very close about him, with their hands always on him in a careful, caressing grip, as though all the while feeling him to make sure he was there. It was like men handling a fish which is still alive and may jump back into the water. But he stood quite unresisting, yielding his arms limply to the ropes, as though he hardly noticed what was happening.

Eight o'clock struck and a bugle call, desolately thin in the wet air, floated from the distant barracks. The superintendent[1] of the jail, who was standing apart from the rest of us, moodily prodding the gravel with his stick, raised his head at the sound. He was an army doctor, with a grey toothbrush moustache and a gruff voice. "For God's sake hurry up, Francis", he said irritably. "The man ought to have been dead by this time. Aren't you ready yet?"

Francis, the head jailer, a fat Dravidian in a white drill suit and gold spectacles, waved his black hand. "Yes sir, yes sir", he bubbled. "All iss satisfactorily prepared. The hangman iss waiting. We shall proceed."

"Well, quick march, then. The prisoners can't get their breakfast till this job's over."

We set out for the gallows. Two warders marched on either side of the prisoner, with their rifles at the slope; two others marched close against him, gripping him by arm and shoulder, as though at once pushing and supporting him. The rest of us, magistrates and the like, followed behind. Suddenly, when we had gone ten yards, the procession stopped short without any order or warning. A dreadful thing had happened—a dog, come goodness knows whence, had appeared in the yard. It came bounding among us with a loud volley of barks, and leapt round us wagging its whole body, wild with glee at finding so many human beings together. It was a large woolly dog, half Airedale, half pariah. For a moment it pranced round us, and then, before anyone could stop it, it had made a dash for the prisoner, and jumping up tried to lick his face. Everyone stood aghast, too taken aback even to grab at the dog.

"Who let that bloody brute in here?" said the superintendent angrily. "Catch it, someone!"

A warder, detached from the escort, charged clumsily after the dog, but it danced and gambolled just out of his reach, taking everything as part of the game. A young Eurasian jailer picked up a handful of gravel and tried to stone the dog away, but it dodged the stones and came after us again. Its yaps echoed from the jail walls. The prisoner, in the grasp of the two warders, looked on incuriously, as though this was another formality of the hanging. It was several minutes before someone managed to catch the dog. Then we put my handkerchief through its collar and moved off once more, with the dog still straining and whimpering.

It was about forty yards to the gallows. I watched the bare brown back of the prisoner marching in front of me. He walked clumsily with his bound arms, but quite steadily, with that bobbing gait of the Indian who never straightens his knees. At each step his muscles slid neatly into place, the lock of hair on his scalp danced up and down, his feet printed themselves on the wet gravel. And once, in spite of the men who gripped him by each shoulder, he stepped slightly aside to avoid a puddle on the path.

It is curious, but till that moment I had never realised what it means to destroy a healthy, conscious man. When I saw the prisoner step aside to avoid the puddle, I saw the mystery, the unspeakable wrongness, of cutting a life short when it is in full tide. This man was not dying, he was alive just as we were alive. All the organs of his body were working—bowels digesting food, skin renewing itself, nails growing, tissues forming—all toiling away in solemn foolery. His nails would still be growing when he stood on the drop, when he was falling through the air with a tenth-of-a-second to live. His eyes saw the yellow gravel and the grey walls, and his brain still remembered, foresaw, reasoned—reasoned even about puddles. He and we were a party of men walking together, seeing, hearing, feeling, understanding the same world; and in two minutes, with a sudden snap, one of us would be gone— one mind less, one world less.

The gallows stood in a small yard, separate from the main grounds of the prison, and overgrown with tall prickly weeds. It was a brick erection like three sides of a shed, with planking on top, and above that two beams and a crossbar with the rope dangling. The hangman, a grey-haired convict in the white uniform of the prison, was waiting beside his machine. He greeted us with a servile crouch as we entered. At a word from Francis the two warders, gripping the prisoner more closely than ever, half led half pushed him to the gallows and helped him clumsily up the ladder. Then the hangman climbed up and fixed the rope round the prisoner's neck.

We stood waiting, five yards away. The warders had formed in a rough circle round the gallows. And then, when the noose was fixed, the prisoner began crying out on his god. It was a high, reiterated cry of "Ram! Ram! Ram! Ram!" not urgent and fearful like a prayer or a cry for help, but steady, rhythmical, almost like the tolling of a bell. The dog answered the sound with a whine. The hangman, still standing on the gallows, produced a small cotton bag like a flour bag and drew it down over the prisoner's face. But the sound, muffled by the cloth, still persisted, over and over again: "Ram! Ram! Ram! Ram! Ram!"

The hangman climbed down and stood ready, holding the lever. Minutes seemed to pass. The steady, muffled crying from the prisoner went on and on, "Ram! Ram! Ram!" never faltering for an instant. The superintendent, his head on his chest, was slowly poking the ground with his stick; perhaps he was counting the cries, allowing the prisoner a fixed number—fifty, perhaps, or a hundred. Everyone had changed colour. The Indians had gone grey like bad coffee, and one or two of the bayonets were wavering. We looked at the lashed, hooded man on the drop, and listened to his cries—each cry another second of life; the same thought was in all our minds: oh, kill him quickly, get it over, stop that abominable noise!

Suddenly the superintendent made up his mind. Throwing up his head he made a swift motion with his stick, "Chalo!" he shouted almost fiercely.

There was a clanking noise, and then dead silence. The prisoner had vanished, and the rope was twisting on itself. I let go of the dog, and it galloped immediately to the back of the gallows; but when it got there it stopped short, barked, and then retreated into a corner of the yard, where it stood among the weeds, looking timorously out at us. We went round the gallows to inspect the prisoner's body. He was dangling with his toes pointed straight downwards, very slowly revolving, as dead as a stone.

The superintendent reached out with his stick and poked the bare brown body; it oscillated slightly. "*He's* all right", said the superintendent. He backed out from under the gallows, and blew out a deep breath. The moody look had gone out of his face quite suddenly. He glanced at his wrist-watch. "Eight minutes past eight. Well, that's all for this morning, thank God."

The warders unfixed bayonets and marched away. The dog, sobered and conscious of having misbehaved itself, slipped after them. We walked out of the gallows yard, past the condemned cells with their waiting prisoners, into the big central yard of the prison. The convicts, under the command of warders armed with lathis, were already receiving their breakfast. They squatted in long rows, each man holding a tin pannikin, while two warders with buckets marched round ladling out rice; it seemed quite a homely, jolly scene, after the hanging. An enormous relief had come upon us now that the job was done. One felt an impulse to sing, to break into a run, to snigger. All at once everyone began chattering gaily.

The Eurasian boy walking beside me nodded towards the way we had come, with a knowing smile: "Do you know, sir, our friend (he meant the dead man), when he heard his appeal had been dismissed, he pissed on the floor of his cell. From fright.—Kindly take one of my cigarettes, sir. Do you not admire my new silver case, sir? From the boxwalah, two rupees eight annas. Classy European style."

Several people laughed—at what, nobody seemed certain.

Francis was walking by the superintendent, talking garrulously: "Well, sir, all hass passed off with the utmost satisfactoriness. It wass all finished—flick! like that. It iss not always so—oah, no! I have known cases where the doctor wass obliged to go beneath the gallows and pull the prissoner's legs to ensure decease. Most disagreeable!"

"Wriggling about, eh? That's bad", said the superintendent.

"Ach, sir, it iss worse when they become refractory! One man, I recall, clung to the bars of hiss cage when we went to take him out. You will scarcely credit, sir, that it took six warders to dislodge him, three pulling at each leg. We reasoned with him. 'My dear fellow', we said, 'think of all the pain and trouble you are causing to us!' But no, he would not listen! Ach, he wass very troublesome!"

I found that I was laughing quite loudly. Everyone was laughing. Even the superintendent grinned in a tolerant way. "You'd better all come out and have a drink", he said quite genially. "I've got a bottle of whisky in the car. We could do with it."

We went through the big double gates of the prison, into the road. "Pulling at his legs!" exclaimed a Burmese magistrate suddenly, and burst into a loud chuckling. We all began laughing again. At that moment Francis' anecdote seemed extraordinarily funny. We all had a drink together, native and European alike, quite amicably. The dead man was a hundred yards away.[2]

ERIC A. BLAIR

1. Spelt as 'superintendant' in *The Adelphi* throughout; as here in *The New Savoy*.
2. See 'As I Please,' 61, 15 November 1946, *3115*, for further reflections upon hanging. See also *The Road to Wigan Pier*, 'I watched a man hanged once' (*CW, V*, 136–7).

109. To Dennis Collings

16 August 1931   Handwritten

At 1B Oakwood Rd   Golders Green   N.W

Dear Dennis,[1]

I said I would write to you. I haven't anything of great interest to report yet about the Lower Classes, & am really writing to tell you about a ghost I saw in Walberswick cemetery. I want to get it on paper before I forget the details. See plan below.

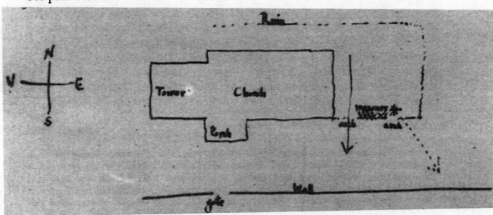

Above is W'wick church as well as I can remember it. At about 5.20 pm on 27.7.31 I was sitting at the spot marked*, looking out in the direction of the dotted arrow. I happened to glance over my shoulder, & saw a figure pass along the line of the other arrow, disappearing behind the masonry & presumably emerging into the churchyard. I wasn't looking *directly* at it & so couldn't make out more than that it was a man's figure, small & stooping, & dressed in lightish brown; I should have said a workman. I had the impression that it glanced towards me in passing, but I made out nothing of the features. At the moment of its passing I thought nothing, but a few seconds later it struck me that the figure had made no noise, & I followed it out into the churchyard. There was no one in the churchyard, & no one within possible distance along the road—this was about 20 seconds after I had seen it; & in any case there were only 2 people in the road, & neither at all resembled the figure. I looked into the church. The only people there were the vicar, dressed in *black*, & a workman who, as far as I remember, had been sawing the whole time. In any case he was too tall for the figure. The figure had therefore vanished. Presumably an hallucination.

I have been up in town since the beginning of the month. I have made arrangements to go hop-picking, but we shan't start till the beginning of September. Meanwhile I've been busy working. I met recently one of the editors of a new paper[2] that is to start coming out in October, & I hope I shall be able to get some work from them—not enough to live on, of course, but enough to help. I've been making just a few enquiries among the tramps. Of the three friends I had before, one is believed to have been run over & killed, one has taken to drink & vanished, one is doing time in Wandsworth. I met a man today who was, till 6 weeks ago, a goldsmith. Then he poisoned his right forefinger, & had to have part of the top joint removed; that means he will be on the road for life. It is appalling what small accidents can ruin a man who works with his hands. Talking of hands, they say hop-picking disables your hands for weeks after—however, I'll describe that to you when I've done it.

Have you ever looked into the window of one of those Bible Society shops? I did today & saw huge notices 'The cheapest Roman Catholic Bible 5/6d. The cheapest Protestant Bible 1/–', 'The Douay version *not* stocked here' etc. etc. Long may they fight, I say; so long as that spirit is in the land we are safe from the R.C.'s—this shop, by the way, was just outside St Paul's. If you are ever near St Paul's & feel in a gloomy mood, go in & have a look at the statue of the first Protestant bishop of India, which will give you a good laugh. Will write again when I have news. I am sending this to S'wold.

Yours
Eric A Blair

1. Dennis Collings (1905–) was a friend of Orwell's from the time the Blair family moved to Southwold in 1921; Collings's father became the Blair family doctor. Collings grew sisal in Mozambique, 1924–27; read anthropology at Cambridge, 1928–31; and was appointed assistant curator of the Raffles Museum, Singapore, when he joined the Colonial Service in 1934. That year he married Eleanor Jaques, with whom Orwell corresponded. He contributed to *Orwell Remembered*, 76–83. See Shelden, 156, 192; U.S.: 142–43, 174–75.
2. *Modern Youth.*

110. To Dennis Collings

Thursday night, [27 August 1931]   Handwritten

[A lodging-house in Southwark Bridge Road]

Dear Dennis,

Please excuse pencil & bad writing, as I am writing this in a lodging house. It is a 7d kip—& looks it, I may say—in Southwark, & I believe the only one at the price in London. We go down for the hopping tomorrow morning: 2d tram to Bromley, & hike the rest.

I have had an interesting 2 days camping in Trafalgar Square. It has, at this time of year, a floating population of 200 or so. You can make yourself fairly comfortable against the north wall & can get tea all day long, as a coffee shop nearby will give you boiling water free or 1d for a billyful (billies are called 'drums' by the way). I was there all yesterday & was to have spent the night in St Martin's Church, but as you had to queue up for an hour to get a decent place we decided to stay in the square. You take my tip & *never* sleep in Trafalgar Square. We were tolerably comfortable till midnight, except that once in 5 or 10 minutes the police came round waking those who were asleep

& making anyone who was sitting on the ground stand up. Every ten minutes it would be, 'Look out, mates, 'ere comes the flattie (policemen). Take up thy bed & walk' etc. And then the police: 'Now then, get off of that. If you want to sit, sit on the benches' etc. There were only benches for 40 out of the 200, but we got *some* rest, as we kipped down again the moment the policeman had passed. After midnight the cold was glacial. Perhaps a dozen people managed to sleep, the rest walked the streets, with an occasional sit-down for a rest— this for 4 consecutive hours. At 4 am someone managed to get hold of a big pile of newspaper posters & brought them along to use as blankets. ''Ere y'are, mate tuck in the fucking eiderdown. Don't we look like fucking parsons in these 'ere surplices? 'Ere, I got "Dramatic appeal from the Premier" round *my* neck. That ought to warm yer up, oughtn't it?' etc. We made ourselves into large newspaper parcels, & were comparatively warm, tho' still not warm enough to sleep, apart from the police. I doubt whether more than 10 or 20 of the 200 people slept a wink during the night. At 5 we all went to Stewart's coffee shop in St Martin's Lane, where it is understood that you can sit from 5 am to 9 am for a 2d cup of tea—or even for less, for often 2 or 3 fellows who had only 2d between them clubbed together & shared a cup of tea. You were allowed to sleep with your head on the table till 7 am, after which the proprietor woke you up. This is the absolutely regular routine of Trafalgar Square "sleepers". Two of the fellows I was with had had 7 consecutive weeks of it & some people do it all the year round. They make up the sleepless night by naps during the morning. The rules about what you may & may not do in Trafalgar Square are curious, & should interest you as an anthropologist. Till noon you can do what you like (even shave in the fountains) except that the police wake you if they see you asleep. From noon to 9 pm you can sit on the benches or the pedestals of the statues, but are moved on if you sit on the ground. After 9 pm you are also moved on from the pedestals of the statues. Between 9 pm & midnight the police wake those who are asleep every 5 minutes, after midnight every half hour. For all this no ostensible reason.

About 8 pm last night a woman came up crying bitterly. It appeared that she was a tart & someone had poked her & then cleared off without paying the fee, which was 6d. It appeared that of the dozen or so women among the 200 in the square, half were prostitutes; but they were the prostitutes of the unemployed, & usually earn so little that they have to spend the night in the Square. 6d. is the usual fee, but in the small hours when it was bitter cold they were doing it for a cigarette. The prostitutes live on terms of perfect amity with the other down & out women. In Stewart's coffee shop this morning, however, an old girl who had slept in Covent Garden was denouncing 2 tarts, who had earned enough to get a few hours in bed & then a good breakfast. Each time they ordered another cup of tea she was yelling, 'There's another fuck! That's for that fucking negro you let on for a tanner' etc.

Today went much as yesterday & tonight, as we have a long day before us, I decided on getting a bed. My mates have gone to St Martin's Church, preferring to spend their money on a meat breakfast. This place is an apalling° squalid cellar, as hot as hell & the air a¹ sort of vapour of piss, sweat & cheese.

A pale youth, some kind of labourer but looking consumptive, keeps declaiming poetry in front of the fire. Evidently he is genuinely fond of it. You should hear him declaiming:

> 'A voice so thrilling ne'er was 'eard
> In Ipril from the cuckoo bird,
> Briking the silence of the seas
> Beyond the furthest 'Ebrides' etc.[2]

Also speaks of himself as 'sicklied o'er with the pile cast of care'. I should love to hear him recite 'O holy hope & high humility'. I have met other curious types of whom I will write to you when I have time. Also about the prevalence of homosexuality in London, & stowaways. The songs I have heard this time are 'Alleluia, I'm a bum', which I believe is American. Also one about

> 'Tap, tap, tapetty-tap,
> I'm a perfect devil for that,
> Tapping 'em 'ere, tapping 'em there,
> I've been tapping 'em everywhere.'

Tap = beg. Perhaps an old music hall song?

I hope this letter has not been too inconsequent & illegible. I will write when I have further news & a more comfortable place to write in. If you don't hear within a fortnight it probably will mean I've been pinched for begging, as the mates I'm going with are hardened 'tappers' & not above petty theft.

Yours
Eric A Blair

1. a] of
2. Stanza 2 of Wordsworth's 'The Solitary Reaper'.

III. Hop-Picking Diary

25 August–8 October 1931   Orwell's typsecript (typed 10 October 1931)

This is the first of many diaries written by Orwell. They are all printed here in sloped, or inclined, roman type, to provide immediate identification, and, except for some Domestic Diaries, are in chronological order. When a letter or other item and a diary entry have the same date, the diary entry is placed last.

<u>25.8.31:</u> *On the night of the 25th I started off from Chelsea with about 14/– in hand, and went to Lew Levy's kip in Westminster Bridge Road. It is much the same as it was three years ago, except that nearly all the beds are now a shilling instead of ninepence. This is owing to interference by the L.C.C. who have enacted (in the interests of hygiene, as usual) that beds in lodging houses must be further apart. There is a whole string of laws of this type relating to lodging houses, * but there is not and never will be a law to say that*

---

* *For instance, Dick's cafe in Billingsgate. Dick's was one of the few places where you could get a cup of tea for 1d, and there were fires there so that anyone who had a penny could warm himself for hours in the early mornings. Only this last week the L.C.C. closed it on the ground that it was unhygienic* [Orwell's note]. L.C.C. was the London Country Council.

the beds must be reasonably comfortable. The net result of this law is that one's bed is now three feet from the next instead of two feet, and threepence dearer.

26.8.31: The next day I went to Trafalgar Square and camped by the north wall, which is one of the recognized rendezvous of down and out people in London. At this time of year the square has a floating population of 100 or 200 people (about ten per cent of them women), some of whom actually look on it as their home. They get their food by regular begging rounds (Covent Garden at 4 am. for damaged fruit, various convents during the morning, restaurants and dustbins late at night etc.) and they manage to 'tap' likely-looking passers by for enough to keep them in tea. Tea is going on the square at all hours, one person supplying a 'drum', another sugar and so on. The milk is condensed milk at 2½d a tin. You jab two holes in the tin with a knife, apply your mouth to one of them and blow, whereupon a sticky greyish stream dribbles from the other. The holes are then plugged with chewed paper, and the tin is kept for days, becoming coated with dust and filth. Hot water is cadged at coffee shops, or at night boiled over watchmen's fires, but this has to be done on the sly, as the police won't allow it. Some of the people I met on the square had been there without a break for six weeks, and did not seem much the worse, except that they are all fantastically dirty. As always among the destitute, a large proportion of them are Irishmen. From time to time these men go home on visits, and it appears that they never think of paying their passage, but always stow away on small cargo boats, the crews conniving.

I had meant to sleep in St Martin's Church, but from what the others said it appeared that when you go in you are asked searching questions by some woman known as the Madonna, so I decided to stay the night in the square. It was not so bad as I expected, but between the cold and the police it was impossible to get a wink of sleep, and no one except a few hardened old tramps even tried to do so. There are seats enough for about fifty people, and the rest have to sit on the ground, which of course is forbidden by law. Every few minutes there would be a shout of 'Look out, boys, here comes the flattie!' and a policeman would come round and shake those who were asleep, and make the people on the ground get up. We used to kip down again the instant he had passed, and this went on like a kind of game from eight at night till three or four in the morning. After midnight it was so cold that I had to go for long walks to keep warm. The streets are somehow rather horrible at that hour; all silent and deserted, and yet lighted almost as bright as day with those garish lamps, which give everything a deathly air, as though London were the corpse of a town. About three o'clock another man and I went down to the patch of grass behind the Guards' parade ground, and saw prostitutes and men lying in couples there in the bitter cold mist and dew. There are always a number of prostitutes in the square; they are the unsuccessful ones, who can't earn enough for their night's kip. Overnight one of these women had been lying on the ground crying bitterly, because a man had gone off without paying her fee, which was sixpence. Towards morning they do not even get sixpence, but only a cup of tea or a cigarette. About four somebody got hold of a number of newspaper posters, [1] and we sat down six or eight on a bench and packed ourselves in enormous paper parcels, which kept us fairly warm till Stewart's cafe in St Martin's Lane opened. At Stewart's you can sit from five till nine for a cup of tea (or sometimes three or four people even share a cup between them) and you are allowed to sleep with your head on the table till seven; after that the proprietor wakes you. One meets a very mixed crowd there—tramps, Covent Garden porters, early business people, prostitutes— and there are constant quarrels and fights. On this occasion an old, very ugly woman, wife of a porter, was violently abusing two prostitutes, because they could afford a better breakfast than she could. As each dish was brought to them she would point at it and shout accusingly, 'There goes the price of another fuck! We don't get kippers for breakfast, do we, girls? 'Ow do you think she paid for them doughnuts? That's that there negro that 'as 'er for a tanner' etc. etc., but the prostitutes did not mind much.

27.8.31: At about eight in the morning we all had a shave in the Trafalgar Square fountains, and I spent most of the day reading Eugenie Grandet, which was the only book I had brought with me. The sight of a French book produced the usual remarks—'Ah, French? That'll be something pretty warm, eh?' etc. Evidently most English people have no idea that there are French books which are not pornographic. Down and out people seem to read exclusively books of the Buffalo Bill type. Every tramp carries one of these, and they have a kind of circulating library, all swapping books when they get to the spike.

That night, as we were starting for Kent the next morning, I decided to sleep in bed and went to a lodging house in the Southwark Bridge Road. This is a sevenpenny kip, one of the few in London, and looks it. The beds are five feet long, with no pillows (you use your coat rolled up), and infested by fleas, besides a few bugs. The kitchen is a small, stinking cellar where the deputy sits with a table of flyblown jam tarts etc. for sale a few feet from the door of the lavatory. The rats are so bad that several cats have to be kept exclusively to deal with them. The lodgers were dock workers, I think, and they did not seem a bad crowd. There was a youth among them, pale and consumptive looking but evidently a labourer, who was devoted to poetry. He repeated

> 'A voice so thrilling ne'er was 'eard
> In Ipril from the cuckoo bird,
> Briking the silence of the seas
> Beyond the furthest 'Ebrides'

with genuine feeling. The others did not laugh at him much.

28.8.31: The next day in the afternoon four of us started out for the hop-fields. The most interesting of the men with me was a youth named Ginger, who is still my mate when I write this. He is a strong, athletic youth of twenty six, almost illiterate and quite brainless, but daring enough for anything. Except when in prison, he has probably broken the law every day for the last five years. As a boy he did three years in Borstal, came out, married at eighteen on the strength of a successful burglary, and shortly afterwards enlisted in the artillery. His wife died, and a little while afterwards he had an accident to his left eye and was invalided out of the service. They offered him a pension or a lump sum, and of course he chose the lump sum and blued it in about a week. After that he took to burglary again, and has been in prison six times, but never for a long sentence, as they have only caught him for small jobs; he has done one or two jobs which brought him over £500. He has always been perfectly honest towards me, as his partner, but in a general way he will steal anything that is not tied down. I doubt his ever being a successful burglar, though, for he is too stupid to be able to foresee risks. It is all a great pity, for he could earn a decent living if he chose. He has a gift for street selling, and has had a lot of jobs at selling on commission, but when he has had a good day he bolts instantly with the takings. He is a marvellous hand at picking up bargains and can always, for instance, persuade the butcher to give him a pound of eatable meat for twopence, yet at the same time he is an absolute fool about money, and never saves a halfpenny. He is given to singing songs of the Little Grey Home in the West type, and he speaks of his dead wife and mother in terms of the most viscid sentimentality. I should think he is a fairly typical petty criminal.

Of the other two, one was a boy of twenty named Young Ginger, who seemed rather a likely lad, but he was an orphan and had had no kind of upbringing, and lived the last year chiefly on Trafalgar Square. The other was a little Liverpool Jew of eighteen, a thorough guttersnipe. I do not know when I have seen anyone who disgusted me so much as this boy. He was as greedy as a pig about food, perpetually scrounging round dust-bins, and he had a face that recalled some low-down carrion-eating beast. His manner of talking about women, and the expression of his face when he did so, were so loathsomely obscene as to make me feel almost sick. We could never persuade him to wash more of himself than his nose and a small circle round it, and he mentioned quite casually that he had several different kinds of louse on him. He too was an orphan, and had been 'on the toby' almost from infancy.

I had now about 6/–, and before starting we bought a so-called blanket for 1/6d and cadged several tins for 'drums'. The only reliable tin for a drum is a two-pound snuff tin, which is not very easy to come by. We had also a supply of bread and margarine and tea, and a number of knives and forks etc., all stolen at different times from Woolworth's. We took the twopenny tram as far as Bromley, and there 'drummed up' on a rubbish dump, waiting for two others who were to have joined us, but who never turned up. It was dark when we finally stopped waiting for them, so we had no chance to look for a good camping place, and had to spend the night in long wet grass at the edge of a recreation ground. The cold was bitter. We had only two thin blankets between the four of us, and it was not safe to light a fire, as there were houses all round; we were also lying on a slope, so that one rolled into the ditch from time to time. It was rather humiliating to see the others, all younger than I, sleeping quite soundly in these conditions, whereas I did not close my eyes all night. To avoid being caught we had to be on the road before dawn, and it was several hours before we managed to get hot water and have our breakfast.

29.8.31: When we had gone a mile or two we came to an orchard, and the others at once went in and began stealing apples. I had not been prepared

217

for this when we started out, but I saw that I must either do as the others did or leave them, so I shared the apples; I did not however take any part in the thefts for the first day, except to keep guard. We were going more or less in the direction of Sevenoaks, and by dinner time we had stolen about a dozen apples and plums and fifteen pounds of potatoes. The others also went in and tapped whenever we passed a baker's or a teashop, and we got quite a quantity of broken bread and meat. When we stopped to light a fire for dinner we fell in with two Scotch tramps who had been stealing apples from an orchard nearby, and stayed talking with them for a long time. The others all talked about sexual subjects, in a revolting manner. Tramps are disgusting when on this subject, because their poverty cuts them off entirely from women, and their minds consequently fester with obscenity. Merely lecherous people are all right, but people who would like to be lecherous, but don't get the chance, are horribly degraded by it. They remind me of the dogs that hang enviously round while two other dogs are copulating. During the conversation Young Ginger related how he and some others on Trafalgar Square had discovered one of their number to be a 'Poof', or Nancy Boy. Whereupon they had instantly fallen upon him, robbed him of 12/6d, which was all he had, and spent it on themselves. Evidently they thought it quite fair to rob him, as he was a Nancy Boy.

We had been making very poor progress, chiefly because Young Ginger and the Jew were not used to walking and wanted to stop and search for scraps of food all the time. On one occasion the Jew even picked up some chipped potatoes that had been trodden on, and ate them. As it was getting on in the afternoon we decided to make not for Sevenoaks but for Ide Hill spike, which the Scotchmen had told us was better than it is usually represented. We halted about a mile from the spike for tea, and I remember that a gentleman in a car nearby helped us in the kindest manner to find wood for our fire, and gave us a cigarette each. Then we went on to the spike, and on the way picked a bunch of honeysuckle to give to the Tramp Major. We thought this might put him in a good temper and induce him to let us out next morning, for it is not usual to let tramps out of the spike on Sundays. When we got there however the Tramp Major said that he would have to keep us in till Tuesday morning. It appeared that the Workhouse Master was very keen on making every casual do a day's work, and at the same time would not hear of their working on Sunday; so we should have to be idle all Sunday and work on Monday. Young Ginger and the Jew elected to stay till Tuesday, but Ginger and I went and kipped on the edge of a park near the church. It was beastly cold, but a little better than the night before, for we had plenty of wood and could make a fire. For our supper, Ginger tapped the local butcher, who gave us the best part of two pounds of sausages. Butchers are always very generous on Saturday nights.

30.8.31: Next morning the clergyman coming to early service caught us and turned us out, though not very disagreeably. We went on through Sevenoaks to Seal, and a man we met advised us to try for a job at Mitchell's farm, about three miles further on. We went there, but the farmer told us that he could not give us a job, as he had nowhere where we could live, and the

Government inspectors had been snouting round to see that all hop-pickers had 'proper accommodation'. (These inspectors,* by the way, managed to prevent some hundreds of unemployed from getting jobs in the hop-fields this year. Not having 'proper accommodation' to offer to pickers, the farmers could only employ local people, who lived in their own houses.) We stole about a pound of raspberries from one of Mitchell's fields, and then went and applied to another farmer called Kronk, who gave us the same answer; we had five or ten pounds of potatoes from his fields, however. We were starting off in the direction of Maidstone when we fell in with an old Irishwoman, who had been given a job by Mitchell on the understanding that she had a lodging in Seal, which she had not. (Actually she was sleeping in a toolshed in somebody's garden. She used to slip in after dark and out before daylight.) We got some hot water from a cottage and the Irishwoman had tea with us, and gave us a lot of food that she had begged and did not want; we were glad of this, for we had now only 2½d left, and none too much food. It had now come on to rain, so we went to a farmhouse beside the church and asked leave to shelter in one of their cowsheds. The farmer and family were just starting out for evening service, and they said in a scandalised manner that of course they could not give us shelter. We sheltered instead in the lych-gate of the church, hoping that by looking draggled and tired we might get a few coppers from the congregation as they went in. We did not get anything, but after the service Ginger managed to tap a fairly good pair of flannel trousers from the clergyman. It was very uncomfortable in the lych-gate, and we were wet through and out of tobacco, and Ginger and I had walked twelve miles; yet I remember that we were quite happy and laughing all the time. The Irishwoman (she was sixty, and had been on the road all her life, evidently) was an extraordinarily cheerful old girl, and full of stories. Talking of places to 'skipper' in, she told us that one cold night she had crept into a pigsty and snuggled up to an old sow, for warmth.

When night came on it was still raining, so we decided to find an empty house to sleep in, but we went first to buy half a pound of sugar and two candles at the grocer's. While I was buying them Ginger stole three apples off the counter, and the Irishwoman a packet of cigarettes. They had plotted this beforehand, deliberately not telling me, so as to use my innocent appearance as a shield. After a good deal of searching we found an unfinished house and slipped in by a window the builders had left open. The bare floor was beastly hard, but it was warmer than outside, and I managed to get two or three hours' sleep. We got out before dawn, and by appointment met the Irishwoman in a wood nearby. It was raining, but Ginger could get a fire going in almost any circumstances, and we managed to make tea and roast 1.9.31: some potatoes. When it was light the Irishwoman went off to work, and Ginger and I went down to Chambers' farm, a mile or two away, to ask for work. When we got to the farm they had just been hanging a cat, a thing I never heard of anyone doing before. The bailiff said that he thought he could give us a job, and told us to wait; we waited from eight in the morning

* Appointed by the Labour Government [Orwell's note].

till one, when the bailiff said that he had no work for us after all. We made off, stealing a large quantity of apples and damsons, and started along the Maidstone road. At about three we halted to have our dinner and make some jam out of the raspberries we had stolen the day before. Near here, I remember, they refused at two houses to give me cold water, because 'the mistress doesn't allow us to give anything to tramps.' Ginger saw a gentleman in a car picnicking nearby, and went up to tap him for matches, for he said, that it always pays to tap from picnickers, who usually have some food left over when they are going home. Sure enough the gentleman presently came across with some butter he had not used, and began talking to us. His manner was so friendly that I forgot to put on my cockney accent, and he looked closely at me, and said how painful it must be for a man of my stamp etc. Then he said, 'I say, you won't be offended, will you? Do you mind taking this?' 'This' was a shilling, with which we bought some tobacco and had our first smoke that day. This was the only time in the whole journey when we managed to tap money.

We went on in the direction of Maidstone, but when we had gone a few miles it began to pour with rain, and my left boot was pinching me badly. I had not had my boots off for three days and had only had about eight hours sleep in the last five nights, and I did not feel equal to another night in the open. We decided to make for West Malling spike, which was about eight miles distant, and if possible to get a lift part of the way. I think we hailed forty lorries before we got a lift. The lorry drivers will not give lifts nowadays, because they are not insured for third party risks and they get the sack if they have an accident. Finally we did get a lift, and were set down about two miles from the spike, getting there at eight in the evening. Outside the gates we met an old deaf tramp who was going to skipper in the pouring rain, as he had been in the spike the night before, and they would confine him for a week if he came again. He told us that Blest's farm nearby would probably give us a job, and that they would let us out of the spike early in the morning if we told them we had already got a job. Otherwise we should be confined all day, unless we went out 'over the wall'—i.e. bolted when the Tramp Major was not looking. Tramps often do this, but you have to cache your possessions outside, which we could not in the heavy rain. We went in, and I found that (if West Malling is typical) spikes have improved a lot since I was last in.★ The bathroom was clean and decent, and we were actualy° given a clean towel each. The food was the same old bread and marg, though, and the Tramp Major got angry when we asked in good faith whether the stuff they gave us to drink was tea or cocoa.† We had beds with straw palliasses and plenty of blankets, and both slept like logs.

In the morning they told us we must work till eleven, and set us to scrubbing out one of the dormitories. As usual, the work was a mere formality. (I have never done a stroke of real work in the spike, and I have never met anybody who has.) The dormitory was a room of fifty beds, close

★ No: a bit worse if anything [Orwell's note].
† To this day I don't know which it was [Orwell's note].

together, with that warm, faecal stink that you never seem to get away from in the workhouse. There was an imbecile pauper there, a great lump of about sixteen stone, with a tiny, snouty face and a sidelong grin. He was at work very slowly emptying chamberpots. These workhouses seem all alike, and there is something intensely disgusting in the atmosphere of them. The thought of all those grey-faced, ageing men living a very quiet, withdrawn life in a smell of W.Cs, and practising homosexuality, makes me feel sick. But it is not easy to convey what I mean, because it is all bound up with the smell of the workhouse.

At eleven they let us out with the usual hunk of bread and cheese, and we went on to Blest's farm, about three miles away; but we did not get there till one, because we stopped on the way and got a big haul of damsons. When we arrived at the farm the foreman told us that he wanted pickers and sent us up to the field at once. We had now only about 3d left, and that evening I wrote home asking them to send me 10/–; it came two days later, and in the mean time we should have had practically nothing to eat if the other pickers had not fed us. For nearly three weeks after this we were at work hop-picking, and I had better describe the different aspects of this individually.

X *2.9.31 to   Hops are trained up poles or over wires about 10 feet high, 19.9.31:   and grown in rows a yard or two apart. All the pickers have to do is to tear them down and strip the hops into a bin, keeping them as clean as possible of leaves. In practice, of course, it is impossible to keep all the leaves out, and the experienced pickers swell the bulk of their hops by putting in just as many leaves as the farmer will stand for. One soon gets the knack of the work, and the only hardships are the standing (we were generally on our feet ten hours a day), the plagues of plant lice, and the damage to one's hands. One's hands get stained as black as a negro's with the hop-juice, which only mud will remove,† and after a day or two they crack and are cut to bits by the stems of the vines, which are spiny. In the mornings, before the cuts had reopened, my hands used to give me perfect agony, and even at the time of typing this (October 10th) they show the marks. Most of the people who go down hopping have done it every year since they were children, and they pick like lightning and know all the tricks, such as shaking the hops up to make them lie loose in the bin etc. The most successful pickers are families, who have two or three adults to strip the vines, and a couple of children to pick up the fallen hops and clear the odd strands. The laws about child labour are disregarded utterly, and some of the people drive their children pretty hard. The woman in the next bin to us, a regular old-fashioned East Ender, kept her grandchildren at it like slaves.—'Go on, Rose, you lazy little cat, pick them 'ops up. I'll warm your arse if I get up to you' etc. until the children, aged from 6 to 10, used to drop down and fall asleep on the ground. But they liked the work, and I don't suppose it did them more harm than school.

* The passage between crosses (at least the substance of it) has been used for an article in the Nation [Orwell's note. The second X is six paragraphs later]. For the article, see 116.
† Or hop-juice, funnily enough [Orwell's note].

As to what one can earn, the system of payment is this. Two or three times a day the hops are measured, and you are due a certain sum (in our case twopence) for each bushel you have picked. A good vine yields about half a bushel of hops, and a good picker can strip a vine in about 10 minutes, so that theoretically one might earn about 30/– by a sixty hour week. But in practice this is quite impossible. To begin with, the hops vary enormously. On some vines they are as large as small pears, and on others hardly bigger than peas; the bad vines take rather longer to strip than the good ones—they are generally more tangled—and sometimes it needs five or six of them to make a bushel. Then there are all kinds of delays, and the pickers get no compensation for lost time. Sometimes it rains (if it rains hard the hops get too slippery to pick), and one is always kept waiting when changing from field to field, so that an hour or two is wasted every day. And above all there is the question of measurement. Hops are soft things like sponges, and it is quite easy for the measurer to crush a bushel of them into a quart if he chooses. Some days he merely scoops the hops out, but on other days he has orders from the farmer to 'take them heavy', and then he crams them tight into the basket, so that instead of getting 20 bushels for a full bin one gets only 12 or 14—i.e. a shilling or so less. There was a song about this, which the old East End woman and her grandchildren were always singing:

Our lousy hops!
Our lousy hops!
When the measurer he comes round,
Pick 'em up, pick 'em up off the ground!
When he comes to measure
He never knows where to stop;
Ay, ay, get in the bin
And take the fucking lot!'

From the bin the hops are put into 10-bushel pokes which are supposed to weigh a hundredweight and are normally carried by one man. It used to take two men to hoist a full poke when the measurer had been taking them heavy.

With all these difficulties one can't earn 30/– a week or anything near it. It is a curious fact, though, that very few of the pickers were aware how little they really earned, because the piece-work system disguises the low rate of payment. The best pickers in our gang were a family of gypsies, five adults and a child, all of whom, of course, had picked hops every year since they could walk.[2] In a little under three weeks these people earned exactly £10 between them—i.e., leaving out the child, about 14/– a week each. Ginger and I earned about 9/– a week each, and I doubt if any individual picker made over 15/– a week. A family working together can make their keep and their fare back to London at these rates, but a single picker can hardly do even that. On some of the farms nearby the tally, instead of being 6 bushels to the shilling, was 8 or 9, at which one would have a hard job to earn 10/– a week.

When one starts work the farm gives one a printed copy of rules, which are designed to reduce a picker more or less to a slave. According to these rules the farmer can sack a picker without notice and on any pretext whatever, and pay him off at 8 bushels a shilling instead of six—i.e. confiscate a quarter of his earnings. If a picker leaves his job before the picking is finished, his earnings are docked the same amount. You cannot draw what you have earned and then clear off, because the farm will never pay you more than two thirds of your earnings in advance, and so are in your debt till the last day. The binmen (i.e. foremen of gangs) get wages instead of being paid on the piecework system, and these wages cease if there is a strike, so naturally they will raise Heaven and earth to prevent one. Altogether the farmers have the hop-pickers in a cleft stick, and always will have until there is a pickers' union. It is not much use to try and form a union, though, for about half the pickers are women and gypsies, and are too stupid to see the advantages of it.

As to our living accommodation, the best quarters on the farm, ironically enough, were disused stables. Most of us slept in round tin huts about 10 feet across, with no glass in the windows, and all kinds of holes to let in the wind and rain. The furniture of these huts consisted of a heap of straw and hop-vines, and nothing else. There were four of us in our hut, but in some of them there were seven or eight—rather an advantage, really, for it kept the hut warm. Straw is rotten stuff to sleep in (it is much more draughty than hay) and Ginger and I had only a blanket each, so we suffered agonies of cold for the first week; after that we stole enough pokes to keep us warm. The farm gave us free firewood, though not as much as we needed. The water tap was 200 yards away, and the latrine the same distance, but it was so filthy that one would have walked a mile sooner than use it. There was a stream where one could do some laundering, but getting a bath in the village would have been about as easy as buying a tame whale.

The hop-pickers seemed to be of three types: East Enders, mostly costermongers, gypsies, and itinerant agricultural labourers with a sprinkl-ing of tramps. The fact that Ginger and I were tramps got us a great deal of sympathy, especially among the fairly well-to-do people. There was one couple, a coster and his wife, who were like a father and mother to us. They were the kind of people who are generally drunk on Saturday nights and who tack a 'fucking' on to every noun, yet I have never seen anything that exceeded their kindness and delicacy. They gave us food over and over again. A child would come to the hut with a saucepan: 'Eric, mother was going to throw this stew away, but she said it was a pity to waste it. Would you like it?' Of course they were not really going to have thrown it away, but said this to avoid the suggestion of charity. One day they gave us a whole pig's head, ready cooked. These people had been on the road several years themselves, and it made them sympathetic.—'Ah, I know what it's like. Skippering in the fucking wet grass, and then got to tap the milkman in the morning before you can get a cup of tea. Two of my boys were born on the road' etc. Another man who was very decent to us was an employee in a paper factory. Before this he had been vermin-man to ——, and he told me that the dirt and vermin in ——'s kitchens, even [their headquarters], passed belief. When he worked at ——'s branch in T —— Street, the rats were so numerous that it was not safe to go into the kitchens at night unarmed; you had to carry a revolver.[3] After I had mixed with these people for a few days it was too much fag to go on putting on my cockney accent, and they noticed that I talked 'different'.

As usual, this made them still more friendly, for these people seem to think that it is especially dreadful to 'come down in the world'.

Out of about 200 pickers at Blests° farm, 50 or 60 were gypsies. They are curiously like oriental peasants—the same heavy faces, at once dull and sly, and the same sharpness in their own line and startling ignorance outside it. Most of them could not read even a word, and none of their children seemed ever to have gone to school. One gypsy, aged about 40, used to ask me such questions as, 'How far is Paris from France?' 'How many days' journey by caravan to Paris?' etc. A youth, aged twenty, used to ask this riddle half a dozen times a day.—'I'll tell you something you can't do?'— 'What?'— 'Tickle a gnat's arse with a telegraph pole.' (At this, never-failing yells of laughter.) The gypsies seem to be quite rich, owning caravans, horses etc. yet they go on all the year round working as itinerant labourers and saving money. They used to say that our way of life (living in houses etc.) seemed disgusting to them, and to explain how clever they had been in dodging the army during the war. Talking to them, you had the feeling of talking to people from another century. I often heard a gypsy say, 'If I knew where so and so was, I'd ride my horse till it hadn't a shoe left to catch him'—not a 20th century metaphor at all. One day some gypsies were talking about a noted horse-thief called George Bigland, and one man, defending him, said: 'I don't think George is as bad as you make out. I've known him to steal Gorgias' (Gentiles') horses, but he wouldn't go so far as to steal from one of us.'

The gypsies call us Gorgias and themselves Romanies, but they are nicknamed Didecais (not certain of spelling). They all knew Romany, and occasionally used a word or two when they didn't want to be understood. A curious thing I noticed about the gypsies—I don't know whether it is the same everywhere—was that you would often see a whole family who were totally unlike one another. It almost seems to countenance the stories about gypsies stealing children; more likely, though, it is because it's a wise child etc.

One of the men in our hut was the old deaf tramp we had met outside West Malling spike—Deafie, he was always called. He was rather a Mr F.'s aunt[4] in conversation, and he looked just like a drawing by George Belcher,[5] but he was an intelligent, decently educated man, and no doubt would not have been on the road if he could hear. He was not strong enough for heavy work, and he had done nothing for years past except odd jobs like hopping. He calculated that he had been in over 400 different spikes. The other man, named Barrett, and a man in our gang named George, were good specimens of the itinerant agricultural labourer. For years past they had worked on a regular round: Lambing in early spring, then pea-picking, strawberries, various other fruits, hops, 'spud-grabbing', turnips and sugar beet. They were seldom out of work for more than a week or two, yet even this was enough to swallow up anything they could earn. They were both penniless when they arrived at Blest's farm, and I saw Barret° work certainly one day without a bite to eat. The proceeds of all their work were the clothes they stood up in, straw to sleep on all the year round, meals of bread and chese° and bacon, and I suppose one or two good drunks a year. George was a dismal devil, and took a sort of worm-like pride in being underfed and overworked, and always tobying from job to job. His line was, 'It doesn't do for people like us to have fine ideas'. (He could not read or write, and seemed to think even literacy a kind of extravagance.) I know this philosophy well, having often met it among the dishwashers in Paris. Barrett, who was 63, used to complain a lot about the badness of food nowadays, compared with what you could get when he was a boy. — 'In them days we didn't live on this fucking bread and marg, we 'ad good solid tommy. Bullock's 'eart. Bacon dumpling. Black pudden. Pig's 'ead.' The glutinous, reminiscent tone in which he said 'pig's 'ead' suggested decades of underfeeding.

Besides all these regular pickers there were what are called 'home-dwellers'; i.e. local people who pick at odd times, chiefly for the fun of it. They are mostly farmers' wives and the like, and as a rule they and the regular pickers loathe one another. One of them, however, was a very decent woman, who gave Ginger a pair of shoes and me an excellent coat and waistcoat and two shirts. Most of the local people seemed to look on us as dirt, and the shopkeepers were very insolent, though betwee[n] us we must have spent several hundred pounds in the village.

One day at hop-picking was very much like another. At about a quarter to six in the morning we crawled out of the straw, put on our coats and boots (we slept in everything else) and went out to get a fire going—rather a job this September, when it rained all the time. By half past six we had made tea and fried some bread for breakfast, and then we started off for work, with bacon sandwiches and a drum of cold tea for our dinner. If it didn't rain we were working pretty steadily till about one, and then we would start a fire between the vines, heat up our tea and knock off for half an hour. After that we were at it again till half past five, and by the time we had got home, cleaned the hop juice off our hands and had tea, it was already dark and we were dropping with sleep. A good many nights, though, we used to go out and steal apples. There was a big orchard nearby, and three or four of us used to rob it systematically, carrying a sack and getting half a hundredweight of apples at a time, besides several pounds of cobnuts. On Sundays we used to wash our shirts and socks in the stream, and sleep the rest of the day. As far as I remember I never undressed completely all the time we were down there, nor washed my teeth, and I only shaved twice a week. Between working and getting meals (and that meant fetching everlasting cans of water, struggling with wet faggots, frying in tin-lids etc.) one seemed to have not an instant to spare. I only read one book all the time I was down there, and that was a Buffalo Bill. Counting up what we spent I find that Ginger and I fed ourselves on about 5/– a week each, so it is not surprising that we were constantly short of tobacco and constantly hungry, in spite of the apples and what the others gave us. We seemed to be forever doing sums in farthings to find out whether we could afford another half ounce of shag or another two-pennorth of bacon. It wasn't a bad life, but what with standing all day, sleeping rough and getting my hands cut to bits, I felt a wreck at the end of it. It was humiliating to see that most of the people there looked on it as a holiday—in fact, it is because hopping is regarded as a holiday that the pickers will take such *starvation wages. It gives one an insight into the lives of farm labourers, too, to realise that according to their standards hop-picking is hardly work at all.*

One night a youth knocked at our door and said that he was a new picker and had been told to sleep in our hut. We let him in and fed him in the morning, after which he vanished. It appeared that he was not a picker at all, but a tramp, and that tramps often work this dodge in the hopping season, in order to get a kip under shelter. Another night a woman who was going home asked me to help her get her luggage to Wateringbury station. As she was leaving early they had paid her off at eight bushels a shilling, and her total earnings were only just enough to get herself and family home. I had to push a perambulator, with one eccentric wheel and loaded with huge packages, two and a half miles through the dark, followed by a retinue of yelling children. When we got to the station the last train was just coming in, and in rushing the pram across the level crossing I upset it. I shall never forget that moment—the train bearing down on us, and the porter and I chasing a tin chamberpot that was rolling up the track. On several nights Ginger tried to persuade me to come and rob the church with him, and he would have done it alone if I had not managed to get it into his head that suspicion was bound to fall on him, as a known criminal. He had robbed churches before, and he said, what surprised me, that there is generally something worth having in the Poorbox. We had one or two jolly nights, on Saturdays, sitting round a huge fire till midnight and roasting apples. One night, I remember, it came out that of about fifteen people round the fire, everyone except myself had been in prison. There were uproarious scenes in the village on Saturdays, for the people who had money used to get well drunk, and it needed the police to get them out of the pub. I have no doubt the residents thought us a nasty vulgar lot, but I could not help feeling⁶ that it was rather good for a dull village to have this invasion of cockneys once a year.

1. *posters* is handwritten substitution for *parcels*.
2. *walk*]*work*
3. Names deleted on legal grounds.
4. Mr F.'s aunt is the aunt of Flora Finching's deceased husband in *Little Dorrit* by Dickens. Left in Flora's care, she was known simply as 'Mr F.'s Aunt.' Her major characteristics are described as 'extreme severity and grim taciturnity; sometimes interrupted by a propensity to offer remarks in a deep warning voice, which, being totally uncalled for by anything said by anybody, and traceable to no association of ideas, confounded and terrified the mind.' One interjection might have had special appeal for Orwell, who had lived at Henley-on-Thames as a child: 'Mr F.'s Aunt, after regarding the company for ten minutes with a malevolent gaze, delivered the following fearful remark. "When we lived at Henley, Barnes's gander was stole by tinkers" ' (chapter 13).
5. George Belcher (1875–1947) was a Royal Academician. His books of drawings included *Characters* (1922), *Taken from Life* (1929), and *Potted Char* (1933).
6. *help feeling*]*feel*

112. To Dennis Collings

4 September 1931   Handwritten

Mereworth   Kent

Dear Dennis,

I hope this does *not* find you as it leaves me, for we are slopping about here in the most apalling° seas of slush, unable to work & with no occupation but trying to start fires with wet wood. I have been here since the first & only done one full day's work. I had an interesting time coming down. Four of us set out with about 4/– between us, & until the 3rd we only had another 1/– between us, so you can imagine how we lived. The first day we got as far as Bromley, camped in a field & went on to Ide Hill. There 2 of us went into the spike, & my mate & I camped in a wood. The next day we went on through Sevenoaks to Seal, & walked about 10 miles from farm to farm trying to find a job. Finally we slept in an unfinished house, then went on to West Malling &, as it was pouring with rain, slept in the spike for the night. Next day we came down here & got a job. We got most of our food on the way by begging, & did not go short of anything except tobacco, but the cold & discomfort of sleeping out of doors are worse than you would believe. I have kept notes of all this in my diary, & later I will amplify these & send you a copy if it would interest you.

The mate I am with is an interesting type. Aged 26, has been 3 years in Borstal, 2 years in the army, 3 times in prison, married & widowed. He is & looks the typical petty burglar, but is really a very likeable fellow.

As to this hopping, it is a bloody swindle & only goes on because there is a large supply of casual labourers ready to do almost anything, & the East Enders rather like the trip to the country. The rate of pay here is 1/– for six bushels of hops. The working day is 9 or 10 hours, in which time an exceptionally skilful picker can pick about 20 bushels—i.e. 3/4d. My only full day I managed by half killing myself to pick 10 bushels, & hope to work up to 15 bushels a day later. On some farms the rate of payment is actually 1/– for 8 bushels. A law has recently been passed compelling farmers to give their hoppickers proper accommodation, which makes one wonder what sort of accommodation they got before. Here 4 of us live in a tin hut about 12 feet across, with no glass in the windows, letting in the rain & draughts on all sides, & furnished only with a large heap of straw. Here you shudder till about 5.45 am, then up, get a fire going & make tea, hurry out to the fields & pick till 12.30, when you knock off for half an hour for lunch. Then you pick again till about 5, then have more battles with fires, shave & get your supper, & so to bed at about 9 o'clock. All this for about 15/– a week. Still it is rather fun for a short while, & I shall at any rate be able to make a saleable newspaper article out of it.

I hope to write you a more interesting letter when I have got somewhere comfortable to sit (I have not sat in a chair for about 10 days), but for the moment here are one or two pieces of practical wisdom I have garnered. Treasure them, for who knows when you may be on the road yourself.

When boiling water over a wood fire, if you put a chip of wood in the water it will remove some of the smoky taste.

The only reliable tin for a billy (known as a 'drum') is a snuff tin, preferably a 2 lb. one. They are not easy to come by, as most tobacconists don't keep snuff.

You can always beg meat from a butcher on Saturday nights.

When sleeping in the open, it is warmer to take your coat off & put it over you than to wear it.

As to new words, here are some, but I think they are rather current slang than actual dialect words.

Drum up, to   =   to make a fire.
Toby, a   =   a tramp. (Also 'to toby', etc.)
Chat, a   =   a louse.
Pony, a   =   a shit.
Skipper, to   =   to sleep in the open.
Get   =   ? Word (noun) of abuse, but meaning uncertain.

By the way, I had thought that the 'rhyming slang' was quite extinct, but one occasionally hears it used here. 'A dig in the grave' for a shave, 'the hot cross bun' for the sun, etc. Give the enclosed to your father if you remember. It might interest him. I will write again later.

Yours
Eric A Blair

P.S. I have made further enquiries about the custom tramps used to have of marking doors where they had begged, to indicate what sort of reception they got. It appears to be quite extinct, & none of the tramps I have met have heard of it.

113. Hop-Picking Diary

<u>19.9.31:</u>   *On the last morning, when we had picked the last field, there was a queer game of catching the women and putting them in the bins. Very likely there will be something about this in the Golden Bough. It is evidently an old custom, and all harvests have some custom of this kind attached to them. The people who were illiterate or therabouts° brought their tally books to me and other 'scholars' to have them reckoned up, and some of them paid a copper or two to have it done. I found that in quite a number of cases the farm cashiers had made a mistake in the addition, and invariably the mistake was in favour of the farm. Of course the pickers got the sum due when they complained, but they would not have if they had accepted the farm cashier's reckoning. Moreover, the farm had a mean little rule that anyone who was going to complain about his tally book had to wait till all the other pickers had been paid off. This meant waiting till the afternoon, so that some people who had buses to catch had to go home without claiming the sum due to them. (Of course it was only a few coppers in most cases. One woman's book, however, was added up over £1 wrong.)*

Ginger and I packed our things and walked over to Wateringbury to catch the hoppickers' train. On the way we stopped to buy tobacco, and as a sort of farewell to Kent, Ginger cheated the tobacconist's girl of fourpence, by a very cunning dodge. When we got to Wateringbury station about fifty hoppers were waiting for the train, and the first person we saw was old Deafie, sitting on the grass with a newspaper in front of him. He lifted it aside, and we saw that he had his trousers undone and was exhibiting his penis to the women and children as they passed. I was surprised—such a decent old man, really; but there is hardly a tramp who has not some sexual abnormality. The Hoppers' train was ninepence cheaper than the ordinary fare, and it took nearly five hours to get us to London—30 miles. At about 10 at night the hop-pickers poured out at London Bridge station, a number of them drunk and all carrying bunches of hops; people in the street readily bought these bunches of hops, I dont know why. Deafie, who had travelled in our carriage, asked us into the nearest pub and stood us each a pint, the first beer I had had in three weeks. Then he went off to Hammersmith, and no doubt he will be on the bum till next year's fruit-picking begins.

On adding up our tally book, Ginger and I found that we had made just 26/- each by eighteen days' work. We had drawn 8/- each in advances (or 'subs' as they are called), and we had made another 6/- between us by selling stolen apples. After paying our fares we got to London with about 16/- each. So we had, after all, kept ourselves while we were in Kent and come back with a little in pocket; but we had only done it by living on the very minimum of everything.

19.9.31 to 8.10.31: Ginger and I went to a kip in Tooley Street, owned by Lew Levy who owns the one in Westminster Bridge Road. It is only seven-pence a night, and it is probably the best sevenpenny one in London. There are bugs in the beds, but not many, and the kitchens, though dark and dirty, are convenient, with abundant fires and hot water. The lodgers are a pretty low lot—mostly Irish unskilled labourers, and out of work at that. We met some queer types among them. There was one man, aged 68, who worked carrying crates of fish (they weigh a hundredweight each) in Billingsgate market. He was interested in politics, and he told me that on Bloody Sunday in '88 he had taken part in the rioting and been sworn in as a special constable on the same day. Another old man, a flower seller, was mad. Most of the time he behaved quite normally, but when his fits were on he would walk up and down the kitchen uttering dreadful beast-like yells, with an expression of agony on his face. Curiously enough, the fits only came on in wet weather. Another man was a thief. He stole from shop counters and vacant motor cars, especially commercial travellers' cars, and sold the stuff to a Jew in Lambeth Cut. Every evening you would see him smartening himself up to go 'up West'. He told me that he could count on £2 a week, with a big haul from time to time. He managed to swoop the till of a public house almost every Christmas, generally getting £40 or £50 by this. He had been stealing for years and only been caught once, and then was bound over. As always seems the case with thieves, his work brought him no good, for when he got a large sum he blued it instantly. He had one of the ignoblest faces I ever saw, just like a hyena's; yet he was likeable, and decent about sharing food and paying debts.

Several mornings Ginger and I worked helping the porters at Billingsgate. You go there at about five and stand at the corner of one of the streets which lead up from Billingsgate into Eastcheap. When a porter is having trouble to get his barrow up, he shouts 'Up the 'ill!' and you spring forward (there is fierce competition for the jobs, of course) and shove the barrow behind. The payment is 'twopence an up'. They take on about one shover-up for four hundredweight, and the work knocks it out of your thighs and elbows, but you don't get enough jobs to tire you out. Standing there from five till nearly midday, I never made more than 1/6d. If you are very lucky a porter takes you on as his regular assistant, and then you make about 4/6d a morning. The porters themselves seem to make about £4 or £5 a week. There are several things worth noticing about Billingsgate. One is that vast quantities of the work done there are quite unnecessary, being due to the complete lack of any centralised transport system. What with porters, barrowmen, shovers-up etc, it now costs round about £1 to get a ton of fish from Billingsgate to one of the London railway termini. If it were done in an orderly manner, by lorries, I suppose it would cost a few shillings. Another thing is that the pubs in Billingsgate are open at the hours when other pubs are shut. And another is that the barrowmen at Billingsgate do a regular traffic in stolen fish, and you can get fish dirt cheap if you know one of them.

After about a fortnight in the lodging house I found that I was writing nothing, and the place itself was beginning to get on my nerves, with its noise and lack of privacy, and the stifling heat of the kitchen, and above all the dirt. The kitchen had a permanent sweetish reek of fish, and all the sinks were blocked with rotting fish guts which stank horribly. You had to store your food in dark corners which were infested by black beetles and cockroaches, and there were clouds of horrible languid flies everywhere. The dormitory was also disgusting, with the perpetual din of coughing and spitting—everyone in a lodging house has a chronic cough, no doubt from the foul air. I had got to write some articles, which could not be done in such surroundings, so I wrote home for money and took a room in Windsor Street near the Harrow Road. Ginger has gone off on the road again. Most of this narrative was written in the Bermondsey public library, which has a good reading room and was convenient for the lodging house.

—— ooOoo ——

NOTES.

New words (i.e. words new to me) discovered this time.

Shackles . . . . broth or gravy.
Drum, a . . . . . a billy can. (With verb to drum up meaning to light a fire.)
Toby, on the . . on the tramp. (Also to toby, and a toby, meaning a tramp. Slang Dictionary gives the toby as the highroad.)

Chat, a . . . . . . .a louse. (Also chatty, lousy. S.D. gives this but not a chat.)
Get, a . . . . ? (Word of abuse, meaning unknown.)[2]
Didecai, a . . . . . a gypsy.
Sprowsie, a . . . . a sixpence.
Hard-up . . . . . . tobacco made from fag ends. (S.D. gives a hard-up as a
man who collects fag ends.)
Skipper, to . . . . to sleep out. (S.D. gives a skipper as a barn.)
Scrump, to . . . . to steal.
Knock off, to . . .to arrest.
Jack off, to . . . . to go away.
Jack, on his . . . . on his own.
Clods . . . . coppers[1]

Burglars' slang.

A stick, or a cane a jemmy. (S.D. gives stick.)
Peter a . . . . . . .a safe. (In S.D.)
Bly,* a . . . . . . .an oxy-acetylene blowlamp

Use of the word 'tart' among the East Enders. *This word now seems
absolutely interchangeable with 'girl', with no implication of 'prostitute'.
People will speak of their daughter or sister as a tart.*

Rhyming slang. *I thought this was extinct, but it is far from it. The hop-
pickers used these expressions freely: A dig in the grave, meaning a shave.
The hot cross bun, meaning the sun. Greengages, meaning wages. They also
used the abbreviated rhyming slang, e.g. 'Use your twopenny' for 'Use your
head.' This is arrived at like this: Head, loaf of bread, loaf, twopenny loaf,
twopenny.*

Homosexual vice in London. *It appears that one of the great rendezvous is
Charing Cross underground station. It appeared to be taken for granted by
the people on Trafalgar Square that youths could earn a bit this way, and
several said to me, 'I need never sleep out if I choose to go down to Charing
Cross.' They added that the usual fee is a shilling.*

*. *I forgot to mention that these lamps are hired out to burglars. Ginger said that he had paid
£3.10.0 a night for the use of one. So also with other burglars' tools of the more elaborate
kinds. When opening a puzzle-lock, clever safe-breakers use a stethoscope to listen to the click
of the tumblers* [Orwell's note].

1. Clods . . .coppers] *interlinear insertion.*
2. Presumably the contemporary 'git' (roughly, as in 'you git,' an ignorant fool). Compare the
Scots, 'gyte' (pronounced 'git'), formerly used for a child.

114. To Dennis Collings

Monday night, [12 October 1931]   Handwritten

2 Windsor St   London W.9

Dear Dennis,

Herewith the narrative[1] of my adventures. Much of it repeats what I have told you before, but I wanted a full account for my own future reference. Keep it for me, will you? You will excuse carbon copy & bad typing. Please show it to Mr Pullein,[2] who wanted to hear about my experiences. Also to Eleanor Jaques if she would care to see it, but don't let it go any further. Please also (I am assuming you are in S'wold) tell them both[3] I will write to them soon.

The above will be my adress° till further notice. I am pretty busy, as I am getting stories etc to do for the new paper Modern Youth. (A poisonous name for a poisonous paper—& the things I write for them are also poisonous, but one must live.)

Yours
Eric A Blair

P.S. A shop near here sells mandrakes, but I'm afraid they won't have been procured in the correct manner. Remind me sometime to tell you an interesting thing about werwolves.°[4]

1. The Hop-Picking Diary.
2. Collett ('Uncle Colin') Cresswell Pulleyne, a barrister from Yorkshire, was a friend of Blair and Collings in Southwold. Orwell had some difficulty in spelling this name correctly.
3. Orwell's parents.
4. This letter is adorned with several doodles, three including the syllables 'Med,' 'Ten,' and 'Scand,' but the writing and drawings do not look like Orwell's work.

115. From a letter to Brenda Salkeld

[October 1931?][1]

I have been doing a good deal of work, & hope to do a good deal more for the new paper 'Modern Youth', tho' I'm afraid they won't give me a regular job. It is to appear on the 29th, & from the advance copy I have seen looks a pretty poisonous rag—something for the young business man who is not yet tired, but will be later in life. They only commission me to do stupid things, but we must live, of course. I don't know what the paper's chances of survival are, but I should say good as—at any rate, they have pots of money.

1. This excerpt was quoted by Brenda Salkeld in a letter to Ian Angus, 7 April 1963. The rest of the letter has not survived, as she confirmed, 25 March 1984.

116. 'Hop-Picking,'[1]
The New Statesman and Nation,[2] 17 October 1931

"A holiday with pay." "Keep yourself all the time you're down there, pay your fare both ways and come back five quid in pocket." I quote the words of two experienced hop-pickers, who had been down into Kent almost every season since they were children, and ought to have known better. For as a matter of fact hop-picking is far from being a holiday, and, as far as wages go, no worse employment exists.

I do not mean by this that hop-picking is a disagreeable job in itself. It entails long hours, but it is healthy, outdoor work, and any able-bodied person can do it. The process is extremely simple. The vines, long climbing plants with the hops clustering on them in bunches like grapes, are trained up poles or over wires; all the picker has to do is to tear them down and strip the hops into a bin, keeping them as clean as possible from leaves. The spiny stems cut the palms of one's hands to pieces, and in the early morning, before the cuts have reopened, it is painful work; one has trouble too with the plant-lice which infest the hops and crawl down one's neck, but beyond that there are no annoyances. One can talk and smoke as one works, and on hot days there is no pleasanter place than the shady lanes of hops, with their bitter scent—an unutterably refreshing scent, like a wind blowing from oceans of cool beer. It would be almost ideal if one could only earn a living at it.

Unfortunately, the rate of payment is so low that it is quite impossible for a picker to earn a pound a week, or even, in a wet year like 1931, fifteen shillings. Hop-picking is done on the piece-work system, the pickers being paid at so much a bushel. At the farm where I worked this year, as at most farms in Kent, the tally was six bushels to the shilling—that is, we were paid twopence for each bushel we picked. Now, a good vine yields about half a bushel of hops, and a good picker can strip a vine in ten or fifteen minutes; it follows that an expert picker might, given perfect conditions, earn thirty shillings in a sixty-hour week. But, for a number of reasons, these perfect conditions do not exist. To begin with, hops vary enormously in quality. On some vines they are as large as small pears, on others no bigger than hazel nuts; the bad vines take as long to strip as the good ones—longer, as a rule, for their lower shoots are more tangled—and often five of them will not yield a bushel. Again, there are frequent delays in the work, either in changing from field to field, or on account of rain; an hour or two is wasted in this manner every day, and the pickers are paid no compensation for lost time. And, lastly, the greatest cause of loss, there is unfair measurement. The hops are measured in bushel baskets of standard size, but it must be remembered that hops are not like apples or potatoes, of which one can say that a bushel *is* a bushel and there is an end of it. They are soft things as compressible as sponges, and it is quite easy for the measurer to crush a bushel of them into a quart if he chooses. As the hop-pickers often sing—

> When he comes to measure,
> He never knows where to stop;

> Ay, ay, get in the bin,
> And take the bloody lot!

From the bin the hops are put into pokes, which are supposed when full to weigh a hundredweight, and are normally carried by one man. But it often needs two men to handle a full poke, when the measurer has been "taking them heavy."

With these working conditions a friend and myself earned, this September, about nine shillings a week each. We were new to the job, but the experienced pickers did little better. The best pickers in our gang, and among the best in the whole camp, were a family of gypsies, five adults and a child; these people, spending ten hours a day in the hop-field, earned just ten pounds between them in three weeks. Leaving the child out of account (though as a matter of fact all the children in the hop-field work) this was an average of thirteen and fourpence a week each. There were various farms nearby where the tally was eight or nine bushels to the shilling, and where even twelve shillings a week would have been hard to earn. Besides these starvation wages, the hop-picker has to put up with rules which reduce him practically to a slave. One rule, for instance, empowers a farmer to sack his employees on any pretext whatever, and in doing so to confiscate a quarter of their earnings; and the picker's earnings are also docked if he resigns his job. It is no wonder that itinerant agricultural labourers, most of whom are in work ten months of the year, travel "on the toby" and sleep in the casual ward between jobs.

As to the hop-pickers' living accommodation, there is now a whole tribe of Government officials to supervise it, so presumably it is better than it used to be. But what it can have been like in the old days is hard to imagine, for even now the ordinary hop-picker's hut is worse than a stable. (I say this advisedly: on our farm the best quarters, specially set apart for married people, *were* stables.) My friend and I, with two others, slept in a tin hut ten feet across, with two unglazed windows and half a dozen other apertures to let in the wind and rain, and no furniture save a heap of straw: the latrine was two hundred yards away, and the water tap the same distance. Some of these huts had to be shared by eight men—but that, at any rate, mitigated the cold, which can be bitter on September nights when one has no bedding but a disused sack. And, of course, there were all the normal discomforts of camp life; not serious hardships, but enough to make sure that when we were not working or sleeping we were either fetching water or trying to coax a fire out of wet sticks.

I think it will be agreed that these are thoroughly bad conditions of pay and treatment. Yet the curious thing is that there is no lack of pickers, and what is more, the same people return to the hop-fields year after year. What keeps the business going is probably the fact that the Cockneys rather enjoy the trip to the country, in spite of the bad pay and in spite of the discomfort. When the season is over the pickers are heartily glad—glad to be back in London, where you do not have to sleep on straw, and you can put a penny in the gas instead of hunting for firewood, and Woolworth's is round the corner—but still, hop-picking is in the category of things that are great fun when they are over. It figures in the pickers' mind as a holiday, though they are working hard all the time and out of pocket at the end. And besides this there is the piece-work system, which disguises the low rate of payment; for "six bushels a shilling" sounds much more than "fifteen shillings a week." And there is the tradition of the good times ten years ago, when hops were dear and the farmers could pay sixpence a bushel; this keeps alive the tales about "coming home five quid in pocket." At any rate, whatever the cause, there is no difficulty in getting people to do the work, so perhaps one ought not to complain too loudly about the conditions in the hop-fields. But if one sets pay and treatment against work done, then a hop–picker is appreciably worse off than a sandwich-man.

ERIC BLAIR

1. Adapted from Orwell's Hop-Picking Diary; see *111*.
2. *The New Statesman* was founded 12 April 1913; it incorporated *Nation and Athenaeum*, 28 February 1931. *Nation* had been founded as *The Speaker*, 4 January 1890; the name was changed 2 March 1907; it absorbed *The Athenaeum*, founded 2 January 1828, on 19 February 1921. Orwell contributed more than twenty items to *The New Statesman and Nation*, mainly reviews, but including 'Hop-Picking,' 'Common Lodging Houses' (*141*), and a short article on Charles Reade (*671*).

117. To T. S. Eliot

30 October 1931   Handwritten

2 Windsor Street   London W. 9

Dear Mr Eliot,[1]
I am writing to you personally, as Richard Rees tells me that he has spoken to you on my behalf. I have just read a rather interesting French novel called A la Belle de Nuit,[2] by Jacques Roberti. It is the story of a prostitute, quite true to life so far as one can judge, & most ruthlessly told, but not a mere exploitation of a dirty subject. It seems to me worth translating, & if Messrs. Faber & Faber would like to try a translation I think I could do the job as well as most people. I don't pretend to have a scholarly knowledge of French, but I am used to mixing in the kind of French society described in the novel, & I know French slang, if not well, better than the majority of Englishmen. I don't know whether such a book would sell, but I believe Zola's novels sell in England, & this author seems to have some resemblances to Zola.

Perhaps you will let me know whether Messrs. Faber & Faber would like to hear more of this? If they would like to see the book I can send it along, or translate a few pages as a specimen. I see that the translation rights are reserved, but I suppose that could be fixed up if it were decided to translate.

Yours truly
Eric Blair

1. T. S. Eliot was a director of the publishing firm Faber & Faber at this time.
2. Orwell did not always underline titles or enclose them within quotation marks.

118. To Brenda Salkeld

Saturday night, [October 1931]   Handwritten

2 Windsor St.   W. 9[1]

Dearest Brenda,

Thank you so much for your letter, which persuades me that you have not quite forgotten me after all. I am going to leave the above adress,° as there is a yapping dog here which gets on my nerves, but I will let you know my new one, & in any case they will forward a letter if you write here. Modern Youth have postponed publication till the 19th as their printers went bankrupt. I have finished the things I was doing for them & have been able to make a start with my new novel. I am also trying to persuade some publishers to let me translate a French novel for them. I'm afraid they'll junk it (it is the life history of a prostitute & extremely realistic; I should think reading it would put any girl off the primrose path) but it is worth trying. By the way, did you say you collected signatures? I have T. S. Eliot's signature if you want it. He is reader to these publishers.

This afternoon, wanting to be in a gloomy frame of mind in order to get on with what I was writing, I went into Kensal Rise[2] cemetry°. The inscriptions on the tombstones sent me into such paroxysms of laughter that all gloom was gone for the day. One gentlemen, I remember, "entered into Heaven in a happy & peaceful reliance upon the merits of his Saviour." The thought entered my mind that all these tombstones & epitaphs are, after all, a last attempt on the part of the corpse to get himself noticed & talked about, & that really an epitaph which gives one a good laugh accomplishes this better than another. When you see some huge hideous slab of granite you know that the dead creature underground is saying in effect "you SHALL notice me", but something comic would be much more to the point. If I ever get time to compose my epitaph I shall take care to make it an amusing one. Funerals also ought to be comic, though for another reason. I mean because death would cease to be horrible if one could see it as something funny.

Have you read anything interesting? I got hold of an interesting book called "What was the Gunpowder Plot?" by John Gerard S.J. Of course the S.J.[3] makes you look askance, but the book was written back in the 'nineties before the present barrage of R.C. propaganda had reached its height. The thesis is that the Gunpowder Plot was a sort of Zinovieff Letter[4] scheme got up by Cecil[5] & Co. as propaganda against the Catholics. His documentary evidence, which of course I can't judge, seems very strong, & in any case if you think of it there is strong a priori presumption against such a story being true. For example, how could anyone have dug a mine under the House of Parliament undetected, much more smuggled in 18 barrels of powder? I also read General Spears' "Liaison 1914", quite interesting, & Coulton's "Mediaeval Scene", a popularisation of his books on the Middle Ages. Coulton is a man at whose name all good Catholics make the sign of the evil eye. Also "Guilty but Insane"[6]—atrociously written but interesting matter.

It is glorious weather here. These autumn days, when the sun only overcomes the mist after a fearful struggle, remind me of an old man getting over his yearly attack of flu. I forget whether I mentioned that simile to you, but it is an idea that would make a good rondeau. And talking of rondeaux, I saw in a notice of the Public Health people the delightful remark "Consumptives should refrain from kissing." What a good refrain for a ballade—but I can only think of 3 rhymes to it & one of these is unprintable.

I hope Dennis gave you my ms. I told him to. Write soon. I do so like seeing your handwriting on the envelope.

With love
Eric

1. It is not known when Orwell left Windsor Street; on 6 January, he wrote to Leonard Moore from the Fierzes' house in Golders Green.
2. An error for Kensal Green. See G. K. Chesterton's reference in 'The Rolling English Road': 'Before we go to Paradise by way of Kensal Green.'
3. The Society of Jesus (Jesuits).
4. Grigory Yevseyevich Zinovyev (1883–1936) was one of the architects of the Russian Revolution of 1917. With Stalin and Kamenev, he was instrumental in preventing Trotsky from succeeding Lenin. He later fell out of favour, was expelled from the Communist Party and readmitted more than once, and was executed in 1936. In 1924, a letter allegedly from him as chairman of the Communist International (the Comintern) was published in the London press. It supported subversive activity, and, though a forgery, played a part in the fall of the first Labour government of Britain. It was the archetypal 'red scare.'
5. Sir Robert Cecil (1563?–1612); 1st Earl of Salisbury, 1605), Chief Minister to King James I of England. It has been argued that he acted as agent provocateur to the Gunpowder Plot conspirators in 1605.
6. Unidentified. *Guilty but Insane*, a legal book by Professor G. W. Keeton, did not appear until 1961. Orwell may refer to Sefton Kyle's novel *"Guilty, but—,"* published by Herbert Jenkins in 1927; cheap edition, January 1930. Jenkins also published *Guilty but Not Insane*, by J. C. Lenehan, but no edition before 1938 has been traced.

119. To T. S. Eliot

4 November 1931   Handwritten

2 Windsor.° St.   W. 9

Dear Mr Eliot,

Thank you for your letter—I am sending "A la Belle de Nuit" under a separate cover. As I said, I think it ought to have more chance in England than most French novels.[1] If Messrs. Faber & Faber ever want any other French books translated, I should be very much obliged if they would give me a trial. I am anxious to get hold of some work of this kind, & I think I could do it as well as the average translator.

Yours truly
Eric A Blair

1. Neither Faber & Faber nor any other publisher commissioned this translation from Orwell. A translation by Samuel Putnam was published in New York as *Without Sin* in 1932.

120. To Christy & Moore [Leonard Moore]

[November–December 1931][1] Handwritten

At The Kiln Wisboro' Green nr. Billingshurst Sussex

Dear Sir,

Mrs Sinclair Fierz[2] tells me that she has spoken to you about me, & that you would like to see some of my work. I doubt whether I have anything in hand at the moment which will be of the smallest use to you, but I am sending two short stories[3] which you *might* be able to use. There is also the ms. of a book, about which I think Mrs Fierz spoke to you, but I am sending that to Faber & Faber. I recently did 2 short stories for the periodical "Modern Youth", which I now hear has collapsed. If I can get the ms. of these stories back I will send them to you, as I think they should both be easily[4] saleable. Please communicate with me at

2 Queen St
Southwold
Suffolk.

Yours faithfully
Eric A Blair

P.S. I should think these stories would want retyping if they were to be tried on any magazines—They have been by me a long time & one has been sent to a magazine who rejected it. I am sending them for you to have a look at, however.

1. This was written to the man who was to become Orwell's literary agent in 1932, Leonard Moore of Christy & Moore. From the reference to *Modern Youth's* collapse (which it had not done when he wrote to Dennis Collings and Brenda Salkeld; see *114* and *115*), this letter must be later than 12 October 1931. *Modern Youth* failed because the printer's bills were not paid; and because the printer seized all the copy, Orwell became an innocent victim of their action (Crick, 219). Copies of *Modern Youth* have not been traced. Leonard Moore died in January 1959.
2. Mrs Mabel Sinclair Fierz; see *102, n. 1.*
3. One was 'An Idiot,' the return of which was requested by Orwell in a letter to Moore on 6 January 1932; see *121.*
4. easily] equally.

1932

121. To Leonard Moore

6 January 1932   Handwritten

At. 1B Oakwood Rd   Golders Green   N.W

Dear Sir,

Thanks very much for your letter. I am sorry you had the trouble of reading those stories, which I did not think would be of much use to you. Will you please send me as soon as possible, at the above adress,° the story called An Idiot? I want to give it to the Adelphi, who will print it for me.[1] As to the other, shy it away, as it is worth nothing. I am going to make an effort during this week to recover the two stories I did for Modern Youth. It appears that the printers siezed° them, as Modern Youth's account with them was not paid. I don't know, but it seems to me that they have no rights over these manuscripts, which cannot have been the property of Modern Youth, since the° none of the authors were paid. If so be that I *can't* get the ms. back, I will re-do the stories from memory when I get an opportunity. One of them I think I have a copy of somewhere, the other—unfortunately the more saleable one—I shall have to rewrite entirely. However, I will try the printers.

I haven't heard from Fabers about that book.[2] If they *do* accept it, which I am afraid is unlikely, I will put them in touch with you. But if they won't have it I doubt whether anyone else would, as it was sent to T. S. Eliot with a personal recommendation from a friend of his.[3] Also, the Adelphi will print bits of it if the publishers reject it, so I shall make a bit that way. Could you by any chance put me in touch with anyone who wants either translation or annotation done? I know French thoroughly & Spanish pretty well, & I have specialised knowledge on one or two subjects.

Yours faithfully
Eric A Blair

1. 'An Idiot' was not published in *The Adelphi* or elsewhere. The typescript has not been traced.
2. *Down and Out in Paris and London.* An account of the progress of this book towards its publication is in Crick, 223–34, and Stansky and Abrahams, I, 263–69.
3. Presumably Richard Rees, then editor of *The Adelphi*; see *124*.

122. To T. S. Eliot

Wednesday, [17 February 1932]   Handwritten postcard; dated from postmark

Westminster Chambers   Westminster Bridge Rd.   S.E

Dear Mr Eliot,
I rang you up today about a ms. of mine[1] & you were kind enough to say you would have a look at it shortly. I forgot to say, if you are writing any time before *Saturday*, could you please send it to the above adress°?[2]

Yours truly
Eric A Blair

1. *Down and Out in Paris and London.*
2. Faber & Faber's register notes that 'A Scullion's Diary' by E. Blair was received on 14 December 1931 and rejected on 25 February 1932; see Crick, 605, n. 44.

123. The Hawthorns Private School

About 14 April 1932, Orwell started work as a teacher at The Hawthorns, a small private school for boys in Station Road (later renamed Church Road), Hayes, Middlesex. He worked there until the end of the summer term of 1933, and in September 1933 began teaching at Frays College, Uxbridge, Middlesex. While at The Hawthorns, Orwell wrote and produced a school play, an experience that provided material for *A Clergyman's Daughter*. The play has survived; see *154*. For Orwell's time at The Hawthorns, see Crick, 220–23 and especially the note on 606–07, which comments on the account given in Stansky and Abrahams, I, 262 and II, 23–35. The school, as it was in 1984 (Fountain House Hotel), is illustrated in Thompson, 38. See also Shelden, 171–72; U.S.: 156.

124. To Leonard Moore

26 April 1932   Typewritten; handwritten postscript

The Hawthorns   Station Rd.   Hayes   Middlesex

Dear Mr Moore,
Thank you for your letter. The history of the ms. "Days in London and Paris" is this. About a year and a half ago I completed a book of this description, but shorter (about 35000 words), and after taking advice I sent it to Jonathan Cape. Cape's said they would like to publish it but it was too short and fragmentary (it was done in diary form), and that they might be disposed to take it if I made it longer. I then put in some things I had left out, making the ms. you have, and sent it back to Capes,° who again rejected it. That was last September. Meanwhile a friend who was editor of a magazine

had seen the first ms., and he said that it was worth publishing and spoke about it to T. S. Eliot, who is a reader to Faber and Faber. Eliot said the same as Cape's— i.e. that the book was interesting[1] but much too short. I left the ms. you have with Mrs Sinclair Fierz and asked her to throw it away, as I did not think it a good piece of work, but I suppose she sent it to you instead. I should of course be very pleased if you could sell it, and it is very kind of you to take the trouble of trying. No publishers have seen it except Faber's and Cape's. If by any chance you *do* get it accepted, will you please see that it is published pseudonymously, as I am not proud of it. I have filled up the form you sent, but I have put in a clause that I only want an agent for dealings with publishers. The reason is this. I am now very busy teaching in a school, and I am afraid that for some months I shan't be able to get on with any work except occasional reviews or articles and I get the commissions for these myself. But there is a novel[2] that I began some months ago and shall go on with next holidays, and I dare say it will be finished within a year: I will send it to you then. If you could get me any French or Spanish books to translate into English I would willingly pay you whatever commission you think right, for I like that kind of work. There is also a long poem describing a day in London which I am doing, and it *may* be finished before the end of this term. I will send you that too if you like, but I should not think there is any money for anybody in that kind of thing. As to those stories[3] you have I should shy them away, as they are not really worth bothering with.

Yours truly
Eric A Blair

P.S. I tried to get Chatto & Windus to give me some of Zola's novels to translate, but they wouldn't. I should think somebody might be willing to translate Zola—he has been done, but atrociously badly.[4] Or what about Huysmans? I can't believe "Sainte Lydwine de Schiedam" has been translated into English. I also tried to get Faber's to translate a novel called "A la Belle de Nuit", by Jacques Roberti. It is very good but apallingly° indecent, & they refused it on that ground. I should think somebody might take it on—do you know anybody who isn't afraid of that kind of thing? (The book isn't pornographic, only rather sordid.) I could get hold of the copy I had & send it if necessary. I could also translate old° French, at least anything since 1400 A.D.

1. interesting] too interesting
2. *Burmese Days.*
3. These stories do not appear to have survived.
4. Zola's novels had been published in England by Henry Vizetelly (1820–1894), who also established the Mermaid Series of Dramatists and published translations of Dostoevski, Flaubert, and Tolstoy. The publication in English of Zola's *La Terre* (though 'amended') led to Vizetelly's being fined and in 1889 jailed on the charge of obscenity. The caution of British publishers at the time Orwell was starting to appear in print is not therefore unreasonable. See Textual Note to *A Clergyman's Daughter, CW,* III.

125. Review of *The Civilization of France* by Ernst Robert Curtius; translated by Olive Wyon

The Adelphi, May 1932

This book is an attempt to sum up, from a purely cultural, non-political point of view, the special contribution that France makes to civilisation. It is written by a German, and a terrifically learned one, but its general attitude to life and thought is quite of the English stamp. In effect Herr Curtius's criticism of France is that a German finds the French intelligence very much *smaller* than his own, though more perfected and perhaps more adult, rather as one might feel if one met a man from antiquity face to face. Thus "a Hegel, a Schopenhauer, a Nietzsche are unthinkable in France. They would destroy the garden of civilization° and the realm of humanity. The sense of infinity cannot live freely within French philosophy." In other words, French culture is classical and anthropocentric, and to those outside the classical tradition it looks rather like a strait-waistcoat, though an exceedingly elegant one. This is the sum of Herr Curtius's conclusions, and, apart from the scholarship shown, it is very much what would be said by any well-informed Englishman.

However, the real interest in a comparison between different countries lies in the historical question. Granted that French thought is by nature classical and static, and that France now contrasts with England or Germany far more than she did in the eighteenth century, how did the difference arise? Herr Curtius traces it partly to Rome (the French being the conscious inheritors of the Roman culture), and partly to special racial characteristics which the French derive from their mixed ancestry. No doubt these have had their influence, but surely recent life, especially recent economic life, is more important than remote Celts and Latins? If one looks at the history of the nineteenth century one sees that France, with her settled agricultural life and unsettled politics, could not possibly have developed the same culture as a truly modern country. Throughout that century countries like England were being urbanised and regimented with enormous speed, and at the same time the mass of the people were being more and more dispossessed; while France, until very recently, was really living in an earlier age—an age of weak government, strong public opinion, and comparatively wide distribution of property. Even now the French are far more nearly a race of peasants than we are. And peasants as a rule have perfect taste but few new ideas, and they are utterly incurious about Nature—a character which agrees with the general character of French literature. The ruling impression that one gets from living in France is that the French are not essentially different from ourselves, but simply, for good and evil, a little behind the times.

Apart from matters of taste, there are other French traits which can be explained simply as non-modern habits of thought. Take for instance the enthusiasm for justice, which Herr Curtius rightly names as a French characteristic, and which is really a symptom of old-fashioned radicalism. A few days before Sacco and Vanzetti were executed[1] I was standing on the steps of one of the English banks in Marseilles, talking to the clerks, while an immense procession of working people streamed past, bearing banners inscribed *"Sauvons Sacco et Vanzetti!"* etc. It was the kind of thing that one might have seen in England in the eighteen forties, but surely never in the nineteen twenties. All these people—tens of thousands of them—were genuinely indignant over a piece of injustice, and thought it quite natural to lose a day's wages in order to say so. It was instructive to hear the clerks (English) saying "Oh well, you've got to hang these blasted anarchists," and to see their half-shocked surprise when one asked whether Sacco and Vanzetti were guilty of the crime for which they had been condemned. In England, a century of strong government has developed what O. Henry called "the stern and rugged fear of the police" to a point where any public protest seems an indecency. But in France everyone can remember a certain amount of civil disturbance, and even the workmen in the bistros talk of *la revolution*— meaning the next revolution, not the last one. The highly socialised modern mind, which makes a kind of composite god out of the rich, the government, the police and the larger newspapers, has not been developed—at least, not yet.

One says not *yet*, because it is a question whether France will keep the special place which she now holds in civilisation. Herr Curtius sees national culture chiefly as a matter of tradition, and he thinks that the French tradition is too strong and too self-sufficing to change. On the other hand, if it is economic life that decides the colour of men's thoughts, then the French mind is bound to change, and that rapidly. Since the war France has definitely become an industrial country, and the processes that we connect with industrialism—for instance, the desertion of the land by the younger peasants and the destruction of the small trader—have at least begun. Given a continuance of this, what seem to be the most deeply-rooted French characteristics may vanish. Herr Curtius notices, for instance, the French lack of colour-prejudice, and sets this down to some special racial quality which is lacking in Englishmen and Germans. Yet the Englishman of the eighteenth century seems to have had very little colour-prejudice; therefore the growth of this nasty emotion is in some way connected with our recent history, and for all we know the French will soon possess it to the full Kipling-power. The French intellect as we now know it is typified by, perhaps, La Fontaine; yet surely the type would change after a century of up-to-date mechanical civilisation? Perhaps in A.D.2000 the French will be producing their Wordsworth, their Dr. Bowdler, their Whitman, their General Booth—or anyone else who, at this moment, would seem flagrantly un-French.

One of Herr Curtius's opinions is specially worth noticing, and that is that the Catholic Church is steadily gaining power in France, and has won what amounts to a victory over the State; bad news, but not surprising after what we have seen of the Church's recuperative powers in England.

For an account of French literature and thought, and a brief history of France on the non-political side, this book is useful and interesting. The translation seems to be excellent.

ERIC BLAIR

1. They were executed on 22 August 1927. Orwell was returning from Burma.

126. To the Editor, *The New English Weekly*[1]

5 May 1932

Sir,—May I draw attention to some remarks about the late Ivar Kreuger,[2] made by Sir Arthur Salter in one of his radio lectures on The Problem of World Government?

The 'Listener' for March 23 quotes Sir Arthur Salter as follows: "Since I gave my last talk the world is poorer by an incalculable loss. In the sphere of economic and financial organisation, Mr. Ivar Kreuger was, in my belief, the greatest man of our age, both in achievement and in intrinsic personal quality. He had constructed with creative vision, with unrivalled ability, with stupendous success," etc., etc. Those who listened-in on that night will agree that the "Listener" gives only the feeblest idea of Sir Arthur's panegyric, which lasted for five or ten minutes, and was delivered in lachrymose tones and in a style that recalled Cleopatra lamenting over the corpse of Antony.[3]

Now that "the greatest man of our age" is discovered to have committed, among other things, a little matter of forgery involving £21,000,000, perhaps comment is superfluous. But I should like to point out that Sir Arthur Salter is an acknowledged financial expert, and that he made these remarks in an official lecture to a circle of study-groups, whom he was supposed to be leading, via the League of Nations, to one of Mr. H. G. Wells' Utopias.

Eric A. Blair

1. The *New English Weekly: A Review of Public Affairs, Literature and the Arts* was founded by A. R. Orage (1873–1934) on 21 April 1932 and edited by him until his death. Philip Mairet then took over the editorship. It was amalgamated with *The New Age*, which Orage had founded in 1907, and which he edited until 1922, on 22 December 1938. Publication ceased with Vol. 35, no. 24, 22 September 1949. Orwell reviewed frequently for it until 1940, and it published his 'In Defence of the Novel' and 'Spilling the Spanish Beans' (two parts).
2. Ivar Kreuger (1880–1932), Swedish financier who tried to monopolise the production of matches, committed suicide in Paris on 12 March 1932. It was later found that he had falsified his accounts. Many of the subsidiary companies under his control were bankrupted as a result.
3. See *104, n. 2.*

127. Review of *The Spirit of Catholicism* by Karl Adam; translated by Dom Justin McCann, O.S.B.

New English Weekly, 9 June 1932

This is a notable book, and well worth reading, though it contains too many sentences of this type:

"Since the community and not the individual is the bearer of the spirit of Jesus, and since its visibility consists especially in the manifestation of this essential unity, therefore the visible organism of the Church postulates for its visibility a real principle of unity in which the supra-personal unity of all the faithful obtains perceptible expression and which supports, maintains and protects this unity."

It is hard work to dredge a meaning out of such morasses of words, but no one who is interested in the present revival of Catholicism will find the trouble wasted.

What distinguishes this book from the current drizzle of Catholic propaganda is that it is more or less non-controversial. Our English Catholic apologists are unrivalled masters of debate, but they are on their guard against saying anything genuinely informative. Few of them have any object beyond self-justification; their writings, therefore, are either a stream of cheery insult at biologists and Protestant historians, or an attempt to bluff the fundamental difficulties of faith out of existence. Father Adam does not proceed on these lines. He is not trying to prove any particular adversary a fool but rather to show what goes on inside the Catholic soul, and he hardly bothers to argue about the philosophical basis of faith. It is interesting to compare his book with some English book of similar tendency—for instance, with Father Martindale's recent book, "The Roman Faith." The contrast between the Catholic who simply believes, and the convert who must for ever be justifying his conversion, is like the contrast between a Buddha and a performing fakir. Father Martindale, being committed to the statement that faith is essentially reasonable, can neither stand up to his difficulties nor ignore them. Consequently he evades them, with considerable nimbleness. He sails over the theory of evolution in a sort of logical balloon-flight, with common sense flung overboard for ballast; he dodges past the problem of evil like a man dodging past his creditor's doorway—and so on. Father Adam, who has started by saying that faith is not to be approached in the same spirit as "the profane sciences," has no need of these tricks. With a creed that is safe from "profane" criticism, he is in a very strong position; it gives him the chance to develop his own ideas, and to say something constructive and interesting.

What, then, can the non-Catholic, learn from this book about the Catholic faith? Well, in one sense nothing, for there can be little real contact of mind between believer and unbeliever. As Father Adam says, "the Catholic of a living faith, and he alone, can make this investigation" (into the nature of Catholicism), and the others, with their ill-will or ignorantia invincibilis or what-not, are self-excluded. Nevertheless, in an objective way, something can be learned, or rather, relearned, namely, the Hebrew-like pride and exclusiveness of the genuine Catholic mind. When Father Adam writes of the Communion of the Saints, one gets an impression of the Church not so much as a body of thought as of a kind of glorified family bank—a limited company paying enormous dividends, with non-members rigidly excluded from benefits. Here are Father Adam's words:

"The Saints during their mortal life amassed beyond the measure of their duty a store of wealth . . . this wealth of the Saints is that 'treasure of the Church,' that sacred family inheritance, which belongs to all members of the body of Christ, and which is at the service especially of sick and feeble members."

The smallest shareholder draws his bonus on the profits made by Augustine or Aquinas. The point is missed if one forgets that the "family"

247

means the Church and the Church alone; the rest of humanity, stray saints apart, being so much negligible matter, for whom there can be nothing save a slightly rigid pity, for extra ecclesiam nulla salus, and "dogmatic intolerance," as Father Adam puts it, "is a duty to the infinite truth." Father Adam allows that non-Catholics of good will have been known to exist here and there; but these in reality are Catholics without knowing it, since any virtue that exists outside the Church must be held to have proceeded, "invisibly," *from* the Church. And apart from special mercies, which are by no means to be counted on, "all pagans, Jews, heretics and schismatics have forfeited eternal life and are destined to everlasting fire."

This is quite straightforward, and much more impressive than what we get from our English Catholic apologists. These, with their public-school methods of controversy, have given so strong an impression of not being in earnest that hardly a soul in England bothers to hit back at them. Nearly all our anti-clerical feeling is directed at the poor, unoffending old Church of England. If ever a word is raised against Rome, it is only some absurd tale about Jesuit intrigues or babies' skeletons dug up from the floors of nunneries. Very few people, apart from the Catholics themselves, seem to have grasped that the Church is to be taken seriously. Books of this kind, therefore, written with genuine learning and free from silly-cleverness, are of great value.

[Unsigned][1]

1. See *131*.

128. To Leonard Moore

10 June 1932   Handwritten

The Hawthorns   Hayes   Middlesex

Dear Sir,
I am told that the Clarendon Press often want books annotated & have a certain amount of difficulty in finding people who are competent & will do this conscientiously. I would be very glad to get hold of a book to annotate, if they would give it me. Perhaps it might be worth trying them?[1]

Yours faithfully
Eric A Blair

1. Annotated in Moore's office: '11.0 tomorrow (Friday).'

129. To Eleanor Jaques

Tuesday, [14 June 1932]   Handwritten; dated from postmark

The Hawthorns   Hayes   Middlesex

Dear Eleanor,[1]
How do things go with you? I hope your father is better, & that you have got
your garden into shape. I have been teaching at the above foul place for nearly
two months. I don't find the work uninteresting, but it is very exhausting, &
apart from a few reviews etc. I've hardly done a stroke of writing. My poor
poem, which was promising not too badly, has of course stopped dead. The
most disagreeable thing here is not the job itself (it is a day-school, thank
God, so I have nothing to do with the brats out of school hours) but Hayes
itself, which is one of the most godforsaken places I have ever struck. The
population seems to be entirely made up of clerks who frequent tin-roofed
chapels on Sundays & for the rest bolt themselves within doors. My sole
friend is the curate—High Anglican but not a creeping Jesus & a very good
fellow. Of course it means that I have to go to Church, which is an arduous
job here, as the service is so popish that I don't know my way about it & feel
an awful B.F. when I see everyone bowing & crossing themselves all round
me & can't follow suit. The poor old vicar, who I suspect hates all this
popery, is dressed up in cope & biretta & led round in procession with candles
etc., looking like a bullock garlanded for sacrifice. I have promised to paint
one of the church idols (a quite skittish-looking B.V.M, half life-size, & I
shall try & make her look as much like one of the illustrations in La Vie
Parisienne as possible) & to grow a marrow for the harvest festival. I would
"communicate" too, only I am afraid the bread might choke me. Have you
read anything interesting lately? I read for the first time Marlowe's Faustus, &
thought it rotten, also a mangy little book on Shakespeare trying to prove
that Hamlet = Earl of Essex,[2] also a publication called The Enemy of
Wyndham Lewis (not the professional R.C[3]), who seems to have something
in him, also something of Osbert Sitwell, also some odes of Horace, whom I
wish I hadn't neglected hitherto—otherwise nothing, not having much time
or energy. Mrs. Carr[4] sent me two books of Catholic apologetics, & I had
great pleasure in reviewing one of them[5] for a new paper called the New
English Weekly. It was the first time I had been able to lay the bastinado on a
professional R.C. at any length. I have got a few square feet of garden, but
have had rotten results owing to rain, slugs & mice. I have found hardly any
birds' nests—this place is on the outskirts of London, of course. I have also
been keeping a pickle-jar aquarium, chiefly for the instruction of the boys, &
we have newts, tadpoles, caddis-flies etc. If when you are passing, if you ever
do, the pumping station at the beginning of the ferry-path, you see any eggs
of puss-moths on the poplar trees there, I should be awfully obliged if you
would pick the leaves & send them me by post. I want some, & have only been
able to find one or two here. Of course I don't mean make an expedition
there, I only mean if you happen to be passing. What is Dennis[6] doing these
days? I want to consult him about an extraordinary fungus that was dug up

here, but of course he never answers letters. I may or may not come back to S'wold for the summer holidays. I want to get on with my novel[7] and if possible finish the poem I had begun, & I think perhaps it would be best for me to go to some quiet place in France, where I can live cheaply & have less temptation from the World, the Flesh & the Devil than at S'wold. (You can decide which of these categories you belong to.) By the way, if you are ever to be in London please let me know, as we might meet, that is if you would like to. Please remember me to your parents, also to Mr and Mrs Pullein[8] if you see them.

Yours
Eric A Blair

P.S. In case you see Dennis, you might tell him the fungus was like this (below.) It was dug up underground.

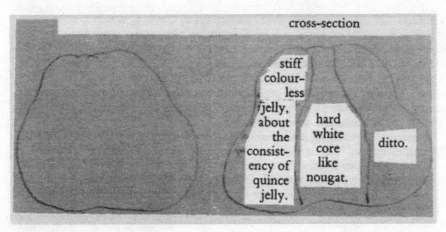

About this size & very like
an apple in shape, but dead
white, & flabby to the touch.

P.P.S. I trust this adress° is all right.

1. Eleanor Jaques (?–1962) and her family arrived in Southwold from Canada in 1921. They were for a time next-door neighbours of the Blairs in Stradbroke Road. She and Orwell became friends and she is mentioned in Orwell's 12 October 1931 letter to Dennis Collings, whom she married in 1934. See Shelden, 175, 192; U.S.: 159, 174–75.
2. Probably *The Essential Shakespeare* by J. Dover Wilson (1932).
3. D. B. Wyndham Lewis; see *688, n. 2.*
4. A Southwold friend of Orwell and Eleanor Jaques.
5. *The Spirit of Catholicism*; see *127.*
6. Dennis Collings.
7. *Burmese Days.*
8. Collett Cresswell Pulleyne and his mother.

130. To Eleanor Jaques

Sunday, [19 June 1932]   Handwritten; dated from postmark

The Hawthorns   Station Rd.   Hayes   Middlesex

Dear Eleanor,

I am sorry I did not after all ring up this morning, but when I did not hear from you till Saturday I arranged to take some of the boys out & your letter only arrived afterwards. Also I am not very near a telephone here. I hope you had not been counting on going out today. Let me know if you *are* staying in town, & if so we can arrange to go out again. Thanks so much for sending the jumping bean, which, however, got crushed in the post, poor little thing. I duly went fishing yesterday, but it was rotten—at least there were fish there, but they won't bite in this hot clear weather, & I only got one mangy little tench during the whole day. I am going to try near Uxbridge, & I believe the fishing in the Thames near Hampton Court is not so bad, & that would be nearer for you if you are staying in London. I found a few birds' nests while we were fishing, & the water-birds there were quite interesting to watch.

Let me hear from you soon,

Yours
Eric A Blair

131. To the Editor, *The New English Weekly*

30 June 1932

Following Orwell's review of *The Spirit of Catholicism* (127), Father C. C. Martindale, S.J. (1879–1963), a famous preacher on the staff of Farm Street Church, London, wrote in the *New English Weekly*, 23 June 1932, that Orwell had cited a phrase, 'all pagans . . . have forfeited eternal life' as though it were 'a quotation from Dr Adam himself.' Martindale argued that it was 'an expression from the Council of Florence' and that Karl Adam's 'lucid explanation' was what 'anyone who knows the subject would say.' He complained that Orwell's allusions to his book, *The Faith of the Roman Church*, indicated 'an equal carelessness, or an inability to perceive what is being spoken of . . . neither ill-manners nor imperception matter much: disingenuousness does: and that is the lightest charge that can be laid against his use of the quotation mentioned above.' He argued that Orwell had treated his book as if it were 'a justification of the Catholic faith—apologetics if not propaganda—whereas it was a statement expanded no more than what was needed for intelligibility.' There was, he said, no need for him to discuss the 'problem of evil' and he denied that he sailed over the theory of evolution.

Sir,—Father Martindale, in your issue of the 23rd inst., calls my review of "The Spirit of Catholicism" disingenuous. I see nothing disingenuous in attributing to Father Adam a view which he himself heartily endorses; and as for his "explanation," I think I indicated fairly enough the extent to which he tones down the ferocity of extra ecclesiam nulla salus. The rest of Father Martindale's letter depends upon the claim that his own book, "The Faith of the Roman Church," is not a book of propaganda. And this claim, as any fair-minded person will admit after reading the book, is—may I say "disingenuous"?

Eric A. Blair

132. To Leonard Moore

1 July 1932   Handwritten lettercard

The Hawthorns   Church Road   Hayes.   Middx.

Dear Mr Moore,

Thank you for your letter—I went & saw Mr Gollancz[1] at the time named, & he gave me a full account of the alterations he wants made in the book.[2] Names are to be changed, swearwords etc. cut out, & there is one passage which is to be either changed or cut out—a pity, as it is about the only good bit of writing in the book, but he says the circulating libraries would not stand for it. I am going to let him have the ms. back in about a week. I did not say anything about the book having no commercial value, & he seemed to think fairly well of it, so perhaps you will be able to get good terms from him.

Yours truly
Eric A. Blair

1. Victor Gollancz (1893–1967; Kt. 1965) was Orwell's first publisher. Educated at Oxford, he taught at Repton for two years, introducing a civics class that brought him into conflict with the headmaster, Dr Geoffrey Fisher (later Archbishop of Canterbury); he was sacked in 1918 and worked on minimum-wage legislation and edited 'The World of Today' series for Oxford University Press. In 1921, he joined Benn Brothers, publishers of trade journals and a few books. He became managing director of a separate company, Ernest Benn Ltd, in 1923, which he developed successfully. In October 1927, he established his own publishing house. His first book, Susan Glaspell's *Brook Evans*, was published on 19 April 1928; in his first year, sixty-four books were published on a diversified list. Although a member of the Labour Party and born into an orthodox Jewish family, he was later to describe himself as a Christian socialist. His most well-known achievement was the formation of the Left Book Club. It was under this imprint that *The Road to Wigan Pier* was published in March 1937. See *Gollancz: The Story of a Publishing House, 1928–1978*, by Sheila Hodges (1978), and Peter Lewis, *George Orwell: The Road to 1984*, 64.

2. *Down and Out in Paris and London.*

133. To Leonard Moore

6 July 1932   Handwritten

The Hawthorns   Church Road   Hayes.   Middx.

Dear Mr Moore,

I am sending herewith the ms. which I told Mr Gollancz I would let him have back in about a week. I have made the alterations of names etc. that he asked for, & I think there is now nothing that can cause offence. The passage between pp. 6 & 13 that was objected to cannot be altered very radically. I have crossed out or altered the phrases that seemed to show too definitely what was happening & perhaps like this it might pass inspection. If not, I think the only thing to do is to remove Chap. II in toto, as Chap. III follows fairly consecutively from Chap. I.

As to a title (Mr. Gollancz said the present one will not do) I suggest putting at the start the quotation

> "The Lady Poverty was fair,
> But she hath lost her looks of late"
> (Alice Meynell)

& calling the book "The Lady Poverty" or "Lady Poverty". If this will not do I will think of another title.

I think if it is all the same to everybody I would prefer the book to be published pseudonymously. I have no reputation that is lost by doing this, & if the book has any kind of success I can always use the same pseudonym again.

Perhaps you will be kind enough to tell Mr Gollancz all this?

Yours truly
Eric A Blair

134. To Eleanor Jaques

Friday, [8 July 1932]   Handwritten; dated from postmark

The Hawthorns   Church Road   Hayes.   Mddx.

Dear Eleanor,

Please do write & tell me you were not hurt at my not after all coming to meet you that Sunday—you did not write & I thought it might be that. I should be so sorry if you became angry with me. I would gladly have come if I could.

How is S'wold? Nothing happens here. I have had a small controversy with Fr. Martindale, S.J. & he wrote & told Mrs Carr he would like to meet me, as I was deeply in error & he could put me right. I must meet him sometime if possible.

Is there any hope of your coming up to town again? I *may* be in S'wold during the first week or two of the holidays—not certain. Please remember me to your parents, & write & tell me you are not incensed with me.

Yours
Eric A Blair

135. 'Clink'

[August 1932]

The events narrated in 'Clink'[1] started on Saturday, 12 December 1931 (or possibly a week later). The text is printed from Orwell's typescript. See Richard Rees, *George Orwell: Fugitive from the Camp of Victory*, 144.

This trip was a failure, as the object of it was to get into prison, and I did not, in fact, get more than forty eight hours in custody; however, I am recording it, as the procedure in the police court etc. was fairly interesting. I am writing this eight months after it happened, so am not certain of any dates, but it all happened a week or ten days before Xmas 1931.

I started out on Saturday afternoon with four or five shillings, and went out to the Mile End Road, because my plan was to get drunk and incapable, and I thought they would be less lenient towards drunkards in the East End. I bought some tobacco and a "Yank Mag" against my forthcoming imprisonment, and then, as soon as the pubs opened, went and had four or five pints, topping up with a quarter bottle of whisky, which left me with twopence in hand. By the time the whisky was low in the bottle I was tolerably drunk—more drunk than I had intended, for it happened that I had eaten nothing all day, and the alcohol acted quickly on my empty stomach. It was all I could do to stand upright, though my brain was quite clear—with me, when I am drunk, my brain remains clear long after my legs and speech have gone. I began staggering along the pavement in a westward direction, and for a long time did not meet any policemen, though the streets were crowded and all the people pointed and laughed at me. Finally I saw two policemen coming. I pulled the whisky bottle out of my pocket and, in their sight, drank what was left, which nearly knocked me out, so that I clutched a lamp-post and fell down. The two policemen ran towards me, turned me over and took the bottle out of my hand.

They: " 'Ere, what you bin drinking?" (For a moment they may have thought it was a case of suicide.)

I: "Thass my boll whisky. You lea' me alone."

They: "Coo, 'e's fair bin bathing in it!—What you bin doing of, eh?"

I: "Bin in boozer 'avin' bit o' fun. Christmas, ain't it?"

They: "No, not by a week it ain't. You got mixed up in the dates, you 'ave. You better come along with us. We'll look after yer."

I: "Why sh'd I come along you?"

They: "Jest so's we'll look after you and make you comfortable. You'll get run over, rolling about like that."

I: "Look. Boozer over there. Less go in 'ave drink."

They: "You've 'ad enough for one night, ole chap. You best come with us."

I: "Where you takin' me?"

They: "Jest somewhere as you'll get a nice quiet kip with a clean sheet and two blankets and all."

I: "Shall I get drink there?"

They: "Course you will. Got a boozer on the premises, we 'ave."

All this while they were leading me gently along the pavement. They had my arms in the grip (I forget what it is called) by which you can break a man's arm with one twist, but they were as gentle with me as though I had been a child. I was internally quite sober, and it amused me very much to see the cunning way in which they persuaded me along, never once disclosing the fact that we were making for the police station. This is, I suppose, the usual procedure with drunks.

When we got to the station (it was Bethnal Green, but I did not learn this till Monday) they dumped me in a chair & began emptying my pockets while the sergeant questioned me. I pretended, however, to be too drunk to give sensible answers, & he told them in disgust to take me off to the cells, which they did. The cell was about the same size as a Casual Ward cell (about 10 ft. by 5 ft. by 10 ft° high), but much cleaner & better appointed. It was made of white porcelain bricks, and was furnished with a W.C., a hot water pipe, a plank bed, a horsehair pillow and two blankets. There was a tiny barred window high up near the roof, and an electric bulb behind a guard of thick glass was kept burning all night. The door was steel, with the usual spy-hole and aperture for serving food through. The constables in searching me had taken away my money, matches, razor, and also my scarf—this, I learned afterwards, because prisoners have been known to hang themselves on their scarves.

There is very little to say about the next day and night, which were unutterably boring. I was horribly sick, sicker than I have ever been from a bout of drunkenness, no doubt from having an empty stomach. During Sunday I was given two meals of bread and marg. and tea (spike quality), and one of meat and potatoes—this, I believe, owing to the kindness of the seargeant's° wife, for I think only bread and marg, is provided for prisoners in the lock-up. I was not allowed to shave, and there was only a little cold water to wash in. When the charge sheet was filled up I told the story I always tell, viz. that my name was Edward Burton,[2] and my parents kept a cake-shop in Blythburgh, where I had been employed as a clerk in a draper's shop; that I had had the sack for drunkenness, and my parents, finally getting sick of my drunken habits, had turned me adrift. I added that I had been working as an outside porter at Billingsgate, and having unexpectedly "knocked up" six shillings on Saturday, had gone on the razzle. The police were quite kind, and read me lectures on drunkenness, with the usual stuff about seeing that I still had some good in me etc. etc. They offered to let me out on bail on my own recognizance, but I had no money and nowhere to go, so I elected to stay in custody. It was very dull, but I had my "Yank Mag", and could get a smoke if I asked the constable on duty in the passage for a light—prisoners are not allowed matches, of course.

The next morning very early they turned me out of my cell to wash, gave me back my scarf, and took me out into the yard and put me in the Black Maria. Inside, the Black Maria was just like a French public lavatory, with a row of tiny locked compartments on either side, each just large enough to sit down in. People had scrawled their names, offences and the lengths of their sentences all over the walls of my compartment; also, several times, variants on this couplet—

> "Detective Smith knows how to gee;
> Tell him he's a cunt from me."

("Gee" in this context means to act as an agent provocateur.) We drove round to various stations picking up about ten prisoners in all, until the Black Maria was quite full. They were quite a jolly crowd inside. The compartment doors were open at the top, for ventilation, so that you could reach across, and somebody had managed to smuggle matches in, and we all had a smoke. Presently we began singing, and, as it was near Christmas sang several carols. We drove up to Old Street Police Court singing—

> "Adeste, fideles, laeti triumphantes,
> Adeste, adeste ad Bethlehem" etc.

which seemed to me rather inappropriate.

At the police court they took me off and put me in a cell identical with the one at Bethnal Green, even to having the same number of bricks in it—I counted in each case. There were three men in the cell beside° myself. One was a smartly dressed, florid, well-set-up man of about thirty five, whom I would have taken for a commercial traveller or perhaps a bookie, and another a middle-aged Jew, also quite decently dressed. The other man was evidently a habitual burglar. He was a short rough-looking man with grey hair and a worn face, and at this moment in such a state of agitation over his approaching trial that he could not keep still an instant. He kept pacing up and down the cell like a wild beast, brushing against our knees as we sat on the plank bed, and exclaiming that he was innocent—he was charged, apparently, with loitering with intent to commit burglary. He said that he had nine previous convictions against him, and that in these cases, which are mainly of suspicion, old offenders are nearly always convicted. From time to time he would shake his fist towards the door and exclaim "Fucking toe-rag! Fucking toe-rag!", meaning the "split" who had arrested him.

Presently two more prisoners were put into the cell, an ugly Belgian youth charged with obstructing traffic with a barrow, and an extraordinary hairy creature who was either deaf and dumb or spoke no English. Except this last all the prisoners talked about their cases with the utmost freedom. The florid, smart man, it appeared, was a public house "guv'nor" (it is a sign of how utterly the London publicans are in the claw of the brewers that they are always referred to as "governors", not "landlords"; being, in fact, no better than employees), & had embezzled the Christmas Club money. As usual, he was head over ears in debt to the brewers, and no doubt had taken some of the money in hopes of backing a winner. Two of the subscribers had discovered this a few days before the money was due to be paid out, and laid an information. The "guv'nor" immediately paid back all save £12, which was also refunded before his case came up for trial. Nevertheless, he was certain to be sentenced, as the magistrates are hard on these cases—he did, in fact, get four months later in the day. He was ruined for life, of course. The brewers would file bankruptcy proceedings and sell up all his stock and furniture, and he would never be given a pub licence again. He was trying to brazen it out in front of the rest of us, and smoking cigarettes incessantly from a stock of Gold Flake packets he had laid in—the last time in his life, I dare say, that he would have quite enough cigarettes. There was a staring, abstracted look in his eyes all the time while he talked. I think the fact that his life was at an end, as far as any decent position in society went, was gradually sinking into him.

The Jew had been a buyer at Smithfields for a kosher butcher. After working seven years for the same employer he suddenly misappropriated £28, went up to Edinburgh—I don't know why Edinburgh—and had a "good time" with tarts, and came back and surrendered himself when the money was gone. £16 of the money had been repaid, and the rest was to be repaid by monthly instalments. He had a wife and a number of children. He told us, what interested me, that his employer would probably get into trouble at the synagogue for prosecuting him. It appears that the Jews have arbitration courts of their own, & a Jew is not supposed to prosecute another Jew, at least in a breach of trust case like this, without first submitting it to the arbitration court.

One remark made by these men struck me—I heard it from almost every prisoner who was up for a serious offence. It was, "It's not the prison I mind, it's losing my job." This is, I believe, symptomatic of the dwindling power of the law compared with that of the capitalist.

They kept us waiting several hours. It was very uncomfortable in the cell, for there was not room for all of us to sit down on the plank bed, and it was beastly cold in spite of the number of us. Several of the men used the W.C., which was disgusting in so small a cell, especially as the plug did not work. The publican distributed his cigarettes generously, the constable in the passage supplying lights. From time to time an extraordinary clanking noise came from the cell next door, where a youth who had stabbed his "tart" in the stomach—she was likely to recover, we heard—was locked up alone. Goodness knows what was happening, but it sounded as though he were chained to the wall. At about ten they gave us each a mug of tea—this, it appeared, not provided by the authorities but by the police court missionaries—and shortly afterwards shepherded us along to a sort of large waiting room where the prisoners awaited trial.

There were perhaps fifty prisoners here, men of every type, but on the whole much more smartly dressed than one would expect. They were strolling up and down with their hats on, shivering with the cold. I saw here a thing which interested me greatly. When I was being taken to my cell I had seen two dirty-looking ruffians, much dirtier than myself and presumably drunks or obstruction cases, being put into another cell in the row. Here, in the waiting room, these two were at work with note-books in their hands, interrogating prisoners. It appeared that they were "splits", and were put into the cells disguised as prisoners, to pick up any information that was going—for there is complete freemasonry between prisoners, and they talk without reserve in front of one another. It was a dingy trick, I thought.

All the while the prisoners were being taken by ones & twos along a corridor to the court. Presently a sergeant shouted "Come on the drunks!" and four or five of us filed along the corridor and stood waiting at the entrance of the court. A young constable on duty there advised me—

"Take your cap off when you go in, plead guilty and don't give back answers. Got any previous convictions?"

"No."

"Six bob you'll get. Going to pay it?"

"I can't, I've only twopence."

"Ah well, it don't matter. Lucky for you Mr Brown isn't on the bench this morning. Teetotaller he is. He don't half give it to the drunks. Coo!"

The drunk cases were dealt with so rapidly that I had not even time to notice what the court was like. I only had a vague impression of a raised platform with a coat of arms over it, clerks sitting at tables below, and a railing. We filed past the railing like people passing through a turnstile, & the proceedings in each case sounded like this—

"Edward-Burton-drunk-and-incapable-Drunk?-Yes-Six-shillings-move-on-NEXT!"

All this in the space of about five seconds. At the other side of the court we reached a room where a sergeant was sitting at a desk with a ledger.

"Six shillings?" he said.

"Yes."

"Going to pay it?"

"I can't."

"All right, back you go to your cell."

And they took me back and locked me in the cell from which I had come, about ten minutes after I had left it.

The publican had also been brought back, his case having been postponed, and the Belgian youth, who, like me, could not pay his fine. The Jew was gone, whether released or sentenced we did not know. Throughout the day prisoners were coming and going, some waiting trial, some until the Black Maria was available to take them off to prison. It was cold, and the nasty faecal stench in the cell became unbearable. They gave us our dinner at about two o'clock—it consisted of a mug of tea and two slices of bread and marg. for each man. Apparently this was the regulation meal. One could, if one had friends outside get food sent in, but it struck me as damnably unfair that a penniless man must face his trial with only bread and marg. in his belly; also unshaven—I, at this time, had had no chance of shaving for over forty eight hours—which is likely to prejudice the magistrates against him.

Among the prisoners who were put temporarily in the cell were two friends or partners named apparently Snouter and Charlie, who had been arrested for some street offence—obstruction with a barrow, I dare say. Snouter was a thin, red-faced, malignant-looking man, and Charlie a short, powerful, jolly man. Their conversation was rather interesting.

Charlie:[3] "Cripes, it ain't 'alf fucking cold in 'ere. Lucky for us ole Brown ain't on to-day. Give you a month as soon as look at yer."

Snouter (bored, and singing):

> "Tap, tap, tapetty tap,
> I'm a perfect devil at that;
> Tapping 'em 'ere, tapping 'em there,
> I bin tapping 'em everywhere—"

Charlie: "Oh, fuck off with yer tapping! Scrumping's what yer want this time of year. All them rows of turkeys in the winders, like rows of fucking soldiers with no clo'es on—don't it make yer fucking mouth water to look at 'em. Bet yer a tanner I 'ave one of 'em afore tonight."

Snouter: "What's 'a good? Can't cook the bugger over the kip-'ouse fire, can you?"

Charlie: "Oo wants to cook it? I know where I can flog (sell) it for a bob or two, though."

Snouter: " 'Sno good. Chantin's the game this time of year. Carols. Fair twist their 'earts round, I can, when I get on the mournful. Old tarts weep their fucking eyes out when they 'ear me. I won't 'alf give them a doing this Christmas. I'll kip indoors if I 'ave to cut it out of their bowels."

Charlie: "Ah, *I* can sling you a bit of a carol. 'Ymns, too. (He begins singing in a good bass voice)—

> "Jesu, lover of my soul,
> Let me to thy bosom fly—"

The constable on duty (looking through the grille): "Nah then, in 'ere, nah then! What yer think this is? Baptist prayer meeting?"

Charlie (in a low voice as the constable disappears); "Fuck off, pisspot. (He hums)—

> "While the gathering waters roll,
> While the tempest still is 'igh!

You won't find many in the 'ymnal as I can't sling you. Sung bass in the choir my last two years in Dartmoor, I did."

Snouter: "Ah? Wassit like in Dartmoor now? D'you get jam now?"

Charlie: "Not jam. Gets cheese, though, twice a week."

Snouter: "Ah? 'Ow long was you doing?"

Charlie: "Four year."

Snouter: "Four years without cunt—Cripes! Fellers inside'd go 'alf mad if they saw a pair of legs (a woman), eh?"

Charlie: "Ah well, in Dartmoor we used to fuck old women down on the allotments. Take 'em under the 'edge in the mist. Spud-grabbers they was—ole trots seventy year old. Forty of us was caught and went through 'ell for it. Bread and water, chains—everythink. I took my Bible oath as I wouldn't get no more stretches after that."

Snouter: "Yes, you! 'Ow come you got in the stir lars' time then?"

Charlie: "You wouldn't 'ardly believe it, boy. I was narked—narked by my own sister! Yes, my own fucking sister. My sister's a cow if ever there was one. She got married to a religious maniac, and 'e's so fucking religious that she's got fifteen kids now. Well, it was 'im put 'er up to narking me. But I got

259

it back on 'em *I* can tell you. What do you think I done first thing, when I come out of the stir? I bought a 'ammer, and I went round to my sister's 'ouse and smashed 'er piano to fucking matchwood. I did. 'There', I says, 'that's what you get for narking me! You mare', I says" etc. etc. etc.

This kind of conversation went on more or less all day between these two, who were only in for some petty offence & quite pleased with themselves. Those who were going to prison were silent and restless, and the look on some of the men's faces—respectable men under arrest for the first time—was dreadful. They took the publican out at about three in the afternoon, to be sent off to prison. He had cheered up a little on learning from the constable on duty that he was going to the same prison as Lord Kylsant.[4] He thought that by sucking up to Lord K. in jail he might get a job from him when he came out.

I had no idea how long I was going to be incarcerated, & supposed that it would be several days at least. However, between four and five o'clock they took me out of the cell, gave back the things which had been confiscated, and shot me into the street forthwith. Evidently the day in custody served instead of the fine. I had only twopence and had had nothing to eat all day except bread and marg., and was damnably hungry; however, as always happens when it is a choice between tobacco and food, I bought tobacco with my twopence. Then I went down to the Church Army shelter in the Waterloo Road, where you get a kip, two meals of bread and corned beef and tea and a prayer meeting, for four hours work at sawing wood.

The next morning I went home,[5] got some money, and went out to Edmonton. I turned up at the Casual Ward about nine at night, not downright drunk but more or less under the influence, thinking this would lead to prison—for it is an offence under the Vagrancy Act for a tramp to come drunk to the Casual Ward. The porter, however, treated me with great consideration, evidently feeling that a tramp with money enough to buy drink ought to be respected. During the next few days I made several more attempts to get into trouble by begging under the noses of the police, but I seemed to bear a charmed life—no one took any notice of me. So, as I did not want to do anything serious which might lead to investigations about my identity etc., I gave it up. The trip, therefore, was more or less of a failure, but I have recorded it as a fairly interesting experience.

—— ooOoo ——

1. Clink is a cant word for a prison, from the Clink, one-time prison in the London borough of Southwark dating from the sixteenth century.
2. When choosing a pseudonym for the publication of *Down and Out in Paris and London*, Orwell told Leonard Moore that he always used the name P. S. Burton; see *148*. Blythburgh is a mile or so inland from Southwold.
3. *Charlie*] *Snouter*
4. Lord Kylsant (1863–1937), a Conservative M.P., Chairman of the Royal Mail Steam Package Company, and with large shipbuilding interests, was sentenced to twelve months' imprisonment in 1931 for circulating a false prospectus. His personal guilt was never entirely established in the public mind.
5. His lodgings at 2 Windsor Street, Paddington, near St Mary's Hospital. The house has been demolished; part of the estate is illustrated in Thompson, 31.

136. To Leonard Moore

4 August 1932   Handwritten lettercard

36 High Street   Southwold   Suffolk.

Dear Mr Moore,
The above adress° will find me at any time during August or September.

Yours sincerely
Eric A Blair

137. To Leonard Moore

12 August 1932   Handwritten

36 High St   Southwold   Suffolk.

Dear Mr Moore,
Many thanks. I am returning the signed agreement herewith. Thank you also
for the booklet which you sent before, & which I read with great interest. By
the way, Gollancz does not say anything about the *title* of the book (which
was left open) nor the pseudonym I am to use. I previously suggested to him
the title "Lady Poverty" or "The Lady Poverty" (referring to a poem of Alice
Meynell's), but it now occurs to me that "In Praise of Poverty" would be the
best title. I will also think of a good pseudonym—I suppose the thing is to
have an easily memorable one—which I could stick to if this book had any
success.

Yours sincerely
Eric A Blair

P.S. I have just looked thro' the agreement again. I see that it says (Clause I)
"new & original work". The substance of one chapter in the book appeared a
year or two ago as an article in the Adelphi.[1] I also sent the New Statesman
about Xmas an article on Common Lodging Houses[2] which repeats some of
what is said in another chapter, but tho' they accepted it & sent a proof they
have never printed it, I don't know why: they may do so later. Does this
matter? I think I did mention to Gollancz something about this. In any case, I
don't think it would interfere with the book in any way.

E.A.B

1. 'The Spike'; see *104*.
2. 'Common Lodging Houses' was to appear in *The New Statesman and Nation*, 3 September
1932; see *141*.

138. To Eleanor Jaques

Thur., [18 August 1932]   Handwritten lettercard; dated from postmark

36 High St   Southwold

Dearest Eleanor,

Do not forget *Tuesday*, 2.15 pm by Smith's bookshop. And, as you love me, do not *change your mind* before then.[1] If you are at church on Sunday, pray for good weather on Tuesday. If it *does* rain, can you meet me same time & place after all, & we will go somewhere or other. Till then, all my love.

Eric

P.S. Please send me a line to reassure me that you have not changed your mind.

1. What would normally be full points, or periods, are quite clearly small dashes in this letter-card. This is a frequent characteristic of Orwell's handwriting at this time—perhaps especially when in haste. A full point has been adopted here and elsewhere, to avoid giving a false impression.

139. Review of *Persephone in Hades* by Ruth Pitter[1]

The Adelphi, September 1932

This is something slightly out of the common; a poem done in classical style; but a genuine classical style, not the mincing archaism which sometimes goes by that name. Take such a passage as—

>   unreconciled
> To winter, all the stricken forest lies
> Sodden with weeping, and with frenzy torn:
> The fields lie barren, the dishevelled vine
> Scourges the propping elm.

This is perfectly in the spirit of *surtout point de zèle*, with all the adjectives deliberately chosen to avoid cheap effect; yet it is not an imitation, but rather a development—a descendant, as it were, in the direct line from Pope. Such a poem arouses mixed feelings. One is bound to admire its metrical accomplishment, and yet one cannot help feeling that nowadays there is something altogether too refined, something bloodless, about the classical style. The fact is that the whole tradition of formalism and *surtout point de zèle* was created for minds quite different from our own. In its most vital periods classicism is always accompanied by, perhaps springs from, an earthy and even blackguardly outlook which is not natural to modern men. There is hardly an eighteenth century author whom one can read without feeling instinctively that he had a family of natural children, and was capable of intriguing for a sinecure. In any individual case this might not hold, but the men of the eighteenth century did draw some of their strength from their lack of spirituality; they avoided Marie Corelli-ism by being below it as well as by being above it. A modern Englishman is never utterly unspiritual, and he is deliberately throwing away a part of his mind if he sticks to classicism. Still, there is a reward for mastering the classical technique—in itself a notable feat. One can see the reward here; a sort of cold, crystal clearness which almost chills at the time, and yet is likely to stick by one when gaudier things vanish. And in lines like these—

> willow pale,
> With wealthy yellow for the thronging bees,
> And sweet though barren silver.

Anyone who has an ear must recognise the genuine thing. This is an unusual poem, and technically an admirable one.

ERIC BLAIR

1. Ruth Pitter (1897–1992; CBE, 1979) was a poet and friend of the Blairs, especially of Marjorie. She lived in Mall Chambers, Kensington when Orwell's mother was living there; see *34, n. 1.* In 1928, Pitter and a friend found Orwell a room with Mrs. Edwin Craig at 22 Portobello Road, next door to her Walberswick Peasant Pottery Co. Ltd. Thompson illustrates both houses (23) and no. 20, where lived a builder with whom she was not on speaking terms; see 'As I Please,' 26, 26 May 1944, *2478.* See also Crick, 178–79; Shelden, 130–31; U.S.: 118–20; Thompson, 13–14. Portobello Road runs from Notting Hill Gate at its south end to a little southeast of Kensal Green Cemetery. Pitter's memories of Orwell appear in *Orwell Remembered*: 'Like a Cow with a Musket' (her description of Orwell's early attempts to write) and 'We cruel girls laughed' (68–75). Orwell reviewed her book *The Spirit Watches* in *The Adelphi* in February 1940; see *589.* See also *204, n. 5.*

140. Review of *Byron and the Need of Fatality* by Charles du Bos; translated by Ethel Colburn Mayne

The Adelphi, September 1932

This book is a study of the underlying causes of Byron's incest with his half-sister, and as far as one can judge—for only a specialist could keep track of the vast quantities of Byronic literature—an exceptionally penetrating one. M. du Bos' thesis is that Byron committed incest, besides other far worse actions, because he was one of those men who must needs feel themselves the creatures of destiny. He created a sort of myth in which he was the central character, and in which he was doomed, like Oedipus, to commit some appalling and inescapable crime. It took the form of incest, perhaps because of a family tradition of inbreeding, which M. du Bos says had always had a morbid fascination for Byron. The story is an absorbing one, and when it deals with the short married life of the Byrons—Byron hated his wife from the start, and took care to let her learn that he had committed incest—it reaches genuine tragedy. The only person whose behaviour is not fully explained is Augusta Leigh, the half-sister. She seems not to have been a vicious woman, but she must have been vague and pliable to the point of idiocy. (Her way of referring to a liaison with her half-brother was, "I have been most unfortunate in all my nearest connections.") Perhaps, at the start,

263

she hardly understood what she was doing; at any rate, it is clear that the blame was wholly Byron's.

Nevertheless, though M. du Bos is very fair to Byron, there is one thing in his favour which he leaves unsaid. It is that the whole business of the incest was a fairly trivial matter. Byron's subsequent behaviour to his wife was abominable, but the incest *in itself* was not an outrageous case. Augusta Leigh was only Byron's half-sister—M. du Bos, after an introductory passage, refers to her throughout as "the *sister*"; this is rather misleading—and they had been brought up separately. In certain societies (among some of the ancient Greeks, for instance) marriage with non-uterine sisters has been an accepted custom; it is not, therefore, forbidden by any radical instinct. Moreover, M. du Bos' narrative makes it clear that Byron had no feeling of perversion in what he did. It is true that with his "need of fatality" he was glad of this chance to damn himself. Incest smelt of hell-fire (a great disinfectant, and, to spirited natures, a great provocative) and therefore it appealed to him; but there was evidently a quite natural attraction as well—in fact, on M. du Bos' showing, Augusta was the only woman who ever did attract Byron greatly. He made a deadly sin out of his personal tastes, as normal men make a virtue out of *their* personal tastes. It is unfair, and could even prejudice sound judgment of his poetry, to regard him as a cold-blooded pervert.

This is worth remembering, because there are spiritually two Byrons, and the business of the incest obscures the one who matters to posterity. Byron, as M. du Bos says, was "born in two halves." One half is the Byron of *Manfred*—the "fated being," with his beauty, his superhuman wickedness and all the rest of it—for whose sake, according to Samuel Butler, all right-minded girls used once to weep at the mention of Missolonghi. And the other half is the Byron of *Don Juan*, with unparalleled qualities both as man and poet—unparalleled, that is, in the century since his death. For is there not something especially lacking in our own age, and especially to be honoured, in the sane, earthbound, bawdy spirit of *Don Juan*? And still better is the enthusiasm for justice and honesty which led Byron into sympathy with all rebels—with the French revolutionists, with the Luddite rioters, with Napoleon against the kings of Europe, with the Greeks against the Turks. In a far more corrupt age than Byron's, who has produced a poem anything like *The Vision of Judgement*?

> "He had written praises of a regicide,
> He had written praises of all kings whatever,
> He had written for republics far and wide,
> And then against them bitterer than ever.
> For pantisocracy he once had cried
> Aloud—a scheme less moral than 'twas clever;
> Then grew a hearty anti-Jacobin—
> Had turn'd his coat—and would have turn'd his skin."[1]

This of the then poet laureate, and *mutatis mutandis* it might be said of about half our modern political journalists. But how very unmodern it would be to say it! Similarly with *The Isles of Greece*—almost the only good English patriotic poem, though the patria in the case happens not to be England. Romantic nationalism means very little to-day, but the underlying mood of *The Isles of Greece*, and the peculiar clear ring of its oratory, are permanently valuable. The contrast between the manliness, the fundamental decency of Byron's best poems, and his behaviour towards women, brings out the truth of M. du Bos' remark that Byron was "born in two halves."

This is a fair-minded, discerning book, very interesting to anyone who wants to see the whole story of Byron, his wife and his half-sister thoroughly thrashed out. M. du Bos has been especially happy in his translator, herself author of a well-known life of Lady Byron.

ERIC BLAIR

1. In *The Vision of Judgement* (1822), Byron parodied Robert Southey's *Vision of Judgement*, published the preceding year. In his Preface, Southey castigated 'the Satanic school' which 'they'—'men of diseased hearts and depraved imaginations'—had set up. The plural form only slightly disguised the attack as being directed at others as well as Byron. Byron's satire is an attack on philistinism as exemplified by Southey, Poet Laureate from 1813. Orwell quotes stanza 97. His punctuation is not quite correct: there were semicolons at the ends of lines 1, 2, and 4, and a comma after 'Aloud.'

141. 'Common Lodging Houses'

The New Statesman and Nation, 3 September 1932

Common lodging houses, of which there are several hundred in London, are night-shelters specially licensed by the LCC. They are intended for people who cannot afford regular lodgings, and in effect they are extremely cheap hotels. It is hard to estimate the lodging-house population, which varies continually, but it always runs into tens of thousands, and in the winter months probably approaches fifty thousand. Considering that they house so many people and that most of them are in an extraordinarily bad state, common lodging houses do not get the attention they deserve.

To judge the value of the LCC legislation on this subject, one must realise what life in a common lodging house is like. The average lodging house ("doss house", it used to be called) consists of a number of dormitories, and a kitchen, always subterranean, which also serves as a sitting-room. The conditions in these places, especially in southern quarters such as Southwark or Bermondsey, are disgusting. The dormitories are horrible fetid dens, packed with anything up to a hundred men, and furnished with beds a good deal inferior to those in a London casual ward. Normally these beds are about 5 ft 6 in. long by 2 ft 6 in. wide, with a hard convex mattress and a cylindrical pillow like a block of wood; sometimes, in the cheaper houses, not even a pillow. The bed-clothes consist of two raw-umber-coloured sheets, supposed to be changed once a week, but actually, in many cases, left on for a month, and a cotton counterpane; in winter there may be blankets, but never enough. As often as not the beds are verminous, and the kitchens invariably swarm with cockroaches or black beetles. There are no baths, of course, and no room where any privacy is attainable. These are the normal and accepted conditions in all ordinary lodging houses. The charges paid for this kind of accommodation vary between 7d and 1/1d a night. It should be added that, low as these charges sound, the average common lodging house brings in something like £40 net profit a week to its owner.

Besides the ordinary dirty lodging houses, there are a few score, such as the Rowton Houses and the Salvation Army hostels, that are clean and decent. Unfortunately, all of these places set off their advantages by a discipline so rigid and tiresome that to stay in them is rather like being in jail. In London (curiously enough it is better in some other towns) the common lodging house where one gets both liberty and a decent bed does not exist.

The curious thing about the squalor and discomfort of the ordinary lodging house is that these exist in places subject to constant inspection by the LCC. When one first sees the murky, troglodytic cave of a common lodging-house kitchen, one takes it for a corner of the early nineteenth century which has somehow been missed by the reformers; it is a surprise to find that common lodging houses are governed by a set of minute and (in intention) exceedingly tyrannical rules. According to the LCC regulations, practically everything is against the law in a common lodging house. Gambling, drunkenness, or even the introduction of liquor, swearing, spitting on the floor, keeping tame animals, fighting—in short, the whole social life of these places—are all forbidden. Of course, the law is habitually broken, but some of the rules are enforceable, and they illustrate the dismal uselessness of this kind of legislation. To take an instance: some time ago the LCC became concerned about the closeness together of beds in common lodging houses, and enacted that these must be at least 3 ft apart. This is the kind of law that is enforceable, and the beds were duly moved. Now, to a lodger in an already overcrowded dormitory it hardly matters whether the beds are 3 ft apart or 1 ft; but it does matter to the proprietor, whose income depends upon his floor space. The sole real result of this law, therefore, was a general rise in the price of beds. Please notice that though the space between the beds is strictly regulated, nothing is said about the beds themselves— nothing, for instance, about their being fit to sleep in. The lodging-house keepers can, and do, charge 1/– for a bed less restful than a heap of straw, and there is no law to prevent them.

Another example of LCC regulations. From nearly all common lodging houses women are strictly excluded; there are a few houses specially for women, and a very small number—too small to affect the general question— to which both men and women are admitted. It follows that any homeless man who lives regularly in a lodging house is entirely cut off from female society—indeed, cases even happen of man and wife being separated owing to the impossibility of getting accommodation in the same house. Again, some of the cheaper lodging houses are habitually raided by slumming parties, who march into the kitchen uninvited and hold lengthy religious services. The lodgers dislike these slumming parties intensely, but they have no power to eject them. Can anyone imagine such things being tolerated in a hotel? And yet a common lodging house is only a hotel at which one pays 8d a night instead of 10/6d. This kind of petty tyranny can, in fact, only be defended on the theory that a man poor enough to live in a common lodging house thereby forfeits some of his rights as a citizen.

One cannot help feeling that this theory lies behind the LCC rules for common lodging houses. All these rules are in the nature of interference-legislation—that is, they interfere, but not for the benefit of the lodgers. Their emphasis is on hygiene and morals, and the question of comfort is left to the lodging-house proprietor, who, of course, either shirks it or solves it in the spirit of organised charity. It is worth pointing out the improvements that could actually be made in common lodging houses by legislation. As to cleanliness, no law will ever enforce that, and in any case it is a minor point. But the sleeping accommodation, which is the important thing, could easily be brought up to a decent standard. Common lodging houses are places in which one pays to sleep, and most of them fail in their essential purpose, for no one can sleep well in a rackety dormitory on a bed as hard as bricks. The LCC would be doing an immense service if they compelled lodging-house keepers to divide their dormitories into cubicles and, above all, to provide comfortable beds; for instance, beds as good as those in the London casual wards. And there seems no sense in the principle of licensing all houses for "men only" or "women only", as though men and women were sodium and water and must be kept apart for fear of an explosion; the houses should be licensed for both sexes alike, as they are in some provincial towns. And the lodgers should be protected by law against various swindles which the proprietors and managers are now able to practise on them. Given these conditions, common lodging houses would serve their purpose, which is an important one, far better than they do now. After all, tens of thousands of unemployed and partially employed men have literally no other place in which they can live. It is absurd that they should be compelled to choose, as they are at present, between an easy-going pigsty and a hygienic prison.[1]

ERIC BLAIR

1. A fortnight after the publication of this article, a letter to the editor of *The New Statesman and Nation* by Theodore Fyfe, of Cambridge, was published. He described himself as an architect who had worked for the London County Council on the construction of a 'lodging home of the better kind.' He thought that the L.C.C.'s management of common lodging houses ('a festering sore,' until they took over) 'worthy of all praise' and concluded: 'They would be the first to admit that much more might be done, but . . . the common lodging house is not the only evil under the sun.' On 19 October 1932, Orwell expressed his annoyance to Eleanor Jaques at not having seen Fyfe's letter, so that he might respond to it (see *145*); it was not until she had sent it to him in her letter of 13 December 1932 that he saw what Fyfe had written; see *152*.

142. To Brenda Salkeld

Sunday, [September 1932]   Handwritten

The Hawthorns   Church Rd   Hayes, Mdx

Dearest Brenda

I am writing as I promised, but can't guarantee an even coherent letter, for a female downstairs is making the house uninhabitable by playing hymn-tunes on the piano, which, in combination with the rain outside & a dog yapping somewhere down the road, is rapidly qualifying me for the mental home. I hope you got home safely & didn't find the door barred against you. I reached home just on the stroke of midnight. It was ever so nice seeing you again & finding that you were pleased to see me, in spite of my hideous prejudice against your sex, my obsession about[1] R.C.s, etc.

I have spent a most dismal day, first in going to Church, then in reading the Sunday Times, which grows duller & duller, then in trying to write a poem which won't go beyond the first stanza, then in reading through the rough draft of my novel,[2] which depresses me horribly. I really don't know which is the more stinking, the Sunday Times or the Observer. I go from one to the other like an invalid turning from side to side in bed & getting no comfort whichever way he turns. I thought the Observer would be a little less dull when Squire[3] stopped infesting it, but they seem deliberately to seek out the dullest people they can get to review the dullest books. By the way, if you are by any chance wanting to impose a penance upon yourself, I should think you might try Hugh Walpole's recent 800-page novel.[4]

I hope you will read one or two of those books I mentioned to you.[5] By the way, I forgot to mention, what I think you told me before you had not read, Dr Garnett's (not Richard or Edward Garnett) The Twilight of the Gods.[6] If you haven't read that, it's a positive duty to do so. The story the title is taken from is far from being the best, but some of the others, such as "The Purple Head" are excellent. I suppose you have read Mark Twain's Life on the Mississippi? And J. S. Haldane's Possible Worlds? And Guy Boothby's Dr Nikola? And Mrs Sherwood's The Fairchild Family? All these are in different ways a little off the track (Dr Nikola is a boy's sixpenny thriller, but a first rate one) & I can recommend all of them. H. L. Mencken's book In Defence of Women would probably be amusing, but I haven't read it. I see Wyndham Lewis (not D. B. Wyndham Lewis, a stinking RC) has just brought out a book called Snooty Baronet, apparently a novel of sorts. It might be interesting. All I've ever read of his was a queer periodical called The Enemy, & odd articles, but he's evidently got some kick in him—whether at all a sound thinker or not, I can't be sure without further acquaintance. The copy of The Enemy I read was all a ferocious attack, about the length of an average novel, on Gertrude Stein—rather wasted energy, one would say.

Well, au revoir, for I have really no news. I will write again in a week or so & hope I shall then be in a more cheerful mood. I hope you will not have too unbearable a term—

With much love
Eric

1. about] & against
2. *Burmese Days.*
3. John C. Squire (1884–1958; Kt., 1933), journalist, essayist, poet, and literary editor of *The New Statesman and Nation*, 1913–19, founded the *London Mercury* and edited it, 1919–34. He also edited the English Men of Letters series.
4. *The Fortress.*
5. For books Orwell recommended to Brenda Salkeld in the 1930s, as reported to Howard Fink, see *166. The Twilight of the Gods* and *Dr Nikola* are included in his list.
6. Dr. Richard Garnett (1835–1906) was a librarian and author. His *Twilight of the Gods and Other Tales*, published in 1888 and augmented in 1903, was described as 'cynical apologues.'

143. To Eleanor Jaques

Monday, [19 September 1932]   Handwritten

"The Hawthorns"   Church Rd.   Hayes   Mdx.

Dearest Eleanor,
You will think it very neglectful of me not to have written all this time, but I have hardly known whether I am on my head or my heels since arriving. Now, however, things have shaken down a bit. I have started the term's work, also been to church yesterday—sitting behind a moribund hag who stinks of mothballs & gin, & has to be more or less carried to & from the altar at communion; I suppose the truth is the poor old wretch is more or less in articulo mortis & is communicating as frequently as possible lest the Devil should happen to slip in at some moment when she is in mortal sin, & carry her off to the hottest part of Hell. I have managed to put in an hour or two at my own work, also frantically busy with a play the boys are to act at the end of the term.[1] Also reading a book called "Belief in God" by Bishop Gore— late Bishop of Oxford, who confirmed me,[2] & seemingly quite sound in doctrine tho' an Anglican.

How horrible & wintry the weather has turned these last two days. On the whole we had excellent weather at S'wold, & I cannot remember when I have ever enjoyed any expeditions so much as I did those with you. Especially that day in the wood along past Blythburgh Lodge—you remember, where the deep beds of moss were. I shall always remember that, & your nice white body in the dark green moss. Do come up to London soon if you can. It would make so much difference having someone like you about the place, even if we could only meet occasionally & then only walk about the streets & picture galleries. I am going to make one or two expeditions in partibus infidelium[3] later in the winter—but nothing very interesting this time, only to see how the Embankment sleepers get on in winter.

Please remember me to your parents, also Dennis[4] & the Pulleins.[5] I will write again soon, when I have more leisure & more news.

With all my love
Eric

1. 'King Charles II'; see *154.*
2. Bishop Charles Gore (1853–1932) was Bishop of Oxford from 1911 to 1919. He wrote a

number of books, including *Belief in God* (1921), and *Belief in Christ* (1922). For Orwell's preparation for confirmation, see *35, n. 3.*

3. in partibus infidelium: in the lands of unbelievers; here, into uncivilized parts.

4. Dennis Collings.

5. Collett Pulleyne and his family in Southwold.

144. Review of *Phantom Fame* by Harry Reichenbach

The Adelphi, October 1932

These are the confessions of an American publicity agent. He started his career in the old pre-cinema days of the travelling carnivals when pickpockets employed by the management robbed the "suckers" while the conjuror was giving his performance, and the carnival doctor exhibited hired tapeworms as samples of his skill. Later on he rose to the world of the million-dollar filmstars, and when America entered the war he took a leading part in the cowardly campaign of propaganda organised by Lord Northcliffe. Two anecdotes are worth repeating for the light they throw on the modern mind. One, that when Gloria Swanson was at the height of her fame she had her dressing-room set on wheels, because she was too lazy to walk sixty yards to the studio stage. The other, that Reichenbach once gave publicity to a restaurant by putting in the window a bowl of water labelled "The only living Brazilian invisible fish." The book is excellent fun, but it could do with a glossary for the use of English readers.

145. To Eleanor Jaques

Wed. night, [19 October 1932]   Handwritten

"The Hawthorns"   Church Rd   Hayes   Mdx.

Dearest Eleanor,

I am glad to hear you had a nice time on the broads, even tho' the motor boat was not too docile. I have been unutterably busy & am half exhausted already. I am going up to town for a night or two on the 28th—intend going out on to the Embankment that night to see how the sleepers out get on at this time of year. Is there any chance of your being up in town by then? And when you *are* coming up, what will your adress° be? We simply must meet if it can be managed.

The papers this morning report quite serious rioting in Lambeth round the City Hall.[1] It was evidently *food*-rioting, as the bakers' shops were looted. That points to pretty serious conditions & there may be hell to pay in the winter if things are as bad as that already. I expect, tho', just enough will be done to prevent anything violent happening. I know the quarter where it happened so well—I dare say some of my friends took part in it.

I was sorry to hear about poor old Crick[2] being run in over the entertainment tax tickets—another sign of the bad times of course. I hope people in the town aren't being beastly to him about it? I heard from Denis Collings the other day, asking me to go & stay with him at Cambridge at the half term. I would have liked to, but it is hard for me to get away, & there are, tho' I did not tell him so, two or three people at Cambridge whom I'm not anxious to meet. By the way, if you see the Pulleynes (*do* they spell their name like that? I'm never sure) any time, I would be awfully obliged if you would get from them an° ms. of mine they have describing some adventures last Xmas. It's not very interesting but Brenda Salkeld is anxious to see it & I'd take it very kindly if you would send it to her—I hope it would not be too much trouble? Don't let your parents see the ms.,[3] as it has bad words in it. My novel[4] is making just a little progress. I see now more or less what will have to be done to it when the rough draft is finished, but the longness & complicatedness are terrible. I've done no other writing, except part of a mucky play the boys are to act later. I am told that there was a letter in the New Statesman some weeks back, attacking me for an article I'd written for them.[5] So annoying—I never saw it, & not to reply to an attack looks as tho' one admitted being wrong, which I'm sure I wasn't there in any major fact. I take in the Church Times regularly now & like it more every week. I do so like to see that there is life in the old dog yet—I mean in the poor old C. of E. I shall have to go to Holy Communion soon, hypocritical tho' it is, because my curate friend is bound to think it funny if I always go to Church but never communicate. What is the procedure? I have almost forgotten it. As far as I remember you go up to the rail & kneel down, but I don't remember whether there are any responses to make. You have to go fasting, do you not? And what about being in mortal sin? I wish you would prompt me. It seems rather mean to go to H.C. when one doesn't believe, but I have passed myself off for pious & there is nothing for it but to keep up the deception.

Dearest Eleanor, it was so nice of you to say that you looked back to your days with me with pleasure. I hope you will let me make love to you again some time, but if you don't it doesn't matter, I shall always be grateful to you for your kindness to me. Write soon & let me know your news, & above all if & when you are coming up to town. By the way, the other day I saw a man— Communist, I suppose—selling the Daily Worker,[6] & I went up to him & said, "Have you the D.W.?"—He: "Yes, sir." Dear old England!

With love
Eric

1. Should be County Hall. The extensive rioting in the Lambeth area of London on Tuesday, 18 October 1932, was described in the *Brixton Free Press* of 21 October under the headline 'Police Charge Riotous Unemployed.' See Thompson, 34. Shops were looted, police were attacked, and dozens of rioters were arrested. There were also demonstrations near St Thomas's Hospital, at St George's Circus, and in Murphy Street, a march from Brixton to the Public Assistance Commission in Brook Street on Thursday, 20 October, and from 27 to 30 October serious clashes in central London to protest against unemployment.
2. Crick was the proprietor of the local cinema at Southwold, where Orwell's father attended every new film. Entertainment tax was first levied on 1 August 1918 as a wartime measure, but it was continued thereafter.
3. 'Clink'; see *135*.

4. *Burmese Days.*
5. See *141, n. l.*
6. The *Daily Worker* represented Communist Party views and policies, 1 January 1930 to 23 April 1966; incorporated in the *Morning Star* from 25 April 1966. It was suppressed by government order 22 January 1941 to 6 September 1942.

146. To Leonard Moore

15 November 1932   Handwritten

"The Hawthorns"   Church Rd.   Hayes   Mdx.

Dear Mr Moore,

Many thanks for your letter & the two sets of proofs,[1] which arrived yesterday. As there are *two* proofs, I do not fully understand whether I am intended to correct the one bearing reader's objections with a view to answering those objections, & the other for misprints etc., or whether I need only correct one. I have begun doing *both* corrections in the copy with the reader's remarks, & hope this will do. I can let you have the proof back in about a week—I can't manage it before, as I am terribly rushed at present.

I have no objection to the title, but do you think that "X" is a good pseudonym? The reason I ask is that if this book doesn't flop as I anticipate, it might be better to have a pseudonym I could also use for my next one. I leave this to you & Mr Gollancz to decide.

The novel[2] is not getting on badly, in the sense that I am fairly pleased with what is now done, but it moves slowly, as I have practically no time to work. I did a good deal to it during the holidays & some at the beginning of the term, but at present, besides teaching, I am kept busy producing a school play,[3] which means making costumes etc. besides rehearsing. I *hope* to get the book done by the summer, but can't promise.

I hope that you & Mrs Moore are well.

Yours sincerely
Eric A Blair

1. Of *Down and Out in Paris and London.*
2. *Burmese Days.*
3. 'King Charles II'; see *154.*

147. To Eleanor Jaques

18 November 1932   Handwritten

"The Hawthorns"   Church Rd.   Hayes   Mdx.

Dearest Eleanor,

Thanks so much for your letter. It was so delightful to hear from you again & know that you are up in London & we can meet. My only *good* days for going up to town are Fridays & Saturdays. I could meet you on either Friday or

Saturday of next week any time after 4 pm Could you manage either of those days? If *not*, I could manage either Wednesday or Tuesday as you suggest, but it would have to be after 6 pm Please let me know, also where you would like to meet.

I am sorry to hear about your ankle & the operation. I hope, however, that the ankle will be permanently better now? I have been having an apallingly° busy time, & for several weeks past have not set pen to paper except to correct some proofs of my book.[1] Besides all the usual school work, I have had to write & produce a play—am now in the throes of rehearsing it—& what is worst of all, have had to make most of the suits of armour etc. for the boys to act it. For the last few weeks I have been suffering untold agonies with glue & brown paper etc. Also painting a cigarette box for the Church Bazaar, which I very rashly undertook to gild—will never try that job again. Also suffering from a devilish cold, & correcting proofs. My book is to come out in early Jan., I think. Gollancz wants to call it "The Confessions of a Down & Out". I am protesting against this as I don't answer to the name of down & out, but I will let it go if he thinks seriously that it is a taking title.

By the way, I have half an idea that Macbeth will be on at Sadler's Wells next Sat. If they have a matinée, would you like to go to it? I so adore Macbeth.[2] In a moment I will go upstairs & see if I can find the Sadler's Wells programme, & then I can find out if it is on on that day. If so, I could probably get away early, as there isn't much to do on Saturdays. If there is no matinée, *perhaps* I could go to the evening performance, but it is a little difficult because it means sleeping the night in London.

I have just found the programme. It says there is a matinée of Macbeth on Sat. the 26th November at 2.30 at the *Old Vic*. That is rather convenient— much more get-at-able than the other theatre. Do tell me you can come. And let me know where to meet. The Old Vic is in the Waterloo Rd, some distance south of the river. Till I hear from you, au revoir.

With love
Eric

1. *Down and Out in Paris and London.*
2. *Macbeth* opened on Monday, 21 November 1932. It was produced by Harcourt Williams (1880–1957), who was responsible for nearly fifty productions of Shakespeare's plays at the Old Vic between 1929 and 1934. Malcolm Keen (1887–1970) played Macbeth, and Margaret Webster (1905–1972) was Lady Macbeth. An illustration of a scene with Keen and Webster is in Thompson, 39. On 17 October 1943, Orwell produced a talk following a drastically shortened version of the play for the BBC's Eastern Service.

148. To Leonard Moore

Sat.[1] [19 November 1932]   Handwritten

"The Hawthorns"   Church Rd.   Hayes   Mdx.

Dear Mr Moore,

Many thanks for your letter. I sent off the proof with the printer's queries on it yesterday. I made a few alterations & added one or two footnotes, but I think I arranged it so that there would be no need of "over-running". I will send on the other proof as soon as possible.

As to a pseudonym, the name I always use when tramping etc. is P. S. Burton,[2] but if you don't think this sounds a probable kind of name, what about

> Kenneth Miles,
> George Orwell,
> H. Lewis Allways.

I rather favour George Orwell.[3]

I would rather not promise to have the other book[4] ready by the summer. I could certainly do it by then if I were not teaching, but in this life I can't *settle* to any work, & at present particularly I am rushed off my feet. I have got to produce a school play, & I have not only had to write it, but I have got to do all the rehearsing &, worst of all, make most of the costumes. The result is that I have practically no leisure.

I should like very much to come out & see you & Mrs Moore some time. I can get to Gerrards Cross quite easily from here, but I have unfortunately forgotten your home adress.° Perhaps you could let me know it? I could come over some Sunday afternoon—Sunday the 4th Dec.,[5] for instance, if you would be at home then?

Yours sincerely
Eric A. Blair

P.S. [at top of letter] As to the *title* of the book. Would "The Confessions of a Dishwasher" do as well? I would *rather* answer to "dishwasher" than "down & out", but if you and Mr G.[6] think the present title best for selling purposes, then it is better to stick to it.

1. This undated letter, as for a number of others, can be placed from the receipt stamp used in Moore's office. The use of this evidence is not again mentioned.
2. In 'Clink' (see *135*), he had the name Edward Burton put down on the charge sheet and he used the name Burton for a character in his play 'King Charles II' (see *154*).
3. In the BBC radio broadcast about the magazine *The Adelphi*, first transmitted 6 July 1958, and produced by Rayner Heppenstall, Sir Richard Rees recalled Orwell's fear that if his real name appeared in print 'an enemy might get hold of [it] and work some kind of magic on it.' In *George Orwell: Fugitive from the Camp of Victory*, Rees elaborated on this: Orwell had told him that it 'gave him an unpleasant feeling to see his real name in print because "how can you be sure your enemy won't cut it out and work some kind of black magic on it?" Whimsy, of course; but even Orwell's genuine streak of old-fashioned conventionality sometimes bordered on whimsy and you could not always be quite certain if he was serious or not' (44).
4. *Burmese Days*.
5. See letter to Eleanor Jaques, *151*.
6. Victor Gollancz.

149. To Leonard Moore

Mon., [21 November 1932]   Handwritten postcard; dated from postmark

"The Hawthorns" Church Rd. Hayes Mdx.

After returning the proof of "The confessions of a down & out"° I find that there were 2 mistakes I left uncorrected. They are:

Page 46, end of line 8—semi-colon after "sad" should be changed to a comma.

Page 274, end of bottom line—comma after "elsewhere" should be changed to a full stop.[1]

Eric A. Blair

1. Both corrections were made before the first edition was printed. See *CW*, I, 32, line 15, and 205, line 34.

150. To Eleanor Jaques

Tue., [22 November 1932]   Handwritten

"The Hawthorns" Church Rd. Hayes Mdx.

Dear Eleanor,

In haste. I'm afraid I can't manage so early as 1 o'c on Sat. Could you meet me at the Old Vic itself at about 2 pm I have some things to see to in the morning & doubt being able to get away before 12.30 pm I suppose you know where the Old Vic is? In the Waterloo road, just near Waterloo Station.[1]

With love
Eric

1. Enclosed was a small newspaper advertisement for a complete course in painting and designing modern furniture, for 5s 6d, obtainable from Dorothy Smith, Interior Decorator, 14 Cursitor Street, London, E.C.4.

151. To Eleanor Jaques

Wed., [30 November 1932]   Handwritten

"The Hawthorns" Church Rd. Hayes Mdx.

My dearest Eleanor,

I would have written before if I had had time, to tell you how much I enjoyed seeing you again & to ask whether you will be able to come out again. If we had even passable weather, how would it be to go out some Sunday into the country, where we could go for a long walk & then have lunch at a pub? London is depressing when one has no money. I couldn't go this Sunday, as I have to go & see some people at Gerrard's Cross,[1] but some other, perhaps. Let me know.

I hope Mrs L. is paying her debts & not being too exacting. I am living in a sort of nightmare—schoolwork, rehearsing boys for their parts in the play, making costumes, & playing football. No writing of any description, of course. The friend who was going to lend me "Ulysses" has at last got his copy back, & I shall go up to town one day to collect it, if I can manage it. If I do, I will let you know beforehand & we could meet for tea if you were anywhere in that part of London. Please send that ms.[2] back sometime—no hurry though. Also that letter you cut out of the *Nation*.[3] I like to know everything that is said by my enemies.

How I wish you were here. Whatever happens you must get some kind of job in London so that we can meet from time to time. I shall be a little less penniless next term, I hope. I am so looking forward to the holidays, tho' I'm afraid I shan't have too much time. When we were together you didn't say whether you were going to let me be your lover again. Of course you can't if Dennis[4] is in S'wold, but otherwise? You mustn't if you don't want to, but I hope you will. Write soon.

With much love
Eric

1. Leonard Moore and his wife; see letter to Moore, 19 November 1932, *148*.
2. 'Clink'; see *135*.
3. Theodore Fyfe's letter to *The New Statesman and Nation*; see *145*.
4. Dennis Collings.

152. To Eleanor Jaques

Tue., [13 December 1932]   Handwritten

"The Hawthorns" Church Rd Hayes Mdx.

Dearest Eleanor,
Many thanks for your last letter. I have had not an instant to write. I hope all goes well with you? Are you selling any stockings? And do your clients behave properly? I was in Trafalgar Square only yesterday, because I'd had to run up to London, but it was such short notice that I couldn't write to let you know, & I didn't know any adress° except your Roehampton one, otherwise we might have met. A pity.

Can you by any chance come out with me this *Sunday* 18th? (w.p.[1] of course, but given even tolerable weather I should love to go for a walk somewhere.) For instance if you could take a ticket to Uxbridge from Paddington & let me know the time, I could get in at Hayes & we could go on to Uxbridge & have a good long walk, & get lunch at Denham or somewhere[2]—I hardly know the country but could consult a map. I hope it will be possible. Also, a friend of mine in London has some time shortly coming to stay with him a person who he says is most exciting—an old man who lives the life of a vagabond in order to conform with the Sermon on the Mount. He said if the old man arrived before I went away, to come in & see him, & I said I would like to bring a friend, so if all the times fitted we might go there some evening. In any case I must try & arrange a meeting with you somehow before I leave London. I leave here about the 22nd, I think. What date are you going down? Perhaps we could travel together. Let me know your news & your plans, & your adress° if you have changed it. I must stop now or I shall miss the post.

With much love
Eric

P.S. Thanks ever so for sending that letter from the *Nation*. A very feeble attack I thought—not worth answering.[3]

1. Weather permitting.
2. Compare the excursion made by Gordon Comstock and Rosemary to Burnham Beeches in *Keep the Aspidistra Flying*, chapter VII.
3. Theodore Fyfe's letter to *The New Statesman and Nation*; see *145*.

153. To Eleanor Jaques

Mon., [19 December 1932]   Handwritten lettercard; dated from postmark;
addressee from address[1]

[1]"The Hawthorns"   Church Rd.   Hayes   Mdx.

In haste. I will meet you as you say on *Wednesday*, 3.30 pm outside National Gallery. Also on Friday, I would like to travel down with you, & for that am even ready to start out in the middle of the night as you propose. Let's make quite sure about the times, however, because last time I took the Eclipse I was left in the soup thro' their starting from a different place & at a different time without warning anybody.

Till Wednesday, au revoir & love.

Eric

1. Orwell spelt Eleanor's surname 'Jacques' on the address side of the lettercard.

154. 'King Charles II'

[September–December 1932]   Typewritten; handwritten annotations

Orwell's correspondence from 19 September 1932 makes frequent reference to the work he was doing in producing a school play he had written. This activity clearly dominated his Christmas term. There are many parallels between this play and the play, *Charles I*, Dorothy produces in *A Clergyman's Daughter*, in particular his 'suffering untold agonies with glue & brown paper etc.,' as he wrote to Eleanor Jaques, 18 November 1932. (See *A Clergyman's Daughter*, *CW*, III, last two paragraphs of 84 and final paragraph of the novel, 296–97). He refers to his 'miserable school play' in a letter to Leonard Moore but, in what is doubtless self-depreciation, he does admit it 'went off not badly' (23 December).

It was presumably presented about the 20 December. The play was again performed at Hayes on 4 April 1992, by Compass Arts Theatre.

The play survives because one of the participants, Geoffrey W. Stevens, kept his copy; his name, in Orwell's hand, is at the top of the second and third leaves. This typescript was bought in 1988 by Bill Blair, of Connecticut (no relation to Orwell), who kindly allowed it to be included here and provided some information about the physical characteristics of the script. See also William T. Blair, 'George Orwell's "King Charles II": An Early Criticism of Revolutionary Government,' *Review of English Studies*, 41 (1980), 370–73.

There are fifteen leaves. The first three are typed; the remaining twelve, numbered 3 to 14 (making two pages numbered 3), are from wax stencils of the Gestetner (or similar) system. The first two leaves were typed on typing paper and the third on lined school-essay paper; these three measure 8 by 10 inches. The other pages are on foolscap (13 by 8¼ inches). The different modes of production and the two page threes indicate that the opening of the play was rewritten at a late stage, after copies of the script had been run off, perhaps to establish the setting more clearly. The date, '1651,' is not clear and has sometimes been misread as '1661'; see Crick, 232. Speech headings have been set in italic for greater clarity. The sound effects in the margins of the first two pages are in Orwell's hand. Simple mistypings have been corrected; otherwise the words of the script are as reproduced here.

Orwell takes some licence with fact. The first act is on the night of the Battle of Worcester, 23 August 1651. Act II is set in Bristol the following day, to which Will Hodge has been brought, as a prisoner, some sixty miles, and from which Charles escapes by boat to France. In fact, Charles was hunted for nearly six weeks, hiding, according to a legend Orwell ignores, in an oak tree near Worcester while Cromwell's troops searched for him in nearby fields.

The characters, in order of speaking, are:

Landlord of an inn near Worcester
Mr Giles, the oldest inhabitant of the village
George Burton, a labourer
Lucy, the landlord's daughter
Sir Edward Mortimer, a cavalier fleeing from the battle
Sir James Digby, a cavalier fleeing from the battle
Charles II, King of England, seeking to escape to France
Will Hodge, apprentice to the landlord
Captain Chambers, 17th Regiment, Parliamentary Army
Thin Roundhead soldier
Fat Roundhead soldier   A Father
A Boy, his son   A Man.

KING CHARLES II.

ACT I

Scene: An inn near Worcester. It is the evening of the Battle of Worcester, 1651. Present in the inn are the landlord, Mr. Giles, the oldest inhabitant of the village, his granddaughter, Lucy, and George Burton, a labourer.

Mr G. (setting down his mug).   You've been a-watering that beer again, landlord!

Landlord. No, not I.

[BOOM] *Mr G.* It don't taste the same as it did when I were a boy. I mind the time, in good Queen Bess's reign—(A booming noise. All except Mr G. look towards the window.)

Burton. Hark! Did you hear that? The guns!

[BOOM]

HORSES *Mr G.* What's that, eh? (Another boom.) I'm a little hard of hearing these
coming nearer] days.

Lucy. (standing looking out of window) Oh, grandpa! There's men coming down the road on horseback, with swords in their hands!

Mr G. What?

Landlord (shouting in Mr G.'s ear) The guns! From the battle. Charles's army and Cromwell's have been fighting ever since the morning. We shall know who's won in half an hour.

[Horses stop] *Mr G.* Ah, the battle? A lot of foolishness! We didn't have these here civil wars and rebellions when I was a young man. I mind the time—(A sudden
[FIRING] burst of firing outside.)

[FIRING *Lucy.* Oh, grandpa! They're fighting! (Jumps down and runs to her
SHOUTING grandfather for protection. Loud noise of fighting outside—banging,
CLASHING shouting, clashing of swords etc. Landlord bars door on left of stage.)
HORSES]
Burton. Here! Let's get out of this!

[Ditto, not *Landlord.* By the looks of things, Charles is beaten and his army's
quite so loud [SCREAM]
scattered. (Scream from outside.) Listen to that! They're cutting some poor fellow's throat down there, in the street. This is no place for the child. You'd best get out the back way, Mr Giles, as quick as you can.

Mr G. (as more firing sounds) Here, help me up, one of you! I can't skip
[FIRING] about like you young fellows, with the rheumatics in my bones. (More
[BULLET] firing. A bullet comes in through the window and rattles against the wall.)

Burton. Here! I'm off! (Exit hurriedly by right door).

Landlord (helping Mr G. up) Come on, Mr Giles. Get the child out of this.
[FIRING] (Mor° firing, a little further off.)

[HORSES *Lucy.* Oh, grandpa! I'm frightened!
getting
further off.] *Landlord.* Don't you be afraid, dear; they're going away now. Go out the back away° and across the fields. You'll be safe there. (Exeunt Mr G. and
[KNOCK] Lucy. As they go there is a bang on the left door.)

Landlord. Who's there? (Takes sword from wall.)

Voice without. Friends!

Landlord.   Roundhead or Cavalier?

Voice without.   Cavaliers. We come from the battle. Open, for God's sake!

(Landlord puts back sword and opens door. Enter Sir Edward Mortimer, supporting Sir James Digby, who is almost falling with exhaustion.)

Landlord.   What! Is it you, Sir Edward Mortimer?
        And you, good old Sir James! I scarcely knew you,
        So thick the dust of battle lies upon you.

Sir E.M.   Look to Sir James; he's spent and all but dead;
        Such days as these are ill for his white hairs.
(They help Sir J.D. to table and sit him in a chair.)

Sir J.D.   Some wine! I shall be better presently.
(Wine is brought and Sir J.D. is revived.)

Landlord.   How went the battle, sir?

Sir E.M.   Lost! All is lost.
        Those guns you hear are Cromwell's guns, now scattering
        The last of Charles's force. There's no hope now
        But that our gracious king may slip his foes
        And journey safe to France.

Sir J.D.   Ay, all is finished,
        And all our labour and our wounds are vain.
        I think a bloodier battle ne'er was fought
        Than this most fatal day of Worcester field.

Sir E.M.   We have had our share. This sword of mine is bloody,
        And here's my own blood on my doublet, too,
        Where one of Cromwell's footmen thrust his pike,
        Bawling "Death to the king!" An inch this way
        And he'd have ended me.

Sir J.D.   This wine revives me.
        Come, Mortimer, we must not waste our time;
        There's much to be arranged. – Listen, good landlord,
        After the fight today, when all was lost,
        Our gracious king, seeing his hopes defeated,
        Rode from the field with thirty faithful men
        To seek a hiding place. And we have word
        That he will travel, alone and in disguise,
        Along this very road.

Landlord.   What, sir, will the king come here?

Sir. E.M.   Yes. We shall meet him here and plan how best
        To keep him hid till we've a ship for France.
        He will be here at any moment now.
        We must make ready. Have you horses here?

Landlord.   We've two, sir.

Sir E.M.   Good – (sound of steps on stair.)

Sir J.D.   Hark! Do you hear that step upon the stair?
It will be he, I doubt not; but stand ready,
Lest this should be some stranger.

(Sir E.M. stands waiting with his hand on his sword. Knock at door.)

Landlord.   Enter!

(Enter a man dressed as Sir E.M. and Sir J.D., but muffled up in his cloak and with his hat pulled over his face. As he reaches the centre of the stage he throws open his cloak and pulls off his hat. It is Charles II.)

Sir J.D. & Sir E.M. (falling on one knee)   The king!

Landlord   (falls on his knees behind them)   Lord have mercy on us! The king!

Charles.   Up,   gentlemen!   We'll spare the ceremonies;
There is no time to waste in kneeling now.
Is all safe here?

Sir J.D.   Yes, sire, for the while.
And comes your Majesty alone?

Charles.   Alone, weaponless and on foot.
My horse is dead. My sword is snapped in two.
My men are scattered through the countryside.
I am a penniless and landless king.
True subjects must you be who would serve such.

Sir J.D.   Heaven send your majesty a better fortune!

Sir E.M. and Landlord.   God save the king!

Charles.   I trust He may.
I hardly know how I have come so far,
With troops of horsemen scouring every road,
Beating the bushes with their swords and crying
'Where went the king?' No matter, I am here,
And we'll take breath awhile and make our plans.
We are safe here, I hope. Whose house is this?

Landlord.   Mine, sire. Your Majesty's poor subject.

Sir E.M.   A loyal fellow, sire, I'll warrant him.

Charles.   Good. Let's to work. Here are my plans (produces map),
     and here
The safest roads are marked; I'll make for Bristol;
A ship waits there, under a loyal captain

Who'll keep me hid till we are safe at sea.
Have you your horses ready, landlord?

Landlord. I'll call the boy, sir. He shall saddle them. (Calls through inner door) Will! Are you there, Will?

Will Hodge. Ay ay, sir!

Sir E.M. That voice again!

(Enter Will Hodge by inner door, where Landlord meets him. Charles and the others are busy with the maps at the table. Landlord takes Will by the shoulders to straighten him up, & pulls some straws out of his hair. Will is a stupid-looking youth, with a broad accent.)

Landlord (in a low voice to Will) Come on, now, straighten yourself up! Try and look like a man. Stand up and don't gape. That's the king over there.

Will (in a much louder voice) The king? Go on, that ain't the king! The king's dead. They cut 'is 'ead off two year ago.

Landlord. The king's son, fool!

Will. Oh, the king's *son*? Why, you said 'e was the king just now.

Landlord. Come on, you fool!

(Pushes him over towards table. As they appear before the others, Sir J.D. and Sir E.M. start up and exclaim in astonishment. Charles also looks up to see what is the matter. Will stands in front of them pulling his forelock.)

Sir E.M. Sire, do you see that face?

Charles.   What?

Sir J.D.   This fellow's face, sire!
The strangest chance that ever yet befell!
This clown – it seems near treasonable to say it—
He is the living image of yourself.
Look at his face sire.

Charles.   What? That's strange.

(Charles has got up, and at the same time Sir E.M. has produced a small mirror from his pocket. He takes Will by the shoulders & holds the mirror up so that Charles may see his own face side by side with Will's.)

Will.   'Ere! What are you doin' of?

Landlord (prodding him in back) Silence, fool!

Charles.   We're strangely like, indeed.

Sir J.D.   Saving your presence, sire, this lad might be

Your own twin brother. His voice, too, is the same,
Though coarse in speech and accent.

Landlord.   All these years
Poor Will has kept my pigs, and never yet
I saw that likeness!

Sir E.M.   Look, sire!

(He has picked up Charles's hat and cloak from the table, and he quickly wraps the cloak round Will and claps the hat on his head.)

Will.   'Ere! What are you dressin' me up for? 'Oo do you think I am?
Guy Fawkes?

Sir E.M.   Look, sire! A very king in seeming.

Charles.   Strange!
Had this but come at any other time,
We'd have rare jests upon it. – But time presses.
Take off that cloak; we can't be fooling now.
Will, haste and saddle your horses. Feed them first,
And hang a store of corn upon each saddle.

Will.   Yessir! (Exit.)

Charles.   Good landlord, bring what food and drink you can;
I must get strength before my journey hence.

Landlord.   I will, sire.

(He is just starting to follow Will when there is a loud bang on the outer door. All start. Another bang, and trampling of feet.)

Landlord.   Who's there?

Voice without.   Open in the name of the law!

Sir J.D. and Sir E.M.   The Roundheads!

(The Landlord runs to the door and shoots the bolt.)

Voice without.   Open in the name of the law!

Landlord.   Who are you that speak?

Voice without.   Captain Chambers, of the seventeenth regiment, with a troop of fifty horse. We seek the traitor Charles Stuart, who fled from the battle and has been traced along this road. Open! (Another bang.)

Charles.   Lost after all! Ah, had I but been gone
Five minutes since!

Sir J.D.   Draw your sword, Mortimer. At least we'll shed
Some Roundhead blood before they take the king.

Voice without.   Open!

Charles.   The game is lost. I can but fight and die.

Sir E.M.   But not alone, sire! While we three can fight,
These Roundheads shall repent they ever came.

Voice without.   Open! (More and louder banging.)

Charles.   I'll sooner die than yield. (Draws his sword, finds it to be
broken, and throws it on the floor.)
Give me that sword that hangs upon the wall;
They shall not serve me as they served my father.

(All this time the banging and trampling without are getting louder.
Landlord hurries for the sword that is hanging on the wall. Meanwhile Sir
E.M. & Sir J.D. have drawn their swords and are standing waiting for the
door to break. As the landlord comes back a thought seems to strike him, and
he halts.)

Landlord.   Sire! Sire! All is not lost! All may be well,
Can we but find the time to do it. Listen,
Will Hodge the prentice boy, whose face and yours
Are liker than two brothers – he shall play
The part of king until the danger's over.
I'll fetch him now; we'll dress him in your clothes
And when the door breaks, as it must ere long,
They'll sieze° him for your majesty. The while,
You, meanly clad, take horse and slip away;
For they'll not care how servants come and go.
Thus all is saved, if Heaven wills it.

Sir E.M.   Most timely thought!

Sir J.D.   Brave plan indeed!

Charles.   O noble landlord!
If ever I do rule this land again,
Thou shalt be duke. Go! There's no time to lose.

(Exit Landlord hurriedly. Louder noise and more shouts without all this
time. The three men are standing at the door, and Sir E.M. & Sir J.D. still
have their swords drawn.)

Sir J.D.   Heaven send this door will stand!

Charles.   It's of strong oak;
'Twill hold five minutes – enough, if we are speedy.

(A much louder crash and sound of splintering.)

Sir E.M.   Ah, they have brought a beam! They'll break it now
Within two minutes. (Runs to inner door and shouts)
Make haste, there! Oh make haste!

(Re-enter Landlord dragging Will by the arm.)

Will. 'Eere, what's all this? There's a 'ole troop of men outside with swords and muskets. (Crash at the door.) They'll 'ave that door off the 'inges if they go on like that. What's it all about, eh?

Landlord. Don't talk, fool! Off with your jerkin!

Will. Why should I – (Landlord begins to pull Will's jerkin over his head.)

Sir J.D. (At door and holding it) Quick, sire, the hinge is yielding! Off with your cloak!

(In frantic haste Will is dressed in Charles's clothes and Charles in Will's. Will exclaims from time to time " 'Ere, what's all this?" etc. The noise outside is growing louder and louder, and there are shouts of "Now, all together, men!" etc. The door is evidently giving way. Landlord and Sir J.D. fling themselves against the door as the exchange of clothes is finished.)

Sir J.D. Fly, fly, your Majesty! And we'll delay them
Till you are clear away.

Sir E.M. (To Will.)   And you, Will, play your part.
You are Charles Stuart now. When they arrest you,
Answer "I am the king". You understand?

Will. I'm to say "You are the king". Is that it, sir?

Sir E.M. No, fool! *You* are the king. If you act well,
There's gold for you; but if not, with this sword
I'll run you through the body. – Fly, your majesty, fly!

Charles. Farewell, good friends. There is no time to speak
My thanks for all that you have done today,
But in a happier time I'll not forget it.
Farewell!

The others. God save the king!

(Exit Charles by inner door. The others except Will Hodge hurry to the table, Sir E.M. & Sir J.D. sit down, and all try to look as innocent as possible. Will is left standing in the middle of the room. At the same moment as Charles disappears, the door breaks. Enter Captain Chambers and two soldiers, one fat, one thin. They present their pistols at Will.)

Captain C. Stand, in the name of the law!

Will. Well, I ain't sitting down, am I?

Captain C. What is your name?

Will. Hi am the king. (Behind his hand to others at table) That's right, ain't it?

Captain C. You are not the king. There is no king in England now. You are the rebel and traitor Charles Stuart. I now arrest you in the name of the law, and your head will be cut off as your father's was. Secure him, men!

(The soldiers approach Will. The thin soldier stands in front of him and the fat soldier behind. Both point their pistols at him.)

Will. Don't you get saying things against my father, my father's never 'ad 'is 'ead chopped off. 'E's one of the most respected men in the parish, my father is.

Thin soldier. Up with your hands!

Will. What for?

Thin soldier. Put up your hands, I said! (Will obeys.)

Captain C. Search him, men. If he has weapons, take them.

Thin soldier. Come, now, Charles Stuart! If you've a pistol, hand it over.

Will (reaches down to take pistol at his belt) 'Ere you are, then.

Fat soldier. Hands up! (Will puts up his hands again.)

Thin soldier. Didn't I tell you to hand over your pistol. (Will begins to lower his hands again.)

Fat soldier. Hands up! (This goes on several times.)

Will. Well, there's no satisfying some people.

Captain C. (reading from a scroll) I publish to all and sundry that Charles Stuart has been proclaimed an outlaw and rebel against the laws of England. He will be removed for instant execution. The penalty for aiding his escape is death. (While he is saying this the fat soldier slips to the table, takes a pull at one of the mugs which are on it, and jumps back to his place in time as the officer looks up.) You, men, guard your prisoner well. I go now to order the troop for his escort. When I call, you will follow with the prisoner.

Soldiers. Yes sir.

Captain C. And remember, you are soldiers of Cromwell's army. See that you behave accordingly. Let me hear of no drinking or riotous behaviour in this low pothouse. You understand.

Fat soldier. Oh yes, sir. We never drink, we don't, sir.

(Exit Captain C.)

Will. 'Ere, 'ow much longer 'ave I got to stand with my 'ands up in the air?

Thin soldier. Just as long as we think good for you.

Will. Well, I'll look a nice fool if my trousers start coming down, won't I?

(Meanwhile the fat soldier is again at the table and has picked up one of the mugs.)

Fat soldier. Well, when the cats° away the mice will play. Better have a drink while we get the chance.

Thin soldier. For shame! Don't you know that drink is a man's worst enemy?

Fat soldier. Well, we're told to love our enemies, aren't we? (drinks)[1]

Will. 'Ere, what was that your captain said? "Instant execution", 'e said. What does that mean – "instant execution"?

Fat soldier. It means having your head chopped off, mate, and pretty quick about it. I've seen 'em – whack! (Makes the motion of a chopper striking his neck, and drinks again.)

Will. But you don't mean as I've got to 'ave my 'ead chopped off? (Lowers his hands and begins feeling at his neck.)

Thin soldier. Up with your hands!

Fat soldier. Cheer up, mate; it don't hurt after the first stroke.

Will. Oh dear, my 'ead feels loose on my shoulders already.

(A shout outside)

Soldiers. Coming, sir! (They begin to march Will out of the room.)

Will. But 'ere, I say! I didn't know as I was letting myself in for this, I didn't!

Fat soldier. Come on, Charles Stuart. You're going to instant execution, you are. Whack!

Will. But I say – (Exeunt soldiers with Will between them.)

Sir E.M. (springing to his feet) All's well!

Landlord. Ay, sir, the king is safe by now.

Sir J.D. With this escape he will get safe to sea.
They'll not find out their error till the morning,
And then, since poor Will Hodge is innocent,
They'll set him free. You have done nobly, landlord;
The king will not forget it.

Sir E.M.   No, nor we.
Here's gold – the best I can in these poor times.

(Hands him money. Sir J.D. does the same. Both move towards door.)

Landlord. Fare you well, sirs.

Sir J.D.   Farewell.
We will to Bristol swiftly as we may;
Please Heaven tomorrow sees the king set free,
The danger over and the ship at sea.

CURTAIN

ACT II

Bristol. A street. About the middle of the stage, a little to the right, a pair of stocks in which Will Hodge is sitting, eating an apple. The two soldiers who took him prisoner the previous night are guarding him, one on either side, armed with pikes. Throughout the act, when no-one else is present the fat soldier lounges about and produces a clay pipe from his pocket, springing to attention again when anybody else appears.)
Enter from the left a crowd, among whom are a father, mother and small boy.

The father. Well, there's been some rare goings-on lately. They say the king escaped from the battle after all and got clear away. They say he's hiding in this town now. If they don't look sharp and catch him he'll slip aboard a ship and be away to France.

Another man. I wouldn't be sorry if he did, either.

Father. Well, don't you go saying it too loud, or you might find yourself dangling from a gallows. They're hanging everyone who helped him to escape, it's said.

Boy. (pointing to Will) What's that man doing there, father?

Father. He's in the stocks, sonny.

Boy. Why did they put him there, then?

Father. Because he's been naughty, I expect.

Boy. Shall I be put in the stocks when I'm grown-up, father?

Father. We'll hope not, sonny.

Boy. Poor man! Let's give him a penny.

Father. It'd take more than a penny to get him out of there, I expect.

(By this time the crowd is half across the stage.)

Fat soldier. (relaxing and rubbing his back) This job don't half give me the crick in the back! Oh Lord, here comes the captain! (Springs to attention again. Enter Captain C. with a scroll in his hand. The soldiers salute. The bystanders listen while Captain C. reads from the scroll.)

Captain C. (reading) "I publish to all and sundry that Will Hodge has been sentenced to death for aiding the rebel Charles Stuart in his escape. He will be publicly exposed in the stocks for the space of one day, and after that taken to the place appointed and hanged by the neck until he is dead. So perish all traitors!" Fix this notice above his head. (Soldiers obey.) And you (to thin soldier), come with me. You, fellow (to fat soldier), guard your prisoner well!

Fat soldier. Yessir! (Exeunt Captain C. and thin soldier.)

Father. There, you see what it is, my boy. He's going to be hung tomorrow.

Boy. Poor man! (As the crowd leaves the stage the boy runs back, drops a penny in Will's lap, and follows his parents.)

Will. (to soldier) What was that your captain said?

Fat soldier. He said you was to be hung by the neck until you was dead. I wouldn't be in your shoes, mate, that I wouldn't.

Will. 'Ung by the neck. 'Ere! I wouldn't like that!

Fat soldier. It ain't what you like, it's what's good for you, see?

Will. But what 'ave I done? Why should I be 'ung?

Fat soldier. Oh, it don't take much to get a man hung nowadays. Lucky for you you wasn't ordered to be drawn and quartered as well.

Will. But it ain't fair! I won't 'ave it! (Struggles.)

Fat soldier. Now then, none of that! If you get up to any tricks, it's my duty to take this here pike and run you through the middle. (Prods him with point of pike.)

Will. Well, do me a kindness and don't do your duty, then.

(Fat soldier springs to attention. Enter from left Charles still in disguise, with Sir J.D. & Sir E.M.)

Charles.   Halt here a moment while we're unobserved.
Listen, Sir James, 'tis best, I think, to part;
No end is served by going three together,
For if they take us, your head falls with mine.
We'll say farewell; make you your own escape,
While I, thus meanly clad, slip to the quay,
Creep past the Roundhead sentries, take a skiff,
And board my vessel like a common sailor.
Once there, I'm safe, but I must make all speed;
In half an hour the tide begins to ebb,
And we must sail ere that.

Sir J.D.   God speed your majesty!
I'd come with you and share your fate, if taken,
But that one man is more observed than three.

Sir E.M.   Could not your majesty devise some signal
Whereby we'll know when you are safely sped?

Charles.   Well thought! I'll have the captain fire his cannon
Soon as the ship has crossed the harbour bar.
Then when you hear the cannon boom, you'll know
That Charles is safe at last.

Sir J.D.	Heaven send we hear that sound!
Charles.	There is one other matter. Good Sir James,
	And you, good Mortimer, receive my pledge
	That when these ills are past, and once again
	I hold my father's throne, your loyal aid
	Shall be rewarded. That good landlord, too,
	He never shall regret the part he played.
	But one thought troubles me. That village boy,
	Will Hodge, he whom the Roundheads took for me,
	What has befallen him? He's safe, I trust?
	I would not wish that he should come to ill.
Sir J.D.	They'll set him free, your majesty, I doubt not,
	He was but ignorant. – Ha! What is this?
	(He sees Will Hodge in stocks.)
Charles.	What is it?
Sir E.M.	(holding Charles back) No, sire, don't show your face! These
	soldiers know you.
	I'll go myself. (Goes up to soldier.)
	(To soldier.) Good fellow who is this?
	What crime has he committed?
Fat soldier.	Traitor, sir. Will Hodge his name is, sir. Going to be hung to-morrow morning, sir.
Sir E.M.	Hanged? Oh, poor wretch! (Hurries back to Charles.) Sire, it is
	poor Will Hodge,
	Condemned to die for aiding your escape.
Charles.	O evil fate! Can we not save him? Ah,
	That I should bring this poor, good soul to death!
Sir J.D.	You can do naught, sire. If yourself were taken,
	It would not change his fate. And a king's life
	Is worth a thousand of such simple yokels.
Charles.	Still, let's do what we can. Look, here is gold;
	Take all I have, there's more aboard the ship,
	And if I'm taken, why, I need no gold.
	Give him it all, for gold unlocks all doors;
	Perchance he'll buy a pardon.
Sir J.D.	I'll see to it.
	And now, sire, let's be gone, for the ship waits,
	And all is ruined if you lose the tide.
	Conceal your face, sire, while we pass the soldier.

(They pass the stocks, Charles hiding his face, and pause by the right hand exit.)

Charles. Now, fare you well, good friends!

Others. Farewell, sire!

Charles. Guard your own safety, both, and let me know
If poor Will Hodge makes his escape or no.
I'll to the quay, and when the cannon roars,
You'll know that Charles is bound for friendly shores.

(Exit.)

Sir J.D. I'll ne'er breathe freely till the cannon sounds.
And now to save Will Hodge. (Approaching soldier) Tell me,
    good fellow,
If I should make some gift to this poor wretch,
Some trifle that will buy him simple comforts,
Is that unlawful?

Soldier. No, sir, not that I knows of.

Sir J.D. (Giving purse to Will)   Take this, poor man. If you must die, at
    least
You'll not die comfortless. (To Sir E.M., as they pass on) And
    now to wait,
And pray that we may hear the cannon roar.
There's twenty minutes yet; if by that time
The gun sounds not, then Charles's doom is sealed.

(Exeunt.)

(Will tips the gold pieces out of the bag and counts them.)

Soldier. Coo! Your luck's in, ain't it?

Will. Luck? A precious lot of use this is to me when I'm going to be 'ung tomorrow morning. I'd give more than that lot to be out of this 'ere. (Points to stocks.)

Soldier. Well, we can have something to pass the time away, any way. Slip us one of them and I'll run off and get a bottle for the two of us.

Will. What? Run off an° leave me, would you? What about your duty as you're always talking about?

Soldier. Oh, we has a bit too much duty in Cromwell's army. It's duty morning, noon and night. – Look out, cover that money up. There's somebody coming.

(Enter from the left a crowd, running, headed by the father, mother and boy who appeared before.)

Father. Quick! This way. The king's down at the harbour, and they say he's getting aboard a ship. He'll be out at sea in another moment if they don't catch him. Come on!

(Exeunt running across stage and shouting. Enter from left Captain C. and thin soldier.)

Captain C.   Run to the quay, fellow! Go like the wind! Bid them stop every ship, board her and search her. I'll follow. Run!

(Exit soldier running across stage. Captain C. follows more slowly. Enter from left Sir J.D. and Sir E.M.)

Sir J.D.   Now speed is all. If Charles's sails are set
Before the Captain's message reach the quay,
Then all is well. We can but wait in hope.
And listen for the gun's report. – Come, we'll go this way.

(Exeunt across stage.)

Soldier.   Well, they've all gone down to the quay. Now's our chance for a quiet bottle. Hand over one of them guineas, won't you?

Will.   No. Think I'm going to hand my money over to you?

Soldier.   Don't be a fool! Have you forgot you're going to be hung tomorrow morning? Your money won't be much use to you at the other end of the drop. Might as well spend it while you get the chance.

Will.   Don't you get calling me a fool!

Soldier.   Well, you are a fool, aren't you? Didnt° they use to call you the village idiot? Why, the bloke at the inn told me as you couldn't even read and write.

Will.   Reading and writing ain't everything. There's plenty of things I can do as you cant,° anyway.

Soldier.   What, for instance?

Will.   Lots of things. Well, for instance, you couldn't turn your toes in same as I'm doing now. (Turns his feet round in the stocks so that his toes meet.)

Soldier.   Course I could! Anybody could. Look here. (Turns his toes in.)

Will.   I meant in the stocks, silly. You couldnt° do it if you was sitting in the stocks same as I am now.

Soldier.   Course I could!

Will.   I bet you you couldn't.

Soldier.   I bet you I could.

Will.   I bet you all this lot you couldn't. (Shakes purse of money.)

Soldier.   Is that a bet?

Will.   Yes.

Soldier.   Come on, then, I'll show you. (Kneels down, produces key and unlocks stocks.) You'll be sorry you was so obstinate in a moment. I'll have that money off of you, and I'll drink a health to your body when it's swinging on the gallows. Come on, get out of my way. (Pushes Will aside and gets into stocks.)

Will. Let's see you do it, then. (Soldier settles himself in stocks. Will picks up key.)

Soldier. There you are, then. (Will locks stocks.) Here! What are you doing?

Will. You'll soon see.

Soldier (shouting)   You let me out of this?°

Will. Let you out, eh? (Laughs.) I may be a fool, but I ain't such a fool as all that, matey.

Soldier (shouting louder)   You let me out of it! (Aims a blow at Will.)

Will (standing just out of his reach)   Now then! Now then! No temper! This is what comes of betting, you see. Ain't there a rule against betting in your army? Let's 'ope this'll be a lesson to you.

Soldier. Help! Help!

(Will throws himself on the soldier, binds him with his scarf, gags him, and muffles him up in his cloak and hat. The soldier makes gurgling noises.)

Will. Well, I'm off. Good bye, soldier. (Chinks his purse of money in the soldier's ear.) Village idiot you called me, was it? Perhaps I ain't the *only* idiot in the world. (Exit, chinking the purse of money.)

(Enter a crowd from the left, headed by Sir J.D. and Sir E.M.)

Sir J.D.   Still the gun has not fired! The time creeps by;
There's scarce five minutes now before the tide.
The chance hangs by a hair. – But what is this?

(They see the soldier alone and muffled up in the stocks. At the same time, enter from the right Captain C. He too sees the soldier.)

Captain C.   What's this? Treason! Where are the guards? (He pulls off the soldier's hat and gag, and sees who it is.) Speak, villain! What's happened? You'll smart for this!

Soldier.   Sir –

(A tremendous explosion. It is the gun of the king's ship firing. Sir E.M. & Sir J.D. wave their hats. Enter from the right a messenger, running.)

Messenger. (to Captain C)   Sir! Sir! The king's escaped! His ship has left the harbour. They fired that shot as they crossed the bar. The soldiers arrived there just a minute too late.

Captain C.   Ten thousand curses!

(Cheer from the crowd.)

Captain C.   Silence, there! Silence, for shame! Is this a time for cheering, when a traitor whose head should have fallen has escaped? Silence, or some of you may hang for it. (To messenger.) Come, fellow, to the harbour. (Exeunt. Another cheer from the crowd.)

The boy.   Oh, father, I am glad the king's escaped!

Father.   Well, I ain't sorry myself.

The boy.[2]   And that poor man that was in the stocks, he's escaped too.

Father.   Well, there's another of them in his place.

A man.   Come on, the king don't escape every day. Let's go and have a drink on it.

Soldier. (as he sees them moving away)   Here, what about me? Where do I come in?

Man.   You don't come in, mate, you stays where you are. I wouldn't be in your shoes when you go up before the general tomorrow morning. He'll order you fifty with the cat o' nine tails, he will.

Soldier.   Oh Lord, why did I join the army?

Sir J.D.   Good people all, this is a joyous time
When our good king, long in most dangerous plight,
Is safe at sea and bound for friendly France.
We'll honour it with song, and silver too
Sir Edward here and I will give you all
To drink good health unto his majesty.
Long may he flourish, and soon come the day
When the usurper Cromwell ends his sway;
Peace, freedom and prosperity shall reign
When England has her own true king again!
Come, sir, if you've a song, let's hear it.

(Song.)

CURTAIN.

1. drinks] *manuscript addition by Orwell*
2. The boy] *manuscript addition by Orwell*

A forty-page, lavishly-illustrated edition of this play, entitled *Król Karol II*, was published in February 2000 by Dom Wydawniczy Bellona, Warsaw. The Polish translation was by Bartolomiej Zborski (who contributes a two-page afterword) and the colour illustrations, nine of which are full page (A4 size), were drawn by Katarzyna and Pavel Glodkowie.

155. To Leonard Moore

Friday, [23 December 1932]   Handwritten

36 High St   Southwold   Suffolk

Dear Mr Moore,

Thanks very much for the advance copies,[1] which have just arrived. I think the get-up is very nice, & they have shown extraordinary cleverness in making it look quite a long book. What does "a recommendation of the Book Society" on the cover mean?

I wonder if it could be arranged that one copy should be sent for review to the Adelphi? They know me & I write for them sometimes, so they would give it a sympathetic review, I expect.

I hope you will have a merry Christmas. Please give my kindest wishes to Mrs Moore. The miserable school play over which I had wasted so much time went off not badly. I am now free till the 18th, & I hope in that time I'll be able to polish up a fair chunk of the novel[2] to the point where you can form an opinion on it.

Yours very sincerely
Eric A Blair

P.S. [at top of letter] I'm going to send this to your home adress° as I expect you won't be at your office for some days.[3]

1. Of *Down and Out in Paris and London*.
2. *Burmese Days*.
3. Annotated in Moore's office: '29/12/32.'

156. To Leonard Moore

24 December 1932   Handwritten

36 High St   Southwold   Suffolk

Dear Mr Moore,

I am sending you a copy of the book separately.[1] I didn't see your letter waiting for me till after I had sent off my previous letter to you. I am returning the postal order—of course the tickets were complimentary tickets, & anyway all is over now—I mean the play is performed & done with.[2] I shall send this to your office, as I don't expect it will arrive for several days.[3] In haste

Eric A Blair

1. Presumably one of the advance copies of *Down and Out in Paris and London* referred to in his letter of 23 December; see *155*.
2. Presumably tickets for the school play.
3. Stamped in Moore's office 28 December 1932 and answered on 30 December.

1933

157. Publication of *Down and Out in Paris and London*

Down and Out in Paris and London was published in London by Victor Gollancz on 9 January 1933; 1,500 copies were printed. Later in the month, 500 additional copies were printed. A third impression (date unknown) of 1,000 copies followed; none were remaindered. The type was distributed on 13 February 1934. Harper & Brothers, in New York, published 1,750 copies on either 30 June 1933, according to Ian Willison, or 25 July 1933, according to Miss Herdman of Harper; see *181* and *177A*. A review appeared in *Books* (U.S.) on 30 July, making the July date more likely. According to Willison, the type was also distributed on 13 February 1934; 383 copies were remaindered. A French translation by R. N. Raimbault and Gwen Gilbert, *La Vache Enragée*,[1] with a preface by Panaït Istrati,[2] was published by Gallimard, in Paris, on 2 May 1935. This edition of 5,500 copies had not been sold out by March 1953. (These details are principally from Willison.) Orwell wrote an introduction for the French edition; see *211* for an English version. Penguin Books published a paper-bound edition of 55,000 copies on 18 December 1940. The contemporary French translation has the title, *Dans la dèche* (an expression Arnold Bennett uses to describe destitution in the French-influenced English in the Paris scenes of *The Old Wives' Tale* (1908): 'Is he also in the ditch?' III, 6, iii).

Orwell's knowledge of *The People of the Abyss* (1903) by Jack London is well established. Whether he knew the work of the Czech-German Egon Erwin Kisch, in *Der Rasende Reporter* (1925), is uncertain. It is a series of short pieces on factual topics connected by thematic cross-references. The first is 'Unter den Obdachlosen von Whitechapel' (Among the Homeless of Whitechapel), an account of a night spent in a Salvation Army hostel in the East End of London.[3] What was factual, what autobiographical, and what fictitious in *Down and Out in Paris and London* was noted by Orwell in a copy of the book given to Brenda Salkeld. She and Michael Shelden, who located the book, kindly made these annotations available. The book is inscribed: 'To Brenda, with best wishes — Eric A Blair 28.12.32.' There are sixteen annotations, keyed here by chapter and page number to *CW*, I:

II, 7: para 'Listen, then': '*Not* autobiography. The fellow really did talk like this, tho'.'

III, 12: first para: 'Succeeding chapters not actually autobiography, but drawn from what I have seen.'

IV, 20: para 'It was now absolutely necessary': 'This is a fairly accurate portrait except for the name.'

V, 24: para 2, against 'Bouillon Zip': 'Bouillon Kub[4]—changed for fear of libel.'

V, 24: para 'The room was an attic': 'All this fairly exact description of actual happenings.'

VI, 32: 'Boris would contribute': 'Exaggerated: but I have seen people living in just this fashion.'

VII, 36: opening lines: 'This all happened.'

VIII, 44: para 'It was through one of these Russian refugees': 'This happened very much as described.'

X, 54: opening lines: 'All as exact as I could make it.'

XV, 82: start of Valenti's story: 'He did tell me this story, tho' not so consecutively.'

XIX, 100: opening lines: 'All the following is an entirely accurate description of the restaurant.'

XXIII, 123: para 'Roucolle died, aged seventy-four': 'More or less true, I believe.'

XXIV, 127: para 'Sleeping in the saloon': 'Quite true.'

XXIV, 128: para 'I was outside in the street': 'This incident is invented to explain trip, but all the experiences described hereafter are authentic.'

XXVI, 141: para 'He led the way': 'Called the "Ramblers' Rest"—High Church organisation.'

XXIX, 160: para 'An old public school boy': 'He wasn't actually an O.E,[5] but from some other well-known school, I forget which.'

1. The title is idiomatic: 'manger de la vache enragée' means 'to suffer great hardship,' or—more appropriately, with reference to Orwell's book—'to rough it.' *La Vache Enragée* was also the title of a satiric monthly journal published in Paris in 1896, for which Toulouse-Lautrec designed a poster.

2. Panaït Istrati (Gherassim Istrati, 1884–1935), Romanian author and translator, wrote in, and translated into, French. He was encouraged by Romain Rolland (1866–1944), who dubbed him 'a Balkan Gorki.' In 1927 he travelled in the USSR, and in 1929 published *Vers l'autre flamme*, three volumes written in collaboration with two others. According to the French translation of the *Small Soviet Encyclopédie Littéraire* (Moscow, 1966), it misrepresented Soviet life to such an extent, because of Istrati's petit-bourgeois conception of liberty, that Rolland and 'all true friends of the USSR' turned their backs on him (from *L'Arc*, Aix-en-Provence, 1983, 86/7, translated from Russian into French by Arthur Rubinstein and Jean Riere, 138). Istrati translated several novels by Upton Sinclair and William Faulkner for French publishers. In his preface to *La Vache Enragée*, he makes a number of comparisons between Gorki and Orwell. He concludes that Orwell's book makes one think, makes one meditate on life's griefs, just as does a novel by Balzac, but without one's having to endure Balzac's tedious detail. Istrati died three weeks before *La Vache Enragée* appeared.

3. See Keith B. Williams, 'The Will to Objectivity: Egon Erwin Kisch's *Der Rasende Reporter*,' *MLR*, 85 (1990), 92–106, an early draft of which was kindly given to the editor by its author. See also Dieter Schlenstedt, *Egon Erwin Kisch: Leben und Werk* (Berlin, 1985); for *Der Rasende Reporter*, see edition published by Verlag Kiepenheuer und Witsch (Köln, 1983).

4. Bouillon Kub was soup in granulated cube form based on beef essence. A famous advertisement of about the time Orwell was writing showed the red cube against a bull's head. The Bibliothèque des Arts Décoratifs, Paris, has a copy, and a colour illustration is in Attilio Rosi, *Posters* (Milan, 1966; London, 1969), dated 1930, though it bears the date 1931 next to the name of the designer, Leonatto Cappiello. The poster also appeared in the background in Truffaut's film *Le Dernier Métro* (1980), set in German-occupied Paris.

5. Old Etonian.

158. To Leonard Moore

17 January 1933   Typewritten

36 High St   Southwold   Suffolk

Dear Mr Moore,

I am returning to Hayes[1] tomorrow (Wednesday), and I thought of looking in at your office on my way through London, about four or half past, and taking a chance of your being still there. I want to bring you about 100 pp. I have not actually completed but got more or less into order of my novel.[2] If you are not there I will leave the ms., with some notes about the extent to which it is done etc.

I have seen a number of notices about the other book,[3] and they were very much better than I had expected, particularly those in the Evening Standard and the Daily Mail. I believe there was a good one in the Morning Post, but I didn't see that one. No libel actions hitherto, I hope? The book was listed in this week's Sunday Express among "best sellers of the week". Does that mean anything definite? I suppose it will be some weeks before you can tell whether it is selling or not.

A week ago I received from your office six copies of a novel called "Hanging Waters" (I think), and I returned them, as I supposed they must have been sent by mistake.[4] I hope they turned up all right.

Yours sincerely
Eric A Blair

1. The district in which the Hawthorns school was situated, about fourteen miles due west of London, four miles southeast of Uxbridge.
2. *Burmese Days*; the phrasing is Orwell's.
3. *Down and Out in Paris and London.*
4. Presumably author's free copies distributed prior to publication, and sent to Orwell by mistake. The author was Keith West (pen name for Kenneth Westmacott Lane); the novel was reviewed in January 1933. It was successful enough to have at least two cheap editions.

159. To Leonard Moore

1 February 1933   Typewritten

The Hawthorns   Church Rd.   Hayes   Mdx.

Dear Mr Moore,

I don't suppose you saw the enclosed rather snooty letter which was in the Times of 31st Jan.[1] It would have been most damaging to let it go unanswered. I enclose herewith a copy of the letter I have sent in reply, and if you have time I wish you would let me know whether this was the right reply to make.

I rang up your office on Saturday on the off chance of finding you there, but they said you were away. I wanted to know what you thought of the first 100 pp. of my novel,[2] that is if you had had time to look at it. I know that as it stands it is fearful from a literary point of view, but I wanted to know whether given a proper polishing up, excision of prolixities & general tightening up, it was at all the sort of thing people want to read about. I should think the[3] fact that it is about Burma and there are so few novels with that setting, might offset the lack of action in the story—it is mostly description, I am afraid; there are to be a murder and a suicide later, but they play rather a subsidiary part.

Yours sincerely
Eric A. Blair

P.S.[4] Thank you for forwarding a volume from a man named Gardner. I am writing to thank him.

1. The letter was from M. Umberto (printed as 'Humbert') Possenti of the Hotel Splendide, 105 Piccadilly, London W1:

   Sir, – I do not want to push myself forward, but I feel that, as no one else in my profession has come out to defend the good name of French *restaurateurs* and hotelkeepers, I have no choice but to do so. In your *Literary Supplement* of January 12 your reviewer, dealing with a recently published book of reminiscences, says that the author "found work as a washer-up in a famous restaurant, gaining there experiences which, he alleges, have made him vow never to eat a meal in a Parisian restaurant as long as he lives." Other papers have quoted the disgusting passage to which your reviewer refers, and in this way the author's allegations have secured a large publicity. In effect he claims to have proved by his experience that the kitchens of Parisian restaurants are filthy. That kitchen which he specially describes is said to be that of "one of the dozen most expensive hotels in Paris"; and it is further said to be "near the Place de la Concorde. . . . The ordinary charge for a night's lodging, not including breakfast, was 200 francs."

   Now, one of my French *confrères* ought to have dealt with this nonsense, but, as no one else has done so and as the allegations are by implication against all other luxury hotels and restaurants in Paris, and, since Paris may now be said to be the nursery of hotel management, against those of London, I am moved, as a *restaurateur* and *hôtelier* of 40 years' experience, to deny in the most emphatic manner possible the truth of what the author says. Such a disgusting state of things as he describes is in such places inconceivable. The kitchens of large and "smart" restaurants have to be clean; the work has to be done in a cleanly and orderly manner or it would not get done at all. Such kitchens, I assert, are cleaner than those of most private houses; they have to be. Moreover, it has long been the custom to allow the curious customer to see over the restaurant's kitchen. Speaking generally, the customer has only to ask the director of any restaurant of the first class to be allowed to see how the work is done and someone is at once detailed to show him round immediately—mind, no previous notice is demanded. To permit the book's statements to appear unchallenged would mean that infinite harm would be done to the London and Paris restaurant trade. By the way, I do not wish to be *méchant*, but in your issue of January 17 I saw with amusement that M. François de la Rochefoucauld, writing in 1784, says in a private letter that in English kitchens "the dirt is indescribable." That was 150 years ago; his experience could not have been great; and he was not attacking institutions in which hundreds of thousands of English pounds are invested.

2. *Burmese Days.*
3. the] that
4. Placed to the right of the valediction and signature. Mr. Gardner has not been identified.

160. To the Editor, *The Times*

11 February 1933

Sir,—

I have read a letter in your columns from M. Humbert Possenti attacking the truthfulness of my book "Down and Out in London and Paris", which was reviewed in your *Literary Supplement* of 12 January.[1] Referring to alleged dirtiness in the service quarters of a Paris hotel M. Possenti says:

> I am moved, as a *restaurateur* and *hôtelier* of 40 years' experience, to deny in the most emphatic manner possible the truth of what the author says. Such a disgusting state of things as he describes is in such places inconceivable. The kitchens of large and "smart" restaurants have to be clean: the work has to be done in an orderly and cleanly manner or it would not get done at all. Such kitchens, I assert, are cleaner than those of most private houses, &c.

M. Possenti seems not to realise that these remarks are quite beside the point. The passages objected to in my book did not refer to Paris hotels in general, but to one particular hotel. And as M. Possenti does not know which hotel this was he has no means of testing the truth of my statements. So I am afraid that, in spite of his 40 years' experience, my evidence in this case is worth more than his.

M. Possenti adds that hotel kitchens could not be seriously dirty, because "speaking generally" it is usual to allow inspection by customers. I do not know how "general" this practice is, but I do know that in our hotel there were places which no customer could possibly have been allowed to see with any hope of retaining his custom. M. Possenti also misquotes me by saying that I had "vowed never to eat a meal in a Parisian restaurant as long as I lived." I said nothing of the kind. What I did say was that I should never again enjoy a meal in a "smart" restaurant—*i.e.* a restaurant in which the food, in order to make it sufficiently elegant in appearance, has to be mauled about by sweaty hands.

By the way, M. Possenti seems to think that I have some patriotic animus against French restaurants as opposed to English ones. Far from it. I wrote about a Paris hotel and restaurant because it was of those that I had direct experience. I had no wish whatever to suggest that in this matter of kitchen dirtiness the French are worse than any other nation.

Yours faithfully,
"George Orwell"

1. On 17 February 1933, *The Times* published a letter from St Clair Thomson of 64 Wimpole St., London, W1, in which he said, 'hotelkeepers and *restaurateurs* would inspire still more confidence if they had a very visible notice inviting clients to inspect the kitchens at any hour, unannounced.' M. Possenti of the Hotel Splendide, Piccadilly, London, in a reply published on 21 February 1933, said that his kitchen would 'without notice, be open to the inspection of those who lunch and dine here—not too many at a time, of course, or the cooks will not be able to get on with their work!' The Splendide is no longer a hotel; for a time it housed the Arts Council of Great Britain. It is not known in which Paris hotel Orwell worked. The Georges V has been suggested; and also the Hôtel Lotti, to which Ashenden is summoned in chapter 7 of

Somerset Maugham's *Ashenden* (1928), a book Orwell recommended to Brenda Salkeld; see *166*. It is also mentioned in chapter two of Evelyn Waugh's *Vile Bodies* (1930). The dates are possibly significant, but the implications can be taken in contrary ways defying positive identification. Sam White (1911–1988), the *Evening Standard*'s Paris correspondent for many years, reported in the issue for 16 June 1967 a conversation he had had with Sonia Orwell in which two other hotels were suggested: the Ritz and the Crillon. Following that conversation, he said, 'It is now clear . . . that the hotel concerned was the Crillon.' Recent holiday guides give all these hotels the highest recommendations.

161. To Eleanor Jaques

18 February 1933   Handwritten

"The Hawthorns"   Church Rd.   Hayes   Mdx.

Dear Eleanor,

If you see the Pulleynes[1] any time I should be awfully obliged if you would ascertain whether the copy of my book I sent them turned up all right. They sent me a postal order to buy a copy for them, but of course I don't know whether it got there or not. Not much news. The agent was very pleased with the 100 pp. of my novel[2] I sent him, & harries me to get on with it. One of my poems in the March Adelphi,[3] I think—at least, I have had a proof of it. I have got a bit of garden & done some digging. Are you coming up to town? I do hope you are & we can meet. Let me know well in advance—I am so fearfully pressed for time here & have to make the most of my week-ends. Excuse this hasty scrawl.

Yours
Eric A Blair

1. Collett Cresswell Pulleyne, a barrister from Yorkshire, and his family are mentioned on a number of occasions in earlier correspondence with Eleanor Jaques and Dennis Collings; see *114, n. 2*. The Pulleynes lived in Southwold.
2. *Burmese Days.*
3. 'Sometimes in the middle autumn days'; see *164*.

162. To Leonard Moore

21 February 1933   Handwritten

"The Hawthorns"   Church Rd.   Hayes   Mdx.

Dear Mr Moore,

Thanks very much indeed, I am certainly very pleased to hear about your deal with Harper's.[1] I suppose they are the same people as run Harper's Magazine? DV,[2] I think I can promise you a further 100 pp. of the novel[3] about as near completion as the last, by the end of this term (ie. in April.)

Yours sincerely
Eric A Blair

1. The contract with Harper & Brothers, New York, to publish *Down and Out in Paris and London*; see 167. *Harper's*, as *Harper's New Monthly Magazine*, founded by the Harper brothers of the publishing house in New York, in 1850, made a feature of serialising English novels.
2. *Deo volente* (God willing).   3. *Burmese Days*.

163. To Eleanor Jaques

Sunday, [26 February 1933]   Handwritten

The Hawthorns   Church Rd.   Hayes   Mdx.

Dearest Eleanor,

How nice to hear from you again & know that you are in the land of the living. I am sorry that job with the fashion-plate artist didn't come to anything. I do hope you will find something to suit you, & don't forget about letting me know when you do come up to town. I am having a beastly cold—my first this winter, I think, but none the less annoying. It was very kind of Dennis to think of writing to the *Times* in my defence. They took their time about printing my letter of reply, & I have since also been criticised in the *Licensed Victuallers Gazette*,[1] but I think they are beneath answering. I think I shall be able to let the agent have the second 100 pp. of my novel by the end of this term. The other book[2] has been disposed of to Harpers—I mean the American rights—& I should think they are pretty good people to deal with. Yes, I met the old vagabond chap, & he was rather interesting. His philosophy seemed to me Buddhist rather than Christian—all about the futility of making any effort & the necessity [of] attaining peace of mind, in other words Nirvana. But he came flying back from Nirvana pretty rapidly when I said something against Carlyle (the old chap is[3] a Scotchman) so evidently the affairs of this world still have their claws in him. He said, what struck me as a sane remark, that he did not counsel anyone else to follow his own example, for everyone must work out his salvation in the way suited to him. This fits in with the Indian saying that there are 84,000 or is it 84,000,000 ways to salvation, & I suppose about double the number to damnation. I have just read a book called "James Joyce & the Plain Reader"[4]—weak trash, which would give the impression that J. was a writer on the Walpole-Priestley level. Also Upton Sinclair's autobiography—ridiculous, but rather fun. I have dug a biggish-sized patch of my garden, but there is still a lot to do & it is difficult to find the time. I wish you were coming up to town this next weekend as I have two or three free days on end—halfterm.

With much love
Eric

1. 17 February 1933.   3. is] was
2. *Down and Out in Paris and London*.   4. By Charles Duff.

164. 'Sometimes in the middle autumn days'

The Adelphi, March 1933

Sometimes in the middle autumn days,
The windless days when the swallows have flown,
And the sere elms brood in the mist,
Each tree a being, rapt, alone,

I know, not as in barren thought,
But wordlessly, as the bones know,
What quenching of my brain, what numbness,
Wait in the dark grave where I go.

And I see the people thronging the street,
The death-marked people, they and I
Goalless, rootless, like leaves drifting,
Blind to the earth and to the sky;

Nothing believing, nothing loving,
Not in joy nor in pain, not heeding the stream
Of precious life that flows within us,
But fighting, toiling as in a dream.

O you who pass, halt and remember
What tyrant holds your life in bond;
Remember the fixed, reprieveless hour,
The crushing stroke, the dark beyond.

And let us now, as men condemned,
In peace and thrift of time stand still
To learn our world while yet we may,
And shape our souls, however ill;

And we will live, hand, eye and brain,
Piously, outwardly, ever-aware,
Till all our hours burn clear and brave
Like candle flames in windless air;

So shall we in the rout of life
Some thought, some faith, some meaning save,
And speak it once before we go
In silence to the silent grave.

Eric Blair

165. To Brenda Salkeld

Friday night, [10? March 1933]   Handwritten

The Hawthorns   Church Rd.   Hayes   Mdx.

Dearest Brenda

Forgive me for not writing for so long, but I have been as usual submerged with work & in the intervals trying to break the back of my garden. Today I nearly broke my own back, using the turfing iron & yesterday gave myself one on the shin with a pickaxe. Have you read Ulysses yet?[1] If you want a good book explaining what James Joyce is about *don't* read "James Joyce for the Plain Reader" by some BF called Duff[2]—it is about the worst piece of criticism I have yet read. I forget if I told you that one thing you have to get used to in Ulysses is that great quantities of it are written in parody—some of the styles that I recognize, & some that I don't. For instance where a little girl of the servant type is thinking it is all in the style of Peg's Paper—rather an elephantine joke, I think. And there is a lot of parody of Homer &, I think, ancient Irish literature, which is sometimes exceedingly funny. You will find the first chapter or two dull, but they have to be read carefully, because everything reappears in dream-form in the great chapter. The only one you could read detached from its context is the last, & even then one wouldn't understand it all without having read the previous ones. It appears that in the chapter where the medical students are talking while the woman has a baby, the successive changes of style symbolise foetal development. I don't know why he does these tricks, nor why he has been so careful to keep the parallelism with the Odyssey so close.

Have you seen any more of your friends who worship Bernard Shaw? Tell them that Shaw is Carlyle & water, that he ought to have been a Quaker (cocoa and commercial dishonesty), that he has squandered what talents he may have had back in the '80's in inventing metaphysical reasons for behaving like a scoundrel, that he suffers from an inferiority complex towards Shakespeare, & that he is the critic, cultured critic (not very cultured but it is what B meant) that Samuel Butler prayed to be delivered from. Say that Shaw's best work was one or two early novels & one or two criticisms he wrote for the Saturday Review when Harris[3] was editor, & that since then it has got steadily worse until its only function is to console fat women who yearn to be highbrows. Say also that he has slandered Ibsen in a way that must make poor old I turn in his grave. Also that Shaw cribbed the plot of "Pygmalion" from Smollett & afterwards wrote somewhere or other that Smollett is unreadable. By the way I hope you are fasting hard, as this is Lent?[4] I have so few excesses of any kind that I have really nothing to give up. Write again soon & tell me all the news. Also if you are coming up to town again anytime. It was so nice at Burnham Beeches & I should love to go there again when the trees are budding.

With much love
Eric

1. During the 1930s, Orwell recommended 'best books' to Brenda Salkeld. She recalled these to Howard Fink many years later; see *166*.
2. Charles Duff. The book was published in 1932.
3. Frank Harris (1865–1931), British-American man of letters and author of *My Life and Loves*, published, mainly privately, in 1925 and for many years banned in Britain and the United States, edited the *Evening News* and *Fortnightly Review* in London and, in the United States, *Pearson's*.
4. Brenda Salkeld (see *107, n. 2*) was a clergyman's daughter.

166. 'Best Books' recommended by Orwell to Brenda Salkeld in the 1930s, as reported to Howard Fink[1]

BARHAM, R.   The Ingoldsby legends.
BOOTHBY, G.   Nikola.[2]
BRONTE, C.   Jane Eyre.
BRONTE, E.   Wuthering heights.
BUTLER, S.   The notebooks.

CHAUCER, G.   "Bits of the Canterbury tales, esp. 'Wife of Bath's Prologue' ".
CONRAD, Joseph.   The secret agent.

DARWIN, Charles.   Voyage of the Beagle.
DICKENS, Charles.   David Copperfield.
DOYLE, Conan.   Sherlock Holmes.

FIELDING, Henry.   Amelia.
FORSTER, E.M.   Passage to India.
FRANCE, Anatole.   L'anneau d'amethyste.
FREEMAN, R.A.   The eye of Osiris (and) various other detective stories.

GARNETT, (Dr.)   The twilight of the Gods.[3]

HARDY, Thomas   The Dynasts.
HUXLEY, A.   Antic hay.

JEFFRIES, R.   The amateur poacher.
JOYCE, James.   Ulysses.[4]

LAWRENCE, D.H.   England, my England.

MAUGHAM, W.S.   Ashenden.[5]
MELVILLE, H.   Typee (or) Moby Dick.
MERIMEE, P.   Carmen.

PETRONIUS, A.   The Satyricon (translation).
POE, E.A.   Tales of mystery and imagination.
PREVOST, A.   Manon Lescaut.

READE, C.   Foul play (or) A Jack of All Trades.
.. ..   Hard cash.

SHAKESPEARE, W. King Lear.
SMOLLETT, T. Peregrine Pickle.
STENDHAL. La Chartreuse de Parme.
SURTEES, R.S. Handley Cross.
SWIFT, J. Gulliver's travels.

THACKERAY, W.M. Vanity fair.
TOLSTOY, L. War and peace.
TROLLOPE, A. Barchester Towers.
TWAIN, Mark. Roughing it.[6]

VOLTAIRE, F. Candide.

ZOLA, E. La Débâcle.

1. This list, doubtless incomplete, is reproduced by permission of Howard Fink.
2. See letter to Brenda Salkeld, *142*.
3. See letter to Salkeld, *142*.　　　　5. See *160, n. 1*.
4. See letters to Salkeld, *165, 176, 186*.　　6. See letter to Salkeld, *204*.

167. To Leonard Moore

Sat. [25 March 1933]　　Handwritten

"The Hawthorns"　Church Rd.　Hayes　Mdx.

Dear Mr Moore,
Many thanks for the contract.[1] I enclose it herewith duly signed. It seems a very good one, & I am greatly obliged to you for getting it for me. Will Harper's want any changes in the book? I think I said some offensive things about Americans in one or two places—I forget.

I am sending for my press-cuttings; all of which I had sent home, & I will forward them to you as soon as possible. I don't think I care for that idea of giving biographical details, after the way I have seen American publishers use them. As to photographs, I am not certain whether my photograph would be a very good advert.

I have been terribly busy, but managed to get through the piece of the novel[2] I set myself & I will let you have pp. 100–200 round about April 15th.

Yours sincerely
Eric A Blair

1. For the publication in the United States of *Down and Out in Paris and London*.
2. *Burmese Days*.

168. Review of *Gogol* by Boris de Schloezer
The Adelphi, April 1933

However little one knows about Gogol—I had better begin by admitting that all I know of Gogol's works is *Dead Souls*, read years ago—this is an interesting book, because of the light it throws on the growth and decay of literary ability.

Gogol was one of those writers who are at first extremely prolific and then wither up like plants in shallow soil. He began early under the encouragement of Pushkin, and with hardly a pause produced one book after another, all the best being in some sort satires on Russian character and institutions. Turgènev considered Gogol's play "The Government Inspector" to be "one of the most destructive (i.e. subversive) that had ever appeared." When Gogol was still young his masterpiece, the first part of *Dead Souls*, was published, and after this, quite abruptly, a change came over him. He repented of all he had done hitherto. He counted it a kind of blasphemy (he was very pious) to have written comic and subversive books. Henceforward he would write books that were ennobling, comforting; books, above all— for in spite of his satires Gogol was a complete reactionary, taking even serfdom for granted—that should reconcile man to his lot. It was to be "Slaves, obey your masters" preached at enormous length in the guise of fiction. The first part of *Dead Souls* had shown humanity at its basest; the second part should show how high, under the twin blessings of the Czardom and the Orthodox Church, humanity could rise.

This project was a total failure. From the very moment of his conversion, so to speak, not only Gogol's comic genius but even his power of writing deserted him. For the remainder of his life, ten years or so, he was entirely sterile. He wandered restlessly from place to place, living on his friends, and struggling in the labyrinth of a dreadful book that never got any further. By degrees he developed a sort of religious paranoia that led him to preach ceaselessly at his friends, mortify himself at the command of a fanatical priest, and once, even, go on a pilgrimage to the Holy Land. The second part of *Dead Souls* was forever "on the point of appearing," and never appeared. Gogol finally threw the manuscript into the fire a few months before his death. He died aged 43, apparently from despair rather than from any recognisable disease. During his last ten years he had produced nothing at all except a sort of *apologia pro vita sua*, mostly in the form of collected letters.

It is not certain what was the nature of Gogol's trouble, but M. de Schloezer traces it to a kind of emotional impotence, or rather to Gogol's increasing awareness of this. Sexually it appears, he was quite impotent, and what was more, he was one of those people who are incapable of any passion, any real *feeling* whatsoever. He did not, M. de Schloezer says, know the meaning of love or affection. Now, Gogol had written a book called *Dead Souls*, and though in the first place "souls" only meant serfs, the title had a curious appropriateness which Gogol himself recognised. All the characters in the book were not merely base, they were also extraordinarily void of any kind of spiritual aliveness—briefly, they were dead souls. Gogol, M. de

Schloezer thinks, grew more and more to realise that he himself was also a dead soul, cut off from real love and real penitence—dead, that is, in the one place where, as a Christian, he wanted to be alive. All his noble and comforting sentiments were humbug, and he knew them to be humbug, because at heart he was not "saved." For the last ten years of his life he struggled against his destiny, trying, as it were, to revivify his dead soul, and failing. This sense of being damned for mere spiritual deficiency, quite apart from any *action*, is common in Calvinistic countries; it is interesting to find it at work in a very orthodox member of the Greek Church.

Had Gogol lived in our own time there would probably have been a horrible tale of starvation to add to that of intellectual failure. But luckily for him, eighteenth century traditions seem to have persisted in Russia as late as his day (1810–1850),[1] and there were plenty of pensions and sinecures for artists of talent. Even so, the story of his efforts to regain his lost skill is a depressing one, here told very lucidly and with great sensitiveness.

Eric Blair

1. Orwell is approximating. Nicolai Gogol lived from 1809–1852.

169. To Leonard Moore

7 April 1933   Handwritten

The Hawthorns   Church Rd.   Hayes   Mdx.

Dear Mr Moore,
I wonder whether you will be in your office on the 15th (Sat. before Easter) or 17th? I would like to see you, if possible, & I will bring the second 100 pp. of my novel at the same time. I shall also be in town on the 12th. but I can't get the 100 pp. ready by then as my typewriter is under repair. Perhaps you could let me know which day would be most convenient to you for me to call; also about what time.

Yours sincerely
Eric A Blair

170. To Leonard Moore

Saturday, [29 April 1933]   Typewritten

36 High St   Southwold   Suffolk

Dear Mr Moore,
I am coming up to London, or rather to Hayes, on Wednesday next. My best time for seeing Miss Herdman[1] would be either Wednesday afternoon between four and five, or Friday evening between five and six, or any time on

Saturday. If, however, none of these would do, I could arrange to come at some other time.

Yours sincerely
Eric A Blair

P.S. I shall be at the above address till Wednesday.

1. Representative of Harper & Brothers, New York; see *181*. An annotation to Orwell's letter made in Moore's office indicates that the meeting was at first arranged for Friday, 5 May 1933, then changed to Wednesday, 3 May, too late for Orwell to attend; see *172*.

171. 'Summer-like for an instant'

The Adelphi, May 1933

Summer-like for an instant the autumn sun bursts out,
And the light through the turning elms is green and clear;
It slants down the path and the ragged marigolds glow
Fiery again, last flames of the dying year.

A blue-tit darts with a flash of wings, to feed
Where the coconut hangs on the pear tree over the well;
He digs at the meat like a tiny pickaxe tapping
With his needle-sharp beak as he clings to the swinging shell.

Then he runs up the trunk, sure-footed and sleek like a mouse,
And perches to sun himself; all his body and brain
Exult in the sudden sunlight, gladly believing
That the cold is over and summer is here again.

But I see the umber clouds that drive for the sun,
And a sorrow no argument ever can make away
Goes through my heart as I think of the nearing winter,
And the transient light that gleams like the ghost of May;

And the bird unaware, blessing the summer eternal,
Joyfully labouring, proud in his strength, gay-plumed,
Unaware of the hawk and the snow and the frost-bound nights,
And of his death foredoomed.

Eric Blair

172. To Leonard Moore

Thursday, [4 May 1933]   Handwritten

The Hawthorns   Church Rd   Hayes   Mdx.

Dear Mr Moore,

I am so sorry about never turning up for the appointment with Miss Herdman yesterday, but I never got your letter till yesterday evening. I was, as I had explained, in Southwold till Wednesday morning, & when I got to Hayes in the evening there was the letter waiting for me, but of course it was long past the time of the appointment. I hope Miss Herdman will not be mortally offended. I am writing to her as well.

Yours sincerely
Eric A Blair

173. To Eleanor Jaques

Thursday, [25 May 1933]   Handwritten

The Hawthorns   Church Rd   Hayes   Mdx.

Dearest Eleanor,

I write this not knowing where you are, but I shall send it to your adress° in Roehampton, hoping they will forward it if necessary. Do please try & come out somewhere with me when you are up in town again. It is such lovely weather, & it would be so delightful to go for a long walk in the country somewhere. If you can't manage a Saturday or Sunday, I can always make an excuse & get away. Or at worst we could meet in town for an afternoon. What are you doing in August? I don't know whether I'll be in S'wold or not—not, if my parents let their house. I am probably leaving this place at the end of the term, but I may go to another rather similar school in Uxbridge, which is near here. Write soon & let me know when you [are] going to be in town & if you can meet me.

With love from
Eric

174. Nellie Limouzin[1] to Orwell

3 June 1933   Typewritten; handwritten addition and postscript

My Dear Eric,

As part of the money I enclose is for renewal of sub. to *Adelphi*, *when* you are up,[2] you might pay it in for me—no hurry—[3] I put a warning note, so that you should not be disappointed on finding that my little present is less than would at first appear. The *A*. will be 7/6, so that, as you ought to get about 23 bob, I think for the 100 francs, that will mean something like 15/−

to 15/6 for yourself—I wish it were more. It will pay the rent of your allotment,[4] which I *hope* has brought you some profit; of course seeds must have cost something, perhaps some manure and also perhaps tools, although I hope you were able to borrow or steal those.

When you have time, I should like to know whether or not you have secured the Uxbridge school[5] and whether at a better salary and other conditions; I earnestly hope there will be no supervision after school hours. I rather fancy from my experience of an afternoon's trip to Uxbridge, that it is about as stinking a hole as Hayes, so I hope that some other advantages will make it a better post for you. I suppose you wouldn't care to try for one of Ruth Pitter's travelling jobs?[6] You said some time ago that she has travellers, but of course they may be dyed-in-the-woolies who travel with other things and do her stuff as an extra line. Avril too seems to be going strong and must have some posts in her gift, but I daresay the assistants get very poorly paid, as A. herself was when she began.

I have begun the *Chartreuse de Parme*, but have read only a few pages as yet, for I saw a reference in some work to *The Prince* and, as I had never read it, I have begun that also and am about half way through it. I suppose you have read it long ago, probably at school. It is rather more historical than I had expected and interesting if only as some kind of picture of the Renaissance period. There is a very long Introduction in the edition I have (a French one of E's.[7]) which annoyed me when I looked at it, but I found it quite enlightening in the end. I don't know whether you dislike introductions; to me they are irritating as a rule, because they hold one from the real text and yet one doesn't like to miss them. But in this edition of *The Prince*, what is more annoying is the addition of foot-notes° by Queen Christine, daughter of Gustavus Adolphus, who appears to have ended her days in Italy. I am also reading an interesting work on Les Dogmes Sexuels;[8] it is a refutation of the generally accepted ideas on sex as regards the contrast between the male and female and is based on biology of which the first long chapter consists, beginning with the single cell etc. Evidently the authoress is a serious scientist.

Here, while attending the Disarmament conferences, they are at the same time preparing for war pretty thoroughly, including the building of subterranean passages. But how on earth can they construct enough to hold the millions of inhabitants? Then they are beginning 'practice' with those hideous gas masks. There was a meeting held—or to be held—in Maisons Lafitte, to propagate this interest in gas masks, but a lot of people broke it up, saying they were against war. By the bye, that was a pretty revolutionary situation at the Oxford Debating soc., when a majority voted against participation in future war, especially the form of the resolution which specially mentioned king and country.[9] To-morrow the anti-fascist Congress opens at the salle Pleyel in Rue du F. St. Honoré. I shall not be surprised at ructions, for the Police have been giving out instructions as to how the delegates are to behave and threatening to deport any who overstep the line of what should be the attitude of the country to other powers etc. etc. Very many socialists are joining and the members of the socl. trade union, the C. G. T.,[10] against the orders of the party bosses; I should not be surprised to hear of a very big split in the French Soc. Party before long, for their treachery is getting a bit too obvious. I see a lot of delegates from England are coming, again a mixed grill.

I must stop here. Don't bother to reply at once if time is altogether too scarce—next week-end will do. And then you can reply as to any *likelihood* of your being able to come to Paris, also as to the books I mentioned in my last letter. Love.

A^t. N

P.S. I hope the Americans won't take umbrage at your remarks on pp. 110 & 111. Perhaps even they aren't quite fair, for those cereals are not really disgusting any more than porridge; in view of your experience of French cooks' methods, they are certainly far less disgusting; so couldn't you soften the passage down for the U.S.A. edition?[11]

1. Elaine ('Aunt Nellie') Adam, née Limouzin, Orwell's aunt, who lived in Paris, see *189, n. 1*
2. Presumably when Orwell came to London.
3. *when you . . . no hurry*] *handwritten marginal insertion*
4. This is the first evidence that Orwell had an allotment, a plot of land rented from the local authority (a system that still continues). For the first indication of his interest in gardening, see *161*. This developed into managing smallholdings in Hertfordshire and on the island of Jura.
5. Frays College, a private school for boys and girls; see *173* and *179, n. 4.*
6. Ruth Pitter, a poet (see *139, n. 1*), ran Walberswick Peasant Pottery Co. Ltd from 24 Portobello Road, next door to where Orwell lodged in 1927–28, before going to Paris.
7. Eugène Adam, Nellie's husband; see *189, n. 1* and *212.*
8. Adrienne Sahnque, *Les Dogmes Sexuels: les influences sociales et mystiques dans l'interpretations traditionnelles des faits sexuels* (Paris, 1932).
9. In February 1933 the Oxford Union passed a motion, 275 to 153, that in no circumstances would it fight for King and Country. The following week, the debating hall was invaded by those angered by the motion; they tore the offending page from the Union's minute book. The Union President said the motion would be reinstated, but a former Union officer, Prince Leonid Lieven, told him, 'Sir, even if you are not prepared to defend your King and Country, might you not have defended the Minute book!' (*Chronicle of the Twentieth Century*, 425). In *The Second World War* (I, 77), Winston Churchill, referring to this 'ever-shameful resolution,' passed under the inspiration of C. E. M. Joad, noted, 'It was easy to laugh off such an episode in England, but in Germany, in Russia, in Italy, in Japan, the idea of a decadent, degenerate Britain took deep root and swayed many calculations' (U.S.: *The Gathering Storm*, 85).
10. La Confédération générale du travail.
11. Writing of those who stayed in big, expensive hotels in Paris of the kind in which he was working, 'mostly Americans, with a sprinkling of English – no French,' Orwell wrote, 'They would stuff themselves with disgusting American "cereals" . . . One customer, from Pittsburg,° dined every night in his bedroom on grape-nuts, scrambled eggs and cocoa' (*Down and Out in Paris and London, CW*, I, 81). The text was not changed for the U.S. edition, not even to change the spelling of Pittsburgh.

175. To Eleanor Jaques

Tuesday, [6 June 1933]   Handwritten

The Hawthorns   Church Rd   Hayes   Mdx.

Dearest Eleanor,

How nice to hear that you can come out with me. I think next Saturday would be best, because if it is Wednesday I can only get away in the morning by inventing sick relatives etc. Let us hope this weather will continue. Where would you like to go? We can either go to Uxbridge & walk along the canal bank, in which case

i.[1] There is a Green Lines° bus that leaves Poland St at 10.30 (but might make sure of exact time) & reaches the Adam & Eve pub at Hayes about 11.15, & I can meet you there & we can go on to Uxbridge: or

ii. There is a train that leaves Paddington at 10.26 & reaches Hayes (by the way don't forget it is Hayes Middlesex: don't get carried away into Kent or somewhere) at 11.1, & I could meet you at Hayes Station & we could take the train, but

iii. I think it would be nicest if we went somewhere where there are *woods*, seeing what the weather is like; eg. to Burnham Beeches. So perhaps the best thing of all would be for me to come up to town & meet you any time & place you like, but preferably at Paddington, because I suppose we should take the train from there. How would it do to say 11 am at the small bookstall at the beginning of platform 1 on Paddington Station?

Please let me know what your ideas are, &, in the mean time, pray for good weather. If by evil chance anything should fall through so that you can't come on Saturday, let me know in time & I can always at a pinch arrange to come out another afternoon.

Love
Eric.

1. Orwell always drew a double underline beneath each lower-case roman numeral and dotted 'v' and 'x' whenever they occurred. These characteristics are to be found in the manuscript drafts of *Nineteen Eighty-Four* (e.g., 178). Neither feature is reproduced here and is not commented upon again.

176. To Brenda Salkeld

Saturday, [? June 1933][1]   Handwritten

The Hawthorns   Church Rd   Hayes   Mdx.

Dearest Brenda

I sent you about two thirds of the rough draft of my novel yesterday. I would have sent it earlier, but it has been with my agent all this time. He is quite enthusiastic about it, which is more than I am; but you are not to think that when finished it will be quite as broken-backed as at present, for with me almost any piece of writing has to be done over and over again. I wish I were one of those people who can sit down and fling off a novel in about four days. There is no news here. I am frightfully busy, suffering from the heat, and exercised about the things in my garden, which are going to dry up and die if this cursed weather doesn't change. I am growing, among other things, a pumpkin, which of course needs much more careful treatment than a marrow. I have read nothing, I think, except periodicals, all of which depress me beyond words. Do you ever see the New English Weekly? It is the leading Social Credit[2] paper. As a monetary scheme Social Credit is probably sound, but its promoters seem to think that they are going to take the main weapon out of the hands of the governing classes without a fight, which is an illusion. A few years ago I thought it rather fun to reflect that our civilisation is doomed, but now it fills me above all else with boredom to think of the horrors that will be happening within ten years—either some appalling calamity, with revolution and famine, or else all-round trustification and Fordification, with the entire population reduced to docile wage-slaves, our lives utterly in the hands of the bankers, and a fearful tribe of Lady Astors[3] and Lady Rhonddas[4] et hoc genus riding us like succubi in the name of Progress. Have you read "Ulysses" yet? It sums up better than any book I know the fearful despair that is almost normal in modern times. You get the same kind of thing, though only just touched upon, in Eliot's poems. With E, however, there is also a certain sniffish "I told you so" implication, because as the spoilt darling of the Church Times he is bound to point out that all this wouldn't have happened if we had not shut our eyes to the Light. The CT annoys me more and more. It is a poor satisfaction even to see them walloping the Romans, because they do it chiefly by descending to their level. I wonder whether it is true, as I have been told, that the CT advertisement columns are full of disguised abortion advertisements? If so it is pretty disgusting in a paper which is in constant pursuit of Bertrand Russell, Barney the Apostate,[5] etc because of their birth control propaganda. By the way did you see Barney's recent pronouncements at the Conference on I forget what, about the undesirable multiplication of the lower classes. His latest phrase is "the social problem class", meaning all those below a certain income. Really you sometimes can't help thinking these people are doing it on purpose. Write soon. I wish you were here now. Have you been bathing yet? I keep putting it off.

With love
Eric A. Blair

1. This letter may antedate the letter to Eleanor Jaques tentatively dated 6 June 1933.
2. The Social Credit movement, based on the ideas of Major C. H. Douglas, claimed that prosperity could be achieved through a reform of the monetary system.
3. Nancy Witcher Astor (1879–1964), wife of the first Viscount Astor, born in Virginia, society and political hostess at Cliveden, the Astor estate on the Thames, was the first woman to take her seat in the House of Commons, 1919–45. She was an eloquent advocate of temperance and women's rights. In the first edition of Coming Up for Air (1939), Orwell included Lady Astor's name among a 'fearful tribe' of 'soul-savers and Nosey Parkers.' Though that name was set for the Secker & Warburg 1948 edition—as the 1947 proof witnesses—it was marked for omission in proof and has not thereafter been included. The omission sign does not appear to be Orwell's, but it might well follow his instructions. Since the name Lord Beaverbrook in

this same list was allowed to stand, fear of an action for libel or defamation could hardly be responsible for the omission. Perhaps Orwell removed the name out of his friendship with David Astor, who did not know of the change. The name is not included in *CW*, VII, 183.

4. Margaret Haig Thomas (1883–1958), second Viscountess Rhondda, was a highly successful businesswoman and ardent believer in the equality of the sexes. She actively edited her own independent weekly, *Time and Tide*, 1928–58.

5. Ernest William Barnes (1874–1953) was a mathematician and modernist churchman, and Bishop of Birmingham, 1924–53. His writings include *Should Such a Faith Offend?* and *Scientific Theory and Religion*.

177. To Leonard Moore

Friday, [16 June 1933]   Handwritten

The Hawthorns   Church Rd.   Hayes.

Dear Mr Moore,

A friend of mine and my parents, Mr C. R. Peters,[1] recently wrote to me asking me if I could introduce him to Gollancz's, as he has written a book that he thinks might interest them. I thought it would be better if I put him in touch with you, as your introduction would no doubt be worth more than mine. Mr Peters is an officer of the Indian Police, and he tells me that his book is a collection of stories based on his experiences. I should think that that ought to be of great interest, and you would know whether Gollancz or some other publisher would be most suitable.

Yours sincerely
Eric A Blair

1. While C. R. Peters served in the Indian Imperial Police, his three sons were educated in England. In 1930 and 1931 Orwell tutored the boys at Southwold during three vacations. Richard Peters (1919–) became professor of the philosophy of education at the University of London, and his account of being coached by Orwell is in *Orwell Remembered*, 90–94. Despite feeling apprehensive about meeting him, he records that Orwell 'captivated us completely within five minutes.' The father's stories seem not to have been published; there is no entry in the British Library Catalogue.

177A. Publication of *Down and Out in Paris and London* in the United States

Harper & Brothers published *Down and Out in Paris and London* on 30 June 1933, or, possibly, on 25 July 1933; see 157. The dust jacket carries the following paragraph 'About the Author,' almost certainly based on material supplied by Orwell. Note the words given in double quotation marks.

'George Orwell was born in India in 1903 and was educated in Eton from 1917 to 1921, "but learned as nearly as possible nothing, chiefly owing to laziness." He served with the Indian Imperial Police for five years but resigned in 1928 chiefly because he disliked putting people in prison for doing the same things which he should have done in their circumstances. Subsequently he has earned his living by schoolmastering and private tutoring, and he has also worked in a Paris hotel, picked hops, pushed a barrow in Billingsgate and done other varied jobs. Soon after he came home from Burma he became interested in the lives of destitute people and began to make expeditions among tramps. It was only after he had done this a number of times that it occurred to him that his experiences could be used for literary purposes. Later on when he was genuinely hard up he was glad to know the ropes in the world of the destitute.'

178. To Eleanor Jaques

7 July 1933 Handwritten

The Hawthorns Church Rd Hayes Mdx.

Dearest Eleanor,
It seems so long since that day I went out with you—actually, I suppose, about a month. This "glorious" weather has been almost the death of me. However, I occasionally manage to get over to Southall & have a swim at the open-air baths, & my garden has done pretty well considering the drought. The only failures I have had were shallots & broad beans, both I fancy due to having been planted too late. I have had enormous quantities of peas, & I am a convert forever to the system of sinking a trench where you are going to grow a row of peas. I hope I shall be in S'wold for part of the summer holidays, but I am afraid it won't be long, because I am going to a new school at Uxbridge next term & they may want me to do some tutoring during the holidays. God send I'll be able to drop this foul teaching after next year. I do hope you'll be in Southwold during the holidays & perhaps we can go & picnic as we did last year. I am so pining to see the sea again. Do try to be in S'wold if you can, & keep some days free for me during the first fortnight in August. I think I shall get home about the 28th of this month. My novel will be about finished by the end of this term, but I don't like large sections of it & am going to spend some months revising it. Please write & tell me what your plans are, & remember me to your parents.

With much love
Eric

179. To Eleanor Jaques

Thursday, [20 July 1933] Handwritten

The Hawthorns Church Rd Hayes Mdx.

Dearest Eleanor,
Do write & tell me if you will be in S'wold during the summer holidays. I am going to be there I think from the 29th inst. to the 18th August, & am so

319

wanting to see you. If you are to be there, try & keep some days free for me, & it would be so nice if we could go & bathe & make our tea like we used to do last year along the W'wick[1] shore. Let me know.

The heat here is fearful, but it is good for my marrows & pumpkins, which are swelling almost visibly. We have had lashings of peas, beans just beginning, potatoes rather poor, owing to the drought I suppose. I have finished my novel, but there are wads of it that I simply hate, & am going to change. They say it will be soon enough if it is done some time at the end of the year. Please G. I get a little spare time in my next job. I went over to see the prize-giving at the school & it looked pretty bloody—the girls' section of the school (which I shall have nothing to do with—perhaps it is for the best) sang the female version of Kipling's "If." I am told that there is also a female version of "Forty years on", which I would give something to get hold of.[2] I have been reading *in* D. H. Lawrence's collected letters. Some of them very interesting—there is a quality about L. that I can't define, but everywhere in his work one comes on passages of an extraordinary freshness, vividness, so that tho' I would never, even given the power, have done it quite like that myself, I feel that he has seized on an aspect of things that no one else would have noticed. In another way, which I can still less explain, he reminds me of someone from the Bronze Age. I think there are some scraps of mine in the August Adelphi[3]—a poem, but I am not sure it is not one you have seen. Au revoir, & write soon.[4]

Much love from
Eric

1. Walberswick, about two miles south of Southwold. Ruth Pitter's pottery, next door to where Orwell lived in 1927, was called the Walberswick Peasant Pottery Co Ltd. See Thompson, 23.
2. 'Forty Years On,' the Harrow school song, written in 1872 by John Farmer, was also sung by many girls' schools; in *Great Days and Jolly Days* (1977), Celia Haddon lists a wide range of girls' schools (21). It was also sung by such coeducational schools as Eccles Grammar. Haddon gives an excellent, well-illustrated account of this phenomenon that so intrigued Orwell. He reverted to this topic in a letter of 1935; see *245*.
3. There was no poem by Orwell in the August issue of *The Adelphi*, though his review of Enid Starkie's *Baudelaire* appeared. His next poem to be published was 'A dressed man and a naked man' in the October number; see *182*.
4. Summer term at The Hawthorns ended on or about 28 July 1933. Orwell then spent three weeks, until 18 August, at his parents' home in Southwold. He did not return for the autumn term at The Hawthorns, which had, in any case, run into financial difficulties, and was later sold. Instead, he went to teach at Frays College, a private school for boys and girls, in Uxbridge, Middlesex, some sixteen miles from central London. See Shelden, 193–94; U.S.: 175–76. A picture is in Thompson, 40.

180. Review of *Baudelaire* by Enid Starkie

The Adelphi, August 1933

This is a biography of Baudelaire, and only incidentally a book of criticism, though it prints a number of the poems, usually in full. It is so detailed and well-documented that it should make any further life of Baudelaire unnecessary in English.

The misery of Baudelaire's life, which has become proverbial, seems to have been even worse than one had imagined. Kind but uncomprehending parents, an appalling mulatto mistress, debts, syphilis, prosecution for obscenity, more debts, complete literary failure, death from general paralysis at the age of forty-six—these are part of the story. Between his duns and his step-father, it was probably Baudelaire's failure to earn either money or a reputation that hit him hardest of all. His chances of success were ruined by the prosecution for obscenity, which caused all the influential critics to boycott him—for literary life in France seems, at least then, to have been characterised by the same slimy careerism as in England. Sainte-Beuve, who was perfectly aware of Baudelaire's talent, steadily refused him any public recognition. Gautier, whom Baudelaire always hailed as his master (it is hard to see why: surely the two men are very unlike?), would not even come to his funeral. Probably no poet of equal talent has ever died so obscure.

Now, when Baudelaire is not only bowed down to by the 'critics, cultured critics' but also swallowed whole by the pious, it is clear that he suffered for not having the special illusions of his own time. His agonised attitude to life, those fearful remorses and despairs, the deadly ennui which is his prevailing theme—how wrong it must all have seemed to the eighteen fifties! To say that we do not so much love our lives as cling to them

> Ainsi qu'un débauché pauvre qui baise et mange
> Le sein martyrisé d'une antique catin—
> (like a poverty-stricken debauchee gnawing the tormented
> breast of an aged prostitute)

this is the real blasphemy of an optimistic age. But we understand it only too well nowadays. His sense of the real horror of debauchery (as opposed to the juicy appeal that the moralists give it), and his "fundamental piety," which Miss Starkie rightly insists upon, are also better appreciated in an age that has had some of the nonsense knocked out of it. What makes Baudelaire so memorable is that he expresses our typical modern moods with such matchless clarity. Reading such poems as, say, "Les Bijoux," or (except for one line) "l'Albatros," one sees that perfection in the handling of words could hardly go further.

Miss Starkie's book is rather amateurishly written ("he little knew" etc.) but it is extremely just and discerning, and displays enormous knowledge of French literary life in the nineteenth century. The publishers claim that it will upset "the Baudelaire legend," presumably meaning that Baudelaire is generally thought of as a mere scoundrel and pornographer. If any such legend still exists, this book should certainly help to end it; it may also save Baudelaire from some of the consequences of being patted on the head by Sir John Squire. The stiff price of eighteen shillings seems inexcusable, considering the very poor paper the book is printed on.

Eric Blair

181. To Leonard Moore

Tuesday, [1 August 1933]   Typewritten

36 High St   Southwold   Suffolk

Dear Mr Moore,

I heard from Miss Herdman, of Harper's, the other day, and she said the American edition of "Down and Out" was coming out on the 25th July.[1] Do you think it would be worth getting the American press-cuttings? If so, could you please ask the press-cutting people to get them? I suppose it means paying another half year's subscription.[2]

I am down here for two or three weeks. I had my first bathe yesterday—the North Sea seems horribly cold after the swimming baths. Please remember me to Mrs Moore.

Yours sincerely
Eric A Blair

1. Willison records the publication of *Down and Out in Paris and London* in New York as on 30 June 1933.
2. Annotated in Moore's office: '*Charge* Burrelles Press Clipping Bureau.'

182. 'A dressed man and a naked man'

The Adelphi, October 1933

A dressed man and a naked man
Stood by the kip-house fire,
Watching the sooty cooking-pots
That bubble on the wire;

And bidding tanners up and down,
Bargaining for a deal,
Naked skin for empty skin,
Clothes against a meal.

"Ten bob it is," the dressed man said,
"These boots cost near a pound,
"This coat's a blanket of itself
"When you kip on the frosty ground."

"One dollar," said the naked man,
"And that's a hog too dear;
"I've seen a man strip off his shirt
"For a fag and a pot of beer."

"Eight and a tanner," the dressed man said,
"And my life-work is yours,
"All I've earned at the end of a life
"Knocking at farmers' doors;

"Turnips, apples, hops and peas,
"And the spike when times are slack,
"Fifty years I've tobied it
"For these clothes upon my back."

"Take seven," said the naked man,
"It's cold and the spikes are shut;
"Better be naked here in kip
"Than dressed in Lambeth Cut."

"One tanner more," the dressed man said,
"One tanner says the word,
"Off comes my coat of ratcatcher
"And my breeches of velvet cord;

"Now pull my shirt over my head,
"I'm naked sole to crown,
"And that's the end of fifty years
"Tobying up and down."

A minute and they had changed about,
And each had his desire;
A dressed man and a naked man
Stood by the kip-house fire.

Eric Blair

183. To Leonard Moore

17 October 1933   Handwritten

Frays College   Harefield Rd.   Uxbridge   Mdx.

Dear Mr Moore,

Many thanks for your letter, enclosing the cuttings, & for the cheque, which I ought to have acknowledged earlier. I am sorry to hear Harper's are disappointed. But I suppose a sale of 1100 copies[1] does not represent an actual loss to them?

The other book[2] will be finished in November—better say the *end* of November. I am sorry to have been so slow, but I am submerged with work in this place. I hope to finish the writing before our half-term, which is about November 3rd, & then I will do the typing as rapidly as possible. I have however already typed 150 pp. of the earlier part. The book is going to be unconscionably long—round about 400 pp. I trust that does not matter? I should be able to cut it if they demanded that.

Yours sincerely
Eric A Blair

1. Harper & Brothers had printed 1,750 copies of *Down and Out in Paris and London*, and, as Stansky and Abrahams put it, to sell no more than 1,100 in those days was 'not as lamentable

. . . as it would seem now.' The type was distributed in February 1934, some nine months after the publication of the U.S. edition, and 383 copies of the book were remaindered in the United States; see Stansky and Abrahams, II, 36–37.

2. *Burmese Days*.

184. To Leonard Moore

Sunday, [26 November 1933]   Typewritten

Frays College   Harefield Rd,   Uxbridge   Mdx.

Dear Mr Moore,

Will you by any chance be at home next Saturday afternoon—the second I think the date is? I finished my novel[1] some time back and have been typing it out in what spare time I can get in this place, and I think I can get it all typed by Saturday. I would like to see you personally if possible, because I want to discuss another project I have.[2] It is almost impossible for me to get up to town during your office hours, but I could come out to Gerrards° Cross by motor bike if you were at home and it wouldn't inconvenience you. Or I could come on Sunday morning if you are in the habit of doing business on Sunday.

I am very dissatisfied with the novel, but it is all about up to the standard of what you saw, and of course I have made all the necessary corrections and tightened it up as well as I could. It will be about 375 pp.—allowing for the fact that I have used wide margins, about 85,000 words.[3] That seems awfully long to me. If the publisher said he would take it subject to cutting I would know where to cut it, but I'd rather not have to, as I am sick of the sight of it. Let's hope the next one will be better.

Yours sincerely
Eric A Blair

P.S. [at top of letter] I am not certain of your address in Gerrards° Cross, tho' I think I could find my way there. If you will be at home, would you let me know the name of your house?

1. *Burmese Days*.
2. Possibly his idea for *A Clergyman's Daughter*, which he began to write on returning to Southwold in the middle of January 1934. See reference to his next novel towards the end of his letter to Brenda Salkeld in December, *186*.
3. *Burmese Days* is about 100,000 words.

185. Review of *Criticisms and Opinions of the Works of Charles Dickens* by G. K. Chesterton

The Adelphi, December 1933

There is one great advantage about Mr. Chesterton's manner of approaching Dickens, and that is that it is not too purely literary. Most modern literary criticism is literary and nothing else—that is, it concentrates on an author's style and thinks it rather vulgar to notice his subject matter. Undoubtedly the influence of this type of criticism has been healthy (it has saved us from Shakespeare the Great Moral Teacher and all that, and from the windy platitudes of the Bernard Shaw era, when duds like Brieux were foisted upon us for the sake of their sermons), but it misses part of the point with such a writer as Dickens. Dickens was essentially a moralist, and he cannot be treated as though he were, say, Flaubert.

Being a moralist, Dickens did not invent his characters merely *as* characters, but rather as embodiments of the human qualities that he liked and disliked. And it is probably the secret of their vitality, that Dickens's likes and dislikes are such as any decent man would share. He was always, when he understood the issue, on the side of the weak against the strong. As Mr. Chesterton says, Dickens "saw that under many forms there was one fact, the tyranny of man over man; and he struck at it when he saw it, whether it was old or new." This is perfectly true. Dickens's view of life was sometimes one-eyed and he was not free from a rather disagreeable petty-bourgeois class-feeling, but on the whole his instincts were sound. It was only when he outraged them he went astray, artistically as well as morally.

The best instance is in *David Copperfield*. As Mr. Chesterton points out, the artistic collapse of *David Copperfield* has an ethical cause. It is perfectly clear that *David Copperfield* is autobiography (imaginative autobiography, of course), and it is equally clear if one looks closely that towards the end Dickens begins telling lies. He wrenches the book out of its natural channel and gives it a conventional happy ending, which is not only unconvincing but also abominably priggish. Dora is made to die of nothing in particular, the improvident and lovable characters are hustled off to Australia, and David marries the insufferable Agnes—a marriage which has, like so many marriages in Victorian fiction, a nasty suggestion of incest. The result is disaster, culminating in the rather horrible saturnalia at the end, in which everything is turned upside down and Dickens temporarily loses not only his comic genius but even his sense of decency. The prison scene in the last chapter is really disgusting. It is worthy of Edgar Wallace. Dickens had some ugly moods upon which Mr. Chesterton evidently does not care to dwell. The essay on *David Copperfield* is, however, an excellent piece of writing, and by a great deal the most interesting thing in the book.

Of course, Mr. Chesterton would not be himself if he did not make Dickens a mouthpiece for various of his own fads. Where Dickens's opinion happens to coincide with Mr. Chesterton's, as for instance upon the subject of the English Poor Law, well and good, that is Dickens's opinion; where it happens not to coincide, as for instance on the subject of the Middle Ages, or the French Revolution, or the Roman Catholic Church, Mr. Chesterton explains that Dickens did not really think that, he only thought he thought it. Dickens is used as a stick to beat all modern novelists and most nineteenth century ones, including Thackeray. (Why are Dickens and Thackeray always compared? They are completely unlike. The novelist among Dickens's contemporaries who most resembled him was Surtees.) Again, some of

Dickens's faults—his morbid love of corpses, for instance – are exalted into virtues because Mr. Chesterton either shares them or feels that he ought to share them. There is an attempt, though it is not as pronounced as it might be, to affiliate Dickens with the Middle Ages—the mythical Middle Ages beloved of Roman Catholics, when peasants were boozy but monogamous, and there was no serfdom and no Holy Inquisition. However, there is one thing which Mr. Chesterton has not said, and which he must be honoured for not saying. He has not said that if Dickens had had a little more brains he would have turned Roman Catholic. Not many of our Catholic apologists would have refrained from saying that. It would be absurd to pretend that Mr. Chesterton is not a Catholic apologist, but at least he has never joined in the great game of pretending that no book by a Protestant author can be readable.

Mr. Chesterton is at his best when he writes about Dickens. He has this in common with Dickens, too, that however much one may disagree with him, and even when one considers him a definitely bad and cheap writer, one cannot help liking him. It would be interesting to see his special method of criticism applied to some of our other major novelists—in particular, to Fielding.

Eric Blair

186. To Brenda Salkeld

Sunday, [10? December 1933]   Typewritten

Frays College   Harefield Road   Uxbridge   Mdx.

Dearest Brenda

Many thanks for your letter of some time back. I have at last a few instants in which I can sit down to reply. I am so glad you got hold of and read "Ulysses" at last. When you say "What do you think Joyce is after?" I should say several things, which it is not very easy to define shortly. In the first place one has got to decide what a novel normally sets out to do. I should say that it sets out first (I am placing these in order of difficulty, the simplest first) to display or create character, secondly to make a kind of pattern or design which any good story contains, and thirdly, if the novelist is up to it, to produce *good writing*, which can exist almost as it were in vacuo and independent of subject. This is very crudely put, but you might see what I mean by the analogy of a picture—not that I am any judge of pictures—which has in the first place a subject (eg. it might be a portrait), secondly a design made up of lines, planes etc and lastly if the painter is really good can give one the greatest pleasure of all by its (so to speak) *texture*—the quality of the brushmarks etc. I think "Ulysses" follows this scheme fairly closely, but the queer and original thing about it is that instead of taking as his material the conventional and highly simplified version of life presented in most novels, Joyce attempts to present life more or less as it is lived. Of course he is not trying *merely* to represent life. When "Ulysses" first came out one heard it said on every side that it was an attempt to describe a day in somebody's life, leaving nothing out, etc etc. It is not that. If one thinks, a complete description of a day, or even of an hour, would be simply an enormous omnium gatherum, quite formless and probably not at all interesting, and in any case would not convey the impression of life at all. Art implies selection and there is as much selection in "Ulysses" as in "Pride and Prejudice". Only Joyce is attempting to select and represent events and thoughts as they occur in life and not as they occur in fiction. Of course he is not altogether successful but the very way in which he sets about it is enough to show how extraordinarily original his mind is. When I first came on "Ulysses" it was some odd chapters in a review, and I happened to strike that passage where Gerty Macdowell is soliloquising. It then seemed to me a sort of elephantine joke to write the whole passage in the style of the Heartsease library, but I now see that you could not possibly display the interior of the girl's mind so well in any other way, except at much greater length. You will remember no doubt how well the horrid little narcissistic touches about her "girlish treasures" and being "lost in dreams" etc were done. Similarly Bloom, Mrs B and Dedalus are all given styles of their own, to display the different qualities of their minds. Dedalus's style is infected with Elizabethan and medieval literature, Mrs B thinks in a sort of formless mess, and Bloom thinks in a series of short phrases, except in the brothel scene, where he is too drunk to know the difference between reality and imagination. There are certain changes of style that I don't see the reason for, eg. the frequent parodies of newspaper reports, and also of Homer or it may be of ancient Irish literature, though some of these are quite amusing. For instance you may remember when Paddy Dignam, the drunkard, is dead, Joyce suddenly breaks into mock-Homeric style with "Fleet was his foot upon the bracken, Dignam of the beamy brow". The scene where the medical students are talking in the pub seems to be done in a series of Parodies of English literature from the earliest times to the present day. This again I don't see the reason for, unless it is because a baby is being born "off" and the change of style symbolises birth, which seems to me rather elephantine. Quite apart from the different styles used to represent different manners of thought, the observation is in places marvellous. For instance, the funeral scene. Compare the thoughts which pass through Bloom's mind with those that pass through the mind of an ordinary character in fiction at a funeral. As to the design itself, so far as I understand it, it doesn't seem to me to be altogether successful. The incidents are clearly based on the "Odyssey". You can identify a lot of them. Bloom is Odysseus, Dedalus is Telemachus, Mrs B is Penelope (complete with suitors), Gertie Macdowell is Nausicaa, Bella what's her name who keeps the brothel is Circe etc. I fancy Joyce's idea in basing it on the "Odyssey" is that he means to say "There is the Bronze Age—here is us". Nevertheless the book does seem to me to split up into a lot of unrelated or thinly related incidents.

I hope you will forgive me for lecturing you at this enormous length. After all you can always stop reading. As to the characters themselves, I think both

327

Dedalus and Bloom are certainly self-portraits—one of Joyce at 22 and the other at 38. I think Bloom is much the more interesting as well as the more successful. Dedalus is the ordinary modern intellectual whose mind is poisoned by his inability to believe in anything, and only different from the English version of the same thing by having been brought up in a Catholic atmosphere and on monkish learning instead of the classical education you get or are supposed to get in England. Bloom on the other hand is a rather exceptionally sensitive specimen of the man in the street, and I think the especial interest of this is that the cultivated man and the man in the street so rarely meet in modern English literature. The man in the street is usually described in fiction either by writers who are themselves intellectually men in the street, tho' they may have great gifts as novelists (eg. Trollope), or by cultivated men who describe him *from outside* (eg. Samuel Butler, Aldous Huxley). If you read the words of almost any writer of the intellectual type, you would never guess that he also is a being capable of getting drunk, picking girls up in the street, trying to swindle somebody out of half a crown, etc. I think the interest of Bloom is that he is an ordinary uncultivated man described from within by someone who can also stand outside him and see him from another angle. Not that Bloom is an absolutely typical man in the street. He has obviously for instance a streak of intellectual curiosity, which sometimes gets him into trouble with his pub friends and his wife. Also there are his sexual abnormalities, which are not those of the average man. I am not sure that purely as a bit of character-drawing Mrs B is not the best of the lot. Buck Mulligan is good. The other minor characters don't seem to me to stand out much, but some of the pub conversations are very good.

As to the actual writing in "Ulysses", it isn't everybody's money, but personally I think it is superb in places. If you look you will see that Joyce is continually holding himself back from breaking out into a species of verse, and at times he does so, and those are the bits I like. The bit where Bloom remembers the time he was making love to his wife on the cliffs before they were married, and where he sees the man eating in that disgusting chop-shop, and then his subsequent thoughts about the butchers' stalls at the market, and the bit in the brothel scene where Bella, who has then turned into a man, tells him about his wife (Bloom's) being unfaithful to him, and where the plaster statuette is talking about the sheet of the "Pink'un"[1] that she was wrapped up in, have haunted me ever since reading them. If you read these aloud you will see that most of them are essentially verse. One of the most remarkable things in the book, to me, is the verse describing the thoughts of somebody's dog—you remember, it starts "The curse of my curses, Seven days every day". He seems to me there actually to have discovered a new rhythmical scheme.

Excuse this long and somewhat didactic letter. The fact is Joyce interests me so much that I can't stop talking about him once I start. I thought you would have read most of the books in that list. You ask whether I was really impressed by "The Dynasts". I wouldn't want to read it again in toto, but I think it attains the end it sets out for, and there are some very fine passages in it. The description of the battle of Waterloo is splendid, though probably historically misleading, but you would miss some of the effect if you hadn't read the rest of the book. Of course wads of it are dull beyond words. I have read nothing lately except a smelly little pamphlet on Plato and Aristotle which doesn't tell you anything much about Plato and Aristotle. I am crushed with work as usual, but hope to be a little freer next week when the examinations we are now doing are over. My novel is with the agent. He seems hopeful about it, but personally I am sick of the sight of it. It is a fearful length—almost Priestley-size. The next one[2] will be better I hope, but I don't suppose I shall be able to start it before the holidays. Is it still impossible for you to come walking with me? You were rather indiscreet to tell your mother I think. If you want to read "Portrait of the Artist", Joyce's earlier book, you can get it out of Smith's. There are good bits in it. The part where the boy passes through a pious stage is written in a subtly loathsome style which is very clever. But it is a commonplace book compared with "Ulysses". Write again soon.

With much love
Eric A Blair

1. The *Sporting Times*, first published in 1865. It was printed on pink paper, and later issues were subtitled 'Otherwise known as the *Pink 'Un.*'
2. *A Clergyman's Daughter*.

187. To Leonard Moore

Thursday, [28 December 1933]   Handwritten

Uxbridge Cottage Hospital[1]

Dear Mr Moore,

Now that I am stronger I can thank you for your great kindness in several times dropping in & enquiring after me, also for your Christmas card. I am hoping to get up in a day or two, & perhaps leave this place in about a week, after which I am going straight down to Southwold.[2] Of course I can't go back to school at the beginning of the term, so I am going to chuck teaching, at least for the while. It is perhaps rather imprudent, but my people are anxious that I should do so, as they are concerned about my health, & of course I shall be able to write my next novel in 6 months or so[3] if I haven't got to be teaching at the same time. I trust all will go well with the one now with the publisher— I suppose we shan't hear till half way through Jan. Please remember me to Mrs Moore.

Yours sincerely
Eric A Blair

1. Illustrated in Thompson, 40. Orwell was admitted to the hospital with severe pneumonia about Christmas.
2. In fact, he spent a couple of days at Faversham House Hotel, Ealing Common, before returning to Southwold in mid-January.
3. *A Clergyman's Daughter* was completed by 3 October 1934, that is, in nine, not six, months.

1934

188. To Leonard Moore

4 January 1934   Handwritten

Uxbridge Cottage Hospital

Dear Mr Moore,
Many thanks for your letter. I am in all probability leaving this place on Monday,[1] & if by any chance you should have any communication for me about then or the following[2] couple of days, my address will be:

Faversham House Hotel
51–53 Hamilton Rd
Ealing Common W.5

My best New Year wishes to yourself & Mrs Moore—if it is not too late. I shall address this to Gerrard's Cross, as it will probably reach you on Saturday.

Yours sincerely
Eric A. Blair

1. Monday was 8 January.   2. following] next

189. To Leonard Moore

16 January 1934   Typewritten

36 High St.   Southwold   Suffolk

Dear Mr Moore,
Do you think any publishing firm would undertake the translation of a French book named "Esquisse d'une Philosophie de la dignite° humaine", by Paul Gille? I think I could get the author to let me translate it if any firm would do it. The author writes to my aunt's husband,[1] who is translating the book into Esperanto(!): "No doubt the connections you have in England would make it possible for you to put me in touch with someone who would undertake the English translation? English is, so to speak, the only great language in which none of my "Esquisse" has appeared . . . (Among others he mentions Italian and Chinese translations) . . . A translation had been undertaken at New York, but some difficulties have arisen which made it impossible for the translator to continue" etc.

I suppose there are firms which go in for books of that description—I take this to be some kind of book of philosophy. I am sending for a copy of it. I

333

don't suppose anything will come of it, but I thought that at any rate it might be worth trying.

Yours sincerely
Eric A Blair

1. Orwell's favourite aunt, Elaine ('Nellie') Limouzin, lived in Paris. Her husband, Eugène Adam, an ardent Esperantist, founded the Sennacieca Asocio Tutmonda (Workers' Esperanto Association of the World) in 1928 (the year Orwell went to live in Paris). He would speak only Esperanto. Orwell's aunt apparently suggested that her nephew translate it into English. Orwell did not translate Gille's book. Eugène Adam left his wife; he committed suicide in Mexico in 1947. Nellie Limouzin died in 1950; see Shelden, 136–38; U.S.: 124–26.

190. To Leonard Moore

Saturday, [27 January 1934]   Typewritten

36 High St   Southwold   Suffolk

Dear Mr Moore,
Many thanks for your letter. It is disappointing about Heinemann's—however, if we can find *somebody* to publish the book,[1] no matter. My best time to see Mr Saxon[2] would be Wednesday at 4.30. I don't know where his office is—perhaps you could let me know? I will try and come in at your office before going to see him, but it is rather difficult to get up to London from here before, say, 2 pm

I have just received a copy of that French book I spoke to you of,[3] and will read it before Wednesday and let you know what it is like. It is quite short, and from the glance I have taken at it, it seems to be a book of anti-materialist, anti-Marxist tendency.

I am much stronger, and have began doing a little work. By the way, I know that Harper's owe me a few royalties[4]—not much, I am afraid, but about £20 or £30. Do you think it would be possible to get anything out of them say next month? It doesn't matter now, but I may be getting rather hard up in a month or two.

Yours sincerely
Eric A. Blair

1. On first reading *Burmese Days*, Gollancz had rejected it for fear of libel. Moore then tried other publishers. It is not known how many, but certainly Heinemann and Cape rejected it.
2. Eugene Saxton, chief editor of Harper & Brothers, New York. He first asked for some alterations in *Burmese Days* for fear of libel.
3. *Esquisse d'une philosophie de la dignité humaine* by Paul Gille; see *189*.
4. For *Down and Out in Paris and London*. There is a large question mark in the margin next to this paragraph, presumably a reminder by Moore to have this checked.

191. To Leonard Moore

2 February 1934   Typewritten

36 High St   Southwold   Suffolk

Dear Mr Moore,
I enclose herewith the slip I spoke to you of, which was to be pasted inside that French book.[1]

I saw Mr Saxton as arranged and we talked for a long time, but he did not say anything very definite. I understood him to say that he would let you know about the novel in a week or two. He asked me how long it would take to make certain changes in the novel, if necessary, and I told him a week. I also asked him about a short biography on Mark Twain, and he advised me to apply to Chatto and Windus, and he said that if I wrote to a man named Raymond in the firm, he (Mr Saxton) would add his reccommendation.° I don't know whether it is really worth asking Chatto's, but there is this, that if they do intend to publish anything about Mark Twain for his centenary next year, they might not find it so easy to get anyone who knew anything about Mark Twain. It was a pity Mr Hamilton[2] was not there. I think if he shows any willingness to publish my book, it would be better to close with him, as I want to get it published in some form or other.

Yours sincerely
Eric A. Blair

1. Presumably *Esquisse d'une philosophie de la dignité humaine* by Paul Gille; see *189, 190*. What the slip was is not known.
2. Hamish Hamilton (1900–1988) directed his own publishing house in London. See *198, 199*.

192. To Leonard Moore

Thursday, [8 February 1934]   Typewritten

36 High St   Southwold   Suffolk

Dear Mr Moore,
Many thanks for your letter, and for the exertions you have been taking over my novel. As soon as I get the ms. from you I will go over it very carefully and make the necessary alterations, which should not, I think, take more than three or four days at most. But with regard to Mr Saxton's remarks about the last two or three pp. of the novel, I am sorry to say I don't agree with him at all. I will cut these out if it is absolutely insisted upon, but not otherwise. I hate a novel in which the principal characters are not disposed of at the end. I will, however, cut out the offending words "it now remains to tell" etc.[1]

Yours sincerely
Eric A Blair

1. These words do not appear at the end of *Burmese Days* in any of its editions.

193. To Leonard Moore

Thursday, [15 February 1934]   Typewritten

36 High St.   Southwold   Suffolk

Dear Mr Moore,

Thanks for your wire and the manuscript.[1] There has been a good deal of flying to and fro of wires etc, because your last letter seemed to imply that the ms. had already been sent off, and when it didn't arrive I was a little nervous that it might have been lost. I wonder if you could be kind enough to inform your office of my present address, as they have been sending things to Uxbridge.[2] I am starting on the alterations, and shall do them along exactly the lines I outlined to you, trusting that will be all right. I think I can promise you the ms. with all alterations made by Tuesday the 20th. Is it then to be shown to Gollancz again, or handed over to Harper's? I shall pin a note to the front page explaining what alterations I have made.

Do you think that translation business is likely to come to anything? I had a letter from the author asking what publishers we were going to try it on. He expresses himself quite satisfied with my translating powers—I suppose the publishers would enquire about that?[3]

Yours sincerely
Eric A. Blair

1. Of *Burmese Days*.
2. Presumably to Frays College, where he had taught until Christmas.
3. Next to this paragraph is a note, made in Moore's office: 'Routledge dec[lined]   Allen & Unwin considering.' This 'translation business' came to nothing.

194. Review of *Critique of Poetry* by Michael Roberts

The Adelphi, March 1934

Mr. Roberts starts his book with a lengthy quotation from Pater—a disinterested action, for nine readers out of ten would close the book hurriedly after one glimpse of that dreaded name. However, one ought not to grumble when one meets with a critic who has a good word for everybody. Most English critics, apart from the publishers' touts who review novels in the Sunday papers, are much keener to prevent one from enjoying the books they disapprove of, than to add to one's enjoyment. The prevailing type of critic is the young gentleman who wants to cut off our supply of Milton, Wordsworth, Shelley and Keats, and deliver us over, bound hand and foot, to Mr. Eliot's frigid and snooty Muse.[1]

There are two interesting things in this book. One is an exposure—its connection with poetic technique is not clear—of Poe's arithmetical errors in *The Gold Bug*. The other is a discussion of the difference between visualising and non-visualising thinkers. It is not generally realised, or is commonly forgotten, that the process of thought differs vastly in different people; some people think chiefly by a series of visual images, others almost entirely abstractly. Mr. Roberts seems to suggest that the visualising type of mind is necessarily a more primitive type than the non-visualising—a very disputable suggestion, for the power of visualisation is possessed *in addition* to the power of abstract thought.[2] But it is interesting to see the subject raised.

E. A. B

1. This might refer to the Cambridge Critics and *Scrutiny*. F. R. Leavis (1895–1978), the editor, wrote on 'Milton's Verse' in Vol. 2, No. 2, 1933 and his revaluation of Wordsworth was published in Vol. 3, No. 3, 1934. His revaluations of Shelley and Keats were not published in *Scrutiny* until Vol. 4, Nos. 2 and 4, 1935–36, and his collection of essays, *Revaluation*, was published only in 1936. Orwell might have had in mind remarks on Wordsworth, Shelley, and Keats made by T. S. Eliot (1888–1965) in *The Use of Poetry and the Use of Criticism* (1933), and there are comments on Milton in his *Homage to John Dryden* (1924), particularly in 'The Metaphysical Poets.' Eliot's first essay devoted specifically to Milton ('A Note on the Verse of John Milton') was not published until *Essays & Studies*, XXI, 1935. So it seems probable that Orwell was thinking of Leavis on Milton, and Eliot on Wordsworth, Shelley, and Keats. An echo of Orwell's response to the kind of criticism found here is in one of his last reviews, that of Leavis's *The Great Tradition* (1948); see *3543*.
2. In *The Mind of a Mnemonist: Little Book about a Vast Memory*, translated from Russian by L. Solotaroff (1987), A. R. Luria shows that this does not appear to be always correct.

195. To Leonard Moore

12 March 1934   Typewritten

36 High St   Southwold   Suffolk

Dear Sir,

Many thanks for the copy of Harper's contract, which I am returning herewith signed. I see that it does not say anything about sending copies to periodicals for review. If and when the book appears in the U.S.A, I should like copies to be sent to at least a dozen English papers which I should name. If Harper's do not agree to this, I could purchase copies myself at trade price and send them. However, this can be arranged when the time comes.

Provided all goes well and Harper's legal adviser does not raise any objections, I wonder if you could be kind enough to ask them to insert at the beginning of the book a note to the effect that "all the characters in this story are entirely imaginary"[1] etc?[2]

Yours faithfully
Eric A. Blair

1. The U.S. edition (the first) notes, 'All characters in this book are fictitious.' Possibly Gollancz's anxieties about libel and defamation had communicated themselves to Orwell. The first English edition carries a much more detailed disavowal; see Textual Note to *Burmese Days*, *CW*, II. Note that Moore is addressed as 'Dear Sir,' not by name.
2. Below the signature is a note in shorthand (doubtful words in square brackets): 'Dear [Thr . . . nd] [Retention] of the American book means that it would get reviewed when the English book comes out.' The sign for 'book' is probably to be read as 'edition.'

196. 'On a Ruined Farm near the His Master's Voice Gramophone Factory'

The Adelphi, April 1934[1]

As I stand at the lichened gate
With warring worlds on either hand—
To left the black and budless trees,
The empty sties, the barns that stand

Like tumbling skeletons—and to right
The factory-towers, white and clear
Like distant, glittering[2] cities seen
From a ship's rail—as I stand here,

I feel, and with a sharper pang,
My mortal sickness; how I give
My heart to weak and stuffless ghosts,
And with the living cannot live.

The acid smoke has soured the fields,
And browned the few and windworn flowers;
But there, where steel and concrete soar
In dizzy, geometric towers—

There,[3] where the tapering cranes sweep round,
And great wheels turn, and trains roar by
Like strong, low-headed brutes of steel—
There is my world, my home; yet why

So alien still? For I can neither
Dwell in that world, nor turn again
To scythe and spade, but only loiter
Among the trees the smoke has slain.

Yet when the trees were young, men still
Could choose their path—the wingèd[4] soul,
Not cursed with double doubts, could fly,
Arrow-like to a foreseen goal;

And they who planned those soaring towers,
They too have set their spirit free;
To them their glittering world can bring
Faith, and accepted destiny;

But none to me as I stand here
Between two countries, both-ways torn,
And moveless still, like Buridan's donkey[5]
Between the water and the corn.

Eric Blair

1. This version was checked against Orwell's typescript; see variants in notes *3* and *4*. The factory is illustrated in Thompson, 39. The poem was selected for *The Best Poems of 1934*, edited by Thomas Moult.
2. Typescript suggests that Orwell considered using 'glistering' here, probably to avoid repetition; see penultimate stanza. He would have had the chance to make the change in proof, but apparently did not wish to do so. His letter to Eleanor Jaques of 18 February 1933 (see *161*) suggests that proofs were sent to contributors, but not long before publication.
3. Comma omitted after 'There' in typescript.
4. wingèd] wingéd *in typescript*
5. Buridan's ass (rather than donkey) died of starvation because, standing midpoint between two kinds of food, it could not decide which was the more attractive and so stood stockstill. This problem is attributed to Jean Buridan, French scholastic philosopher of the fourteenth century.

197. Review of *Further Extracts from the Note-Books of Samuel Butler*, chosen and edited by A.T. Bartholomew

The Adelphi, April 1934

This second selection from the Notebooks is a little disappointing, and it was probably inevitable that it should be so. Butler attached far more importance to his ideas than to purely literary creation, and tending as he did to see confirmation of them everywhere, he was bound to repeat himself. The peculiar charm of the first issue of notes was not so much in any ideas they contained, as in those brief, perfectly told anecdotes about things that Butler had seen and overheard in the streets and public houses. Tiny as they were, some of them had the same mysteriously significant quality as, say, the conversation between the packhorse carriers in the first part of *Henry IV*.[1] No doubt a great many of them were Butler's own invention, but he was in any case an ideal observer of life. He was a good listener, and he had a far more genuine appreciation of common speech than most of the novelists who have exploited it.

There are one or two amusing remarks in this collection. For example:

"I saw a tombstone in Woolwich churchyard with the text, 'The Lord hath need of him.' Remembering the circumstances under which the text was spoken, it seemed to me that the executor of the deceased had hinted that he was an ass rather clearly."

It was typical of Butler's queer mind to link up Matthew xxi 3 with that hackneyed stonemason's blurb. But entries of that kind are few and far between. The great majority of them are intolerably cheap epigrams of the kind that consist in turning some popular saying upside down ("Jesus, with all thy faults I love thee still," etc.)—the kind of thing that was first vulgarised by Shaw and Chesterton, and has since been done to death in the middle articles in the reviews. Either this selection has been badly done, or, what is more likely, all the juice was sucked out of the Notebooks in the previous issue.

On the other hand, this book will have its value for those who are

339

personally interested in Butler. It has the merit of being arranged in chronological order, and it contains a good deal of incidental literary criticism—nothing so good, however, as the celebrated remark about Blake, Dante, Virgil and Tennyson that so enraged Sir Edmund Gosse.[2] A great number of the entries are of a blasphemous and anti-clerical nature, which probably gives a slightly misleading impression. Butler certainly disliked Christ and the teaching of Christ, but it is doubtful whether he seriously objected to Christianity—that is, to the churches. As he himself said somewhere or other, it was "men like Darwin and Huxley" who were his natural enemies, rather than the priests; and in spite of his ambition to photograph a seasick bishop, he obviously had a sneaking affection for the clergy.

This is a scrappy, unsatisfactory book, but, like everything Butler ever wrote, it leaves one with an affection for its author. He is always likeable, even when he is being silly. The book contains a rather charming photograph of Butler, seated at his writing table.

Eric Blair

1. *I Henry IV*, 2.1: the scene at the inn yard at Rochester in the early morning. This not only is an apt comparison but also is indicative of Orwell's concerns. There is perhaps no scene in all of Shakespeare that more sharply delineates the painful and troublous daily round of those at the bottom of the social scale.

2. As the self-proclaimed *enfant terrible* of literature, Samuel Butler (1835–1902) said that he and Henry Festing Jones had 'agreed that Blake was no good because he learnt Italian at 60 in order to study Dante, and we know Dante was no good because he was so fond of Virgil, and Virgil was no good because Tennyson ran him, and as for Tennyson—well, Tennyson goes without saying' (*The Note-Books of Samuel Butler*, selected, arranged and edited by Henry Festing Jones, 1912, 183). Sir Edmund Gosse (1849–1928), one of those instrumental in developing the academic study of English in the later nineteenth century and a prolific author, commented: Butler's 'literary judgments were *saugrenu* to the last extreme. What are we to think of a man who lays it down that'—and he quotes, slightly inaccurately, the passage given above? 'There is no critical meaning in such outbursts; they would be almost imbecile in their aimless petulance if we did not understand that Virgil and Dante and Blake lay in the dark segment of Butler's vision, and that he had not so much formed an adverse opinion of their merits as no opinion at all' ('Samuel Butler,' an essay reprinted in *Aspects and Impressions*, 1922, 69). Orwell was fascinated by Butler's *Note-Books* throughout his life. In 'As I Please,' 34, 21 July 1944 (see *2514*) he wrote that he had read them when he was in Burma. He refers to an anecdote in Bartholomew's edition in his War-time Diary; see *677*.

198. To Leonard Moore

11 April 1934   Typewritten

36 High St   Southwold   Suffolk

Dear Mr Moore,

Many thanks for your letter. Would it be convenient for Mr Hamilton[1] to see me on Friday April the 20th?[2] Or Saturday the 21st, but I expect Friday would be better for him, and the time that would suit me best would be in the afternoon, say not before 4 o'clock. I have got to come up to town some time, and could manage that week-end conveniently. I am very intrigued to know what it is that he wants to talk about. I suppose you haven't heard from Harper's whether their solicitors thought the novel[3] was all right? It has been foul weather here and everything is very backward. My novel[4] is not getting on badly, and I have done more than I expected to do in the time, though of course very roughly as yet.

Yours sincerely
Eric A. Blair

1. From the context of Orwell's letter to Moore of 25 April (see *199*), Hamish Hamilton represented Harper's as well as his own publishing house. Precisely what the project was is not known.
2. Next to 'April 20th' is the annotation '4.30.'
3. *Burmese Days.*
4. *A Clergyman's Daughter.*

199. To Leonard Moore

25 April 1934   Typewritten

36 High St   Southwold   Suffolk

Dear Mr Moore,
Many thanks for your letter. I am returning the contract herewith duly signed.[1] I am naturally extremely pleased that you have been able to arrange for a French translation of Down and Out, and I must thank you very much for all the trouble you have been at over this book. I went to see Mr Hamilton as arranged, but the interview did not come to much, as the project he was suggesting (he asked me not to tell anyone what it was) needed certain specialised knowledge which I have not got. However, I used once to know a man who I think could do what Hamilton wanted, and I said that I would do my best to get in touch with him. Hamilton said that he had not heard about the fate of my novel,[2] but the last he heard was that it was still with their lawyers and they thought it would be all right. He also said that if no English publication was arranged, Harper's intended to sell a certain amount of copies over here.

Yours sincerely
Eric A. Blair

1. The contract was for the French translation of *Down and Out in Paris and London*, published as *La Vache Enragée* by Gallimard, in Paris, on 2 May 1935. The translation was by R. N. Raimbault and Gwen Gilbert. Orwell wrote an introduction for it, dated 15 October 1934; see *211*. For characteristics of this edition, see *157* and *CW*, I, Textual Note.
2. *Burmese Days.*

200. To Leonard Moore

2 May 1934   Typewritten

36 High St   Southwold   Suffolk

Dear Mr Moore,

If we don't hear soon from Harper's about my novel[1] what do you say to cabling? I would like to know soon whether they have come to any decision. I will pay the costs of the cable of course.

Yours sincerely
Eric A. Blair

1. *Burmese Days.*

201. Review of *The Aesthetic of Stéphane Mallarmé* by Hasye Cooperman; *Baudelaire: The Tragic Sophist* by G.T. Clapton

The Adelphi, July 1934

Mr. Cooperman's book consists partly of a decipherment of certain of Mallarmé's poems—not the earlier poems, but the later, unintelligible ones—and partly of an analysis of Mallarmé's symbolism and the relation of his poems to Wagner's music.

To the general reader, the most interesting part of the book will be that dealing with the reasons for Mallarmé's extreme obscurity. Briefly, Mr. Cooperman explains that Mallarmé made his poetry obscure, more or less intentionally, in a search for greater and greater abstraction. On the face of it an intensely and wilfully individual poet, he was really attempting to reach the very opposite of the individual—the absolute. The changes that he made in his poems over a number of years were nearly always in the direction of greater abstractness, and hence of greater vagueness, on the ground that the vague and general word comes nearer to reality (in the Platonic sense) than the concrete and the particular. The vague word, so to speak, *contains* the vivid word. Mr. Cooperman analyses certain of the poems line by line, explaining the reasons for each successive alteration.

This is done with great care and discernment, and is in places distinctly interesting to read, but, frankly, it does not get one very much further; least of all when one comes to poems like "Un Coup de Dés," where Mallarmé leaves out all the conjunctions and plays fearful tricks with punctuation and typography. One sees that to understand Mallarmé it is necessary to be the "ideal reader," of whom there are, perhaps, two in every million people. And, without taking the Squire-Priestley attitude towards "highbrows," one may be forgiven for feeling that there is something wrong somewhere when poets of obvious talent write poems that are virtually unintelligible—poems that are admittedly aimed only at the "ideal reader," and can only be made comprehensible even to him by the enormous researches of scholars. (Mr. Cooperman's bibliography runs to twenty-eight pages.) Probably the truth is that artistic obscurity, so common this last seventy years, is only one of the morbid growths of our decaying civilisation, and is traceable directly to economic causes. The pity is, though of course it is only what one would expect, that artists should succumb to it more or less in proportion as they are gifted.

Mr. Clapton's pamphlet is very readable, but rather perverse. He says on the last page but two: "It is in no spirit of orthodox moral condemnation that I have subjected Baudelaire to this analysis"; whereas in fact the whole pamphlet is one long diatribe of moral condemnation, or something so like it as makes no difference. In substance, his accusation is that Baudelaire was an inconsistent and perhaps even dishonest writer, because he did not play the game of Satanism according to the rules. When it suited him, Mr. Clapton says, he accepted the Christian dualism and turned it upside down as an orthodox Satanist should; but also, when it suited him, he attacked Christian ethics from a *non*-Christian standpoint which made his own *anti*-Christian pose meaningless. This is undoubtedly true, but Mr. Clapton seems not to have reflected that to be a Satanist seven days a week would be like blacking oneself all over to play Othello. Satanism can never be quite as consistent as orthodox Christian belief, because it can never be equally sincere; for no one who believed *literally* in the vindictive God of the Christians would take the risk of defying Him.

But surely Baudelaire's attitude is quite understandable, and, in spite of its apparent inconsistency, defensible? He clung to the ethical and the imaginative background of Christianity, because he had been brought up in the Christian tradition and because he perceived that such notions as sin, damnation, etc., were in a sense truer and more real than anything he could get from sloppy humanitarian atheism. Spiritually the Christian cosmos suited him, though as a rule he preferred to turn it upside down. But, of course, he was not and could not make himself a believer in the same literal sense as the people who go to church on Sunday; so it was natural that he should sometimes attack Christian ethics from without instead of from within.

It is perhaps a rather complicated attitude, but natural enough at a time when religious belief was decaying, and it did not incapacitate Baudelaire as a poet; on the contrary, it was the making of him. But Mr. Clapton seems comparatively uninterested in Baudelaire qua poet, merely paying him a grudging compliment or two on the last page. However, he has obviously made an intimate study of him as a man, and his pamphlet is extremely well-informed, admirably written and of great interest to anyone who knows Baudelaire's poetry and the main facts of his life.

Eric Blair

202. To Brenda Salkeld

27 July 1934   Typewritten

36 High St   Southwold   Suffolk

Dearest Brenda

Many thanks for your last letter. How I wish you were here![1] I am so miserable, struggling in the entrails of that dreadful book[2] and never getting any further, and loathing the sight of what I have done. *Never* start writing novels, if you wish to preserve your happiness. I hope your lecture went off all right. Dennis Collings and Eleanor were married on Monday, but they are not back in Southwold yet. Dennis has got to leave for Malaya in about another ten days. I have had quite a lot of stuff from the garden, but the peas have given out for the time being. We have started eating the cauliflowers, and they are delicious. I am fattening a marrow, but it is a very bad shape and I don't think I shall let it get very large. The beans we sowed have grown to an enormous size, but for some reason there is not much blossom on them, so I have pinched out the tops. I had lunch yesterday with Dr Ede.[3] He is a bit of a feminist and thinks that if a woman was brought up exactly like a man she would be able to throw a stone, construct a syllogism, keep a secret etc. He tells me that my anti-feminist views are probably due to Sadism! I have never read the Marquis de Sade's novels—they are unfortunately very hard to get hold of. Do you remember that afternoon when we had tea with Delisle Burns[4] and I asked him what was the tune of "Malbrouck s'en va-t-en guerre", and he said it was the same as "For he's a jolly good fellow"? And the other night I was passing the King's Head, and the Buffaloes, who were holding one of their secret conclaves in there, were singing it—or rather, as they seemed to be gargling it through pints of beer, what it sounded like was:

> Fo-or-*ee's* a jorrigoo' fellow,
> For-*ee's* a jorrigoo' fellow,
> For-ee's a jorrigoo' fe-ellow—
> And toori oori us![5]

And I could not help thinking again what very peculiar histories tunes have. To think that Napoleon was whistling, at I forget what battle, the same tune as the Buffaloes were singing! And it struck me that an *idea* is very like a tune in this way, that it goes through the ages remaining the same in itself but getting into such very different company. It is an idea that interests me, and I must use it in my next book. I found Vacandard's history of the Inquisition quite interesting. It is a Catholic history, so you can be sure that you are getting, so to speak, the minimum of everything. It appears, though V. himself doesn't mention it, that the pendulum in Poe's story was actually used, though not at such a late date as Poe makes out. Torture was not used in the tribunals of the Inquisition after the middle of the 18th century, but the Pope did not formally abolish it till 1816. Our hedgehog has disappeared. I knew it would be so. It does occasionally come at night (it is somewhere in the next door garden, I think), but we never see it. When are you coming back? I can't stick this place when you are not here. If I were not fairly busy I should go mad here. I shall have to go up to London in October, but not before, I think, as I doubt if I can finish my novel before then. I don't know when the other[6] is coming out—I haven't had the proofs yet, and I don't know how long it will take after I have corrected the proofs. I wish you could come back here and stay somewhere before the end of the holidays. Write soon and tell me what you are doing.

With much love
Eric

1. Although Brenda Salkeld taught in Southwold, she went home for vacations; hence Orwell's wishing she were in Southwold.
2. *A Clergyman's Daughter.*
3. Unidentified.
4. Cecil Delisle Burns (1879–1942) was, at the time, Stevenson Lecturer in Citizenship, University of Glasgow. He worked in the Ministry of Reconstruction, 1917–19, and in the Ministry of Labour, 1919–21. Among his many books are *The Growth of Modern Philosophy* (1909); *Political Ideals* (3rd edition, 1919); *Principles of Revolution* (1920); *Philosophy of Labour* (1925); *Modern Civilization on Trial* (1931); *Horizon of Experience* (1933). Although associated with Glasgow University, he also had an address close to Mabel Fierz's house in Hampstead Garden Suburb, London.
5. Gordon Comstock hears 'beer-choked voices' singing this verse in *Keep the Aspidistra Flying* (1936), *CW*, IV, 79–82.
6. *Burmese Days.*

203. Review of *Poems of Rainer Maria Rilke*, translated from the German by J. B. Leishman

The Adelphi, August 1934

It is practically impossible to get from a verse translation any idea of what the original poem is like, especially when one does not know the language in which it was written. But the chances are that these translations are accurate ones as well as being, in several cases, distinctly good poems in themselves. There is such a lack of rhymes in English, and particularly of rhymes to vitally necessary words ("death," "self," "love," "wound," etc.) that a translator must be before all else an ingenious rhymer. Mr. Leishman certainly satisfies this test. His rhymes are excellent, and he has other qualities as well. This, from the opening poem of the book, has the air of being a really good translation:

> There, where the line of cottages grows thin,
> And the new narrow-chested houses thrust
> Through crazy scaffoldings and choking dust
> To ask each other where the fields begin:
>
> Pale and half-hearted there the spring remains;
> Summer is feverish behind plank and paling;

> Children and cherry-trees are always ailing;
> Autumn alone there something still retains
>
> Distant and reconciling;

Notice the fine, swift-moving rhythm of the second stanza, which remains true to the conventional form and yet avoids the te-tum te-tum effect which is the curse of the English decasyllabic line. Notice also the agreeable assonance between "ailing" and "reconciling." The blank verse poem "Orpheus, Eurydice, Hermes," is a remarkable piece of work, and so is "The Ashanti," whose opening stanzas are vaguely reminiscent of Baudelaire, though marred by the use of the word "lithe."

This is a book which can be read with a good deal of pleasure for its own sake, but it does not leave one much wiser about Rainer Maria Rilke. The chief impression one carries away is that of a vague melancholy—wistfulness, if the word can be used without calling up visions of "Beautiful Joe"—that might belong to any poet in any age or country.

Eric Blair

204. To Brenda Salkeld

Tuesday night, [late August? 1934]   Handwritten

36 High St   Southwold   Suffolk

Dearest Brenda

Many thanks for your letter. I hope you are enjoying yourself more in Ireland than I am in England. When are you coming back? I am going up to town as soon as I have finished the book[1] I am doing, which should be at the end of October. I haven't settled yet where I am going to stay, but somewhere in the slums for choice. A friend wrote offering me the lease of part of a flat in Bayswater, but it would choke me to live in Bayswater. No, I have never seen a tortoise drinking. Darwin mentions that when he was in the Galapagos Is. the big tortoises there which lived on cactuses & things on the higher ground used to come down into the valley once or twice in the year to drink, & the journey took them a day or two. They stored the water in a kind of sack in their bellies. I have been reading some books by Lafcadio Hearn— tiresome stuff, & he idolises the Japanese, who always seem to me such a boring people. I also tried to read Lord Riddell's diary of the Peace Conference & After. What tripe! It is amazing how some people can have the most interesting experiences & then have absolutely nothing to say about them. I went to the pictures last week and saw Jack Hulbert in "Jack Ahoy" which I thought very amusing, & a week or two before that there was quite a good crook film, which, however, my father ruined for me by insisting on telling me the plot beforehand. This week "The Constant Nymph" is on. I haven't been to it, of course, but even when I see the posters it makes me go hot all over to think that in my youth—I think I must have been about 23 when it was published in book form—I was affected by it almost to tears O *mihi praeteritos* etc. I should think that any *critic* who lives to a great age must have many passages in his youth that he would willingly keep dark. There must be, for instance, many critics who in the 'nineties went all mushy over Hall Caine or even Marie Corelli—though M.C isn't so absolutely bad, judging by the only book of hers I ever read. It was called "Thelma" & there was a very licentious clergyman in it who wasn't half bad. Did you, by the way, give me back those books of Swift? It doesn't matter, only I don't want to lose them. Yes, "Roughing It"[2] does "date" a bit, but not enough—because anything worth reading always 'dates.' Do come back soon. I am so miserable all alone. I have practically no friends here now, because now that Dennis & Eleanor are married & Dennis has gone to Singapore,[3] it has deprived me of two friends at a single stroke. Everything is going badly. My novel about Burma made me spew when I saw it in print, & I would have rewritten large chunks of it, only that costs money and means delay as well. As for the novel I am now completing, it makes me spew even worse, & yet there *are* some decent passages in it. I don't know how it is, I can write decent passages but I can't put them together. I was rather pluming myself on having a poem[4] in the "Best Poems of 1934," but I now learn that there are several dozen of these anthologies of the so called best poems of the year, & Ruth Pitter[5] writes to tell me that she is in 4 of this year's batch, including one called "Twenty Deathless Poems." We are getting delicious French beans from the garden, but I am concerned about the pumpkin, which shows signs of ripening though it is not much bigger than an orange. All my fruit has been stolen by the children next door, as I forsaw° it would. The little beasts were in such a hurry to get it that they didn't even wait till it was half ripe, but took the pears when they were mere chunks of wood. Another time I must try a dodge Dr Collings told me, which is to paint a mixture of vaseline & some indelible dye, I forget what, on a few of the fruit that are likely to be taken first & then you can spot who has taken it by the stains on their hands. The town is very full & camps of Girl Guides etc. infesting all the commons. I nearly died of cold the other day when bathing, because I had walked out to Easton Broad not intending to bathe, & then the water looked so nice that I took off my clothes & went in, & then about 50 people came up & rooted themselves to the spot. I wouldn't have minded that, but among them was a coastguard who could have had me up for bathing naked, so I had to swim up & down for the best part of half an hour, pretending to like it. Do come back soon, dearest one. Can't you come & stay with somebody before the term begins? It is sickening that I have to go away just after you come back. Write soon.

With much love
Eric

1. *A Clergyman's Daughter.*
2. By Mark Twain (1872): it describes the author's experiences with silver miners in Nevada a decade earlier. An unsigned review in *Overland Monthly*, June 1872, said its humour was such that it 'should have a place in every sick-room, and be the invalid's chosen companion.'

3. Dennis Collings and Eleanor Jaques married in 1934; he had been made assistant curator at the Raffles Museum in Singapore; see *109*, *n. 1* and *129*, *n. 1*.
4. 'On a Ruined Farm near the His Master's Voice Gramophone Factory'; see *196*.
5. Ruth Pitter (see *139*, *n. 1*) had known Orwell since World War I, and he had stayed in her house from time to time in 1930. He later reviewed two of her books of poetry; see *139* and *589*. In 1937 she won the Hawthornden Prize for Literature and in 1955 was awarded the Queen's Medal for Poetry. Her *Collected Poems* appeared in 1991.

205. To Brenda Salkeld

Wed. night, [early September? 1934]   Typewritten in red

36 High St   Southwold   Suffolk

Dearest Brenda

As you complain about the gloominess of my letters, I suppose I must try and put on what Mr Micawber called the hollow mask of mirth, but I assure you it is not easy, with the life I have been leading lately. My novel[1] instead of going forwards, goes backwards with the most alarming speed. There are whole wads of it that are so awful that I really don't know what to do with them. And to add to my other joys, the fair, or part of it, has come back and established itself on the common just beyond the cinema, so that I have to work to the accompaniment of roundabout music that goes on till the small hours. You may think that this is red ink I am writing in, but really it is some of the bloody sweat that has been collecting round me in pools for the last few days. I am glad to hear you enjoyed yourself in the peninsular, as you are pleased to call it. I shall send this to the London address you gave me, hoping they will keep it for you. The garden isn't doing badly. We had so many cauliflowers that we couldn't eat them up fast enough, so about twenty have run to seed. I have one marrow—the eighth so far—that is almost Harvest Festival size, and I am letting it get ripe to make jam out of. I managed to get my copy of "Ulysses" through safely this time. I rather wish I had never read it. It gives me an inferiority complex. When I read a book like that and then come back to my own work, I feel like a eunuch who has taken a course in voice production and can pass himself off fairly well as a bass or a baritone, but if you listen closely you can hear the good old squeak just the same as ever. I also bought for a shilling a year's issue of a weekly paper of 1851, which is not uninteresting. They ran among other things a matrimonial agency, and the correspondence relating to this is well worth reading. "Flora is twenty one, tall, with rich chestnut hair and a silvery laugh, and makes excellent light pastry. She would like to enter into correspondence with a professional gentleman between the ages of twenty and thirty, preferably with auburn whiskers and of the Established Church." The interesting thing to me is that these people, since they try to get married through a matrimonial agency, have evidently failed many times elsewhere, and yet as soon as they advertise in this paper, they get half a dozen offers. The women's descriptions of themselves are always most flattering, and I must say that some of the cases make me distinctly suspicious—for of course that was the great age of fortune-hunting. You remember that beautiful case in "Our Mutual Friend," where both parties worked the same dodge on each other. I wish you could come back here. However, if you can't it can't be helped. I could not possibly have come to Haslemere. I most particularly want to get this novel done by the end of September, and every day makes a difference. I know it sounds silly to make such a fuss for so little result, but I find that anything like changing my lodging upsets my work for a week or so. When I said that I was going to stay in a slummy part of London I did not mean that I am going to live in a common lodging house or anything like that. I only meant that I didn't want to live in a respectable quarter, because they make me sick, besides being more expensive. I dare say I shall stay in Islington. It is maddening that you cannot get unfurnished rooms in London, but I know by experience that you can't, though of course you can get a flat or some horrible thing called a maisonette. This age makes me so sick that sometimes I am almost impelled to stop at a corner and start calling down curses from Heaven like Jeremiah or Ezra or somebody—"Woe upon thee, O Israel, for thy adulteries with the Egyptians" etc etc. The hedgehogs keep coming into the house, and last night we found in the bathroom a little tiny hedgehog no bigger than an orange. The only thing I could think was that it was a baby of one of the others, though it was fully formed—I mean, it had its prickles. Write again soon. You don't know how it cheers me up when I see one of your letters waiting for me.

With love
Eric

1. *A Clergyman's Daughter.*

206. To Leonard Moore

10 September 1934   Typewritten

36 High St   Southwold   Suffolk

Dear Mr Moore,

One or two friends of mine want to know whether they can buy copies of my novel[1] when it comes out, by writing to Harper's in New York for it. Would Harper's supply them in that case, do you think? I suppose Harper's will send me six copies as usual? And I wonder whether you could be kind enough to order me three copies extra, as there are a lot of people who will want copies. I think they said on the contract I could get copies at cost price or at any rate below selling price.[2] I shall be able to let you have the novel I am doing about the end of the month or early in October, I think. I am not very satisfied with it, as it is rather fragmentary, but there are bits in it that people might find interesting, I hope. By the way there is a poem of mine in some book that is coming out called The Best Poems of 1934. According to our contract this ought to have been done through you, but I didn't write to you about it as there is no money in it—there wouldn't be, it being poetry! I am coming up to

London some time in October, I think, to stay several months. I sent back the proofs of my novel a month or six weeks ago, so I suppose they might get it out at the time they said—that is at the end of this month. When it comes out, will you get me the press-cuttings, please?[3]

Yours sincerely
Eric A. Blair

1. Annotated in Moore's office: ' "Burmese Days" by George Orwell (Harpers) Sep 9, 1934.'
   The ninth was a Sunday; *Burmese Days* was not published until 25 October 1934.
2. Annotated in Moore's office: 'Yes.'
3. Annotated in Moore's office: 'Argus note date pubn.' Argus was a press-cutting agency.

207. To Brenda Salkeld

Tuesday night, [11?[1] September 1934]   Typewritten

36 High St   Southwold   Suffolk

Dearest Brenda,

Many thanks for your letter. I am so glad to hear you have been having such an interesting time, and only wish I could reciprocate, but the most exciting things I have been doing are to plant out cabbages and make hurried trips into Lowestoft and Norwich in search of bulbs. Last time we were in Lowestoft we saw some Jews selling alarm clocks at sixpence each! Even if they had gone for a month you would have fairly good value for your money. My novel is due to come out in New York tomorrow—I don't know that it actually will, but that is the day it is scheduled for. Please pray for its success, by which I mean not less than 4000 copies. I understand that the prayers of clergyman's° daughters get special attention in Heaven, at any rate in the Protestant quarter. I suppose I shall get some copies in about 10 days and some reviews in about 10 days after that. I hope they haven't put quite such a bloody jacket on it as they did last time. I hope to finish the other one about the end of the month, and then I must sit down and plan out my next before going up to London. I am pleased with parts of this one I am doing, and other parts make me spew. I don't believe anyone will publish it or if they do it won't sell, because it is too fragmentary and has no love-interest. When exactly are you coming back to Southwold? Be sure and let me know so that I can keep Sunday free for you, and *please* don't go and tie yourself up with engagements for the whole of the first fortnight so that I never get a chance to see you. I have just been reading Huc's Travels in Tartary and Thibet,° which I can reccommend.° The garden is now looking very bare, as we have taken nearly everything up, but we are putting in bulbs etc. I have started taking snuff, which is very nice and useful in places where you can't smoke. Please write soon and let me know when you are coming. Don't forget what you are to tell me when you come back.

With much love
Eric

P.S. Don't forget to bring back my "Roughing It,"[2] will you? I want it to look up some quotes.

1. *Burmese Days* ('my novel' early in the letter) was to be published in September 1934; see *206, n. 1.* Orwell must, therefore, have written this in September, even though publication was not until 25 October. He hopes to finish 'the other one' (*A Clergyman's Daughter*; note reference to Salkeld's being a clergyman's daughter) about the end of the month. The uncertainty suggests that he wrote well before the month's end. On 3 October he tells Moore he is sending him the typescript of his new novel; see *209.* The likely Tuesdays are 11 and 18 September. By the 18th, Salkeld would probably be back in Southwold for her new term. The letter has therefore been dated 11th September.
2. See letter to Brenda Salkeld, in late August, *204.*

208. To Leonard Moore

Sunday, [23 September 1934]   Typewritten

36 High St   Southwold   Suffolk

Dear Mr Moore,
I was talking yesterday to Mr Jonathan Cape, the publisher, and asked him whether he would like to see "Burmese Days." I shouldn't think there is much likelihood of his taking it, as apart from anything else he tells me he goes to the same lawyer[1] as Gollancz and therefore would probably have the same ideas about what constituted libel. However, he said he would like to have a look at the book. I wonder whether you would be kind enough to send him a copy when we get some from Harper's? He said you were a friend of his, and I expect he would remember his interview with me if you mentioned it.

Yours sincerely
Eric A Blair

1. Harold Rubinstein; see *219, n. 3.*

209. To Leonard Moore

3 October 1934   Typewritten

36 High St   Southwold   Suffolk

Dear Mr Moore,
I am sending my novel "A Clergyman's Daughter" under a separate cover. I will register it, and trust it will arrive all right. I am not at all pleased with it. It was a good idea, but I am afraid I have made a muck of it—however, it is as good as I can do for the present. There are bits of it that I don't dislike, but I am afraid it is very disconnected as a whole, and rather unreal. Possibly you will be able to find a publisher for it. I should be interested to hear your reader's opinion, and what publisher you intend to try it on. In case the point

should come up, the school described in Capter° IV is totally imaginary, though of course I have drawn on my general knowledge of what goes on in schools of that type.

Yes, of course keep a copy of "Burmese Days" when it arrives. By the way, I notice that that anthology of which I told you, in which there is one of my poems, comes from Jonathan Cape.[1] It might be worth mentioning that to him when we show him "Burmese Days." But I don't think it is at all likely that he would publish that book.

Yours sincerely
Eric A Blair

1. 'On a Ruined Farm near the His Master's Voice Gramophone Factory' appeared in *The Best Poems of 1934*; see *196, n. 1*.

210. To Leonard Moore

9 October 1934   Typewritten

36 High St   Southwold   Suffolk

Dear Mr Moore,

Your office forwarded me this morning a letter from the Frenchman who is translating "Down and Out" into French.[1] He said among other things that he would like to see my next book with a view to translating it. I should not think that "Burmese Days" is the kind of thing a French publisher would be interested in, but I think it is worth trying, because this man mentioned that André Malraux wrote a preface or introduction for another English book which he translated. André Malraux is a very well-known writer, and if he could be induced to write a preface the book would, I should say, be much likelier to find a publisher.[2] I know that he himself has written at any rate one novel about the East, and he might for that reason be interested in a book of this kind. I mentioned this to the translator, of course. So I wonder if you could be kind enough to see that he gets a copy when it appears? His name and address are: Monsieur R.N. Raimbault, 12 Rue Bruyère, Le Mans (Sarthe), France. Or perhaps the proper course would be to communicate with the publisher—I don't know. I suppose we shall have to order another copy for this purpose. M. Raimbault wants me to do a preface to "Down and Out," which I will send direct to him to save time.[3] I am coming up to town on Thursday, and will let you know my London address when I have settled down, as I shall probably be in London the whole winter.[4]

Yours sincerely
Eric Blair

1. R. N. Raimbault translated the book with Gwen Gilbert; see *157*.
2. André Malraux (1901–1976) was a novelist, who established himself with *La Condition Humaine* (1933), a tank commander in World War II, and a guerrilla leader during the German occupation of France. A leftist intellectual in the interwar years, he moved significantly to the right after 1945 and was Minister of Information and then of Culture in General de Gaulle's

government. He did not write a forward for the French edition of *Down and Out in Paris and London*, nor, despite having described his experiences in Spain in print (*L'Espoir*, 1937), for *Homage to Catalonia*. See also *3209, n. 1*.
3. Orwell wrote the introduction at once; see *211*.
4. Annotated in Moore's office: 'Called.'

211. Introduction to the French Edition of *Down and Out in Paris and London*

15 October 1934

The original English text of this introduction has not survived. The French text, as published in *La Vache Enragée* in 1935, is given in Appendix 1, *344*. The date is that given by Orwell at the end of the introduction. The translation was made by Shirley Jones, with revisions by Sonia Orwell.

My kind translators have asked me to write a short preface for the French edition of this book. As probably many of my French readers will wonder what chain of events brought me to Paris at the time when the incidents described in this book took place, I think it would be best to begin by giving them a few biographical details.

I was born in 1903. In 1922 I went to Burma where I joined the Indian Imperial Police. It was a job for which I was totally unsuited: so, at the beginning of 1928, while on leave in England, I gave in my resignation in the hopes of being able to earn my living by writing. I did just about as well at it as do most young people who take up a literary career—that is to say, not at all. My literary efforts in the first year barely brought me in twenty pounds.

In the spring of 1928 I set off for Paris so as to live cheaply while writing two novels[1]—which I regret to say were never published—and also to learn French. One of my Parisian friends found me a room in a cheap hotel in a working-class district which I have described briefly in the first chapter of this book, and which any sharp-witted Parisian will doubtless recognise. During the summer of 1929 I had written my two novels, which the publishers left on my hands, to find myself almost penniless and in urgent need of work. At that time it was not illegal—or at any rate not seriously illegal—for foreigners living in France to take jobs and it seemed more natural to me to stay in the city I was in, rather than return to England where, at that time, there were about two and a half million unemployed. So I stayed on in Paris and the events which I describe in this book took place towards the end of the autumn of 1929.

As for the truth of my story, I think I can say that I have exaggerated nothing except in so far as all writers exaggerate by selecting. I did not feel I had to describe events in the exact order in which they happened, but everything I have described did take place at one time or another. At the same time I have refrained, as far as possible, from drawing individual portraits of particular people. All the characters I have described in both parts of the book are intended more as representative types of the Parisian or Londoner of the class to which they belong than as individuals.

I should also add that this book makes no claims to giving a complete picture of life in Paris or London but only to portray one particular aspect. As almost without exception all the scenes and incidents in which I was involved have something repugnant about them it might seem that, without wishing to do so, I have given the impression that I think Paris and London are unpleasant cities. This was never my intention and if, at first sight, the reader should get this impression this is simply because the subject-matter of my book is essentially unattractive: my theme is poverty. When you haven't a penny in your pocket you are forced to see any city or country in its least favourable light and all human beings, or nearly all, appear to you either as fellow sufferers or as enemies. I want to emphasise this point particularly for my French readers because I would be distressed if they thought I have the least animosity towards a city of which I have very happy memories.

At the beginning of this preface I promised to give the reader some biographical details. So, for those it might interest, I will just add that after leaving Paris towards the end of 1929 I earned my living largely by teaching and in a small way by writing. Since the publication in England of *Down and Out in Paris and London*—the book here translated—I have written two novels, the second of which I have, indeed, just completed.[2] The first of these is due to be published in a day or two by a New York publishing house.[3]

George Orwell

1. The manuscript of neither novel survives. Writing to Michael Meyer on 12 March 1949 (see *3570*), Orwell said, 'I simply destroyed my first novel after unsuccessfully submitting it to one publisher, for which I'm rather sorry now.'
2. *A Clergyman's Daughter.*
3. *Burmese Days*, published by Harper & Brothers, 25 October 1934.

212. Booklovers' Corner, 1 South End Road, Hampstead, London, NW3

October 1934–January 1936

On 23 September 1934, Elaine Adam, née Limouzin, Orwell's aunt Nellie, with whom he had stayed in Paris in 1928 and possibly 1929,[1] wrote to her friend Myfanwy Westrope, wife of the owner of Booklovers' Corner, about Orwell: 'I had a letter from Eric yesterday, saying that his second novel was scheduled to come out in New York on the 19th (last Wednesday).[2] He is pretty sick that it can be sold only over there and hopes that "two or three thousand" will go off. He intends finishing his third novel[3] before the end of this month and will then go up to London and "stay some months." I shall give him your address and hope you will be able to see him. I shall advise him to write to you first, for no doubt you are both pretty busy with the shop, the house and I.L.P. work. He may *possibly* be staying in Golder's Green for I know he has a friend there[4] and, if so, he would be "contagious"° to you . . . I must finish now, as I have other letters to write, one to the editor of *Le Temps*, in which paper there is a series of articles running on "Women in the Modern World" and I think they might like one on the Burmese women[5] who really have a unique position among the Eastern women, being the equals of the men. If they would like the article, then Eric could do it very efficiently, with his experience out there.[6] His book being published in America has Burma as the setting.'[7]

Eugène Adam was an important figure in the Esperantist movement, in which the Westropes were also active. According to Mrs. Westrope, 'George Orwell probably learnt a good deal concerning Russia from E. L.'s husband who, as Editor of the *Sennacieca Revuo*, was in close touch with Russian affairs. The latter became a stern opponent of the Stalinist regime, on discovering its true nature—which he designated "Red Fascism"—and he afterwards edited *Herezulo*, described as "an independent review for fighting against all dogmas." '

As a result of this introduction, and because they had met Orwell through the Independent Labour Party, Orwell was offered work and a place to live by Francis G. Westrope and his wife. From about the middle of October 1934 to the end of January 1936 he worked as a part-time assistant at Westrope's shop, Booklovers' Corner. He boarded with the Westropes at 3 Warwick Mansions, Pond Street, in the same block as the bookshop, until mid-February 1935, as did Jon Kimche,[8] another part-time assistant at the shop. Kimche worked in the mornings; Orwell, in the afternoons. Orwell told Brenda Salkeld (see *235*) that Mrs. Westrope was 'the non-interfering sort' of landlady. The novelist Peter Vansittart (1920–) has described meeting Orwell when, as a schoolboy, he went to Booklovers' Corner to purchase *A Damsel in Distress*, but Orwell tried to persuade him to buy *Trader Horn in Madagascar*. Orwell was later to give him his first book to review, and he wrote two 'As I Please' columns for *Tribune*, 4 July and 15 August 1947.[9]

Orwell's experience at Booklovers' Corner provided background material for *Keep the Aspidistra Flying*. See Crick, 249–56; Thompson, 44, for an illustration of the corner as it was in 1984, a pizza house. Kimche's memories of his and Orwell's time at the bookshop are in *Remembering Orwell*, 54–55. In November 1969 Sonia Orwell unveiled a plaque at the site where the bookshop had been, commemorating Orwell's having worked and lived there.

1. Mrs. Westrope explained in a note with this excerpt from Elaine Limouzin's letter (both of which and the note on Eugène Adam are reproduced from a copy supplied by Michael Meredith, The School Library, Eton College, and by the kind permission of the Provost and Fellows) that Orwell 'could have continued to stay' with his aunt and her husband in Paris 'had he not wished to gain experience of the underworld, in preparation for the writing of *Down and Out in Paris and London*. When this book appeared, Elaine sent me a copy, asking me not to judge Eric by its contents as he was "not a bit like his book". This I found to be true later. M.W.' For the Westropes and Booklovers' Corner, see Shelden, 212–16; U.S.: 193–97.
2. *Burmese Days* was not published in September, as Orwell had expected, but on 25 October 1934; see *206, n. 1*.
3. *A Clergyman's Daughter*.
4. Francis and Mabel Fierz; see *102, n. 1*.
5. Orwells' maternal grandfather, of French extraction, had been a teak merchant in Moulmein, Burma. His aunt Nellie had lived in Burma, too.
6. No such article by Orwell has been traced.
7. The letter was written from 14 ave. Corbera, Paris 12[e].
8. Jon Kimche (1909–1994), born in Switzerland, came to know the Westropes through the ILP. He had lived with them for a month or two before, and stayed for a further two months after, Orwell's arrival. In May 1937 he went to Spain to meet Orwell, arriving in the midst of the troubles in Barcelona. He later ran the Socialist Book Centre, was military correspondent for

the *Evening Standard*, 1941–45, and wrote under the name 'Liberator' for *The Observer*, 1942–46. He was acting editor of *Tribune*, 1942–44; and then became Reuter's special correspondent for Spain, Austria, Persia, and the Middle East, 1944–46, before rejoining *Tribune*, as editor from 1946 to January 1948. In an interview with Ian Angus, 5 September 1967, he recalled heated arguments in the *Tribune* office over Palestine, and Orwell's belief that Zionists should be equated with Wardour Street film magnates. He also recalled that Orwell's copy was 'always perfect.' He helped arrange Orwell's journey to Switzerland in the winter of 1949–50. See *Remembering Orwell*, 54–56, 88–89, 94–95, 139–41, 215.

9. Letter to the editor, [24] August 1988.

213. To Leonard Moore

Saturday, [20 October 1934]   Typewritten

3 Warwick Mansions   Pond Street   Hampstead   N.W.

Dear Mr Moore,

Many thanks for the copy of Burmese Days.[1] I have heard from my French translator, who tells me that Andre Malraux is a friend of his and would almost certainly undertake to do a preface for a French translation of it, and also that, as Malraux is on the reading committee of the N.R.F. publishing house,[2] his recommendation would bear weight with them. So will you please send the translator a copy as soon as the others come? I think I gave you his address, but will repeat it in case I didn't. Monsieur R. N. Raimbault, 12 Rue Bruyere, Le Mans (Sarthe), FRANCE. Could you in future communicate with me at the above address and not the one I gave you before,[3] as that one is the address of the shop, and I am not always there?

Yours sincerely
Eric A Blair

1. An advance copy: publication date was 25 October 1934.
2. *La Nouvelle Revue Française*, a journal and publishing house. It published the second volume of Proust's *A la recherche du temps perdu* in 1919, after the relative failure of the first volume, published in 1913 at the author's expense. During the German occupation, the journal became pro-Nazi, under the editorship of Pierre-Eugène Drieu la Rochelle; see *913, n. 8*.
3. Presumably Booklovers' Corner, 1 South End Road, Hampstead. South End Road and Pond Street join at the corner where the bookshop was situated; Orwell lived in the block that included the bookshop.

213A. Publication of *Burmese Days* in the United States

Burmese Days was published in New York by Harper & Brothers on 25 October 1934. There were two printings. The first, I-1, comprised 2,000 copies. The second, K-1, the number of copies of which is not known, was probably issued on 11 December 1934. The type was distributed on 16 February 1935; 976 copies were remaindered; see *246, n. 4*. An edition modified in fear of actions for libel and defamation was published by Gollancz on 24 June 1935; 2,500 copies were printed. A second impression, date unknown, of 500 copies followed. There were no remaindered copies. Type was distributed on 5 May 1936. The original text (with some variants) was first published in England by Penguin Books in May 1944; 60,000 copies were printed. Details of differences between these and other editions are given in *CW*, II, Textual Note. For reactions of reviewers, see Stansky and Abrahams, II, 56–s57 (for U.S.), 115–17 (for British).

214. Review of *Medieval Religion* by Christopher Dawson

The Adelphi, November 1934

It is increasingly difficult for anyone who is not a historical student to know what to think about the Middle Ages. Boileau's *"ces siecles grossiers,"* and the Victorian legends about mail-clad scoutmasters with "knightly growths" on their upper lips, are both equally discredited, and we have nothing very definite to put in their places. But of course the only question that really matters is, had the Middle Ages a spiritual unity and a common European civilisation that we have now lost? Mr. Dawson answers Yes, but very tentatively. He seems to think that the Middle Ages only achieved their synthesis for a brief period during the thirteenth century, and that the seeds of dissolution were present even then.

Much of his book is concerned with cultural development, and, so far as I am able to judge, displays very great erudition. His remarks on the Arab influence, which reached northern Europe via Provence and brought with it the cult of romantic love, are particularly interesting. The essay on Piers Plowman is a good piece of work in itself, but it blinks the fact, which centuries of neglect have proved, that Langland is practically unreadable.

This book is almost entirely lacking in the humbug which we have come to expect as a matter of course from English Roman Catholics. In fact, it might almost have been written by a Frenchman. What a relief to find that even in England there are still Catholic writers who can give us something better than the braying of Belloc[1] and the tittering of Knox.[2]

Eric Blair

1. Hilaire Belloc (1870–1953) was an essayist, novelist, author of many histories, and much verse, mainly comic. He also wrote on military matters as a weekly commentator during both World Wars. He was a Liberal M.P., 1906–10, and an active propagandist for Roman Catholicism.
2. Monsignor Ronald Arbuthnott Knox (1888–1957), Roman Catholic priest, was an essayist, writer of many religious books, and translator of the Bible (the Vulgate text; completed 1955). A convert to Roman Catholicism, he was, for many people, unofficially, a spokesman for the Roman Catholic church. See also *843, n. 1.*

215. To Leonard Moore

14 November 1934   Handwritten

3 Warwick Mansions   Pond St   Hampstead   NW.3

Dear Mr Moore,

Many thanks for your letter—I hope you can read my handwriting—I have left my typewriter down in the shop.

I knew there would be trouble over that novel.[1] However, I am anxious to get it published, as there are parts of it I was pleased with, & I dare say that if I had indicated to me the sort of changes that Mr Gollancz wants, I could manage it. I am willing to admit that the part about the school, which is what seems to have roused people's incredulity, is overdrawn, but not nearly so much so as people think. In fact I was rather amused to see that they say "all that was done away with 30 or 40 years ago" etc, as one always hears that any particularly crying abuse was "done away with 30 or 40 years ago." As to this part, it is possible that if Mr Gollancz agrees, a little "toning down" might meet the bill. I dont° want to bother you with details about this, however.

As to the points about libel, swearwords etc., they are a very small matter & could be put right by a few strokes of the pen. The book does, however, contain an inherent fault of structure which I will discuss with Mr Gollancz, & this could not be rectified in any way that I can think of. I was aware of it when I wrote the book, & imagined that it did not matter, because I did not intend it to be so realistic as people seem to think it is.

I wonder if you could be kind enough to arrange an interview for me with Mr Gollancz?[2] I should think it would take quite an hour to talk over the various points, if he can spare me that much time. I don't particularly mind what day or time I see him, so long as I know a day beforehand so as to let them know at the shop.

I have seen one review of "Burmese Days" in the Herald Tribune. Rather a bad one, I am sorry to say—however, big headlines, which I suppose is what counts.

Yours sincerely
Eric A Blair

P.S. [at top of letter] If you should have occasion to ring up about the interview, my number is Hampstead 2153.[3]

1. Moore received Orwell's letter of 3 October on the 5th; he must have sent *A Clergyman's Daughter* to Victor Gollancz immediately, and Gollancz must have read it quickly for on 9 November he wrote to Moore about his reservations. On 13 November Moore wrote to Gollancz to tell him that 'in view of what you say I think you may like to know that when sending the manuscript to me the author pointed out that "in case the point should come up, the school described in chapter IV is totally imaginary, though of course I have drawn on my general knowledge of what goes on in schools of that type." ' Moore must have sent Orwell details of this and other objections to the novel; this letter is Orwell's response. For problems posed by the text of *A Clergyman's Daughter*, see *CW*, III, Textual Note. See also Crick, 256–58.
2. Annotated in Moore's office: '3.30 Geo Orwell,' presumably for 19 November 1934; see *216*.
3. The telephone number of Booklovers' Corner.

216. To Leonard Moore

20 November 1934   Handwritten

Booklovers' Corner   1, South End Road, Hampstead, N.W.3.[1]

Dear Mr Moore,

Thanks for your letter. I had a talk with Gollancz yesterday, & we decided that it lay between cutting out or "toning down" the part objected to.[2] The former would be easier, but it would I think make the ending of the book too abrupt, so I am going to rewrite that chapter, which will take about a month. I told Gollancz I would send it to him direct.

I am glad M. Raimbault likes "Burmese Days." No, I shouldn't think it would be much use trying it elsewhere. I did, however, hear that Wishart (a publisher I had never heard of)[3] will publish books that other people are afraid of. No pressing°-cuttings yet from New York, I suppose?[4]

Yours sincerely
Eric A Blair

1. This line and '19' of a line for the date are part of a printed letterhead, which also has the telephone number (Hampstead 2153), 'Francis G. Westrope, Bookseller, &c.' and a framed line drawing captioned 'South End Green in 1833, now the Tram Terminus.' This is not again noted.
2. In *A Clergyman's Daughter*.
3. Lawrence & Wishart is still active. Ernest Edward Wishart (1902–1987) founded the publishing house of Wishart & Co shortly after completing a degree in history and law at Cambridge. He published Nancy Cunard's *Negro* and books by Geoffrey Gorer, Roy Campbell, E. M. Forster, Aldous Huxley and Bertrand Russell; from 1925 to 1927 Wishart published *The Calendar of Modern Letters*, edited by Edgell Rickword. Wishart refused to join the Communist Party, but his sympathies were Marxist. In 1935 he merged with Martin Lawrence. They published much left-wing literature, including the complete works of Marx, Lenin, and Stalin. Wishart took less interest in publishing after the outbreak of the World War II; he managed a number of farms in Sussex.
4. Annotated in Moore's office: 'Some have crossed this letter.'

217. Review of *The Ideals of East and West* by Kenneth Saunders

The Adelphi, December 1934

This book consists of a series of lectures on the leading religious systems of the world, delivered to the Pacific School of Religion in Berkeley, California, and it is mainly wind. The most interesting parts of it are various analects from Chinese, Indian, Japanese, and other writings, including a number of popular proverbs. But even here there is a good deal that was not worth reproducing ("A youth, when at home, should be filial, and abroad, respectful to his elders"—Confucius), and I can think of at least three Oriental proverbs that have more meat in them than the great majority of those quoted. The book ends with an imaginary conversation between the representatives of five religions, who vie with one another in sentiments of dreary uplift.

Mr. Saunders's manner of writing is at times so like a parody of the familiar American Wisdom of the East stuff as to arouse the suspicion that he is doing it on purpose. Presumably he is not, but when one encounters, in the poem with which the book opens, a couplet like this:—

> "That Love that transmutes pagan attitudes
> "To something nearer the Beatitudes,"

the suspicion is very hard to escape. This is the kind of book that brings both Asia and America into undeserved discredit.

E. B.[1]

1. Hereafter all Orwell's contributions to *The Adelphi* are signed 'George Orwell' and are not so indicated.

218. To Leonard Moore

10 December 1934   Handwritten

3 Warwick Mansions   Pond St   NW.3

Dear Mr Moore,

I rang you up at about a quarter to one, but you were not in. I heard from M. Raimbault this morning, & he says:

"One of my Italian friends, who is at present director at Paris of a Franco-Italian literary agency which he himself founded, asks me whether I can put him in touch with an English correspondent or representative who is well known among the publishers. It would be a question of disposing—in the same way that Messrs. Christy & Moore do for English works in France—of the translation rights of Italian books, or of the translations themselves. No doubt you have literary relationships in London which would make it easy for you to do this." etc. etc.

Do you think we could do a deal with him in any way? I know of course that there is never much doing in the way of translations in England, but on the other hand I suppose *some* Italian works get translated into English, & I suppose that if this Italian really has a fairly large agency it could be so arranged that every more or less translateable° work reached the English publishers viâ you. That is if you cared to take this business up. Of course *I* can't do much about it, because I haven't the "literary relationships" referred to. Perhaps you could let me know whether you care to here° more of this, & I could write to M. Raimbault.

I received 4 more copies of "Burmese Days" the other day. I wonder if you would let me know what there is to pay for these? That is, when you get the invoice from Harper's? I had better pay for them as I have them, otherwise I shall be owing you such a lot. I cannot now remember how many I asked you to order for me, but it is in my mind that I asked for 2 others besides these 5 (from which these 4 you sent me came.) If I *didn't* order 2 others, would you please order them for me, as there are still 2 people to whom I promised to sell copies & whom I haven't been able to sell them to.

I don't wish to worry you any further, but I wonder whether those press-cutting people are doing their job properly. I notice that the cuttings they send me arrive a month or more after their appearance, & it seems to me that if they keep up to date with the papers it oughtn't to take so long as that. Also they have only sent me 3 actual reviews—all the others were advance ads. inserted by Harpers before the book appeared. Of course I don't know that there have been many more reviews than those 3, but there certainly have been others, as friends of mine who see the American papers have mentioned seeing reviews in the New Yorker etc.

Yours sincerely
Eric A Blair

219. To Victor Gollancz [Ltd?]

17 December 1934   Typewritten

3 Warwick Mansions   Pond Street   Hampstead   NW.3

Dear Sir,

I am sending herewith the MS. of "A Clergyman's Daughter," which I have altered in accordance with your suggestions.[1] I enclose a note of the alterations I have made, together with the reader's[2] and Mr Rubinstein's[3] reports, which you sent on to me. Perhaps you could let me know through my agents (Messrs. Christy and Moore) whether you can now see your way to publishing the book.

Yours faithfully
Eric A. Blair[4]

[Page references are to the original, lost, typescript.]

NOTES ON ALTERATIONS IN "A CLERGYMAN'S DAUGHTER."

P. 45. Have altered the statement that Mr Warburton "tried to rape" Dorothy, as Mr Rubinstein objected to it.

P. 46. and also P. 82. A few lines inserted to make more plausible Dorothy's friendship with Mr Warburton.

P. 50. Reference to Roman Catholic priest cut out.

P. 54–5. Passage objected to on score of unpleasantness cut out.

P. 74. Mistake about book by Bertrand Russell cut out.

P. 137. Have written query in margin, as it struck me that it might be libellous to draw attention to the resemblance between Lord Snowdon and the man in the Don't wear a Truss advertisement.

P. 205. Reference to Sunday Express cut out.

P. 214. A few words giving a too exact idea of the locality of the school have been cut out.

P. 216–220. The interview between Dorothy and Mrs Creevy has been toned down, with a view to making Mrs Creevy out a somewhat less barefaced swindler.

P. 224–229. The description of Dorothy's first lesson at the school has been toned down, with a view to giving a less exaggerated impression of the low standard prevailing in these schools.

P. 230–231. Description of textbooks in use at the school has not been altered, as it is substantially true.

P. 247–256. I have not altered except in minor details the account of Dorothy's difficulties with the children's parents, and the row over "Macbeth," as, making allowance for a slight touch of burlesque, this is the kind of thing that does happen in these schools.

P. 257–261. I have greatly toned down this conversation, in consonance with the alterations on pp. 216–220 and pp. 224–229.

P. 262–265. General remarks on private schools toned down slightly and put in a perhaps more plausible manner. The reader, by the way, objected to my statement that there are about 10,000 private schools in England. I had this figure from one of the weekly papers dealing with education, and it should be verifiable. The statement that these schools, unless "recognized" (and it is not at all easy to get a school "recognized") are not liable to inspection on educational grounds, is absolutely correct.

P. 267. Remarks about lessons toned down, to agree with above.

P. 292, and also P. 265 and 262. I have cut out the suggestion, which Mr Rubinstein objected to, that if Dorothy lost her job she would be on the streets again.

In general, throughout this school part I have toned down, but not cut out altogether, the suggestion that private schools of this type are apt to be more or less of a swindle, existing only to make money and not giving much more than a pretence of education. What I have done in effect is to make the standard at the school somewhat higher than I made it before. I have not altered the character of Mrs Creevy, the proprietress, except in so far as was necessary to fit in with the other changes.

In the final chapter I have made minor alterations, but have not changed the general trend of it. I had myself thought it a very weak ending, but the particular point raised by Mr Rubinstein, that a friendship between a girl like Dorothy and a man like Mr Warburton was incredible, and that it would be unlikely that he would take any interest in her, had not struck me. I hope that the line or two I have put in on P. 46, remarking on the fact that pious and immoral people appear to have a mysterious attraction for one another, will make this relationship more plausible.

—— ooOoo ——

1. Orwell's letter was probably intended for Gollancz rather than for Norman Collins, Deputy Chairman of Victor Gollancz Ltd, who later interviewed Orwell.
2. Gerald Gould (1885–1936) was the reader; his identity would almost certainly not be known to Orwell. He recommended publication, for though the novel presented 'snags and difficulties,' it was 'an extraordinary book' and 'very original.' See Crick, 256. Gould at this time was an influential reviewer for *The Observer*, and a poet, essayist, and former editor of the *Daily Herald*. In Orwell's 1936 essay 'In Defence of the Novel' (see *333*), Gould is typified as

one 'driven ever upwards on a topless ladder of adjectives' when he praises the novels he reviews; and writing to Jack Common in 1938 (see *433*), Orwell pictures himself 'as a sort of Gerald Gould selling my intellectual virtue at constantly-decreasing prices.'
3. Harold Rubinstein (1891–1975) was a distinguished lawyer whose advice was sought by many publishers. He was a perspicacious literary critic, a playwright and author.
4. When Orwell signed his name 'Eric A. Blair,' he frequently put a full point before and after the 'A,' both raised above the line. This practice has not been reproduced.

220. To Leonard Moore

24 December 1934   Handwritten

Booklovers' Corner   1, South End Road, Hampstead, N.W. 3.

Dear Mr Moore,
M. Raimbault writes: "Amato (his Italian friend who runs the international translation business) has asked me whether you will give him the Italian translation rights of "Down & Out" & "Burmese Days." Can you hand these rights over to me—that is, if they have not been disposed of elsewhere? I will do my very best to get your books translated into Italian & to find an opening for them in Italy. I do not know, however, whether your views, which are not exactly Fascist, would be approved of in the country of M. Mussolini," etc.

I take him to mean that Amato wants the translation rights in case any Italian publisher could be got to authorise a translation. I suppose this is all right? No doubt if we put the matter in his hands he would make efforts to get the books translated, tho' I don't suppose that at best this would bring in much money. If you say yes I will write to M. Raimbault & tell him to go ahead & that he or Amato is to communicate with you to fix up about the agreement.

I ought to have written to you some days back to tell you that I sent back the revised MS. of "A Clergyman's Daughter" to Gollancz. I had made a good number of alterations, & sent an explanation of those I had made, but I did not alter it so completely as he seemed to wish. However, perhaps it will be enough to satisfy him. If he won't now publish the novel I think I shall take out the one chapter that pleased me & try to get some magazine to publish it separately.

I am sorry I did not write in time to send Christmas greetings, but, as you may imagine, we have been worked off our feet in the shop.

Please remember me very kindly to Mrs Moore.

Yours sincerely
Eric A. Blair

221. To Leonard Moore

28 December 1934   Handwritten

Booklovers' Corner   1, South End Road, Hampstead, N.W. 3

Dear Mr Moore,

I think the enclosed cheque should about cover what I owe you (somewhere in the neighbourhood of $13) for copies of "Burmese Days." And could you please order me one more copy?[1] I am sorry to keep troubling you, but people are always clamouring for copies. I hope Harper's won't get on to the fact that I have sold 3 or 4 of those I had.

I find that Harper's are not selling "Burmese Days" in Paris. I don't know whether that is because Paris is too near England, but if not, I think they could be certain of selling a few dozen copies there, as there are 3 Anglo-American bookshops, largely patronised by Americans.[2]

Many thanks to you & Mrs Moore for your Christmas card.

Yours sincerely
Eric A. Blair

1. Annotated in margin in Moore's office: 'phoned 31 xii 34.'
2. Annotated in margin in Moore's office: 'phoned Harpers.'

1935

222. To Leonard Moore

9 January 1935   Typewritten

3 Warwick Mansions   Pond Street   Hampstead   NW.3

Dear Mr Moore,
The two enclosed stories were sent me by an aunt of mine.[1] I don't suppose
you can do anything with them, but am sending them just in case you might
be able to, as I said I would do what I could to get them published. If you
don't think they are worth anything, please don't waste any time over them.

I enclose also the account from Harper's which you sent on to me.[2] It seems
to be for more than I sent you. Perhaps you could let me know later what I
still owe you.

I forget whether I told you that I had had and sent back the proofs of the
French version of "Down and Out," and that Raimbault has made a very
good job of it.[3] Would you like a copy of it when it comes out?

Yours sincerely
Eric A. Blair

1. Presumably from Aunt Nellie Limouzin, in Paris.
2. For copies of *Burmese Days* at trade price.
3. It is important to note Orwell's approval of the French translation of *Down and Out in Paris and
   London* in view of his later comments on other translations; for example, that of *Burmese Days*
   into French, which he described as 'VERY BAD' in his notes for his literary executor; see *3728*.

223. To Victor Gollancz [Ltd?]

10 January 1935   Typewritten

3 Warwick Mansions   Pond Street   Hampstead   NW.3

Dear Sir,
I am returning the MS. of "A Clergyman's Daughter" herewith. I think there
is now nothing in it that could possibly be made the subject of an action for
libel. None of the characters are intended as portraits of living individuals,
nor are any of the names those of actual persons known to me. As to the
localities described, they are all imaginary. "Knype Hill" is an imaginary
name and so far as I know no place of that name exists; in the story it is
mentioned as being in Suffolk, but that is all. In the hop-picking part (chapter
2) there is nothing whatever to indicate an exact locality. In Chapter 4
Southbridge is described as a suburb ten or a dozen miles of° London, but

367

there is now nothing to show which side of London it was. As to the reference to a shop called "Knockout Trousers Ltd." in Chapter 2, so far as I know there is no shop of any such name, and the house mentioned in the same part as being a refuge of prostitutes is again totally imaginary. It is stated to have been somewhere off Lambeth Cut. Lambeth Cut is a longish street, but if this is still considered dangerous, I can easily change Lambeth Cut to a fictitious street in the proof. I enclose a note on[1] the alterations, together with Mr Rubinstein's letter, herewith.

Yours faithfully
Eric A. Blair

Note on alterations in "A Clergyman's Daughter."

P. 50. "Barclay's Bank" altered to "the local bank."
P. 73. The remarks "Swine of atheists like Bertrand Russell and Julian Huxley" and "their beastly atheist propaganda" have been allowed to stand, as these are not made in propria persona, but through the mouth of one of the characters. Also, this character is treated ironically and his remarks about Bertrand Russell etc. are in reality favourable to the latter.
P. 74. "He was in the thick of every controversy, especially when the Church Times was at its chosen sport of baiting Modernists and atheists" has been altered to "He was in the thick of every controversy and in the forefront of every assault upon Modernists and atheists."
P. 74. "The fiendish Russell" has been allowed to stand, because though said in propria persona it is obviously said ironically, ie. Russell is only described as "fiendish" because he would appear 'fiendish' to the character (Victor Stone) in question.
P. 75.[2] Mr Rubinstein crossed out the remark that a paper called "The High Churchman's Gazette" had "a remarkable° small circulation." I was not aware that any paper of this name actually existed. However, I have altered "a remarkably small circulation" to "a small and select circulation."
P. 161. "Lambeth public library" altered to "the nearest public library."
P. 166. The same alteration again.
P. 297. "The manager of Barclay's Bank" altered to "the bank manager."

1. on] of
2. '74' crossed out in ink and '75' written in.

224. To Brenda Salkeld

Tuesday, [15 January 1935][1]   Typewritten

3 Warwick Mansions   Pond Street   Hampstead   NW.3

Dear Brenda,

Thanks for your letter. No, I cannot say that Havelock Ellis's signature, as I remember it, struck me as being at all like what I expected.[2] I should have expected him to write a very fine hand and use a thinner nib. We bought recently a lot of books with the authors' signatures in, and some of them containing autograph letters as well, but they were all sold almost at once. One that pleased me was inscribed "From Beverley Nicholls, in all humility." There is a subtle humour in that. I often see autographed letters etc. advertised among the lots at book-auctions. I remember distinctly that in one case a letter from Sheila Kaye-Smith was priced higher than one from Sarah, Duchess of Marlborough (the Queen Anne one.) You often see autographs of Napoleon advertised, but they are usually pretty expensive, and of course they are not letters, only documents signed by him. Towards the end of his life he never seems to have written anything except his signature with his own hand, and apparently his spelling was appalling. I haven't done much to my new novel,[3] but I have written a poem that is to be part of it.[4] Talking of choosing a new pseudonym, I think it would be rather amusing, as so many women writers have chosen male pseudonyms, to choose a female one. Miss Barbara Bedworthy or something like that. With portrait of the author on the jacket. I have been feeling horribly tired, as for a variety of reasons I have been keeping very bad hours lately. On Sunday night I came away from a friend's house late, found there were no sort of conveyances running, had to walk several miles through drizzling rain, and then, to crown all, found myself locked out and had to raise hell before I could wake anybody up and get in. Have you ever seen Fowler's "Modern English Usage?"[5] Fowler is the man who did, or at any rate contributed to, the small Oxford dictionary, and he is a great authority on syntax etc. He is very amusing about such things as the split infinitive. I was also reading a rather amusing pamphlet on Dr Watson, which proved among other things, from internal evidence, that Watson was married twice. Also one or two of D. H. Lawrence's short stories, also Max Beerbohm's "And Even Now," also, for the I don't know how many-th time, Maupassant's "Boule de Suif"[6] and "La Maison Tellier." I suppose you have read both of those? I must stop now. I hope this letter will be duly waiting for you when you arrive and that you will not be in too unbearably depressed a state. Try and come up to town some time during the term and we will meet. Good bye for the present.

Yours
Eric A. Blair

1. Dated approximately from Orwell's hope at its conclusion that his letter will be awaiting Salkeld's arrival at Southwold and that she will not be unbearably depressed—presumably at the start of a new term. A week earlier or later is possible.
2. Salkeld was then collecting autographs, and Orwell was finding some for her.
3. *Keep the Aspidistra Flying*.
4. 'St Andrew's Day, 1935,' printed in *The Adelphi* in November 1935; see *261*. In *Keep the Aspidistra Flying*, it has two word changes and lacks a title. The title was presumably thought appropriate for a November issue of the magazine; St Andrew's feast day is 30 November.
5. *A Dictionary of Modern English Usage*, by H. W. Fowler, was first published in April 1926 and is still not superseded.
6. In September 1946 Orwell proposed to the BBC that he dramatise this story; see *3059*, *3074* and *3095*.

225. To Leonard Moore

22 January 1935   Typewritten

3 Warwick Mansions   Pond Street   Hampstead   NW.3

Dear Mr Moore,

Many thanks for your letter. Naturally I am very pleased to hear that you have made such good terms with Gollancz for "A Clergyman's Daughter." I am afraid he is going to lose money this time, all right. However, we must hope for the best.

I wonder if you can persuade him, if he puts "Books by the same author," or words to that effect, on the front page, to mention "Burmese Days." He probably won't want to, as it was published in anomalous circumstances and not by him, but I want that book, if possible, not to be altogether lost sight of.

Yours sincerely
Eric A. Blair

226. To Leonard Moore

31 January 1935[1]   Handwritten

3 Warwick Mansions   Pond St   Hampstead   NW3

Dear Mr Moore,

Herewith the extra proof copy of "A Clergyman's Daughter." In returning the other I told them I had put "and *Burmese Days*" on the title page & asked them if they would also mention it on the jacket if the latter has not been printed already. If you are seeing them any time I wonder if you could impress upon them that I want this done, provided Mr Gollancz does not object.

Yours sincerely
Eric A Blair

1. Dated 31.5.35 but stamped in Moore's office 31 January 1935. It was then possible for a letter to be posted and delivered on the same day. Orwell may have incorrectly dated it. His 5 is probably no more than anticipation of the last figure of the year.

227. To Victor Gollancz [Ltd?]

1 February 1935   Handwritten

3 Warwick Mansions   Pond St   Hampstead   NW

Dear Sir,

With reference to the attached letter:

i.[1] Yes, "Knype Hill" is imaginary. Of course all these small County towns where "retired" people live are more or less alike, but I have not consciously carricatured any particular town here.

ii. Yes, the church window is quite imaginary.

iii. Ditto the Blifil–Gordon sugar beet refinery, & Ye Old Tea Shoppe. With regard to the latter, however, I had in mind the sort of shop that is to be found in all these places.

iv. Miss Mayfill & Mrs Semprill are quite imaginary.

v. "A politician described as a Roman Catholic Jew." Yes, I do know one M.P. who answers to this description. So I will make the necessary alterations here.

vi. Persons referred to on pp. 64 & 83, also "Victor Stone," all quite imaginary.

vii. "Dorothy" is entirely fictitious &, as I said before, I had no particular farm in mind. I have, however, said what is demonstrably true about the hop-picking industry.

viii. "Mrs Sawyer" is totally imaginary.

ix. In the remark I made an ex-convict make about Dartmoor, I was repeating something I had actually heard said. I do not know whether such punishments as chaining up & a diet of bread & water are actually in use at Dartmoor, but I have certainly heard talk of them. In any case this was not said in propria persona but through the mouth of a character. At the time of the Dartmoor rebellion pamphlets were issued, & even articles in the paper published, making more serious allegations than this. I don't think there is any harm here, but it could be cut out if it is really dangerous.

x. "Carshalton Grange" is a totally imaginary name. I chose it because I wanted a high-sounding name. The suburb I had vaguely in mind when I wrote of "Southbridge" was Hayes, Middlesex. So far as I know there is no school of any such name there.

xi. As to the schoolbooks, I have seen schoolbooks similar to the ones I have described, though, of course, as was necessary in the circumstances, I have parodied them.

xii. There is one other point not referred to by Mr Rubinstein, but which has occurred to me since reading his letter. This is that round about page 185 I have made one character say something to this effect: "I would have gone to St Martin's in the Fields Church [Trafalgar Square][2] only they won't let you in if you are lousy." So far as I know they *do* refuse to let lousy people into St Martin's Crypt, but I have not personally witnessed this—I am going by what the destitute people say. If this is possibly libellous I will alter "St Martin's" to an imaginary name.

Please excuse bad handwriting—[3]

Yours faithfully
Eric A. Blair

1. Until the end of his life, Orwell regularly underlined small roman numerals twice and dotted 'v' (often twice) and 'x' (once), whether alone or in combination. See, for example, *Facsimile of Nineteen Eighty-Four*, 373, for double-dotted 'v' and 381, where each letter of 'vi' is dotted once. The dotting of 'v' and 'x' and the double underlining are not reproduced in this edition.
2. The square brackets are Orwell's.
3. Orwell not infrequently drew attention to what he regarded as the poor quality of his handwriting. It was, almost invariably (as here) businesslike and legible, even when, at the end of his life, he was very ill and writing in bed. See, however, *259, n. 1*.

228. To Victor Gollancz

1 February 1935   Handwritten

[No address]

Dear Mr Gollancz,[1]
I should add to my remarks in the other letter herewith that the biographical
details of the Rector (Dorothy's father) are totally imaginary, & so too are all
the people mentioned on p. 51.

Yours truly
Eric A. Blair

1. For the first time, Orwell addresses Gollancz personally. He may also have intended earlier
letters for Victor Gollancz where 'Ltd' has been shown within square brackets.

229. To Victor Gollancz

2 February 1935   Handwritten postcard

Pond Street   Hampstead   NW3

Dear Mr Gollancz,
With reference to your letter of yesterday, I am afraid the ms. of "Burmese
Days" was destroyed some time back, & I don't possess a copy of the book.
However, I think Mr Moore, my agent, has one, & I will get him to send you
that, or failing that I will send you the one that is in our lending library[1] as
soon as I can get it back from the person who has it now.

Yours sincerely
Eric A. Blair

1. Since *Burmese Days* was not for sale in Britain, presumably Orwell had donated one to the
local library.

230. To Leonard Moore

2 February 1935   Handwritten postcard

3 Warwick Mansions   Pond Street   Hampstead   NW

Dear Mr Moore,
Mr Gollancz writes to say that he would like to see "Burmese Days" yet
again, as he thinks that if time were taken the libellous points might be cleared
up. I don't know whether you have a copy & whether it is available, but if you
have a copy available, would you send it to him? And could you let me know
whether you have sent it or not, as if you haven't a copy to send I will get hold
of the one that is in our lending library & send that.

I think all is well with "A Clergyman's Daughter" now, but yesterday they made me make a few *more* alterations in the already corrected proof.

Yours sincerely
Eric A. Blair

231. To Victor Gollancz [Ltd?]

4 February 1935   Handwritten postcard

3 Warwick Mansions   Pond St   NW.3

[No addressee]

Ref. your letter of the 2nd, in place of CARSHALTON GRANGE, please put RUSHINGTON GRANGE.[1] I don't think this is the name of a real place. "Carshalton" occurs in two consecutive pages, & possibly once again, so it would be as well to make sure that the compositor alters it each time.[2]

E. A. Blair

1. Annotated in Gollancz office: '[? Known   Not Known G.P.O or in *Who's Who*]' and initialled. The first word is unclear; it could be 'House.'
2. At the top left of the postcard 'Ringwood & Peg's Paper' has been written in the corner. Ringwood House was the school owned by Mrs. Creevey in *A Clergyman's Daughter*. For *Peg's Paper*, see 232.

232. To Victor Gollancz [Ltd?]

Wednesday, [6 February 1935]   Handwritten postcard; dated from postmark

[No address]

[No addressee]

Yes, delete "Peg's paper and" as suggested.

E. A. Blair

233. To Victor Gollancz

14 February 1935   Typewritten

77 Parliament Hill   Hampstead   NW.3

Dear Mr Gollancz,

Many thanks for your letter. Naturally I shall be very pleased to see your solicitor about "Burmese Days," and will do my best to give him all the information he requires. Perhaps you will be kind enough to give me about two days° notice when I am to see him, so that I can make sure of getting away from the shop where I work.

I wonder if you would inform your office that my address will be the above till further notice.[1]

Yours sincerely
Eric A. Blair

1. Last paragraph annotated, 'Notify all departments.' Orwell had moved to 77 Parliament Hill (which runs at right angles to South End Road, where Booklovers' Corner is No.1) in Mrs. Rosalind Obermeyer's flat, until the end of July or early August 1935; see *250*. Mrs. Obermeyer, in March 1935, introduced him to Eileen O'Shaugnessy, his wife-to-be; see *253, n. 1*. She and Eileen were reading for master's degrees in psychology at University College London. The house is in Thompson, 46. Also see Crick, 262; Stansky and Abrahams, II, 88ff; Shelden, 223; U.S.: 202–3.

234. To Leonard Moore

14 February 1935   Typewritten

77 Parliament Hill   Hampstead   NW.3

Dear Mr Moore,
Here with° Gollancz's letter re. "Burmese Days." I wonder if you could tell your office that my address will be the above till further notice? It may be that I shall have to change my lodgings again later, in which case I will let you know, but in any case I shall be here about a month.

Yours sincerely
Eric A. Blair

235. To Brenda Salkeld

16 February 1935   Handwritten

Booklovers' Corner   1, South End Road, Hampstead, N.W.3.

Dearest Brenda,
Isn't it sickening, I can't keep the room I am in at present for more than a few weeks.[1] It was let to me on the understanding that I should have to give it up if somebody offered to take it & another room that are beside it together,[2] & now somebody has done so. So I shall have fresh miseries of house-hunting, & probably shan't find another place where I shall be so comfortable & have so much freedom. My present landlady[3] is the non-interfering sort, which is so rare among London landladies. When I came she asked me what I particularly wanted, & I said, "The thing I most want is freedom." So she said, "Do you want to have women up here all night?" I said, "No," of course, whereat she said, "I only meant that I didn't mind whether you do or not." Not much is happening here.

Gollancz, who has re-read "Burmese Days," wrote enthusiastically about it & said he was going to have it thoroughly vetted by his lawyer, after which the latter was to cross-examine me on all the doubtful points. I hope the lawyer doesn't report against it as he did last time. You notice that all this happened a year ago, & I do not know what has made G. change his mind again. Perhaps some other publisher has wiped his eye by publishing a novel about India, but I don't seem to remember any this year. Rees[4] got me a lot more signatures for you, which I will send when I can find them, but at present I have mislaid them. I am living a busy life at present. My time-table is as follows: 7 am get up, dress etc, cook & eat breakfast. 8.45 go down & open the shop, & I am usually kept there till about 9.45. Then come home, do out my room, light the fire etc. 10.30 am—1 pm I do some writing. 1 pm get lunch & eat it. 2 pm—6.30 pm I am at the shop. Then I come home, get my supper, do the washing up & after that sometimes do about an hour's work. In spite [of] all this, I have got more work done in the last few days than during weeks before when I was being harried all day long. I hope G. *does* publish "Burmese Days," as apart from the money (& my agent has tied him down with a pretty good contract) it will tide over the very long interval there is going to be between "A Clergyman's Daughter" & the one[5] I am writing now. I want this one to be a work of art, & that can't be done without much bloody sweat. My mother writes me that she isn't going away after all, so I will come down to S'wold for a week-end as soon as I can, but it will have to be when my employer's wife is up & about again. Write soon.

With much love
Eric

1. By 'more than a few weeks' Orwell was not referring to a few weeks more, but to the total time he had been able to spend in the Westropes' flat.
2. The phrasing is Orwell's.
3. Mrs. Myfanwy Westrope.
4. Richard Rees; see *95*.
5. *Keep the Aspidistra Flying*.

236. To Victor Gollancz

19 February 1935   Telegram

Gollancz telegraphed Orwell on 19 February 1935: 'Can you come here discuss Burmese° two thirty Friday twenty second.' Orwell replied from Belsize Park (Post Office) that same day:

YES CERTAINLY = BLAIR +

What transpired at that meeting is, in part, told in Orwell's letter to Leonard Moore of 22 February 1935; see *238*. It is possible to reconstruct something else that occurred and to suggest that something said to have occurred did not take place.

An American reader of *Burmese Days*, John R. Hall, of the Democrat-News Printing Company, Marshall, Missouri, wrote to Orwell on 5 February 1935 to tell him how much he had enjoyed the novel; he enclosed a review he had written. On the back of that letter is a sketch map with, in Orwell's hand, notes of topographical and name changes required by Harold Rubinstein, the lawyer, keyed to the pagination of the U.S. edition of *Burmese Days*.

It is probable that Orwell took this flattering letter to the meeting to encourage Gollancz to publish *Burmese Days*. He drew on the back of it the sketch map of Kyauktada, the scene of the events in *Burmese Days*, probably to assist him in delocalising it from Katha, a real town. That sketch map, with its notes, follows; see *237*. It is also the frontispiece in this edition of *Burmese Days*, *CW*, II. A full account of the sketch map and the process of identification is given in *CW*, II, Appendix, 302–08.

Stansky and Abrahams give a detailed account of this meeting (II, 58–60). However, this gives a different account from the brief one by Orwell in his letter to Moore. Orwell says he saw 'Gollancz and his solicitor,' but Stansky and Abrahams, drawing on what was 'recalled by Collins long afterwards,' state that it had been arranged that 'Blair should come to the Gollancz office to discuss the problem with Norman Collins (1907–82), Deputy Chairman of the firm.' Collins, from 1929 to 1931, had been assistant literary editor of the *News Chronicle* and 'had begun his own literary career as a writer with *The Facts of English Fiction*, and in 1934 had followed it with a novel, *Penang Appointment*.' He became a director of Gollancz in 1934; see Stansky and Abrahams, II, 58.

Collins recalled in detail the questions he had asked Orwell and Orwell's answers—mostly that the facts and characters of *Burmese Days* were all drawn from life. Their meeting 'had its elements of comedy.' Stansky and Abrahams conclude, 'Eventually, however—if not that afternoon—he accepted the seriousness of the problem as it was put to him.' They then say: 'In the light of Blair's sweeping claims to Collins, it comes as something of an anti-climax to discover that the changes were only three in number, a matter of new names for certain characters: most importantly, the evil Burmese magistrate U Po Kyin became U Po Sing, and Dr Veraswami became Dr Murkhaswami' (60). In a footnote, they explain that in later editions the names of the characters were restored 'and the American and English editions have since that time been identical.'

Closer examination shows that the changes are much more extensive; see Textual Note to the *CW* edition of *Burmese Days*. The role Collins describes himself as playing is more puzzling. There was hardly time for an earlier meeting. Orwell wrote on 14 February to say he would be pleased to see Gollancz's solicitor, and Gollancz telegraphed him on the 19th. The meeting was on the 22nd, and six days later Orwell sent in his alterations.

A clue may be found in the mode of address Orwell adopted for his letter of 28 February when sending the alterations; see *239*. From 1 February, he had begun to address his letters to Gollancz 'Dear Mr Gollancz.' The letter of the 28th begins 'Dear Sir.' It seems most likely that Gollancz and Rubinstein conducted the meeting with Orwell (probably mainly the latter, since Orwell mentions 'changes specifically asked for by Mr Rubinstein') with Norman Collins in attendance. It might have been arranged that Orwell send the alterations to Collins, who would then see the book through the press.

How much of the conversation Collins reported actually took place can only be guessed at; what seems certain from the tone of Orwell's letter to Moore of 22 February (see *238*)—'a few trifling alterations which will not take more than a week'—is that it is not correct to interpret his attitude as 'not yet ready to cooperate,' as in Stansky and Abrahams, II, 59.

The illustration is approximately 87% of the size of the original.

237. Orwell's Sketch Map of Kyauktada, *Burmese Days*

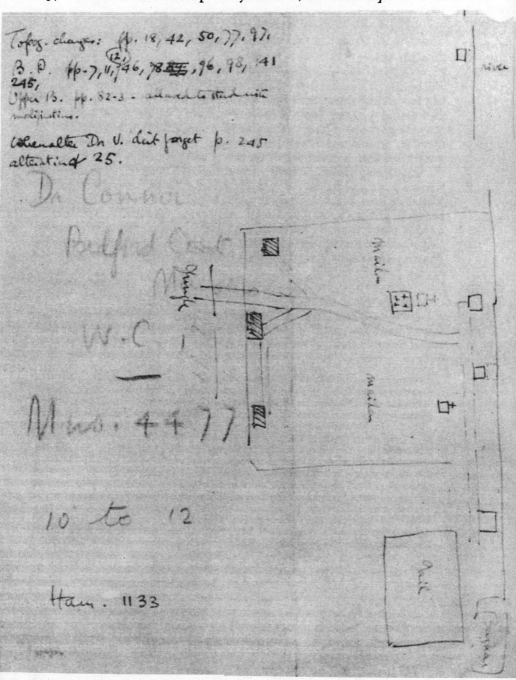

238. To Leonard Moore

22 February 1935   Typewritten; handwritten postscript

77 Parliament Hill   Hampstead   NW.3

Dear Mr Moore,

I saw Gollancz and his solicitor this afternoon and had a long talk, and you will be glad to hear that they are quite ready to publish BURMESE DAYS, subject to a few trifling alterations which will not take more than a week. Gollancz says that if A CLERGYMAN'S DAUGHTER succeeds, he thinks of publishing BURMESE DAYS about June,[1] otherwise he would publish it in September or October. So this will nicely tide over what will otherwise be a very long interval between A CLERGYMAN'S DAUGHTER and my next.

I was talking last night with a friend named Rayner Heppenstall[2] who writes a good deal for the Adelphi. He tells me that he does reviews for the Yorkshire Post, and that if they would send him A CLERGYMAN'S DAUGHTER, he would give it a boost. I wonder if one could arrange this? I gather that he reviews pretty regularly for them, but has not much choice of what books they send him. Perhaps one could send a copy to the Yorkshire Post with the remark "This might interest Mr Heppenstall," or words to that effect?

Yours sincerely
Eric A. Blair

P.S. [to right of page] I did ask G's office to let me have an advance copy of "A Clergyman's Daughter" if possible. Perhap[s] I could give this to Heppenstall if he could arrange° with his paper.

1. It was published on 24 June 1935.
2. Rayner Heppenstall (1911–1981), novelist, critic, and crime historian, shared a flat with Orwell later in 1935, though the arrangement was not wholly successful; see *250, n. 2*. Despite coming to blows, they remained lifelong friends and worked together on radio programmes. Heppenstall was a feature writer and producer for the BBC, 1945–65, and a drama producer, 1965–67. He produced Orwell's adaptation of *Animal Farm* for radio in 1947; an adaptation of it by Peter Duval Smith in 1952; his own revision of Orwell's version in 1957. He also commissioned and produced Orwell's 'The Voyage of the *Beagle*' in 1946. His *Four Absentees* (1960) has reminiscences of Orwell; the relevant portions are reprinted in *Orwell Remembered*, 106–15. A touch of his character can be gathered from his exasperation at the sentimental outpourings about Joan of Arc; as recalled by John Weightman, he 'once wrote an article entitled, if I remember rightly, "That Awful Girl", in which he presented Joan as a European disaster, because she invented French nationalism at a time when France and England, in spite of their differences, still had a chance of developing into a single community' ('Myth for all Seasons,' *The Observer*, 30 August 1981). For Orwell's description of Heppenstall, see *242*; see also Shelden, 225; U.S.: 204–05.

239. To Victor Gollancz [Ltd]
28 February 1935   Typewritten

77 Parliament Hill   Hampstead   NW.3

Dear Sir,[1]
I am sending back separately the American copy of BURMESE DAYS, in which I have made the alterations asked for. I trust all will now be well. A detailed statement of the changes I have made is herewith. As to the note on the changes in the names, which was to explain the fact that two oriental characters bore unreal names, I should be greatly obliged if this could be put *opposite the front page* where it will be sure of being seen. Otherwise, if anyone from India or Burma gets hold of the book and sees an incorrect name in the very first line, he will naturally be prejudiced against the book. Will it be necessary to break up this copy for the purpose of setting the type? If so, it does not matter, but if it is kept intact I should like it back, as I have only one copy of the American edition.

I have just received the six complimentary copies of A CLERGYMAN'S DAUGHTER, for which many thanks.

Yours faithfully
Eric A. Blair

[Page references are to the first, the U.S., edition.]

Alterations to BURMESE DAYS.

The following changes specifically asked for by Mr Rubinstein have been made:

p. 19. The date 1910 has been got rid of. Similarly on p. 365, the date 1926 has been altered to 19—.

p. 28. Name Pereira altered to Walters.

p. 33. Reference to importing rickshaw specially from Rangoon has been cut out.

p. 39. "Parody of a fifth-rate story in Blackwood's" altered to "fifth-rate parody of a story in Blackwood's." Further down: "whisky, Blackwood's and the Bonzo pictures" altered to "whisky, Lancashire cotton shirts and public-school humbug."

p. 96. The words (of scoutmasters) "homosexuals almost to a man" cut out.

p. 366. Reference to Mandalay General Hospital cut out.

p. 367. The name Macdougall cut out.

In addition, the following general changes have been made:
1. With reference to the possible identification of the imaginary town of Kyauktada with the real town of Katha. I have been unable to obtain a map of Katha, but I have searched my memory and made out a fairly clear picture of it. It was something like my description of Kyauktada, except that a. I had put the cemetery beside the church, which it was not in Katha, b. I had put in a pagoda which did not exist at Katha, and c. I had described the Club as

379

having a garden that ran down to the river, whereas that at Katha, as well as I can now remember, was not actually *on* the river, though near it. To make things more vague, I have now made the following changes: a. All direct and indirect statements about Kyauktada being in *Upper* Burma have been cut out or altered. It is admitted to be somewhere within striking distance of Mandalay, but it is not stated in which direction. The only remarks about *Upper* Burma that have been left in are on pp. 82–3. I let these stand as they referred to an earlier period of the hero's life and had nothing to do with Kyauktada. b. "The Irrawaddy" has throughout been changed to "the river." c. I have altered, eg. on p. 209, one or two remarks describing vegetation etc. which would only be found in the far north of Burma. Incidentally, I have found one or two places where I believe I have mixed up the flora and fauna of Upper and Lower Burma, and I have let these stand. d. I have cut out or altered a number of remarks such as "he turned to the right" etc. which would make the topography of Kyauktada too similar to that of Katha. These changes will be found on pp. 18, 42, 50, 77, 97. e. Katha was a railway terminus, and I had described Kayauktada as a terminus. I have now altered this to "junction."

2. As to names. The name U Po Kyin has been altered throughout to U Po Sing. This is not a possible Burmese name, but I fancy it will sound sufficiently like one to pass muster with the majority of readers. The name Dr Veraswami has been altered to Dr Murkhaswami. I consulted the oriental languages man at the British Museum, who gave me this name as a good Sanscrit name which *sounds* all right but which could not actually belong to any real individual.

The name Lackersteen has been altered throughout to Latimer. I dont,° of course, know for certain that there was *not* somebody named Latimer in Burma, but I never heard of one, whereas I did, as I said, once hear of somebody called Lackersteen.

As to the names of officials mentioned in the book—Macgregor, Westfield, Maxwell and Verrall. The events of the story are supposed to be taking place in 1926, though I have now cut out this date and it can only be inferred in a roundabout way if at all. The British Museum does not possess a Burma Civil List for 1926, but they had one for 1929, which was the nearest date. I have been through this and cannot find any of the names I have used.

The name of the native paper has been changed from the Burmese Patriot to the Burmese Sinn Feiner. I don't think this is a possible name, and at the same time it gives the right implication to an English reader.

I have been carefully through the book and tried to change the above names wherever they occurred, but I suppose I may have missed one or two. Perhaps the compositors could be instructed to make the necessary changes if there are any that I have missed.

A note such as Mr Gollancz asked for, on the changes in the names, is attached.

—— ooOoo ——

1. The letter may have been intended for Gollancz, but more probably for Norman Collins; see *236*. There is one page missing: the note on the changes in the names of U Po Kyin (altered to U Po Sing) and Dr Veraswami (which became Dr Murkhaswami). It was doubtless sent as copy for setting with the rest of the book. Such a note appears in the Gollancz edition. For this, and the effects of the changes listed, see Textual Note to *Burmese Days*, *CW*, II. See also letter of 15 November 1946 to Dr W. M. C. Harrowes, *3117*.

240. Review of *Caliban Shrieks* by Jack Hilton

The Adelphi, March 1935

This is the first review to be signed 'George Orwell.'

This witty and unusual book may be described as an autobiography without narrative. Mr. Hilton lets us know, briefly and in passing, that he is a cotton operative who has been in and out of work for years past, that he served in France during the latter part of the War, and that he has also been on the road, been in prison, etc., etc.; but he wastes little time in explanations and none in description. In effect his book is a series of comments on life as it appears when one's income is two pounds a week or less. Here, for instance, is Mr. Hilton's account of his own marriage:

"Despite the obvious recognition of marriage's disabilities, the bally thing took place. With it came, not the entrancing mysteries of the bedroom, nor the passionate soul-stirring emotion of two sugar-candied Darby and Joans, but the practical resolve that, come what may, be the furnisher's dues met or no, the rent paid or spent, we—the wife and I—would commemorate our marriage by having, every Sunday morn, ham and eggs for breakfast. So it was we got one over on the poet with his madness of love, the little dove birds, etc."

There are obvious disadvantages in this manner of writing—in particular, it assumes a width of experience which many readers would not possess. On the other hand, the book has a quality which the objective, descriptive kind of book almost invariably misses. It deals with its subject *from the inside*, and consequently it gives one, instead of a catalogue of facts relating to poverty, a vivid notion of what it *feels* like to be poor. All the time that one reads one seems to hear Mr. Hilton's voice, and what is more, one seems to hear the voices of the innumerable industrial workers whom he typifies. The humorous courage, the fearful realism and the utter imperviousness to middle-class ideals, which characterise the best type of industrial worker, are all implicit in Mr. Hilton's way of talking. This is one of those books that succeed in conveying a frame of mind, and that takes more doing than the mere telling of a story.

Books like this, which come from genuine workers and present a genuinely working-class outlook, are exceedingly rare and correspondingly important. They are the voices of a normally silent multitude. All over England, in every industrial town, there are men by scores of thousands whose attitude to life, if only they could express it, would be very much what

Mr. Hilton's is. If all of them could get their thoughts on to paper they would change the whole consciousness of our race. Some of them try to do so, of course; but in almost every case, inevitably, what a mess they make of it! I knew a tramp once who was writing his autobiography. He was quite young, but he had had a most interesting life which included, among other things, a jail-escape in America, and he could talk about it entrancingly. But as soon as he took a pen in his hand he became not only boring beyond measure but utterly unintelligible. His prose style was modelled upon *Peg's Paper* ("With a wild cry I sank in a stricken heap," etc.), and his ineptitude with words was so great that after wading through two pages of laboured description you could not even be certain what he was attempting to describe. Looking back upon that autobiography, and a number of similar documents that I have seen, I realise what a considerable literary gift must have gone to the making of Mr. Hilton's book.

As to the sociological information that Mr. Hilton provides, I have only one fault to find. He has evidently not been in the Casual Ward since the years just after the War, and he seems to have been taken in by the lie, widely published during the last few years, to the effect that casual paupers are now given a "warm meal" at mid-day. I could a tale unfold about those "warm meals." Otherwise, all his facts are entirely accurate so far as I am able to judge, and his remarks on prison life, delivered with an extraordinary absence of malice, are some of the most interesting that I have read.

241. To Christy & Moore Ltd[1]

1 March 1935   Handwritten postcard

77 Parliament Hill   NW.3

[No addressee]
Many thanks for the 6 copies of "A Clergyman's Daughter." I sent the copy of 'Burmese Days.'° with corrections, to Mr Gollancz yesterday.

E A. Blair

1. Addressed to 'Christie° & Moore Ltd. Literary Agents,' at 222 Strand, London, not personally to Leonard Moore.

242. To Brenda Salkeld

7 March 1935   Typewritten

77 Parliament Hill   Hampstead   NW.3

Dearest Brenda
Just a line to thank you for your nice letter and to tell you that I sent off your copy of "A Clergyman's Daughter" last night. As you will see, it is tripe, except for chap 3, part 1, which I am pleased with, but I don't know whether

you will like it. It is billed to come out on Monday next, so don't show it to anyone before that, will you? I am glad to say my agent has made very good terms for "Burmese Days." It was curious that you should mention that review of Joad's book, because Heppenstall, the man who wrote it, stayed at my place the night before last—in fact he was having breakfast with me when I was reading your letter. I did *not* tell him what you said about "second-rate highbrows." As a matter of fact, he is very nice—a Yorkshireman, very young, twenty four or five I should say, and passionately interested in the ballet. He reviews books on the ballet for Time and Tide, I think. As to people having no "sympathy," I should think that anyone who had sympathy with a person like Joad would have something seriously wrong with them. I cannot tell you how I am looking forward to coming down next weekend. I do hope it won't fall through. No, I *don't* feed entirely on things that don't need cooking. I have bought a small gas-stove called a Bachelor Griller, and you can grill, boil and fry on it, but not bake. As a matter of fact I can cook not too badly, and I have already given a dinner-party to three people all at once and cooked everything myself. But of course I haven't much time, because I still have to go to the shop for about an hour in the morning besides the afternoon, and it is a struggle to get in three hours a day at my writing. The other night I went to the Coliseum to see the so-called Blackbirds[1]—a troop of negro[2] actors—and was bored stiff. I mean if I get time to go and see George Robey as Falstaff.[3] I dare say he could do the part if he would sink his own personality. I have bought an awfully nice set of chessmen—wood, not ivory, but they are beautiful big pieces, weighted, and the white ones are real boxwood. The other day my employer was at a house buying books, and they offered him these chessmen, and he bought them for a *shilling*. We were going to put them in the window at ten shillings, but I bought them in for seven and six instead. They would cost thirty shillings new, I should say. I must say I do see some queer interiors when I go out to fetch books that we buy. The other day I went to a house inhabited by an old woman and her middle-aged daughter, and I was just about to look at the books when every light in the house fused. Of course these two women were helpless, so with that chivalry which you have so often noticed in me I spent half an hour crawling about among the rafters with candles and bits of ginger-beer wire, mending the fuse. I have been reading a lot of back numbers of the Criterion—a paper I don't normally see, as it costs seven and sixpence, but we bought some among some books. I must say that for pure snootiness it beats anything I have ever seen. Here is T. S. Eliot on the servant-problem as seen from the Anglo-Catholic standpoint:

> "I do not like the situation (i.e. of having only one servant). . . . I should prefer to employ a large staff of servants, each doing much lighter work but profiting by the benefits of the cultured and devout atmosphere of the home in which they lived."

That bit about the cultured and devout atmosphere reminds me, as Samuel Butler said of a cracked church bell he heard somewhere, of the smell of a bug.[4]

I must stop now. You will see if you read "A Clergyman's Daughter" that I have employed you as a collaborator in two places. Write again soon. With love.

Eric

1. One of a series of all-black shows originally produced by Lew Leslie in New York and advertised as the 'World's Funniest and Fastest Revue—Glorifying the American Negro' (as Ziegfeld's follies claimed to glorify 'the American Girl'). Amongst its principals were Adelaide Hall and Bill ('Bojangles') Robinson. British impresario Charles Cochran brought the show to the London Pavilion in 1926.
2. Orwell was later to require a capital N for this word. See 'As I Please,' 2, 10 December 1943, *2391*, and Textual Note to *CW*, II, *Burmese Days*.
3. George Robey (1869–1954), an outstanding music-hall and revue artiste, played Falstaff in *I Henry IV*, 28 February 1935, at Her Majesty's Theatre, London. Although not uniformly praised, several critics, including James Agate and Herbert Farjeon, liked his interpretation. He later played Falstaff in Laurence Olivier's film of *Henry V* (1944), in an interpolated scene.
4. Henry Festing Jones, editor of *The Note-Books of Samuel Butler* (1912) was visiting Butler's friend Charles Gogin, who lived opposite St Pancras Church, when the bells struck up: 'The tonic bell on which the tune concluded was the most stuffy and out of tune. Gogin said it was like the smell of a bug' (246). Orwell reviewed *Further Extracts from the Note-Books of Samuel Butler*, chosen and edited by A. T. Bartholomew, in 1934; see *197*.

242A. Publication of *A Clergyman's Daughter*

A Clergyman's Daughter was published by Victor Gollancz Ltd on 11 March 1935; 2,000 copies were printed. The type was distributed on 20 March 1936. The U.S. edition was published by Harper & Brothers, 17 August 1936. According to Gollancz, 500 sets of sheets were provided for this: according to Harper, 1,000 sets. Of these, 256 were remaindered. See Willison.

243. To Leonard Moore

27 March 1935   Typewritten

77 Parliament Hill   Hampstead   NW.3

Dear Mr Moore,

Many thanks for your cheque for £51.2.9.[1] The enclosed[2] was sent me by the American Treasury Dep.t.° I cannot cope with this kind of thing. I seem to remember that a deduction for American Income Tax was made on Harper's royalty statement, but perhaps it would be better to let this claim drop rather than have to mess about with affidavits etc.

I have received a good many cuttings about "A Clergyman's Daughter" and they are better than I had expected. I don't suppose it will have sold many copies, though. I wonder if you have received Gollancz's second spring or summer list? We never get his catalogues at the shop, but another bookseller told me that the spring or summer list, whichever it is, includes a very striking advance notice of "Burmese Days," which I should like to see if you happen to have a copy to spare.

My next book[3] is getting on fairly well, though slowly. I expect it will take me all of this year. If you want to have an advance wad of it to show to Gollancz, I expect I can let you have one about June.

Yours sincerely
Eric A. Blair

1. See also *255* and *262*.
2. Presumably a claim form for a refund of tax paid on royalties. Orwell's total income in the United States would be insufficient to be taxed.
3. *Keep the Aspidistra Flying*.

244. To Leonard Moore

[13 April 1935]   Handwritten; dated from postmark

Booklovers' Corner, 1 South End Road, Hampstead, N.W.3.

Dear Mr Moore,
I wonder if you could find out for me whether Gollancz has any copies of "Down & Out" left over, which he would sell off at remainder price. We could sell a few copies in the shop if we could get them cheap, as it is sometimes advertised for in trade papers.

Yours sincerely
Eric A. Blair

P.S. [to left on card] The reviews of "A Clergyman's Daughter" were much better than I expected, especially the Mail & the Herald.[1]

1. The *Daily Mail* was politically to the right; the *Daily Herald*, to the left. Although the political views of these national newspapers would not necessarily be reflected in book reviews, the combination of good reviews in two papers of different political persuasions may have been particularly pleasing to Orwell.

245. To Brenda Salkeld

7 May [1935]   Typewritten: handwritten postscript

77 Parliament Hill   Hampstead   NW.3

Dearest Brenda,
I am afraid this will not reach St Felix[1] before you do, as I only got your letter this evening—I suppose the posts were late owing to the jubilee.[2] I went down to Brighton, for the first time in my life, for Sunday and Monday.[3] I went there with disagreeable apprehensions, but consoling myself by thinking that sooner or later I was sure to want to mention a trip to Brighton in a novel. However, I was rather agreeably surprised, and I didn't, in any case, spend much time by the sea shore, but went inland and picked bluebells etc. I found a number of nests, including a bullfinch's with four eggs, and by the way about a week ago I found a tit's nest, but I couldn't get at it, though I

385

saw the bird go off the nest, as it was in the middle of a thorn bush. The crowds in Brighton weren't so bad, but of course it was an awful business getting back on Sunday,[4] the train being so packed that people were hanging out of the windows. On Saturday night I was down in Chelsea, and it took me two hours to get back to Hampstead, the whole centre of London was so blocked with taxis full of drunken people careering round, singing and bellowing "Long live the King!" What surprised me was that most of them were very young—the last people whom you would expect to find full of patriotic emotion; but I suppose they just welcomed the excuse for making a noise. That night I had been to see Rees, really to borrow some money off him, as I had forgotten Monday was a bank holiday and had not got any money out of the bank, but he was at some sort of Socialist meeting and they asked me in and I spent three hours with seven or eight Socialists harrying me, including a South Wales miner who told me— quite good-naturedly, however—that if he were dictator he would have me shot immediately. I have done quite a lot of work, but oh! what mountains there are to do yet. I don't know that I shall be able to let you have that piece[5] to see in June after all, but I will some time—when it is fit to be seen, I mean. I am now getting to the stage where you feel as though you were crawling about inside some dreadful labyrinth. I don't know that I have read much. I read D. H. Lawrence's "Women in Love," which is certainly not one of his best. I remember reading it before in 1924—the unexpurgated version that time— and how very queer it seemed to me at that age. I see now that what he was trying to do was to create characters who were at once symbolical figures and recognizable human beings, which was certainly a mistake. The queer thing is that when he concentrates on producing ordinary human characters, as in "Sons and Lovers" and most of the short stories, he gets his meaning across much better as well as being much more readable. I have also been glancing into some numbers of "The Enemy," the occasional paper Wyndham Lewis used to run, which we have in the shop. The man is certainly insane. I have hit on a wonderful recipe for a stew, which is the following: half a pound of ox-kidney, chopped up small, half a pound of mushrooms, sliced; one onion chopped very fine, two cloves of garlic, four skinned tomatoes, a slice of lean bacon chopped up, and salt, the whole stewed very gently for about two and a half hours in a very little beef stock. You eat it with sphagetti° or rather coquillettes. It is a good dish to make, as it cooks itself while you are working. I have been deriving a lot of pleasure from some numbers of the Girls'° Own Paper of 1884 and 1885. In the answers to correspondents two questions crop up over and over again. One, whether it is ladylike to ride a tricycle. The other, whether Adam's immediate descendents° did not have to commit incest in order to carry on the human species. The question of whether Adam had a navel does not seem to have been agitated, however.

I must stop now, as I don't think I have any more news. As to your presentiment, or "curious feeling" about me, you don't say when exactly you had it. But I don't know that I have been particularly unhappy lately—at least, not more than usual.

With much love and many kisses
Eric

P.S. [at top of first page] Near Brighton I passed Roedean School. It seemed to me that even in holiday time I could feel waves of snobbishness pouring out of it, & also aerial music to the tune of the female version of "Forty Years On" & the Eton "Boating Song."[6] Do you play them at hockey, or did they write to you "St Felix, who are you?"

1. St Felix School for Girls, Southwold, where Salkeld was the gym mistress.
2. The Silver Jubilee of King George V.
3. The Bank Holiday on Monday, 6 May, was given to mark the Jubilee.
4. Orwell must mean Monday.
5. Presumably a portion of *Keep the Aspidistra Flying*. In his letter to Moore of 14 May 1935 (*246*), Orwell says he intended to write what became a novel as a book of essays; the 'piece' referred to was perhaps one of these essays in process of transformation into a different genre.
6. See *179, n. 2.*

246. To Leonard Moore

14 May 1935   Typewritten

77 Parliament Hill   Hampstead   NW.3

Dear Mr Moore,
Many thanks for your letter. Naturally I am very pleased to hear that Mr Gollancz speaks so nicely of me.[1] Thanks also for sending the copies of the Czech translation of "Down and Out." Of course I can't judge what kind of translation it is, but at any rate they have got it up quite nicely. I have made arrangements, or I am now making them, to lecture to a literary society in Essex some time this autumn.[2] When the time comes I will instruct them to pay them° my fee through you. I mention this, as it is a line of business which might possibly be worked up at some later time. The novel I am doing[3] isn't getting on too badly, though rather slowly, as it is only quite recently that I really got into my stride. I had intended, as you know, to do it in the form of a book of essays, but changed it to a novel. I expect it will take me all this year. I am not going to rush it, as I am rather pleased with it as a conception and want very much to make a good job of it. I wonder whether you have heard how "Burmese Days" sold in America? I shouldn't think it would sell more than about 1500 copies.[4]

Yours sincerely
Eric A. Blair

1. On 9 May, Moore wrote to Orwell to say that the type of *Down and Out in Paris and London* was being distributed, since there was to be no reprint. Victor Gollancz had also told Moore that, though rights to the book would now revert to Orwell, 'this must not be interpreted, of course, to mean any weakening in all my interests in Blair for, in my opinion, he is likely to be in years to come one of the half dozen most important authors on our lists.' Moore hoped this would encourage Orwell 'to get on with' his next book.
2. On 16 October, Orwell spoke to the South Woodford Literary Society, before an audience of four or five hundred people; see *258*.
3. *Keep the Aspidistra Flying*.
4. There were two printings, 2,000 copies and an unknown number; see *213A*. In February 1935,

976 copies were remaindered. If the second printing was also 2,000 copies, then 3,024 copies would have been sold. It seems unlikely to have been fewer than 1,500, if there was need for a second printing so soon after the first. See Stansky and Abrahams, II, 56–57, which ignores the second printing and assumes that only 1,024 copies were sold or distributed for review.

246A. Publication of *Burmese Days* in England

The first English edition of *Burmese Days* was published by Victor Gollancz Ltd on 24 June 1935; see *213A*. The text was considerably modified from that published in New York on 25 October 1934; see *CW*, II, Textual Note.

247. To Leonard Moore

15 July 1935   Typewritten

77 Parliament Hill   Hampstead   NW.3

Dear Mr Moore,

I was talking yesterday to a retired Indian Civil Servant from Burma who had read "Burmese Days" and said it had interested him, and he said he was sending a copy to a friend in Burma. It occurred to me that we could probably sell quite a lot of copies in Burma, and also India, and I wondered whether Mr Gollancz was making any arrangements to do this. There are quite extensive libraries and bookshops out there. Also it would be well worth sending a copy for review to the Rangoon Gazette and Rangoon Times, and perhaps to one or two of the Indian papers. Of course for all I know Mr Gollancz has done all this already, but I thought I would mention it, just in case it had not been done.

The copies of the French translation (only two) were sent to me direct by the translator. They have printed it quite nicely. I am sorry to say that Panaït Istrati, who wrote the introduction, died almost immediately afterwards,[1] before I could thank him. The translator tells me that Malraux has been too busy to read "Burmese Days," because he has been occupied with this international conference of literary men, but he intends to do so shortly and will propose it to the N.R.F. if it interests him.[2]

Yours sincerely
Eric A. Blair

1. Panaït Istrati died on 16 April 1935; *La Vache Enragée* was published on 2 May 1935; see *157*.
2. See letter to Moore, 9 October 1934 (*210*), for the proposal that Malraux write a 'preface' for *Burmese Days*.

248. Review of *The Victorians and their Books* by Amy Cruse

The Adelphi, August 1935

This is a meandering, gorbellied book, but it contains a lot of useful information. Its purpose, from which it digresses rather too often, is to tell one what books were being read at each period of the Victorian Age, and what people were saying about them.

There are several facts which a survey of this kind forces upon one's attention. One, of course, is the complete cultural severance of nineteenth-century England from Europe. During the whole period there does not seem to have been a single foreign book, unless one counts American books and the Bible, which made any impression at all on the wider public. Another fact, rather less obvious perhaps, is that hysteria about books and the over-rating of trumpery writers—in fact, the book-ramp—was at least as prevalent then as now. This is particularly noticeable with regard to novels. It may be rather hard to believe after a course of Walpole and Gould[1] but the Victorians took their novels quite as seriously as we do. Men and women alike devoured them with child-like eagerness. The wounded officers in the hospitals of the Crimea clamoured for the works of Charlotte M. Yonge. Macaulay "cried as though his heart would break" (his own phrase) over *Dombey and Son*. And even the busiest people seem to have found time not only to read novels but also to write lengthy reviews of them in private letters to their friends. On every popular novel of the period Miss Cruse quotes long, serious comments by the most unexpected people, from Swinburne to Gladstone, and from Florence Nightingale to Edward Fitzgerald. Even the Queen made public pronouncements on novels occasionally. Moreover, reputations were much more durable in those days. It was not then, as now, a case of "That's genius—that was!"[2] Once you were established as a Great Writer you remained Great at least until all your early admirers were dead. Indeed, the Great were nailed so firmly to their pedestals that some of the most spurious of them are sticking there even now.

Another point, a small one but worth noticing, is the change in the sense of decency. Admittedly the period between, say, 1840 and 1890 was a squeamish period—though there are some excellent dirty jokes in Surtees and Marryat; but our own age is equally squeamish in a different way. For the Victorians, though scared by the obscene, were at any rate not scared by the macabre. The generation which thought *Jane Eyre* a dangerous book could swallow Poe's *Tales*, and the description of the death of Krook in *Bleak House*, almost without a murmur. There would probably be a fearful outcry now if Poe's *Tales* had just appeared for the first time. The sense of decency varies, of course, from country to country as well as from age to age.

This is a book whose whole interest lies in its subject matter. It is badly written, clumsily put together, and marred by indiscriminate enthusiasm. Miss Cruse has a particular affection for those slimy Low Church scout-masters, Charles Kingsley and Tom Hughes. However, even here she disinters facts which are of interest. In particular, there is one phrase she records which beautifully sums up the nineteenth-century middle-class

Protestant mentality. This is where Kingsley refers to the Appennine mountains as the "Popish Appennines."

1. It was Gerald Gould, poet and reviewer for *The Observer*, who, in his capacity as chief reader for Victor Gollancz, had (unknown to Orwell) recommended the publication of *A Clergyman's Daughter*; see 219, n. 2.
2. Orwell adapts a contemporary slogan for Shell petrol: 'That's Shell – that was!'

249. Review of *Twenty Thousand Streets under the Sky* by Patrick Hamilton; *The Proceedings of the Society* by Katharine M. Williams; *I Lie Alone* by R. G. Goodyear

New English Weekly, 1 August 1935

Here are three novels all endeavouring, in very different ways, to present a picture of "real life." I think the best way I can deal with them is to mention them in descending order of length—which is also, as it happens, ascending order of merit.

"Twenty Thousand Streets under the Sky" is an enormous novel—to be exact, it is a trilogy, but bound into one cover—describing the not very complicated relations between a literary young man bartender, a good-hearted barmaid who loves the bartender in vain, and a worthless little prostitute who does the bartender out of his money. Here, I think, is a fair sample:

> "In their journey from the table to the door Jenny said nothing about Turkish Delight. In fact, she was scrupulously careful not to even *look* Turkish Delight—possibly too careful. At any rate, in Tom's imagination, it seemed that if he did not get Turkish Delight the entire evening was endangered. For it was an axiom that, amid all the varied delights that generous nature showered, to Turkish Delight Jenny was most consistently faithful."

There are 753 pages, all of them round about this level. The style, it will be seen, is what one may call the masticatory style—that is, the style that comments on everything, à la Bennett, instead of making plain statements. Mr. Hamilton's more immediate master, however, is obviously Priestley. He has set out, sincerely enough, to write a novel about "real life," but with the Priestleyan assumption that "real life" means lower-middle class life in a large town and that if you can pack into your novel, say, fifty-three descriptions of tea in a Lyons Corner House, you have done the trick. The result is what one might expect: a huge well-meaning book, as shapeless and inert as a clot of frog-spawn.

However, "Twenty Thousand Streets under the Sky" is good of its rather unappetising kind. It is perfectly self-consistent and contains nothing wilfully cheap or false. And whatever one may think of its quality, there can be no two opinions about its quantity; 753 pages for eight and sixpence is good value. Mr. Priestley contributes an introduction, thus giving the lie to a well-known epigram of Mr. Yeats.[1]

"The Proceedings of the Society" is shorter, and its subject matter is more genteel. As a matter of fact it is not really a novel, but a series of stories and sketches dealing with the members of a literary society in a South of England watering-place. These people are the most depressing Struldbrugs° I have read about for a long time. Without exception they lead lives of unutterable futility, and nearly all of them are so old as to have no active memories later than the reign of King Edward. Personally, I doubt whether even the members of the Bournemouth Literary Society (is it Bournemouth?) are quite as bad as they are pictured here. But Miss Williams has clearly a bias in favour of the depressing. Nothing lurid, of course—no heads stuck in gas ovens or anything of that kind; merely the peaceful, deadly depression of people who are now old and have never even been alive. Over it all there hangs the atmosphere of genteel decay; residential hotels, fixed annuities, false teeth, galoshes and bath chairs. Life unlived—that is Miss Williams's theme essentially.

It is curious, but the cult of disillusionment in books of this type has a certain resemblance to the old Christian cult of self-mortification. The *ideal rongeur* has merely changed its shape. Instead of being the ideal Christian sanctity, it is now the ideal—equally unattained by most people—of a life fully lived. In Baudelaire's day you woke in the brothel and lamented your lost innocence. Now, on the other hand, you are wheeled in your bath chair down the Bournemouth parade, thinking with mingled desolation and relief of the adultery you failed to commit in '97. It is perhaps a spiritual come-down. But this is a distinctly readable book. It is typically a woman's book (it owes a little to Katherine Mansfield, perhaps) in its mixture of sentimentality and disillusionment. The fourth story, "Remembering Ethel," is a very good story—excellently conceived and sufficiently well executed.

"I Lie Alone" is much narrower in its range. In fact, it is hardly more than a full-length portrait of a single character, Lyddie Gossett, a peculiarly graceless and soulless old maid. Lyddie's true character is revealed only by degrees, and rather subtly. At the beginning one imagines that she is going to be the typical dear old hen of fact and fiction—the dear "motherly" old soul who makes quince jelly and cowslip wine and sews patchwork quilts for the poor. As the story goes on, however, it becomes clearer and clearer that she is an entirely worthless slut whose every thought turns on food or drink, usually food. Throughout the book, on almost every page, she is either devouring, planning or recovering from some sordid "tasty" meal; or else she is sinking, flannel-nightgowned, into the stuffy embraces of a feather bed. Mr. Goodyear is very ruthless in his descriptions. No *preux chevalier*, I feel, would write like this about a lady:

> "Groping in the hot darkness, she belched. 'Cucumber,' she said, and patted her breast.
> "A warm, fruity perfume spread through the room as she lovingly cut the cake. A faint steam rose from the dark slices."

Towards the end the book becomes more of a narrative, and perhaps deteriorates a little. Lyddie's father, for whom she has kept house all her life,

391

dies, and his pension with him. Of course such a woman as Lyddie is incapable either of saving money or of keeping a job. She sponges on one relative after another, goes to pieces, drinks more and more, and at last dies miserably in the public infirmary. A squalid story, but interesting. After reading it one sees more clearly than before why gluttony was included among the seven deadly sins. The book's originality lies rather in its subject-matter than in its treatment. The actual writing, as can be seen from the extract I have given above, is undistinguished. This book is recommended by the Book Guild.

1. 'But was there ever dog that praised his fleas?' from 'To a Poet, who would have me praise certain bad Poets, Imitators of his and mine.'

250. To Christy & Moore[1]

4 August 1935   Typewritten

50 Lawford Road   Kentish Town   NW5.

Dear Sir,
Please note that my address will be as above until further notice.[2]

Yours faithfully
Eric A. Blair

1. Addressee identified from the rubber stamp used to date receipt of this letter.
2. Orwell had moved from Parliament Hill to a working-class suburb about a mile and a half from Booklovers' Corner. The flat (see Thompson, 47) was rented in Orwell's name but shared with Michael Sayers (1912–), who contributed short stories and reviews to *The Adelphi*, and Rayner Heppenstall, see *238*. The relationship was not wholly satisfactory, Orwell and Heppenstall even coming to blows; see Heppenstall's *Four Absentees*, 83–86; also *Orwell Remembered*, 106–15. However, they remained friends and later worked together on BBC broadcasts. Sayers was described by Orwell in a letter of 21 April 1949 (see *3603*) to Ruth Fischer (author of *Stalin and German Communism*) as a 'a very out-at-elbow young Irish poet' in 1935. In 1938 he went to America, to work as English play editor for Norman Bel Geddes; see *Four Absentees*, 94. He returned in 1945, having 'changed in the most astonishing way, turning into a fat prosperous business-man. . . . He was very pro-USSR.' Orwell lived at Lawford Road until the end of January 1936, when he stopped working at Booklovers' Corner. See *257, n. 4.*

251. To Leonard Moore

6 September 1935   Typewritten

50 Lawford Rd.   Kentish Town   NW.

Dear Mr Moore,
Many thanks for your letter. Naturally I would like to do the serial for the News Chronicle[1] if possible, but I am not absolutely certain that I could manage it. The difficulty is not so much as to length, subject etc., as that a serial requires some dramatic qualities which are not much in my line.

However, if as you say they will say definitely yes or no on the strength of a first instalment and synopsis, perhaps one could come to an arrangement without wasting too much time on it. Suppose I sent you a first instalment in two or three weeks' time? If they like it, I can go on with it; if they say no, I can drop it and there is only about a week's work wasted. But I would like to know whether in case of their accepting they would want the remaining instalments immediately. Because if they would, I should have to write the whole thing before submitting it, and that means a month's work, probably. On the other hand, if they accepted on the strength of the first instalment and were willing to wait, say, three weeks for the other four, all would be well. The point is that if I do this serial it will put my novel back a month or so, and naturally I don't want to do that for nothing.

Yours sincerely
Eric A. Blair

1. *News Chronicle* was politically aligned to the Liberal Party's viewpoint. In his column 'As I Please,' 30, 23 June 1944, Orwell described its politics as 'a very pale pink—about the colour of shrimp paste, I should say, but still pink'; see *2492*. It ceased publication on 17 October 1960, when it was merged with the right-wing *Daily Mail*.

252. To Leonard Moore

12 September 1935   Typewritten

50 Lawford Rd.   Kentish Town   NW.

Dear Mr Moore,
Thanks for your letter. I will let you have the first instalment and synopsis in a week or ten days. It is a story I have had in my head a long time, and I think I can make it just about the right length. I am afraid they may think it rather a squalid story—however, I will see to it that there is nothing verbally offensive.

Yours sincerely
Eric A. Blair

253. To Rayner Heppenstall

Tuesday night, [24 September 1935]   Typewritten

50 Lawford Rd.   Kentish Town   NW.

Dear Rayner,
Many thanks for letter. I hope the enclosed MS. is what you wanted. I infer from what you would no doubt call your handwriting that you were taught script at school; the result is that I can't read a single word of the manuscript part of your letter, so I may not have followed your instructions exactly.

I am suffering unspeakable torments with my serial, having already been at it four days and being still at the second page. This is because I sat down and wrote what was not a bad first instalment, and then upon counting it up found it was 3500 words instead of 2000. Of course this means rewriting it entirely. I don't think I am cut out for a serial-writer. I shall be glad to get back to my good old novel where one has plenty of elbow room. I have three more chapters and an epilogue to do, and then I shall spend about two months putting on the twiddly bits.

Even if my serial doesn't come to anything, and I don't expect it to, I intend taking a week or so off next month. My people have asked me to come down and stay with them, and if I can get my sister to drive me over, as I don't think I can drive her present car, I will come over and see you. I don't know that part of the country, but if it is like ours it must be nice this time of year.

I forwarded a letter this evening which had urgent proofs on it. I hope it gets to you in time, but it had already been to your old address. You ought to let editors and people know that you have changed your address.

You are right about Eileen.[1] She is the nicest person I have met for a long time. However, at present alas! I can't afford a ring, except perhaps a Woolworth's one. Michael[2] was here last night with Edna[3] and we all had dinner together. He told me he has a story in the anthology of stories that is coming out, but he seemed rather down in the mouth about something. I was over at the Fierz'[4] place on Sunday and met Brenda[5] and Maurice[6] whom no doubt you remember, and they were full of a story apparently current among Communists to the effect that Col. Lawrence[7] is not really dead but staged a fake death and is now in Abyssinia. I did not like Lawrence, but I would like this story to be true.

Au revoir. Please remember me to the Murrys.[8]

Yours
Eric A. Blair

1. Eileen O'Shaughnessy (1905–1945) was to marry Orwell on 9 June 1936. They had met in 1925, according to Lettice Cooper (*PEN Broadsheet*, No. 17, Autumn 1984), at a party, when she was, she once said, 'Rather drunk, behaving my worst, very rowdy.' Before George left the house he said to a friend, 'The girl I want to marry is Eileen O'Shaughnessy.' Since Orwell was in Burma in 1925, this must refer to the party Mrs. Rosalind Obermeyer gave at 77 Parliament Hill in March 1935. Mrs. Obermeyer, who introduced them (see *233, n.1*), records that Orwell said to her, 'Now *that* is the kind of girl I would like to marry!' (Crick, 267). Lettice Cooper worked with Eileen Blair at the Ministry of Food during the war. Eileen, she recalls, was 'of medium height, a little high-shouldered, she was very pretty, and had what George called a cat's face, blue eyes and near black hair. She moved slowly, she always looked as if she was drifting into a room with no particular purpose there. She had small, very shapely hands and feet. I never saw her in a hurry, but her work was always finished up to time. . . . Eileen's mind was a mill that ground all the time slowly but independently. Diffident and unassuming in manner she had a quiet integrity that I never saw shaken' (*PEN Broadsheet*). She was born in South Shields (her father was a Collector of Customs), graduated from Oxford in 1927, and then, among other jobs, she worked as a teacher at a school in Taplow, acted as a reader for Dame Elizabeth Cadbury, worked for the Archbishop's Advisory Board for Prevention and Rescue Work, ran a secretarial and typing agency, tried free-lance journalism, and helped her brother, Laurence, a surgeon and chest specialist, to prepare his work for publication. At the time she met Orwell she was reading for a master's degree in psychology at University College London; see *257*, and *257, n. 5*. See also Stansky

and Abrahams, II 104–08; Crick, 267–70; Shelden, 227–31; U.S.: 207–10. Lydia Jackson's reminiscences are in *Orwell Remembered*, 66–68.
2. Michael Sayers; see *250, n. 2.*
3. Unidentified.
4. Francis and Mabel Fierz, at whose home in Golders Green Orwell often found refuge when he first came to London; see *102*, n. 1.
5. Brenda Eason Verstone (1911–) studied art at the Chelsea School of Art and then worked as a journalist for trade publications concerned with paper and packaging.
6. Maurice Oughton was a leading aircraftman in the Royal Air Force in 1942, when he published a slim volume of poems, *Out of the Oblivion*, which includes his picture.
7. T. E. Lawrence ('Lawrence of Arabia'), who had died as a result of a motor-cycle accident on 19 May 1935.
8. Heppenstall was staying with John Middleton Murry in Norfolk.

254. Review of *Captain Conan* by Roger Vercel; *Private Life of a Successful Man* by W. F. Casey; *Song o' Sixpence* by T. Thompson; *Criss-Cross* by Don Tracy; *Keep it Quiet* by Richard Hull

New English Weekly, 26 September 1935

The chief need of the reviewer to-day is a new set of adjectives. This is not merely because all the strongest adjectives in the dictionary ("terrific," "startling," "unforgettable," etc.: but there are two or three which have not yet been discovered, and it is better to keep quiet about them) have been so vulgarized that no decent person can use them any longer. It is also because, as things are at present, books which are gulfs apart in real merit are praised or dispraised in almost exactly the same words. If one is reviewing a novel by, say, Dell or Deeping,[1] it will not do to write it off, snootily and unhelpfully, as a piece of tripe. One has got to take it seriously, which means applying to it the same terms as one would apply to Stendhal or even to Shakespeare. This is like weighing a flea on a spring-balance intended for a whale. Any honest reviewer would have to admit that *Gulliver's Travels* and *The Adventures of Sherlock Holmes* are both of them very good books. He might even go further and describe both of them as terrific, startling, unforgettable, etc. And yet obviously there is a certain distinction—a distinction which ought to be made clearer than most reviewers succeed in making it. Failing those badly-needed adjectives, which we are not likely to get, the best solution would be to arrange a more accurate classification for the novels themselves. They should be divided rigidly into grades, like the various grades of the Legion of Honour. "A brilliant novel of the ninth class," or "A disgracefully bad first-class novel"—that is the kind of classification we need.

I mention this because it happens that all the novels on my present list are of extremely low standard. One can differentiate between them and say that this one is good and that one is bad, but all of them are good or bad in a very small way; they belong definitely to the lower grades. *Captain Conan*, which is a translation from the French, might be admitted into the fourth or fifth class of novels, perhaps. It is a story of the French army of occupation in Roumania and Bulgaria immediately after the War. The central character, Captain Conan, is at once a hero and a disgusting brute. He is a natural warrior, the kind of man whose ideal is a lifetime of campaigning with short interludes of boozing and lechery. Having fought through the War with great distinction and passionate enjoyment, he manages to prolong it unofficially for several months after it is over. At last, however, he is demobilized, and at the end of the book we are given a brief, rather pathetic glimpse of him a dozen years later. Peace has been the ruin of him, of course. At thirty-five or so he is a fat, broken, henpecked man, dying of ennui and cirrhosis of the liver. The style is jerky and impressionistic, and so, no doubt, is the style of the original. But there is an important fact that the translator has not grasped. This is that in translating dialogue from a foreign language one must either translate literally, and exploit the foreignness for what it is worth, or disregard accuracy and make the characters talk like English people. He wavers between Gallicisms and English slang, with the result that all the dialogue is like this:

"Look here," he spluttered, "a grenade isn't a tangerine, you know. If they're served out, they're intended to be used; and to lay a trap with them for the man for whom they're meant—that, my friend, say what you like, is the stuff!"

No human being in any age or country ever talked quite like that.

Private Life of a Successful Man is a book of a more familiar stamp. The hero, Margrove, is a typical modern "great man"—the kind of man the American business colleges try to persuade you to believe that you can be. He is the owner of innumerable enterprises, including "Culture, Ltd.", and he cherishes a supposed resemblance to Napoleon. Needless to say, his private life is empty and unsatisfying. His wife looks down on him, his other women bore him, etc., etc. (How much more original it would be, and how much more horrifying, to depict a "great man" who was *not* disappointed by his "greatness"!) The author has evidently had an opportunity of studying Lord Northcliffe at close quarters. But his novel will not bear comparison with another novel written on the same theme a dozen years ago—it is forgotten now, perhaps, but it was a good novel—the late W. L. George's *Caliban*.

For a brief moment, at the beginning of *Song o' Sixpence*, when I came upon the sentence " 'Midst the browns and purples of this stark landscape he was spiritually at home," I thought I was in for "dark" earth and deflorations behind haystacks. However, *Song o' Sixpence* is not that kind of book. It is more like a biography of a very unpretentious kind. It ambles along in such a pedestrian manner that one feels sure all the time there must be a "plot" coming presently; but the "plot" never arrives. The hero, Zach Kay, is a Lancashire boy who runs away from home, falls in with a pedlar, launches out on his own and makes a fortune very easily and unconvincingly. (He does it mainly by selling coughdrops.) Presently, he marries his housekeeper, or rather she marries him—there is much "pawky" humour here, if "pawky" is the correct Lancashire word—he becomes a town councillor and then a mayor, loses his wife, loses his money, and finally, at the age of about fifty, goes back to the road as a pedlar. It is quite an agreeable story, and I am sure all north-country readers will be delighted by the barbarous lingo in which the characters talk.

"Ah wor wondering," said Zach timorously, "if Ah dar' ax yo're Sally to be housekeeper for me. Ah'd pay her weel. An' hoo could have a neet or two off if hoo's getten a felly."

And again:

"He'll fetch thee owt tha wants fro' the town," she said, "he's a willin' lad, an' he hasn't a tit in his stable as couldn't poo' a elephant up a broo."

That should go straight to the Lancastrian heart, should it not? I rather object to it, I feel sure that there is quite enough north-country dialect in real life without letting it get into novels.

The two other books on the list are crime-stories. *Criss-Cross* is American and "tough." The "tough" American books would make one exclaim that Hemingway has a lot to answer for, were it not that their very number suggests that Hemingway is merely a sympton and not a cause. The probability is that one of these days the "tough" school of literature will vanish so suddenly that Hemingway will not even have time to be debunked. *Keep it Quiet* is English and gentlemanly. But as for the dust-wrapper of this book, all I can say is that I should have thought Faber's were above that kind of thing.

1. About the time he wrote this review, Orwell was also writing *Keep the Aspidistra Flying*, in which he described the novels of Ethel M. Dell and Warwick Deeping as 'garbage.' This description was cut by the publisher. It is restored in this edition; see *CW*, IV, Textual Note for 7/34.

255. To Leonard Moore

30 September 1935   Typewritten

50 Lawford Rd.   Kentish Town   NW.

Dear Mr Moore,

Many thanks for your cheque for £9–2–9.[1]

I am sending herewith the first instalment, as promised. I have spent a week of agony over the beastly thing, but have small hopes that it will be any use. It is too much out of my line. The story I had in mind is potentially a good one, but I can't do with having to cram things into such short length as that. Still, I suppose it is just worth showing it to the News Chronicle people. As to the synopsis, I was not exactly certain what kind of synopsis they wanted. When a serial is printed they usually give a very short synopsis relating the bare outline of the events that have happened, but I did not think that would be much use to a person who wanted an idea of what the story would be like. So I have written a synopsis of five or six pages, giving a fairly complete résumé of the story and trying to convey some of the spirit of it. In the event of their accepting, which I am afraid I don't think likely, I can do them a synopsis of the ordinary kind if required.[2]

I had a letter from Gollancz, harrying me about my novel.[3] He says he must have it by the end of the year, to come out at the end of February. I think I can just about manage that. If this serial came to anything, I would take about three weeks off from the bookshop, to give me extra time. By the way, the sooner they can let me know yes or no about the serial, the better.

I wonder whether, since the News Chronicle have shown this much interest in me, it would be possible to get them to give me some books to review later? Apart for° the reviews I have done for some years past in the Adelphi. I have begun reviewing most of the novels for the New English Weekly. Financially this does one no good, but it is probably a bit of an advert. Recently a publisher wrote saying he would like me to review a novel he had published as he had seen my reviews in the N.E.W.

Yours sincerely
Eric A. Blair

1. Orwell was evidently receiving royalty payments half-yearly (a common practice). He acknowledged receiving £51.2.9 on 27 March 1935 (see *243*) and on 8 November 1935 asked Moore if any royalties were due; see *262*.
2. The *News Chronicle* was then publishing a five-part serial every week from Monday to Friday, each by a different author. At least some stories were announced as specially written for the series. Orwell's synopsis and instalment were apparently rejected; see *262*.
3. *Keep the Aspidistra Flying.*

256. Review of *The Life and Times of Henry Crabb Robinson* by Edith J. Morley

The Adelphi, October 1935

Henry Crabb Robinson was born in 1775 and died in 1867, and had an eventful though dilettante life. He was a newspaper correspondent in Germany, and later in Spain, during the Napoleonic War, and he was acquainted with Goethe, with various other German poets, and with practically every English literary man of any eminence during the first half of the nineteenth century. It is therefore improbable that he was quite such a tedious person as this book makes him appear. It is one of those omnium gatherum books which are made up mostly of extracts from letters and diaries, but which contain enough interpolated matter to bring them under the heading of biography. The qualities needed in a biographer are piety and wit. Professor Morley has piety in abundance. She shows an almost morbid interest in everything Henry Crabb Robinson said and did, and follows up doubtful meanings in his letters with a minuteness worthy of a school text-book. Students of modern literary pathology will be interested by the footnote on page 53.[1]

Henry Crabb Robinson's diaries and reminiscences are shortly to be published at greater length, and they will probably be of some interest when they appear, for he seems to have been a fairly typical Englishman of his time. He belonged to the puritanical monied class which was rising on the ruins of the old aristocracy, and which was liberal in the sense that it rather liked shaking its fist at any tyrant who was safely distant. He began, like Wordsworth, with an enthusiasm for the French Revolution, and ended up with the ineradicable anti-French prejudice which was produced in so many Englishmen by the long war with France. He was also keenly interested in the scientific inventions of his time, and carefully recorded his impressions on taking chloroform (he was one of the first people in England to do so) and on travelling in a railway train in 1833. The accounts of the chloroform and the railway journey, and the information that safety razors were already in use in 1849, are the only things I carry away from Professor Morley's book with any sense of profit.

1. The footnote elucidates 'a cargo "of caravanzes, a kind of bean" ' in the text and reads: 'Crabb Robinson's spelling and explanation. *O.E.D.* gives calavance, obs., with several variants, not including his. The original English forms were *garvance, caravance*, and the derivation is uncertain. It is a name for certain varieties of pulse, and may ultimately be connected with Gk. ερέβινθος, meaning chick-pea, though this is very doubtful.'

257. To Rayner Heppenstall

5 October 1935   Typewritten

50 Lawford Rd.   Kentish Town   NW.

Dear Rayner,

I managed to dig out your things, but only "apres plaingtz° et pleurs at° angoisseux gemissements."[1] I trust they are the right ones. I sent off my bloody serial-instalment and synopsis about a week ago, but don't expect them to accept it. It is too much out of my line. If they *do* accept, I shall take about three weeks off, and shall probably go and stay somewhere near London where I can be in country air but come up to town once a week to see to the shop.[2] If they *don't*, I shall in any case take a week off, and shall probably come down to S'wold, in which case I will come over and see you. I am very happy to have got back to my novel,[3] which is going not badly. I haven't seen Michael[4] for some time. Eileen says she won't marry me as yet (of course you won't repeat these things I tell you about E. etc.) as she is not earning any money at present and doesn't want to be a drag on me. However, that will arrange itself later when she has finished her course at London University,[5] and besides perhaps I shall be earning more next year. On the other hand by next year we may all have been blown sky-high. I was down at Greenwich the other day and looking at the river I thought what wonders a few bombs would work among the shipping. Last night I went with Geoffrey Gorer[6] to see Greta Garbo in "Anna Karenina"—not too bad. Please remember me to the Murrys.

Yours
Eric

399

1. 'after years / Of anguish'd moanings and laments' . . . From François Villon (1431–1463), *Le Testament*, stanza 12, lines 1–2; translated by Norman Cameron.
2. Booklovers' Corner.
3. *Keep the Aspidistra Flying*.
4. Michael Sayers, who had been sharing the flat at 50 Lawford Road with Orwell and Heppenstall. For Heppenstall's account of life there, see 'The Shooting Stick,' *Twentieth Century*, April 1955, 367–73, e.g.: 'Now, I am afraid that Paul [Michael Sayers] and I tended to exploit Orwell. I think Paul always sooner or later paid his rent. I paid mine when I could, but I did not do my share of the washing-up, and Orwell always got breakfast. He was the cook anyway, and I did go out for the beer. We both *liked* Orwell, but he was ten years older than us, so that we came near to viewing him as an eccentric old boy. We also found his preoccupations insufficiently highbrow . . . ' (368).
5. Eileen O'Shaughnessy completed her course work in June 1936 but did not finish the thesis necessary for the award of a master's degree. Her thesis was concerned with measuring the imagination of schoolchildren and had been undertaken on the advice of Professor Cyril Burt; see Crick, 268.
6. Geoffrey Gorer (1905–1985) was a social anthropologist and author of many books, including *Africa Dances* (1935), *The American People: A Study in National Character* (revised, New York, 1964), and *Death, Grief and Mourning in Contemporary Britain* (1965). On 16 July 1935, he had written to Orwell, about *Burmese Days*: 'It is difficult to praise without being impertinent; it seems to me you have done a necessary and important piece of work as well as it could be done.' They met and remained lifelong friends.

258. Report on Lecture 'Confessions of a Down and Out'

South Woodford Literary Society, 16 October 1935

Arrangements for this lecture were made in May 1935 (see *246*), and Orwell wrote to Moore in May 1936 (see *309*) that it 'passed off all right.' It had 'some such title as "Confessions of a Down & Out." ' Some 400 to 500 people attended, and Orwell was delighted and surprised by the response; see *259, 260*. The *Woodford Times* gave this report on the lecture in its issue of 25 October 1935 under the head 'Confessions of a "Down and Out." '

Mr. Orwell commenced by saying that by "destitution" he did not mean someone out of work and drawing the dole or parish relief, but those who really did not know where the next meal was coming from—the tramps who frequented the casual wards of workhouses. He gave a vivid description of terrible conditions under which these people existed; the life on the road, when their only way of getting a meal was by begging or petty theft; conditions in the casual ward, where they had to spend the night on a stone floor with three blankets for their bed and covering; shut in, without a light, for twelve or thirteen hours; the bad food, consisting of little else than bread and margarine and tea, and a piece of cheese and perhaps two hot boiled potatoes or parsnips for dinner. The result of this poor food on the health of men was obvious—they looked healthy when seen from a distance, because they were sunburnt, but they were really very unhealthy and constantly undernourished. The total amount of food which a man received in twenty-four hours in a casual ward was 1½ lbs. of very inferior bread, 2 ozs. margarine, 2 ozs. cheese, one quart of tea, and possibly two potatoes or parsnips.

They were also very much at the mercy of the weather as they were obliged to keep on the move, the law forbidding them to visit the same casual ward more than twice in a month. If a tramp once got wet, he usually stayed wet for several days, in addition to which, he couldn't make a fire in really heavy rain to cook any food which he might have been able to obtain.

Mr. Orwell also spoke at some length on the other evils of this system, its causes, and possible remedies, and said that many people were apt to regard a destitute man as a rogue who needed discouraging as much as possible, and he did not think much could be done in the way of improvement until people realised that they were human beings like the rest of the community, driven by force of circumstances to lead this wretched life.

259. To Rayner Heppenstall

Friday, [18 October 1935]   Handwritten

50 Lawford Rd.   Kentish Town

Dear Rayner,
In haste. Herewith things—trust they are the right ones. Still can't find pouch.[1] Coming down to S'wold on Sunday to stay till Friday. Will come across & see you if poss. It depends on buses as I can't drive my sister's present car—however I will manage it somehow. I haven't heard about my serial— probably it will all turn out a frost. Novel struggling towards its end. Lecture on Wed. went over *big*. Was surprised to find how easy it is.

Yours
Eric

1. In the light of Orwell's strictures about Heppenstall's handwriting (see *253*), this hasty note is written in a manner that might almost seem to be repaying Heppenstall in kind. The word transcribed here as 'pouch' (tobacco-pouch?) is uncertain.

260. To Leonard Moore

Saturday, [26 October 1935]   Handwritten

50 Lawford Rd.   Kentish Town   NW.5

Dear Mr Moore,
Many thanks for your letter. I really hardly expected the serial business to° much. I will however go & see Miss Gosse[1] as suggested some time next week.

I forget if I told you my lecture on the 16th went off quite successfully. There was an audience of 400 or 500 people & they seemed quite interested, & the secretary asked me to come again next year. This suggested to me that we might perhaps try to get some more lecture engagements—this year it would be too late, I suppose, as one has to book up during the summer for the winter months—& perhaps it would be a useful sideline.

If you are communicating with the press-cutting people any time, I wonder if you could ask them not to send me cuttings of my own contributions to magazines?

My novel is a bit behind, but I think I shall just manage to finish it by the end of the year. A Frenchman writes asking whether we would like "La Vache Enragée" translated into English!

Yours sincerely
Eric A. Blair

1. Commissioning editor for the *News Chronicle*.

261. 'St Andrew's Day, 1935'

The Adelphi, November 1935[1]

Sharply the menacing wind sweeps over
The bending poplars, newly bare,
And the dark ribbons of the chimneys
Veer downward; flicked by whips of air,

Torn posters flutter; coldly sound
The boom of trams and the rattling of hooves,
And the clerks who hurry to the station
Look, shuddering, over the Eastern rooves,

Thinking, each one, "Here comes the winter!
"Please God I keep my job this year!"
And bleakly, as the cold strikes through
Their entrails like an icy spear,

They think of rent, rates, season tickets,
Insurance, coal, the skivvy's wages,
Boots, schoolbills, and the next instalment
Upon the two twin beds from Drage's.[2]

For if in careless summer days
In groves of Ashtaroth we whored,
Repentant now, when winds blow cold,
We kneel before our rightful lord;

The lord of all, the money-god,
Who owns us, blood and hand and brain,
Who gives the roof that stops the wind,
And, giving, takes away again;

Who marks with jealous, watchful care
Our thoughts, our dreams, our secret ways,
Who picks our words and cuts our clothes
And maps the pattern of our days;

Who chills our anger, curbs our hope,
And buys our lives and pays with toys,
Who claims as tribute broken faith,
Accepted insults, muted joys;

Who binds with chains the poet's wit,
The navvy's strength, the soldier's pride,
And lays the sleek, estranging shield
Between the lover and his bride.

1. In a letter to Brenda Salkeld in January (see *224*), Orwell said he had written a poem that was to be part of his new novel, *Keep the Aspidistra Flying*. It was first printed in *The Adelphi* under a title not used in the novel. The choice of title may have been an afterthought (possibly not Orwell's) and suggested by the issue in which the poem appeared. Differences between the poem in *The Adelphi* (and here) and at the end of Section VII of *Keep the Aspidistra Flying* are (*Adelphi* first):

line 8: Eastern] eastern		25: marks] spies
15: schoolbills,] school-bills		25: care] care,
22: owns us,] rules us		27: clothes] clothes,

2. Drage's was a chain of furniture stores.

262. To Leonard Moore

8 November 1935   Typewritten

50 Lawford Rd.   Kentish Town   NW.5

Dear Mr Moore,

Many thanks for your two letters and for sending back those Ms. I rang up Miss Gosse, and it seems she wanted me to do something about unemployment etc. For the moment I am rather tired of that subject besides being very busy with my novel, but I have an idea for my next book which, if it came to anything, might be useful to the News Chronicle incidentally.

I wonder if it would be possible to get Mr Gollancz to let me have something in advance? I am very hard up,[1] so much so that I shall shortly have difficulty in paying my rent etc.,[2] and I particularly don't want to be worried about money at this moment when I am struggling with the closing stages of my novel. I don't know whether there are any royalties coming to me, very likely not, as I haven't seen any statements of sales, but perhaps he would advance me something on my present novel if I typed out and sent a substantial wad of it. I should be greatly obliged if you would find out.

The reason why I was amused at the Frenchman suggesting an English translation of LA VACHE ENRAGEE° is that this is the French title of Down and

403

Out.° He evidently hadn't read the book but had heard bits of it on the radio. I suppose if we were clever we would have sold him the translation rights for a trifle.

Yours sincerely
Eric Blair

1. The surviving correspondence for 1935 shows that from his writing Orwell received £51.2s 9d in March and £9.2s.9d in September. This letter was annotated, in Moore's office, that 2s. 11d was 'unearned' for *Down and Out in Paris and London*; in other words, royalties had been advanced over sales to the extent of slightly less than 15p. in contemporary coinage. For *A Clergyman's Daughter*, the amount 'unearned' was £5.13.3. It is likely that these payments represent earnings from these two books and *Burmese Days* for this period, against which must be set at least $13 for copies of *Burmese Days* he had purchased; see *221* and *222*. The total of £60.5s.6d would be in addition to his modest pay as a part-time bookshop assistant and the small sums he might have received for reviewing and his lecture of 16 October. To put this sum in perspective, comparison might be made with the weekly wage of the Barnsley miner, 'Mr G,' which averaged £2.10s (see Wigan Pier Diary, *294*, *13.3.36*) or the annual salary of the South Yorkshire Branch miners' secretary, Mr. H. Wilde, of £260 (see *294*, *15.3.36*). For £30 plus received in April 1936, see his letter to Moore of 18 April 1936, *302*.
2. Without the contributions of Sayers and Heppenstall, Orwell was now finding the rent an increased burden.

263. Review of *Tropic of Cancer* by Henry Miller; *The Wolf at the Door* by Robert Francis

New English Weekly, 14 November 1935

Modern man is rather like a bisected wasp which goes on sucking jam and pretends that the loss of its abdomen does not matter. It is some perception of this fact which brings books like *Tropic of Cancer* (for there will probably be more and more of them as time goes on) into being.

Tropic of Cancer is a novel, or perhaps rather a chunk of autobiography, about Americans in Paris—not the monied dilettante type, but the out-at-elbow, good-for-nothing type. There is much in it that is remarkable, but its most immediately noticeable and perhaps essential feature is its descriptions of sexual encounters. These are interesting not because of any pornographic appeal (quite the contrary), but because they make a definite attempt to get at real facts. They describe sexual life from the point of view of the man in the street—but, it must be admitted, rather a debased version of the man in the street. Nearly all the characters in the book are habitués of the brothel. They act and describe their action with a callous coarseness which is unparalleled in fiction, though common enough in real life. Taken as a whole, the book might even be called a vilification of human nature. As it may justly be asked what good is done by vilifying human nature, I must amplify the remark I made above.

One result of the breakdown of religious belief has been a sloppy idealization of the physical side of life. In a way this is natural enough. For if there is no life beyond the grave, it is obviously harder to face the fact that birth, copulation, etc., are in certain aspects disgusting. In the Christian centuries, of course, a pessimistic view of life was taken more or less for granted. "Man that is born of woman hath but a short time to live and is full of misery," says the Prayer Book, with the air of stating something obvious. But it is a different matter to admit that life is full of misery when you believe that the grave really finishes you. It is easier to comfort yourself with some kind of optimistic lie. Hence the tee-heeing brightness of *Punch*, hence Barrie and his bluebells, hence H. G. Wells and his Utopiæ infested by nude school-marms. Hence, above all, the monstrous soppification of the sexual theme in most of the fiction of the past hundred years. A book like *Tropic of Cancer*, which deals with sex by brutally insisting on the facts, swings the pendulum too far, no doubt, but it does swing it in the right direction. Man is not a Yahoo, but he is rather like a Yahoo and needs to be reminded of it from time to time. All one asks of a book of this kind is that it shall do its job competently and without snivelling—conditions that are satisfied in this case, I think.

Probably, although he chooses to describe ugly things, Mr. Miller would not answer to the name of pessimist. He even has passages of rather Whitmanesque enthusiasm for the process of life. What he seems to be saying is that if one stiffens oneself by the contemplation of ugliness, one ends by finding life not less but more worth living. From a literary point of view his book is competent, though not dazzlingly so. It is firmly done, with very few lapses into the typical modern slipshoddy. If it attracts critical attention it will no doubt be coupled with *Ulysses*, quite wrongly. *Ulysses* is not only a vastly better book, but also quite different in intention. Joyce is primarily an artist; Mr. Miller is a discerning though hardboiled person giving his opinions about life. I find his prose difficult to quote because of the unprintable words which are scattered all over it, but here is one sample:—

"When the tide is on the ebb and only a few syphilitic mermaids are left stranded in the muck the Dome looks like a shooting gallery that's been struck by a cyclone. Everything is slowly dribbling back to the sewer. For about an hour there is a death-like calm during which the vomit is mopped up. Suddenly the trees begin to screech. From one end of the boulevard to the other a demented song rises up. It is the signal that announces the close of the exchange. What hopes there were are swept up. The moment has come to void the last bagful of urine. The day is sneaking in like a leper. . . . "

There is a fine rhythm to that. The American language is less flexible and refined than the English, but it has more life in it, perhaps. I do not imagine that in *Tropic of Cancer* I have discovered the great novel of the century, but I do think it a remarkable book, and I strongly advise anyone who can get hold of a copy to have a look at it.[1]

With *The Wolf at the Door* we are on more familiar ground. In a way it is the exact opposite of *Tropic of Cancer*, for it comes under the heading of "literature of escape." The question always is, of course, where are you escaping to? In this case it is to the fantastic but very detailed universe inhabited by a small child. The story, which Mr. Havelock Ellis, who contributes an introduction, declared to be essentially "a dream," is about a peasant girl, child of desperately poor parents, in northern France soon after the war of 1870. I can best indicate its quality by a quotation:—

"I placed my books, *The Office of the Dead* and *Selected Thoughts from Bossuet*, in front of my seat, and as we knelt the little board reached level with my teeth. Should prayers last too long, I would suck the red off the *Selected Thoughts*, and my lips coloured themselves crimson. That Sunday I bit the wood, I remember particularly the taste of that Chantecroix wood, smacking of resin and covered with the grease of our little hands – and I broke one of my front teeth. . . . "

This kind of thing goes on, in a monstrous turbid stream almost without paragraphs, [for] four hundred pages. There are two things that strike one. First, that one would not expect such a shapeless book from a French writer; second, that shapeless or no it has undoubted power in it. On every page and almost in very line there are little touches like that of the child sucking the colour off the prayer-book, and as a whole the book is a marvel of imaginative reconstruction. Those who like the atmosphere-of-childhood stuff (nothing soppy, either—no tinkling through the Wendy glades) will revel in it. It is hard not to feel that the author could do better if he would trouble to cut and revise. But I am nervous of saying this, partly because all the French critics seem to have hailed the book as a masterpiece, partly because I have not read it in the original.

As to the translation, except for the dialogue, that never-escaped pitfall, it reads so unlike a translation that one may presume it to be a very good one.

1. The Alderman Library, University of Virginia, has a typescript of the portion of this review that deals with *Tropic of Cancer* among its Henry Miller papers. This is not Orwell's typescript but a copy of the printed review.

1936

264. To Leonard Moore

17 January 1936   Handwritten postcard

1 South End Road   Hampstead   NW.3

Dear Mr Moore,

I handed my novel in to Mr Gollancz personally on Wednesday.[1] I would have sent it viâ you as usual, but it was already late & as it had your label on it I thought it would be all right. I heard from Mr Gollancz this morning to say he liked it & was sending it to be vetted by his solicitor.

I have left my address at Lawford Rd., & am not certain where I shall settle down next, but could you send all communications to the above address? They will always be forwarded from there.

Yours sincerely
Eric A Blair

1. The 17th was a Friday, so *Keep the Aspidistra Flying* was delivered to Gollancz on Wednesday, 15 January.

265. 'Rudyard Kipling'

New English Weekly, 23 January 1936

Rudyard Kipling[1] was the only popular English writer of this century who was not at the same time a thoroughly bad writer. His popularity was, of course, essentially middle-class. In the average middle-class family before the War, especially in Anglo-Indian families, he had a prestige that is not even approached by any writer of to-day. He was a sort of household god with whom one grew up and whom one took for granted whether one liked him or whether one did not. For my own part I worshipped Kipling at thirteen, loathed him at seventeen, enjoyed him at twenty, despised him at twenty-five and now again rather admire him. The one thing that was never possible, if one had read him at all, was to forget him. Certain of his stories, for instance *The Strange Ride, Drums of the Fore and Aft* and *The Mark of the Beast*, are about as good as it is possible for that kind of story to be. They are, moreover, exceedingly well told. For the vulgarity of his prose style is only a surface fault; in the less obvious qualities of construction and economy he is supreme. It is, after all (see the "Times Literature° Supplement"), much easier to write inoffensive prose than to tell a good story. And his verse, though it is almost a by-word for badness, has the same peculiarly memorable quality.

> "I've lost Britain, I've lost Gaul,
> "I've lost Rome, and, worst of all,
> "I've lost Lalage!"

may be only a jingle, and *The Road to Mandalay* may be something worse than a jingle, but they do 'stay by one.' They remind one that it needs a streak of genius even to become a by-word.

What is much more distasteful in Kipling than sentimental plots or vulgar tricks of style, is the imperialism to which he chose to lend his genius. The most one can say is that when he made it the choice was more forgivable than it would be now. The imperialism of the 'eighties and 'nineties was sentimental, ignorant and dangerous, but it was not entirely despicable. The picture then called up by the word "empire" was a picture of overworked officials and frontier skirmishes, not of Lord Beaverbrook and Australian butter. It was still possible to be an imperialist and a gentleman, and of Kipling's *personal* decency there can be no doubt. It is worth remembering that he was the most widely popular English writer of our time, and yet that no one, perhaps, so consistently refrained from making a vulgar show of his personality.

If he had never come under imperialist influences, and if he had developed, as he might well have done, into a writer of music-hall songs, he would have been a better and more lovable writer. In the rôle he actually chose, one was bound to think of him, after one had grown up, as a kind of enemy, a man of alien and perverted genius. But now that he is dead, I for one cannot help wishing that I could offer some kind of tribute—a salute of guns, if such a thing were available—to the story-teller who was so important to my childhood.

1. The death of Rudyard Kipling (born 1865) on 18 January 1936 was the occasion for this essay. For Orwell's longer essay on Kipling, published in *Horizon*, February 1942, see *948*.

266. Review of *Night Pieces* by Thomas Burke; *Jagged Skyline* by Mary Dunstan; *Full Circle* by Hilda Lewis; *The Lively Lady* by Kenneth Roberts; *War Paint* by F. V. Morley; *Long Shadows* by Lady Sanderson; *Who Goes Home?* by Richard Curle; *Gaudy Night* by Dorothy Sayers; *The Queen of Spies* by Major Thomas Coulson; *Bright Armour* by Monica Salmond

New English Weekly, 23 January 1936

When is a novel not a novel?

Take almost any serial from "Peg's Paper" or "Violet's Paper," paragraph it in a civilised manner, give it a sophisticated title (this is done by choosing a title that ought to have a "the" in it and then leaving out the "the"), and it will be found to be quite indistinguishable from four-fifths of the things that pass as novels nowadays. As a matter of fact, several of the books on my present list are rather worse than "Peg's Paper," because they are just as infantile and vulgar and have much less vitality. However, with ten books to review I have no space for a jeremiad on the present state of English fiction. So here goes.

Mr. Burke's *Night Pieces* are ghost stories of a rather mild kind. I don't think Mr. Burke is at his best with the supernatural, but *Yesterday Street* is not a bad story. Miss Dunstan's *Jagged Skyline* is romantic—Alps and long-lost half-brothers. *Full Circle* is a very long novel of the miniature saga type, covering two or three generations. It is about Jews, but as these Jews are apparently not kosher and not persecuted for their Jewishness, it might just as well be about Gentiles. There is the inevitable family feud, the inevitable Romeo-Juliet motif, and the inevitable reconciliation when it is too late. A dull, stodgy novel, fairly competently written.

The Lively Lady and *War Paint* are both of them historical novels dealing with approximately the same period—the period of the Napoleonic War. *The Lively Lady* is written by an American. It is blood and thundery stuff about privateering in the war of 1812, and is chiefly interesting as showing that the old-fashioned, nineteenth-century type of American bumptiousness ("The libation of freedom must sometimes be quaffed in blood," etc.) is still going strong. *War Paint*, though written by an Englishman, is also about Americans. It is an exceedingly naïve adventure story, and at the same time a sort of Chelsea Hospital for superannuated jokes. For my own part I don't object to old jokes—indeed, I reverence them. When sea-sickness and adultery have ceased to be funny, Western civilization will have ceased to exist. But with the plot of a story it is a rather different matter; there, I think, we have a right to expect something new. I would like to draw Mr. Morley's attention to a certain chapter in the middle of his book and to a certain story of Conan Doyle's entitled *The Striped Chest*.

After this we take a dive into the sewers of literature. I see no reason to be polite to a book like *Long Shadows*. It is tripe. One quotation should be enough:

" . . . the house was folded in the silence of night, while towards it, all unseen in the darkness, came the spirit of the past, stirred from its long rest and bringing who can say what joy and sorrow to those on whom its shadow should fall?"

Who Goes Home? is perhaps a very little better. It is a mystery-story, and it does work up a faint flicker of interest as to what is going to happen. But what English! It is amazing that people can go on turning out books year after year and yet continue to write so badly. Here for example is a sentence (it has points of interest for the social historian) explaining why the villain was a villain:

"Gore's background was austere and bourgeois, but perhaps long ago there had been some frustrated poet in the family, to say nothing of some would-be swindler or worse, and perhaps their influence had mysteriously fused in him."

The moral would seem to be, never frustrate a poet.

I do not share the opinion expressed in the "Observer" that *Gaudy Night* puts Miss Sayers "definitely among the great writers," but there is no doubt that as far as literary ability goes she is out of the class of the other writers I am considering here. Yet even she, if one looks closely, is not so far removed from "Peg's Paper" as might appear at a casual glance. It is, after all, a very ancient trick to write novels with a lord for a hero. Where Miss Sayers has shown more astuteness than most is in perceiving that you can carry that kind of thing off a great deal better if you pretend to treat it as a joke. By being, on the surface, a little ironical about Lord Peter Wimsey and his noble ancestors, she is enabled to lay on the snobbishness ("his lordship," etc.) much thicker than any overt snob would dare to do. Also, her slickness in writing has blinded many readers to the fact that her stories, considered as detective-stories, are very bad ones. They lack the minimum of probability that even a detective-story ought to have, and the crime is always committed in a way that is incredibly tortuous and quite uninteresting. In *Gaudy Night* Harriet Vane has at last succumbed to Lord Peter's advances. So it is time that Lord Peter, who is now forty-five, settled down and gave up detection. But needless to say he won't. He and his title are a lot too profitable for that. A little bird in a yellow jacket has just whispered to me that next year there will be another corpse in the library and Lord Peter and Harriet (Viscountess Wimsey?) will be off on a fresh quest.

My last two books are not novels, but books about the War. *The Queen of Spies* is the story of Louise de Bettignies, a celebrated spy of the Allies who died in captivity and who, according to Major Coulson, was responsible for warning the French general staff that the great German attack of 1916 was to be directed at Verdun. As usual, bad writing triumphs over interesting material. Major Coulson really ought to steer clear of this kind of thing (it has a paragraph to itself in the book): "Those wounds of the heart, they hurt no less because we cover them with a smile!"

Bright Armour is the history of the experiences of a V.A.D. It is interesting, because it is a plain record of fact, presented by somebody who would probably be incapable of invention. The English is of a badness passing belief. Here is one example:

"I felt keen sorrow at parting with my brilliant hunter Schoolgirl without even seeing her—how bitter it would have been if the whole sum of things had not been so acute."

How could a sum be acute? It sounds like a mixture of arithmetic and geometry. Amateur writers would save themselves and their readers a lot of trouble if they would grasp the very simple rule that one ought never to use the passive voice where the active will do. Lady Salmond seems to take a positive delight in using the passive. Thus when she wants to say that she saw some Zeppelins overhead she says "They were perceived in the dark sky," leaving it uncertain who "perceived" them.

Plenty of people, I imagine would find *Bright Armour* interesting, because it has something definite to relate and gives one an idea of what the War was like from a nurse's point of view. I imagine, too, that detective-story fans will not let *Gaudy Night* pass unread. But as for the other books on this list—no!

267. Changes to Avoid Libel in *Keep the Aspidistra Flying*

Orwell's letter to his agent, Leonard Moore, of 17 January says that the manuscript of *Keep the Aspidistra Flying* was handed in 'to Mr Gollancz' on 15 January, and that Gollancz was 'sending it to be vetted by his solicitor'; see *264*; Harold Rubinstein wrote his report on 20 January, having, evidently, worked through the weekend on vetting the text (according to *Who's Who*, his 'recreation' was 'homework').

Orwell responded on 23 January, although his enclosed notes are dated 21 January; see *268*. The addressee of this letter is not known: Orwell simply wrote 'Dear Sir.' It is probable that Victor Gollancz was not being addressed, for, even though Orwell was put out at having to make changes, he by now addressed Gollancz by name.

Stansky and Abrahams believe Norman Collins handled this matter: 'The novel was scheduled for publication at the beginning of March 1936. Proofs were in hand in January. And then belatedly, someone at Gollancz seems to have subjected the text to the closest scrutiny, for all at once a crisis over the possibility of libel erupted. . . . Once again Orwell found himself in conference with Norman Collins, to whom he had taken a firm dislike—the aftermath, no doubt, of that earlier similar conference over *Burmese Days*—discussing the potentially actionable points that would have to be altered. As before, Orwell yielded to reason—what could one do?' (II, 133)

This may be what happened, though Collins's part in the conference on *Burmese Days* has been exaggerated. The train of events is more complicated.

A letter of 29 January signed by Dorothy Horsman, a director of Victor Gollancz Ltd (see *269, n.1*), told Orwell (whom she addresses as Eric Blair) that she had sent his letter to Rubinstein, and was now sending him Rubenstein's comments, with copies of pages 304, 4 and 6 (her order) of the typescript, for comment and/or alteration. Orwell's reply of 31 January is written on Miss Horsman's letter; see *269*.

The manuscript was presumably then sent for composition, and Orwell went off to the north.

Just over a fortnight later, on 17 February, Collins wrote a conciliatory letter to Orwell asking him to consider further changes. Quite possibly the printer alerted the publisher to danger, for he would be equally liable to punishment under what Collins described as 'the extraordinary laws of this peculiar country.' Collins stressed that he had discussed every point raised 'with Mr Gollancz and we have brought the number of changes down to an irreducible minimum.'

The letter was addressed to 72 Warrington Lane, Wigan. Orwell replied the next day, but from 22 Darlington Street; see *279*. That was no sooner sent than Orwell was asked to make further changes, in the advertising slogans. His telegram of 19 February said this was impossible, see *281*. On 24 February, having already corrected the proofs, he addressed to Gollancz a further series of changes, mainly of advertising matter, in response to a letter from Collins. The same day, he wrote to Moore expressing his anguish at having to make the changes in proof by using the same number of letters; see *284*. Moore received the letter on 25 February and on the 26th wrote to Collins, including the first paragraph of Orwell's letter in its entirety and commenting: 'As you will see, he is by no means unreasonable and I hope next time you will not send the book to press until everything that needs to be done has been done to the typescript.' Collins, playing fair, marked the letter to be seen by Gollancz.

What happened was clearly hard on Orwell, though it is easy today to underestimate the genuine basis for the publisher's anxieties. He simply could not afford even to win a libel or defamation suit, never mind lose one. As Collins put it in his letter to Orwell on 17 February, 'you may have noticed that no fewer than four books have been withdrawn during the past week or so' as a result of actions for libel. It is apparent that there is no question of Collins and Orwell being locked in conference: all was conducted by correspondence.

Certainly Orwell did not get on easily with Collins in years to come, and the seeds for their antipathy were evidently watered by this exchange. See Orwell's letter to Jack Common of 17 March *(295)*, in which he blamed the alterations on Collins.

What really is behind the bitterness Orwell felt is that he had, psychologically, put *Keep the Aspidistra Flying* out of his mind, as any author will do. That changes were belatedly required was bad enough, but perhaps what made the request much more trying was the contrast between seemingly pettifogging legalisms and the harsh reality of what Orwell was seeing in Wigan and his awakening to a world so much harsher than that of Gordon Comstock and the trivialities of Roland Butta. The contrast between the changes he typed out on 24 February and his diary entry for that day—during which he visited the aptly named Crippen mine—is striking. It was hardly surprising that he expressed a sense of outrage when writing to Moore. Details of textual changes are given in *CW*, IV,. 279–87. See also Sheila Hodges, *Gollancz: The Story of a Publishing House, 1928– 1978* (1978), 106–07, especially 107: 'Libel was generally something of a nightmare with Orwell's books. It was not that he was deliberately difficult—on the contrary; but he seems to have had great difficulty in grasping either what constitutes libel in this country, even when the legal position had been clearly explained to him, or the very real dangers involved. *Keep the Aspidistra Flying*, a fierce attack on the evils of mass advertising, is a case in point. The novel was already in page proof before it emerged, quite by accident, that Orwell had been wrong in assuring Gollancz that the firms he took to task in the book were imaginary, or, in those cases where they were real, that he had changed the names so materially that identification was impossible.'

Among Orwell's papers was a copy of an impersonal letter, signed by Victor Gollancz, addressed 'Dear Sir or Madam,' on the subject of libel. This opened by saying that, because some authors were not very clear about the law of libel, an outline of its provisions was being provided. It explained how a living person might be able to claim he or she had been libelled, and also how a company might be libelled. The letter concluded: 'If, in the case of your own book (which we have just accepted for publication) you have any doubt about these points, you should communicate with us at once before the book is set up in type.' It is not possible to tell whether Orwell received this letter in January 1936, after *Keep the Aspidistra Flying* had been accepted and he had assured Gollancz that the firms he took to task were imaginary, or whether he received it after *Coming Up for Air* was delivered in the spring of 1939. It is possible the letter was drafted as a result of Gollancz's experience in publishing *Keep the Aspidistra Flying*.

268. To Victor Gollancz Ltd

23 January 1936   Typewritten

At. 1 South End Road   Hampstead   NW.3[1]

Dear Sir,

Herewith are notes on the alterations I have made in KEEP THE ASPIDISTRA FLYING.[2] I trust all will now be well. If not, I shall be in London for another week, possibly a little less, and could see you if required.

I am sending the MS. under separate registered cover.

Yours faithfully
Eric A. Blair

21.1.36

With ref. to the attached.[3]

p. 4, 6. The only real slogans among those quoted on p. 6 are "Are you a Highbrow? Dandruff is the reason" and "Pyorrhea? Not me!" I suppose it is O.K. to quote these so long as one doesn't comment to the effect that the claims they make are untrue? So I have cut out "exhorting you to rot your guts with this or that synthetic garbage" on p. 4. I don't think that "Foul, bloody things"[4] on p. 6 amounts to comment, does it?

As to the imaginary product "Bovex." Of course I intend one of the meat-extracts that are on the market, but not any particular one. There are Bovril, Oxo, Beefex, Exox and I believe one other, but there isn't one called Bovex. Surely this is safe enough? Now that the remark about "garbage" is cut out there is no comment on the quality of the things advertised, only a protest against the whole business of advertisement.

p. 9. Have got the° rid of the word "garbage."

p. 14. This is the sort of comment one makes anywhere in a review.

p. 25. By "papery smoke" I meant smoke tasting of paper. I have altered it to "acrid smoke."

p. 29. *All* the characters are quite imaginary. Could put the usual note to this effect at the beginning if desired.

p. 48. The epitaph is quite imaginary. As to the name, it seems to me there is the same danger about all names.

pp. 65–66. These are the *sort* of advertisements you see in Peg's Paper, Violet's Paper etc. The only ones I have actually seen are "The Truth about Bad Legs" and "Drink Habit conquered in Three Days." Surely one has the right to quote these if one doesn't comment? I have cut out the implied comment in "descended to" and "sneaky." The "Drink Habit conquered" people were among those exposed in "Secret Remedies."

pp. 67, 73. Reference to Clark's College cut out. Also the word "arse-wipers" cut out as it might be objected to.

p. 120. See note on p. 29.

p. 163. "Defiled with" (posters) altered to "dotted with."

pp. 183–185. I altered certain passages here in Mr Gollancz's office and I think he has now no objection.

p. 250. Have altered this so that no particular locality is pointed to. My late employer is *not* "the original of Mr McKechnie." But in any case he has no objection.

p. 263. See note on p. 29. So far as I know there is no bookshop in the Waterloo Road and in any case it is an unlikely locality for a "rare" bookshop. But I took care not to say in what part of the Waterloo Road (which is a long road) the bookshop was.

p. 273. See note on p. 29.

p. 304. I have dealt with this in connection with pp. 4, 6.[5]

p. 323. Reference to Drage's and Times Furnishing Co. cut out.

1. This letter is written as from Booklovers' Corner. Between this date and the end of January, Orwell gave up his flat at 50 Lawford Road, Kentish Town, because he was about to journey north, to Wigan, on 31 January.
2. See Textual Note to *CW*, IV. for details of changes made.
3. Meaning 'attached' to this letter.
4. On page 6 of the typescript sent to Orwell for reference, these three words are marked for deletion; the deletion sign is probably not Orwell's. A further attempt was made to obtain his approval for this deletion on 11 March 1936; see *292*.
5. But see *269, n.2.*

269. To Dorothy Horsman

[31 January 1936]   Handwritten

Dorothy Horsman[1] wrote to Orwell on 29 January 1936, enclosing Rubinstein's reply to Orwell's letter of 23 January and copies of pages 4, 6, and 304; she asked for Orwell's comments. What concerned Rubinstein was that the Bovex advertisement referred to on 304 of the typescript (*CW*, IV, 257) was 'on entirely different lines from the Bovex advertisement quoted in the earlier pages,' 4 and 6 (*CW*, IV, 4, 5).[2] Orwell, evidently in great haste, since he was leaving for his journey north on the 31st, simply annotated Miss Horsman's letter as follows and returned all the correspondence to her.

This is perfectly all right. The advert. on p. 304 is not based on any identifiable advert. or any real advert. whatever. I don't think there is the slightest need to alter it.

I am leaving London today, but letters addressed to 1 South End Road, Hampstead NW.3, will be forwarded.

E A. Blair

1. Dorothy Horsman had been Victor Gollancz's secretary at Ernest Benn Ltd. When Gollancz founded his own company in October 1927, Horsman joined him as production manager. 'She was a tower of strength, working early and late and dealing calmly and with immense efficiency, until her retirement in 1961, with every detail of the production, as she did with the thunderstorms that frequently broke over her head.' She became a director, and when Gollancz was ill in the summer of 1943, was appointed joint assistant managing director. (See Sheila Hodges, *Gollancz*, 17, 21, and 155.)
2. The doggerel ballad Orwell wrote for the advertisement showing 'a horribly eupeptic family, with grinning ham-pink faces' (*CW*, IV, 257) was a genre popular in the advertising of the time. The description of the family and the ballad were allowed to stand.

270. *The Road to Wigan Pier* Diary

31 January–25 March 1936

Orwell kept a diary and made a large number of notes to assist him in writing *The Road to Wigan Pier*. These notes, mainly drawn from printed sources, are in Appendix 2, see *345* to *355*. The diary is not given en bloc; each day is placed in chronological order with surviving letters of the period and the review published in *New English Weekly* of 5 March. This enables the irritations arising from changes demanded in *Keep the Aspidistra Flying* to be associated directly with the events of the day on which he responded, as does his letter to Moore of 24 February 1936; see *284*.

When a letter and a diary entry have the same date, the entry is placed last, following the convention that a diary is written last thing at night. The entries, here in sloped, or inclined, roman type, are from a typewritten text, probably made by Orwell, after his move to Wallington in April (see *297, n. 1*), from entries handwritten at the time of the events described. It is possible that he typed them during his 'tour,' using the typewriter on which he typed his letters, but the typescript is in two separately paginated sections (1–36 for 31 January to 5 March inclusive; 1–25, with the heading 'Diary,' for the remainder), so later typing is more probable. The manner of the change to 'slum Corporation houses' (see *287, n. 6*) suggests Orwell's typing, but the footnote added to the entry of 18 March 1936 (see *296*) might lend support to typing by someone else, or by Orwell and another (Eileen ?). The more important handwritten emendations to the typescript, all in Orwell's hand, are given in the notes. Spelling and typing idiosyncracies that may be Orwell's have not been changed (but are marked with °); minor typing slips have been corrected silently as elsewhere. For the financial arrangements for this journey, see *341*.

Orwell drew a map of this journey. As a help in relating with each other the places he visited, it is given first here, although it must have been prepared later.

For this period, see Crick, 277–312; Stansky and Abrahams, II, 133–96 and, in *Orwell Remembered*: Humphrey Dakin, 'The Brother-in-Law Strikes Back'; Joe Kennan, 'With the Wigan Miners'; May Deiner, 'A Visit to Liverpool'; Sydney Smith, 'On a Street Corner in Wigan'; 'Jack Common's Recollections' (which cover a longer period). *The World of George Orwell* contains Ian Hamilton's 'Along the Road to Wigan Pier' (illustrated). Peter Lewis illustrates the original Wigan Pier and Orwell's first lodgings in Wigan (72 Warrington Lane) in *George Orwell: The Road to 1984*. See also Beatrice Campbell, *Wigan Pier Revisited: Poverty and Politics in the 1980s* (1983).

271. Orwell's Sketch Map of his Journey to the North

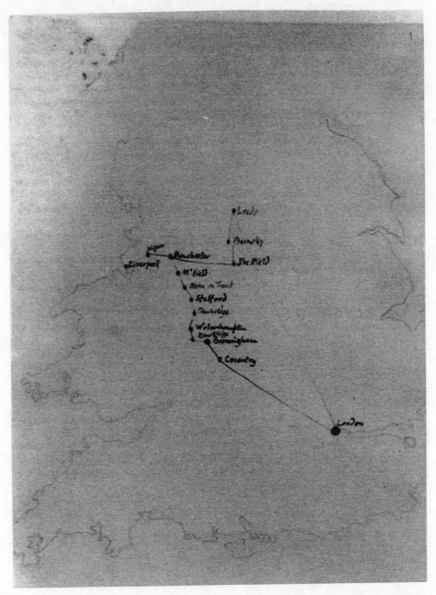

272. *The Road to Wigan Pier Diary*

31.1.36. *To Coventry by train as arranged, arriving about 4 pm. Bed and Breakfast house, very lousy, 3/6. Framed certificate in hall setting forth that (John Smith) had been elected to the rank of Primo Buffo. Two beds in room—charge for room[1] to yourself 5/–. Smell as in common lodging houses. Half-witted servant girl with huge body, tiny head and rolls of fat at back of neck curiously recalling ham-fat.*
1.2.36. *Lousy breakfast with Yorkshire commercial traveller. Walked 12 miles to outskirts of Birmingham, took bus to Bull Ring (very like Norwich Market) and arrived 1 pm. Lunch in Birmingham and bus to Stourbridge. Walked 4-5 miles to Clent Youth Hostel. Red soil everywhere. Birds courting a little, cock chaffinches and bullfinches very bright and cock partridge making mating call. Except for village of Meridew, hardly a decent house between Coventry and Birmingham. West of Birmingham the usual villa-civilization creeping out over the hills. Raining all day, on and off.*

Distance walked, 16 miles. Spent on conveyances, 1/4. On food, 2/3.
2.2.36. *Comfortable night in hostel, which I had to myself. One-storey wooden building with huge coke stove which kept it very hot. You pay 1/– for bed, 2d for the stove and put pennies in the gas for cooking. Bread, milk etc. on sale at hostel. You have to have your own sleeping bag but get blankets, mattress and pillows. Tiring evening because the warden's son, I suppose out of kindness, came across and played ping-pong with me till I could hardly stand on my feet. In the morning long talk with the warden who keeps poultry and collects glass and pewter. He told me how in France in 1918, on the heels of the retreating Germans, he looted some priceless glass which was discovered and looted from him in turn by his divisional general. Also showed me some nice pieces of pewter and some very curious Japanese pictures, showing clear traces of European influence, looted by his father in some naval expedition about 1860.*

Left 10 am., walked to Stourbridge, took bus to Wolverhampton, wandered about slummy parts of Wolverhampton for a while, then had lunch and walked 10 miles to Penkridge. Wolverhampton seems frightful place. Everywhere vistas of mean little houses still enveloped in drifting smoke, though this was Sunday, and along the railway line huge banks of clay and conical chimneys ("pot-banks.") Walk from W'ton to Penkridge very dull and raining all the way. Villa-civilization stretches almost unbroken between the two towns. In Penkridge about 4.30 halted for cup of tea. A tiny frouzy parlour with a nice fire, a little wizened oldish man and an enormous woman about 45, with tow-coloured bobbed hair and no front teeth. Both of them thought me a hero to be walking on such a day. Had tea with them en famille. About 5.15 left and walked another couple of miles, then caught buss° the remaining 4 miles to Stafford. Went to Temperance Hotel thinking this would be cheap, but bed and breakfast 5/–. The usual dreadful room and twill sheets greyish and smelly as usual. Went to bathroom and found commercial traveller developing snapshots in bath. Persuaded him to remove them and had bath, after which I find myself very footsore.

Distance walked, about 16 miles. Spent on conveyances, 1/5. On food, 2/8½.

<u>3.2.36.</u> *Left 9 am. and took bus to Hanley. Walked round Hanley and part of Burslem. Frightfully cold, bitter wind, and it had been snowing in the night; blackened snow lying about everywhere. Hanley and Burslem about the most dreadful places I have seen. Labyrinths of tiny blackened houses and among them the pot-banks like monstrous burgundy bottles half buried in the soil, belching forth smoke. Signs of poverty everywhere and very poor shops. In places enormous chasms delved out, one of them about 200 yards wide and about as deep, with rusty iron trucks on a chain railway crawling up one side, and here and there on the almost perpendicular face of the other, a few workmen hanging like samphire-gatherers, cutting into the face with their picks apparently aimlessly, but I suppose digging out clay. Walked on to Eldon and lunch at pub there. Frightfully cold. Hilly country, splendid views, especially when one gets further east and hedges give way to stone walls. Lambs here seem much more backward than down south. Walked on to Rudyard Lake.*

Rudyard Lake (really a reservoir, supplying the pottery towns) very depressing. In the summer it is a pleasure resort. Cafes, houseboats and pleasure-boats every ten yards, all deserted and flyblown, this being the off-season. Notices relating to fishing, but I examined the water and it did not look to me as though it had any fish in it. Not a soul anywhere and bitter wind blowing. All the broken ice had been blown up to the south end, and the waves were rocking it up and down, making a clank-clank, clank-clank—the most melancholy noise I ever heard. (Mem. to use in novel some time and to have an empty Craven A packet bobbing up and down among the ice.)

Found hostel, about 1 mile further on, with difficulty. Alone again. A most peculiar place this time. A great draughty barrack of a house, built in the sham-castle style— somebody's Folly—about 1860. All but three or four of the rooms quite empty. Miles of echoing stone passages, no lighting except candles and only smoky little oilstoves to cook on. Terribly cold.

Only 2/8d left, so tomorrow must go into Manchester (walk to Macclesfield, then bus) and cash cheque.

Distance walked, 12 miles. Spent on conveyances 1/8. On food, 2/8½d.

<u>4.2.36.</u> *Got out of bed so cold that I could not do up any buttons and had to [go] down and thaw my hands before I could dress. Left about 10.30 am. A marvellous morning. Earth frozen hard as iron, not a breath of wind and the sun shining brightly. Not a soul stirring. Rudyard lake (about 1½ miles long) had frozen over during the night. Wild ducks walking about disconsolately on the ice. The sun coming up and the light slanting along the ice the most wonderful red-gold colour I have ever seen. Spent a long time throwing stones over the ice. A jagged stone skimming across ice makes exactly the same sound as a redshank whistling.*

Walked to Macclesfield, 10 or 11 miles, then bus to Manchester. Went and collected letters, then to bank to cash cheque but found they were shut—they shut at 3 pm here. Very awkward as I had only 3d in hand. Went to Youth Hostel headquarters and asked them to cash cheque, but they refused, then to

Police Station to ask them to introduce me to a solicitor who would cash a cheque, but they also refused. Frightfully cold. Streets encrusted with mounds of dreadful black stuff which was really snow frozen hard and blackened by smoke. Did not want to spend night in streets. Found my way to poor quarter (Chester Street), went to pawnshop and tried to pawn raincoat but they said they did not take them any longer. Then it occurred to me my scarf was pawnable, and they gave me 1/11d on it. Went to common lodging house, of which there were three close together in Chester Street.

Long letter from Rees advising me about people to go and see, one of them, luckily, in Manchester.

Distance walked, about 13 miles. Spent on conveyances, 2/–. On food, 10d.

<u>5.2.36.</u> *Went and tried to see Meade but he was out. Spent day in common lodging house. Much as in London. 11d for bed, cubicles not dormitories. The "deputy" a cripple as they seem so often to be. Dreadful method here of making tea in tin bowls. Cashed cheque in morning but shall stay tonight in lodging house and go and see Meade tomorrow.*

6–10.2.36. *Staying with the Meades[2] at 49 Brynton Rd., Longsight, Manchester. Brynton Rd. is in one of the new building estates. Very decent houses with bathrooms and electric light, rent I suppose about 12/– or 14/–. Meade is some kind of Trade Union Official and has something to do with the editing of Labour's Northern Voice—these are the people who do the publishing side of the Adelphi. The M.s have been very decent to me. Both are working-class people, speak with Lancashire accents and have worn the clogs in their childhood, but the atmosphere in a place like this is entirely middle-class. Both the M.s were faintly scandalised to hear I had been in the common lodging house in Manchester. I am struck again by the fact that as soon as a working man gets an official post in the Trade Union or goes into Labour politics, he becomes middle-class whether he will or no. ie. by fighting against the bourgeoisie he becomes a bourgeois. The fact is that you cannot help living in the manner appropriate and developing the ideology appropriate to your income (in M's case I suppose about £4 a week.) The only quarrel I have with the M.s is that they call me "comrade." Mrs M., as usual, does not understand much about politics but has adopted her husband's views as a wife ought to; she pronounces the word "comrade" with manifest discomfort. Am struck by the difference of manners even as far north as this. Mrs M. is surprised and not altogether approving when I get up when she enters the room, offer to help with the washing-up, etc. She says, "Lads up here expect to be waited on."*

M. sent me across to Wigan to see Joe Kennan, an electrician who takes a prominent part in the Socialist movement. Kennan also lives in a decent Corporation house (Beech Hill Building Estate) but is more definitely a working man. A very short, stout, powerful man with an extraordinarily gentle, hospitable manner and very anxious to help. His elder child was upstairs in bed (scarlet fever suspected) the younger on the floor playing with soldiers and a toy cannon. Kennan smiles and says, "You see—and I'm supposed to be a pacifist." He sent me to the N.U.W.M.[3] shelter with a letter to the secretary asking him to find me a lodging in Wigan. The shelter is a dreadful ramshackle little place but a godsend to these unemployed men as it is warm and there are newspapers etc. there. The secretary, Paddy Grady, an unemployed miner. A tall lean man about 35, intelligent and well-informed and very anxious to help. He is a single man getting 17/– bob° a week and is in a dreadful state physically from years of underfeeding and idleness. His front teeth are almost entirely rotted away. All the men at the N.U.W.M very friendly and anxious to supply me with information as soon as they heard I was a writer and collecting facts about working-class conditions. I cannot get them to treat me precisely as an equal, however. They call me either "Sir" or "Comrade."

1. *room*] *bed; handwritten emendation*
2. Frank Meade was an official of the Amalgamated Society of Woodworkers. He ran the Manchester office of *The Adelphi* and was business manager of *Labour's Northern Voice*, organ of the Independent Socialist Party.
3. National Unemployed Workers' Movement.

273. To Christy & Moore

11 February 1936   Handwritten

72 Warrington Lane   Wigan   Lancs.

Dear Sir,
The above will be my address till further notice (probably for about the next four weeks.)[1]

Yours faithfully
Eric A. Blair

1. This was the home of Mr. and Mrs. Hornby (illustrated in Lewis, 51). According to Crick their real names were John and Lily Anderton (281).

274. *The Road to Wigan Pier* Diary

<u>11.2.36.</u> *Staying at 72 Warrington Lane, Wigan. Board and lodging 25/– a week. Share room with another lodger (unemployed railwayman), meals in kitchen and wash at scullery sink. Food all right but indigestible and in monstrous quantities. Lancashire method of eating tripe (cold with vinegar) horrible.*
   The family. Mr Hornby, aged 39, has worked in the pit since he was 13. Now out of work for nine months. A largish, fair, slow-moving, very mild and nice-mannered man who considers carefully before he answers when you ask him a question, and begins, "In my estimation." Has not much accent. Ten years ago he got a spurt of coal dust in his left eye and practically lost the sight of it. Was put to work "on top" for a while but went back to the pit as he

could earn more there. Nine months ago his other eye went wrong (there is something called "nyastygmus"[1] or some such name that miners suffer from) and he can only see a few yards. Is on "compensation" of 29/– a week, but they are talking of putting him on "partial compensation" of 14/– a week. It all depends whether the doctor passes him as fit for work, though of course there would not be any work, except perhaps a job "on top," but there are very few of these. If he is put on partial compensation he can draw the dole until his stamps are exhausted.

Mrs Hornby. Four years older than her husband. Less that 5 feet tall. Toby-jug figure. Merry disposition. Very ignorant—adds up 27 and 10 and makes it 31. Very broad accent. There seem to be 2 ways of dealing with the "the" here. Before consonants it is often ommitted° altogether ("Put joog on table," etc.) before vowells° it is often incorporated with the word. eg. "My sister's in thospital"—th as in thin.

The son "our Joe," just turned 15 and has been working in the pit a year. At present is on night shift. Goes to work about 9 pm returns between 7 and 8 am, has breakfast and promptly goes to bed in bed vacated by another lodger. Usually sleeps till 5 or 6 pm He started work on 2/8 a day, was raised to 3/4, ie. £ a week. Out of this 1/8 a week comes off for stoppages (insurance etc.) and 4d a day for his tram fares to and from the pit. So his net wage, working full time, is 16/4 a week. In summer, however, he will only be working short-time. A tallish, frail, deadly pale youth, obviously much exhausted by his work, but seems fairly happy.

Tom, Mrs Hornby's cousin, unmarried and lodging there—paying 25/– a week. A very hairy man with a hare-lip, mild disposition and very simple. Also on night shift.

Joe, another lodger, single. Unemployed on 17/–*a week. Pays 6/– a week for his room and sees to his own food. Gets up about 8 to give his bed up to "our Joe" and remains out of doors, in Public Library etc., most of day. A bit of an ass but has some education and enjoys a resounding phrase. Explaining why he never married, he says portentously, "Matrimonial chains is a big item." Repeated this sentence a number of times, evidently having an affection for it. Has been totally unemployed for 7 years. Drinks when he gets the chance, which of course he never does nowadays.

The house has two rooms and scullery downstairs, 3 rooms upstairs, tiny back yard and outside lavatory. No hot water laid on. Is in bad repair—front wall is bulging. Rent 12/– and with[2] rates 14/–. The total income of the Hornbys is:

Mr Hornby's compensation	29/– a week	
Joe's wages	16/4	"
Tom's weekly payment	25/–	"
Joe's ditto	6/–	"
Total	£3-16-4.	

* 15–? [Orwell's handwritten footnote]

Payment of rent and rates leaves £3-2-4. This has to feed 4 people and clothe and otherwise provide for 3.* Of course at present there is my own contribution as well but that is an abnormality.

Wigan in the centre does not seem as bad as it has been represented—distinctly less depressing than Manchester. Wigan Pier said to have been demolished. Clogs commonly worn here and general in the smaller places outside such as Hindley. Shawl over head commonly worn by older women, but girls evidently only do it under pressure of dire poverty. Nearly everyone one sees very badly dressed and youths on the corners markedly less smart and rowdy than in London, but no very obvious signs of poverty except the number of empty shops. One in three of registered workers said to be unemployed.

Last night to Co-Op hall with various people from the N.U.W.M. to hear Wal Hannington³ speak. A poor speaker, using all the padding and cliches of the Socialist orator, and with the wrong kind of cockney accent (once again, though a Communist entirely a bourgeois), but he got the people well worked up. Was surprised by the amount of Communist feeling here. Loud cheers when Hannington announced that if England and U.S.S.R went to war U.S.S.R would win. Audience very rough and all obviously un-employed (about 1 in 10 of them women) but very attentive. After the address a collection taken for expenses—hire of hall and H.'s train-fare from London. £1-6-0 raised—not bad from about 200 unemployed people.⁴

You can always tell a miner by the blue tattooing of coal dust on the bridge of his nose. Some of the older men have their foreheads veined with it like Roquefort cheese.

<u>12.2.36.</u> *Terribly cold. Long walk along the canal (one-time site of Wigan Pier) towards some slag-heaps in the distance. Frightful landscape of slag-heaps and belching chimneys. Some of the slag-heaps almost like mountains—one just like Stromboli. Bitter wind. They had had to send a steamer to break the ice in front of the coal barges on the canal. The bargemen were muffled to the eyes in sacks. All the "flashes" (stagnant pools made by the subsidence of disused pits) covered with ice the colour of raw umber. Beards of ice on the lock gates. A few rats running slowly through the snow, very tame, presumably weak with hunger.*

---

* *The H.s are well-off by local standards* [Orwell's handwritten footnote].

1. Eye astigmatism?
2. with] *handwritten insertion*
3. Walter Hannington (1895–) was a leader of the NUWM and author of *Unemployed Struggles 1919–1936* and *The Problem of the Distressed Areas*, which was published by the Left Book Club in November 1937. Like *The Road to Wigan Pier*, it had a centre section of thirty-two plates. Reg Reynolds, one of Orwell's pacifist friends (see *1060, n. 1*), writing of his sympathy with the Hunger Marchers, observed that when they arrived at Hyde Park Corner, London, they 'did not look at all hungry—least of all that stout Communist, Wal Hannington, who led them' (*My Life and Crimes*, 1956, 106).
4. £1.6s equals 312 old pence; 130 new pence.

275. To Leonard Moore

13 February 1936   Handwritten

72 Warrington Lane   Wigan   Lancs.

Dear Mr Moore,

I don't know whether you have had a proof of "Keep the A. flying"—you said you would want one for purposes of dealing with American publishers. Gollancz sent me two sets, owing to uncertainty about my address, so I am forwarding one copy to you. I haven't corrected it & may make a few alterations to the text, but only minor ones.

When it comes out I suppose I shall get 6 copies as usual. Could you get me 3 extra copies at cost price? Did anything transpire about the copies of "A Clergyman's Daughter" with Harper's? Or perhaps they haven't published it yet?[1]

The above address will find me for the next 3 or 4 weeks. I am having a most interesting time & picking up a lot of information.

Yours sincerely
Eric A. Blair

1. It was published by Harper & Brothers in New York on 17 August 1936.

276. *The Road to Wigan Pier* Diary

13.2.36.   *Housing conditions in Wigan terrible. Mrs H. tells me that at her brother's house (he is only 25, so I think he must be her half brother, but he has already a child of 8), 11 people, 5 of them adults, belonging to 3 different families, live in 4 rooms, "2 up 2 down."*

All the miners I meet have either had serious accidents themselves or have friends or relatives who have. Mrs Hornby's cousin had his back broken by a fall of rock—"And he lingered seven year afore he died and it were a-punishing of him all the while"—and her brother in law fell 1200 feet down the shaft of a new pit. Apparently he bounced from side to side, so was presumably dead before he got to the bottom. Mrs H. adds: "They wouldn't never have collected t'pieces only he were wearing a new suit of oilskins."

277. To Cyril Connolly

14 February 1936   Handwritten

72 Warrington Lane   Wigan   Lancashire

Dear Connolly,[1]

I was sorry I missed seeing you again before leaving London. When is your novel[2] coming out? I will write to the Obelisk Press[3] (by the way you might tell me their address) & ask for a copy, & then I expect I can either review it or

425

get it reviewed for the New English Weekly. Not that that gives one much of a boost, but every little helps. Possibly also the Adelphi, but this I doubt, as they now fight shy of everything that hasn't a political implication.

I am living here with a family of coal-miners, employed & unemployed. After staying a month in Lancs. I intend to go on to Yorkshire or Durham or both & have a look at the mines & miners there. I haven't been down any coal mines yet but am arranging to do so. The miners here are very nice people, very warm-hearted & willing to take one for granted. I would like to stay a good long time in the North, 6 months or a year, only it means being away from my girl & also I shall have to come back & do some work after about a couple of months. I am just correcting the proofs of my novel,[4] which should be out in about a month I suppose; otherwise not doing any work, as it is impossible in these surroundings.

I suppose you heard about Alan Clutton-Brock's wife?[5] A bad job, & he has two small kids, too.

Yours
Eric A. Blair

P.S. [at top, to the left] This address will find me for about 3 weeks, not longer.[6]

1. Cyril Connolly was a friend of Orwell's since their time at St Cyprian's and Eton; see *1, n. 1*.
2. *The Rock Pool*. Reviewed by Orwell in the *New English Weekly*, 23 July 1936; see *321*.
3. Obelisk Press was a publishing house run from Paris between the two World Wars by Jack Kahane (see *600, n. 51*). He published books in English for the continental market, many of which, considered too risky for English publishers to handle, became minor classics. See also *565, 12.8.39, n. 2*.
4. *Keep the Aspidistra Flying*.
5. Alan Francis Clutton-Brock (c. 1903–1976) was a contemporary of Orwell's at Eton, art critic of *The Times*, and from 1955 to 1958 Slade Professor of Fine Art at Cambridge. His wife had been killed in a car accident.
6. In fact, Orwell left 72 Warrington Lane the next day, when Mrs. Hornby was taken ill and went into hospital. Lodgings were found for Orwell over the infamous tripe shop described in *The Road to Wigan Pier* (chapter 1). This is usually taken to be at 22 Darlington Street, Wigan; see Crick, 282, which gives supporting evidence. However, Sydney Smith (b. 1909) argues that it was 35 Sovereign Street; lodgers lived in 33, next door. See *Orwell Remembered*, 136–39, for Smith's memories and the headnote, in which Crick mentions the different address. In the absence of more positive evidence, he considers 22 Darlington Street to be the setting for the opening of *The Road to Wigan Pier*. Orwell addressed his letters from 22 Darlington Street.

278. *The Road to Wigan Pier* Diary

15.2.36. *Went with N.U.W.M. collectors on their rounds with a view to collecting facts about housing conditions, especially in the caravans. Have made notes on these, Q.V.[1] What chiefly struck me was the expression on some of the women's faces, especially those in the more crowded caravans. One woman had a face like a death's head. She had a look of absolutely intolerable misery and degradation. I gathered that she felt as I would feel if I were coated all over with dung. All the people however seemed to take these conditions quite for granted. They have been promised houses over and over again but nothing has come of it and they have got into the way of thinking that a livable house is something absolutely unattainable.*

Passing up a horrible squalid side-alley, saw a woman, youngish but very pale and with the usual draggled exhausted look, kneeling by the gutter outside a house and poking a stick up the leaden waste-pipe, which was blocked. I thought how dreadful a destiny it was to be kneeling in the gutter in a back-alley in Wigan, in the bitter cold, prodding a stick up a blocked drain. At that moment she looked up and caught my eye, and her expression was as desolate as I have ever seen; it struck me that she was thinking just the same thing as I was.[2]

Changing lodgings as Mrs H. is ill with some mysterious malady and ordered into hospital. They have found lodgings for me at 22 Darlington Rd.,[3] over a tripe shop where they take in lodgers.[4] The husband an ex-miner (age 58) the wife ill with a weak heart, in bed on sofa in kitchen. Social atmosphere much as at the H.s but house appreciably dirtier and very smelly. A number of other lodgers. An old ex-miner, age about 75, on old age pension plus half a crown weekly from parish (12/6 in all.) Another, said to be of superior type and "come down in the world," more or less bedridden. An Irish ex-miner who had shoulder blade and several ribs crushed by a fall of stone a few years ago and lives on disability pension of about 25/– a week. Of distinctly superior type and started off as a clerk but went "down pit" because he was big and strong and could earn more as a miner (this was before the War.) Also some newspaper canvassers. Two for John Bull,[5] distinctly motheaten, ages about 40 and 55, one quite young and was for four years in rubber firm in Calcutta. Cannot quite make this lad out. He puts on Lancashire accent when talking to the others (he belongs locally) but to me talks in the usual "educated" accent. The family apart from the Forrests themselves consists of a fat son who is at work somewhere and lives nearby, his wife Maggie who is in the shop nearly all day, their two kids, and Annie, fiancée of the other son who is in London. Also a daughter in Canada (Mrs F. says "at Canada.") Maggie and Annie do practically the whole work of the house and shop. Annie very thin, overworked (she also works in a dress-sewing place) and obviously unhappy. I gather that the marriage is by no means certain to take place but that Mrs F. treats Annie as a relative all the same and that Annie groans under her tyranny. Number of rooms in the house exclusive of shop premises, 5 or six and a bathroom-W.C. Nine people sleeping here. Three in my room besides myself.

Struck by the astonishing ignorance about and wastefulness of food among the working class people here—more even than in the south, I think. One morning when washing in the H.s' scullery made an inventory of the following food: A piece of bacon about 5 pounds. About 2 pounds of shin of beef. About a pound and a half of liver (all of these uncooked.) The wreck of a monstrous meat pie (Mrs H. when making a pie always made it in an enamelled basin such as is used for washing up in. Ditto with puddings.) A dish containing 15 or 20 eggs. A number of small cakes. A flat fruit pie and a "cake-a-pie" (pastry with currants in it.) Various fragments of earlier pies. 6 large loaves and 12 small ones (I had seen Mrs H. cook these the night before.)

427

Various odds and ends of butter, tomatoes, opened tins of milk etc. There was also more food keeping warm in the oven in the kitchen. Everything except bread habitually left about uncovered and shelves filthy. Food here consists almost entirely of bread and starch. A typical day's meals at the H.s'. Breakfast (about 8 am): Two fried eggs and bacon, bread (no butter) and tea. Dinner (about 12.30 pm): A monstrous plate of stewed beef, dumplings and boiled potatoes (equal to about 3 Lyons portions) and a big helping of rice pudding or suet pudding. Tea (about 5 pm): A plate of cold meat, bread and butter, sweet pastries and tea. Supper (about 11 pm): fish and chips, bread and butter and tea.

16.2.36. *Great excitement because a couple who stayed here for a month about Xmas have been arrested (at Preston) as coiners and it is believed they were making their false coins while here. The police inspector here for about an hour asking questions. Mrs F. tells of snooping round their room while they were out and finding a lump of something like solder under the mattress and some little pots like egg-cups only larger. Mrs F. agreed instantly to everything the police inspector suggested, and when he was upstairs searching the room I made two suggestions and she agreed to those too. I could see she had made up her mind they were guilty on hearing they were unmarried. When the inspector had written out her statement it came out that she could not read or write (except her signature), though her husband can read a little.*

One of the canvassers' beds is jammed across the foot of mine. Impossible to stretch my legs out straight as if I do so my feet are in the small of his back. It seems a long time since I slept between linen sheets. Twill sheets even at the M.s. Theirs (the M.s') was the only house I have been in since leaving London that did not smell.

17.2.36. *The newspaper-canvassers are rather pathetic. Of course it is a quite desperate job. I fancy what John Bull do is to take on people who make frantic efforts and work up a little more or less spurious business for a while, then sack them and take on more, and so on. I should judge these men each make £2 or £3 a week. Both have families and one is a grandfather. They are so hard up that they cannot pay for full board but pay something for their rooms and have a squalid little cupboard of food in the kitchen, from which they take out bread, packets of marg. etc and cook themselves meals in a shamefaced manner. They are allocated so many houses each day and have to knock at every door and book a minimum number of orders. They are at present working some swindle on behalf of John Bull by which you get a "free" tea set by sending two shillings worth of stamps and twenty four coupons. As soon as they have had their food they start filling up blank forms for the next day, and presently the older one falls asleep in his chair and begins snoring loudly.*

Am struck, though, by their knowledge of working-class conditions. They can tell you all about housing, rents, rates, state of trade etc. in every town in the north of England.

---

1. 'Which see.' For Orwell's notes on the caravan dwellers, see 346, *Wigan, Housing*.

2. For a slightly different version of this 'epiphany,' see *The Road to Wigan Pier*, *CW*, V, 14–15, where Orwell describes himself as seeing the woman from a train bearing him away from the 'monstrous scenery of slag-heaps.'
3. 'Rd.' typed in error for Street.
4. *lodgers*] *lodgings*; *handwritten emendation*
5. *John Bull* was a popular weekly founded in 1906 and initially edited by Horatio Bottomley (1860–1933), who, describing himself during World War I as 'The Soldier's Friend,' campaigned for Ramsay MacDonald (later prime minister) to be imprisoned; but it was Bottomley who was imprisoned, for fraud. His journal specialised in sensationalism and competitions for relatively large prizes. Publication ceased in 1960.

279. To Norman Collins

18 February 1936   Handwritten

On 17 February, Norman Collins, as Deputy Chairman of Victor Gollancz Ltd, wrote to Orwell requesting more changes in *Keep the Aspidistra Flying*. Orwell annotated Collins's letter and returned it to Victor Gollancz himself on 24 February; see *283* for his annotations. He replied to Collins as follows:

22 Darlington Street   Wigan   Lancs

Dear Sir,

With reference to your letter, I will do what I can short of ruining the book altogether. But there are one or two things I cannot possibly change:

i. References to "Mr McKechnie". "Mr McKechnie" is *not* a portrait of any real person. As I had been working in a bookshop I thought the idea might cross Mr Gollancz's mind that I intended a portrait of my late employer, & for this reason alone I said it might be better if my employer O.K'd the passages referring to the bookshop. It was not because any portrait was intended, but merely to set Mr Gollancz's mind at rest. In the book "Mr McKechnie" is described as an old man with white hair & beard who is a teetotaller & takes snuff.

My late employer (Mr F. G. Westrope, 1 South End Rd. Hampstead NW.3) is a middle-aged clean-shaven man who is not a teetotaller & never takes snuff. In any case I know him far too well to suppose he would take any action even if he imagined himself to be caricatured. If you really wish I will get him to furnish a written undertaking not to bring a libel action.

ii. The word "sod." I really cannot cut this out. I have used it in all my books before. A book like, for instance, Robert Graves's "Goodbye to All That," which was a best-seller, used "sod" freely.

iii. The passage about "Come here, not a bad mouth," etc. I can't see any harm in this. Of course if the public read dirty meanings into it, so much the worse, but you can read dirty meanings into anything.

The above address will find me for the next 10 days.

Yours faithfully
Eric A Blair

280. *The Road to Wigan Pier* Diary

<u>18.2.36.</u> In the early morning the mill girls clumping down the cobbled street, all in clogs, make a curiously formidable sound, like an army hurrying into battle. I suppose this is the typical sound of Lancashire. And the typical imprint in the mud the outline of a clog-iron, like one half of a cow's hoof. Clogs are very cheap. They cost about 5/– a pair and need not wear out for years because all they need is new irons costing a few pence.

As always and everywhere, the dress peculiar to the locality is considered plebeian. A very down in the mouth respectable woman, at one of the houses I visited with the N.U.W.M. collectors, said:

"I've always kept myself decent-like. I've never worn a shawl over my head—I wouldn't be seen in such a thing. I've worn a hat since I was a girl. But it don't do you much good. At Christmas time we was that hard put to it that I thought I'd go up and try for a well-wisher. (Hamper given away by some charitable organisation.) When I got up there the clergyman says to me, 'You don't want no well-wisher;' he says. 'There's plenty worse than you. We knows many a one that's living on bread and jam,' he says. 'And how do you know what *we're* living on?' I says. He says, 'You can't be so bad if you can dress as well as that,' he says—meaning my hat. I didn't get no well-wisher. If I'd ha' gone up with a shawl over my head I'd ha' got it. That's what you get for keeping yourself respectable."

281. To Gollancz [Ltd?]

19 February 1936

11.55   19 FEB   36   WIGAN
ABSOLUTELY IMPOSSIBLE MAKE CHANGES SUGGESTED WOULD MEAN COMPLETE REWRITING AM WIRING AGENT[1] = BLAIR +

1. There is no record of the telegram to Moore regarding changes demanded for *Keep the Aspidistra Flying*.

282. *The Road to Wigan Pier* Diary

<u>19.2.36.</u> When a "dirt-heap" sinks, as it does ultimately, it leaves a hummocky surface which is made more so by the fact that in times of strikes the miners dig into some of these places in search of small coals. One which is used as a playground looks like a choppy sea suddenly frozen. It is called locally "the flock mattress." The soil over them is grey and cindery and only an evil-looking brownish grass grows on them.

This evening to a social the N.U.W.M had got up in aid of Thaelmann's[1] defence-fund. Admission and refreshments (cup of tea and meat pie) 6d.

About 200 people, preponderantly women, largely members of the Co-Op, in one of whose rooms it was held, and I suppose for the most part living directly or indirectly on the dole. Round the back a few aged miners sitting looking on benevolently, a lot of very young girls in front. Some dancing to the concertina (many of the girls confessed that they could not dance, which struck me as rather pathetic) and some excruciating singing. I suppose these people represented a fair cross-section of the more revolutionary element in Wigan. If so, God help us. Exactly the same sheeplike crowd—gaping girls and shapeless middle-aged women dozing over their knitting—that you see everywhere else. There is no turbulence left in England. One good song, however, by an old woman, I think a cockney, who draws the old age pension and makes a bit by singing at pubs, with the refrain:

> *"For you can't do that there 'ere,*
> *"No, you can't do that there 'ere;*
> *"Anywhere else you can do that there,*
> *"But you can't do that there 'ere."*

<u>*20.2.36.*</u> *This afternoon with Paddy Grady to see the unemployed miners robbing the "dirt-train," or, as they call it, "scrambling for the coal." A most astonishing sight. We went by the usual frightful routes along the colliery railway line to fir-tree sidings, on our way meeting various men and women with sacks of stolen coal which they had slung over bicycles. I would like to know where they got these bicycles—perhaps made of odd parts picked off rubbish dumps. None had mudguards, few had saddles and some had not even tyres. When we got to the big dirt-heap where the trainloads of shale from that pit are discharged, we found about 50 men picking over the dirt, and they directed us to the place further up the line where the men board the train. When we got there we found not less than 100 men, a few boys, waiting, each with a sack and coal hammer strapped under his coat tails. Presently the train hove in sight, coming round the bend at about 20 mph. 50 or 70 men rushed for it, seized hold of the bumpers etc. and hoisted themselves onto the trucks. It appears that each truck is regarded as the property of the men who have succeeded in getting onto it while it is moving. The engine ran the trucks up onto the dirt-heap, uncoupled them and came back for the remaining trucks. There was the same wild rush and the second train was boarded in the same manner, only a few men failing to get on to it. As soon as the trucks had been uncoupled the men on top began shovelling the stuff out to their women and other supporters below, who rapidly sorted out the dirt and put all the coal (a considerable amount but all small, in lumps about the size of eggs) into their sacks. Further down the "broo" were the people who had failed to get onto either train and were collecting the tiny fragments of coal that came sliding down from above. You do not, of course, when you are boarding[2] the train, know whether you are getting onto a good truck or not, and what kind of truck you get is entirely luck. Thus some of the trucks, instead of being loaded with the dirt from the floor of the mine, which of course contains a fair quantity of coal, were loaded entirely with shale. But it appears, what I had never heard of before, that among the shale, at any rate*

in some mines, there occurs an inflammable rock called "cannel" (not certain of spelling) which makes fairly good fuel. It is not commercially valuable because it is hard to work and burns too fast, but for ordinary purposes is good enough. Those who were on the shale trucks were picking out the "cannel," which is almost exactly like the shale except that it is a little darker and is known by splitting horizontally, almost like slate. I watched the people working until they had almost emptied the trucks. There were twenty trucks and something over 100 people were at work on them. Each, so far as I could judge, got about 1/2 cwt. of either coal or "cannel." This performance sometimes happens more than once a day when several dirt-trains are sent out, so it is evident that several tons of fuel are stolen every day.

The economics and ethics of the whole business are rather interesting. In the first place, robbing the dirt-train is of course illegal, and one is technically trespassing by being on the dirt-heap at all. Periodically people are prosecuted—in fact in this morning's "Examiner" there was a report of 3 men being fined for it. But no notice is taken of the prosecutions, and in fact one of the men fined was there this afternoon. But at the same time the coal company have no intention of using the coal etc. that is thrown out among the dirt, because it would not repay the cost of sorting. If not stolen, therefore, it would be wasted. Moreover, this business saves the company the expense of emptying the trucks, because by the time the coal-pickers have done with them they are empty. Therefore they connive at the raiding of the train—I noticed that the engine-driver took no notice of the men clambering onto the trucks. The reason for the periodical prosecutions is said to be that there are so many accidents. Only recently a man slipped under the train and had both legs cut off. Considering the speed the train goes at, it is remarkable that accidents do not happen oftener.

The most curious vehicle I saw used for carrying away coal was a cart made of a packing case and the wheels from two kitchen mangles.

Some of this coal that is stolen is said to be on sale in the town at 1/6 a bag. 21.2.36. The squalor of this house is beginning to get on my nerves. Nothing is ever cleaned or dusted, the rooms not done out till 5 in the afternoon, and the cloth never even removed from the kitchen table. At supper you still see the crumbs from breakfast. The most revolting feature is Mrs F. being always in bed on the kitchen sofa. She has a terrible habit of tearing off strips of newspaper, wiping her mouth with them and then throwing them onto the floor. Unemptied chamberpot under the table at breakfast this morning. The food is dreadful, too. We are given those little twopenny readymade steak and kidney pies out of stock. I hear horrible stories, too, about the cellars where the tripe is kept and which are said to swarm with black beetles. Apparently they only get in fresh supplies of tripe at long intervals. Mrs F. dates events by this. "Let me see, now. I've had in three lots of froze (frozen tripe) since then," etc. I judge they get in a consignment of "froze" about once in a fortnight. Also it is very tiring being unable to stretch my legs straight out at night.

1. Ernst Thaelmann (1886–1944), a transport worker, was Chairman of the German Communist Party from 1925. A member of the Reichstag, 1924–33, he ran for the presidency in 1932 against Hindenburg and polled five million votes. He was arrested in 1933, but his trial was postponed several times. In October 1936 Berlin announced he would be detained for life without a trial. Officially reported killed in an air raid, he was shot by the Nazis in August 1944 at Buchenwald. Germans fighting for the Republic in Spain formed themselves into a Thaelmann Centuria (later Brigade).
2. *boarding*] *loading; typewritten emendation*

283. To Victor Gollancz

24 February 1936   Typewritten

22 Darlington Street   Wigan, Lancs.

Dear Mr Gollancz,

I enclose herewith a note on the alterations I have made to "Keep the Aspidistra etc." together with Mr Collins's letter.[1] I trust it will now be all right. It seems to me that these alterations spoil the book altogether; however, perhaps that is better than being prosecuted for libel. I have not made any alterations other than those specially demanded, ie. have not corrected the printer's errors, so these alterations will have to be added to the ones I made previously and which are in the other proof-copy. I hope I have not failed to make the alterations all through, but if there is any page where I have failed to cut out the offending "Roland Butta," no doubt the compositor will notice it. I am sending back the proof under a separate cover. The above address will find me till Saturday.

Yours sincerely
Eric A. Blair

NOTE ON ALTERATIONS.

Pp. 10. 12 etc. "Roland Butta" altered all through to "Corner Table." This has the same number of letters and to some extent preserves the effect of Lyons teashops etc. without referring to any real advertisement.
P. 12. "Are you a Highbrow? Dandruff is the Reason" and "Pyorrhoea? Not me!" cut out and "Asthma was choking her!" and "Curve Cut – the Smoke for Outdoor Men" (both imaginary) substituted.
P. 68. "The Truth about Bad Legs" cut out and "New Hope for the Ruptured" substituted.
P. 71. "Are you a Highbrow? etc." cut out and "Kiddies Clamour for their Breakfast Crisps" substituted.
P. 148. "Drage furniture" altered to "hire-purchase furniture." Impossible to equalise letters here.
P. 207. "Roland Butta" altered to "the movies."
P. 287. "The cheap but lousy picture house in the Westminster Bridge Road" altered to 'a . . . ditto . . . near etc."
P. 303. "Guinness is good for you," "Night Starvation etc.," "Halitosis is

ruining his career," "Pyorrhea?° Not me!" and "Are you a Highbrow?" etc., all cut out and "Get that waist-line back to normal!", "Prompt relief for feeble kidneys," "Asthma was choking her!" and "Are *you* ashamed of you° undies?" (all imaginary) substituted.

In the alterations to pp. 12 and 303 I have equalised the letters but have altered the order entirely and have stuck in slips of paper showing how it should read. I hope the compositor will get this right.

The only real advertisement now left in the book is "Have a Camel." I left this in because it is quite inoffensive and because it is an American advertisement and therefore unlikely to get us into trouble. If desired it can be cut right out (it is on p. 302) but I would rather it were left in.[2]

I have not altered the swearwords etc. objected to, for reasons explained in my previous letter.

1. Letter of 17 February 1936; see *279*. Orwell annotated the letter as follows. In the margin beside a request that 'Roland Butta' and 'those two revolting advertisements for Dandruff and pyorrhoea' be changed to something entirely imaginary, he wrote, 'altered,' as he did next to the requests that the advertisement about 'bad legs' be changed and the reference to Drage's furniture store on 148 be altered to something like 'Hire Purchase' (though Drage's elsewhere was allowed to stand). He also marked 'altered' against a request that the 'lousy picture-house in the Westminster Bridge Road' be changed from 'in' to 'near' and that the advertisements on 302 and 303 be fictitious. These alterations are in the Textual Note to *Keep the Aspidistra Flying, CW*, IV, 4/9, 5/13, 5/15, 55/8, 126/21, 249/23, and 263/1–7. In three places he resisted. By the paragraph about Mr. McKechnie, he wrote, 'Not altered. Have explained this earlier'; by 'frequent use of the word "sod" ' (which, though he admitted it sounded utterly grotesque, Collins feared 'will chop off a sale of several hundreds'), he wrote 'not altered.' The third item not changed is revealing. Collins in a postscript—not, perhaps, an afterthought, but because he did not wish a woman to type out his anxieties—wrote. 'I wd. propose also to omit "Come here. Not a bad mouth. Come here" on 228 [197/6–7] for reasons wh. it wd. be easier to explain in conversation than in writing!' which he initialled. Orwell annotated this, 'Not altered. Cannot see any dirty meaning here.' This last passage and 'sod,' specifically at 5/4 (mentioned by Collins), were allowed to stand, and Gollancz risked Westrope's feeling ridiculed in McKechnie and suing. Westrope did not sue. Did Orwell perhaps not see the point Collins was making about 197/6–7?
2. This was cut out. See Textual Note, *CW*, IV. 262/6–15 *or* 16–26.

284. To Leonard Moore

24 February 1936   Handwritten

22 Darlington Street   Wigan   Lancs.

Dear Mr Moore,

Many thanks for your letter. I have made the alterations Gollancz asked for and sent back the proof and I trust it will now be all right. It seems to me to have utterly ruined the book, but if they think it worth publishing in that state, well and good. Why I was annoyed was because they had not demanded these alterations earlier. The book was looked over and O.K.'d by the solicitor as usual, and had they *then* told me that no reminiscence (it was in most cases only a reminiscence, not a quotation) of actual advertisements was allowable, I would have entirely rewritten the first chapter and modified several others. But they asked me to make the alterations when the book was in type and asked me to equalise the letters, which of course could not be done without spoiling whole passages and in one case a whole chapter. On the other hand to rewrite the whole first chapter when it was in type would have meant an immense addition to expenses, which obviously I could not ask Gollancz to bear. I would like to get this point clear because I imagine the same trouble is likely to occur again. In general a passage of prose or even a whole chapter revolves round one or two key phrases, and to remove these, as was done in this case, knocks the whole thing to pieces. So perhaps another time we could arrange with Gollancz that all alterations are to be made while the book is in typescript.[1]

If you manage to get an American publisher to accept the book, I wonder whether you could see to it that what he prints is the version first printed, without these subsequent alterations?[2] I should like there to be one unmutilated version of it in existence.

The above address will find me till Saturday.

Yours sincerely
Eric A Blair

1. See 267.
2. *Keep the Aspidistra Flying* was not published in the United States until after Orwell's death. Harcourt, Brace and Company issued it in 1956, and the text as revised for Gollancz was followed.

285. *The Road to Wigan Pier* Diary

24.2.36. *Yesterday went down Crippen's mine with Jerry Kennan,*[1] *another electrician friend of his, two small sons of the latter, two other electricians and an engineer belonging to the pit, who showed us round. The depth to the cage bottom was 300 yards. We went down at 10.30 and came up at 1.30, having covered, according to the engineer who showed us round, about 2 miles.*

As the cage goes down you have the usual momentary qualm in your belly, then a curious stuffed-up feeling in your ears. In the middle of its run the cage works up a tremendous speed (in some of the deeper mines they are said to touch 60 mph. or more) then slows down so abruptly that it is difficult to believe you are not going upwards again. The cages are tiny—about 8 feet long by 3½ wide by 6 high. They are supposed to hold 10 men or (I think) about a ton and a half of coal. There were only six of us and two boys, but we had difficulty in packing in and it is important to face in the direction you are going to get out the other end.

Down below it was lighter than I expected, because apart from the lamps we all carried there were electric lights in the main roads. But what I had not expected, and what for me was the most important feature all through, was the lowness of the roof. I had vaguely imagined wandering about in places rather like the tunnels of the Underground; but as a matter of fact there were

435

very few places where you could stand upright. In general the roof was about 4 ft. or 4 ft. 6 ins high, sometimes much lower, with every now and again a beam larger than the others under which you had to duck especially low. In places the walls were quite neatly built up, almost like the stone walls in Derbyshire, with slabs of shale. There were pit-props, almost all of wood, every yard or so overhead. They are made of small larch trees sawn to the appropriate length (from the quantity used I see now why people laying down plantations almost always plant larch) and are simply laid on the ends of the upright props, which are laid on slabs of wood, thus.:

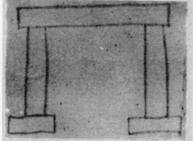

and not fixed in any way. The bottom slabs gradually sink into the floor, or, as the miners put it, "the floor comes up," but the weight overhead keeps the whole thing in place. By the way the steel girders used here and there instead of wooden props had buckled, you got an idea of the weight of the roof. Underfoot is thick stone dust and the rails, about 2½ ft. wide, for the trolleys. When the path is down hill miners often slide down these on their clogs, which, being hollow underneath, more or less fit onto the rails.

After a few hundred yards of walking doubled up and once or twice having to crawl, I began to feel the effects in a violent pain all down my thighs. One also gets a bad crick in the neck, because though stooping one has to look up for fear of knocking into the beams, but the pain in the thighs is the worst. Of course as we got nearer the coal face the roads tended to get lower. Once we crawled through a temporary tunnel which was like an enlarged rat hole, with no props, and in one place there had been a fall of stone during the night—3 or 4 * tons of stuff, I should judge. It had blocked up the entire road except for a tiny aperture near the roof which we had to crawl through without touching any timber. Presently I had to stop for a minute to rest my knees, which were giving way, and then after a few hundred yards more we came to the first working. This was only a small working with a machine worked by two men, much like an enlarged version of the electric drills [2] used for street mending. Nearby was the dynamo (or whatever it is called) which supplied the power through cables to this and the other machines; also the comparatively small drills (but they weigh 50 lbs. each and have to be hoisted onto the shoulder) for drilling holes for blasting charges; also bundles of miners' tools locked together on wires like bundles of keys, which is always done for fear of losing them.

We went a few hundred yards further and came to one of the main workings. The men were not actually working here, but a shift was just coming down to start work about 250 yards further on. Here there was one of

---

* Jerry Kennan said 20 or 30. I don't know which of us would be best judge [Orwell's handwritten footnote].

the larger machines which have a crew of 5 men to work them. This machine has a revolving wheel on which there are teeth about a couple of inches long set at various angles; in principle it is rather like an immensely thickened circular saw with the teeth much further apart, and running horizontally instead of vertically. The machine is dragged into position by the crew and the front part of it can be swivelled round in any direction and pressed against the coal face by the man working it. Two men called "scufters" shovel the coal onto a rubberbelt conveyor which carries it through a tunnel to the tubs on the main road, where it is hauled by steam haulage to the cages. I had not realised before that the men operating the coal-cutter are working in a place rather less than a yard high. When we crawled in under the roof to the coal face we could at best kneel, and then not kneel upright, and I fancy the men must do most of their work lying on their bellies. The heat also was frightful—round about 100 degrees F. so far as I could judge. The crew keep burrowing into the coal face, cutting a semi-circular track, periodically hauling the machine forward and propping as they go. I was puzzled to know how that monstrous machine—flat in shape, of course, but 6 or 8 feet long and weighing several tons, and only fitted with skids, not wheels—could have been got into position through that mile or so of passages. Even to [3] drag the thing forward as the seam advances must be [4] a frightful labour, seeing that the men have to do it practically lying down. Up near the coal face we saw a number of mice, which are said to abound there. They are said to be commonest in pits where there are or have been horses. I don't know how they get down into the mine in the first place. Probably in the cages, but possibly by falling down the shaft, as it is said that a mouse (owing to its surface area being large relative to its weight) can drop any distance uninjured.

On the way back my exhaustion grew so great that I could hardly keep going at all, and towards the end I had to stop and rest every fifty yards. The periodical effort of bending and raising oneself at each successive beam was fearful, and the relief when one could stand upright, usually owing to a hole in the roof, was enormous. At times my knees simply refused to lift me after I had knelt down. It was made worse by the fact that at the lowest parts the roof is usually on a slope, so that besides bending you have to walk more or less sideways. We were all pretty distressed except the engineer taking us round, who was used to it, and the two small boys, who did not have to bend to any extent; but I was by a good deal the worst, being the tallest. I would like to know whether any miners are as tall as I am, and if so, whether they suffer for it. The few miners whom we met down the pit could move with extraordinary agility, running about on all fours among the props almost like dogs.

After we had at last emerged and washed off the more obtrusive dirt and had some beer, I went home and had dinner and then soaked myself for a long time in a hot bath. I was surprised at the quantity of dirt and the difficulty of getting it off. It had penetrated to every inch of my body in spite of my overalls and my clothes underneath those. Of course very few miners have baths in their homes—only a tub of water in front of the kitchen fire. I *should say it would be quite impossible to keep clean without a proper bathtub.*

In the room where we changed our clothes there were several cages of canaries. These have to be kept there by law, to test the air in cases of explosion. They are sent down in the cage, and, if they do not faint, the air is all right.

The Davy lamps give out a fair amount of light. There is an air intake at the top but the flame is cut off from this by a fine gauze. Flame cannot pass through holes of less than a certain diameter. The gauze therefore lets the air in to sustain the flame but will not let the flame out to explode dangerous gases. Each lamp when full will burn for 8–12 hours, and they are locked, so that if they go out down the pit they cannot be relighted. Miners are searched for matches before going down the pit.

1. Joe ('Jerry') Kennan (dates unknown) was an unemployed collier at this time and an activist in the Independent Labour Party. He maintained that the lodgings at 72 Warrington Lane were spotlessly clean, despite Orwell's strictures and 'that Orwell left it for the tripe shop in order to find something worse' (headnote to 'With the Wigan Miners,' Joe Kennan's memories in *Orwell Remembered*, 130). Whether spotless or not, Orwell's hurried departure tallies with Mrs. Hornby's illness as reported by Orwell; see 277, *n.6*. Kennan, perhaps understandably, resented not being sent an autographed copy of *The Road to Wigan Pier* (133).
2. Orwell presumably had in mind pneumatic drills.
3. to] the; *handwritten emendation*
4. be] the; *handwritten emendation*

286. To [Christy & Moore][1]

27 February 1936   Handwritten

22 Darlington Street, Wigan, Lancs.

Dear Sir,
From Sunday (29th)[2] the following address will find me:

21 Estcourt Avenue,[3]
Headingly,
Leeds,
Yorkshire.

Yours faithfully
Eric A. Blair

1. No addressee, but the letter is impressed with the receipt stamp used in Leonard Moore's office.
2. The 29th was actually a Saturday; perhaps the Leap Year confused Orwell.
3. The home of Marjorie, Orwell's elder sister, and her husband, Humphrey Dakin. Dakin (1896–1970), who married Marjorie in July 1920, was a civil servant who worked for the National Savings Committee. Orwell visited them from time to time 'to get some writing done and to be looked after by his sister. Humphrey seemed to resent this and there was tension between the two men. Humphrey plainly viewed him as a work-shy drop-out, though Marjorie continued to help her brother' (headnote to 'The Brother-in-Law Strikes Back,' *Orwell Remembered*, 127–30). On his journey north, Orwell stayed with the Dakins 5–11 and 26–30 March 1936.

287. *The Road to Wigan Pier* Diary

<u>27.2.36.</u>   *On Wednesday (25th) went over to Liverpool to see the Deiners[1] and Garrett.[2] I was to have come back the same night, but almost as soon as I got to Liverpool I felt unwell and was ignominiously sick, so the Deiners insisted on putting me to bed and then on my staying the night.[3] I came back yesterday evening.*

I was very greatly impressed by Garrett. Had I known before that it is he who writes under the pseudonym of Matt Lowe in the Adelphi and one or two other places, I would have taken steps to meet him earlier. He is a biggish hefty chap of about 36, Liverpool-Irish, brought up a Catholic but now a Communist. He says he has had about 9 months' work in (I think) about the last 6 years. He went to sea as a lad and was at sea about 10 years, then worked as a docker. During the War he was torpedoed on a ship that sank in 7 minutes, but they had expected to be torpedoed and had got their boats ready, and were all saved except the wireless operator, who refused to leave his post until he had got an answer. He also worked in an illicit brewery in Chicago during Prohibition, saw various hold-ups, saw Battling Siki[4] immediately after he had been shot in a street brawl, etc. etc. All this however interests him much less than Communist politics. I urged him to write his autobiography, but as usual, living in about 2 rooms on the dole with a wife (who I gather objects to his writing) and a number of kids, he finds it impossible to settle to any long work and can only do short stories. Apart from the enormous unemployment in Liverpool it is almost impossible for him to get work because he is blacklisted everywhere as a[5] Communist.

He took me down to the docks to see dockers being taken on for an unloading job. When we got there we found about 200 men waiting in a ring and police holding them back. It appeared that there was a fruit ship which needed unloading and on the news that there were jobs going there had been a fight between the dockers which the police had to intervene to stop. After a while the agent of the company (known as the stevedore, I think) emerged from a shed and began calling out the names or rather numbers of gangs whom he had engaged earlier in the day. Then he needed about 10 men more, and walked round the ring picking out a man here and there. He would pause, select a man, take him by the shoulder and haul him foreward,° exactly as at a sale of cattle. Presently he announced that that was all. A sort of groan went up from the remaining dockers, and they trailed off, about 50 men having been engaged out of 200. It appears that unemployed dockers have to sign on twice a day, otherwise they are presumed to have been working (as their work is mainly casual labour, by the day) and their dole docked for that day.

I was impressed by the fact that Liverpool is doing much more in the way of slum-clearance than most towns. The slums are still very bad but there are great quantities of Corporation houses[6] and flats at low rents. Just outside Liverpool there are quite considerable towns consisting entirely of Corporation houses, which are really quite livable and decent to look at, but having as usual the objection that they take people a long way from their work. In the centre of the town there are huge blocks of workers' flats imitated from those in Vienna. They are built in the form of an immense ring, five stories high, round a central courtyard about 60 yards across, which forms a playground for children. Round the inner side run balconies, and there are wide windows on each side so that everyone gets some sunlight. I was not able to get inside any of these flats, but I gather each has either 2 or 3 rooms,* kitchenette and bathroom with hot water. The rents vary from about 7/– at the top to 10/– at the bottom. (No lifts, of course.) It is noteworthy that the people in Liverpool have got used to the idea of flats (or tenements, as they call them) whereas in a place like Wigan the people, though realising that flats solve the problem of letting people live near their work, all say they would rather have a house of their own, however bad it was.

There are one or two interesting points here. The re-housing is almost entirely the work of the Corporation, which is said to be entirely ruthless towards private ownership and to be even too ready to condemn slum houses without compensation. Here therefore you have what is in effect Socialist legislation, though it is done by a local authority. But the Corporation of Liverpool is almost entirely Conservative. Moreover, though the re-housing from the public funds is, as I say, in effect a Socialist measure, the actual work is done by private contractors, and one may assume that here as elsewhere the contractors tend to be the friends, brothers, nephews etc. of those on the Corporation. Beyond a certain point therefore Socialism and Capitalism are not easy to distinguish, the State and the capitalist tending to merge into one. On the other side of the river, the Birkenhead side (we went through the Mersey tunnel) you have Port Sunlight, a city within a city, all built and owned by the Leverhulme soap works. Here again are excellent houses at fairly low rents, but, as with publicly-owned property, burdened by restrictions. Looking at the Corporation buildings on the one side, and Lord Leverhulme's buildings on the other, you would find it hard to say which was which.

Another point is this.[7] Liverpool is practically governed by Roman Catholics. The Roman Catholic ideal, at any rate as put forward by the Chesterton-Beachcomber[8] type of writer, is always in favour of private ownership and against Socialist legislation and "progress" generally. The Chesterton type of writer wants to see a free peasant or other small-owner living in his own privately owned and probably insanitary cottage; not a wage-slave living in an excellently appointed Corporation flat and tied down by restrictions as to sanitation etc. The R.Cs in Liverpool, therefore, are going against the supposed implications of their own religion. But I suppose that if the Chestertons et hoc genus grasped that it is possible for the R.Cs to capture the machinery of local and other government, even when it is called Socialist, they would change their tune.

No clogs or shawl over head in Liverpool. Returning by car, noticed how abruptly this custom stops a little west of Wigan.†

* presumably 3—living room & 2 bedrooms [Orwell's handwritten footnote].
† It is said by everyone in Wigan that clogs are going out. Yet in the poorer quarters I person in 2 seems to me to wear clogs, & there are (I think) 10 shops which sell nothing else [Orwell's footnote].

Am trying to arrange to return to London by sea if G. can get me a passage on a cargo boat.

Bought two brass candlesticks and a ship in a bottle. Paid 9/– for the candlesticks. G. considered I was swindled but they are quite nice brass.

1. May and John Deiner (dates unknown) ran the Liverpool branch of *The Adelphi* circle. John was a telephone engineer. Orwell was introduced to them by either Middleton Murry or Richard Rees. He arrived very ill, and the Deiners took care of him. He talked of making the return journey to London by sea from Liverpool, so he might experience conditions at sea. Owing to his illness, he saw less of Liverpool than he had hoped. There is a charming memoir of Orwell by May Deiner in *Orwell Remembered*, 134–36.
2. George Garrett was an unemployed seaman with whom Orwell got on very well. He wrote for *The Adelphi*, and short stories under the pseudonym 'Matt Lowe,' from *matelot*, the term naval ratings use to this day to describe themselves. He had spent much of the 1920s in America and was a member of the Industrial Workers of the World, a revolutionary industrial union nicknamed the Wobblies. Later he made use of his ability to imitate an American accent convincingly by playing small parts requiring that skill in plays presented at the Merseyside Unity Theatre, including the role of Agate Keller in Clifford Odets's *Waiting for Lefty*. In his last Literary Notebook, Orwell quoted from an essay by Garrett on Conrad's *The Nigger of the Narcissus* that had appeared in *The Adelphi* in June 1936; see *3725*.
3. The Deiners insisted that Orwell stayed in bed for three days (Crick, 285). *Orwell Remembered*, 134, headnote, states that he was with the Deiners for four or five days.
4. Battling Siki, Senegalese boxer who unexpectedly knocked out the great French champion Georges Carpentier, early in 1922, to take the light heavyweight championship of the world. He lost the title shortly afterward to the Irishman Mike McTigue. His attempt to make his name as a boxer in the United States was unsuccessful, and one morning he was found shot dead in a back street of New York. The Siki-Carpentier fight was filmed and shown widely round Europe in 1922. Orwell could easily have seen this film in the months before he left for Burma.
5. *as a*] *typescript has* as as
6. *Corporation houses*] *slum Corporation houses; first word typed and crossed out—perhaps an instance of self-correction while typing*
7. *this*] *which; typewritten emendation*
8. G. K. Chesterton, in whose journal, *G. K.'s Weekly*, Orwell's first professional writing in English appeared ('A Farthing Newspaper,' 29 December 1928; see *80*). The 'Beachcomber' column in the *Daily Express* was started in 1924 by J. B. Morton (1893–1979), also a Roman Catholic. Orwell makes frequent pejorative references to the 'Beachcomber' column. See 'As I Please,' 30, 23 June 1944, *2492*, for a more considered comparison of Chesterton and Morton.

288. To Richard Rees

29 February 1936   Typewritten

22 Darlington Street   Wigan, Lancs.

Dear Richard,

I thought you might like a line to hear how I am getting on in partibus infidelium.[1] Your introductions were of the greatest value to me, especially that to Meade, who put me in touch with a friend at Wigan who was exactly what I wanted. I have been here nearly three weeks and have collected reams of notes and statistics, though in what way I shall use them I haven't made up my mind yet. I have been living and associating almost entirely with miners, largely unemployed of course. The lads at the N.U.W.M. have been of great service to me and everyone has been most willing to answer questions and show me over their houses. I have gone into the housing question rather minutely, because it is a very urgent one here and I gather in most places in the north. I have only been down one coal mine so far but hope to go down some more in Yorkshire. It was for me a pretty devastating experience and it is a fearful thought that the labour of crawling as far as the coal face (about a mile in this case but as much as 3 miles in some mines), which was enough to put my legs out of action for four days, is only the beginning and ending of a miner's day's work, and his real work comes in between. Have you ever been down a mine? I don't think I shall ever feel quite the same about coal again.

I went over and saw the Deiners and Garrett earlier this week. Unfortunately I was ill while there and so not at my best, but I had some long talks with G. and was greatly impressed by him. Had I known before that he was "Matt Lowe," I should have taken steps to meet him earlier. I am leaving Wigan on Monday, going to stay a couple of nights at Sheffield to meet your friend Brown,[2] then on to Leeds to stay a day or two with my sister till I can find some miner's house to stay at in Barnsley. I may also go up to Durham for a little while but I am not sure—the trouble is that this travelling is rather expensive. I am coming back to town about the end of March and then perhaps may be able to do some work again—impossible, of course, in these surroundings. I am arranging to take a cottage at Wallington near Baldock in Herts, rather a pig in a poke because I have never seen it, but I am trusting the friends who have chosen it for me, and it is very cheap, only 7/6 a week. My novel[3] ought to be out in a few weeks. There was the usual last-minute stew about libel, this time, unfortunately, after it was in proof so that I had to spoil a whole chapter with alterations. This business of libel is becoming a nightmare—it appears that there now exist firms of crook solicitors who make a regular income by blackmailing publishers. However I hope I may get an American edition of my novel printed unmutilated.

Meade said something about your coming up north a little later, but I expect it will be after I have returned home. Let me know about your movements.

Yours
Eric A. Blair

1. in partibus infidelium] in regions of unbelievers; see 'these barbarous regions,' 295.
2. William (or James?) Brown, an unemployed man who contributed Marxist articles to The Adelphi; see 289.
3. Keep the Aspidistra Flying.

289. The Road to Wigan Pier Diary

2.3.36. At 154 Wallace Road, Sheffield.
Thick snow everywhere on the hills as I came along. Stone boundaries between the fields running across the snow like black piping across a white

dress. Warm and sunny, however. For the first time in my life saw rooks copulating.[1] On the ground, not in a tree. The manner of courtship was peculiar. The female stood with her beak open and the male walked round her and it appeared as though he was feeding her.

Memories of Wigan: Slagheaps like mountains, smoke, rows of blackened houses, sticky mud criss-crossed by imprints of clogs, heavy-set young women standing at street corners with their babies wrapped in their shawls, immense piles of broken chocolate in cut-price confectioners' windows.

3.3.36. This house: Two up two down, living room about 14' by 12', parlour rather smaller. Sink and copper in living room, no gas fire, outside W.C. Rent with rates about 8/6. 2 cellars as well.[2] Husband is out of work (P.A.C.[3]—was previously store-keeper at a factory which closed down and discharged its whole staff), wife works as a char at 6d an hour. One kid aged 5.

James Brown: age 45 but looks less. Has malformed right hand, also one foot. This was inherited and he fears it is transmissible, so will not marry. Owing to this has never had much in the way of regular work. Was with a circus for some years as groom, clown and "Wild West" rider—he could apparently handle the bridle with his damaged hand. Now lives alone and for some reason gets no dole, only something from the parish and help from his brother. Has a single room with only an open fireplace, no oven, to cook on. Is terribly embittered and declares that feeling of actual hatred for the bourgeoisie, even personal hatred of individuals, is necessary to any genuine Socialist. Is nevertheless a good fellow and very anxious to help. Mixed up with his political feelings is the usual local patriotism of the Yorkshireman and much of his conversation consists of comparison between London and Sheffield to the detriment of the former. Sheffield is held to lead London in everything, eg. on the one hand the new housing schemes in Sheffield are immensely superior, and on the other hand the Sheffield slums are more squalid than anything London can show. I notice that apart from the usual hatred between the Northerner and the Southerner, there is also hatred between the Yorkshireman and the Lancashireman, and also internecine hatred between the various Yorkshire towns. No one up here seems to have heard of any place in the south of England except London. If you come from the south you are assumed to be a cockney however often you deny it. At the same time as the Northerner despises the Southerner he has an uneasy feeling that the latter knows more of the arts of life and is very anxious to impress him.

Had a very long and exhausting day (I am now continuing this March 4th) being shown every quarter of Sheffield on foot and by tram. I have now traversed almost the whole city. It seems to me, by daylight, one of the most appalling places I have ever seen. In whichever direction you look you see the same landscape of monstrous chimneys pouring forth smoke which is sometimes black and sometimes of a rosy tint said to be due to sulphur. You can smell the sulphur in the air all the while. All buildings are blackened within a year or two of being put up. Halting at one place I counted the factory chimneys I could see and there were 33. But it was very misty as well as smoky—there would have been many more visible on a clear day. I doubt whether there are any architecturally decent buildings in the town. The town is very hilly (said to be built on seven hills, like Rome) and everywhere streets of mean little houses blackened by smoke run up at sharp angles, paved with cobbles which are purposely set unevenly to give horses etc. a grip. At night the hilliness creates fine effects because you look across from one hillside to the other and see the lamps twinkling like stars. Huge jets of flame shoot periodically out of the rooves of the foundries (many working night shifts at present) and show a splendid rosy colour through the smoke and steam. When you get a glimpse inside you see enormous fiery serpents of red-hot and white-hot (really lemon-coloured) iron being rolled out into rails. In the central slummy part of the town are the small workshops of the "little bosses," ie, smaller employers who are making chiefly cutlery. I don't think I ever in my life saw so many broken windows. Some of these workshops have hardly a pane of glass in their windows and you would not believe they were inhabitable if you did not see the employees, mostly girls, at work inside.

The town is being torn down and rebuilt at an immense speed. Everywhere among the slums are gaps with squalid mounds of bricks where condemned houses have been demolished and on all the outskirts of the town new estates of Corporation houses are going up. These are much inferior, at any rate in appearance, to those at Liverpool. They are in terribly bleak situations, too. One estate just behind where I am living now, at the very summit of a hill, on horrible sticky clay soil and swept by icy winds. Notice that the people going into these new houses from the slums will always be paying higher rents, and also will have to spend much more on fuel to keep themselves warm. Also, in many cases, will be further from their work and therefore spend more on conveyances.

In the evening was taken to a Methodist Church where some kind of men's association (they call it a Brotherhood)[4] meet once a week to listen to a lecture and have discussions. Next week a Communist is speaking, to the evident dismay of the clergyman who made the announcements. This week a clergyman who spoke on "Clean and Dirty Water." His lecture consisted of incredibly silly and disconnected ramblings about Shaw's "Adventures of a Black Girl etc." Most of the audience did not understand a word of it and in fact hardly[5] listened, and the talk and the questions afterwards were so unbearable that Brown and I slipped out with his friend Binns to see the latter's back to back house, on which I took notes. B. says that most of the members of this Brotherhood are unemployed men who will put up with almost anything in order to have a warm place where they can sit for a few hours.

Accent in Sheffield not so broad as in Lancashire. A very few people, mostly miners I think, wear clogs.

1. All editions of *The Road to Wigan Pier* have 'rooks treading' except *CW*, V; see 16, line 16. The second proof had 'rooks courting,' but even that was regarded as too explicit. According to Eileen Blair's letter of 17 January 1937, Orwell had originally written 'copulating,' as here in his diary.

2. '*2 cellars as well*' is a handwritten addition. Space was left for this addition, so possibly the original could not be read and this was inserted later.

3. Public Assistance Committee of the local authority.

4. In *Nineteen Eighty-Four*, O'Brien explains that those who have read Goldstein's Testament 'will be full members of the Brotherhood,' which opposes the State (*CW*, IX, 182).

5. *hardly*] *fair hardly; first word typed and crossed out*

290. Review of *Esther Waters* by George Moore; *Our Mr. Wrenn* by Sinclair Lewis; *Dr. Serocold* by Helen Ashton; *The Owls' House* by Crosbie Garstin; *Hangman's House* by Donn Byrne; *Odd Craft* by W. W. Jacobs; *Naval Occasions* by Bartimeus; *My Man Jeeves* by P. G. Wodehouse; *Autobiography*, 2 vols., by Margot Asquith

New English Weekly, 5 March 1936

The Penguin Books are splendid value for sixpence[1] so splendid that if the other publishers had any sense they would combine against them and suppress them. It is, of course, a great mistake to imagine that cheap books are good for the book trade. Actually it is just the other way about. If you have, for instance, five shillings to spend and the normal price of a book is half-a-crown, you are quite likely to spend your whole five shillings on two books. But if books are sixpence each you are not going to buy ten of them, because you don't want as many as ten; your saturation-point will have been reached long before that. Probably you will buy three sixpenny books and spend the rest of your five shillings on seats at the "movies." Hence the cheaper books become, the less money is spent on books. This is an advantage from the reader's point of view and doesn't hurt trade as a whole, but for the publisher, the compositor, the author and the bookseller it is a disaster.

As for the present batch of Penguin Books—the third batch of ten—far and away the best of them, of course, is *Esther Waters*. I do not know Moore's work very well, but I cannot believe that he ever did anything better than this. It was written by a man whose fingers were all thumbs and who had not learned some of the most elementary tricks of the novelist, for instance, how to introduce a new character, but the book's fundamental sincerity makes its surface faults almost negligible. Moore's great advantage as a novelist lay in not having an over-developed sense of pity; hence he could resist the temptation to make his characters more sensitive than they would be in real life. *Esther Waters* is in the same class as *Of Human Bondage*—both of them books which are stuffed full of literary faults but which are not likely to drop out of favour.

Sinclair Lewis's *Our Mr. Wrenn* is a weak early work which hardly seems worth reprinting. Presumably it was chosen because the copyright of *Babbit*[*t*] or *Elmer Gantry* would have been too expensive. *Dr. Serocold* is good of its kind—it describes a day in the life of a country doctor—and must not be judged by its appalling last sentence. According to Miss E. M. Delafield, the only cases that doctors in fiction ever attend are confinements. Miss Ashton, who is a doctor herself, has evidently noticed this tendency and avoided it. Crosbie Garstin I cannot do with, nor with Donn Byrne—the latter, I think, still has a biggish reputation, but he was too like a professional Irishman for my taste. It would be interesting to know whether W. W. Jacobs keeps his popularity. On his low level he is as good a short-story writer as we have had. His stories look as though they grew together. But their range is tiny, and they depend upon the Punch-like notion that a working-class person, as such, is a figure of fun and possesses no sense of honour. I should expect a Communist to describe *Odd Craft* as ideologically poisonous, which indeed it is.

I suppose I ought not to be rude to *Naval Occasions*, which I greatly enjoyed when I was a little boy just before the war. Those were the great days of the Navy's popularity. Small boys wore sailor suits, and everyone belonged to something called the Navy League and had a bronze medal which cost a shilling, and the popular slogan was "We want eight (dreadnoughts) and we won't wait!" Bartimeus, I fancy, aspired to be the Kipling of the Navy and merely succeeded in being a rather more naïve and likeable Ian Hay. It was a pity not to choose a better Wodehouse book than *My Man Jeeves*, which was the first of its series and contains at least one story which has since been reissued in a better form. Still, it was a great day for Mr. Wodehouse when he created Jeeves, and thus escaped from the realm of comedy, which in England always stinks of virtue, into the realm of pure farce. The great charm of Jeeves is that (although he did pronounce Nietzsche to be "fundamentally unsound") he is beyond good and evil.

Finally, there are the two volumes of Lady Asquith's autobiography. This, I admit, I have never been able to read *in toto*, either now or when it first appeared. If you are born into one of our governing families and spend your life in political circles, you are bound to meet interesting people, but you don't, it seems, necessarily learn to write decent English. I remember that some French novelist, describing a letter he had received from a lady of title, said: "Her style was that of a concierge."

In my capacity as reader I applaud the Penguin Books; in my capacity as writer I pronounce them anathema. Hutchinsons are now bringing out a very similar edition, though only of their own books, and if the other publishers follow suit, the result may be a flood of cheap reprints which will cripple the lending libraries (the novelist's foster-mother) and check the output of new novels. This would be a fine thing for literature, but it would be a very bad thing for trade, and when you have to choose between art and money—well, finish it for yourself.

1. John Lane's Penguin Books were launched on 30 July 1935 with ten books. Orwell reviewed the third batch of ten, published 5 March 1936. J. E. Morpurgo comments on this review in *Allen Lane: King Penguin, a Biography* (1979): 'George Orwell . . . held views which might have led him to welcome a series which was intended to offer the joys of book-collecting to the masses; at very least, he should have noticed the decent austerity of Penguin design, so very different from the "beastly Rackhamesque" book jackets which he detested for their "elvish children tripping Wendily through a bluebell glade". Instead he floundered, first

considering the list book by book and then, if for some eccentric reasons, calling upon the gods to damn the whole project. . . . For all his aggressive waspishness Orwell's literary opinion of the list was generally sound' (100–01). In the light of this assessment, it is ironic that the first paragraph of Orwell's review was reprinted in *The Bookseller*. 26 July 1975, under the title 'Penguin celebrate with Orwell,' to mark forty years of Penguin Books. The reference to Rackhamesque book jackets is to *Keep the Aspidistra Flying, CW*, IV, 3.

291. *The Road to Wigan Pier* Diary

<u>5.3.36.</u> *At 21 Estcourt Avenue, Headingley, Leeds.*[1]
I left Sheffield at 10.30 this morning, and in spite of its being such a frightful place and of the relief of getting back into a comfortable house, I was quite sorry to leave the Searles. I have seldom met people with more natural decency. They were as kind to me as anyone could possibly be, and I hope and trust they liked me. Of course I got their whole life-history from them by degrees. Searle is 33 and was an only child. When a youth he joined the Army and was in the Ordnance Corps (or whatever it is called) with the army of occupation in Palestine and in Egypt. He has vivid memories of Egypt and wishes he was back there. Since then he has only had short-lived jobs, eg. as store-keeper and check-weighman at various works, also as railway (outside) porter. Mrs. S. comes from a somewhat more prosperous family, as her father till only a few weeks ago★ was in a good job at £5 a week and also made something on the side by making fishing rods. But it was a very large family (11) and she went into service. She married S. when he was on the dole, against the opposition of her family. At first they could not get a house,[2] and lived in a single room, in which two children were born and one died. They told me they had only one bed for the family and had to "lay out" the dead baby in the perambulator. Finally, after frightful difficulty (one reason for this is that private landlords are not too keen on[3] letting to people on the dole and there is a certain amount of bribery of agents) they got this house, of which the rent is about 8/6. Mrs. S. earns about 9/– a week from her charing. Exactly what deduction is made for this from S's dole I don't know, but their total income is 32/6. In spite of which I had great difficulty in getting them to accept enough for my keep while there – they wanted to charge only 6/–for full board and lodging from Monday night to Thursday morning. They keep the house very clean and decent, have a bit of garden, though they can't do much with it, as it has factory chimneys on one side and the gas works on the other, besides being poor soil, and are very fond of one another. I was surprised by Mrs S's grasp of the economic situation and also of abstract ideas—quite unlike most working-class women in this, though she is I think not far from illiterate. She does not seem resentful against the people who employ her—indeed she says they are kind to her—but sees quite clearly the essential facts about domestic service. She told me how the other day as she waited at the lunch table she calculated the price of the food on the table (for 5

★ *He died very suddenly & his wife has now no resources except the old age pension & an insurance policy* [Orwell's handwritten footnote].

persons for one meal) and it came to 6/3 – as much as the P.A.C. allows her child for a fortnight.

Brown was very good and took my request to "show me over Sheffield" even too seriously, so that from morning to night I was being rushed from place to place, largely on foot, to see public buildings, slums, housing estates etc. But he is a tiresome person to be with, being definitely disgruntled and too conscious° of his Communist convictions. In Rotherham we had to have lunch at a slightly expensive restaurant because there didn't seem to be any others except pubs (B. is TT.), and when in there he was sweating and groaning about the "bourgeois atmosphere" and saying he could not eat this kind of food. As he declares that it is necessary to literally hate the bourgeoisie, I wondered what he thought of me, because he told me at the very start I was a bourgeois and remarked on my "public school twang." However, I think he was disposed to treat me as a sort of honorary proletarian, partly because I had no objection to washing in the sink etc., but more because I seemed interested in Sheffield. He was very generous and though I had told him at the start that I was going to pay for his meals etc. while we were together, he would always go out of his way to spare me expense. It seems that he lives on 10/– a week—I had this from Searle: exactly where B's 10/– comes from I don't know—and the rent of his room is 6/–. Of course it would not be possible to subsist on the remainder, allowing for fuel. You could only keep alive[4] on 4/– a week (see attached)[5] if you spent nothing on fuel and nothing on tobacco or clothes. I gather B. gets meals from time to time from the S's and other friends, also from his brother who is in comparatively good employ. His room is decent and even cultured-looking, as it has bits of "antique" furniture which he has made himself, and some crude but not disagreeable pictures, mostly of circuses, which he has painted. Much of his bitterness obviously comes from sexual starvation. His deformity handicaps him with women, his fear of transmitting it has stopped him from marrying (he says he would only marry a woman past the childbearing age), and his inability to earn money makes it more impossible still. However, at one of the Adelphi summer schools[6] he picked up with some schoolmistress (aged 43) who I gather is his mistress when opportunities permit and who is willing to marry him, only her parents oppose it. The Searles say he has improved greatly since taking up with this woman—before that he used to have fits occasionally.

We had an argument one evening in the Searles' house because I helped Mrs S. with the washing-up. Both of the men disapproved of this, of course. Mrs S. seemed doubtful. She said that in the North working-class men never offered any courtesies to women (women are allowed to do all the housework unaided, even when the man is unemployed, and it is always the man who sits in the comfortable chair), and she took this state of things for granted, but did not see why it should not be changed. She said that she thought the women now-a-days, especially the younger women, would like it if men opened doors for them etc. The position now-a-days is anomalous. The man is practically always out of work, whereas the woman occasionally is working. Yet the woman continues to do all the housework and the man not a handsturn, except carpentering and gardening. Yet I think it is instinctively felt by both sexes that the man would lose his manhood if, merely because he was out of work, he became a "Mary Ann."

One particular picture of Sheffield stays by me. A frightful piece of waste ground (somehow, up here a piece of waste ground attains a squalor that would be impossible even in London), trampled quite bare of grass and littered with newspaper, old saucepans etc. To the right, an isolated row of gaunt four-room houses, dark red blackened by smoke. To the left an interminable vista of factory chimneys, chimney behind chimney, fading away into a dim blackish haze. Behind me a railway embankment made from the slag of furnaces. In front, across the piece of waste ground, a cubical building of dingy red and yellow brick, with the sign, "John Grocock, Haulage Contractor."

Other memories of Sheffield: stone walls blackened by smoke, a shallow river yellow with chemicals, serrated flames, like circular saws, coming out from the cowls of the foundry chimneys, thump and scream of steam hammers (the iron seems to scream under the blow), smell of sulphur, yellow clay, backsides of women wagging laboriously from side to side as they shove their perambulators up the hills.

Mrs Searle's recipe for fruit loaf (very good with butter) which I will write down here before I lose it:

1 lb flour. 1 egg. 4 oz. treacle. 4 oz. mixed fruit (or currants). 8 oz. sugar. 6 oz. margarine or lard.

Cream the sugar and margarine, beat the egg and add it, add the treacle and then the flour, put in greased tins and bake about 1/2 to 3/4 hour in a moderate oven.

Also her '54321' recipe for sponge cake:

5 oz. flour, 4 oz. sugar, 3 oz. grease (butter best), 2 eggs, 1 teaspoonful baking powder. Mix as above and bake.

The first numbered section of the diary, pages 1 to 36, concludes here. The second numbered section, pages 1 to 25, is headed 'Diary' in Orwell's handwriting.

7.3.36. Staying till next Wed. with M. and H. at 21 Estcourt Avenue, Headingley. Conscious all the while of difference in atmosphere between middle-class home even of this kind and working-class home. The essential difference is that here there is elbow-room, in spite of there being 5 adults and 3 children, besides animals, at present in the house. The children make peace and quiet difficult, but if you definitely want to be alone you can be so—in a working-class house never, either by night or day.

One of the kinds of discomfort inseparable from a working-man's life is waiting about. If you receive a salary it is paid into your bank and you draw it out when you want it. If you receive wages, you have to go and get them in somebody else's time and are probably kept hanging about and probably expected to behave as though being paid your wages at all was a favour. When Mr Hornby at Wigan went to the mine to draw his compensation, he had to go, for some reason I did not understand, on two separate days each week, and was kept waiting in the cold for about an hour before he was paid. In addition the four tram journeys to and from the mine cost him 1/–, reducing his compensation from 29/–weekly to 28/–. He took this for granted, of course. The result of long training in this kind of thing is that whereas the bourgeois goes through life expecting to get what he wants, within limits, the working-man always feels himself the slave of a more or less mysterious authority. I was impressed by the fact that when I went to Sheffield Town Hall to ask for certain statistics,[7] both Brown and Searle— both of them people of much more forcible character than myself—were nervous, would not come into the office with me, and assumed that the Town Clerk would refuse information. They said, "He might give it to you, but he wouldn't to us." Actually the Town Clerk was snooty and I did not get all the information I asked for. But the point was that I assumed my questions would be[8] answered, and the other two assumed the contrary.

It is for this reason that in countries where the class hierarchy exists, people of the higher class always tend to come to the front in times of stress, though not really more gifted than the others. That they will do so seems to be taken for granted always and everywhere. NB. to look up the passage in Lissagaray's History of the Commune describing the shootings after the Commune had been suppressed. They were shooting the ringleaders without trial, and as they did not know who the ringleaders were, they were picking them out on the principle that those of better class than the others would be the ringleaders. One man was shot because he was wearing a watch, another because he 'had an intelligent face.' NB. to look up this passage.

Yesterday with H. and M. to Hawarth° Parsonage, home of the Brontes and now a museum. Was chiefly impressed by a pair of Charlotte Bronte's cloth-topped boots, very small, with square toes and lacing up at the sides. 9.3.36.   Yesterday with H. and M. to their cottage at Middlesmoor, high up on the edge of the moors. Perhaps it is only the time of year, but even up there, miles from any industrial towns, the smoky look peculiar to this part of the country seems to hang[9] about anything. Grass dull-coloured, streams muddy, houses all blackened as though by smoke. There was snow everywhere, but thawing and slushy. Sheep very dirty—no lambs, apparently. The palm was out and primroses putting out new shoots: otherwise nothing moving.

1. Home of Orwell's elder sister. Marjorie, and her husband, Humphrey Dakin; see 286, n. 3.
2. house] house, in which; last two words typed and crossed out
3. on] handwritten over to
4. alive] alive if you; last two words typed and crossed out
5. 'attached' is this from News of the World. 1 March 1936 (also in The New Statesman and Nation): LIVING ON 4S A WEEK: MAN'S DESCRIPTION OF HOW HE DOES IT. Following the disclosures in the News of the World of parents who have to bring up big families on tiny incomes, a correspondent draws our attention to the case of a man who spends less than 4s a week on food.
    His week's supply and its cost is as follows:—

	s.	d.
3 Wholemeal loaves	1	0
½ lb. Margarine		2¼
½ lb. Dripping		3
1 lb. Cheese		7
1 lb. Onions		1½
1 lb. Carrots		1½
1 lb. Broken biscuits		4
2 lb. Dates		6
1 Tin evaporated milk		5
10 Oranges		5
Total cost	3	11½

The man, Mr W. Leach, of Lilford Road, London, S.E., adds that he would prefer to boil the carrots to eating them raw "but, of course, to boil the water would cost too much." [In contemporary coinage, 3s 11½d is 20p; these items cost about £8.80 in November 1993.]

6. *summer schools] handwritten interlinear insertion*
7. See Statistical Information Provided by Medical Officer of Health, Sheffield, *351.*
8. *would be] would be asked fo°; last two words typed and crossed out*
9. *hang] hand; d overwritten by g*

292. To Victor Gollancz Ltd

11 March 1936   Typewritten; handwritten list

21 Estcourt Avenue   Headingley   Leeds

Dear Sir,

With reference to the attached letters, I have made all the alterations suggested by Mr Rubinstein.[1] I have left the other references to the other real advertised products mentioned by the Fanfare Press, as Mr Rubinstein states that they do not seem to matter in the context. I think I have made the necessary alterations all through, but in case of my having let the original words remain standing in any case, I suppose the compositors will see to this. A statement of the alterations I have made is herewith.

Communications sent to the above address will always be forwarded to me.

Yours faithfully
Eric A. Blair

P.S. I am sending the proof back under separate cover.

Ref. attached.

P. 6. "Foul, bloody things" deleted.[2]

P. 25. "Acrid" altered to "soothing." It cannot very well stand without an adjective, but I suppose there is no objection to saying that Players' cigarettes are "soothing"?[3]

P. 66. "Drink Habit Conquered in Three Days" altered to "Earn Five Pounds a Week in Your Spare Time." This is not an identifiable advertisement.

E A. Blair

1. Libel lawyer acting for Victor Gollancz Ltd; see *219, n. 3.*
2. For Orwell's initial response to the objection to these words, see *268.*
3. The objection to Orwell's describing the taste of Player's Weights (a cheap brand of cigarettes) as 'papery' was made early, and Orwell changed it to 'acrid'; see *268.* To meet renewed legal objections, the description was changed so that it became complimentary. Orwell's comment is, of course, ironic. *CW*, IV, 21, line 11, restores 'papery.'

293. To Leonard Moore

11 March 1936   Typewritten

21 Estcourt Avenue   Headingley   Leeds

Dear Mr Moore,

Many thanks for your letter and the proof. I am sending the latter back to Gollancz direct, to save time. I hope and trust there will be no further objections now. I have made all the alterations suggested by Mr Rubinstein but have left the others mentioned by the Fanfare Press which Mr Rubinstein says "do not seem to matter in the context." I may mention that some of the products stated by the Fanfare Press to be real products were ones I had invented myself with no notion that anything of that name was actually on the market. One or two of the things they mentioned could not very well be altered, eg. they mention the reference to Drage's, which occurs in the poem in the middle of the book *as a rhyme,* and therefore obviously could not be changed. In any case it has been in print already (in the "Adelphi".) But I presume that Mr Rubinstein's suggestions cover what is[1] necessary.

I wonder if I could get hold of a proof copy of Alec Browne's° forthcoming book "The Fate of the Middle Classes," which Gollancz is publishing. I think I could undertake to do a short review of it either for the Adelphi[2] or the New English Weekly, but actually I want it in connection with the book I am projecting now, as by its title it seems to be discussing a matter I shall have to touch on. I never buy new books nowadays and I might not be able to get it from the library, but I don't want to put Gollancz to the expense of a bound copy, so if he could let me have a proof copy I should be greatly obliged.[3]

Yours sincerely
Eric A. Blair

1. is] *typed as* it
2. Annotated in Moore's office: 'phoned Gollancz 12/3/36.'
3. See letter to Jack Common. *295.* The review was published in *The Adelphi* in May 1936; see *308.* Alec Brown's last name had no e.

294. *The Road to Wigan Pier* Diary

11.3.36.   On the last two evenings to "discussion groups"—societies of people who meet once a week, listen-in to some talk on the radio and then discuss it. Those at the one on Monday were chiefly unemployed men and I believe these "discussion groups" were started or at any rate suggested by the Social Welfare people who run the unemployed occupational centres. That on Monday was decorous and rather dull. Thirteen people including ourselves (one woman besides M.), and we met in a room adjoining a public library. The talk was on Galsworthy's play "The Skin Game" and the discussion kept to the subject until most of us adjoined to a pub for bread and cheese and beer afterwards. Two people dominated the assembly, one a huge bull-headed man named Rowe who contradicted whatever the last speaker had said and involved himself in the most appalling contradictions, the other a youngish, very intelligent and extremely well-informed man named Creed. From his refined accent, quiet voice and apparent omniscience, I took him for a librarian. I find he keeps a tobacconist's shop and was previously a commercial traveller. During the War he was imprisoned as a conscientious objector. The other meeting was at a pub and the people were of higher standing. The arrangement is that M. and H. go there taking the portable radio, and the publican, who is a member of the group, lets them have a room for the evening. On this occasion the talk was called "If Plato lived Today," but actually no one listened-in except M. and myself—H. has gone to Bedford. When the talk was over the publican, a Canadian with a very bald head, a market gardener who was already the worse for drink, and another man, rolled in and there began an orgy of drinking from which we escaped with difficulty about an hour later. Much talk on both nights about the European situation and most people saying (some of them with ill-dissembled hope) that war is certain. With two exceptions all pro-German.

Today to Barnsley to fix up about a place to stay. Wilde, secretary of the South Yorkshire Branch of the Working Men's Club & Institute Union, has fixed it all up for me. The address is 4 Agnes Avenue. The usual 2 up 2 down house, with sink in living room, as at Sheffield. The husband is a miner and was away at work when we got there. House very disorganised as it was washing day, but seemed clean. Wilde, though kind and helpful, was a very vague person. He was a working miner till 1924 but as usual has been bourgeois-ified. Smartly dressed with gloves and umbrella and very little accent—I would have taken him for a solicitor from his appearance.

Barnsley is slightly smaller than Wigan—about 70,000 inhabitants—but distinctly less poverty-stricken, at any rate in appearance. Much better shops and more appearance of business being done. Many miners coming home from the morning shift. Mostly wearing clogs but of a square-toed pattern different from the Lancashire ones.

13.3.36.   At 4 Agnes Terrace,° Barnsley.

This house is bigger than I had imagined. Two rooms and tiny larder under the stairs downstairs, 3 or 4* rooms upstairs. 8 people in the house—5 adults and 3 children. Front room which should be parlour is used as bedroom. Living room, about 14 by 12, has the usual kitchener, sink and copper. No gas stove. Electric light in all rooms save one. Outside W.C.

---

* 3 [Orwell's handwritten footnote].

The family. Mr Grey, a short powerful man, age about *45*, with coarse features, enlarged nose and a very fatigued, pale look. He is rather bald, has his own teeth (unusual in a working class person of that age) but they are very discoloured. A bit deaf, but very ready to talk, especially about technicalities of mining. Has worked in the pit ever since a small boy. On one occasion was buried by a fall of earth or stone—no bones broken, but it took ten minutes to dig him out and two hours to drag him to the cage. He tells me no machinery (stretchers etc.) exists for conveying injured men away from the scene of accidents. Obviously some kind of stretcher running on the trolley rails could be contrived, but this would involve stopping all the haulage of coal while it was being done. So injured men have to be carried to the cage by helpers who are themselves bending double and can only get them along very slowly. Mr G. works at removing the coal onto the trucks after it is cut—"scufting" I think it is called. He and his mate are paid piece-work 2/2 per ton—1/1 each. On full time his wages average £2–10–0 a week. His stoppages amount to 6/11. He works at Darton, about 4 miles away and goes there by bus.[1] Journeys cost 6d a day. So his net wages on full time are about £2–0–0 a week.

Mrs G. is about 10 years younger,* motherly type, always cooking and cleaning, accent less broad than her husband's. Two little girls, Doreen and Ireen (spelling?) aged 11 and 10. The other lodgers are a widowed joiner, employed on the woodwork at the new dog-track, and his son aged about 11, and a professional singer who is going to sing at one of the pubs. All the larger pubs in Barnsley employ singers and dancers (some of these very immoral according to Mrs G.) more or less constantly.

The house is very clean and decent and my room the best I have had in lodgings up here. Flanelette sheets this time.

14.3.36.   Much talk last night with Mr G. about his War experiences. Especially about the malingering he saw going on when he was invalided with some injury to his leg, and the astute ways the doctors had of detecting it. One man feigned complete deafness and successfully kept it up during tests lasting two hours. Finally he was told by signs that he would be discharged and could go, and just as he was passing through the door the doctor said casually "Shut that door after you, would you?" The man turned and shut it, and was passed for active service. Another man feigned insanity and got away with it. For days he was going round with a bent pin on a bit of string, pretending to be catching fish. Finally he was discharged, and on parting with G. he held up his discharge papers and said "This is what I was fishing for." I was reminded of the malingering I saw in the Hopital° Cochin in Paris, where unemployed men used to remain for months together on pretence of being ill.[2]

Beastly cold again. Sleet this morning. But yesterday as I came on the train they were ploughing and the earth looked much more spring-like; especially in one field where the earth was very black, not like the usual clay soil hereabouts, and as the ploughshare turned it over it looked like chocolate fudge being sliced up with a knife.

---

* *Actually their ages are 50 & 38* [Orwell's handwritten footnote].

I am very comfortable in this house but do not think I shall pick up much of interest in Barnsley. I know no one here except Wilde, who is thoroughly vague. Cannot discover whether there is a branch of the N.U.W.M. here. The public library is no good. There is no proper reference library and it seems no separate directory of Barnsley is published.

15.3.36. Last night with Wilde and others to the general meeting of the South Yorkshire Branch of the Working Men's Club & Institute Union, held at one of the clubs in Barnsley. About 200 people there, all busily tucking into beer and sandwiches, though it was only 4.30 pm—they had got an extension for the day. The club was a big building, really an enlarged pub with one big hall which could be used for concerts etc., and in which the meeting was held. It was a bit stormy in parts, but Wilde and the chairman had them pretty well in hand and were complete masters of all the usual platform phraseology and procedure. I notice from the balance sheet that W.'s salary is £260 per annum.[3] Before this I had never realised the number and importance of these working men's clubs, especially in the North and especially in Yorkshire. These at this meeting consisted of pairs of delegates sent by all the clubs in South Yorkshire. There would have been I should say 150 delegates, representing therefore 75 clubs and probably about 10,000 members. That is in South Yorkshire alone. After the meeting I was taken to have tea in the committee room with about 30 of what were, I gathered, some of the more important delegates. We had cold ham, bread and butter, cakes and whisky which everyone poured into their tea. After that with W. and the others went down to the Radical and Liberal Club in the middle of the town, where I have been before. There was a sort of smoking concert going on, as these clubs, like the pubs, all engaged singers etc. for the week-ends. There was quite a good knockabout comedian whose jokes were of the usual twins-mother-in-law-kippers type, and pretty steady boozing. Wilde's accent becomes much broader when he is in these surroundings. It appears that these clubs were first started as a kind of charitable concern in the mid-nineteenth century, and were, of course, Temperance. But they escaped by becoming financially self-supporting and have developed, as I say, into sort of glorified co-operative pubs. Grey, who belongs to the Radical and Liberal Club, tells me his subscription is 1/6d a quarter and all drinks are 1d or 2d a pint cheaper than at the pubs. Youths under 21 are not admitted and (I think) women cannot be members but can go there with their husbands. Most of the clubs are avowedly non-political, and in this and in the fact that the members are mostly of the more prosperous working-class type—comparatively few unemployed—one can foresee the germs of a danger that they will be politically mobilised for anti-socialist purposes.

Talking with a man who was previously a miner but now works as a labourer for the Corporation. He was telling me about the housing conditions in Barnsley in his childhood. He grew up in a back to back house in which there were 11 people (two bedrooms, I suppose) and you not only had to walk 200 yards to get to the lavatory, but shared it with, in all, 36 people.

Have arranged to go down the Grimethorpe pit next Saturday. This is a very up-to-date pit⁴ and possesses certain machinery that does not exist anywhere else in England. Also to go down a "day hole" pit on Thursday afternoon. The man I spoke to told me it was a mile to the coal face, so if the "travelling" is bad I shan't go the whole way—I only want to see what a "day hole" is like and am not going to incapacitate myself like last time.

When G. comes back from the pit he washes before having his food. I don't know whether this is usual, but I have often seen miners sitting down to eat with Christy Minstrel faces—completely black except very red lips which become clean by eating. When G. arrives he is as black as ink, especially his scalp—for this reason miners usually wear their hair short. He pours out a large basin of hot water, strips to the waist and washes himself very methodically, first his hands, then his upper arms, then his forearms, then his chest and shoulders, then his face and head. Then he dries himself and his wife washes his back. His navel is still a nest of coal-dust. I suppose from the waist down he must normally be quite black. There are public baths and the miners go to them but as a rule not more than once a week—one cannot be surprised at this, as a miner has not much time between working and sleeping. Miners' houses with bathrooms, other than the new Corporation ones, are practically unknown. Only a few colliery companies have baths at the pit-heads.

I notice that G. does not eat very much. At present, working on the afternoon shift, he has the same breakfast as I have (an egg and bacon, bread—no butter—and tea) and has a light lunch, such as bread and cheese, about half past twelve. He says he cannot do his work if⁵ he has eaten too much. All he takes with him to the pit is some bread and dripping and cold tea. This is the usual thing. The men do not want much in the stifling air down there, and besides, they are not allowed any time off for eating. He gets home between 10 and 11 pm, and it is then that he has his only heavy meal of the day.

<u>16.3.36.</u> *Last night to hear Mosley speak at the Public Hall, which is in structure a theatre. It was quite full—about 700 people I should say. About 100 Blackshirts on duty, with two or three exceptions weedy-looking specimens, and girls selling "Action"⁶ etc. Mosley spoke for an hour and a half and to my dismay seemed to have the meeting mainly with him. He was booed at the start but loudly clapped at the end. Several men who tried at the beginning to interject questions were thrown out, one of them—who as far as I could see was only trying to get a question answered—with quite unnecessary violence, several Blackshirts throwing themselves upon him and raining blows on him while he was still sitting down and had not attempted any violence. M. is a very good speaker. His speech was the usual claptrap— Empire free trade, down with the Jew and the foreigner, higher wages and shorter hours all round etc. etc. After the preliminary booing the (mainly) working-class audience was easily bamboozled by M. speaking from as it were a Socialist angle, condemning the treachery of successive governments towards the workers. The blame for everything was put upon mysterious international gangs of Jews who are said to be financing, among other things, the British Labour Party and the Soviet. M.'s statement re. the international situation: "We fought Germany before in a British quarrel; we are not going*

to fight them now in a Jewish one" was received with loud applause. Afterwards there were questions as usual, and it struck me how easy it is to bamboozle an uneducated audience if you have prepared beforehand a set of repartees with which to evade awkward questions. eg. M. kept extolling Italy and Germany, but when questioned about concentration camps etc. always replied "We have no foreign models; what happens in Germany need not happen here." To the question, "How do you know that your own money is not used to finance cheap foreign labour?" (M. having denounced the Jewish financiers who are supposed to do this), M. replied, "All my money is invested in England," and I suppose comparatively few of the audience realised that this means nothing.

At the beginning M. said that anyone ejected would be charged under the public meetings act. I don't know whether this was actually done, but presumably the power to do so exists. In connection with this the fact that there are no police on duty inside the building is of great importance. Anyone who interrupts can be assaulted and thrown out and then charged into the bargain, and of course the stewards, ie. M. himself, are the judges of what constitutes an interuption.° Therefore one is liable to get both a hammering and a fine for asking a question which M. finds it difficult to answer.

At the end of the meeting a great crowd collected outside, as there was some public indignation about the men who had been thrown out. I waited for a long time in the crowd to see what would happen, but M. and party did not emerge. Then the police managed to split the crowd and I found myself at the front, whereupon a policeman ordered me away, but quite civilly. I went round to the back of the crowd and waited again, but still M. did not appear and I concluded he had been sneaked out by a back door, so went home. In the morning at the Chronicle office, however, I was told that there had been some stone-throwing and two men had been arrested and remanded.

G. changed this morning onto the early morning shift. He gets up at 3.45 am and has to be at work, ie. at the coal face, at 6. He gets home about 2.30 pm His wife does not get up to get his breakfast and he says few miners will allow their wives to do so. Also that there are still some miners who if they meet a woman on their way to work will turn back and go home. It is considered bad luck to see a woman before going to work. I presume this only applies to the early morning shift.

1. bus]tram; *handwritten emendation*
2. Orwell spent 7–22 March in this hospital in 1929. He wrote about the experience in 'How the Poor Die,' *Now*, n.s. 6, November 1946; see *3104*.
3. A copy of the agenda for the 14 February Branch Council meeting and the printed Statement of Accounts for year ending 31 December 1935 are among Orwell's notes. In addition to Wilde's salary, £52 was paid to a clerk.
4. pit]and; *handwritten emendation*
5. if] *handwritten insertion*
6. *Action* was the journal of the British Union of Fascists. On 9 July 1936, Orwell was asked by Mrs. Hastings Bonora if she could quote from the Trafalgar Square scene of *A Clergyman's Daughter* in a review of *Victoria of England* she was writing for *Action*. She hoped he was not

violently anti-Fascist and would 'consequently say CERTAINLY NOT.' Evidently that was what Orwell did say, because on 14 July she wrote to him, 'Even if you disapprove of the Fascist ideal, you must still recognise the point we all have in common—the welfare of the unfortunate "Down and Outs." ' In a final letter, 24 July, she claimed that her party at least had a programme, 'but you have never put forward a single suggestion for ameliorating the lot of our "Misérables." '

295. To Jack Common

17 March 1936   Typewritten

4 Agnes Terrace   Barnsley, Yorks.

Dear Common,[1]

Would you like a short review of Alec Browne's° book "The Fate of the Middle Classes"? Or is someone else doing it for you? I have scrounged a free copy and it seems not an uninteresting book, at any rate it is on an important subject and I thought I might, eg., do a few lines for the Adelphi Forum[2] on it.

I have been in these barbarous regions for about two months and have had a very interesting time and picked up a lot of ideas for my next book[3] but I admit I am beginning to pine to be back in the languorous South and also to start doing some work again, which of course is impossible in the surroundings I have been in. My next novel[4] ought to be out shortly. It would have been out a month ago only there was one of those fearful last-minute scares about libel and I was made to alter it to the point of ruining it utterly. What particularly stuck in my gizzard was that the person who dictated the alterations to me was that squirt Norman Collins. Do you want a copy sent to the Adelphi? If you think you could get it reviewed I will have them send a copy, but not if you haven't space to spare. I went to the Adelphi offices[5] in Manchester and saw Higginbottom[6] several times, also Meade with whom I stayed several days. I may tell you in case you don't know that there are fearful feuds and intrigues going on among the followers of the Adelphi and I will tell you about these when I see you. I didn't say anything of this to Rees when I wrote, because I thought his feelings might be hurt.

What about the international situation? Is it war? I think not, because if the government have any sense at all they must realise that they haven't got the country behind them. I think things will remain uneasily in statu quo and the war will break out later, possibly this autumn. If you notice wars tend to break out in the autumn, perhaps because continental governments don't care to mobilise until they have got the harvest in.

I heard Mosley[7] speak here on Sunday. It sickens one to see how easily a man of that type can win over and bamboozle a working class audience. There was some violence by the Blackshirts, as usual, and I am going to write to the Times about it, but what hope of their printing my letter?[8]

I shall be at the above address till about the 25th, after that returning to London, by sea if I can manage it. Hoping to see you some time after that,

Yours
Eric A. Blair

1. Jack Common (see 95), who had worked in a solicitor's office, a shoe shop, and as a mechanic, was co-editor of *The Adelphi*, 1935–36. Crick calls him 'one of the few authentic English proletarian writers,' and tells of Common's first meeting with Orwell (204). Though there was a certain tension between them, they remained friends. Common's books included *The Freedom of the Streets*, described by Crick as 'straight-talking or garrulous polemic' (354), *Kiddar's Luck*, and *The Ampersand*. Found among his papers was a manuscript written some time in the late 1950s called 'Orwell at Wallington'; see *Orwell Remembered*, 139–43. It concludes: 'Years later I realised that no pub ever knew my friend as "Eric", let alone "George."'
2. *The Adelphi* Forum was described by the editor as being 'open for short topical comments and for the expression of opinion which may be entirely different from our own.'
3. *The Road to Wigan Pier.*
4. *Keep the Aspidistra Flying.*
5. On the initiative of some of Middleton Murry's northern admirers, the printing and publishing organisation of *The Adelphi* was taken over by the Workers' Northern Publishing Society in Manchester. In the early 1930s Murry found himself at the head of a breakaway segment of the Independent Labour Party known as the Independent Socialist Party—a short-lived phenomenon. It was from these *Adelphi* supporters that, when Orwell was commissioned to write a book on working-class conditions in the north, Richard Rees gave him names as contacts.
6. Sam Higenbottam (1872–) was a contributor to *The Adelphi*, a Socialist, and author of *Our Society's History* (1939), an account of the Amalgamated Society of Woodworkers.
7. Sir Oswald Mosley, Bt. (1896–1980), was successively a Conservative, Independent, and Labour M.P. In 1931 he broke away from the Labour Party to form the 'New Party.' Later he became fanatically pro-Hitler and turned his party into the British Union of Fascists. His followers were known as Blackshirts. He was interned early in the war.
8. Orwell wrote the letter, but *The Times* did not publish it. He also sent it to the *Manchester Guardian*. His diary for 20.3.36 (see 296) concludes, 'I hardly expected the Times to print it, but I think the M.G. might, considering their reputation.'

296. *The Road to Wigan Pier* Diary

<u>18.3.36.</u> *The Barnsley public baths are very bad. Old-fashioned bathtubs, none too clean, and not nearly enough of them. I judged by the appearance of the place there were at most 50 baths*—this in a town of 70–80 thousand inhabitants, largely miners, not one of whom has a bath in his own house, except in the new Corporation houses.*

Some curious coincidences. When I went to see Len Kaye he recommended me to see Tommy Degnan, to whom I had also been recommended by Paddy Grady at Wigan. But what was more curious still, D. was one of the men who were thrown out at Mosley's meeting, though not the one I actually saw

---

* *Actually 19!* [Orwell's handwritten footnote].

thrown out. I went round to see D. last night and had some difficulty in finding him. He lives in a dreadful barn of a place called Garden House, which is an old almost ruinous house which half a dozen unemployed men have taken and made a sort of lodging house of. D. himself is not unemployed, though at the moment "playing" because a few days before the hammering he got at M.'s meeting he was slightly crushed by a fall of stone in the mine. We went out to look for the man whom I actually saw thrown out, as I want to get particulars and see his bruises before writing to the papers about it, but couldn't find him, and I am to see him today. Then in the street we ran across another man whom I saw thrown out. The latter's ejection was an interesting instance of the way any upset can be misrepresented and turned to advantage by a demagogue of the type of Mosley. At the time of the uproar at the back of the hall, this last man—name Hennesy,* I think—was seen to rush on to the stage, and everyone thought he had gone there to shout something out and interrupt M.'s speech. It struck me at the time as curious that though on the stage he didn't shout anything out, and the next moment, of course, the Blackshirts on the platform seized him and bundled him out. M. shouted out, "A typical example of Red tactics!" It now appears what happened was this. Hennesey saw the Blackshirts at the back of the hall bashing D., and couldn't get to him to help him because there is no aisle up the middle; but there was an aisle up the right hand side, and the only way he could get to this was over the stage. D. after being thrown out was charged under the Public Meetings Act, but H. not. I don't know yet whether the other man, Marshall, was. The woman who was thrown out—this was somewhere at the back and I didn't see it—was hit on the head with a trumpet and was a day in hospital. D. and H. were in the Army together and H. was wounded in the leg and D. taken prisoner when the Vth Army was defeated in 1918. D., being a miner, was sent to work in the Polish mines. He said all of them had pit-head baths. H. says the French ones have them too.

G. told me a dreadful story of how a friend of his, a "dataller", was buried alive. He was buried under a fall of small stone, and they rushed to him and, though they could not get him out completely, they got his head and shoulders free so that he could breathe. He was alive and spoke to them. At this moment they saw that the roof was coming down again and had to take to flight themselves. Once again he was buried, and once again they managed to get to him and uncover his head, and again he was alive and spoke to them. Then the roof came down again, and this time they did not get him out for some hours, after which, of course, he was dead. But the real point of the story, from G.'s point of view, was that this man had known beforehand that this part of the mine was unsafe and likely to bury him: "And it worked on his mind to that extent that he kissed his wife before he went to work. And she told me afterwards that it was the first time in years he'd kissed her."

---

* His name is Firth, I got it as Hennessey because he was introduced to me as Hellis Firth. (Ellis Firth—people here very capricious about their H's.) [Orwell's handwritten footnote]. The variations in spelling Hennessey are Orwell's. For Firth's weekly budget, see 349.

There is a very old woman—a Lancashire woman—living near here who in her day has worked down the pit, dragging tubs of coal with a harness and chain. She is 83, so I suppose this would be in the seventies.

19.3.36. In frightful exhaustion after going down the "day hole," as, of course, when the time came I had not the strength of mind to say I did not want to go as far as the coal face.

I went down with the "deputy" (Mr Lawson) about 3 pm. and came up about 6.15 pm. L. said we had covered not quite 2 miles. I must say that I got on perceptibly better than at Wigan, either because the going was a little better, as I think it was—probably one could stand upright about one third of the way—or because L., who is an old man, moderated his pace to mine. The chief feature of this pit, apart from its being a "day hole," is that it is infernally wet in most places. There were quite considerable streams running here and there, and two enormous pumps have to be kept running all day and most of the night. The water is pumped up to ground level and has made a considerable pool, but curiously enough it is clear clean water—even drinkable, L. said—and the pool was quite ornamental with waterhens swimming about on it. We went down when the morning shift came up, and there are comparatively few men on the afternoon shift for some reason I did not understand. When we got to the coal face the men were there with the coal-cutter, which was not running at the moment, but they set it running to show me. The teeth on a revolving chain—in principle it is an enormously tough and powerful band-saw—cut in underneath the coal face, after which huge boulders of coal can be easily tumbled out and broken up with picks before being loaded[1] onto the tubs. Some of these boulders of coal, not yet broken up, were about 8 feet long by two thick by four high—the seam is four feet six, I think—and must have weighed many tons.* As it cuts the machine travels backwards or forwards, as desired, along the coal face, on its own power. The place where these men, and those loading the broken coal onto the tubs, were working,[2] was like hell. I had never thought of it before, but of course as the machine works it sends forth clouds of coal dust which almost stifle one and make it impossible to see more than a few feet. No lamps except Davy lamps of an old-fashioned pattern, not more than two or three candle-power, and it puzzled one to see how these men can see to work, except when there are a number of them together. To get from one part of the coal face to another you had to crawl along awful tunnels cut through the coal, a yard high by two feet wide, and then to work yourself on your bottom over mountainous boulders of coal. Of course in doing this I dropped my lamp and it went out. L. called to one of the men working and he gave me his[3] lamp. Then L. said "You'd better cut yourself a bit of coal as a memento" (visitors always do this), and while I was cutting out a piece of coal with the pick, I knocked my second lamp between the two of us, which was disconcerting and brought it home to me how easily you could lose yourself down there if you didn't happen to know the roads.

* A cubic yard of coal said to weight 27 cwt [1,372 kg.] [Orwell's handwritten footnote].

We passed tubs, carrying props etc., going to and fro on the endless belt, which is worked by electricity. The tubs only move at 1½ miles an hour. All the miners at this pit seem to carry sticks, and they gave me one which was a great help. They are about two foot six long and hollowed out just below the knob. At moderate heights (4 ft to 5 ft) you keep your hand on the knob, and when you have to bend really low you grip the stick by the hollow. The ground under foot was as mucky as a farm yard in many places. They say the best way to go is to keep one foot on the trolley-rail and the other on the sleepers, if you can find them. The miners going down the roads run, bent double of course, in places where I could barely stagger. They say it is easier to run than walk when you have the hang of it. It was rather humiliating that coming back, which we did by the most direct route, took me three quarters of an hour and only takes the miners a quarter of an hour. But we had gone to the nearest working, only about half way to the end. Those who work at the furthest working take nearly an hour to get to their work. This time I was given one of the new crash helmets which many, though not all miners, now wear. To look at they are very like a French or Italian tin hat, and I had always imagined they were made of metal. Actually they are of a kind of compressed fibre and very light. Mine was a bore because it was too small and fell off when I bent very low. But how glad of it I was! Coming back when I was tired and could not bend much I must have bashed my head twenty times— once hard enough to bring down a huge chunk of stone—but felt absolutely nothing.*

Walked home with L. to Dodworth as I could get the bus more easily there. He has a two-mile walk with some pretty stiff hills going to and from work, in addition to the walk inside the mine when he gets there. But I suppose as "deputy" he doesn't do much manual work. He has worked in this mine 22 years and says he knows it so well that he never even needs to look up [to] see when there is a beam coming.

Birds all singing. Tiny pink buds on the elms that I had never noticed before. Many female flowers on the hazels. But I suppose as usual the old maids will be cutting them all off for Easter decorations.

When I sit typing the family, especially Mrs G. and the kids, all gather round to watch absorbedly, and appear to admire my prowess almost as much as I admire that of the miners.

20.3.36.   Talking with Firth (see notes on his house.) He gets 32/– a week from the U.A.B.[5] Mrs F. is a Derbyshire woman. Two kids, ages 2 years 5 months and 10 months. They are fairly sturdy as yet and it is evidently the case that these kids do much better in infancy than later, as for about their first three years they get help from the Infants' Welfare Clinic. Mrs F. gets three packets of baby's food (dried milk) a week and also a little Nestle's milk. On one occasion she got an allowance of 2/– a week for a month to buy eggs for the elder child. While there we sent out for some beer. I noted both the F.s let the children drink a little beer out of their glasses. Another kid was in and out of the house mothering the F. baby. Her father was murdered four years ago. The widowed mother gets an allowance of 22/– a week, I do not know from what source, on which she has to keep herself and 4 children.

I did not know before, what F. told me, that when the mines have baths at the pithead these are built not by the company but by the miners themselves, out of the Welfare Fund to which every miner subscribes. This is the case at any rate round here—must try and find out if it is so everywhere. It is by the way another argument against the statement that miners do not want or appreciate baths. One reason why not all pits have baths is that when a pit is anywhere near being worked out it is not considered worth while to build baths.

I forgot to mention that in the day-hole at Wentworth the pit props, owing to the damp, had strange fungi exactly like cotton wool growing on them. If you touched them they went all to nothing, leaving a nasty smell. It appears that a Lancashire miner, instead of slinging his lamp round his neck, has a band above the elbow and hangs the lamp from that.

Today G. earned little or nothing. The coal-cutter had broken down so there was no coal for him to fill into the tubs. When this happens those on piece-work get no compensation, except a shilling or two for odd jobs called bye-work.

I see the Manchester Guardian has not printed my letter re. Mosley and I suppose they never will. I hardly expected the Times to print it, but I think the M.G. might, considering their reputation.

21.3.36. This morning went down the Grimethorpe pit. Not exhausting this time, because in order not to clash with the visit of some students from the Technical College we went to the nearest working, only about 1/4 mile and little bending.

The depth of the mine, at least at the part we went to, is a little over 400 yards. The young engineer who took me thought the cages average 60 mph. when going down, in which case they must touch 80 or more at[6] their fastest. I think this must be an exaggeration, but they certainly travel faster than the average railway train. The especial feature of this pit is the "skip wagon," by which the coal is sent straight up in special cages instead of being sent up, much more laboriously, in tubs. The full tubs come slowly along an inclined rail and are controlled by men at the sides with brakes. Each tub halts for a moment on a weighing machine and its weight is entered up, then the tubs move on and move two at a time into a kind of container which grips them underneath. The container then turns right over, spilling the coal down a shute into the cage below. When the cage has got 8 tons, ie. about 16 tubs, in it, it goes out and the coal is spilt down a similar chute on the surface. Then it goes along conveyor belts and over screens which automatically sort it, and is washed as well. The coal which is being sold to factories etc. is shot straight into goods trucks on the railway line below and then weighed truck and all, the weight of the truck being known. This is the only pit in England which works this system—all others send the coal up in the tubs, which takes much more time and needs more tubs. The system has been worked for a long time in Germany and U.S.A. The Grimethorpe pit turns out about 5000 tons of coal a day.

This time I saw the fillers actually working at the coal face, and now having seen the different operations of coal-getting, except blasting, in progress separately, I understand more or less how it is done. The coal-cutter travels along the face cutting into the bottom of the ledge of coal to the depth of 5 feet. Then the coal can be tumbled out in boulders with picks, or—as here, the Grimethorpe coal being very hard—is first loosened with blasting charges and then extracted. Then the fillers (who have also extracted it) load it onto the conveyor belt which runs behind them and carries it to a chute from which it runs into the tubs. Thus:

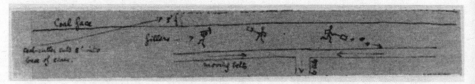

Reduced to approximately two-thirds original size

As far as possible the three operations are done in three separate shifts. The coal-cutter works on the afternoon shift, the blasting is done on the night shift (when the minimum number of people are in the pit), and the fillers extract the coal on the morning shift. Each man has to clear a space[7] 4 or 5 yards wide. So, as the seam of coal is about a yard high and the cutter has undermined it to a depth of 5 feet, each man has to extract and load onto the belt (say) 14 x 5 x 3 cubic feet of coal, equals 210 cubic feet, equals nearly 8 cubic yards of coal. If it is really the case that a cubic yard of coal weighs 27 cwt., this would be well over 10 tons—ie. each man has to shift nearly a ton and a half an hour. When the job is done the coal face has advanced 5 feet, so during the next shift the conveyor belt is taken to pieces, moved 5 feet forward and reassembled, and fresh props are put in.

The place where the fillers were working was fearful beyond description. The only thing one could say was that, as conditions underground go, it was not particularly hot. But as the seam of coal is only a yard high or a bit more, the men can only kneel or crawl to their work, never stand up. The effort of constantly shovelling coal over your left shoulder and flinging it a yard or two beyond, while in a kneeling position, must be very great even to men who are used to it. Added to this there are the clouds of coal dust which are flying down your throat all the time and which make it difficult to see any distance. The men were all naked except for trousers and knee-pads. It was difficult to get through the conveyor belt to the coal face. You had to pick your moment and wriggle through quickly when the belt stopped for a moment. Coming back we crawled onto the belt while it was moving; I had not been warned of the difficulty of doing this and immediately fell down and had to be hauled off before the belt dashed me against the props etc. which were littered about further down. Added to the other discomforts of the men working there, there is the fearful din of the belt which never stops for more than a minute or so.

Electric lights this time—no Davy lamps used in the pit except for testing for gas. They can detect the presence of gas by the flame turning blue. By the height to which the flame can be turned while still remaining blue, they have a rough test of the percentage of gas in the atmosphere. All the roads we went through, except one or two galleries used for short cuts, were high and well-built and even paved underfoot in places. I have at last grasped the reason for the doors one passes through from time to time. The air is sucked out of one entry by fans and goes in of its own accord at another entry. But if not prevented it will come back by the shortest route instead of going all round the mine. Hence the doors, which stop it from taking short cuts.

Excellent baths at the pit. They have no less than 1000 h. & c. shower baths. Each miner has two lockers, one for his pit clothes and one for his ordinary clothes (so that the pit clothes shall not dirty the others.) Thus he can come and go clean and decent. According to the engineer, the baths were built partly by the Miners' Welfare, partly by the royalty owners, and the company also contributed.

During this week G. has had two narrow escapes from falls of stone, one of which actually grazed him on its way down. These men would not last long if it were not that they are used to the conditions and know when to stand from under. I am struck by the difference between the miners when you see them underground and when you see them in the street etc. Above ground, in their thick ill-fitting clothes, they are ordinary looking-men,° usually small and not at all impressive and indeed not distinguishable from other people except by their distinctive walk (clumping tread, shoulders very square) and the blue scars on their noses. Below, when you see them stripped, all, old and young, have splendid bodies, with every muscle defined and wonderfully small waists. I saw some miners going into their baths. As I thought, they are quite black from head to foot. So the ordinary miner, who has not access to a bath, must be black from the waist down six days a week at least.

I have been wondering about what people like the Firths have to eat. Their total income is 32/– a week. Rent 9/0½d. Gas say 1/3. Coal (say 3 cwt. @ 9d)) 2/3. Other minor expenses (eg. F. keeps up his Union payments) say 1/–. That leaves 18/6. But Mrs F. gets a certain amount of baby-food free from the Clinic, so say the baby only costs 1/– a week beyond this. That leaves 17/6. F. smokes at any rate some cigarettes, say 1/– (6 packets of Woodbines a week.) That leaves 16/6 a week to feed 2 adults and a girl aged 2 years, or about 5/6 per week per head. And this takes no account of clothes, soap, matches etc. etc. Mrs F. said they fed chiefly on bread and jam. If I can do so delicately I must ask F. to give me a fairly exact account of their meals for one day.

22.3.36.   Kaye says his father, a collier (now too old for work), always washed the top half of his body and his feet and legs to above the knees. The rest of his body was only washed at very long intervals, the old man believing that washing all over led to lumbago.

Communist meeting in the Market Place disappointing. The trouble with all these Communist speakers is that instead of using the popular idiom they employ immensely long sentences full of "despite" and "notwithstanding" and "be that as it may" etc. in the Garvin[8] strain—and this in spite of always speaking with broad provincial or cockney accents—Yorkshire in this case. I suppose they are given set speeches which they learn by heart. After the visiting speaker Degnan got up to speak and was a much more effective speaker—he speaks very broad Lancashire and though he can talk[9] like a leading article if he wants to he doesn't choose. The usual crowd of men of all ages gaping with entirely expressionless faces and the usual handful of women a little more animated than the men—I suppose because no woman would go to a political meeting unless exceptionally interested in politics. About 150 people. Collection taken for the defence of the young men arrested in the Mosley affair and realised 6/–.

Wandering round Barnsley Main Colliery and the glassworks along the canal with F. and another man whose name I did not get. The latter° mother had just died and was lying dead at home. She was 89 and had been a midwife for 50 years. I noted the lack of hypocrisy with which he was laughing and joking and came into the pub to have a drink etc. The monstrous slag-heaps round Barnsley Main are all more or less on fire under the surface. In the darkness you can see long serpentine fires creeping all over them, not only red but very sinister blue flames (from sulphur) which always seem on the point of going out and then flicker up again.

I notice that the word "spink" (for a great tit, I think, but at any rate some small bird) is in use here as well as in Suffolk.

23.3.36.   At Mapplewell. Houses about the worst I have seen, though we did not manage to get into the very worst ones, which were one-roomed or two-roomed cabins of stone, about 20' by 15' by 15' high, or even less, and practically ruinous. Rent of these, some of which are property of colliery, said to be about 3/–. In the row called Spring Gardens we found public indignation because the landlords have served about half the row with notices to quit for arrears of, in some cases, only a few shillings. (Firth, in Barnsley, has a notice to quit though only about 5/– in arrear and paying this off at 3d per week.) The people took us in and insisted on our seeing their houses. Frightful interiors. In the first one (see notes) old father, out of work of course, obviously horribly bewildered by his notice to quit after 22 years tenancy and turning anxiously to F. and me with some idea that we could help him. The mother rather more self-possessed. Two sons aged about 24, fine big men with powerful well-shaped bodies, narrow faces and red hair, but thin and listless from obvious undernourishment and with dull brutalised expressions. Their sister, a little older and very like them, with prematurely lined face, glancing from F. to me, again with the idea that perhaps we might help. One of the sons, taking no notice of our presence, all the while slowly peeling off his socks in front of the fire; his feet almost black with sticky dirt. The other son was at work. The house terribly bare—no bedclothes except overcoats etc.—but fairly clean and tidy. At the back children playing about in the muck, some of them, aged 5 or 6, barefoot and naked except for a sort of shift. F. told the tenants if the notice to quit was persisted with to come into Barnsley and see him and Degnan. I told them the landlord was only bluffing and to hold their ground and if he threatened taking it to court to threaten in return to sue him for lack of repairs. Hope I did the right thing.

I have glanced at Brown's novel.[10] *It is b——s.*

25.3.36.   Men along the private line leading to Gauber pit unloading trucks of slack. They say the mine "can't get shut o' t'slack" and are laying it by. This is regarded as a sinister sign. If the pits are storing slack already they will soon be running short time. The men get 4d a ton for unloading the slack. A truck holds about 10 tons, so they have to unload 3 trucks to make a day's wage.

I think the dirtiest interiors I see, more than any of the various kinds of squalor—the piles of unwashed crocks, the scraps of miscellaneous food all over the lino-topped table, the dreadful rag mats with the crumbs of years trodden into them—the things that oppress me most are the scraps of newspaper that are scattered all over the floor.

G. is quite badly ill with bronchitis. He stayed away from work yesterday, then this morning, when still obviously ill, insisted on going to work.

Returning to Leeds tomorrow, then on to London on Monday [30 March].

1. *loaded] lowere (beginning of lowered); typed and crossed out*
2. *were working,] handwritten emendation*
3. *his] my; typewritten emendation*
4. *a quarter of] handwritten insertion*
5. Unemployment Assistance Board. See *347*, 'Notes on Houses, No. 12 Albert Street East,' and *CW*, V, 85–86.
6. *at] typed as that*
7. *space] ledge; typed and crossed out*
8. J. L. Garvin (1868–1947) was the right-wing editor of *The Observer*, 1908–42.
9. *talk] speak; typed and crossed out*
10. *Daughters of Albion* (1935) by Alec Brown, described by Orwell as 'a huge wad of mediocre stuff' in his review of *The Novel Today* by Philip Henderson in the *New English Weekly*, 31 December 1936; see *342*.

297. To Leonard Moore

1 April 1936   Typewritten

As from. The Stores   Wallington   Near Baldock   Herts.[1]

Dear Mr Moore,

Herewith the two manuscripts I told you of. I don't think personally the idea of dramatising "Burmese Days" is much good, but it might be worth while getting an expert opinion.

As to the other, "Trying to make Sense of It."[2] If, as is possible, you don't feel you can do anything with it, you might let me have it back and I will send it to Gollancz myself—this, if you had turned it down, would probably only be a formality, but I did promise the author I would send it to Gollancz and would not like him to feel I had not done what I could.

I knew there was something else I wanted to ask you. When "Keep the Aspidistra" comes out, could you ask G. to send a copy to the New English Weekly. I dare say ordinarily he wouldn't, but they say they would like to review it and I expect it is worth while.[3]

Yours sincerely
Eric A. Blair

1. Orwell leased The Stores at Wallington (some thirty-five miles north of London) and moved in on 2 April 1936. In the *Cambridge Weekly News*, 24 November 1988, Pam Dajda describes the cottage and its restoration by current owner Les Kitto; in 1 December, she gives memories of local people who knew Orwell and his wife. The cottage, she says, was rented from Orwell's aunt Nellie Limouzin (Mrs. Adam) for 7s 6d a week. (Eileen arranged for a copy of *The Road to Wigan Pier* to be sent to Mrs. Adam at The Stores in her letter to Leonard Moore of 11 February 1937; see *361*). However, Orwell writes of the landlord as male (see *300*), and Shelden has identified him as a Mr. Dearman (260; U.S.: 236–7). The cottage had been built in the sixteenth century. It had 'a 3 ft 9 in high front door and deep step leading straight into what was the old village shop. The narrow, twisting elm stairway, so unusual it is listed [for preservation], and combination of low ceilings and strategically placed beams are a constant obstacle to the tall and unwary.' The Albertine rose Orwell bought for sixpence in 1936, and about which he wrote evocatively in 'As I Please,' 8, 21 January 1944, still flourished; see *2410*. See also Crick, 295–98; Stansky and Abrahams, II, 175–82; and, for those who knew the Blairs at The Stores, *Remembering Orwell*, 114–19.
2. This is probably something by William Brown, whom Orwell had met in Sheffield (see *288* and *289*), which Orwell tried to get published. There are two undated letters from Brown to Orwell, written from 29 High St, Sevenoaks, Kent, to which he had moved from Sheffield. These thank 'Dear comrade Blair' for his help but regret he was 'unsuccessfull° with my manuscript.' Brown had married on 8 August, and his wife was trying to get work as a teacher. He offers a bed and a welcome for Orwell if he is in that part of the country. Sevenoaks, said Brown, was 'dead in the heart of Feudalism.'
3. The last paragraph has been ticked in Moore's office, indicating that this was done.

298. To Jack Common

3 April 1936   Typewritten

The Stores   Wallington

Dear Common,

I received an unsigned letter which from internal evidence I decided must be from you. I moved into the above yesterday and find myself pretty comfortable, so I think I shall dig myself in, that is if the landlord doesn't raise the rent on me. Of course it isn't what you might call luxurious, but it is as good as one could expect for 7/6 a week so near London. The garden is potentially good but has been left in the most frightful state I have ever seen. I am afraid it will be a year before I can get it nice. As you see by the address this used to be the village shop. The people who had it went bankrupt over a model farm and there has been no shop in the village for a year, so I am thinking of reopening it. Of course there couldn't be much profit in a village of 50–100 inhabitants, especially as vans come from Baldock (three miles away) several times a week, but I don't think I could actually lose money as I have got to pay the rent of the house in any case. At present I am sending out feelers, on the one hand trying to make sure my landlord doesn't double the rent the day after I have bought a new bacon-slicer, on the other making enquiries among the villagers to see whether they would like to have a shop here again. I am a bit vague about how one gets in touch with the wholesalers for a "general" shop, but I suppose it isn't more complicated than a bookshop. If I do open it will be only for certain stated hours so as not to interfere with my work.

I'll send along a review of Brown's book[1] as soon as I can settle to work again, also I'll see that the Adelphi get a copy of my novel.[2] It ought to be out in a few weeks and would have been out a month ago if it had not been for all that bollox about libel. I collected some interesting material for my new book[3] while in Yorkshire and Lancashire, and only hope I shall be able to make use of it. It is a pity I just missed Rees, who is now in Lancashire somewhere I believe. The feuds I observed among the Adelphi followers seemed to centre round two causes. One was that people in each area in the north seem to be savagely jealous of people from other areas and their jealousy takes the form of declaring that theirs is the only genuine distressed area and the others don't know what poverty means. Besides this Brown at Sheffield told me that at the Adelphi summer schools people from the middle classes and genuine working-class people didn't get on together and he and other working-class people were annoyed by patronising airs put on by some of the others. How much truth there was in this I can't say. All the trouble seemed to centre round Brown and Bert Jones. Brown, though at heart a very good fellow and very generous, is rather a difficult person, chiefly owing to his deformity.

When I have got the house and garden into some kind of trim and started to do a little work again, I will come over and see you—I'll give you plenty of notice beforehand. It is a cross-country journey but not far if one did it on a push-bike. Have you got a car or anything nowadays? I would like it if you [could] come over here some time.

Yours
Eric A. Blair

1. *The Fate of the Middle Classes* by Alec Brown.
2. *Keep the Aspidistra Flying.*
3. *The Road to Wigan Pier.*

299. To Leonard Moore
11 April 1936   Typewritten

The Stores   Wallington   Nr. Baldock   Herts.

Dear Mr Moore,

Many thanks for the six copies of "Keep the Aspidistra." When some more become available would you please order three more and charge them to me.[1]

I think I asked you before if a copy could be sent to the New English Weekly. I would also like one to be sent to the Adelphi, as they too said they wanted to review it. Of course it may be that Gollancz doesn't want to whack out free copies to these obscure papers, in which case I will order a couple more copies myself to send to them, as I think it is worth getting some serious (though not necessarily favourable) reviews in papers where I am known.[2]

As to that book of which Gollancz sent me a free copy, I did reviews of it for the Adelphi and N.E.W., and doubtless they will appear in due course.[3]

I am now fairly settled here, am making out the scenario for my new book,[4] and shall be beginning it in a day or two.

Yours sincerely
Eric A. Blair

1. This paragraph is marked with a heavy cross, probably indicating action taken as Orwell requested.
2. This paragraph is marked with a heavy tick, again probably indicating action taken. Richard Rees 'puffed it for the *Adelphi*' and Cyril Connolly 'gave the book a warm but critical welcome in *The New Statesman and Nation*' (Crick, 299).
3. Brown's *The Fate of the Middle Classes*. A review was published in *The Adelphi* in May 1936 (see *308*), and another, unsigned, in the *New English Weekly*, 30 April 1936 (see *307*).
4. *The Road to Wigan Pier*.

300. To Jack Common

Thursday, [16? April 1936]   Typewritten

The Stores,   Wallington, Nr. Baldock.

Dear Common,

Thanks for yours. I have now seen my landlord and it is O.K. about the rent, so I have definitely decided to open the shop and have spread the news among the villagers to some extent. I should certainly be very obliged if you would find out about the wholesalers. I didn't know you had your shop still. I believe there are some wholesalers of the kind at Watford, Kingford or Kingston or some such name. I don't know whether, seeing that I shall only want tiny amounts at a time (apart from the smallness of the village I haven't much storage room), they will make any trouble about delivery. I intend, at first at any rate, to stock nothing perishable except children's sweets. Later on I might start butter and marg. but it would mean getting a cooler. I am not going to stock tobacco because the pubs here (two to about 75 inhabitants!) stock it and I don't want to make enemies, especially as one pub is next door to me. I am beginning to make out lists, though whether any one wholesaler will cover the lot I am not certain. I suppose what I shall start off° will be about twenty quids' worth of stuff. Are these people good about giving credit? What I would like to do would be to give a deposit of about £5 and then pay quarterly. I suppose my bank would give me a reference. It is a pity in view of this that I have just changed my branch because the Hampstead branch were getting quite trustful and told me I could overdraw, though I never asked them. I shall want besides stock one or two articles of shop equipment, such as scales, a bell etc. There are some that go with this place but my landlord has them and he is the sort of person who takes a year before he hands anything over. I have got to tidy up the shop premises and repaint, but if I can click with the wholesalers I should be ready to open up in about 3 weeks.

Yes, this business of class-breaking is a bugger. The trouble is that the socialist bourgeoisie, most of whom give me the creeps, will not be realistic and admit that there are a lot of working-class habits which they don't like and don't want to adopt. E.g. the typical middle-class socialist not only doesn't eat with his knife but is still slightly horrified by seeing a working man do so. And then so many of them are the sort of eunuch type with a vegetarian smell who go about spreading sweetness and light and have at the back of their minds a vision of the working class all T.T., well washed behind the ears, readers of Edward Carpenter[1] or some other pious sodomite and talking with B.B.C. accents. The working classes are very patient under it all. All the two months I was up north, when I spent my entire time in asking people questions about how much dole they got, what they had to eat etc., I was never once socked on the jaw and only once told to go to hell, and then by a woman who was deaf and thought I was a rate-collector. This question has been worrying me for a long time and part of my next book is to be about it.

I will get over when I have a bike or something. If you come over here, either let me know so that there shall be food, or take your chance—but there'll always be *something*, of course. The garden is still Augean (I have dug up twelve boots in two days) but I am getting things straight a little. It is awful to think that for nearly three months I have not done a stroke of work. Getting and spending we lay waste our powers.[2] However I have wads of notes which give me the illusion of not having wasted my time.

Yours
Eric A. Blair

1. Edward Carpenter (1844–1929) was a socialist writer and social reformer whose works include *Towards Democracy* (1883) and *The Intermediate Sex: A Study of Some Transitional Types of Men and Women* (1908).
2. Line 2 of Wordsworth's sonnet, the first line of which is 'The world is too much with us; late and soon' (1807).

301. To Cyril Connolly

Friday, [17? April 1936][1]   Handwritten

The Stores   Wallington, Nr. Baldock   Herts.

Dear Connolly,

The above is now my permanent address, for when your novel[2] comes out. As you see by the address this used to be the village shop. There is now no shop, only vans from Baldock, so I am going to reopen it when I have got the place in order & arranged what wholesalers to deal with. I shan't make much out of it but I ought to make my rent & a little over. Of course I shall have to rationalise it so that it doesn't interfere with my work.

I think you said you had a car so perhaps you might care to come over some time, eg. a Sunday, & perhaps your wife would care to come too. It is about 35 miles from London & might not be a bad run on a fine day. If you do come any time, let me know beforehand lest I should have let myself run out of food, always a danger in these small villages. This is quite a nice little cottage, but with absolutely no conveniences, & if I stay here long, as I dare say I shall, I shall put them in by degrees. The garden is a pigsty at present, but I am doing my best with it. I ought to be all set to open the shop in about 3 weeks. My novel should be out soon—would have been out a month ago only there was that b——x about libel. I went & saw Raymond Mortimer[3] but he was very busy so I grabbed two review copies, one of which turns out to be rather good, & departed.

Yours
Eric A. Blair

1. Orwell told Moore, 2 May 1936, that the shop was due to open on 11 May, and here he says 'in about 3 weeks.' Since *Keep the Aspidistra Flying* was published on 20 April, this was probably written about 17 April.
2. *The Rock Pool*, reviewed by Orwell in the *New English Weekly*, 23 July 1936, see *321*.
3. Raymond Mortimer (1895–1980; CBE, 1955) was a critic and literary editor of *The New Statesman and Nation*. See Orwell's letter to him of 9 February 1938, *424* and also *2022, n. 1*.

302. To Leonard Moore

Saturday, [18 April 1936]   Typewritten

The Stores   Wallington   Nr. Baldock, Herts.

Dear Mr Moore,
Is the enclosed O.K., do you think? I am not certain what he means when he says (p. 2 of letter) "I should wish to receive some remuneration for my adaptation and collaboration" etc.[1] Of course if he means he would expect to receive a share of any royalties that were earned, naturally this would be only proper. On the other hand if he wants me to pay him in advance for adapting the book, nothing doing, of course. Perhaps you would let me know what you think of this letter.

I believe I forgot to acknowledge the cheque for £30 odd you sent me some time back, for which many thanks.[2] I am just starting on my new book and have written the first page or two.[3]

Yours sincerely
Eric A. Blair

1. Presumably the proposed adaptation of *Burmese Days* for the stage; see *297*.
2. The regular twice yearly payment of royalties. See *262, n. 1* for royalties received in that year.
3. In his letter to Richard Rees of 20 April (see *304*), Orwell says he has not begun his new book but is 'all set to do so.' Because he tells Moore in this letter he is 'just starting' his new book, this letter might seem to be later than the one to Rees. However, it is stamped as having been received in Moore's office on 20 April. It may be that 'starting' refers to the scenario Orwell mentions in his letter to Moore of 11 April (see *299*), rather than the text of the book proper.

303. Publication of *Keep the Aspidistra Flying*

Keep the Aspidistra Flying was published by Victor Gollancz Ltd on 20 April 1936. The print run was 3,000, of which 2,500 were bound; 2,256 were sold, at home and overseas, of which 484 were offered as a cheap edition at 3s 6d (instead of 7s 6d) on 16 March 1942. Willison records that 422 of the cheap edition were sold. The type was distributed on 1 May 1936. As a result of German bombing, 500 sets of sheets and, presumably, 244 bound copies were destroyed. The novel was first published in the United States by Harcourt, Brace and Company in December 1956 (Willison and Gollancz records).

304. To Richard Rees

20 April 1936   Typewritten

The Stores   Wallington   Nr. Baldock, Herts.

Dear Richard,

Thanks for your card. Clitheroe,[1] which I vaguely associate with cotton shirts, seems rather a melancholy place to spend the summer in, but everyone to his taste. I have been here about a fortnight, and as you see by the address it has been the village store, and as there is now no shop here (only a tiny village of about 50-75 inhabitants) I am going to reopen it as a "general" shop when I have fixed up with some wholesalers. Jack Common, who has something to do with a shop of the kind I believe, is going to advise me. I haven't as yet done much about it because I have been too busy battling with the garden, which though small has been left in an unspeakable state. It will be about a year before I can make it really nice. It is quite a nice cottage and very cheap, but no conveniences; I shall put these in by degrees if I stay, as I think I shall. I intend opening the shop in the afternoons only, so as to leave me my mornings to work in. I don't expect to make much out of it but I ought to make my rent and a bit over. Wallington is about 35 or 40 miles from town but you can get there fairly quickly if you bike to Hitchin.

I haven't begun my new book yet but am all set to do so. It is not going to be a novel this time. Do you know John Strachey[2] personally? I was at school about the same time as him but didn't know him° I would like to have a talk with him about Mosley with him° some time if I run across him. I heard Mosley[3] speak in Barnsley and his speech though delivered with an excellent platform technique was the most unutterable bollox, but I heard Strachey state in a speech once that Mosley was a very able man. I suppose Strachey has known Mosley intimately, and I would like to know whether M. is sincere in what he says or whether he is deliberately bamboozling the public.

I am going to bike over and see Common some day this week. It is about 8-10 miles. I asked them to send a copy of my new book to the Adelphi—don't know whether they have done so. I also sent a copy to Mrs Meade[4] because I had promised them a copy and M. asked me privately to send it to his wife, but this is troubling me, because I feel she might think herself

473

obliged to read it and it might bore her. If you are with them you could drop a hint to the effect that presentation copies are not meant to be read. It is still beastly cold and everything very late. I have found no nests except thrushes and blackbirds and have not heard the cuckoo or seen a swallow—I usually see my first about the 14th. The blackthorn is out and there are plenty of primroses and cowslips but the hedges are still very bare. If you want to be quiet some time come and stay here, because it is a good place to be quiet if you don't mind the primitiveness, which is bearable at any rate in summer, and there is a nice room you could have.

Yours
Eric A. Blair

1. Clitheroe is a town in Lancashire twenty-eight miles north of Manchester.
2. John Strachey (1901–1963) was a political theorist and Labour M.P., 1929–31. He stood as a candidate for Mosley's New Party, 1931, but shortly after became caught up in the new, widespread enthusiasm for Communism. His book *The Coming Struggle for Power* (1932) was the most influential exercise in Marxism produced by the English Left. He was Labour Minister of Food, 1945–50, and Secretary of State for War, 1950–51.
3. Oswald Mosley; see *295, n. 7.*
4. Wife of Frank Meade, who ran the Manchester office of *The Adelphi.* Orwell stayed with them 6–10 February; see *272.*

305. Review of *Bastard Death* by Michael Fraenkel; *Fast One* by Paul Cain; *The Golden Violet* by Joseph Shearing; *A Different Woman* by Muriel Hine; *The Nursing Home Murder* by Ngaio Marsh and H. Jellett.

New English Weekly, 23 April 1936

Some time ago I reviewed a very unusual book called "Tropic of Cancer," and I suggested that its particular attitude to life derived ultimately from the modern notion that death is an *end* and not the gateway to a new lease of life. The book I have before me this week, also by an American, deals more directly with the same subject—in fact, death is its avowed theme.

Unfortunately, I find "Bastard Death," as a whole, almost unintelligible.[1] "Tropic of Cancer," apart from a certain discursiveness, was cast more or less in ordinary novel form. "Bastard Death" is hardly a novel at all. It consists of a series of separate paragraphs with no very apparent connection between them—in effect, tiny essays—which are perhaps the bones of a possible novel. Here are two or three of them taken at random:—

"I hurry through the streets stark, my sight swollen—an ancient blight upon me. I dare not look into the faces of things . . . of men, women, children, dogs, cats, birds, trees, water, houses. For suffering has conceived indecently."

"The light thins and shrinks, it walks over the hills, nostalgia rankling in it—the pain of distance, of otherness."

"To be strong, to remain in this strength now, the depth cannot be plumbed, the mystery, the sacredness. Now is self-realization, self-completion death."

This, you see, is difficult, and it is not made easier by the explanatory notes, like chapter-headings, that are placed here and there in the margin. I wish I could say that I understood more of this book than individual passages here and there, but I do not. What the author seems to me to be attempting is, in the first place, to reach a fuller awareness of death—a completer realization of death as an absolute (the only absolute we know); secondly, to strip his mind of ordinary mental processes until a point is reached at which thought can begin anew. That is about all I can say—in fact my only function as reviewer is to point this book out to people with minds more abstract than my own. I will take a chance and say that it *is* a remarkable book, and the opinion of Henry Miller, whose writing I do understand and who contributes an introductory letter to this book, confirms me in this.

"Fast One" is also an American book, but of a somewhat different type. The blurb describes it as "a whirlwind of doublecrossing, ambush and murder." Here is a specimen paragraph:—

"The little man came into the room quickly and kicked the side of Kells's head very hard. Kells relaxed his grip on Rose and Rose stood up. He brushed himself and went over and kicked Kells'° head and face several times. His face was dark and composed and he was breathing hard. He kicked Kells very carefully, drawing his foot back and aiming, and then kicking very accurately and hard."

This kind of disgusting rubbish (hailed as "genius" when it comes in a slightly more refined form from Hemingway) is growing commoner and commoner. Some of the threepenny "Yank Mags" which you buy at Woolworth's now consist of nothing else. Please notice the sinister change that has come over an important sub-department of English fiction. There was, God knows, enough physical brutality in the novels of Fielding, Meredith, Charles Reade, etc., but

"our masters then
Were still, at least, our countrymen,"

In the old-style English novel you knocked your man down and then chivalrously waited for him to get up before knocking him down again; in the modern American version he is no sooner down than you take the opportunity of jumping on his face. Unfortunately I have not space here to discuss this question of assault and battery in English fiction. I can only state in passing that it is not, as Bernard Shaw seems to suggest in the preface to "Cashel Byron's Profession," traceable to sadism, but to a subtler and more ignoble cause.

"The Golden Violet" is the story of Angelica Cowley, a female tripe-novelist of the thirties, who marries an odious Jamaica° planter, takes a lover who turns out to be a mulatto, murders her husband at an opportune moment, marries the governor of Jamaica and at the end is once again writing improving novels for young ladies. On the whole rather a good novel; it is a little too like pastiche in places, but the atmosphere of Jamaica is very well rendered.

475

"A Different Woman" is tripe and slightly pernicious tripe. Carla, the heroine, is married to a selfish husband, one of those heartless brutes who expect their wives to keep house with only three servants. She has a most alluring lover called Alaric (by their Christian names ye shall know them: and he had "an arresting face, because of its lean strength and a faint melancholy, which vanished when he smiled"), but the elopement at the end doesn't happen, because Alaric is killed in a motoring accident. However, he returns for a brief visit in spirit form and conducts Carla round the love-nest which they are both to inhabit when she too has passed Beyond the Veil.

"The Nursing Home Murder" is a fairly competent detective story. The motive for the murder and the manner of committing it are both thoroughly dull, but the trail is well covered up and there are plenty of red herrings to choose from. The murdered man is the Home Secretary, and among the red herrings there is the usual gang of Communists or Anarchists, called indifferently one or the other. You see, in England in 1936 it is still quite normal to imagine that a Communist and an Anarchist are the same thing. There are some people whom *nothing* will ever move, except high explosives.

1. On 14 February 1936, Michael Fraenkel (1896–1957) wrote to Orwell to say that he had seen Orwell's review of Henry Miller's *Tropic of Cancer*; see *263*. He thought Orwell 'seemed to have gone so much further with Miller's book than most reviewers. You don't spend most of your time proving or disproving its pornography. . . . You get down to . . . its inherent content.' He asks if Orwell would care to review his last book, *Bastard Death*, which 'attempts to give an articulate expression to this body of ideas—this body of despair—which marks so much of our more significant contemporary literature.' Orwell presumably asked him to send the book, subtitled *The Autobiography of an Idea* (published in Paris and New York in 1936). On 3 May 1936, Fraenkel wrote a friendly letter in response to the review. When he saw it, he said, he had smiled. 'What else could I do? You are so disarmingly frank. You say you do not understand the book. There may be something the matter with the book; but surely there is nothing the matter with you. You are what you are, not an abstract thinker, as you say, apparently at home in a physical reality. The rather transcental° quality of the thought and writing of *Bastard Death* must have seemed considerably removed to you.' He goes on, 'But really, Blair, I say something quite simple,' and he then attempts to explain what it is.

306. To Leonard Moore

Saturday, [25 April 1936]   Typewritten: handwritten postscript

The Stores   Wallington   Nr. Baldock   Herts

Dear Mr Moore,

Many thanks for your letter and the press-cuttings.[1] Most of the latter seem bad—there was an awful one from the Observer and I saw one not much better in the Mail. However, I hardly expected anything else.

You won't forget the three extra copies of "Keep the A.", will you? As I have promised them to various people who are clamouring for copies.

As to that project of dramatising "Burmese Days," if it comes to anything I would like the chap to give it a better title. I forget just what his title was but it was a very weak one. Something like "Black Man's Burden" would be better, I should say.

Yours sincerely
Eric A. Blair

P.S. Books just arrived—many thanks. Also for cheque.[2]

1. Reviews of *Keep the Aspidistra Flying*.
2. Possibly a second cheque, but more probably repeated thanks for the cheque for '£30 odd' mentioned in an earlier letter; see *302*.

307. Review of *The Fate of the Middle Classes* by Alec Brown[1]

New English Weekly, 30 April 1936

Aristocracy can only exist while aristocratic poverty is thinkable. Hence the phrase "nor no poor knight" in that strangely accurate prophecy in "King Lear."[2] Once it is taken for granted that a knight must have at least £1000 a year or stop being a knight, aristocracy gives way to plutocracy.

In England, for centuries past, our so-called aristocracy has been recruited by successive waves of scoundrels who have enriched themselves upon the current swindle and whose position depends solely upon money. The typical member of the House of Lords is a money-lender disguised as a crusader, with a stout wadding of bank-notes under his coat of mail. But a little lower in the social scale the money-principle has not altogether triumphed, and throughout sections of the middle class there has lingered the notion of *gentility* as something superior to and not purchasable by money. This is a point that the Communist, with his eyes glued to "economic realities," is inclined and perhaps wants to miss. Mr. Brown, as an orthodox Communist, explains class solely in terms of money and thus lumps into the middle class everyone who lives neither on dividends nor on a weekly wage. By this definition everyone from the successful professional man to the village cobbler is "middle class," the only differences between them being differences of income; and (for instance) a clergyman, a retail butcher, a sea-captain and a bookie would all have approximately the same attitude to life if their incomes happened to be the same. Actually, as everyone knows, men of similar economic status may differ enormously if they are differently affected by the concept of *gentility*. Thus, in England, an Army officer with £600 a year would die rather than admit a grocer of the same income to be his equal. It is this particular form of snobbery which, when the middle class have learned to act together, may pave the way for some form of Fascism.

For the rest, Mr. Brown's is an interesting book, written in a lively though rather slapdash style, and containing a masterly account of the change-over from industrial capitalism to finance-capitalism.

1. This was one of several books reviewed anonymously under the title 'Reviews.' Orwell wrote another, but signed, review for *The Adelphi* of May 1936; see *308*.
2. From the Fool's prophecy, *King Lear*, 3.2. 79–92.

308. Review of *The Fate of the Middle Classes*, by Alec Brown

The Adelphi, May 1936

It is interesting and rather depressing to see such a complex thing as the English class-system expounded by an orthodox Communist. It is like watching somebody carve a roast duck with a chopper. Mr. Brown, resolutely ignoring everything except economic status, lumps into the middle class the entire block of the population between the dividend-drawers on the one hand and the wage-slaves on the other. The lawyer, the publican, the retail grocer, the clergyman, the smallholder and the village cobbler are all, it seems, "middle class," and Mr. Brown discusses now this type, now that, as though there were no serious distinction between them except the size of their incomes. It is a method of classification about as useful as dividing the population into bald men and hairy men.

In reality the most important fact about the English class-system is that it is *not* entirely explicable in terms of money. The money-relationship on which the Communist rightly insists is interpenetrated by a sort of spurious caste-system. There is no aristocracy in England and in the last resort money will buy anything; yet the aristocratic tradition persists and people are willing to act on it. Hence the fact that every manufacturer or stockbroker who has made his pile sets up an alibi as a country gentleman; hence also the fact that a man with £3 a week who can pronounce his aitches regards himself—and is regarded by other people, to some extent—as the superior of a man with £10 a week who can't. This last fact is enormously important, for it is because of this that the aitch-pronouncing section of the population tend to side with their natural enemies and against the working class, even when they grasp the economic side of the question fairly clearly. The statement that "every ideology is a reflection of economic circumstances" explains a good deal, but it does not explain the strange and sometimes heroic snobbishness that is found in the English middle classes.

The best thing in this book is the explanation—repeated rather too often— of the change that has come over British capitalism since it ceased to export goods and began to export capital. The writing, as in Mr. Brown's other books,[1] is vigorous but slipshod, and there are some exaggerations which might have been avoided. For instance, it is absurd to say that "a quarter of our population is definitely starving," unless by 'definitely starving' you merely mean underfed. The analysis of Mr. H. G. Wells, chosen as a typical middle-class writer, is brilliantly done, but, once again, it fails to take account of the stratifications within the middle class itself.

1. In his diary for 23 March 1936 (see *296*), Orwell wrote, 'I have glanced at Brown's novel [*Daughters of Albion*]. It is b———s.' He reviewed *The Fate of the Middle Classes* also, anonymously, in *New English Weekly*; see *307*.

309. To Leonard Moore

2 May 1936   Handwritten

The Stores   Wallington   Near Baldock   Herts

Dear Mr Moore,

With reference to the attached.[1] I suppose "the new book" they refer to (paragraph 2) is "A Clergyman's Daughter"? All I can say about the sources of it is that the passages relating to hop-picking & to nights spent in Trafalgar Square were drawn directly from my own experience, & that the part about the third-rate girls' school was imaginatively reconstructed from my own experiences in third-rate boys' schools. I see they say they will not repeat photographs they have had before. Perhaps you could send them a pull from that one I had taken for the lecturing people, or send them the block if necessary? It was quite a good photo & it would be rather a nuisance to have another taken. As to "notes dealing with any interest or activity", would it be considered a picturesque detail to say that George Orwell is just setting up a village "general" shop in Hertfordshire? (I am opening up on the 11th.) Also that he is thinking very seriously about getting married.

I don't know when is the time to book lectures for the winter, but do you think those people at South Woodford (the South Woodford Literary Society) would like me to lecture to them again? Perhaps you could approach them? I lectured there last October[2] & so far as I could see it passed off all right. I lectured on some such title as "Confessions of a Down & Out", & I could give a sort of comparison talk to that on life among the coal-miners, using the material I have recently acquired. Conceivably this lecture, & the other, might be worked off on more lecture societies than one. When I lectured I found it seemed to come fairly easy to me & I wouldn't mind doing some more of it if opportunities arose, as naturally I am anxious to earn all I can.

I suppose after the perfectly awful reviews I have had it will not be easy to get an American edition of "Keep the Aspidistra"?[3] But the ones in the Sunday Times, Manchester Guardian, Daily Herald, Morning Post & Time & Tide were all right.

Weather is better here & I am getting my garden, which was a wilderness of tin cans when I came here, into better trim.

Yours sincerely
Eric A. Blair

P.S. I forget whether I mentioned this before. That American who talked of making a dramatic version of "Burmese Days" mentioned a title, but it struck me (I don't remember it now) as a very weak one. If this project comes to anything I would suggest the title "Black Man's Burden."

1. On 23 April 1936, the London office of Harper & Brothers wrote to Orwell asking him for publicity notes and new photographs to help promote his 'new book.'
2. See *258*.
3. Orwell was right: *Keep the Aspidistra Flying* was not published in the United States until December 1956.

310. Review of *We Are Betrayed* by Vardis Fisher; *David and Joanna* by George Blake; *Surprise Item* by Nicolai Gubsky; *The Phoenix' Nest* by Elizabeth Jenkins

Time and Tide, 23 May 1936

Why is it that the typical English novel is staid to the point of primness and the typical American novel is bursting with noise, "action" and physical violence? Ultimately, I think, because in America the tradition of nineteenth-century freedom is still alive, though no doubt the reality is as dead as it is here.

In England life is subdued and cautious. Everything is governed by family ties, social status and the difficulty of earning a living, and these things are so important that no novelist can forget them. In America they either do not operate or it is the convention for novelists to leave them out. Hence the hero of an American novel is presented not as a cog in the social machine, but as an individual working out his own salvation with no inhibitions and no sense of responsibility. If he feels like going to Seattle or setting up a peanut-stand or divorcing his wife in favour of a soul-mate, he can do so provided he has the money—and when the time comes he always does seem to have the money. Vridar Hunter, the young man in *We are Betrayed*, is supposed to be suffering from the after-effects of his "dark and dreadful childhood," but he is in fact master of his destiny to an extent unthinkable in England. He is the usual young rustic—a Mormon by upbringing—who has brains and has come to the city to be educated and is trying to "write." He has made an imprudent marriage while still at college. In rapid succession he becomes a soldier, a garage mechanic, a bootlegger, a lecturer in English literature and the janitor of a block of flats; between whiles he is working away at his novel, studying philosophy and theology and getting mixed up in drinking bouts and bloody affrays about nothing in particular. The one thing he never quite manages to do is to get free of his wife. She is pretty and silly and is devoted to him, and he, unfortunately, is devoted to her. He makes desperate efforts to be unfaithful to her, but almost always flinches at the critical moment. It is, apparently, necessary for the good of his soul that he should get rid of her, and the two children he has begotten are more or less irrelevant.

" . . . . Duty for you is buying food and diapers and sticking to your wife at any cost."

"And what does it mean to you?"

"Honesty with myself . . . ."

Etc. etc. etc. Neither Vridar nor the author appear to recognize any other responsibility. In the end Vridar does not really succeed in freeing himself from his wife; he merely worries her into suicide. The final scenes—the suicide, the desperate unavailing efforts to bring the dead woman round, the horrors of the morgue and the crematorium—are appalling, and written with splendid vigour.

A very able book, and it is an achievement in itself to keep one's interest centred, through 350 pages, on such a half-baked little beast as the hero. But, like so many American novels, it gets its effect largely by enormous omissions.

David and Joanna is also, in a different way, a tale of young people struggling to work out their salvation. A youth and a girl take flight from their depressing relatives and from the ugliness and poverty of industrial Glasgow, and spend a whole summer together in the Highlands, gloriously unmarried. This, of course, is the kind of thing that never lasts long. Presently winter is coming on and a child is due to be born; they come home and submit to be married, and shades of the prison house in the shape of a safe job begin to close upon David. Joanna, however, is still secretly plotting escape. She resolves that after the child is born they will throw up the safe job, go back to the Highlands, get a croft and somehow exist outside the hateful industrial world. Whether she or the author realize quite what kind of life this would mean, I greatly doubt. Mr. Blake writes nicely, but I wish he were not so fond of the word "trig."

Surprise Item is the story of an unbelievably indefinite young man. At the end of the book, as at the beginning, he has failed to discover what he wants. All he knows is that he does not want to be what in fact he is—a member of the upper classes with a small private income. After losing several jobs and divorcing his dull upper-class wife, he drifts into the Communist party, only to drift out of it again on discovering what the higher-up Communists are really like. The author's attitude to Communism is ambiguous. He allows the story to be interrupted by long tirades, some of them very ably written, in favour of Communism, but he represents the politics of the party as a mixture of terrorism and treachery, and leaves it uncertain whether he approves or not.

Those who know how well Miss Jenkins tells a "straight" story will be rather sorry to see her attempting a historical novel, a form which has always rather the air of a *tour de force* or even of an exercise. This tale of theatre-life in the reign of Queen Elizabeth ambles along very gently, so gently that even the death of Marlowe, stabbed in a tavern brawl, with which it culminates, seems almost peaceful. The principal male character is an actor who is making a great hit in the plays of Marlowe, Kyd and Greene. With great strength of mind Shakespeare is not mentioned.

311. To Geoffrey Gorer

Sat., [23 May 1936][1]   Handwritten

The Stores   Wallington   Nr Baldock   Herts

Dear Gorer,

Many thanks for your kind offices re. Time & Tide. They gave me some novels to review. I would have written to you before only as usual I lost your letter with the address & it didn't turn up till this morning. I have had the shop open nearly a fortnight. I took 19/– the first week, this week will be 25/– or 30/ –. That is turnover & the profit on it about pays the rent. I think the business could be worked up to £3 or so. It is very little trouble & no hanging about like in a bookshop. In a grocer's shop people come in to buy something, in a bookshop they come in to make a nuisance of themselves.

I am getting married very shortly[2]—it is fixed for June 9th at the parish church here. This is as it were in confidence because we are telling as few people as possible till the deed is done, lest our relatives combine against us in some way & prevent it. It is very rash of course but we talked it over & decided I should never be economically justified in marrying so might as well be unjustified now as later. I expect we shall rub along all right—as to money I mean—but it will always be hand to mouth as I don't see myself ever writing a best-seller. I have made a fairly good start on my new book.

I was glad to see your book[3] got such good reviews. I saw a very good one in the Times. The book itself I haven't seen yet. When you were in that part of the world did you go to Singapore by any chance? I have a great friend there at the Raffles Museum, Dennis Collings his name is, an anthropologist & very gifted in various strange ways—for instance he can do things like forging a medieval sword so that you can't tell it from a real one. I read your Notes by the Way[4] with great interest. What you say about trying to study our own customs from an anthropological point of view opens up a lot of fields of thought, but one thing to notice about ourselves is that people's habits etc. are formed not only by their upbringing & so forth but also very largely by books. I have often thought it would be very interesting to study the conventions etc. of *books* from an anthropological point of view. I don't know if you ever read Elmer Rice's "A Voyage to Purilia." It contains a most interesting analysis of certain conventions—taken for granted & never even mentioned—existing in the ordinary film. It would be interesting & I believe valuable to work out the underlying beliefs & general imaginative background of a writer like Edgar Wallace. But of course that's the kind of thing nobody will ever print.

Thank God it has rained at last, after 3 weeks drought, & my vegetables are doing fairly well.

Yours
Eric A. Blair

1. In *CEJL*, I, this letter (item 80) followed that to John Lehmann of 27 May 1936. However, in his letter to Moore of 2 May (which has since come to light), Orwell says he expects to open his shop on 11 May (see *309*); here, the shop has been open for nearly a fortnight. That suggests Saturday, 23 May, for this letter, the day his review appeared in *Time and Tide*.
2. To Eileen O'Shaughnessy.
3. *Bali and Angkor.*
4. Properly, 'Notes on the Way,' *Time and Tide*, 23 May 1936.

312. To John Lehmann

27 May 1936   Handwritten

The Stores   Wallington   Near Baldock   Herts.

Dear Mr Lehmann,[1]
I waited before answering your letter, as a friend in London was endeavouring to get me a copy of "New Writing," but evidently she hasn't succeeded yet. What I was going to say was, I am writing a book at present and the only other thing I have in mind is a sketch, (it would be about 2000–3000 words), describing the shooting of an elephant.[2] It all came back to me very vividly the other day & I would like to write it, but it may be that it is quite out of your line. I mean it might be too lowbrow for your paper & I doubt whether there is anything anti-Fascist in the shooting of an elephant! Of course you can't say in advance that you would like it, but perhaps you could say tentatively whether it is at all likely to be in your line or not. If not, then I won't write it; if you think it might interest you I will do it & send it along for you to consider. I am sorry to be so vague but without seeing a copy of 'New Writing' I can't tell what sort of stuff it uses.

Yours very truly
George Orwell

1. John Lehmann (1907–1987) was a writer and publisher, founder and editor of *New Writing*, a literary magazine committed to anti-Fascism, 1936–46 (under various titles). He edited *Penguin New Writing*. 1940–50, *Orpheus*, 1948–49, and *London Magazine*, 1954–61. See also *506, n. 6.*
2. 'Shooting an Elephant' (see *326*) was published in the autumn of 1936; see also *326, n. 1.*

313. To Leonard Moore

8 June 1936   Handwritten

The Stores   Wallington   Nr. Baldock   Herts.

Dear Mr Moore,
Just a line to let you know I am being married tomorrow—very quietly, at the parish church here.
I have done quite a lot of my new book[1] & I suppose it will be done about the usual time. "New Writing" which is published twice yearly by Lane asked me to do something for them. I am writing them a shortish sketch[2]—whether it is quite in their line I am not certain. I just tell you this because according to our contract I am supposed to deal with *publishers* viâ you & this is issued by a publisher tho' it is really a periodical. I suppose you don't know whether "Keep the A." sold decently?[3] The reviews on the whole were awful but several people told me they tried to take it out of libraries & there was a waiting list, which is a good omen, I suppose.
Garden is not doing badly in spite of the drought. I have managed to get hold of another bit of ground, so another year I can grow vegetables there &

have flowers in this garden. The shop is turning over about 30–35 shillings a week & the profit on this just pays my rent for me, which is a help. I dare say it will increase later.

Yours sincerely
Eric A. Blair

1. *The Road to Wigan Pier.*
2. Presumably 'Shooting an Elephant,' published in autumn 1936.
3. Annotated in Moore's office: 'Very rough 1700 inc Col (approx 300) think slight improvement on previous book.' 'Very rough' and 'approx' are doubly underlined. 'Col' is short for 'Colonies,' the book-trade term for Commonwealth countries. For final figures, see *303*.

314. To Anthony Powell

8 June 1936   Handwritten

The Stores   Wallington   Nr. Baldock   Herts.

Dear Mr Powell,[1]
I must apologise for not writing earlier to thank you for your letter & "Caledonia." I liked the latter very much. It is so rare now a days° to find anyone hitting back at the Scotch cult. I am glad to see you make a point of calling them "Scotchmen", not "Scotsmen" as they like to be called. I find this a good easy way of annoying them.[2]

Yes, the reviewers are awful, so much so that in a general way I prefer the ones who lose their temper & call one names to the silly asses who mean so well & never bother to discover what you are writing about.

Please forgive me for not writing earlier. I have been away, but even so I delayed.

Yours truly
George Orwell

1. Anthony Powell (1905–2000) was a novelist and editor. With *A Question of Upbringing* (1951), he began his novel series *A Dance to the Music of Time*. This letter stems from one he wrote to Orwell on 18 May 1936 expressing his approval of *Keep the Aspidistra Flying*, which he preferred to *Burmese Days* and *Down and Out in London and Paris*° 'altho' the latter stands alone as a document.' He referred to the 'extraordinary imbecility of most of the reviews I have seen of the book.' He enclosed his *Caledonia: a fragment*, a verse pastiche of an eighteenth-century satire, privately printed in about 100 copies in 1934. See also *2656, n. 1*.
2. Orwell did later change his attitude. In 'As I Please,' 75A, 27 February 1947, he wrote that it was 'only the most ordinary politeness to do what is asked of one' – that is, call them 'Scotsmen'; see *3176*.

315. Marriage

On 9 June 1936, Orwell and Eileen O'Shaughnessy (see *253, n. 1*) were married in the church at Wallington. See Crick, 303–04; Shelden, 265–67; U.S.: 242–43.

316. To Denys King-Farlow

9 June 1936   Handwritten

The Stores   Wallington   Nr. Baldock   Herts

Dear King-Farlow,[1]
Of course I remember you. But have you changed your name back to King-Farlow? It was Nettleton most of the time you were at Eton. I only got your letter this morning. It was forwarded by Cyril Connolly, who has been away. I'm afraid I can't possibly come along on the 11th, much as I would like to, first of all because it's always difficult for me to get away from here, secondly because like the chap in the N.T. I have married a wife & therefore I cannot come. Curiously enough I am getting married this very morning—in fact I am writing this with one eye on the clock & the other on the Prayer Book, which I have been studying for some days past in hopes of steeling myself against the obscenities of the wedding service. When exactly I'll be up in Town I don't know. This place as you see by the address used to be the village "general" shop, & when I came here I re-opened it as such—the usual little shop stocking groceries, sweets, packets of aspirins etc. It doesn't bring in much but it does pay my rent for me, & for a literary gent that is a consideration. On the other hand it makes it very difficult to get away from here. But if you are ever passing anywhere near, do drop in. It's not much off your track if you are going anywhere in a north-easterly direction or eg. to Cambridge. I should always be at home, except on Saturday afternoons & sometimes on Sundays, & should love to see you again.

I am not in touch with many of the Etonians of our time. Connolly came to see me once in town & he has been very kind in reviewing my books. I used to see Alan Clutton-Brock[2] in 1928—just recently his wife was killed in a motor smash. It was sad about poor Godfrey Meynell.[3] I went & stayed at Cambridge with Gow[4] when I came back from Burma at the end of '27, but though he was very kind it seemed to me I had moved out of his orbit & he out of mine. I suppose most of the others we knew are dons, civil servants & barristers. I hear you have been in the U.S.A. a long time & are very rich & flourishing. I have had a bloody life a good deal of the time but in some ways an interesting one. Please excuse this untidy scrawl.

Yours
Eric A. Blair

1. Denys King-Farlow, a fellow Colleger at Eton and in the same Election (see *29, n. 2*), renewed acquaintance with Orwell in 1936.
2. For Alan Clutton-Brock, see *277, n. 5*.
3. Godfrey Meynell, a contemporary at Eton, had joined the army and was killed on the North West Frontier of India leading his native troops in action. He was posthumously awarded the Victoria Cross.
4. A.S.F. Gow had been Orwell's classical tutor at Eton; see *35*. His picture is in Lewis, 38.

317. To John Lehmann

12 June 1936   Handwritten

The Stores   Wallington   Nr. Baldock   Herts

Dear Mr Lehmann,

Many thanks for the copy of "New Writing,"[1] which I read with great interest. I liked Isherwood's story extremely,[2] & I think it is a splendid thing that there should be at any rate one periodical which has room for long-short stories. I enclose that sketch[3] I mentioned to you. As I say the incident had stuck in my mind & I wanted to write it, but whether it will be quite in your line I am not certain. If not, perhaps I might be able to do something more suitable for some later issue of "New Writing."

Yours sincerely
George Orwell

1. The first number of *New Writing*, which Lehmann edited, was published in April 1936. See Orwell's earlier letter to Lehmann, *312*.
2. Christopher Isherwood (1904–1986) came to prominence in the 1930s with novels centred on Berlin: *Mr Norris Changes Trains* (1935) and *Goodbye to Berlin* (1939). He also wrote verse dramas, including *The Dog Beneath the Skin* (performed in 1935) and *On the Frontier* (1938), with W. H. Auden (see *507, n. 4*). He emigrated to the United States in 1939 and became a U.S. citizen in 1946. The story Orwell so enjoyed was 'The Nowaks.'
3. 'Shooting an Elephant'; see *326*.

318. Review of *Treasure Trek* by James Stead; *Sun on Summer Seas* by Major S. E. G. Ponder; *Don Gypsy* by Walter Starkie

Time and Tide, 11 July 1936

When Mr. Stead, author of *Treasure Trek*, joined the Sacambaya Exploration Company in 1928, it was on the strength of a story so fantastically improbable that only a born adventurer would have paid a moment's attention to it. The story ran that some Jesuits at a remote monastery in the mountains of Bolivia had buried an immense treasure of gold and jewels and afterwards been deported from the country. This was at the end of the eighteenth century, and apparently the leaders of the expedition expected to find the treasure still lying there undisturbed. They must have had very trusting natures. You or I or other low-minded people would have reflected that if the Jesuits had really buried the treasure they might just possibly have gone back and fetched it away afterwards.

Money was wanted for the expedition, and, says Mr. Stead, it "*poured* in." Men were also wanted, and candidates were warned that they were going to a country where the insects would eat them alive, where there would be practically nothing to eat, where they would almost certainly die of blackwater fever if they were not killed by bandits, and where in any case they would break their backs with digging; nevertheless there were four hundred "pleading" applications. Finally twenty men were selected, and when the expedition got to Bolivia it was even worse than they had expected, because of the frightful labour of getting their machinery to the scene of the operations. Anyone who has been in a roadless country will know what that means. They had to drag, by human muscle, pieces of machinery weighing several tons each over mountains that were scarcely passable even for mules. When they had at last reached the supposed site of the treasure they dug frantically for four months, when the rains descended and made further work impossible. By that time they had dug the heart out of a fair-sized mountain, and, needless to say, no treasure had materialised. The expedition broke up, and Mr. Stead took the first boat to Canada and got a job in the trout fisheries. It must be a fine thing to have such an energetic nature as that.

Mr. Stead's further adventures—in Canada, where he found a copper mine which turned out to be valueless because no transport was available, and in Guatemala, where he set out to find the lost treasures of Montezuma and blew a hole in his left hand with a rifle which exploded by accident—are also interesting, though not quite so much so as the first part of the book. As with many books of this kind, interesting subject-matter has to struggle with the most atrocious writing. Expeditions which go exploring and treasure-hunting are always careful to take with them a full complement of doctors, engineers, entomologists and so forth; it is a pity they do not also make a practice of taking at least one trained literary man who could afterwards describe their adventures in decent English.

Major Ponder was transferred from Hong Kong to Malta, and instead of following the direct route he applied for seven months' leave and travelled eastward, via Australia, New Zealand, America and England. The result is an extremely "light," fairly readable travel-book. It deals mainly with hotels and the ordinary show-places, and it does not arouse—at any rate in me—any very ardent desire to follow in Major Ponder's footsteps. This would be a good book with which to while away half an hour in a hotel lounge, but the high price is inexcusable,[1] presumably it is due to the photographs, which, though good enough of their kind, are quite commonplace.

Don Gypsy recounts "the further adventures of a musical picaroon mounted on a frisky hobby-horse." It is all about Spain and raggle-taggle gypsies and picturesqueness generally, even to the extent of a frontispiece of Arthur Rackham. If you like picturesqueness, here is your meat; if you feel about it as I do, here is your poison. The photographs, however, are excellent.

1. Sixteen shillings. The other two books cost 12s 6d and 10s 6d. A novel at that time generally cost about 7s 6d.

319. Review of *Indian Mosaic* by Mark Channing

The Listener, 15 July 1936

This review, Orwell's first for *The Listener*—for which he was paid £1 11s 6d—is not signed. It appears in a section entitled 'The Listener's Book Chronicle.' *The Listener,* published by the British Broadcasting Corporation, first appeared 16 January 1929. Its literary editor from 1935 to 1959 was J. R. Ackerley (1896–1967).

For an average Englishman in India the basic fact, more important even than loneliness or the heat of the sun, is the strangeness of the scenery. In the beginning the foreign landscape bores him, later he hates it, in the end he comes to love it, but it is never quite out of his consciousness and all his beliefs are in a mysterious way affected by it. Mr. Channing knows this, and throughout his story—for it is in a loose sense a story, a history of his 'spiritual pilgrimage' towards Hinduism—he keeps the physical scene before one's eyes.

Mr. Channing is, or was, an officer of the Indian Army. Probably it was fortunate for him that he was in the Supply and Transport Corps and not in an ordinary regiment, for it allowed him to travel widely and to get away from the atmosphere of the barracks and the European clubs. It is interesting to watch his development from a thoughtless youngster contemptuous of 'natives' and chiefly interested in shooting, into a humble student of Persian literature and Hindu philosophy. One of the paradoxes of India is that the Englishman usually gets on better with the Moslem than the Hindu and yet never entirely escapes the appeal of Hinduism as a creed. But as a rule his response to it is unconscious—a mere pantheistic tinge in his thoughts— whereas Mr. Channing has studied Yoga at the feet of a guru and believes that we have far more to learn from India than she from us. He does not, however, believe India to be capable of self-government, and his book ends with a queerly naive mixture of mystical reverence and Kiplingesque imperialism.

To enjoy this book one need not share Mr. Channing's beliefs or take too seriously his accounts of magical happenings. There is a geographical element in all belief—saying what seem profound truths in India have a way of seeming enormous platitudes in England, and *vice versa.* Perhaps the fundamental difference is that beneath a tropical sun individuality seems less distinct and the loss of it less important. But even those with no interest in Hinduism will value this book for its vivid pictures of camps, forests and bazaars, saints, soldiers and animals—pictures which at first seem arbitrarily selected but in the end fall into a coherent and sometimes beautiful pattern.

320. Review of *Tempest Over Mexico* by Rosa E. King; *Rolling Stonemason* by Fred Bower

Time and Tide, 18 July 1936

Reading books like *Tempest Over Mexico* and *Rolling Stonemason*, one is reminded of Conrad's remark that adventures don't happen to adventurous people.

The authors of both these books have known the worst extremities of hunger, danger and homelessness, and both of them are the kind of people who would greatly prefer to live a quiet life if it were possible. Mrs. King, an Englishwoman living in Mexico, had established first a teashop and then a flourishing hotel in the town of Cuernavaca when the Mexican Revolution broke out in 1911. Her children's livelihood and education depended on the hotel, and she refused to abandon it in spite of the six years of almost continuous fighting which raged round and often in the town. Even when she was in comparative safety in Mexico City she insisted on going back to her hotel just at the moment when Cuernavaca was about to be cut off by the rebels and submitted to the horrors of a long siege. When everything had been eaten and scores of people were dying every day of starvation, the general in command decided to evacuate the town with the whole civil population. There followed a frightful retreat through the mountains, with scarcely any food, water or baggage animals, and with the rebels attacking the column night and day and murdering the stragglers. Mrs. King was lucky enough not to be hit by a bullet, but she was badly injured by a dead mule loaded with ammunition falling on top of her, and would not have survived if a young Mexican officer who had befriended her had not lifted her on to his horse. When finally they got to a place of safety, the column, which had started out—men, women and children—eight thousand strong, was reduced to two thousand.

When the Federals had recaptured Cuernavaca, Mrs. King managed to get back to her hotel, to find, of course, that it was in ruins. In any case she never got it back, for the new government handed it over to another owner. She seems, however, to bear no resentment against anybody, and has something good to say even of the most notoriously brutal figures of the Revolution. Even when the rebels were doing their best to slaughter her she found time to reflect that their cause (that of the dispossessed Indians against the feudal landowning class) was a just one and that "in their place I should have acted as they did." Indeed, the lack of bitterness is one of the most remarkable things in a very remarkable book.

Mr. Fred Bower is a stonemason and was brought up, mainly, in the slums of Liverpool, but he has travelled a great deal in foreign countries, particularly in America, working at his trade and lecturing on Socialism. Once again one sees how devotion to a cause will lead the most peaceably-inclined person into adventure. Mr. Bower's life, in between jobs, has been a series of street affrays (it is not so long since it was very unsafe to preach Socialism in America), trouble with the police, penniless periods when he had to jump trains or tramp the roads in search of work, and comfortless journeys across the Atlantic, sometimes as a fireman, sometimes as an unpaid cattle-hand, and once or twice with a forged passport. Finally, at the age of sixty-two, he ended up with silicosis accelerated by malnutrition, and is now living, or existing, on ten shillings a week from the National Health Insurance fund. For years past he has saved rent by living in various caravan residences (in one case a derelict Black Maria) from which the local health officers periodically eject him. What is noticeable is that he seems completely happy. He finds life on ten shillings a week at any rate endurable, and the prospect of dying from exposure hardly troubles him at all. He has had two objects in life, one, to do a good job as a mason, the other, to work for Socialism, and, as he says, "I have no regrets." Incidentally he has assured himself of a queer kind of immortality by planting a copy of the *Clarion* and a revolutionary speech of his own composition deep in the foundations of Liverpool Cathedral.

One of the few encouraging results of universal education is that, at rather rare intervals, books written from a genuinely working-class standpoint are beginning to appear. Jack Hilton's *Caliban Shrieks* was one such book, Private Richard's° *Old Soldier Sahib*[1] was another, and this is a third. Some day, perhaps, working-class writers will learn to write in their own dialect instead of standard South English, and then we shall have a new class of literature which will drive much that is pretentious and silly out of existence.

1. *Old-Soldier Sahib*, by Frank Richards, Second Battalion, Royal Welch Fusiliers, was published in 1936.

321. Review of *The Rock Pool* by Cyril Connolly; *Almayer's Folly* by Joseph Conrad; *The Wallet of Kai Lung* by Ernest Bramah; *Anna of the Five Towns* by Arnold Bennett; *Mr. Fortune, Please* by H. C. Bailey; *The Rocklitz* by George R. Preedy

New English Weekly, 23 July 1936

As Mr. Cyril Connolly is almost the only novel-reviewer in England who does not make me sick, I opened this, his first novel, with a lively interest.

The usual thing to say about a first novel is that it shows great promise but the author has not got his subject-matter completely under control. With Mr. Connolly's novel I should say it is just the other way about. The treatment is mature and skilful—the book looks as if it had been worked at over a period of years—but the subject-matter, especially considering that this is a first novel, is tiresome. The story is a kind of modernization of the myth of Hylas. A young Englishman of the su-superior, monied and cultured type, an Old Wykehamist and a thoroughly ineffectual ass—a 1930 version, really, of the Bernard Shaw Englishman—lands up in one of those dreadful colonies of expatriates calling themselves artists which were dotted all over France during the nineteen-twenties. He decides that he will study them in a detached, scientific way, as one might study the fauna of a rock pool. But behold! detachment is not so easy as he thinks. Almost instantly he has fallen into the pool and been dragged down to the level of its inhabitants, or even lower if that were possible. Before long he is drinking, cadging and lechering exactly like the rest of them, and on the last page he is left gazing at the world through a mist of Pernod but dimly feeling that his present degradation is better than respectable life in England.

There are two reasons why subject-matter such as this is unsatisfactory. In the first place one can hardly approach a novel about artists' colonies on the Mediterranean without reflecting that Norman Douglas and Aldous Huxley did that kind of thing a long time ago and probably better. A more serious objection is that even to want to write about so-called artists who spend on sodomy what they have gained by sponging betrays a kind of spiritual inadequacy. For it is clear that Mr. Connolly rather admires the disgusting beasts he depicts, and certainly he prefers them to the polite and sheeplike Englishman; he even compares them, in their ceaseless war against decency, to heroic savage tribes struggling against Western civilization. But this, you see, only amounts to a distaste for normal life and common decency, and one might equally well express it, as so many do, by scuffling beneath the moulting wing of Mother Church. Obviously, modern mechanized life becomes dreary if you let it. The awful thralldom of money is upon everyone and there are only three immediately obvious escapes. One is religion, another is unending work, the third is the kind of sluttish antinomianism—lying in bed till four in the afternoon, drinking Pernod—that Mr. Connolly seems to admire. The third is certainly the worst, but in any case the essential evil is to think in terms of *escape*. The fact to which we have got to cling, as to a lifebelt, is that it *is* possible to be a normal decent person and yet to be fully alive. Mr. Connolly seems to suggest that there are only two alternatives: lie in bed till four in the afternoon, drinking Pernod, or you will infallibly surrender to the gods of Success and become a London social-cum-literary backstairs-crawler. The orthodox Christian tries to pitchfork you with a very similar dilemma. But both dilemmas are false and unnecessarily depressing.

I criticize Mr. Connolly's subject-matter because I think he could write a better novel if he would concern himself with more ordinary people. But I do not mean to imply that this book is not worth reading. Actually, during the past year I have only read about two *new* books that interested me more, and I doubt if I have read even one that was more amusing. Presumably it was refused publication in England because of the law of libel—there is no indecency in it. The Obelisk Press do a great service by publishing the books that cannot be published over here. It is a pity they think it necessary to pretend in their blurbs and catalogues that they are specialists in pornography.

This time the Penguin Books have not been so well selected as formerly. Out of all Conrad's books, why choose "Almayer's Folly"? There is nothing memorable in it except a certain underlying feeling which one might not detect unless one had lived in the East. It was written when Conrad's English was far from perfect—it is not merely that he employs the foreign idioms that persisted in his prose till far later, but that he had not yet grasped the vulgarity of certain cliché expressions, so that the book teems with phrases like "that astute individual." At present Conrad is out of fashion, ostensibly because of his florid style and redundant adjectives (for my part I like a florid style: if your motto is "Cut out the adjectives," why not go a bit further and revert to a system of grunts and squeals, like the animals?), but actually, I suspect, because he was a gentleman, a type hated by the modern intelligentsia. He is pretty certain to come back into favour. One of the surest signs of his genius is that women dislike his books. But "Almayer's Folly" is only indirectly interesting, because it was Conrad's first book and because of the anecdote about Galsworthy which I suppose is not worth repeating.[1]

The much-praised "Wallet of Kai Lung" seems to me tedious. Probably it owes part of its reputation to having been praised by Belloc, who has damned all modern books but mysteriously excepted four or five. It would have been better to have reprinted Ernest Bramah's excellent detective stories, "Max Carrados" and "The Eyes of Max Carrados." Together with those of Conan Doyle and R. Austin Freeman they are the only detective stories since Poe that are worth re-reading. Incidentally, Ernest Bramah is an example of a rarer bird than the Phoenix, the modest literary man. He hated publicity, and though he made a great popular success with his books he managed to live so obscurely that no one except a few close friends ever discovered what name his pseudonym covered.[2] "Anna of the Five Towns" is a minor work of Arnold Bennett and at this date not worth reading. "Mr. Fortune, Please" is an awful book, of a silliness passing belief, and "The Rocklitz" is a historical novel of a kind I cannot read but which would probably be all right if you know anything about the history of Germany. But on the whole the Penguin Books are keeping up their high level. There are some very good ones in the next batch of ten, and in bulk on my mantelpiece they are as inoffensive to the eye as any sixpenny books could conceivably be.

1. John Galsworthy (1867–1933) and Conrad (1857–1924) were friends. They met when Galsworthy sailed on the *Torrens*, of which Conrad was Chief Officer, in 1893. Conrad was 'a capital chap, though queer to look at,' Galsworthy wrote, and he had 'a fund of stories on which I draw freely.' *Nostromo* was dedicated to Galsworthy. In 'Joseph Conrad: A Disquisition,' *Fortnightly Review*, April 1908, Galsworthy described Conrad's first three novels (the first being *Almayer's Folly*) as 'supercharged; they gleamed, they were luxuriant, like the tropics where their scenes were laid; they had a certain animal delight in their abundance; they rioted' (*Conrad; The Critical Heritage*, edited by Norman Sherry, 1973, 206). In *Castles in Spain and Other Screeds* (1927), Galsworthy wrote that 'only one expression adequately describes the sensations of us who read *Almayer's Folly* in 1894. We rubbed our eyes. Conrad was critically accepted from the very start' (80); and, 'one has only to read Conrad's first book, *Almayer's Folly*, to perceive that he started out on a path of his own, with a method quite peculiar to himself, involuted to a dangerous degree, perhaps, and I can trace no definite influence on him by any writer' (89). No more specific anecdote about Conrad and Galsworthy has been traced.
2. His full name was Ernest Bramah Smith (1869?–1942). *The Wallet of Kai Lung* was first published in 1900. On 4 August 1936, he wrote to Orwell to thank him for his kind reference to the Max Carrados series. Very charmingly, Bramah said that Orwell's opinion of *The Wallet of Kai Lung* cannot diminish his thanks, because he cannot dispute that Orwell has 'very good grounds' for his 'lack of interest'!

322. Lecture, 'An Outsider Sees the Distressed Areas'

The Adelphi Summer School, 4 August 1936

The Adephi Summer School was held at the Adelphi Centre (see *327, n. 4*), Langham, near Colchester, 1–28 August 1936. On each of the four Saturdays, John Middleton Murry gave an introductory talk, and on each Friday summarised the week's conclusions. There were seven or eight talks each week (usually one a day). Orwell, on Tuesday of the first week, 4 August, gave a talk entitled 'An Outsider Sees the Distressed Areas.' Others who spoke that week were Steve Shaw, 'Problems of a Working-class Socialist'; Herbert Read, 'The Function of Art in Modern Society'; Grace Rogers, 'Society and the Family'; J. Hampden Jackson, 'Public Schools'; N. A. Holdaway, 'The Unity of Theory and Practice'; and Geoffrey Sainsbury, 'Humanity and Civilisation.' In the following three weeks, those who gave talks included Reinhold Niebuhr, Max Plowman, Karl Polanyi, John Strachey, and Jack Common (on 'Proletarian Theology'). Rayner Heppenstall acted as chairman for Orwell's talk, and in the second week spoke on 'Material or Spiritual Crisis?' There was a study group each week on a different subject; in the week Orwell spoke, Holdaway conducted the group on 'A New Approach to Economics.'

From the account Heppenstall gives in *Four Absentees* (chapter 15), it would seem that Orwell attended for only a short time. He writes that Orwell 'was coming down to give one of the morning lectures.' After the lecture (for which no text survives) they 'withdrew to the Shepherd and Dog.' Despite their fight eight months earlier (see *250, n. 2*), an incident neither mentioned, they 'settled down to the position of old friends' (125). Murry wrote in his diary, according to Heppenstall, that 'Rayner gave an embarrassing lecture . . . which made me so acutely ashamed for him that I could not look at his face while he delivered it.' Heppenstall maintains that in his lecture he 'anticipated a number of ideas and actual phrases which Murry himself adopted in his ensuing pacifist phase' (127).

See Crick, 305, especially for his discounting of Richard Rees's claim that Orwell intervened in discussions, producing 'breathtaking Marxist paradoxes and epigrams,' and Stansky and Abrahams, II, 182–85. For Charlie Doran's statement that by the time he fought in Spain, Orwell had not read Marx, see *386, n. 1*. See also headnote to *3733* regarding Marxist items in Orwell's collection of pamphlets.

322A. Review of *News from Tartary* by Peter Fleming; *The Abyssinia I Knew* by General Virgin; *Canoe Errant on the Nile* by Major R. Raven-Hart

Time and Tide, 15 August 1936

A journey by train or car or aeroplane is not an event but an interregnum between events, and the swifter the vehicle the more boring the journey becomes. The nomad of the steppe or the desert may have to put up with every kind of discomfort, but at any rate he is living while he is travelling, and not, like the passengers in a luxury liner, merely suffering a temporary death. Mr. Peter Fleming, who set out from Pekin and travelled on horseback across

Sinkiang and down into India via the Pamirs (a distance of well over two thousand miles) knows how to make this clear. His account of the frightful discomforts of the journey—the icy winds, the constant hunger, the impossibility of washing and the struggles with galled camels and exhausted ponies—so far from making one shudder and thank God for *confort moderne*, simply fill one with acute pangs of envy.

"We travelled for seventeen days with the Prince of Dzun. . . . There is something very reassuring about a big caravan. . . . There it wound, stately, methodical, through the bleak and empty land, 250 camels pacing in single file. At the head of it, leading the first string, usually rode an old woman on a white pony, a gnarled and withered crone whose conical fur-brimmed hat enhanced her resemblance to a witch. Scattered along the flanks, outriders to the main column, went forty or fifty horsemen. . . . The little ponies were dwarfed by the bulging sheepskins which encased their masters. Everyone carried, slung across his back, an ancient musket or a matchlock with a forked rest, and a few of the Chinese had repeating carbines, mostly from the arsenal at Taiyuanfu and all of an extremely unreliable appearance. Some people wore broadswords as well."

The journey needed not only toughness but also supreme tact and cunning, for it was made through more or less forbidden territory and neither Mr. Fleming nor his companions (a girl) had a proper passport. There was also the language difficulty and the difficulties caused by some curious gaps in the equipment of the expedition. They had, for example, two portable type-writers (a frightful thing to have to drag across Central Asia) but only one frying pan. For food they had to depend largely on what they could shoot, and their only effective weapon was a .22 rook rifle. Mr. Fleming took the rifle in preference to a shotgun because it made less noise and the ammunition was less bulky; but it was a bold thing to do, for a rifle is not much use unless your game will obligingly sit still to be shot at. By the way, Mr. Fleming describes himself as killing an antelope with the .22 rifle at 400 yards. He says he paced the distance out; I can't help thinking (I only whisper this) that he may have taken rather short paces.

Mr. Fleming seems to have set out on the journey mainly for fun but partly to find out what was happening in Sinkiang. His conclusion is that the U.S.S.R. already controls part of the province and has designs on the rest, less from its own sake than as a strategic jumping-off place against Japanese expansion. It is noticeable that he seems to disapprove rather strongly of the U.S.S.R.'s new imperialistic ambitions. It is a queer tribute to the moral prestige of Communism that we are always rather shocked when we find that the Communists are no better than anybody else.

I prophesy without misgivings that this book will be a best-seller. Parts of it are very badly written—why do writers of travel-books spend so much time in trying to be funny?—but the fascinating material would outweigh far worse faults. The real achievement was not to write the book but to make the journey. And the photographs, mostly taken by Mr. Fleming himself, are so good and so numerous as to make twelve and sixpence a very low price for the book.

The Abyssinia I Knew is not a very good title for General Virgin's book (it is translated from the Swedish by Miss Naomi Walford), for the author only spent a year in Abyssinia, in the official post of military adviser to the Emperor. He has put together a rather scrappy book consisting partly of an account of everyday life in the country, partly of a résumé of the recent history of Abyssinia, and partly of a discussion of the events leading up to the Italo-Abyssinian war. The latter part, of course, is the most interesting. It is doubtful whether anyone in England ever seriously believed in the justice of the Italian cause, for the ony argument put forward by pro-Italians has been to the effect that two blacks make a white; however, the facts revealed in this book make the issue even clearer than before. Incidentally the absurd tale, put abroad by Mr. Shaw and others, that the Abyssinians would have surrendered without resistance if they had not thought the League would support them by force, is authoritatively contradicted.

Canoe Errant on the Nile is a pleasant account of what must be a very pleasant method of travel—that is, wandering down the Nile in a canoe and stopping now and again to examine the Nubian temples which are un-get-at-able in any other way. Major Raven-Hart is chiefly interested in Egyptology, about which he writes with enthusiasm sometimes amounting to passion. At the end he gives a complete list of the equipment he carried. It would be useful to anyone making a similar journey; but what a waste of opportunity to travel all that way by river and not even take a fishing rod!

323. To Henry Miller

26–27 August 1936   Typewritten

The Stores   Wallington   Nr. Baldock   HERTS.

Dear Miller,[1]

Many thanks for your letter. It made me feel rather bad all the same, because I had been meaning for weeks to write to you and had been putting it off. Well, "Black Spring" arrived all right and I liked part of it very much, especially the opening chapters, but I do think, and shall say in reviewing it, that a book like "Tropic of Cancer," dealing with events that happened or might have happened in the ordinary three-dimensional world, is more in your line. I liked "Tropic of Cancer" especially for three things, first of all a peculiar rhythmic quality in your English, secondly the fact that you dealt with facts well known to everybody but never mentioned in print (eg. when the chap is supposed to be making love to the woman but is dying for a piss all the while), thirdly the way in which you would wander off into a kind of reverie where the laws of ordinary reality were slipped just a little but not too much. You do this also in "Black Spring," eg. I like very much your meditation beginning in a public urinal on pp. 60–64, but I think on the whole you have moved too much away from the ordinary world into a sort of Mickey Mouse universe where things and people don't have to obey the rules of space and time. I dare say I am wrong and perhaps have missed your drift altogether, but I have a sort of belly to earth attitude and always feel uneasy when I get away from the ordinary world where grass is green, stones hard etc. It is also, I know, pretty bloody when you have written one unusual book to be blamed for not writing another exactly like it. But I don't want you to think there wasn't a lot in "Black Spring" that I enjoyed. The quality of the prose is fine too, especially that passage I referred to before about the dung and the angels. When I read a piece like that I feel as you feel when you are galloping a really good horse over ground where you don't have to look out for rabbit holes. I will do what I can in the way of reviews. The Adelphi told me I could do a short bit on it, but they are soon going to become a quarterly, and I shall also do it for the New English, but they have shut up shop for August as they always do, so the reviews[2] will be a bit late I expect, but I suppose in your case that doesn't matter so much as with the ordinary twopenny halfpenny novel that is genius for a week and then is sold off as a remainder. I have got to go and milk the goat now but I will continue this letter when I come back.

27.8.36.   I am glad you managed to get hold of a copy of "Down and Out." I haven't one left and it is out of print, and I was going to send you a copy of the French translation (I suppose it was the English version you saw) when I got your letter. Yes, it was published in America too but didn't sell a great deal. I don't know what sort of reviews it got in France—I only saw about two, either because the press-cutting people didn't get them or because I hadn't arranged to have copies sent out with flattering letters to leading critics, which I am told you should do in France. Some others of my books have also been published in America. My second book, "Burmese Days," was published there before being published in England, because my publisher was afraid the India Office might take steps to have it suppressed. A year later my English publisher brought out a version of it with various names etc. altered, so the American edition is the proper one. That is the only one of my books that I am pleased with—not that it is any good qua novel, but the descriptions of scenery aren't bad, only of course that is what the average reader skips. My third book, "A Clergyman's Daughter," which came out in England about a year ago, was published in America last week. That book is bollox, but I made some experiments in it that were useful to me. My last book, "Keep the Aspidistra Flying," won't, I imagine be published in America, because it is a domestic sort of story with an entirely English theme and the American public are getting restive about what I believe is called "British sissy-stuff." I noticed also when I worked in the bookshop that it is harder and harder to sell American books in England. The two languages are drifting further and further apart.

Yes, I agree about English poverty. It is awful. Recently I was travelling among the worst parts of the coal areas in Lancashire and Yorkshire—I am doing a book[3] about it now—and it is dreadful to see how the people have collapsed and lost all their guts in the last ten years. I reviewed Connolly's novel for the N.E.W., but though it amused me I didn't think a lot of it. It surprised me that he should be in such a stew about the book "dating"—as though every book worth reading didn't "date!" I see from the blurb on

"Black Spring" that you got a pretty good write-up from Eliot & Co, also that I am mentioned among them. That is a step up for me—the first time I have been on anybody else's blurb. So no doubt I shall be Sir Eric Blair yet.[4] Write if or when you feel inclined.

Yours
Eric A. Blair

1. Henry Miller (1891–1980) was an American author then living in Paris whose novels, because of their explicitness, were at first banned in Britain and the United States but published on the Continent. *Tropic of Cancer* (1934) is set in a period and milieu of Paris not dissimilar from that in Orwell's *Down and Out in Paris and London*. *Black Spring* (1936) is concerned with his childhood in Brooklyn. After *Tropic of Capricorn* (1939), he returned to the United States.
2. Orwell's review of Miller's *Black Spring* appeared in the *New English Weekly* in September; see 325.
3. *The Road to Wigan Pier.*
4. See Gordon Comstock's sneering bestowal of a knighthood on John Drinkwater in *Keep the Aspidistra Flying*; *CW*, IV, 138, line 5, and Textual Note.

324. Review of *The Black Tents of Arabia* by Carl R. Raswan; *Secret Africa* by Lawrence Green; *In Lightest Africa and Darkest Europe* by P. B. Williams; *Going Native* by Eric Muspratt; *Aerial Odyssey* by E. Alexander Powell
Time and Tide, 12 September 1936

Everyone remembers the long simile in *Paradise Lost*[1] that ends with the lines:

> *The barren plains*
> *Of Sericana, where Chineses drive*
> *With sails and wind their cany waggons light.*

The peculiar charm of this passage is that it evokes, almost like a physical pain, the nostalgia for distant times and places with which people in our age delight in torturing themselves. It is quite probable that this is a pernicious emotion, but we are all acquainted with it and we never take seriously a travel-book that fails to arouse it.

By this test *The Black Tents of Arabia* succeeds, short and scrappy though it is. It is a curious book. The author—a German, apparently, though his book is written in perfect English and there is no indication of a translator—has spent twenty years in the remoter parts of Arabia, buying Arab stallions for European studs and living in complete intimacy with the Bedouins. He has been baptized blood-brother to a Ruala chieftain, has taken part in raids and mass-migrations, starved in the desert, speared wolves, eaten lizards and locusts and had his hair perfumed with gazelle-dung by Bedouin maidens. His book is full of strange lore about camels, Arab horses, hunting and hawking (apparently even gazelles are hunted with the falcon), and it contains a love-story which starts off in romantic Arabian Nights style but has such a grisly ending that one feels certain it must be authentic. If you want to find yourself pining for the deserts of Inner Arabia and thoroughly discontented with your office job and the 8.15 to Town, this is probably the book you are looking for.

Secret Africa, on the other hand, is the kind of travel-book which is amusing for a little while but which has not enough "atmosphere" to awaken feelings of nostalgia. The author is one of those lucky people who can afford to travel round the world collecting improbable stories—"weird and fascinating mysteries," as the blurb on the dust-jacket puts it. The clinical methods of African witch-doctors, the mass-suicides of False Killer Whales, the longevity of Bushmen and Hottentots, diamond-thefts, dodos, liqueurs, snakes, scorpions, murder-trees and tarantulas are some of the subjects he touches on. Personally I rather enjoy learning that the dodo became extinct because imported pigs ate its eggs, that baboons will take to flight at the sight of a man but are not afraid of women, and that the Bushmen of South Africa store fat in their buttocks against lean times and frequently live to be 120 years old; and I hope some of these stories are true, because I shall probably repeat them.

The other African book of my list, *In Lightest Africa and Darkest Europe*, is very "light" indeed. It is a facetious account, rather in the Ian Hay manner, of the author's experiences as a trooper in the British South African Police, as a soldier in the Great War and afterwards as a prospector. I found it tiresome, but as all profits from it are to be donated to the British Legion, one can admire the author's generosity even if one fails to admire his literary style.

Going Native is disappointing. It does, however, chronicle two remarkable achievements—sailing across the North Atlantic in a 30-ton yawl, and living for several weeks on a real desert island, the kind of desert island everyone has always wanted, with palm trees, springs of fresh water, wild goats which let themselves be caught and milked, and glassy seas full of tropical fishes. A book like that ought to be enthralling; but unfortunately it is full of long rambling digressions which appear to have been written at great speed and are mostly about Mr. Muspratt's less conclusive love affairs. This is a pity, for it is obvious everywhere that Mr. Muspratt has real literary gifts and could write a much better book if he chose.

Aerial Odyssey describes an air-journey round the Caribbean Sea, and also illustrates the shortcomings of aeroplane-travel. You can get from place to place at enormous speed, but you see nothing while you are travelling, and even when you land you don't see much because very often you have only a quarter of an hour before the aeroplane takes off again. The author (an American) is obviously indebted to guide-books for much of his material. It must be very nice to be able to travel by air-liner, but I don't think you ought to call that kind of journey an Odyssey. If Odysseus had left Troy in an aeroplane instead of a galley he would have been home in half an hour, and Penelope would have been spared at least three causes for jealousy.

1. Orwell quotes Book 3, lines 437–39; the long simile to which he refers starts at line 431.

325. Review of *Black Spring* by Henry Miller; *A Passage to India* by E. M. Forster; *Death of a Hero* by Richard Aldington; *The Jungle* by Upton Sinclair; *A Hind Let Loose* by C. E. Montague; *A Safety Match* by Ian Hay

New English Weekly, 24 September 1936

When Henry Miller's "Tropic of Cancer" appeared a year ago I approached it with caution because, like a lot of other people, I did not wish to seem or to be impressed by mere obscenity. But I realize now, from the intensity with which it has stayed in my mind, that I underpraised it, and I would like to mention it again before dealing with his new novel, "Black Spring."

The interest of "Tropic of Cancer" was that it cast a kind of bridge across the frightful gulf which exists, in fiction, between the intellectual and the man-in-the-street. English fiction on its higher levels is for the most part written by literary gents about literary gents for literary gents; on its lower levels it is generally the most putrid "escape" stuff—old maids' fantasies about Ian Hay male virgins, or little fat men's visions of themselves as Chicago gangsters. Books about ordinary people behaving in an ordinary manner are extremely rare, because they can only be written by someone who is capable of standing both inside and outside the ordinary man, as Joyce for instance stands inside and outside Bloom; but this involves admitting that you yourself *are* an ordinary person for nine-tenths of the time, which is exactly what no intellectual ever wants to do. "Tropic of Cancer" was a smaller book than "Ulysses." It was not primarily a work of art and it made no attempt to analyse different states of consciousness. But in one way it bridged the gap between the thinking and the unthinking man more successfully than "Ulysses," in that it was not complicated by feelings of horror and repentance. The average sensual man was not used as a kind of confession-box, like Eliot's Sweeny,° but taken for granted. The book's standpoint was really that of Whitman, but without Whitman's American puritanism (which escapes notice because disguised as a kind of nudist uplift) or his American bumptiousness. It was a notable effort to get the thinking man down from his chilly perch of superiority and back into contact with the man-in-the-street; it was only incidentally a pity, perhaps, that the street in question should be the Rue de la Harpe.

"Black Spring" is a book of different scope. It no longer deals with recognizable events of ordinary life, or rather it uses them only as nuclei round which spins a kind of Mickey Mouse universe where things do not have to happen according to the ordinary laws of space and time. Each chapter or each passage starts off with a fragment of reality which is so to speak blown out into a balloon of fantasy. I take one example more or less at random:—

". . . Men and women promenading on the sidewalks: curious beasts, half-human, half-celluloid. Walking up and down the Avenue half-crazed, their teeth polished, their eyes glazed. The women in beautiful garbs, each one equipped with a cold-storage smile. . . . Smiling through life with that demented, glazed look in the eyes, the flags unfurled, the sex flowing sweetly through the sewers. I had a gat with me and when we got to Forty-Second Street I opened fire. Nobody paid any attention. I mowed them down right and left, but the crowd got no thinner. The living walked over the dead, smiling all the while to advertise their beautiful white teeth."

You see here how something that is or might be a description of ordinary reality slides away into pure dream. There is no need to get bogged up in metaphysical discussions about the meaning of "reality." The point is that words are here being used to invade what is really the province of the film. A Mickey Mouse film breaks the rules of common sense more violently than any book ever written, yet because it is seen it is perfectly intelligible. Try to describe it in words and you will fail; worse, nobody will listen to you. The truth is that the written word loses its power if it departs too far, or rather if it stays away too long, from the ordinary world where two and two make four. A tendency to put his day-dreams on paper was apparent in Henry Miller's earlier book, and I think he has been led further in that direction by the remarkable power over words which enables him to slide from reality to fantasy and from urinals to angels without the smallest appearance of effort or incongruity. From a technical point of view this book is an advance on the other. At worst his prose can be flat and full of rhymes, like the passage I quoted above, but at its best it is astonishing. As usual I cannot quote any of the best passages, because of the unprintable words, but if you can get hold of a copy, have a look at the passage between pages 50 and 64, for instance. It is the kind of prose which, when I read it, makes me feel that I should like to fire a salute of twenty-one guns.

I advise anyone who can get hold of this book to read it, and if you happen to have a copy of the first edition, hold it tight, for it may be worth money some day. But I still prefer the earlier book, and I wish that Mr. Miller would chronicle some more of the adventures of his disreputable friends, for which task he seems so admirably suited.[1]

There is some good stuff in the last issue of the Penguin Library. "A Passage to India" is not the perfect novel about India, but it is the best we have ever had and the best we are likely to get, for it is only by some improbable accident that anyone capable of writing a decent novel can be got to stay in India long enough to absorb the atmosphere. I was too young to fight in the war and therefore my opinion about it is valueless, but "Death of a Hero" has always seemed to me to be much the best of the English war books, at least of those describable as novels. The Soviet Government seem to have thought the same when they authorised its translation into Russian. It is a tribute to the book's vitality that the realistic descriptions of the fighting do not clash too violently with the preposterous burlesque of the first part. "The Jungle" is good if you like facts—and you can be sure they are authentic facts, for no one has ever got away with a libel action against Upton Sinclair. "A Hind Let Loose," on the other hand, like all Montague's books, is tiresome and empty. He was one of those "deliciously witty" writers who are all sparkle and no taste, like soda-water.

I shan't quote from "A Safety Match," but I will quote, from the blurb,

what the late Professor Saintsbury wrote to the author on its publication:—
'Let me congratulate you on 'A Safety Match.' *I have read nothing so good for a long time.*"

My italics. Please notice that Saintsbury was probably the most widely-read man in Europe. This shows you what happens to professors of literature when they are so unwise as to write about contemporary books.

1. Miller wrote to Orwell to express his gratitude for this review: 'amazingly sympathetic. Kahane, the publisher, was even more delighted.' He hoped that in time Orwell would take a favourable backward glance at *Black Spring*. The Alderman Library, University of Virginia, has a typescript of the portion of this review that deals with *Black Spring* among its Henry Miller papers. This is not Orwell's typescript but a copy of the printed review.

326. 'Shooting an Elephant'

New Writing, 2, Autumn 1936[1]

In Moulmein, in Lower Burma, I was hated by large numbers of people—the only time in my life that I have been important enough for this to happen to me. I was subdivisional police officer of the town, and in an aimless, petty kind of way anti-European feeling was very bitter. No one had the guts to raise a riot, but if a European woman went through the bazaars alone somebody would probably spit betel juice over her dress. As a police officer I was an obvious target and was baited whenever it seemed safe to do so. When a nimble Burman tripped me up on the football field and the referee (another Burman) looked the other way, the crowd yelled with hideous laughter. This happened more than once. In the end the sneering yellow faces of young men that met me everywhere, the insults hooted after me when I was at a safe distance, got badly on my nerves. The young Buddhist priests were the worst of all. There were several thousands of them in the town and none of them seemed to have anything to do except stand on street corners and jeer at Europeans.

All this was perplexing and upsetting. For at that time I had already made up my mind that imperialism was an evil thing and the sooner I chucked up my job and got out of it the better. Theoretically—and secretly, of course—I was all for the Burmese and all against their oppressors, the British. As for the job I was doing, I hated it more bitterly than I can perhaps make clear. In a job like that you see the dirty work of Empire at close quarters. The wretched prisoners huddling in the stinking cages of the lock-ups, the grey, cowed faces of the long-term convicts, the scarred buttocks of the men who had been flogged with bamboos—all these oppressed me with an intolerable sense of guilt. But I could get nothing into perspective. I was young and ill-educated and I had had to think out my problems in the utter silence that is imposed on every Englishman in the East. I did not even know that the British Empire is dying, still less did I know that it is a great deal better than the younger empires that are going to supplant it. All I knew was that I was stuck between my hatred of the empire I served and my rage against the evil-spirited little beasts who tried to make my job impossible. With one part of my mind I thought of the British Raj as an unbreakable tyranny, as something clamped down, in saecula saeculorum, upon the will of prostrate peoples; with another part I thought that the greatest joy in the world would be to drive a bayonet into a Buddhist priest's guts. Feelings like these are the normal by-products of imperialism; ask any Anglo-Indian official, if you can catch him off duty.

One day something happened which in a roundabout way was enlightening. It was a tiny incident in itself, but it gave me a better glimpse than I had had before of the real nature of imperialism—the real motives for which despotic governments act. Early one morning the sub-inspector at a police station the other end of the town rang me up on the phone and said that an elephant was ravaging the bazaar. Would I please come and do something about it? I did not know what I could do, but I wanted to see what was happening and I got on to a pony and started out. I took my rifle, an old .44 Winchester and much too small to kill an elephant, but I thought the noise might be useful in terrorem. Various Burmans stopped me on the way and told me about the elephant's doings. It was not, of course, a wild elephant, but a tame one which had gone 'must.' It had been chained up as tame elephants always are when their attack of 'must' is due, but on the previous night it had broken its chain and escaped. Its mahout, the only person who could manage it when it was in that state, had set out in pursuit, but he had taken the wrong direction and was now twelve hours' journey away, and in the morning the elephant had suddenly reappeared in the town. The Burmese population had no weapons and were quite helpless against it. It had already destroyed somebody's bamboo hut, killed a cow and raided some fruit-stalls and devoured the stock; also it had met the municipal rubbish van, and, when the driver jumped out and took to his heels, had turned the van over and inflicted violences upon it.

The Burmese sub-inspector and some Indian constables were waiting for me in the quarter where the elephant had been seen. It was a very poor quarter, a labyrinth of squalid bamboo huts, thatched with palm-leaf, winding all over a steep hillside. I remember that it was a cloudy stuffy morning at the beginning of the rains. We began questioning the people as to where the elephant had gone, and, as usual, failed to get any definite information. That is invariably the case in the East; a story always sounds clear enough at a distance, but the nearer you get to the scene of events the vaguer it becomes. Some of the people said that the elephant had gone in one direction, some said that he had gone in another, some professed not even to have heard of any elephant. I had almost made up my mind that the whole story was a pack of lies, when we heard yells a little distance away. There was a loud, scandalized cry of 'Go away, child! Go away this instant!' and an old woman with a switch in her hand came round the corner of a hut, violently shooing away a crowd of naked children. Some more women followed, clicking their tongues and exclaiming; evidently there was something there that the children ought not to have seen. I rounded the hut and saw a man's dead body sprawling in the mud. He was an Indian, a black Dravidian coolie, almost naked, and he could not have been dead many minutes. The people said that the elephant had come suddenly upon him round the corner of the hut, caught him with its trunk, put its foot on his back and ground him into the earth. This was the rainy season and the ground was soft, and his face had scored a trench a foot deep and a couple of yards long. He was lying on his belly with arms crucified and head sharply twisted to one side. His face was coated with mud, the eyes wide open, the teeth bared and grinning with an expression of unendurable agony. (Never tell me, by the way, that the dead look peaceful. Most of the corpses I have seen looked devilish.) The friction of the great beast's foot had stripped the skin from his back as neatly as one skins a rabbit. As soon as I saw the dead man I sent an orderly to a friend's house nearby to borrow an elephant rifle. I had already sent back the pony, not wanting it to go mad with fright and throw me if it smelled the elephant.

The orderly came back in a few minutes with a rifle and five cartridges, and meanwhile some Burmans had arrived and told us that the elephant was in the paddy fields below, only a few hundred yards away. As I started forward practically the whole population of the quarter flocked out of the houses and followed me. They had seen the rifle and were all shouting excitedly that I was going to shoot the elephant. They had not shown much interest in the elephant when he was merely ravaging their homes, but it was different now that he was going to be shot. It was a bit of fun to them, as it would be to an English crowd; besides, they wanted the meat. It made me vaguely uneasy. I had no intention of shooting the elephant—I had merely sent for the rifle to defend myself if necessary—and it is always unnerving to have a crowd following you. I marched down the hill, looking and feeling a fool, with the rifle over my shoulder and an ever-growing army of people jostling at my heels. At the bottom, when you got away from the huts, there was a metalled road and beyond that a miry waste of paddy fields a thousand yards across, not yet ploughed but soggy from the first rains and dotted with coarse grass. The elephant was standing eighty yards from the road, his left side towards us. He took not the slightest notice of the crowd's approach. He was tearing up bunches of grass, beating them against his knees to clean them and stuffing them into his mouth.

I had halted on the road. As soon as I saw the elephant I knew with perfect certainty that I ought not to shoot him. It is a serious matter to shoot a working elephant—it is comparable to destroying a huge and costly piece of machinery—and obviously one ought not to do it if it can possibly be avoided. And at that distance, peacefully eating, the elephant looked no more dangerous than a cow. I thought then and I think now that his attack of 'must' was already passing off; in which case he would merely wander harmlessly about until the mahout came back and caught him. Moreover, I did not in the least want to shoot him. I decided that I would watch him for a little while to make sure that he did not turn savage again, and then go home.

But at that moment I glanced round at the crowd that had followed me. It was an immense crowd, two thousand at the least and growing every minute. It blocked the road for a long distance on either side. I looked at the sea of yellow faces above the garish clothes—faces all happy and excited over this bit of fun, all certain that the elephant was going to be shot. They were watching me as they would watch a conjuror about to perform a trick. They did not like me, but with the magical rifle in my hands I was momentarily worth watching. And suddenly I realized that I should have to shoot the elephant after all. The people expected it of me and I had got to do it; I could feel their two thousand wills pressing me forward, irresistibly. And it was at this moment, as I stood there with the rifle in my hands, that I first grasped the hollowness, the futility of the white man's dominion in the East. Here was I, the white man with his gun, standing in front of the unarmed native crowd—seemingly the leading actor of the piece; but in reality I was only an absurd puppet pushed to and fro by the will of those yellow faces behind. I perceived in this moment that when the white man turns tyrant it is his own freedom that he destroys. He becomes a sort of hollow, posing dummy, the conventionalized figure of a sahib. For it is the condition of his rule that he shall spend his life in trying to impress the 'natives,' and so in every crisis he has got to do what the 'natives' expect of him. He wears a mask, and his face grows to fit it. I had got to shoot the elephant. I had committed myself to doing it when I sent for the rifle. A sahib has got to act like a sahib; he has got to appear resolute, to know his own mind and do definite things. To come all that way, rifle in hand, with two thousand people marching at my heels, and then to trail feebly away, having done nothing—no, that was impossible. The crowd would laugh at me. And my whole life, every white man's life in the East, was one long struggle not to be laughed at.

But I did not want to shoot the elephant. I watched him beating his bunch of grass against his knees, with that preoccupied grandmotherly air that elephants have. It seemed to me that it would be murder to shoot him. At that age I was not squeamish about killing animals, but I had never shot an elephant and never wanted to. (Somehow it always seems worse to kill a *large* animal.) Besides, there was the beast's owner to be considered. Alive, the elephant was worth at least a hundred pounds; dead, he would only be worth the value of his tusks—five pounds, possibly. But I had got to act quickly. I turned to some experienced-looking Burmans who had been there when we arrived, and asked them how the elephant had been behaving. They all said the same thing: he took no notice of you if you left him alone, but he might charge if you went too close to him.

It was perfectly clear to me what I ought to do. I ought to walk up to within, say, twenty-five yards of the elephant and test his behaviour. If he charged I could shoot, if he took no notice of me it would be safe to leave him until the mahout came back. But also I knew that I was going to do no such thing. I was a poor shot with a rifle and the ground was soft mud into which one would sink at every step. If the elephant charged and I missed him, I should have about as much chance as a toad under a steam-roller. But even then I was not thinking particularly of my own skin, only of the watchful yellow faces behind. For at that moment, with the crowd watching me, I was not afraid in the ordinary sense, as I would have been if I had been alone. A white man mustn't be frightened in front of 'natives'; and so, in general, he isn't frightened. The sole thought in my mind was that if anything went wrong those two thousand Burmans would see me pursued, caught, trampled on and reduced to a grinning corpse like that Indian up the hill. And if that happened it was quite probable that some of them would laugh. That would never do. There was only one alternative. I shoved the cartridges into the magazine and lay down on the road to get a better aim.

The crowd grew very still, and a deep, low, happy sigh, as of people who see the theatre curtain go up at last, breathed from innumerable throats. They were going to have their bit of fun after all. The rifle was a beautiful German thing with cross-hair sights. I did not then know that in shooting an elephant one should shoot to cut an imaginary bar running from ear-hole to ear-hole. I ought therefore, as the elephant was sideways on, to have aimed straight at his ear-hole; actually I aimed several inches in front of this, thinking the brain would be further forward.

When I pulled the trigger I did not hear the bang or feel the kick—one never does when a shot goes home—but I heard the devilish roar of glee that went up from the crowd. In that instant, in too short a time, one would have thought, even for the bullet to get there, a mysterious, terrible change had come over the elephant. He neither stirred nor fell, but every line of his body had altered. He looked suddenly stricken, shrunken, immensely old, as though the frightful impact of the bullet had paralysed him without knocking him down. At last, after what seemed a long time—it might have been five seconds, I dare say—he sagged flabbily to his knees. His mouth slobbered. An enormous senility seemed to have settled upon him. One could have imagined him thousands of years old. I fired again into the same spot. At the second shot he did not collapse but climbed with desperate slowness to his feet and stood weakly upright, with legs sagging and head drooping. I fired a third time. That was the shot that did for him. You could see the agony of it jolt his whole body and knock the last remnant of strength from his legs. But in falling he seemed for a moment to rise, for as his hind legs collapsed beneath him he seemed to tower upwards like a huge rock toppling, his trunk reaching skyward like a tree. He trumpeted, for the first and only time. And then down he came, his belly towards me, with a crash that seemed to shake the ground even where I lay.

I got up. The Burmans were already racing past me across the mud. It was obvious that the elephant would never rise again, but he was not dead. He was breathing very rhythmically with long rattling gasps, his great mound of a side painfully rising and falling. His mouth was wide open—I could see far down into caverns of pale pink throat. I waited a long time for him to die, but his breathing did not weaken. Finally I fired my two remaining shots into the spot where I thought his heart must be. The thick blood welled out of him like red velvet, but still he did not die. His body did not even jerk when the shots hit him, the tortured breathing continued without a pause. He was dying, very slowly and in great agony, but in some world remote from me where not even a bullet could damage him further. I felt that I had got to put an end to that dreadful noise. It seemed dreadful to see the great beast lying there, powerless to move and yet powerless to die, and not even to be able to finish him. I sent back for my small rifle and poured shot after shot into his heart and down his throat. They seemed to make no impression. The tortured gasps continued as steadily as the ticking of a clock.

In the end I could not stand it any longer and went away. I heard later that it took him half an hour to die. Burmans were arriving with dahs and baskets even before I left, and I was told they had stripped his body almost to the bones by the afternoon.

Afterwards, of course, there were endless discussions about the shooting of the elephant. The owner was furious, but he was only an Indian and could do nothing. Besides, legally I had done the right thing, for a mad elephant has to be killed, like a mad dog, if its owner fails to control it. Among the Europeans opinion was divided. The older men said I was right, the younger men said it was a damn shame to shoot an elephant for killing a coolie, because an elephant was worth more than any damn Coringhee coolie. And afterwards I was very glad that the coolie had been killed; it put me legally in the right and it gave me a sufficient pretext for shooting the elephant. I often wondered whether any of the others grasped that I had done it solely to avoid looking a fool.[2]

1. John Lehmann, who edited both *New Writing* and *Penguin New Writing*, reprinted 'Shooting an Elephant' in the first issue (November 1940) of the latter. It was broadcast by the BBC Home Service on 12 October 1948. It is not known if this essay is based on an actual occurrence, but note Orwell's 'It all came back to me very vividly' and 'the incident had stuck in my mind' in his letters to Lehmann; see *312* and *317*.
2. Reminiscences of George Stuart, in the Orwell Archive (see headnote to 'Burma, 1922–1927; *63*), record that when a message was brought to the club in Moulmein one Sunday morning, Orwell 'went off in his old Ford to pick up a rifle and went in search of the elephant which was causing great damage on a semi main road and causing danger to life and limb and he shot this elephant.' He was very nonchalant about the whole affair, according to Stuart, but got into serious trouble because the elephant was valuable and because of 'the influence these big firms had over the government.' As a result, Orwell was transferred to Katha. The chief of the police service, Colonel Welbourne, was particularly angry and made a point of denigrating Orwell, saying, for example, that he was a disgrace to Eton: 'Everyone was disgusted with the way he ran Blair down.' See Jeffrey Meyers, *A Reader's Guide to George Orwell*, 71–73, Crick, 165–66, 301–02; Stansky and Abrahams, II, 159–61; Shelden, 115, 117–18; U.S.: 105, 107–08.

327. To Jack Common

5 October 1936   Typewritten

The Stores   Wallington   Nr. Baldock   <u>HERTS.</u>

Dear Comrade Common,

(I hope by the way you share my prejudice against that accursed word "comrade", which has kept many a likely recruit away from the Socialist movement), thanks for yours. I thought "Walls have Mouths" was very good and have given it the best review[1] I could manage in the length, because I thought 800 words was probably the maximum you would have room for. I also take the liberty of sending a poem[2] I had by me and thought you might be able to use. I want some time to do a short note on Henry Miller the American novelist, who in my opinion is something out of the common. I have done reviews of his books in the New English Weekly, but would like to give him a boost anywhere I am allowed, which of course is not in the commercial press, as he comes from a non-advertising publisher.

Yes, do come across any time you feel up to the effort. We are practically always at home, except sometimes on Saturday and Sunday afternoons, and at the end of this month when we are going to stay with my people for a week. It is a pity it is so difficult to get here. Of course you probably *could* get here by bus if you took some circuitous route, eg. via Royston, as there is at any rate occasionally a bus from Royston to Sandon, which is only a couple of miles from here.

Things are prospering tolerably. I have just finished the rough draft of my book and begun on the revision, which will take me till some time in December. It is not a novel this time but a sort of book of essays,[3] but I am afraid I have made rather a muck of parts of it. The goat is giving a quart of milk a day and some of the hens have begun laying. The shop is not doing a great deal but is just about paying our rent for us. I haven't heard from Rees for ages and I want to write to him. Where is he now? Is he still at the Centre?[4] I enjoyed my very short trip there and met some interesting people, and I wished I could have stayed longer especially to hear Holdaway[5] and John Strachey lecture. I was greatly impressed by Large,[6] whom no doubt you know, and my wife almost fell in love with him when he came to tea here.

Please remember me to your wife.

Yours
Eric A. Blair

[Handwritten at top of letter] Or, 'fellow-worker before the Dawn.'

1. Orwell's review of *Walls Have Mouths* by W. F. R. Macartney appeared in *The Adelphi*, November 1936; see *331*.
2. 'A happy vicar I might have been' was published in *The Adelphi*, December 1936; see *335*.
3. Note this description of *The Road to Wigan Pier*.
4. The Adelphi Centre, an offshoot of the magazine, was founded in the summer of 1936 at Langham, Essex. It was intended to be a small self-supporting community with a guest-house for summer schools and conferences designed to promote socialist studies. 'Though less influential [it] was as much a phenomenon of the 1930s as the Left Book Club, but its pedigree, mixing Utopian and Messianic strains, extended back as far as Coleridge and his Pantisocracy, and reflected too the yearnings of D. H. Lawrence . . . for a colony of kindred spirits . . . ' (Stansky and Abrahams, II, 182).
5. N. A. Holdaway, schoolmaster and Marxist theorist, member of the Independent Socialist Party, contributor to *The Adelphi*, was Director of the Adelphi Centre. William Brown (see Orwell's letter to Rees in February, *288*) wrote to Orwell (undated) mentioning that Holdaway 'is certainly worth listening to. Some of those I listened to were not.'
6. E. C. Large was a plant chemist, and author of *The Advance of the Fungi* and a number of novels.

328. Review of *Zest for Life* by Johann Wöller, translated from
the Danish by Claude Napier; *I Took Off My Tie* by Hugh
Massingham

Time and Tide, 17 October 1936

Roughly speaking, no one capable of describing the atmosphere of the tropics
is willing to stay there long enough to absorb it. Hence the rarity of good
novels about the Far East, which can only be written by people who are in
some way anomalous, like Joseph Conrad.

Mr. Wöller is not in the same class as Conrad, but he has points in common
with him. He is a Dane who has spent thirty years in the Dutch service in the
East Indies, he is sodden with memories of Java and Sumatra, and he writes
about them from the angle of someone in touch with European culture. Not
completely in touch, or he would hardly describe Sigrid Undset and G. K.
Chesterton as "two of the most considerable nordic intellects" (incidentally,
how Mr. Chesterton would have hated to be called "nordic"!), but too much
so, probably, to have been quite at home with his fellow-officials over a gin
sling. The underlying theme of the book is the peculiar double homesickness
which is the punishment for deserting your native land. It is really a mistake
to travel—or rather, one should travel only as a sailor or a nomad travels, not
sending roots into foreign places. Live among palm trees and mosquitoes in
savage sunshine, in the smell of garlic and the creaking of bullock-cart
wheels, and you pine for Europe until the time comes when you would
exchange the whole of the so-called beauties of the East for the sight of a
single snowdrop, or a frozen pond, or a red pillar-box. Come back to
Europe, and all you can remember is the blood-red flowers of the hibiscus
and the flying foxes streaming overhead. Yet it seems somehow a pity that
the very concept of home-sickness is presently going to be abolished by the
machine-civilization which makes one part of the world indistinguishable
from another.

By far the best thing in the book is a memory from the author's youth, an
incident—imaginary, but typical of real facts—in the Dutch colonial war of
1900–1912. It describes the torture of a villager who knew, or was supposed
to know, where a rebel chieftain was hiding. Apart from the depth of
imagination with which the scene is pictured, it brings home as a thousand
political pamphlets could not do the inherent evil of imperialism. For the
dreadful thing about the kind of brutalities here described, is that they are
quite unavoidable. When a subject population rises in revolt you have got to
suppress it, and you can only do so by methods which make nonsense of any
claim for the superiority of Western civilization. In order to rule over
barbarians, you have got to become a barbarian yourself. According to Mr.
Wöller, the Dutch are the most humane of the imperialist powers. If so, God
knows what the others can be like.

This is an interesting but rather fragmentary book, and it gives, sometimes
unintentionally, a good picture of what happens to the mind of a sensitive
man when he strays away from the centres of civilization. I have no means of
judging the translation, but I should say it is rather poor.

Mr. Massingham's travel was vertical, not horizontal. Having decided that "the East End is as unknown to us as the Trobriand Islands" (an exaggeration, but not so far from the truth), he took two unfurnished rooms in a tenement house in the worst part of the East End, and got a temporary job as a rent-collector. He could hardly have chosen a better way of getting to know the people, and in fact he got to know them rather too well, for almost immediately, through a misunderstanding, he had to bear the blame of getting an unemployed man sued for his rent. After this he was followed up and down by troops of children chanting "Oo put the brokers in?" stones and rotten apples were flung at him in the street, and in his absence people came into his rooms and stole or smashed his belongings. It was a peculiarly mean persecution, but Mr. Massingham seems to bear no grudges. The throwing of a rotten apple, he says, is no worse than the frigid sniff of a duchess, and after all, you can always throw something back. Later on he managed to live down the false accusation, symbolically took off his tie and was able to meet the East Enders on equal terms and appreciate their real virtues.

The subject-matter of this book is a good deal superior to the writing. Particularly valuable is the portrait of Johnston, the decayed Public School man who lived on the dole and preserved the most viciously anti-working class opinions. Johnston is an important type, for he gives one a glimpse of the fact that when the middle-classes feel the pinch they will turn towards Fascism rather than Socialism.

329. To Leonard Moore

19 October 1936   Typewritten

The Stores   Wallington   Nr. Baldock   <u>HERTS.</u>

Dear Mr Moore,

Many thanks for the cheque for £8-9-0.[1] Do you know if Harper's did anything about procuring me some copies of the American edition of A CLERGYMAN'S DAUGHTER? If you remember, I asked you to buy me a couple if Harper's did not give me any complimentary copies. I would like to have a copy or two, to see what the cover and jacket are like, also because I haven't in any case got a copy of that book. By the way, can you tell me what my contracts with Gollancz provide as to how long he is to keep my books in type? I know he broke up the type of DOWN AND OUT and I think you said he had also broken up the type of A CLERGYMAN'S DAUGHTER, but I thought that if there was anything in the contract about it, it would be a pity to let BURMESE DAYS be broken up before its due time, because after all there is just a possibility of that dramatic version the American is writing coming to something,[2] and in that case the book might be worth reprinting. Perhaps we could suggest something of this sort to Gollancz to persuade him to keep it in type.

I have begun the revision of my book and barring accidents it should be ready in December. Provisionally I am calling it "On the Road to Wigan Pier." It is not a novel but a sort of book of essays.[3] I hope you are well. We are mildly prosperous here, and very busy, what with cleaning out the garden for the winter, looking after the livestock etc. Please remember me to Mrs Moore.

Yours sincerely
Eric A. Blair

1. Orwell acknowledged '£30 odd' on 18 April; with this cheque, his royalties for the year seem to have been rather less than £40, compared with £60.5s.6d in 1935.
2. First referred to in Orwell's letter to Moore of 1 April 1936; see *297*. It came to nothing.
3. Moore quoted the first three sentences of this paragraph in a report to Victor Gollancz of Orwell's progress on this book. He added, 'from the details that he has given me from time to time I have reason to believe that it is extraordinarily good' (5 November 1936). Gollancz's letter of enquiry is dated 29 October.

330. 'Bookshop Memories'

Fortnightly, November 1936[1]

When I worked in a second-hand bookshop—so easily pictured, if you don't work in one, as a kind of paradise where charming old gentlemen browse eternally among calf-bound folios—the thing that chiefly struck me was the rarity of really bookish people. Our shop had an exceptionally interesting stock, yet I doubt whether ten per cent of our customers knew a good book from a bad one. First edition snobs were much commoner than lovers of literature, but oriental students haggling over cheap textbooks were commoner still, and vague-minded women looking for birthday presents for their nephews were commonest of all.

Many of the people who came to us were of the kind who would be a nuisance anywhere but have special opportunities in a bookshop. For example, the dear old lady who "wants a book for an invalid" (a very common demand, that), and the other dear old lady who read such a nice book in 1897 and wonders whether you can find her a copy. Unfortunately she doesn't remember the title or the author's name or what the book was about, but she does remember that it had a red cover. But apart from these there are two well-known types of pest by whom every second-hand bookshop is haunted. One is the decayed person smelling of old breadcrusts who comes every day, sometimes several times a day, and tries to sell you worthless books. The other is the person who orders large quantities of books for which he has not the smallest intention of paying. In our shop we sold nothing on credit, but we would put books aside, or order them if necessary, for people who arranged to fetch them away later. Scarcely half the people who ordered books from us ever came back. It used to puzzle me at first. What made them do it? They would come in and demand some rare and expensive book, would make us promise over and over again to keep it for them, and then would vanish never to return. But many of them, of course, were unmistakeable paranoiacs. They used to talk in a grandiose manner about themselves and tell the most ingenious stories to explain how they had happened to come out of doors without any money—stories which, in many cases, I am sure they themselves believed. In a town like London there are always plenty of not quite certifiable lunatics walking the streets, and they tend to gravitate towards bookshops, because a bookshop is one of the few places where you can hang about for a long time without spending any money. In the end one gets to know these people almost at a glance. For all their big talk there is something moth-eaten and aimless about them. Very often, when we were dealing with an obvious paranoiac, we would put aside the books he asked for and then put them back on the shelves the moment he had gone. None of them, I noticed, ever attempted to take books away without paying for them; merely to order them was enough—it gave them, I suppose, the illusion they were spending real money.

Like most second-hand bookshops we had various sidelines. We sold second-hand typewriters, for instance, and also stamps—used stamps, I mean. Stamp-collectors are a strange silent fish-like breed, of all ages, but only of the male sex; women, apparently, fail to see the peculiar charm of gumming bits of coloured paper into albums. We also sold sixpenny horoscopes compiled by somebody who claimed to have foretold the Japanese earthquake. They were in sealed envelopes and I never opened one of them myself, but the people who bought them often came back and told us how "true" their horoscopes had been. (Doubtless any horoscope seems "true" if it tells you that you are highly attractive to the opposite sex and your worst fault is generosity.) We did a good deal of business in children's books, chiefly "remainders." Modern books for children are rather horrible things, especially when you see them in the mass. Personally I would sooner give a child a copy of Petronius Arbiter than *Peter Pan*, but even Barrie seems manly and wholesome compared with some of his later imitators. At Christmas time we spent a feverish ten days struggling with Christmas cards and calendars, which are tiresome things to sell but good business while the season lasts. It used to interest me to see the brutal cynicism with which Christian sentiment is exploited. The touts from the Christmas card firms used to come round with their catalogues as early as June. A phrase from one of their invoices sticks in my memory. It was: "2 doz. Infant Jesus with rabbits."

But our principal sideline was a lending library—the usual "twopenny no-deposit" library of five or six hundred volumes, all fiction. How the book thieves must love those libraries! It is the easiest crime in the world to borrow a book at one shop for twopence, remove the label and sell it at another shop for a shilling. Nevertheless booksellers generally find that it pays them better to have a certain number of books stolen (we used to lose about a dozen a month) than to frighten customers away by demanding a deposit.

Our shop stood exactly on the frontier between Hampstead and Camden Town, and we were frequented by all types from baronets to bus-conductors. Probably our library subscribers were a fair cross-section of London's reading public. It is therefore worth noting that of all the authors in

511

our library the one who "went out" the best was—Priestley? Hemingway? Walpole? Wodehouse? No, Ethel M. Dell, with Warwick Deeping a good second and Jeffery Farnol, I should say, third. Dell's novels, of course, are read solely by women, but by women of all kinds and ages and not, as one might expect, merely by wistful spinsters and the fat wives of tobacconists. It is not true that men don't read novels, but it is true that there are whole branches of fiction that they avoid. Roughly speaking, what one might call the *average* novel—the ordinary, good-bad, Galsworthy-and-water stuff which is the norm of the English novel—seems to exist only for women. Men read either the novels it is possible to respect, or detective stories. But their consumption of detective stories is terrific. One of our subscribers to my knowledge read four or five detective stories every week for over a year, besides others which he got from another library. What chiefly surprised me was that he never read the same book twice. Apparently the whole of that frightful torrent of trash (the pages he read every year would, I calculated, cover nearly three-quarters of an acre) was stored for ever in his memory. He took no notice of titles or authors' names, but he could tell by merely glancing into a book whether he had "had it already."

In a lending library you see people's real tastes, not their pretended ones, and one thing that strikes you is how completely the "classical" English novelists have dropped out of favour. It is simply useless to put Dickens, Thackeray, Jane Austen, Trollope, etc., into the ordinary lending library; nobody takes them out. At the mere sight of a nineteenth-century novel people say "Oh, but that's *old*!" and shy away immediately. Yet it is always fairly easy to *sell* Dickens, just as it is always easy to sell Shakespeare. Dickens is one of those authors whom people are "always meaning to" read, and, like the Bible, he is widely known at second hand. People know by hearsay that Bill Sykes was a burglar and that Mr. Micawber had a bald head, just as they know by hearsay that Moses was found in a basket of bulrushes and saw the "back parts" of the Lord. Another thing that is very noticeable is the growing unpopularity of American books. And another—the publishers get into a stew about this every two or three years—is the unpopularity of short stories. The kind of person who asks the librarian to choose a book for him nearly always starts by saying "I don't want short stories," or "I do not desire little stories," as a German customer of ours used to put it. If you ask them why, they sometimes explain that it is too much fag to get used to a new set of characters with every story; they like to "get into" a novel which demands no further thought after the first chapter. I believe, though, that the writers are more to blame here than the readers. Most modern short stories, English and American, are utterly lifeless and worthless, far more so than most novels. The short stories which *are* stories are popular enough, *vide* D. H. Lawrence, whose short stories are as popular as his novels.

Would I like to be a bookseller *de métier*? On the whole—in spite of my employer's kindness to me, and some happy days I spent in the shop—no.

Given a good pitch and the right amount of capital, any educated person ought to be able to make a small secure living out of a bookshop. Unless one goes in for "rare" books it is not a difficult trade to learn, and you start at a great advantage if you know anything about the insides of books. (Most booksellers don't. You can get their measure by having a look at the trade papers where they advertise their wants. If you don't see an ad. for Boswell's *Decline and Fall* you are pretty sure to see one for *The Mill on the Floss* by T. S. Eliot.) Also it is a humane trade which is not capable of being vulgarised beyond a certain point. The combines can never squeeze the small independent bookseller out of existence as they have squeezed the grocer and the milkman. But the hours of work are very long—I was only a part-time employee, but my employer put in a 70-hour week, apart from constant expeditions out of hours to buy books—and it is an unhealthy life. As a rule a bookshop is horribly cold in winter, because if it is too warm the windows get misted over, and a bookseller lives on his windows. And books give off more and nastier dust than any other class of objects yet invented, and the top of a book is the place where every bluebottle prefers to die.

But the real reason why I should not like to be in the book trade for life is that while I was in it I lost my love of books. A bookseller has to tell lies about books, and that gives him a distaste for them; still worse is the fact that he is constantly dusting them and hauling them to and fro. There was a time when I really did love books—loved the sight and smell and feel of them, I mean, at least if they were fifty or more years old. Nothing pleased me quite so much as to buy a job lot of them for a shilling at a country auction. There is a peculiar flavour about the battered unexpected books you pick up in that kind of collection: minor eighteenth-century poets, out of date gazeteers, odd volumes of forgotten novels, bound numbers of ladies' magazines of the 'sixties. For casual reading—in your bath, for instance, or late at night when you are too tired to go to bed, or in the odd quarter of an hour before lunch—there is nothing to touch a back number of the *Girl's Own Paper*. But as soon as I went to work in the bookshop I stopped buying books. Seen in the mass, five or ten thousand at a time, books were boring and even slightly sickening. Nowadays I do buy one occasionally, but only if it is a book that I want to read and can't borrow, and I never buy junk. The sweet smell of decaying paper appeals to me no longer. It is too closely associated in my mind with paranoiac customers and dead bluebottles.

1. Extracts from this essay were reprinted in *The Bookseller*, 26 July 1975, under the title 'Penguin celebrates with Orwell,' to mark the fortieth anniversary of the first ten Penguins, on 30 July 1935. As part of their celebrations, Penguin Books reissued eight of Orwell's books. The headnote in *The Bookseller* said the extracts would remind the trade 'that Orwell, too, was a bookseller.' Also reprinted was the opening of Orwell's 1936 review of the third batch of Penguin books; see *290*—an ironic choice in the light of J. E. Morpurgo's description, in his biography of Allen Lane, of the way Orwell 'floundered' in his writing of that review; see *290*, n. 1. *Fortnightly Review*, 1865–1955, was known simply as the *Fortnightly* from July 1934.

331. Review of *Walls Have Mouths* by W. F. R. Macartney, with Prologue, Epilogue and Comments on the Chapters by Compton Mackenzie

The Adelphi, November 1936

This very valuable and absorbingly interesting book—a record of ten years' penal servitude in Parkhurst Prison—brings out two facts about prison life which are not generally appreciated. The first is that the evil thing about the English prison system is not the abuses but the system itself. When you talk to a man who has been in prison, he generally lays emphasis on the bad food, the petty injustices, the cruelty of individual warders, etc., giving the impression that if these minor evils were rectified our prisons would become tolerable, supposing that any prisons could be that. Actually, the cold, rigid discipline of a modern English jail, the solitude, the silence, the everlasting lock-and-key (all of it the work of prison reformers, among the first of whom was Torquemada), is more cruel and far more demoralising than the barbarous punishments of the Middle Ages. Worse than the loss of liberty, worse even than sexual deprivation, is boredom. Mr. Macartney has a good eye for significant detail, and he rubs this fact well home. It is quite usual, he says, at the week-end, to be left in utter solitude for forty-four hours with nothing to read. As a result, the tiniest distractions assume colossal importance. Apparently many of the men in Parkhurst Prison used to procure scraps of glass and secretly grind them into lenses—this must take months to do—and then, with tubes of brown paper, make telescopes with which to look out of their cell windows. Only men who were half mad with boredom would take all that trouble, incidentally risking bread and water for doing so.

The other fact Mr. Macartney makes clear is that in our prison system, as in other departments of English life, all real power is in the hands of one-eyed, permanent officials, who take no notice either of the Government of the moment or of public opinion. Even a prison governor, apparently, is almost powerless against the "screws" who have inherited a brutal system and go on administering it by rule of thumb. It is rather amusing to read about the efforts of the Parkhurst officials to censor the prison library. They were desperately anxious to prevent the convicts getting hold of "subversive" literature, but were far too illiterate to know which books were "subversive" and which were not. The only Home Secretary who seems ever to have made a fight against the cruel inertia of the prison system is Winston Churchill. Clynes, the Labour Home Secretary, actually exerted himself to take away a few of the convicts' privileges. No wonder that most long-term convicts are Tories!

The most dreadful chapter in this book is the one entitled "Notes on Prison Sex Life." It gave me a shock when I read it, for it suddenly revealed to me the meaning of a conversation of years earlier. I once asked a Burmese criminal why he disliked going to jail. He answered with a look of disgust and the single word, "Sodomy." I thought then that he merely meant that among the convicts there were a few homosexuals who pestered the others, but what Mr. Macartney makes clear is that in prison, after a few years, almost *every* man becomes homosexual, in spite of putting up a fight against it. He gives a horrible account of the way in which homosexuality gradually overwhelmed himself, first of all through the medium of his dreams. In a convict prison homosexuality is so general that even the jailors are infected by it, and there are actually cases of jailors and convicts competing for the favours of the same nancy-boy. As for masturbation, it is "referred to openly and indifferently." That is what you condemn a man to when you send him to prison for a long term. And this is the achievement of the dear good reformers (see Charles Reade's *It Is Never Too Late To Mend*) who did away with the promiscuity of the eighteenth century jails.

This is a remarkable book. It is formless and badly written, but packed full of the kind of details that matter. The author is an exceptionally brave, sharp-witted and good-tempered person. He is a Communist (he was given his savage sentence for some ineffectual espionage in the service of the Soviet Government), but not, I fancy, a very orthodox one; he will perhaps not be pleased when I say that he is too decent a human being to be "ideologically" sound. Mr. Compton Mackenzie's prologue and comments might appear at first sight to be unnecessary, but actually they have the effect of pulling the book together and supplying useful corroboration. Probably without Mr. Mackenzie's help the book would not have been published, in which case everyone who cares for decency must be deeply grateful to him.

332. Review of *The Calf of Paper* by Scholem Asch: *Midnight* by Julian Green,[1] translated from the French by Vyvyan Holland

New English Weekly, 12 November 1936

The huge sociological novels which come to us from eastern Europe cannot be criticized except as historical documents, because their authors, consciously or unconsciously, tend to avoid the real problems of the novelist. On the other hand they do an extremely useful work by presenting contemporary history in a readable form, and they can hardly have too much publicity, because anything that brings it home to the Englishman that foreigners really exist and are alive and kicking, especially kicking, is to be welcomed.

I don't think "The Calf of Paper" ought properly to be described as a novel, but I found it immensely interesting and in spite of its length I finished it at a very few sittings. It is a sort of panorama of German society in the hideous period of the inflation. The French are in the Ruhr, the mark is rising like a rocket, speculators are growing rich (they have a beautifully simple system of buying on credit and not paying till the value of the mark falls), the starving people are eating food that would be disdained by pigs, and Hitler and his first small gang of bravos are just beginning to be talked about. All this is presented, *more* Zola, through the histories of two or three more or less interrelated families. The reason why such a book cannot be approached as a work of art is that its method is in reality extremely perfunctory. The author is writing what is essentially a text-book, and he puts in the characters he thinks appropriate very much as one puts ingredients into a cake. He seems to be saying, "Anti-Semitism is just beginning—so we must put in a few families of Jews. And the Nazis are coming up over the horizon—so we'll have a few Nazis. And then, of course, there is the food-shortage—so we'll put in some food-speculators and a starving postman," and so on and so on; but there is not a single scene, character or piece of dialogue which is there because it has forced itself upon him as material *ought* to force itself upon a novelist. This is not an inherent fault of the sociological novel—in fact probably a majority of the novels worth reading are novels-with-a-purpose. Compare Zola, for instance. The scenes of violence Zola describes in *Germinal* and *La Débâcle* are supposed to symbolize capitalist corruption, but they are also scenes. At his best, Zola is not synthetic. He works under a sense of compulsion, and not like an amateur cook following the instructions on a packet of Crestona cake-flour.

Nevertheless, as I have said, "The Calf of Paper" deserves to be read by everybody, if only because it makes clear why the Nazis triumphed and were probably bound to triumph. The only point upon which the author, who is presumably a Jew himself, seems to be in doubt, is the real reason for anti-Semitism. But curiously enough, he supplies a clue, unconsciously, in one of the very few scenes in which a Jew (a young Bolshevik military officer) is held up for our admiration. This scene is a reminder that if you want anti-Semitism explained the best book to read is the Old Testament.

Turn to "Midnight," and you might as well be in a different universe. Here is the most complete and careful avoidance of any contemporary problem— even the time, though vaguely "the present," is not pinned down to any particular decade. In spite of a veneer of naturalism over many of the scenes, the story has about as much relation to real life as one of those German films in which all the actors are silhouettes cut out of black paper.

Here is the plot, if you can call it a plot. In the first chapter there is a meaningless suicide, and a girl of twelve, named Elizabeth, the daughter of the woman who has killed herself, is left homeless. She spends a few hours successively in the houses of three more or less insane aunts, the last of them a sort of Chinese monster, then takes to flight in terror and meets in the street a kind-hearted elderly man who adopts her into his family. There is a lapse of three years, and then Elizabeth is again adopted, this time by a man who has been the lover of her dead mother. The final episode occupies more than half the book and covers a time which is apparently about two days. This episode is pure nightmare all the way through. The house to which Elizabeth has come is a ruinous place in the forest, a sort of appalling asylum inhabited by lunatics of the most varied kinds. The nightmare effect is heightened by the fact that the child has not the vaguest idea how many people the house contains. In the dead of night, overcome about equally by terror and curiosity, she creeps all over the house, peering through keyholes and softly turning door-handles, and encountering some fresh monstrosity in each room. Finally, she meets the only sane person the house contains, a ruffianly peasant boy of about seventeen, and immediately agrees to fly with him. There is a brief burst of pornography, or something approaching it, in which he seduces her, then a murder, an accidental death, another suicide, and the story ends.

If this kind of thing were written at the level of the ordinary English novel you would stop reading after a couple of chapters. But as Mr. Green's mind has in it an unmistakable touch of distinction, you read to the end and then ask yourself, "What the devil is it all *about?*' " I think the answer must be that, finally, it is about nothing.

Obviously it is an attempt to work up an Edgar Allan Poe atmosphere, and in a measure it is successful. At any rate, the feeling of horror and mystery is attained. But there is this important difference, that though Poe is fantastic he is never arbitrary. Even his least naturalistic stories ("The Black Cat," "The Fall of the House of Usher," etc.) are psychologically correct, in the sense that they deal with perfectly intelligible motives. In "Midnight" this is not the case—there is never the slightest reason why any of the things in it should happen. It is, I think, the product of a gifted mind, it contains absolutely no vulgarity or sentimentality, and I am willing to believe that it was written in admirable French; but it is quite meaningless.

I had never before read a novel by Julian Green, and I am glad to have done so, because I feel now that I have his measure. The naturalistic touches in this book are good enough to suggest that he might have been a good novelist along Flaubert-Maupassant lines. As it is he seems to have missed his vocation, probably by being too anxious to fly to the opposite extreme from books like "The Calf of Paper." The truth is that ours is not an age for mysterious romances about lunatics in ruined chateaux, because it is not an age in which one can be unaware of contemporary reality. You can't ignore Hitler, Mussolini, unemployment, aeroplanes and the radio; you can only pretend to do so, which means lopping off a large chunk of your consciousness. To turn away from every-day life and manipulate black paper silhouettes with the pretence that you are really interested in them, is a sort of game of make-believe, and therefore faintly futile, like telling ghost stories in the dark.

1. Julian Hartridge Green (1900–1998) was an American living in Paris. He wrote in French as Julien Green; in English Julian Green. See *600, n. 46.*

333. 'In Defence of the Novel'

New English Weekly, 12 and 19 November 1936

It hardly needs pointing out that at this moment the prestige of the novel is extremely low, so low that the words "I never read novels," which even a dozen years ago were generally uttered with a hint of apology are now *always* uttered in a tone of conscious pride. It is true that there are still a few contemporary or roughly contemporary novelists whom the intelligentsia consider it permissible to read; but the point is that the ordinary good-bad novel is habitually ignored while the ordinary good-bad book of verse or criticism is still taken seriously. This means that if you write novels you automatically command a less intelligent public than you would command if you had chosen some other form. There are two quite obvious reasons why this must presently make it impossible for good novels to be written. Even now the novel is visibly deteriorating, and it would deteriorate much faster if most novelists had any idea who reads their books. It is, of course, easy to argue (*vide* for instance Belloc's queerly rancorous essay[1]) that the novel is a contemptible form of art and that its fate does not matter. I doubt whether that opinion is even worth disputing. At any rate, I am taking it for granted that the novel is worth salvaging and that in order to salvage it you have got to persuade intelligent people to take it seriously. It is therefore worth while to analyse one of the main causes—in my opinion, *the* main cause—of the novel's lapse in prestige.

The trouble is that the novel is being shouted out of existence. Question any thinking person as to why he "never reads novels," and you will usually find that, at bottom, it is because of the disgusting tripe that is written by the blurb-reviewers. There is no need to multiply examples. Here is just one specimen, from last week's "Sunday Times": "If you can read this book and not shriek with delight, your soul is dead." That or something like it is now being written about *every* novel published, as you can see by studying the quotes on the blurbs. For anyone who takes the "Sunday Times" seriously, life must be one long struggle to catch up. Novels are being shot at you at the rate of fifteen a day, and every one of them an unforgettable masterpiece which you imperil your soul by missing. It must make it so difficult to choose a book at the library, and you must feel so guilty when you fail to shriek with delight. Actually, however, no one who matters is deceived by this kind of thing, and the contempt into which novel-reviewing has fallen is extended to novels themselves. When *all* novels are thrust upon you as works of genius, it is quite natural to assume that all of them are tripe. Within the literary intelligentsia this assumption is now taken for granted. To admit that you like novels is nowadays almost equivalent to admitting that you have a hankering after coconut ice or prefer Rupert Brooke to Gerard Manley Hopkins.

All this is obvious. What I think is rather less obvious is the way in which the present situation has arisen. On the face of it, the book-ramp is a quite simple and cynical swindle. Z writes a book which is published by Y and reviewed by X in the "Weekly W." If the review is a bad one Y will remove his advertisement, so X has to hand out "unforgettable masterpiece" or get the sack. Essentially that *is* the position, and novel-reviewing has sunk to its present death largely because every reviewer has some publisher or publishers twisting his tail by proxy. But the thing is not so crude as it looks. The various parties to the swindle are not consciously acting together, and they have been forced into their present position partly against their will.

To begin with, one ought not to assume, as is so often done (see for instance Beachcomber's column, *passim*), that the novelist enjoys and is even in some way responsible for the reviews he gets. Nobody *likes* being told that he has written a palpitating tale of passion which will last as long as the English language; though, of course, it is disappointing not to be told that, because all novelists are being told the same, and to be left out presumably means that your books won't sell. The hack-review is in fact a sort of commercial necessity, like the blurb on the dust-jacket, of which it is merely an extension. But even the wretched hack-reviewer is not to be blamed for the drivel he writes. In his special circumstances he could write nothing else. For even if there were no question of bribery, direct or indirect, there can be no such thing as good novel-criticism so long as it is assumed that *every novel is worth reviewing*.

A periodical gets its weekly wad of books and sends off a dozen of them to X, the hack-reviewer, who has a wife and family and has got to earn his guinea, not to mention the half-crown per vol. which he gets by selling his review copies. There are two reasons why it is totally impossible for X to tell the truth about the books he gets. To begin with, the chances are that eleven out of the twelve books will fail to rouse in him the faintest spark of interest. They are not more than ordinarily bad, they are merely neutral, lifeless and pointless. If he were not paid to do so he would never read a line of any of them, and in nearly every case the only truthful review he could write would be: "This book inspires in me no thoughts whatever." But will anyone pay you to write that kind of thing? Obviously not. As a start, therefore, X is in the false position of having to manufacture, say, three hundred words about a book which means nothing to him whatever. Usually he does it by giving a brief resumé of the plot (incidentally betraying to the author the fact that he hasn't read the book) and handing out a few compliments which for all their fulsomeness are about as valuable as the smile of a prostitute.

But there is a far worse evil than this. X is expected not only to say what a book is about but to give his opinion as to whether it is good or bad. Since X can hold a pen he is probably not a fool, at any rate not such a fool as to imagine that "The Constant Nymph" is the most terrific tragedy ever written. Very likely his own favourite novelist, if he cares for novels at all, is Stendhal, or Dickens, or Jane Austen, or D. H. Lawrence, or Dostoievski— or at any rate, someone immeasurably better than the ordinary run of contemporary novelists. He has got to start, therefore, by immensely lowering his standards. As I have pointed out elsewhere, to apply a decent standard to the ordinary run of novels is like weighing a flea on a spring-balance intended for elephants.[2] On such a balance as that a flea would simply fail to register; you would have to start by constructing another balance which revealed the fact that there are big fleas and little fleas. And this approximately is what X does. It is no use monotonously saying, of book after book, "This book is tripe," because, once again, no one will pay you for writing that kind of thing. X has got to discover something which is *not* tripe, and pretty frequently, or get the sack. This means sinking his standards to a depth at which, say, Ethel M. Dell's "Way of an Eagle" is a fairly good book. But on a scale of values which makes "The Way of an Eagle" a good book,

"The Constant Nymph" is a superb book, and "The Man of Property" is—what? A palpitating tale of passion, a terrific, soul-shattering masterpiece, an unforgettable epic which will last as long as the English language, and so on and so forth. (As for any *really* good book, it would burst the thermometer.) Having started with the assumption that all novels are good, the reviewer is driven ever upwards on a topless ladder of adjectives. And sic itur ad Gould.[3] You can see reviewer after reviewer going the same road. Within two years of starting out with at any rate moderately honest intentions, he is proclaiming with maniacal screams that Miss Barbara Bedworthy's[4] "Crimson Night" is the most terrific, trenchant, poignant, unforgettable, of the earth earthy and so forth masterpiece which has ever, etc., etc., etc. There is no way out of it when you have once committed the initial sin of pretending that a bad book is a good one. But you cannot review novels for a living without committing that sin. And meanwhile every intelligent reader turns away, disgusted, and to despise novels becomes a kind of snobbish duty. Hence the queer fact that it is possible for a novel of real merit to escape notice, merely because it has been praised in the same terms as tripe.

Various people have suggested that it would be all to the good if no novels were reviewed at all. So it would, but the suggestion is useless, because nothing of the kind is going to happen. No paper which depends on publishers' advertisements can afford to throw them away, and though the more intelligent publishers probably realise that they would be no worse off if the blurb-review were abolished, they cannot put an end to it for the same reason as the nations cannot disarm—because nobody wants to be the first to start. For a long time yet the blurb-reviews are going to continue, and they are going to grow worse and worse; the only remedy is to contrive in some way that they shall be disregarded. But this can only happen if somewhere or other there is decent novel-reviewing which will act as a standard of comparison. That is to say, there is need of just *one* periodical (one would be enough for a start) which makes a speciality of novel-reviewing but refuses to take any notice of tripe, and in which the reviewers *are* reviewers and not ventriloquists' dummies clapping their jaws when the publisher pulls the string.

It may be answered that there are such periodicals already. There are quite a number of highbrow magazines, for instance, in which the novel-reviewing, what there is of it, is intelligent and not suborned. Yes, but the point is that periodicals of that kind do not make a speciality of novel-reviewing, and certainly make no attempt to keep abreast of the current output of fiction. They belong to the highbrow world, the world in which it is already assumed that novels, as such, are despicable. But the novel is a popular form of art, and it is no use to approach it with the "Criterion-Scrutiny"[5] assumption that literature is a game of back-scratching (claws in or claws out according to circumstances) between tiny cliques of highbrows. The novelist is primarily a story-teller, and a man may be a very good story-teller (*vide* for instance Trollope, Charles Reade, Mr. Somerset Maugham) without being in the narrow sense an "intellectual." Five thousand novels are published every year, and Ralph Straus[6] implores you to read all of them, or would if he had all of them to review. The "Criterion" probably deigns to notice a dozen. But between the dozen and the five thousand there may be a hundred or two hundred or even five hundred which at different levels have genuine merit, and it is on these that any critic who cares for the novel ought to concentrate.

But the first necessity is some method of *grading*. Great numbers of novels never ought to be mentioned at all (imagine for instance the awful effects on criticism if every serial in "Peg's Paper" had to be solemnly reviewed!), but even the ones that are worth mentioning belong to quite different categories. "Raffles" is a good book, and so is "The Island of Dr. Moreau," and so is "La Chartreuse de Parme,' and so is "Macbeth"; but they are "good" at very different levels: Similarly, "If Winter Comes" and "The Well-Beloved" and "An Unsocial Socialist" and "Sir Lancelot Greaves" are all bad books, but at different levels of "badness." This is the fact that the hack-reviewer has made it his special business to obscure. It ought to be possible to devise a system, perhaps quite a rigid one, of grading novels into classes A, B, C and so forth, so that whether a reviewer praised or damned a book, you would at least know how seriously he meant it to be taken. As for the reviewers, they would have to be people who really cared for the art of the novel (and that means, probably, neither highbrows nor lowbrows nor midbrows, but elastic-brows), people interested in technique and still more interested in discovering what a book is *about*. There are plenty of such people in existence; some of the very worst of the hack-reviewers, though now past praying for, started like that, as you can see by glancing at their earlier work. Incidentally, it would be a good thing if more novel-reviewing were done by amateurs. A man who is not a practised writer but has just read a book which has deeply impressed him is more likely to tell you what it is *about* than a competent but bored professional. That is why American reviews, for all their stupidity, are better than English ones; they are more amateurish, that is to say, more serious.

I believe that in some such way as I have indicated the prestige of the novel could be restored. The essential need is a paper that would keep abreast of current fiction and yet refuse to sink its standards. It would have to be an obscure paper, for the publishers would not advertise in it; on the other hand, once they had discovered that somewhere there was praise that was real praise, they would be ready enough to quote it on their blurbs. Even if it were a very obscure paper it would probably cause the general level of novel-reviewing to rise, for the drivel in the Sunday papers only continues because there is nothing with which to contrast it. But even if the blurb-reviewers continued exactly as before, it would not matter so long as there also existed decent reviewing to remind a few people that serious brains can still occupy themselves with the novel. For just as the Lord promised that he would not destroy Sodom if ten righteous men could be found there, so the novel will not be utterly despised while it is known that somewhere or other there is even a handful of novel-reviewers with no straws in their hair.

At present, if you care about novels and still more if you write them, the outlook is depressing in the extreme. The word "novel" calls up the words "blurb," "genius" and "Ralph Straus" as automatically as "chicken" calls up "bread sauce." Intelligent people avoid novels almost instinctively; as a result, established novelists go to pieces and beginners who "have something to say" turn in preference to almost any other form. The degeneration that must follow is obvious. Look for instance at the fourpenny novelettes that you see piled up on any cheap stationer's counter. These things are the decadent off-spring of the novel, bearing the same relation to "Manon Lescaut" and "David Copperfield" as the lap-dog bears to the wolf. It is quite likely that before long the average novel will be not much different from the fourpenny novelette, though doubtless it will still appear in a seven and sixpenny binding and amid a flourish of publishers' trumpets. Various people have prophesied that the novel is doomed to disappear in the near future. I do not believe that it will disappear, for reasons which would take too long to set forth but which are fairly obvious. It is much likelier, if the best literary brains cannot be induced to return to it, to survive in some perfunctory, despised and hopelessly degenerate form, like modern tomb-stones, or the Punch and Judy show.

1. Hilaire Belloc wrote regularly for a number of journals; some of his essays were collected in a series of books. This reference may be to 'On People in Books,' reprinted in *On Anything* (1920), essays originally in the *Morning Post* and *Morning Leader*. Here and elsewhere, Belloc shows a preference for historical writing over the novel.
2. See also *254*, paragraph 1.
3. Gerald Gould, reviewer for *The Observer*; see *219*, n. 2.
4. Miss Bedworthy appears in *Keep the Aspidistra Flying*, CW, IV, 18 and letter to Brenda Salkeld, 15 January 1935 (*224*). See also Shelden, 216; U.S.: 197.
5. See *194*, n. 1 (March 1934) for the Leavis-*Scrutiny* school of critics.
6. Ralph Straus (1882–1950) was chief fiction reviewer for the *Sunday Times* from 1928 until his death.

334. Review of *Desert Encounter* by Knud Holmboe, translated from the Danish by Helga Holbek; *Coconuts and Creoles* by J. A. F. Ozanne

Time and Tide, 21 November 1936

Knud Holmboe, author of *Desert Encounter*, was murdered by Arab brigands while on his way to Mecca in 1931. This book is an account of a journey across north Africa by motor car in the previous year. In introducing it, Mr. J. H. Driberg, lecturer in anthropology at Cambridge, remarks that in Holmboe "we have lost a potential T. E. Lawrence"—a most unfortunate comparison, for the two men seem to have had nothing in common except a love of the Arabs and a talent for getting on with them.

Holmboe's journey, across territory which was mainly desert, with a perpetually leaking radiator and tyres which punctured every few miles, was a remarkable feat in itself, but what gives his book its particular interest is the fact that he had embraced Mohammedanism and travelled in Arab dress. He was thus able to meet the Arabs, especially the Bedouins, on equal terms and hear what they really thought about their European conquerors. His conclusion seems to be that though the French are not particularly loved, the Italians are the worst colonial administrators the world has seen. They wage continual and ruthless war against the "free" Arabs, even descending to blocking up their wells with concrete, and shooting or hanging almost incredible numbers of so-called rebels who have attempted to defend their ancient grazing-grounds.

> . . . During the French Revolution an average of three people were executed daily in France, which roughly gives twelve hundred people a year. During the time I was in Cyrenaica thirty executions took place daily, which means that about twelve thousand Arabs were executed yearly, not counting those killed in the war or the imported, Eritrean troops on the Italian side . . .

What is especially sinister is that the Italians seem to take no interest in their subject peoples, even a knowledge of Arabic being considered beneath the dignity of an Italian officer. Apparently it is their aim, sometimes openly declared, to exterminate all those who stand in their way. Holmboe is quite ready, however, to admit that the Italians have performed wonderful feats of road-building and town-planning, and that he personally received better treatment at their hands than might have been expected. For though the Italian authorities were naturally suspicious of a white man in Arab dress, they exerted themselves to protect him when he was going through dangerous territory, and on at least one occasion they saved himself and his companions from starving to death in the desert.

This is an impressive book, all the more so because of its *naïveté*. Mussolini's large body of English worshippers would do well to have a look at it. The photographs are indifferent.

Coconuts and Creoles (an unsuitable title, because it leads one to expect a more or less frivolous book) touches on the same subject—colonial maladministration. Here, however, it is not a tale of blocked wells, bombed villages and summary executions, but in the usual British fashion, of sheer well-meaning tactlessness. The author, a clergyman, was for four years a chaplain in the Crown colony of Seychelles, in the Indian Ocean. He gives a carefully documented account of life in the islands, and he makes it quite clear that things are going badly. There is an immense amount of unemployment and mendicancy, the coconut-growing and fishing industries have never been properly developed, officials receive starvation salaries and the police are hopelessly corrupt; prostitution is rampant, there is much religious bigotry and the standard of sexual morals is so low that over 44 per cent. of the children baptised by the author were illegitimate. One underlying evil seems to be that there is no proper educational system. Higher-grade education is in the hands of Marist Brothers, who have succeeded in preventing educational reform by threatening to excommunicate parents who send their children to the Government schools. As a result, the middle-class Creole population, like the Eurasian population in India, is cut off from the chance of earning a decent livelihood.

The author is an Anglican clergyman, and he writes with an unmistakable prejudice against the Roman Catholic Church, for which one must make some allowance. Even so, most of what he says carries conviction. With its innumerable appendices this is rather an *omnium gatherum* book, but it is ably and amusingly written and gives some useful sidelights on a minor problem of Empire. The photographs are very bad.

335. 'A happy vicar I might have been'

The Adelphi, December 1936

A happy vicar I might have been
Two hundred years ago,
To preach upon eternal doom
And watch my walnuts grow;

But born, alas, in an evil time,
I missed that pleasant haven,
For the hair has grown on my upper lip
And the clergy are all clean-shaven.

And later still the times were good,
We were so easy to please,
We rocked our troubled thoughts to sleep
On the bosoms of the trees.

All ignorant we dared to own
The joys we now dissemble;
The greenfinch on the apple bough
Could make my enemies tremble.

But girls' bellies and apricots,
Roach in a shaded stream,
Horses, ducks in flight at dawn,
All these are a dream.

It is forbidden to dream again;
We maim our joys or hide them;
Horses are made of chromium steel
And little fat men shall ride them.

I am the worm who never turned,[1]
The eunuch without a harem;
Between the priest and the commissar
I walk like Eugene Aram;[2]

And the commissar is telling my fortune
While the radio plays,
But the priest has promised an Austin Seven,[3]
For Duggie always pays.[4]

I dreamed I dwelt in marble halls,
And woke to find it true;
I wasn't born for an age like this;
Was Smith? Was Jones? Were you?[5]

1. 'The smallest worm will turn, being trodden on', *3 Henry VI*, 2. 2. 17.
2. Eugene Aram was a schoolmaster of some learning and good repute in Knaresborough, Yorkshire. In 1745 he murdered a man named Clark, but the murder was not discovered until 1758. Aram was arrested while teaching a class, tried, and executed in 1759. Thomas Hood (a favourite of Orwell's) wrote a poem, 'The Dream of Eugene Aram,' published in *The Comic Annual* (though the poem is not humorous) in 1829. Three year later Bulwer Lytton based a novel on the incident. Hood described Aram's walking three times. When he sees one of his pupils readindg 'The Death of Abel,' Aram '. . . took six hasty strides, / As smit with sudden pain,– / Six hasty strides beyond the place, / Then slowly back again.' He sits by the boy and tells him (in fact, his own experience), '. . . how murderers walk the earth / Beneath the curse of Cain,– / With crimson clouds before their eyes, / And flames about their brain.' The last stanza tells how 'Two stern-faced men set out from Lynn / . . . And Eugene Aram walked between, / With gyves upon his wrist.' The second allusion is the most attractive, but the third the most likely; possibly Orwell had both in mind.
3. The Austin Seven was the first successful small family car produced in Britain. The seven refers to the horsepower of its engine.
4. This is a corruption of an advertising slogan for the bookmaker Douglas Stuart: 'Duggie never owes.'
5. The last three stanzas were reprinted in 'Why I Write,' *Gangrel*, 4, Summer 1946; see *3007*.

336. Review of *The Open Air* by Adrian Bell

The Listener, 2 December 1936[1]

An anthology such as *The Open Air*, by Adrian Bell (Faber, 7s. 6d.), which is a series of passages, mainly prose, dealing with country life in its various aspects, brings home to one how completely the old rural culture of England has passed away. The very fact that it is picturesque proves it irrevocable. Perhaps that is why in so many of the writers who have praised country life— George Bourne, George Sturt, Cobbett, even W. H. Hudson—one can feel a hint of make-believe. Mr. Bell has made his anthology focus round two things, craftsmanship and the independence of the labourer. It is curious in how many extracts, from very different writers, the theme of pig-keeping crops up. This is significant, for the decay of pig-keeping in England means something much more serious than Danish bacon for breakfast. Mr. Bell has successfully avoided the obvious, and there are not many passages describing scenery and very few that deal with sport. Incidentally, the quotations from Richard Jefferies might have been better chosen. Jefferies looked at the country with an essentially non-agricultural eye and he is only at his best when he is describing wild animals. When he writes of fishing, for instance, he is inimitable. This book contains comparatively little that is familiar. Open it anywhere and you will almost certainly go on reading. But it would be worth opening for two items alone even if there were nothing else of value in the whole book. One is Gerard Manley Hopkins' lovely poem, 'Felix Randal' in which the rhythm seems to eddy out of the name like smoke out of an ember; the other is a few lines from Lawrence's *Lady Chatterley's Lover* in which the hideous noise of village school-children having a singing-lesson is somehow hit off for ever.

1. This review is unsigned. Orwell was paid £1.1.0d for it.

337. To Leonard Moore

10 December 1936   Typewritten

This is the first of a short series of letters to Moore that have survived in which Orwell makes dispositions for his journey to Spain to fight in the Republican cause. It was received in Moore's office on 11 December and answered the same day. In the light of Orwell's formal authorisation to Moore dated 11 December (see *338*), it may be that Moore sent Orwell a telegram asking for such a declaration to be sent to him rather than given to Eileen, as Orwell here suggests. See Crick, 309–10; Stansky and Abrahams, II, 193–95; Shelden, 274–75; U.S.: 249–50.

The Stores   Wallington   Nr. Baldock   HERTS.

Dear Mr Moore,

I have heard from my bank and they say it will be all right for me to overdraw up to £50 if you guarantee it as you so kindly promised to do. I have also got my passport, so I am ready to depart quite soon. Of course if you *could* get the Herald[1] to commission a few articles or something like that, I should be delighted, so perhaps you could approach them? I suppose they could let us know whether they will or not without much delay?

Of course I don't know in advance how long I shall be away, and possibly communications won't be easy. So I was wondering whether I could make arrangements to leave everything in my wife's charge. There are two points that are likely to arise. In the event of Gollancz accepting my present book, he is sure to ask for some minor alterations which I shan't be here to do, but my wife is perfectly competent to do anything like that, so perhaps I could give her some written authorisation or something like that? In any case I could explain to Gollancz before leaving. Also, if any monies fall due to me, eg. an advance on the present book[2] if published before I came back, I suppose the cheque could be made out in my wife's name so that she could endorse it and pay it in? Of course I don't suppose I shall be away so very long, but it is best to be prepared.

526

I have looked up the stuff I wanted at the Museum,[3] and the book will be typed in ten days or so.[4]

Yours sincerely
Eric A Blair

1. The *Daily Herald* was a newspaper that supported the Labour Party and the trade union movement. Founded 25 January 1911, it ceased publication three months later. A new series was initiated 15 April 1912; became the *Herald* 3 October 1914 to 29 March 1919, and again the *Daily Herald* 31 March 1919 to 14 September 1964. Orwell was not commissioned to contribute.
2. *The Road to Wigan Pier*.
3. The British Museum (now The British Library). Possibly Orwell went there to check facts and figures extracted from Joseph Jones, *The Coal Scuttle* (1936) and from *Colliery Year Book & Coal Trades Directory, 1935*, which Stansky and Abrahams believe he had worked with in the reference library in Wigan (II, 144).
4. Annotated at the top of the letter in Moore's office: 'George Orwell   Keep the Asp | Down & Out | Clergyman's Daughter.'

338. To Christy & Moore Ltd

11 December 1936   Typewritten

Although dated 11 December, this letter was not received in Moore's office until the 18th. As the rapid exchange of letters requesting photographs for *The Road to Wigan Pier* indicates (Collins's letter to the Reverend Gilbert Shaw was sent on 22 December; Shaw replied on the 23rd), this was unlikely to be a result of mail delays (even near Christmas in the 1930s). Because the letter was so important, it was perhaps brought from Hertfordshire by hand. Orwell was there on the 19th; his telegram from Sandon on that day survives and indicates that he was going to London on Monday, the 21st. He had sent the completed typescript of *The Road to Wigan Pier* to Moore by mail on 15 December; it was received by Moore, and acknowledged, on the 16th. Had Orwell been going to London to deliver his letter of authorisation by hand, he would surely have taken the typescript at the same time. Probably the letter was, through an oversight, not posted at once. For the way Moore and Eileen carried out this mandate, see Crick, 309.

The Stores, Wallington, nr. Baldock, HERTS.[1]

Dear Sirs,
During my absence abroad will you please communicate with my wife on all subjects relating to my literary affairs and accept her decision as my own.

In the event of any alterations being required in my manuscript or proofs before publication my wife has my authority to make them on my behalf.

I shall be obliged if you will make payment to my wife any moneys[2] that become due to me during my absence, and her receipt shall be sufficient discharge.

Yours faithfully
Eric A Blair

1. Note that for this formal letter Orwell adopts a different style and punctuates his address fully.
2. In his letter of 10 December, Orwell used the spelling 'monies.'

339. To Leonard Moore

    15 December 1936   Typewritten

The Stores Wallington Nr. Baldock <u>HERTS.</u>

Dear Mr Moore,

Herewith the MS. of "The Road to Wigan Pier." Parts of it I am fairly pleased with, but I should think the chances of Gollancz choosing it as a Left Book Club selection are small,[1] as it is too fragmentary and, on the surface, not very left-wing. Perhaps if it were sent on to him more or less at once he might have a look at it or get someone else to do so before the Xmas holiday, but I suppose we are not likely to hear from him before I leave for Spain, which should be in about a week.

    I have just received a letter from Mrs Clennel Wilkinson, who says she is reader for William Morrow the New York publishers, and she asks me to let her know "whether you have any work in hand which you would care to let me see on behalf of Messrs Morrow with a view to publication in America." I don't think the present book would be of the slightest interest to an American public, but possibly they might consider "Keep the A." I am writing to her to this effect and referring her to you, so perhaps you could get in touch [with] her or with Morrow's.[2]

Yours sincerely
Eric A Blair

1. It was selected; for details, see *341, 362.*
2. Nothing came of this inquiry.

340. To Leonard Moore

    Sat., [19 December 1936]   Handwritten lettercard

Wallington

Dear Mr Moore,

Thanks for your letter. I will be on hand on Monday if Gollancz wants to see me. But I shall be in London, at

24 Croom's Hill
Greenwich S.E. 10[1]

My bank say that guarantee has not reached them yet. I wonder if this could be fixed up as soon as possible, as I want if I can to leave England about Wednesday.[2] In case this letter is delayed, owing to Xmas rush, I will see you or ring up on Monday morning.

Yours sincerely
Eric A. Blair

1. Home of Eileen's brother, Dr. Laurence ('Eric') O'Shaughnessy; see *632, n. 1.*
2. Orwell was issued with Passport No. 157953 on 8 December 1936. This gave his date of birth as 25 June 1902 (instead of 1903). See *3103.*

341. To Victor Gollancz
19 December 1936

On Saturday, 19 December, Victor Gollancz telegraphed Orwell at Wallington to say that it was 'exceedingly important' that they should meet, because 'I think we can make Left Book Club[1] Choice.' He asked Orwell to see him on Monday (the 21st) at any time except 11.30. Orwell replied from Sandon, Hertfordshire:

> 12 NOON MONDAY = BLAIR +

At this meeting it was decided to illustrate *The Road to Wigan Pier*. On Tuesday, Norman Collins sent the first of a series of letters to those who might provide photographs, indicating that it was Clough Williams Ellis, an architect and founder of Portmeirion, who provided some of the names. The names had been written by Gollancz on a piece of blotting paper, which, by a quirk of chance, survives (see p. 530). It was originally intended that there would be forty-eight illustrations, not the thirty-two issued.

Leonard Moore was informed of the result of the meeting in a letter from Gollancz, 24 December 1936 (addressed to 'Gerald' Moore): 'It is highly probable that it will be the Left Book Club Choice for March.' Terms proposed were 10% for the first 2,000 copies of the ordinary trade edition, 15% to 5,000, 20% beyond that figure, and 10% of proceeds from 'Colonials.' On the Left Book Club edition ('if any' is cautiously added in parentheses), the royalty would be 10% of the price of half a crown (12½p). There would be an advance of royalties of £100. The letter concludes by treating *The Road to Wigan Pier* 'as an isolated book,' because, as nonfiction, 'it should come outside the novel contract.' Gollancz asks if there are 'any more to come under the contract.' If there are no more, 'shouldn't we have another agreement?'

Crick records that Orwell received an advance of £500 to enable him to write *The Road to Wigan Pier* and that Orwell told Geoffrey Gorer that he would never have gone north but for that money (Crick, 278). He presumably needed some special inducement, since as recently as 8 November 1935 he had written to Leonard Moore to say that he was 'rather tired' of 'unemployment etc.' as a subject (see 262). However, the sum of £500, which is based only on Geoffrey Gorer's statement, seems excessive and is even more unlikely when added to a formal advance of £100 proposed in the contract terms sent to Leonard Moore on 24 December 1936. Shelden makes no reference to this advance (though privately he has expressed doubts about its size). He simply records that Orwell was to write a book-length treatment of the subject for publication in a trade edition in about a year's time (244; U.S.: 222). An examination of the arithmetic shows that £500 is highly improbable.

Initially only a trade edition was proposed. As late as 24 December 1936—that is, after Orwell had handed in his manuscript—Gollancz had still not decided that a Left Book Club edition should be published, though he thought this was 'highly probable.' Gollancz had a very sensible policy of making only advances certain of being recovered (Hodges, 187); so the advance financial arrangements for *The Road to Wigan Pier* must be considered first in the light of a trade publication alone.

Orwell received an advance of £40 for *Down and Out in Paris and London* (Hodges, 106). The exact sums earned in royalties cannot be absolutely determined, but assuming 10% on the numbers of books printed, and assuming

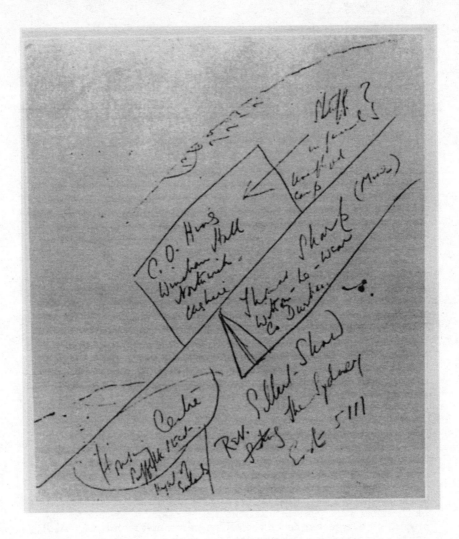

Corner of Victor Gollancz's desk blotter with the names, in his handwriting, of those who might be asked for photographs to illustrate *The Road to Wigan Pier*. When writing to the Reverend Gilbert Shaw, Norman Collins mistakenly addressed the letter to the Reverend Gilbert Sharp—the name noted above Shaw. Reduced to about two-thirds of original size.

all copies were sold, unless some were pulped, and without deducting Orwell's agent's fee (in effect, exaggerating Orwell's earnings), he would have received the following for his first books from Gollancz:

Down and Out:	3,000 @ 8s 6d	= £127.50
Burmese Days:	3,000 @ 7s 6d	= £112.50
A Clergyman's Daughter:	2,000 @ 7s 6d	= £75.00
Keep the Aspidistra Flying:	2,516 @ 7s 6d	= £94.35
	422 @ 3s 6d	= £15.83

The trade edition of *The Road to Wigan Pier* was sold at 10s 6d. The first printing was of 2,000 copies, realising for Orwell £105.00; a further 150 copies were sold, at a royalty of 15%, earning £11.81. Orwell's total earnings from the trade edition thus amounted to £116.81. After Moore had taken his 10%, Orwell would have received a net sum of £105.13—just clearing the advance proposed on 24 December 1936. (Moore's commission may have been as high as 12.125%, for that is the deduction made from £100 payable to Orwell recorded in his Payments Book for 1 September 1945; see *2731, n. 1* and *2736, n. 1*). Of course, Orwell did receive more than that, but from the Left Book Club edition, not envisaged when the supposed advance of £500 was made (although Gollancz may always have had this possibility in mind, as he must have for many books he considered publishing). From the Left Book Club edition, Orwell received 10% on a selling price of 2s 6d, or £550.49; and 10%, presumably, on the 890 copies of Part I sold at 1s 0d, or £4.45. Orwell's total earnings, from the date of publication, 8 March 1937, to 28 November 1939 (the period covered by these figures) was probably £671.75, less the 10% agent's commission, or £604.57. It will be noted that this just covers the supposed advance of £500, as well as the known advance of £100. Spread over the period the money was earned, it brought Orwell a little over £4 per week.

Another way of looking at the amount of Orwell's advance is to interpret it from the point of view of Gollancz's likely return. Before finally deciding on the Left Book Club edition, Gollancz must have expected to cover his immediate costs from the first run of 2,000 copies at 10s 6d per copy. That would bring in £1,050. Orwell's 10% royalty and the £500 would take £605. Booksellers' discounts would take £350 if at 33% (£262.50 at 25%). This would leave Gollancz with £95 (or £182.50) with which to meet other distribution costs, review and author's copies, advertising, overheads, printing and binding, and the cost of thirty-two pages of half-tone plates. Thus, a £500 advance would not enable Gollancz to meet his costs from such a first run. Would Gollancz have calculated on making a heavy loss? Hardly.

It is likely that Orwell needed money to enable him to spend time in the north collecting data. If we compare that £500 with what a miner was then earning— about £2.50 per week—or the secretary of the miners' South Yorkshire Branch— £260 per annum (see *262, n. 1*), that £500 looks remarkably munificent. From August 1941 Orwell was to receive £640 for a year's work for the BBC. Gollancz's supposed £500 would surely have been, at the very least, for a year's work. Writing to Jack Common in April 1936 (see *300*) regarding setting up shop, Orwell sounds hard put to find £20 in order to stock his shelves, rather than like a man who had received £500 a couple of months earlier. Another indication that he was not paid as much as £500 was his need to arrange with his bank an overdraft of up to £50 before leaving for Spain; see *337*. However, were the sum

£50 (sixpence of the 10s 6d per copy of the first run of the book), that would provide Orwell with £6.25 per week for the eight weeks he was actually in the North. Since he was paying about 25s for bed and board at 72 Warrington Lane, that would have left him a fair margin for expenses.

It is suggested, therefore, that Gollancz, initially having in mind only a trade edition, provided Orwell with expense-money to research his book, perhaps £50, and, when the manuscript was delivered, offered an advance that had to be earned out of sales of £100, and later proposed that a Left Book Club edition should also be published.

Crick states that 'Gollancz first tried to persuade Orwell's agent to allow a small public edition of both halves to appear in hard covers, and the large Left Book Club edition to be simply the descriptive first half on Wigan. . . . Moore and Eileen refused to allow this denaturing of the book; and Orwell himself had had time for a preliminary talk with a worried Gollancz. . . . Gollancz got round the difficulty by himself writing an extraordinary introduction to the book' (307–08). Hodges does not mention this in her history of the publishing house. Edwards states in her biography of Gollancz, 'Victor could not bear to reject it, even though his suggestion that the "repugnant" second half should be omitted from the Club edition was turned down. On this occasion Victor, albeit nervously, did overrule C[communist] P[arty] objections in favour of his publishing instinct. His compromise was to publish the book with what Orwell's biographer, Bernard Crick, rightly calls "an extraordinary introduction", full of good criticism, unfair criticism and half-truths' (246–47).

1. The Left Book Club, advertised for the first time in *The New Statesman and Nation*, 29 February 1936, was designed for those 'who desire to play an intelligent part in the struggle *for* World Peace and a better social and economic order, and *against* Fascism.' Books that would normally be sold at from 7s 6d to 25s 0d were to be sold to members at 5s 0d; all books would be original. The three selectors were Victor Gollancz; John Strachey, closely aligned to the Communist Party, though not a member; and Harold Laski, a member of the National Executive of the Labour Party and Professor of Political Science at the London School of Economics, University of London. The Left Book Club was the first of its kind in Britain and was modelled on the Book Society and Collins's Crime Club. Its first two books were published on 18 May 1936, when the club's membership was 9,000; by October 1936 there were 28,000 members. A monthly brochure, *Left Book News*, was issued to members, but was also available, free of charge, to non-members. The club ran for twelve years; its last book was offered in October 1948. See Sheila Hodges, *Gollancz: The Story of a Publishing House 1928–1978*, 117–43, 151, and 124–25 for an illustration of the first advertisement; Ruth Dudley Edwards, *Victor Gollancz: A Biography*, in which each issue of the *News* is noted.

342. Review of *The Novel To-Day* by Philip Henderson

New English Weekly, 31 December 1936

Mr. Philip Henderson's book, "The Novel To-Day," is a survey of the contemporary novel from a Marxist standpoint. It is not a very good book, in fact it can be described as a weaker version of Mirsky's "Intelligentsia of Great Britain," written by someone who has got to live in England and cannot afford to insult too many people, but it is of some interest because it raises the question of art and propaganda which now rumbles like a sort of "noises off" round every critical discussion.

On the last occasion when "Punch" produced a genuinely funny joke, which was only six or seven years ago, it was a picture of an intolerable youth telling his aunt that when he came down from the University he intended to "write." "And what are you going to write about, dear?" his aunt enquires. "My dear aunt," the youth replies crushingly, "one doesn't write *about* anything, one just *writes*." This was a perfectly justified criticism of current literary cant. At that time, even more than now, art for art's sake was going strong, though the phrase itself had been discarded as ninety-ish; "art has nothing to do with morality" was the favourite slogan. The artist was conceived as leaping to and fro in a moral, political and economic void, usually in pursuit of something called "Beauty," which was always one jump ahead. And the critic was supposed to be completely "impartial," *i.e.*, to deal in abstract aesthetic standards which were completely unaffected by his other prejudices. To admit that you liked or disliked a book because of its moral or religious tendency, even to admit noticing that it *had* a tendency, was too vulgar for words.

This is still the official attitude, but it is in process of being abandoned, and especially by the extremists at the opposite poles of thought, the Communist and the Catholic. Both the Communist and the Catholic usually believe, though unfortunately they do not often say, that abstract aesthetic standards are all bunkum and that a book is only a "good" book if it preaches the right sermon. To the Communist, good literature means "proletarian" literature. (Mr. Henderson is careful to explain, however, that this does not mean literature written by proletarians; which is just as well, because there isn't any.) In Henri Barbusse's "One Looks at Russia," for instance, it is stated almost in so many words that a novel about "bourgeois" characters cannot be a good novel. So expressed this is an absurdity, but in some ways it is not a bad position to take up. Any critic who stuck to it consistently would at least do useful work by dragging into the light the (often quite unaesthetic) reasons for which books are liked or disliked. But unfortunately the notion of art for art's sake, though discredited, is too recent to be forgotten, and there is always a temptation to revert to it in moments of difficulty. Hence the frightful intellectual dishonesty which can be observed in nearly all propagandist critics. They are employing a double set of values and dodging from one to the other according as it suits them. They praise or dispraise a book *because* its tendency is Communist, Catholic, Fascist or what-not; but at the same time, they pretend to be judging it on purely aesthetic grounds. Few people have the guts to say outright that art and propaganda are the same thing.

You can see this at its crudest in the so-called book-reviews in some of the Roman Catholic papers, and indeed in religious papers generally. The editorial staff of the "Church Times" gnash their false teeth and quake in their galoshes at the mention of "modern" (*i.e.*, post-Tennysonian) poetry, but strange to say they make an exception of T. S. Eliot. Eliot is a declared Anglo-Catholic, and therefore his poetry, though "modern," has got to be praised. And the Communist critic is hardly more honest. Most of the time

Mr. Henderson is keeping up a pretence of strict critical impartiality, but it is strange how invariably his aesthetic judgments coincide with his political ones. Proust, Joyce, Wyndham Lewis, Virginia Woolf, Aldous Huxley, Wells, E. M. Forster (all of them "bourgeois" novelists) are patted on the head with varying degrees of contempt; Lawrence (proletarian turned bourgeois, which is worse) is viciously attacked; Hemingway, on the other hand, is treated rather respectfully (because Hemingway, you see, is rumoured to be toying with Communism); Barbusse is bowed down to; and a huge wad of mediocre stuff called "Daughters of Albion," by Mr. Alec Brown, gets pages and pages of praise all to itself, because here at last you have real "proletarian" literature—written, like all other "proletarian" literature, by a member of the middle classes.

This kind of thing is very depressing to anyone who cares for the cause of Socialism. For what is it except the most ordinary chauvinism turned upside down? It simply gives you the feeling that the Communist is no better than his opposite number. Nevertheless, these books of Marxist literary criticism have their value for anyone who wants to study the Marxist mind. The basic trouble with all orthodox Marxists is that, possessing a system which appears to explain everything, they never bother to discover what is going on inside other people's heads. That is why in every Western country, during the last dozen years, they have played straight into the hands of their adversaries. In a book of literary criticism, unlike a tract on economics, the Marxist cannot take cover behind his favourite polysyllables; he has got to come out into the open and you can see just what kind of blinkers he is wearing.

I do not recommend this particular book, which is badly written and thoroughly dull all through, but to anyone who has not yet read it I do recommend Mirsky's "Intelligentsia of Great Britain," which was published in 1935. It is a terribly malignant but very able book, and in a distorted way it performs a remarkable feat of synthesis. It is the archetype of Marxist literary criticism. And when you read it you understand—though this, of course, is not what the author intends—why Fascism arose, and why even a quite intelligent outsider can be taken in by the vulgar lie, now so popular, that "Communism and Fascism are the same thing."

On the day before Orwell's review of *The Novel To-Day* was published, he enlisted in the militia of the Workers' Party of Marxist Unification (the POUM) at the Lenin Barracks in Barcelona. He probably left England on Wednesday, 23 December, as he had planned. He travelled via Paris, where he had a seriocomic altercation with a taxi-driver and called on Henry Miller. See Crick, 315–18; Stansky and Abrahams, II, 200–03; Shelden, 274–75; U.S.: 249–50.

343. Wigan Pier

The Road to Wigan Pier was published by Victor Gollancz Ltd on 8 March 1937 in both Left Book Club and trade editions. It was not published in the United States until 1958; see *362*. Although out of chronological order, this is an appropriate place for Orwell's description of Wigan Pier in the BBC programme 'Your Questions Answered,' broadcast on 2 December 1943; see *2384*. He was asked: "How long is the Wigan Pier and what is the Wigan Pier?"

Well, I am afraid I must tell you that Wigan Pier doesn't exist. I made a journey specially to see it in 1936, and I couldn't find it. It did exist once, however, and to judge from the photographs it must have been about twenty feet long.

Wigan is in the middle of the mining areas, and though it's a very pleasant place in some ways its scenery is not its strong point. The landscape is mostly slag-heaps, looking like the mountains of the moon, and mud and soot and so forth. For some reason, though it's not worse than fifty other places, Wigan has always been picked on as a symbol of the ugliness of the industrial areas. At one time, on one of the little muddy canals that run round the town, there used to be a tumble-down wooden jetty; and by way of a joke some nicknamed this Wigan Pier. The joke caught on locally, and then the music-hall comedians got hold of it, and they are the ones who have succeeded in keeping Wigan Pier alive as a byword, long after the place itself had been demolished.[1]

1. Wigan Pier is illustrated in Lewis, 51, with the caption, 'The original pier was used for loading coal onto canal barges. It later became the subject of a music-hall joke. The projecting wooden jetty had already gone when Orwell visited Wigan.' A refurbished warehouse with a decorative railed walkway over the canal was prominently named 'The Orwell Wigan Pier' in the 1980s. The complex houses a museum, restaurants, a public house, and a pier from which barge trips on the canal depart.

APPENDIX 1

344. French Text of Orwell's Introduction to *La Vache Enragée* (*Down and Out in Paris and London*)[1]

Mes dévoués traducteurs m'ont demandé d'écrire une courte préface pour l'édition française de ce livre. Comme il est probable que maint lecteur français se demandera par quel concours de circonstances je me trouvais à Paris à l'époque où se passent les événements que je rapporte, le mieux sera, je pense, de leur donner tout d'abord quelques détails biographiques.

Je suis né en 1903. En 1922, je partis pour la Birmanie, où j'entrai dans la Police Impériale des Indes. C'était un métier qui me convenait aussi peu que possible; aussi, au début de 1928, lors d'un congé que je passais en Angleterre, donnai-je ma démission, dans l'espoir de pouvoir gagner ma vie en écrivant. J'y réussis à peu près aussi bien que la plupart des jeunes gens qui embrassent la carrière des lettres, — autant dire pas du tout. A peine si ma première année de besognes littéraires me rapporta une vingtaine de livres.

Au printemps de 1928, je partis pour Paris, afin de pouvoir vivre à peu de frais le temps d'écrire deux romans, — qui, j'ai le regret de le dire, ne furent jamais publiés, — et, par surcroît, d'apprendre le français. Un de mes amis de Paris me dénicha une chambre dans un hôtel garni d'un quartier ouvrier, que j'ai succinctement décrit au premier chapitre de cet ouvrage, et que tout Parisien quelque peu averti ne manquera sans doute pas de reconnaître. Au cours de l'été de 1929, j'avais écrit mes deux romans, que les éditeurs me laissèrent pour compte, mais je me trouvais presque sans le sou et dans la nécessité urgente de trouver du travail. A cette èpoque, il n'était pas encore interdit, — tout au moins pas strictement interdit, – aux étrangers séjournant en France d'occuper un emploi, et je trouvai plus naturel de rester dans la ville où j'étais plutôt que de rentrer en Angleterre, où il y avait alors environ deux millions et demi de chômeurs. Je demeurai donc à Paris, et c'est à la fin de l'automne de 1929 que se placent les aventures que j'ai racontées.

Quant à la véracité de mon récit, je crois pouvoir affirmer que je n'ai rien exagéré, sinon dans la mesure où tout écrivain exagére, c'est-à-dire en choisissant. Je ne me suis pas cru obligé de relater les faits dans l'ordre même où ils se sont passés, mais tous ceux que j'ai rapportés sont réellement arrivés à un moment ou à un autre. Je me suis toutefois abstenu, autant que possible, de faire des portraits particuliers. Tous les personnages que j'ai décrits dans les deux parties de ce livre ne l'ont été qu'à titre de types représentatifs de la classe de Parisiens ou de Londoniens à laquelle ils appartiennent, et non en tant qu'individus.

Je dois en outre faire remarquer que ce livre n'a pas la prétention de donner une idée complète de la vie à Paris et à Londres, mais seulement d'en décrire l'un des aspects particuliers. Comme les scènes et les événements auxquels je me suis trouvé mêlé ont tous, presque uniformément, quelque chose de répugnant, il est fort possible que j'aie paru, penser sans le vouloir, que Paris et Londres sont des villes abominables. Telle n'a nullement été mon intention, et, si l'on peut, à première vue, s'y méprendre, c'est tout simplement parce que le sujet de mon livre est une chose essentiellement dénuée de charmes: j'ai nommé la pauvreté. Quand vous n'avez pas un sou en poche, vous êtes porté à voir sous son aspect le moins favorable n'importe quelle ville et n'importe quel pays, et tout être humain, ou presque, ne vous apparaît que comme un compagnon de souffrance ou comme un ennemi. Je tenais à préciser ce point surtout pour mes lecteurs parisiens, car je serais navré qu'ils pussent croire que je nourrisse la moindre animosité contre une ville dont je conserve le plus sympathique souvenir.

J'avais promis, au début de cette préface, de donner au lecteur quelques détails biographiques. J'ajouterai donc, pour ceux que cela pourrait intéresser, qu'après mon départ de Paris, à la fin de 1929, j'ai gagné ma vie surtout à enseigner et un peu à écrire. Depuis la publication en Angleterre de *Down and Out in London and Paris*,° le présent volume, j'ai écrit deux autres romans.[2] Je viens de terminer le second.[3] Le premier[4] va paraître dans quelques jours chez un éditeur de New-York.

GEORGE ORWELL.

Londres, 15 octobre 1934.

1. For translation back into English, see *211*.
2. This implies that Orwell thought of *Down and Out in Paris and London* as a novel. However, *romans* could be a translation of either 'novels' or 'books' in Orwell's (lost) original.
3. *A Clergyman's Daughter.*
4. *Burmese Days*, Harper Brothers edn. N.Y.°

APPENDIX 2

345. Orwell's Notes for *The Road to Wigan Pier*

Orwell's preparation for the writing of *The Road to Wigan Pier* was serious, detailed, and varied, even though the time he spent in the north was relatively short. He travelled, observed, asked questions, went to meetings, listened. Some of his experiences he wrote up in the diary published in this volume, but many of the hard facts were assembled in note form, typed, and then annotated. The notes he made were supplemented by digging out information from newspapers, books, and town hall sources.

Although in his letter to Jack Common of 17 March 1936 (see *295*), Orwell says he is anxious 'to start doing some work again, which of course is impossible in the surroundings I have been in,' he is understating, as he frequently did, his efforts and achievements. Stansky and Abrahams point out that there is 'a significant portion of [his] time in Wigan that is not accounted for in his diary,' that in addition to checking the proofs of *Keep the Aspidistra Flying*, he spent some of his time in Wigan Reference Library. They report interviews with two people who saw him there: Carlton Melling, who was in charge of the library, and the novelist John Farrimond (II, 143–44). Orwell also visited the British Museum library late in the course of writing the book, as he told Leonard Moore on 10 December 1936: 'I have looked up the stuff I wanted at the Museum, and the book will be typed in ten days or so.' In fact, only five days later he sent Moore the completed manuscript.

It is impossible to know whether there once were more cuttings, printed sources, and notes, but it is likely that Orwell's notes are complete. There are no obvious gaps and there is a similar pattern to the information provided for Wigan, Barnsley, and Sheffield. It is unlikely that there were notes on Liverpool, because he was ill there, and that city was not a subject in his book. For Liverpool, see Crick, 284–85; Stansky and Abrahams, II, 144–46.

With one exception, all the newspaper cuttings and printed matter refer to the time Orwell was in the north. The exception is a long report of an inquiry into a proposal for slum clearance in the New Street area of Barnsley. This is from the *Barnsley Chronicle*, 24 March 1934, two years earlier.

All Orwell's notes are given here, with illustrations of the pay slips and unemployment forms he collected and referred to in his book. Ellis Firth's Weekly Budget, with Orwell's annotations, is also reproduced. These have an intrinsic interest, and cannot otherwise readily be examined by anyone interested in Orwell's sources and the use he made of them. The newspaper cuttings are not reproduced but references to them and a note of their subject matter are provided. These can be checked in the British Library and some public libraries. For convenience, a contents list, with annotations, where useful, is provided at the end of this headnote.

Some of the material was used by Orwell almost as it stood—Ellis Firth's income and outgoings, for example, though it is only from these notes that we know Firth was the source—and often the modifications made, as in the descriptions of houses and details of pay and deductions, are designed to make his book more readily assimilable. There are, however, some interesting changes. The fact that the houses in Greenough's Row (see Wigan: Additional Notes on Houses) and that on the Welly Estate (see Wigan; Additional Note) were occupied by Catholics was, though noted, omitted from *The Road to Wigan Pier* (see *CW*, V, 49, 62). One fuller example might serve to illustrate Orwell's technique.

The *Barnsley Chronicle* of 24 March 1934 includes this section, headed WIDOW'S PLIGHT in its report of the inquiry into the New Street (Eastern) Slum Clearance Proposal:

'A widow, sixty-three years of age, pleaded to be allowed to retain her four houses in Joseph Street, which were her only means of support. "I had to move from New Street four years ago", she said, "on account of the slum clearance scheme, and I then bought these four cottages in one of which I live. I have worked hard to pay for them, and if you take them from me, I don't know what I shall do".

'Mr Mellor [Barnsley's Chief Sanitary Inspector] detailed the numerous alleged defects of the houses, and the owner declared that she was not in a position to spend a large amount on repairs.'

Orwell's typed notes have this summary: 'One fact that emerges from the New Street inquiry (see cutting) is that the small landlord (old women who have invested their savings in two or three houses) are often the worst landlords because they cannot afford to pay for repairs. (Barnsley, p. 2).'

This is how the report and notes appear in *The Road to Wigan Pier*: '. . . I have noted "Landlord good" or "Landlord bad", because there is great variation in what the slum-dwellers say about their landlords. I found—one might expect it, perhaps—that the small landlords are usually the worst. It goes against the grain to say this, but one can see why it should be so. Ideally, the worst type of slum landlord is a fat wicked man, preferably a bishop, who is drawing an immense income from extortionate rents. Actually, it is a poor old woman who has invested her life's savings in three slum houses, inhabits one of them and tries to live on the rent of the other two—never, in consequence, having any money for repairs' (*CW*, V, 52).

One comparison of Orwell's use of his sources shows a possible misunderstanding by him. He remarks in his book that the pay slips of the colliers often note a deduction for a dead miner's widow, called a 'death stoppage.'

CONTENTS OF NOTES for *The Road to Wigan Pier*

An asterisk indicates that the item is not reproduced here.

Additional Note (on Corporation Houses, Miners)
Additional Notes on Houses

*2. Newspaper Cutting: *Daily Despatch*, 29 February 1936: 'The Lancashire cotton manufacturing industry is faced with a wage fight during the next few months.' Details of earnings of 4,235 weavers in the Preston area. Average earnings £1 6s 4¾d (= £1.32p) a week; average wage for entire cotton-weaving industry is estimated at 32s 6d (= £1.62½p). Details in note at the beginning of Section V of *The Road to Wigan Pier*, *CW*, V, 69.

3. Barnsley (typed notes)
   Population
   Local Industries
   Vital Statistics
   Housing (with printed details from official report)
   Unemployment Occupational Centre (run by Council of Social Service)
   Unemployment
   Religion (from official report)
   Public Buildings
   Corporation Baths
   Notes on Houses

*4a. Annual Accounts to 31 December 1935 of South Yorkshire Branch of the Working Men's Club and Institute Union, Ltd.

*4b. Notice of Branch Council Meeting of South Yorkshire Branch of the Working Men's Club and Institute at Highstone Road Working Men's Club, Worsbro' Common, Barnsley, 14 March 1936, with Agenda

5. Pay Slips for Two-Man Team, Woolley Collieries, 5 and 12 March 1935, 2 April 1935, 7 January 1936, one undated; one Miner's Check Note, December 1936 (1935?)

6. Ellis Firth's Weekly Budget, with Orwell's annotations

*7. Newspaper Cutting: *Barnsley Chronicle*? Illustration of glass-blowers with caption: 'THIRSTY WORK, blowing babies' feeding bottles. Some of the workmates of these Barnsley glass-blowers drink a gallon of beer a shift.'

*8. Newspaper Cutting: *Barnsley Chronicle*, 24 March 1934. Detailed report of a public inquiry into Barnsley Corporation's application for the confirmation of New Street (Eastern) Clearance Order etc, 'ordering the demolition of buildings described in the Schedules' with 'A scathing indictment of Barnsley's slums in the New Street area . . . made by the Town Clerk . . . in outlining the Corporation case'

9. Sheffield (typed notes)
   Population
   Health
   Employment
   Housing
   Typical Sheffield Back to Back House[s]

*10. Programme for 1–8 March 1936 at Victoria Hall, Methodist Church (Sheffield Mission Headquarters), with words of twelve hymns

11. Statistical Information Provided by Medical Officer of Health, Sheffield, 10 March 1936, addressed to E. Blair, 154 Wallace Road, Sheffield, 3

12. Copy of Report of City of Sheffield by W. Asbury (Councillor) on Out-Door Relief, 25 June 1935

13. Unemployment Assistance Board Award Form for J. W. Binns, Sheffield, January 1936

*14. Newspaper Cutting: *Sheffield Telegraph*, 5 March 1936. 'Council's Attitude Towards Shops on Housing Estates. Allegation of Playing Into Hands of 'Certain Interested People'. Plea for Government Work for City'

*15. Newspaper Cutting: *The Times*, 11 March 1936. 'Safety in Coal-Mines. The Personal Factor. Appointment of Special Officials Urged'

*16. Newspaper Cutting: *The Times*, 12 March 1936. 'Diet and Health. Effect of Income and Nutrition. Nation's Expenditure on Food.' A review of a report of the Committee of the League of Nations on 'Food, Health, and Income: A Survey of Adequacy of Diet in Relation to Income,' published by Macmillan.

17. Re Coal-Mining. Figures Taken from *The Coal Scuttle* by Joseph Jones

18. Figures Taken from the *Colliery Year Book & Coal Trades Directory for 1935*

346. WIGAN

POPULATION. Given in 1935 as 86,186. In 1931 census report as 85,356. Excess of births over deaths about, 5[1] per thousand per year, so there has not been much loss by migration. In 1931 report, males 41,313. Females 44,044. Excess of females over males 2731. Population over 14 given (1931) as 64,871, of which males 31,097, females 33,774. ie. number of children equals 20,485, and excess of females is almost entirely in adult population.

HEALTH. See Health Officer's report. But note: Birth rate 17.42, death rate 12.4. Birth rate for whole of England 14.8, death rate 11.8. Wigan has second highest birth rate for Lancs. and about 7th highest death rate. Highest death rate in Wigan (Victoria Ward) 17.07. St. Patrick and St. Thomas Wards (said to be poorest quarters) 15.05 and 13.86. Lowest in town (West Pemberton—better class residential) 7.48, ie. about half St. Patrick's.
General health in Wigan appears fairly good. Physique a little sturdier than in London. Struck by the badness of everyone's teeth—have hardly seen a working class person with good teeth. Even teeth of the very young have a curiously frail look and are of the wrong colour (semi-translucent.) In the Hornbys' household (average age about 36) none except Joe (aged 15) had any teeth of their own. Was told here as elsewhere that as you could get false teeth from your health insurance it was considered an economy to do so. General opinion seems to be that it is best to "get shut of" your teeth as soon as possible. Deformities on the other hand not common.
Number of pubs in Wigan proper, 160. Equal to about 1 to 540 of population. Drunkenness nevertheless not common. Large proportion of pubs are beer houses and the smaller ones constantly changing hands. Few free houses.

Number of (retail) sweetshops 147, equal to about 1 to 590 of population. This apparently does not include tobacconists etc. who sell sweets. Struck by immense number of cut-price sweetshops, much cheaper and nastier than London.

Local bread mostly very bad. Immense sales of cheap readymade meat pies. Fruit and vegetables nowhere very good. Favourite local dishes tripe (eaten cold with vinegar) and cowheel. Less teashops than in southern towns. Unemployed are said to eat very largely tinned meat.

EMPLOYMENT. 1931 census report gives local industries as follow: Mining 7,708 (118 females.) Textiles (not dress) and cellulose, 5,386, mainly women. Manufacture of machinery 2,139. Manufacture of clothing (not knitted) 2,438, mainly women. Transport and communication, 1,966. In business 5,133, about a quarter women. Also minor industries: pottery, woodworking, paper-making etc. In building trade 1,124, almost all men. Unoccupied and retired given as 22,665 (only 2,482 of these men: ie. the others are wives and daughters of those in work.) Unemployed given as 7,708.

Unemployment has grown greatly in last four years. Round figure given by Labour Exchange for this time of year is 10,000 wholly unemployed and "temporarily stopped." This includes those on P.A.C. but not workhouse paupers. Rough figures are:

Men wholly unemployed.............. 8300.
Temporarily stopped .... 3 to 400.
Women both classes .... 1500.
                                        ‾‾‾‾‾‾
                        about 10,000.

Total insured population is about 26,000 men, 10,000 women. Therefore at this time of year about 1 in 3.6 of the insured population is out of work. In the summer (when the pits are producing less coal) proportion rises to about 1 in 3. These figures however do not take account of dependents of unemployed. They should probably be multiplied by something between 3 and 4 to allow for wives and children of registered unemployed. Therefore at any moment at least 30,000 people (rather more than 1 in 3 of population) are drawing or living on the dole. According to officers at Labour Exchange, there has been a "steady core" of about 4,500 miners unemployed for the last 7 years.

Rates of benefit are as follow:

1. "Full Benefit" (ie. until stamps are exhausted):

Single man .... 17/– per week.
Wife .... 9/–.
Each child below 14 .... 3/–.

(Therefore in typical family of parents and 3 children of whom 1 is above 14, total income would be 32/– per week, plus anything brought in by eldest child. Rent for family of this size would seldom[2] be less than 7/6 per week.)

2. U.A.B. (Unemployment Assistance Board, for those who have exhausted their stamps and are on transitional benefit before being turned over to the parish):

Single man	15/– per week.
Man and wife	24/–.
Children 14–18	6/–.
ditto 11–14	4/6.
ditto 8–11	4/–.
ditto 5–11	3/6.
ditto 3–5	3/–.

(Apparently no allowance for infants. NB. that a quarter of this is regarded as rent with a minimum of 7/6 per week. ie. if a man is paying less than a quarter of his dole as rent, or less than 7/6 if his income is 30/– or below, a corresponding amount is deducted from his benefit. In the typical family considered above, total income might be 31/6 plus eldest child's wages if in work, or 37/6 if not in work. A quarter of this would have to be paid as rent.)

3. P.A.C. (Public Assistance Board – local rates aided by central fund.)

Single man	12/6 per week.
Man and wife	23/–.
Eldest child	4/–.
Any other child	3/–.

(Therefore in the typical family above, total income would be 33/– a week, or 29/– plus anything brought in by eldest child if in work. In addition to the above, coal allowance of 1/6 a week (rather less than price of 1 hundredweight) is granted for six weeks before and six weeks after Christmas. P.A.C. rates were recently lower, I think only 19/– for man and wife, but have been raised owing to a struggle by the N.U.W.M.—or so the latter claim.)

Means-test enforcement is said to be strict and question of rent carefully investigated. There is said to be much spying and tale-bearing, when, for instance, somebody is taking in a lodger, in which case a deduction would be made from his benefit if it were known. Meade told me of a case where a deduction was made because a room used to be rented to a travelling dentist one night a week for 3/–. One of the men at the "caravans" told me that he was seen feeding a neighbour's chickens and it was reported that he was drawing wages for this and he had difficulty in refuting it.*

It may be taken that the average family in which there is no one in work is living on an income of round about 30/–, of which a quarter goes on rent. This is to say that the average person has to be fed, clothed, warmed and otherwise cared for for about 6 or 7 shillings a week.

Evidently there are cases of abuse of the dole. Sometimes young unmarried men who are in reality living at home get an accomodation° address in order that they may represent themselves as independent and draw 17/– or 15/– as the case may be.*

* Typescript has an asterisk here and again two paragraphs down; and a footnote: 'See over page.' This, in Orwell's hand, reads: 'As usual, there is extraordinary variation in the different cases. eg. in this house alone: old Jack, superannuated miner aged 75, lives on his old age pension of 10/– plus 2/6 from the parish. He has a home, ie. a married son or daughter (not certain which) & used to live there till the Means Test came in. But now, under the Means Test, they would get less dole if it were known they had a paying lodger, so he has to turn out into lodgings.

Of single unemployed men, some live in lodging houses. There are 10 common lodging houses in town housing 400–500 people. Most men of this kind live in a rented room for which they pay 5/– or 6/– a week and see to their own food. Of course in lodgings of this kind they are not encouraged to stay indoors, hence large numbers of them always hanging about the streets. They are not however very much in evidence because the police move them on if they congregate in large bunches. Their chief haunts are, 1. the Public Library newspaper room, where there are never less than 50 men, sometimes much more. 2. Several free billiards halls. 3. (for members) the N.U.W.M. shelter. 4. (above all) the movies. These are extraordinarily cheap and unemployed men avowedly go there to keep warm. You can always get a seat for 4d and at matinees at many picture houses for 2d.

Besides the above classes there is a fairly large number of disabled miners living on "compensation" pensions from the mines. "Compensation" usually seems to be something under 30/– a week, but some are paid a lump sum down. If their compensation falls below a certain sum (I think about 15/–) they can draw the dole. Also the usual old people living on the old age pension, eg. in the house I am in now there is an old man living solely on his 10/– a week pension.* He is more or less bedridden and only goes out once a week to draw his pension. He hands his 10/– weekly over to Mrs F. and she "does for" him. I see his meals going up and he does not get much beyond bread and butter, tea and an occasional cake.

On the whole, there is not so much overt poverty in Wigan as one might expect. The most obvious sign of poverty is the poorness of the shops and the extraordinary number of shops that are derelict—in some streets about 1 in 3. Everyone is badly dressed but few noticeably ragged; clogs very common but no bare feet. Less obviously down-and-out people than in London. It is said that no one here spends the night in the streets and there is no derelict and as it were unaccounted-for population, except the casual paupers passing through. There are however a few people squatting in abandoned ruinous houses, for which they pay no rent, near the coal pits. In the time I have been here (a fortnight) I have not seen a beggar, though there are said to be a few. Few if any prostitutes. Last year there were 7 or 8 prosecutions for this during the whole year. In effect what you have here is a population living on the dole and getting to take it for granted. The people have now grasped that it is not their fault they are unemployed (this is markedly different from 8 years ago) and are coming to look on drawing the dole as the same as having a job.

HOUSING. In the census report of 1931, total number of occupied houses given as 18,573, or 82,704 rooms. Equals average of a little over 4 people per house or just over 1 per room. Taking half or even two thirds of

'On the other hand: Mr F., who keeps this place, has the tripe-shop, which presumably brings in profit, & also takes in lodgers up to the number of about 9, paying varying amounts from 25/– a week downwards. Also sells teas, casual meals, cigarettes etc. etc. On top of this he has the impertinence to draw the dole & has never been found out.'

* Two of these in this house. But they also receive 2/6 a week from the parish. In Manchester & Salford 5/– [Orwell's handwritten footnote].

these to be bedrooms, it is clear very few people here sleep in a room of their own. At date of census the number of families was given as (NB. almost certainly understated) 1,617 in excess of number of dwellings. Present number of houses not exactly procurable, but since 1931 990 houses are given as having been built and perhaps 100 demolished. Excess of families over houses should now therefore be somewhere in neighbourhood of 700 or 800 plus the number in caravans (see below.) Number of houses built during 1934 was 589, 284 by private enterprise and 304 by the Corporation. Great numbers of houses are condemned and theoretically the people from these houses are given Corporation houses instead, but there are never enough of these and the condemned houses remain standing. Probably in the whole town there are several thousand *families* (not individuals) who cannot get a livable house because there is not such a thing to be had.

Some typical houses I inspected were the following:*

In Wallgate Quarter. Rows of "One up, one down" houses. This means one room upstairs and one room downstairs. Under the stairs there is an alcove measuring about 5 feet by 5 feet and serving for larder, scullery and coalhole. Kitchen measures about 12 feet by 10, and room upstairs corresponds to it. Open fireplace with oven at the side (all houses in Wigan have this) in kitchen. Tiny yard and outside lavatory at back. Rent 4/9, rates 2/6— total 7/3. Rows of others as above, but instead of the alcove there was a recess about 2 feet deep containing the sink—no room for larder etc. Lavatories are common to several houses† and are in little sheds in the alley behind. These houses have no back doors. To go to the lavatory you have to go out by the front door and round the end of the block–50 or 100 yards if you live in the middle of the street. Rent 3/2, rates 2/- —total 5/2.

Rows of others with no alcove at all, merely a sink in the kitchen just inside the front door. No back door. Rent 3/9, rates 3/- —total 6/9.

I was told these conditions are typical all over Wigan. One result of having no back doors is that the women habitually throw refuse out into the gutters in front. Most of the houses I inspected were in fairly good repair, but some I have passed without going inside are almost falling to pieces. A great many houses in the town have sunk owing to subsidence of old mining workings below. Many windows are as much as 20 degrees out of true, and, of course, it is impossible to open them. This taken for granted locally and looked upon as a joke. Out of 20 or 30 houses I have inspected, only 1 (the one I am in now, which is a 7-room house) has a bathroom. No hot water laid on in any of the houses, though when building them it would have been simple to instal a boiler behind the fireplace. People who have a house of any description cling to it however inconvenient it is, and some I spoke to had been in their houses 20 or 30 years. I notice they do not as a rule complain of their landlords but say they are quite well treated.

* See also additional notes on houses [Orwell's handwritten footnote].

† Great majority of houses have their own lavatory [Orwell's handwritten footnote].

The worse° feature here are the colonies of caravans. The number of these is given in the Health Report as 180, and I visited colonies of them amounting to about 100. They are batches of old gypsy caravans, tramcars, buses etc dumped on pieces of waste ground and each inhabited by a family. Interior measurements vary between 6' by 5' by 6' high and about 15' by 6' by 6' high. Some of them are not even constructed of wood but are simply old wagons with semi-circular slats on top over which canvas is stretched, so that you have only canvas between you and the outer air. All have a tiny cottage kitchener inside. As for water, there is a hydrant common to the whole colony. In some I inspected the inhabitants had to walk 150 yards to fetch water. There are no sanitary arrangements at all. The people make what arrangements they can (most of them construct little huts in the tiny patch of ground surrounding their caravan) and once a week dig a deep hole in which they bury their refuse. Some I suppose are inhabited by a single individual, but I did not see one in which there were less than 2 people, and most of the families were fairly large. One, measuring about 12 or 15 feet long, had 7 people living in it. Conditions inside these places have to be seen to be grasped. It is almost literally impossible to turn round, and all the people, especially the children, are unspeakably dirty. All the caravan-dwellers said that in winter they had to keep their fires alight all night to keep warm, and the damp, of course, soaks up through the floor. I was shown mattresses (this was about 11 am.) which were wringing wet. There is never room for more than one or at most two beds, and with families of almost-adult children this raises fresh problems. In one caravan there were a mother, a father, a son and a daughter, the two last round about 18 years old. The mother slept with the daughter and the son with the father—they were plainly afraid of incest. A question I would have liked to ask, but had not the nerve, was what happens in these places when anyone dies. Rents, according to size of caravan, vary from 5/– a week to 8/– including water.

This state of affairs is not due to poverty but to housing shortage, since these rents are about the same as for houses; only the houses are not available. The Health Report only mentions them in a very discreet manner and the Census Report makes what is evidently a deliberate falsification with regard to them. "Structurally separate dwellings of 1 room" occupied by 1 family are given as only 25. But the Health Report now admits to 180, and in 1931 there were presumably more, since this business has admittedly been going on since 1919 and some effort has been made to get the people out into houses. The importance of this lies in the fact that there are said to be caravan-colonies in all the Lancashire towns. By ommitting° mention of these the census report enormously understates the number of families living in one room.

There are not many "back to back" houses in Wigan. I have only seen one row of them.

One mitigation of bad housing conditions is that fuel is cheap. Coal is 1/11 a hundredweight for "best" (2/7d in London) and I think you can get coal of sorts for 1/6. There is also immense and constant thieving of coal from the "dirt-trains." (See diary.) I gather that several tons of coal and "cannel" a day are stolen by the unemployed. Coal cannot be stolen directly from the pits by the working miners, but they steal short lengths of pit-props for kindling wood and to some extent collaborate with the men who rob the "dirt-trains" by allowing as much coal as possible to remain among the dirt.

RELIGION. No exact figures obtainable. Number of churches and chapels of all denominations in Wigan proper seems to be about 40 with about 60 clergy–the numbers are possibly a very little above this. This means allowing about 1 church or chapel to about 2000 or 2500 of the population. Even allowing for the fact that the Catholic churches have a number of successive Masses on Sundays, it is clear that not half the population make any kind of observance. As to numbers of the different denominations, the Anglicans have about 12 churches with 22 clergy, the Catholics about 6 with 17 clergy, the rest belong to various sects. Nonconformity however is said not to be preponderant here. The biggest community are the Catholics with the Anglicans a fairly good second. Large numbers of the population are of Irish descent and Irish names are common though they all speak with the Lancashire accent.

ADDITIONAL NOTES.

Melbourne Street (Wallgate quarter.)
2 up 2 down. Living room 12–14 ft. by 9 ft. Boiler. No gas stove. No cellar. Coal hole. Windows will open but not very well. Chimneys bad. Floor of W.C. frequently flooded, either by leaking roof or overflow of cistern. Landlord refuses repairs. When I came in, husband was scrubbing floor, wife, in poor health, sitting in rocking chair, very down in the mouth and rather dirty. 3 persons (parents and son) in house, all adults. Father is on Means Test, ditto son, the latter only receiving 12/6 as he lives at home. ie. total income of family 36/6 a week. Father worked 42 years in pit. Has lost middle finger of right hand but for some reason got no compensation. Rent 4/1½, rates 2/2. Have been in this house over 30 years. Asked whether would like corporation house; no, because too far out of town. "These houses'd be all right only he (landlord) won't do nothing to 'em." House is very dark.

Victoria Street, fronting on Melbourne Street (further down from above.)
Back to back. 2 up 2 down. Living room 12 ft by 10 ft. No coal hole, only small recess in kitchen. Boiler. Gas stove. No cellar. Windows refuse to open. Chimney smokes. Landlord refuses repairs. 6 people in house, two parents, 4 children, of whom 2 are aged 25 and 15. Clean decent people and not despondent. Rent 5/–, rates 2/6. The Victoria Street side of these back to back houses a filthy miry alley. Some people have to walk about 50 yards to reach lavatory.

Clayton Street. 2 up 2 down. Living room 14 ft by 10 ft. Gas stove. Boiler. Coal hole. Walls let in damp. 2 parents and 1 child in house. Husband on dole, wife works 9 hours a day in spinning mill. Net wages 21/– a week. House very dark—scullery dark enough to need lamp all day. Landlord not too good. Rent 5/4, rates 3/6. Some similar houses in this row are rent 6/–.

In the houses opposite, walls bulging to an extent one would hardly believe. Some have recently been re-faced, but begin bulging anew. Doors and windows hanging at strange angles.

York Street. 3 up and 2 down. Living room about 14 ft. each way. Boiler. Coal hole under stairs. House very dark, but dry. Windows will open. Good landlord. 3 persons in house, of decent type and cheerful. Husband gets dole of 24/–, son, aged about 18, works down pit, for net wage (after stoppages and bus fares) of about 25/–. Miners who work at this pit* are obliged to buy their coal from the company—ie. to take out part of their wages in coal—at 1/6 a bag. Said to be very bad coal. Rent of house 5/4, rates 3/4. They are in arrears with rent and paying off arrears at rate of 2d a week. Landlord has never been known to evict. This appropos° of an old woman down a neighbouring street who kept a little fish shop, was evicted and sold up for her rent and has now disappeared none knows where.

The "Unemployed Leader", October 1935, states:

Great majority of houses in Wigan have no baths.
502 families of 1-10 occupy only 1 room.
2,284 families occupy two rooms per family. (540 of these families consist of 5-12 persons.)
2,699 families occupy 3 rooms per family. (322 of these families consist of 7–15 persons.)
Number of persons living in overcrowded conditions in Wigan is 10,000.
Number of houses needed to relieve overcrowding is 1143.
Number of caravan–dwellers (ie. families) 188 as against 80 in 1932.
Number of back to back houses 160.
Number of houses "scheduled" (not stated whom by) as unfit for human habitation, 2,099.
Infant mortality rate 110 per thousand.
Maternal mortality rate 9 per thousand.

NB. to check as far as possible with figures in health report.

ADDITIONAL NOTE

CORPORATION HOUSES: Great disagreement about these. Jerry Kennan's house in the Beech Hill Estate is as follows:
Downstairs: Large living room with kitchener fireplace (oven at side), boiler behind fire, cupboards and fixed dresser, composition floor. Small hallway. Largish kitchen.
Upstairs: 2 largish bedrooms, 1 small (suitable for boxroom or bedroom at pinch.) Bathroom-W.C. with hot and cold water.
In the kitchen up-to-date electric cooker, hired from Corporation at much the same rate as gas-cooker. Electric laundering machine (automatic wringer

* ditto with most pits. I don't know whether they can enforce this, though [Orwell's handwritten footnote].

in aluminium tank and automatic mangle) costing about £20, purchasable on hire-purchase at 2/3 per week. This company is financially backed by the Corporation. Electricity is fairly cheap.

Smallish garden. These vary, but mostly a little smaller than an allottment.°

Rent 11/3 inclusive. Bus fare into town 2d.

Houses appear well-built and convenient and are quite agreeable to look at. Various restrictions. eg. Not to keep poultry or pigeons, take in lodgers, sublet or start any kind of business, without permission of Corporation. Gather that this is easily accorded in the case of lodgers but would be refused in the case of keeping poultry or keeping shop. Kennan is very satisfied with house and proud of it. Houses are all well kept. Corporation are good about repairs but keep tenants up to the mark with regard to keeping place tidy etc.

On the other hand, Welly Estate Corporation Houses:

Downstairs: Living room, about 14' by 10'. Kitchen a good deal smaller than this. Tiny larder under stairs. Small but fairly good bathroom. (Did not see W.C.—probably outside.) Gas stove. Electric light.[3]

Upstairs: Best bedroom about 12 by 10 with tiny fireplace. Another same size without fireplace. Another tiny one—7' by 6'. Best bedroom has small wardrobe let into wall.

Small garden – about 20 yards by 10.

Number in family 6. Parents, son aged 19, daughter 22, daughter 13, son 8. Catholics. None in work except eldest son. For those on P.A.C, as here, when rent is over ¼ income allowance is made.

Rent 10/3 inclusive. Rather more than a mile from town—no bus, I think. People are very discontented with house. Complaints are as follow:

House is cold, draughty and damp. Fireplace in living room gives out no heat and makes room very dusty—attributed to its being set too low. Fireplace in best bedroom so tiny as to be useless. Smallest bedroom practically useless as such. Walls upstairs cracking already (Verified this myself.) Middle bedroom and living room very dark. Doors do not fit too well. Owing to uselessness of small bedroom, 5 are sleeping in 1 bedroom (2 beds), 1 (the son, I suppose) in the other. Notice that these people were previously in filthy house in town which I inspected recently and made every effort to get out of it. Now want to get back. Gather from their and others' remarks that the Corporation houses seem chilly and unhomelike, partly because they are far from town, partly because this lot are set on top of a windy hill. This lot certainly are jerry-built but it is probably the proximity and stuffiness that these people miss more than anything, especially in winter. Gardens here all neglected. NB. Nearly all the people living in this estate are unemployed.[4]

MINERS. 8 or 10 coal mines in and about Wigan. The deepest about 1000 yards. The most up-to-date said to be the Maypole and Rose Bridge, which I have not seen. The only one I have seen hitherto is Crippen's, which is old-fashioned but said not to be worse than the generality. Depth of Crippen's about 300 yards (more to the deepest workings, I think), and distance from cage to present coal face about three quarters of a mile. This last is apparently an average distance. In some mines it is 3 miles. The important thing here is that at any rate in an old-fashioned mine this distance from the cage to the coal face has got for the most part to be covered bending double, sometimes crawling. 3 miles would take quite an hour and a half to do this way. Mines vary greatly in temperature. Crippen's is dry and rather hot—I judged the temperature in the hottest place to be about 100 degrees. Some are much hotter than this, some very cold, some very wet. Miners are all used to walking doubled up and can do it very fast without apparent fatigue, but don't pretend to like it. They almost always *work* lying down or at best kneeling, but prefer this because they say that a "high face" is usually unsafe. (See diary for account of Crippen's pit.)

Present rates of wages are:

Coal-getter............................ 10/11d a day.
Dataller .... 8/9d a day.

Rates for piece-work not exactly obtainable, but said to average about 1/4 a ton. It is only in a few pits that the coal-getters are paid on piece-work. The dataller (man who attends to the roofing) would of course always get a fixed wage. Working full time, therefore, a coal-getter's wage would be at most £3-5-6, a dataller's £2-12-6, a boy's wage round about £1 a week. Stoppages amount to about 5/–, thus:

Hire of lamp (6d a week) .... 6 d
Insurance (unemployment & health) 1/5
Pick-sharpening .... –/6
Check-weighman .... –/9
Infirmary .... –/2
Hospital .... –/1
Benevolent fund .... –/6
Union fees .... –/6
Total 4/5d

But on top of this there are bus fares. The mines are all on the outskirts of Wigan but owing to the housing shortage the miners have to live wherever they can and there are few cottages near the mines. Nearly all the men live in Wigan. The buses (owned by the corporation) are neither very good nor very cheap. (No such thing as a 1d fare in Wigan—the least is 1½d.) An average week's payment for bus-fares would be 2/–. Therefore there is about 6/6d to come off a miner's wage each week. When on part-time he pays the same stoppages except perhaps for the check-weighman (man paid by the miners themselves to see that weighing is fairly done) which is sometimes remitted for those on part-time.

The time of one shift is 7½ hours. The important thing to notice that this is time spent *at the coal face*, ie. the time spent in getting there has to be added on. It is nothing out of the way for this to take 3 hours, so that the usual time spent at work is round about 10 hours. Add to this the time spent in getting to and from home, and it is about 11 hours.

Cannot yet obtain at all exactly the amount of coal extracted by 1 miner in a year. According to the Samuel Commission a miner in 1913 was only producing about 300 tons a year. Not stated whether this referred to actual coal-getters or to all concerned (datallers, electricians, men who work the cage etc.) but presumably the latter. At present it seems that a team of 35 men working one of the big machines, given good coal, may turn out 450 tons of coal in a day. But one has got to add onto these the datallers etc., bringing the number up to about 60–65. Of course this average would not be kept up, owing to the variation in coal and the fact that many mines run part-time in summer. But it is clear that the average output per man might be somewhere in the neighbourhood of 1000 tons per year. NB. to get more exact figures. Number of miners killed 1927–1934 given as 7839. ie. 1118.4 per year. Number of injuries for same period given as 1,200,042. ie. 121,434.5 per year. Number of miners actually at work about 750,000. (NB. to get more exact figure.) Therefore about 1 miner in 700★ is killed every year and about 1 in 7† injured. But have not hitherto succeeded in discovering how many of these injuries are serious. Injuries means injuries reported and the miners are instructed to report all injuries, even minor ones. The causes of accidents are 1. Falls of stone. These are very frequent and the reason why they do not lead to more injuries is that experienced miners can generally tell by tapping whether the roof is safe. Also the pit-props give warning by creaking. In Crippen's mine we saw here and there "pot holes"—circular holes in the roof from which a lump of stone, usually big enough to kill a man, had suddenly shot out. 2. Explosions, due to gas. The gas is said to be ignited by a pick striking sparks from stone, or by fusing of electric wires, or by "gob fires." These are fires that break out spontaneously in damp coal dust, which apparently gets hot in the same manner as a hot-bed. When they break out they are stifled with sand or bricked over, but are always liable to break out afresh. 3. Heavy falls of stone which cut off isolated parties of men. 4. Falls due to carelessness in blasting. Blasting is only supposed to be done when there is no one working, eg. on Sundays, but in order to save time is often done at other times. It is only done to loosen the coal but may on occasion bring the roof down. The charges are touched off by an electric wire at a distance, but have been known to go off prematurely. 5. Accidents to the cage. The distance to be descended is anything from 100 to 1000 yards. The one I went down in did 300 yards in about ½ a minute, ie. an average speed of about 12 mph.,[5] but it slowed down greatly towards the end and was probably touching 30 or 40 in the middle. Some in the deeper mines are said to touch 60 mph. or even more. The man working the cage has an indicator which shows him how fast it is working, but it is possible for him to make a mistake and there have been many deaths in this way. Apart from accidents miners are said to be healthy, except for those who start off with a tendency to tuberculosis, in which case the dust they are constantly breathing does for

★ 900 (J. Jones) [Orwell's handwritten footnote].
† 6 (J. Jones) [Orwell's handwritten footnote]. Orwell's calculations are incorrect. He takes 1927–34 as seven years. That means 1,119.86 killed per year and 171,434.6 injured. Of 750,000 miners, that is 1 in 670 killed per year and 1 in 4.37 injured. Were this an eight-year period it would be 1 in 765 killed and 1 in 5 injured per year.

them. Their lungs are said to be quite black. Many miners suffer from rheumatism, owing to violent changes of temperature and working in a cramped position. It is noticeable that the rate of accidents do° not decrease although the number of men engaged decreases—ie, proportionately there are more accidents. All miners concur in saying that this is due to speeding-up and that much of the new machinery is unsafe, at any rate with the Lancashire coal. For example, with the new coal cutters they have to cut 6 feet into the face before re-propping, and they say this is too far for safety. All say also that the steel girders now largely used are less safe than the wooden props. The latter creak when they are giving way but the steel girders are liable to fly out without warning.

<u>Baths.</u> Only 2 of the local mines have baths at the pit-head. In the miners' cottages there is probably not 1 in 50 that has a bath.

<u>ADDITIONAL NOTES ON HOUSES.</u>

(All in Scholes quarter.)

Street of 5-room houses, 3 up 2 down, rent and rates 9/1.

2 up 2 down, with tiny scullery. Paper etc. in very bad repair. 1 cellar. No back door or yard. Landlord refuses repairs. Rent 6/6, rates 3/9.

2 up 2 down, front room fairly large—about 16 by 10. Six houses share back yard with one lavatory each. Very bad repair. Terribly bare interiors upstairs. Bare floors, ricketty iron bedsteads covered only with old overcoats and other rags. Rent 4/1, rates 2/9.

2 up 1 down. Hole under stairs for coal. Back door but no back yard. No scullery. Sink in living room. Very bad repair. Floor (of stone) sinking and uneven. Windows will only open a few inches. No boiler. Rent 4/-, rates 2/6.

<u>Condemned.</u> 2 up 2 down. Gas stove. No boiler. Rooms about 12 by 10. Very bad repair and landlord refuses repairs. Tenant has been in this house 38 years. Opposite these a shocking little row of back to back houses which I did not succeed in entering. Almost all windows patched either with paper or boards. Horrible miry alley about 8 feet wide and tumbledown W.Cs. Landlords apparently always refuse repairs when house is condemned.

<u>Condemned.</u> 1 up 1 down. Rooms about 15 by 15. No scullery. Coal hole under stairs. Boiler. Floor going lopsided and no windows will open. Decently dry. Good landlord. Rent 3/8, rates 2/6.

2 up 2 down and pantry as well. Share a yard with a number of other houses. Gas boiler. Rooms about 14 by 12. Dry. No windows will open. Rent 10/-, rates 3/6.

2 up 1 down and coal hole. Terribly squalid interior. Old woman at first got it into hr° head that we were from the Corporation and intended to bully her about overcrowding etc., and gave us tremendous ticking off.[6] "I don't want you buggers nosing round 'ere. I've lived in this 'ouse and I'll be buried from it. I'm not going to let no bugger turn me out," etc. Presently relented and gave us the information we wanted. Four generations living in this house. Catholics. The woman's mother, aged 97, evidently wrong in the head, sat

looking on with expressionless face. Furniture falling to pieces and everything very dirty. Rent 3/4½, rates 2/1.

2 up 2 down. Backyard. Coal hole. Walls are falling absolutely to pieces. Water comes into upstairs rooms in quantities. Downstairs windows will not open. Floor lopsided. Bad landlord. Rent 6/–, rates 3/6.

Greenough's Row. Uncertain whether these houses are condemned or not. Some tenants say yes, some no. They were inspected a few days ago. 1 up 1 down and kitchen. Front room 13 by 8. Walls coming away and water comes in. Back windows will not open, front windows will. Landlord has not done repairs for a long time past. 10 in family—8 children very near together in age. The people have recently been warned that they will be evicted for overcrowding, but the Council have got to find them another house first. Catholics (all in this row seem to be Catholics.) Landlord has not done repairs for a long time past. Rent 4/–, rates 2/3.

Next door. Same arrangement but smaller front room. Water comes in upstairs. Windows will open but are loose. One blew out recently. Catholics but "Religion won't feed you." Landlord refuses repairs. Rent 4/6, rates 2/3.

Further up street. 2 up 1 down. Walls good. 4/– rent, 2/6 rates.

Next door. 2 up 1 down. Share backyard with 4 others. Windows will open. Back kitchen lets in water when it rains. Asked landlord for repairs and "'e larfed at me." Rent 4/2, rates 2/6.

Next door. Same arrangement. 6 in family. No complaints except some defect in chimney. Also the common lavatories are a few feet behind the back door, and in front just across street (15 feet wide) are lavatories of next row of houses, so you have them behind[7] you and in front of you. Rent 5/–, rates 2/6.

Next door. End house. The end houses have rooms a little bigger so are a bit higher in rent. No complaints here—people actually enthusiastic about this house (in good repair except back bedroom which lets in damp) because they have recently escaped into it from the first house in the row, in which they had lived for years. This house is said not only to let in quantities of water but to be sinking rapidly and kitchen floor so askew that you could hardly stand up straight. The woman's father is now living alone in that house. "I couldn't bear to live with him no longer. He's got like a cancer in his mouth and it was a-punishing me to live with him." These people very bitter about the idea of condemning houses and putting the tenants into Council houses which are 3/– or 4/– a week more. Rent here 5/–, rates 2/6.

Owing to the cramped back yards, all the people in this row throw refuse into the street, which is littered with tealeaves, bread etc.

1. 5] 4
2. seldom] never; *handwritten emendation*
3. Gas stove. Electric light.] *handwritten addition*
4. NB. Nearly . . . unemployed.] *handwritten addition*
5. 12 mph.] 10 mph. Despite Orwell's recalculation and the handwritten alteration he made, the speed is still incorrect. A mile is 1,760 yards, so 300 yards in half a minute is a mile in 3 minutes; that is 20 mph.
6. off] *handwritten addition*
7. behind] before

347. BARNSLEY

POPULATION. Mid-1934 (estimated) 71,350. At 1931 census 71,522. (M.O.[1] questions the first figure.) Excess of births over deaths during period 1931–34, 1,834. Also in same period number of inhabited houses increased by 600. By figures given, population must have shrunk by emigration 2016 in period 1931–34. (M.O. says 1400 ??) At any rate there must have been some shrinkage from this cause. Area of town 6,036 acres. Equals density of 10.2 per acre. Equals density of 6528 per square mile.
Number of inhabited houses end of 1934, 17719. Equivalent to 4.02 persons per house. Number of rooms not obtainable, probably averages round about 4 per house.

LOCAL INDUSTRIES. Coal mining, iron-working, glass, linen, paper, shirts.

VITAL STATISTICS. Birth rate 1934, 19.20 (increase of 1.89 on previous year.) Death rate 1934 11.35 (decrease on previous year, rate not obtainable.) Against this, Birth rate for England and Wales 14.8. Death rate for E. and W., 11.8.
Birth rate (Barnsley) in 1923, 24.91 (shrinkage of .5% 1923–1934.)
Average Birth rate for 10 years 1914–1923, 26.68. (Has shrunk about .7% as against average of 1914–23.)
Death rate in 1923, 13.36 (decrease of .201% 1923–34.)
Average death rate for 10 years 1914–23, 18.3. (has decreased by about .7% as against period 1914–23.)
Taking period 1901–1934, Birth rate has shrunk from 36.24 to 19.20, death rate from 22.15 to 11.35, infant mortality from 192 (per thousand) to 64.
   Variation between wards (p.104 of M.O's report). Highest birth rate (Monk Bretton) 32.31. Lowest (West) 16.04. Highest death rate not obtainable. Highest infant mortality (South-East) 130. Lowest (North – also has second lowest birth rate) 33.

HOUSING. (See pp. 56–7 of M.O's report.) Number of houses erected during 1934 326, 35 of these by the Corporation. Number in 1935 not obtainable but presumably about the same or less as there does not seem to be any great activity in building. M.O's report of 1934 gives number of "dwelling-houses found to be in a state so dangerous or injurious to health as to be unfit for human habitation" as 601; and number of (other) houses "found not to be in all respects reasonably fit for human habitation" as 3,346. As against this, *one* house was demolished during 1934. Number demolished during 1935 not obtainable, but probably exceeds 200. During this period the condemnation and destruction of the New Street area (see newspaper cutting attached) was gone through with. The houses in question here numbered 270. Not all have been demolished yet but none are inhabited. There is a waiting list of over 2000 applicants for Corporation houses. All or nearly all of the earth W.Cs in Barnsley have been converted. Virtually no working class houses, other than Corporation houses, have baths or hot water laid on. The public baths have only 19 men's slipper baths (for a population of 70,000!) When the demolition of the New Street area was discussed, the surveyor considered that about 10 of the 270 houses had baths or hot water, but I am told that these were merely shops or other not strictly working class houses. All houses in Barnsley now have their own W.C. (almost always outdoor, of course.) Number of Common Lodging Houses not obtainable but said by M.O's report to be decreasing. Number of houses let off in rooms, on the other hand, said to be increasing. This is of some importance as it suggests that under pressure of poverty people are becoming less particular about having a house of their own and therefore might be more easily reconciled to living in flats.

It is noticeable that demolition and re-housing, when undertaken at all, is done with great ruthlessness. There is a row still in progress about the purchase for building purposes of California Gardens. This is a block of allotments in the New Street area which belongs to a private owner (the Rector of Barnsley, I think) and has been under cultivation, largely intensive cultivation, for something like 100 years. It is admitted that many of the tenants have brought their patch to a high state of cultivation, that they have sunk much capital in greenhouses etc., and that some of them are partly dependent for their living on sale of tomatoes. Nevertheless the Corporation are bent on purchasing the land and intend to offer the tenants no compensation, except that they are to be given fresh allotments elsewhere— these, of course, raw soil which will need years of cultivation before it is worth much.

The following figures are from the Barnsley Chronicle of March 24th 1934:

Number of applicants waiting for houses, 2420.
Estimated number of houses required for re-housing purposes, 2500.
Number Corporation has actually erected (ie. by 1934) 451.
One thing said to increase the cost of land is the mineral rights, which are almost always owned separately from the surface land.
One fact that emerges from the New Street enquiry (see cutting) is that the small landlord (old women who have invested their savings in two or three houses) are often the worst landlords because they cannot afford to pay for repairs.

MUNICIPAL HOUSING ESTATES[3]

'The County Borough of Barnsley Authority has sixteen schemes with a total complement of 2,667 houses. Upon the inception of Municipal Housing Estates in 1921 the initial Schemes commenced were Racecommon Road Estate (49), Huddersfield Road and Gawber Road Estate (282), and Wilthorpe Estate (140), built under the Housing (Assisted) Schemes Act of 1919. The completion of this section was followed by the erection of further houses under the Housing Acts of 1923 and 1924 in various parts of the borough. A Slum Clearance Scheme was carried out, called the New Street (Western) Area Improvement Scheme. The number of houses that were demolished was 139 and the number of tenants re-housed in alternative accommodation under the Re-Housing Act of 1925 was 110. In addition the Minister of Health has confirmed the New Street (Eastern) Clearance Area, The Drake's Yard Clearance Area and the Oakwell Yard Clearance Area, and is at present considering representations in respect of the Westgate and Shambles Street Clearance Areas, Days Court Old Mill Clearance Area, Keel Yard, Stairfoot Clearance Area, and the Carlton Road and Wakefield Road Clearance Area. The borough also own thirty-four small cottage houses in Taylor Row, pre-war built and acquired for highways development at a future date.

'APPLICATIONS FOR HOUSE TENANCIES. The Applications for Tenancies Register has been revised from time to time and at the present there is a waiting list of unclassified applications totalling 2,112.

'CLASSES OF HOUSES. The various types of houses built are:

Total		SCHEMES				
		1919	1923	1924	Re-Hsg.	Gen. Fund
149	Parlour (brick)	139	4	6	—	—
62	" (concrete)	62	—	—	—	—
2,151	Non-par. 3 bedroom	270	710	1,051	120	—
271	Non-par. 2 bedroom	—	—	252	19	—
34	Taylor Row	—	—	—	—	34
2,667	Total	471	714	1,309	139	34

'Table showing number of houses erected in the following areas: Old Borough, Ardsley, Monk Bretton.

Areas	Parlour (brick)	Parlour (concrete)	TYPE Non-parlour 3 bedroom	Non-parlour 2 bedroom	Total
Old Borough	149	62	327	34	572
Ardsley	—	—	680	30	710
Monk Bretton	—	—	1144	241	1385
Total	149	62	2151	305	2667'

Unemployment Occupational Centre (run by Council of Social Service.)
Premises at Milton House, Wellington Street. Premises consist of large hall, small office, basement with furnaces and about four large work-rooms on upper floor. Was previously warehouse of wholesale grocery firm. Rent £1 a week. Besides this there is coke for heating, electric light and other expenses. Total expenses said to be £6 a week.

Number of members on books 500. Active members 360, all men—no boys. Subscription is 1d a week. Evidently the concern is financed by some charitable organisation which may or may not be aided by the Government but is at any rate encouraged by it. There are voluntary helpers who organise and teach handicrafts.

There are classes in Woodworking, Basket-work, Sea-grass work, Cobbling, hand-loom weaving, physical training, Dramatics, rug-making, hair-cutting, upholstering etc. In each subject there is a "leader," who has usually learned his craft at the centre and then instructs others. Apparently the classes in each subject take place on one or at most two evenings a week.

The primary idea is to give unemployed men something to do and a place to go to. Secondarily to let them make furniture, mend shoes etc. for themselves at a low price. It is not or not primarily the object to make things for sale. The men can purchase materials on the instalment system. eg. if a man wants to make a book-case he applies for what wood is needed and gets free use of tools and work-room, paying for the wood at so much a week. Behind this one can discern the motive to keep unemployed men quiet by giving them the illusion of being busy; also to keep them out of the pubs. But I cannot be sure about this till I have seen some of the voluntary helpers.

Went round the work-rooms, in which there were not any classes going on at the moment, however. A fairly good carpentering room with a sufficiency of tools but rather poor ones. Some of the things the men had made were not bad. There is to be an exhibition of things made at these centres at Sheffield shortly. The whole place was decently warm and roomy and unemployed men must be glad to have a place like that to go to. But I did not like the mien of the men who took me round. They were of the submissive type and one of them said rather unctuously that men who had this place to come to "hardly ever went to the public."

This is said to be one of the biggest and most successful centres in England. As the membership is small considering the town's population (probably somewhere about 10,000* registered unemployed) I gather the movement as a whole has not been a success. At Wigan I was told that the men at the centre there were set to making meat-safes which were sold not for their benefit (did not verify this but heard it from two sources), after which the membership dropped off.

NB. It is a pity the facilities for carpentering etc. in these places cannot be incorporated in some genuinely pro-working class movement such as the N.U.W.M.[3]

UNEMPLOYMENT. No exact figures obtainable, but hear on all sides that it amounts to about one third of registered workers (counting in U.A.B. and P.A.C.) ie. probably about 8000. Will increase greatly in summer when mines start short time. Accurate figures later.

RELIGION.[4] 'Until recent divisions consequent upon rapid growth of population, Barnsley consisted of two parishes—St. Mary (the mother church) and St. George. St. George's Church is in Pitt Street. Other Anglican churches are situated as follows: St. John's, Duke Street; St. Peter's, Doncaster Road; St. Edward the Confessor, Kingstone; Christ Church, Ardsley; St. Luke's, Worsborough Common; St. Paul's, Monk Bretton; as well as three mission churches. Other places of worship in the town are:

* More like 8000] *handwritten note.*

Roman Catholic—Church of the Holy Rood, George Street; *Congregational*—Regent Street, Farrar Street, and Sheffield Road; *Baptist*—Sheffield Road and Racecommon Road; *Methodist*—Doncaster Road, Heelis Street, Huddersfield Road, Honeywell, and Pitt Street, Worsborough Common, and Monk Bretton; Blucher Street, Old Town, and Sheffield Road, Ardsley, Monk Bretton, and Worsborough Common; Westgate and Buckley Street, Ardsley; Blucher Street, Ardsley, and Smithies; *Society of Friends*— Huddersfield Road (Adult School in Wellington Street); *Catholic Apostolic*— Blenheim Road; *Plymouth Brethren*— Princess Street; *Salvation Army*— Wellington Street; *New Church (Swedenborgian)*—Parker Street; *Christadelphian*—York Street.'

R.Cs have recently completed new church or chapel. Religion said to retain its hold only on old and middle-aged. But practice of sending children to Sunday school seems general. A few cinemas allowed to open on Sundays, but only in aid of charities.

PUBLIC BUILDINGS. . . . 'The foundation stone was laid on Thursday, 21st April, 1932, by the then Mayor, Councillor R.J. Plummer, and the building was formally opened by H.R.H. the Prince of Wales, K.G., on Thursday, 14th December, 1933. . . . . from the designs of Messrs. Briggs and Thornley, Architects, Liverpool. The Contractors were Messrs. T. Wilkinson and Sons, of Sheffield (foundation); Mr Chas. Smith (stonework up to ground floor); Messrs W. Thornton and Sons, Liverpool (superstructure.) The cost of the site (including demolition) was £12,445; the cost of the building was £136,252."

From "The Official Guide to Barnsley", issued by authority of the Barnsley Town Council. NB. that total cost of new Town hall was £148,697 and was incurred at a time when the town admittedly needed *over 2000* houses, not to mention public baths.

Corporation Baths. 9 men's slipper baths, 6 women's, 1 foam bath with 2 cooling rooms, 2 swimming baths, laundry etc. Charge for slipper bath, men 6d, women 4d. Unemployed are allowed baths free on certain days.

NOTES ON HOUSES.

No. 12 Albert Street East.[5] 3 up 2 down. Front room (parlour type) 15′ by 12′, back room (kitchen) about 12′ by 10′. Back room has kitchener but is almost uninhabitable owing to damp. Front room rather damp also. Cellar. No cupboard under stairs. Outside WC. Door between two downstairs rooms has fallen off hinges. Two of upstairs rooms very damp. One has no gasjet, one has gasjet not in working order. Rent 9/0½d. Family, parents and two kids age 2 years 5 months and 10 months. Total income 32/- plus some baby food from Infants Welfare Clinic. No coal allowance as income is from U.A.B. not P.A.C. Family possesses two beds but not enough bedding to cover them in winter, so sleep all four in one bed. Gas (for lighting only) reckoned as 1/3 a week. Through friend in work family are able to purchase coal at 9d a cwt.

Spring Gardens, Mapplewell. 2 up 1 down. Living room about 14' by 12'. Kitchener. Sink in living room. 1 cupboard. Gas lighting (1d in slot.) Plaster cracking and in places has peeled off walls. No shelves in oven. Gas said to leak slightly.

Upstairs. Two rooms each 10' by 8,' arranged thus: Stairs have no banister at side marked AB, so that by stepping carelessly out of bed one may fall 10 feet onto stones. Dry. Dryrot in planks through which one can see into downstairs rooms. One bedroom has gasjet, one not. Four beds altogether (for 6 persons) but "one bed does nowt," presumably for lack of bedclothes. Only old overcoats etc on bed.

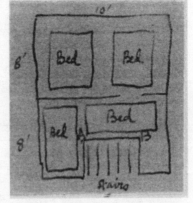

House infested with bugs, but "I keeps 'em down with sheep-dip." Reasonably clean and tidy as far as can be in circumstances. 6 persons in house, all adults, two working. Rent 5/–. About £11 in arrears ("strike rent") and for some weeks past have been paying extra 1/– a week towards arrears. Landlord (woman) now refuses this and has served order to quit. Tenants have been in house 22 years.

Earth road past these cottages like a muckheap and said to be almost impassable in winter. Tiny garden. Stone lavatories at ends of gardens in semi-ruinous condition.

Another, two doors away. 2 up 2 down. Living room with sink and kitchener about 16' by 12'. Scullery about one third of size of this, without ceiling— only rafters. These let in water to such an extent as to make the room useless except as lumber room. All woodwork of kitchen rotting away and doors loose in° hinges.

2 upstairs rooms in much the same condition.

Rent 5/3. Tenant has been 23 years in house, now under orders to quit for arrears ("strike rent.")

House in indescribable state of filth (tenant's own doing) and furniture falling to pieces.

No. 32 Wilthorpe Crescent. Corporation house built 1921–2 under re-housing scheme. Non-parlour type.

Downstairs. Living room 16' by 13' with kitchener and cupboards. Scullery about 12' by 10' with copper, sink and draining board. Bathroom (h. and c.) and small pantry. All these have unplastered walls.

Upstairs. 1 large room with fireplace and room for 2 beds. Another about 12' by 10' with fireplace. Another about 8' by 7' without fireplace. All these rooms plastered and papered.

Electric light. W.C. and coal-hole at back of house (to be reached from outside.) Garden somewhat smaller than allotment. Poor soil. 1½d ride from town.

Rent including rates 12/3. Electricity paid for at flat rate of 8d per week plus ½d per unit (comes to 3/9 for a fortnight in winter.)
House dry and Corporation good about repairs. Tenant very satisfied.

No 23 Blucher Street. 2 up 1 down and cellar.
Downstairs. Living room about 15 square with kitchener, sink and copper. Gas lighting. Room very dark (gas estimated at 3d a day.) Walls sound. Back yard shared with whole row.
Upstairs. Rooms smaller. Not complained of.
Family living on dole. Landlord not complained of. Constant disagreeable smells, especially in summer, from incinerator almost opposite.
Rent 6/6½ including rates.

No 27 Blucher Street. 3 up 2 down and 2 cellars. (Considered the best house in street.)
Downstairs. Living room about 14' square with kitchener. Small kitchen with copper. Gas lighting (gas estimated at 6d a day—NB. this is lighter than the other house.)
Upstairs rooms not complained of.
Rent 8/5 including rates. Walls sound. Landlord not complained of.
Midden in back yard (very smelly in summer) has to be shared with 10 houses. Drain in gutter in front constantly overflowing and floods pavement. Corporation fail to put this right in spite of reports of it. Otherwise, no complaints.

Wortley Street. 2 up 1 down.
Downstairs. Living room about 12 by 10 with kitchener, sink and copper. Sink worn almost flat and constantly overflowing. Coal hole under stairs extending into a sort of tiny outhouse, semi-ruinous. Walls not too sound. Room very dark. Gas estimated at 4d a day.
Upstairs. Really 1 large room partitioned into two. Room nearest stairs has no door. Gas light in both rooms, fireplace in one. Walls in very bad state. Front wall of back room cracked right through. Window frames coming to pieces and have to be stuffed with bits of wood. 3 beds in these rooms. No bedclothes except overcoats, miscellaneous rags etc. Rain comes through walls in several places.
Sewer runs under house and stinks in summer. Corporation "says they can't do nowt." 6 people in house, 2 parents and 4 children aged 15, 14, 8 and 6. Youngest but one attending Queen's Rd. Hospital, TB. suspected. Bugs very bad—"We can't sleep in summer, there's that many of them."
Rent 5/3 including rates.

Haig's Yard, Providence Street. 1 up 1 down and cellar.
Downstairs. Living room about 16' by 10' with kitchener, copper and sink. Walls fairly dry. Almost too dark to read by daylight. Gas estimated at 3d a day. Cellar door extremely dangerous.

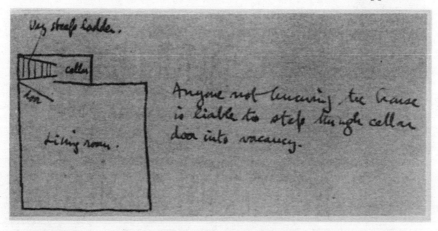

[Handwritten note and drawing on verso of typed notes]

Rent 5/– including rates. Landlord not bad. 3 persons in house, 2 adults (men) and 1 child.

Peel Street (Worsboro' Common.) Back to Back. 2 up 2 down.
Living room about 10 feet square with kitchener, copper and sink. Other room about same size, perhaps intended as parlour, used as bedroom. Large cellar.* 70 yards walk to lavatory. Living room very dark, the other a little less so. Used 16/6 worth of gas in 6 weeks, or about 4½d a day.
Size of upstairs room as below. 3 beds. No bedding except old coats etc. Bugs very bad – "You can't keep 'em down when it's 'ot."
Rent 5/7½ including rates. Landlord not complained of.
8 people in house. (4 beds altogether), 2 parents, 2 adult girls, (eldest 27), 1 young man and 3 children. Father and mother have 1 bed, son has another and remaining 5 share the other two.
It is said that there is always someone ill in this family. Indescribable squalor in downstairs rooms and smell of upstairs rooms almost unbearable.

1. Medical Officer.
2. Printed slip from official report. Orwell annotated this, 'See also additional notes on houses.'
3. NB. It is a pity . . . N.U.W.M.] *handwritten addition*
4. From printed official report. The listing of Methodist chapels is reproduced as given in the original.
5. This was Ellis Firth's house; see *Wigan Pier Diary, 296, 20.3.36,* and *CW,* V, 85–86 for income and expenditure details.

* These are 1 time weavers' houses [Orwell's footnote].

348. Pay Slips for Two-Man Team, Woolley Collieries

Woolley is about five miles northwest of Barnsley. Orwell used these pay slips in his calculation of Ellis Firth's budget; see *349*. The pay slips are approximately two-thirds the size of the originals; the Check Note is about the same size.

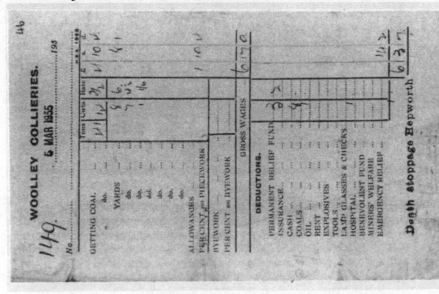

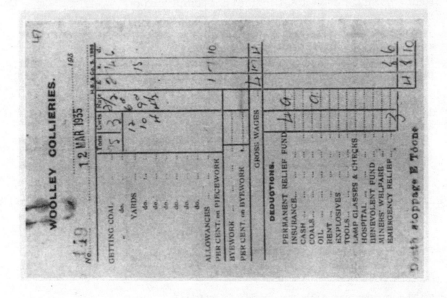

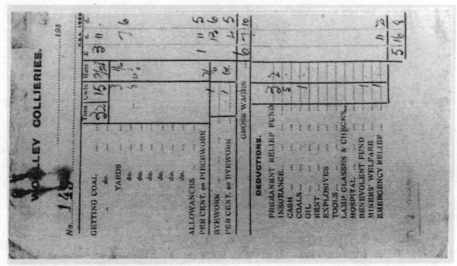

Woolley Colliery Miner's Check Note.
A corf was originally a miner's basket, but
is now a tub or trolley.

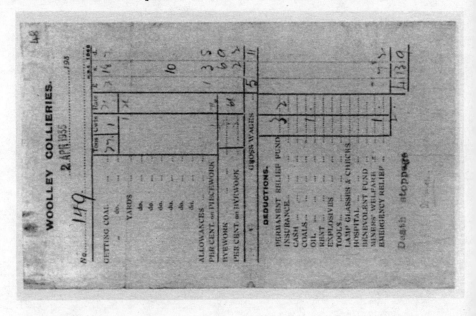

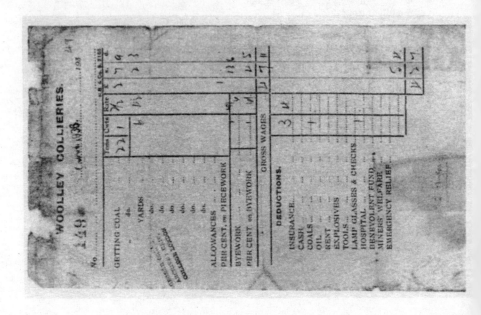

349. Ellis Firth's Weekly Budget

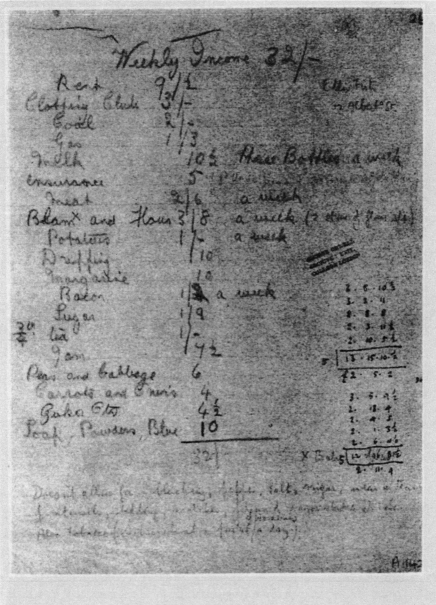

Transcription of Ellis Firth's Weekly Budget

Orwell's annotations are in italic. For his use of this budget, see *The Road to Wigan Pier*, *CW*, V, 85–86; for his use of calculations of weekly earnings, see V, 36–39. Firth's budget, and other examples of costs and conditions given by Orwell, can very usefully be compared with those in the survey of Lambeth published by the Fabian Women's Group in 1913 and conveniently available in *Round About a Pound a Week*, by Mrs. Pember Reeves, Wakefield, 1978.

Weekly Income 32/-

Rent	9/$\frac{1}{2}$[1]		*Ellis Firth*
Clothing Club	3/-		*12 Albert S^t.*
Coal	2/-		
Gas	1/3		
Milk	10$\frac{1}{2}$ three Bottles a week		3. 8.10$\frac{1}{2}$[6]
ensurance°	5 (*3^d Union fees & 2^d*		3. 3.11
	insurance on ^{2}/children)		2. 8. 8
Meat	2/6 a week		2. 3.11$\frac{1}{2}$
Blam★ and Flour	3/8 a week (*2 stone of flour 3/4*)[2]		2.10. 5$\frac{1}{2}$
Potatoes	1/- a week		5 13.15.10$\frac{1}{2}$
Dripping	10		£2.15.2
Margarine	10		
Bacon	1/2 a week		3. 5. 9$\frac{1}{2}$[7]
Sugar	1/9		2.18. 4
$\frac{3}{4}$lb tea	1/-		2. 4. 5
Jam	7$\frac{1}{2}$		2. 1. 3$\frac{1}{4}$
Peas and Cabbage	6		2. 6.10$\frac{1}{2}$
Carrots and Onions	4		5 12.16. 8$\frac{3}{4}$
Quker Ots[3]	4$\frac{1}{2}$		2.11. 4
Soap, Powders, Blue[4]	10		
	32/-		

★ *Balm = Yeast*

Doesn't allow for—blacking, pepper, salt, vinegar, wear & tear of utensils, bedding, matches, firewood, razor blades etc. etc. Also tobacco. (reckoned at a packet of Woodbines[5] a day.)

1. 9s 0$\frac{1}{2}$d, or just over 45p.
2. Twenty-eight pounds in weight, or approximately 12.7 kg. Mrs. Firth, like so many north country housewives until World War II, baked her own bread, about two two-pound loaves a day.
3. Quaker Oats, a proprietary brand used chiefly to make porridge.
4. 'Blue' was added to washing to counteract the tendency of whites to yellow. Despite their poverty, the Firths were prepared to spend money on keeping their clothes clean and bright.
5. A cheap brand of cigarettes (about twopence for a packet of ten) made by W. D. & H. O. Wills; the equivalent of the Player's Weights smoked by Gordon Comstock in *Keep the Aspidistra Flying*.
6. The calculations are the sum of the five pay slips from March 1935 to January 1936 (see *348*) which are referred to in *The Road to Wigan Pier* (*CW*, V, 36–38) divided by five to show average weekly earnings and average take-home pay after deductions. Each pay slip is for a partnership of two men, so the sums have to be divided by two. See *n*. 7 and *CW*, V, 230.

7. This set of figures is the amount remaining after deductions. The first amount, £3 5s 9½d, is meant to be half of the £6 3s 7d paid on 5 March 1935, or £3 1s 9½d. Orwell overestimates the average net earning. Instead of £2 11s 4d, as calculated in *The Road to Wigan Pier*, it should be £2 10s 6¼d, a reduction of 4s 7½d, not 3s 10d; see *CW*, V, 38, 230.

350. SHEFFIELD.

<u>Population:</u> at time of census (1931) 511,742. In 1934, 520,950. Increase of 9208 in 3 years. Excess of births over deaths is between 2 and 3, therefore normal increase would be something under 5000. So there has been a little immigration.

<u>Health:</u> See attached but am trying to get further figures. It is claimed (no figures available) that Sheffield has highest abortion rate of any city in England. W. Asbury (Councillor) states: "In the 7 years from 1927–1934, abortion accounted for 22.4% of deaths from puerperal sepsis. In 1934 it accounted for 59.4% of deaths from puerperal sepsis. Number of abortions treated in the City General Hospital have° increased from 6 per annum in 1912 to 337 in 1934." Making all allowance for abortions now being less often concealed, the last figure points to great increase in abortion. It is also said (again no figures available) that there are 20,000 couples living together unmarried in Sheffield. At the same time sexual starvation owing to unemployment is said to be rife and both insanity and suicide very common. Suicide rate is not published but am trying to get from M.O.
The commonest industrial disease, tuberculosis, especially in those engaged in knife-grinding (breathing dust all the while.)

<u>Employment:</u> Trade brisk at present owing to the war in Abyssinia. The peak figure for unemployment was in 1930, when it touched 60,000. This is statutory benefit only and does not include those on poor relief, but at that time (I presume) there would have been comparatively few on poor relief. By 1932 this had dropped to 54,000. To each of these one has got to add those on poor relief, bringing the totals up to (say) 80,000. The figures on 20th May 1935 (published by Corporation) were:

Unemployed:
Men 30,000
Women .... 3,790.
Lads .... 1,122.
Total .... 35,795.   (This total corresponds to the 60,000
                                              and 54,000.)

Poor relief:
Indoor 1,706
Outdoor .... 36,208.
Total .... 37,914.

Grand total: 73,709. This was the total on 20th May 1935. Now, owing to increased trade in armaments, may be presumed to be less. A round figure might be 60,000. Multiplying by 3 as usual, this makes 180,000, ie. a little over 1 person in 3 either drawing or living on the dole.

Housing: Rehousing is going on at vast speed. Practically the entire central area of Sheffield, barring a few main streets, is slum, and this is all condemned and being replaced as fast as possible. There are bare patches everywhere where houses have been demolished. The new housing estates are at present all on the outskirts. A few blocks of Corporation flats have been built in the centre of the town, and more will be built when this portion has been further demolished. It is estimated that in all 100,000 houses will be built, spread over a number of years, of course. With a town of 500,000 population, this practically means rehousing the whole town. It also means complete redistribution of population and difficulties arising from this because of people finding difficulty in living near their work. It is said that there are still 30,000 back to back houses in Sheffield, and that 65% of the old type houses have neither bath room nor hot water laid on. (No accurate figures here. Have applied to M.O. for number of back to back houses and rate at which Corporation houses are being built.) See attached for account of Corporation houses and back to back house.

TYPICAL SHEFFIELD BACK TO BACK HOUSE.

13/2 Thomas St. Sheffield.
2 up 1 down. ie. it is a 3-storey house with 1 room on each floor. Living room about 12' or 14' by 10'. Cellar below. Sink in living room. Kitchener and gas-ring (no gas stove.) Electric light, penny in the slot, electricity working out at 5d a unit. Owing to its situation this is a dark house and the inmates claim that they spend 6d a day on electricity. This I think must be exaggeration.
First floor bedroom about 15' by 12' and the top one the same. Top one has no door but gives on open stairs. Walls in top rooms are simply coming to bits and oozing damp on all sides. Also to less extent in living room.
Rent 6/6 all in.
There are 6 in family, parents and 4 kids. Husband, by trade a knife-grinder, is T.B. One child in hospital, the others look healthy enough. Total present income is 38/– per week. The threatened reduction to 32/6 (see attached U.A.B. sheet) is arrived at thus: Statutory benefit for this sized family is 39/–. 3/– is deducted for meal allowance to children at school. (4 children, and they are given 2 meals a day, ie. 48 meals @ 1d a meal–query why not 4/–?) and 3/6 off for rent because on P.A.C. rent should be one quarter of allowance. Binns's rent is therefore assessed at 10/– and he is only paying 6/6. That is, total deduction 6/6, leaving 32/6. At present only 1/– is deducted, but the full cut is liable to be restored.
The Binns have been 7 years in this house. Would move, but no house available. Do not want Corporation house because of the enormously greater rent (10/– or 12/–.)

Wybourn Estate new (experimental) type of Corporation houses.
4 up 2 down plus bathroom and WC.
<u>Downstairs:</u> Living room about 19' by 13', kitchen somewhat smaller. Large cupboard in kitchen. Gas stove. Boiler behind living room fire. Bathroom. WC. separate. Gas lighting (NB. all other estates have electricity.)
<u>Upstairs:</u> largest bedroom 14 by 12, two others slightly smaller, smallest only 8' by 7'. Two bedrooms have fireplaces.
Garden about size of allotment. Top soils had been shaved off and cinders etc substituted. Tenant had had to make soil.
These houses are about 3½ years old. Walls are good and Corporation good about repairs. Regulations as usual but I gather are less firmly enforced on these very large housing estates. This particular house 20 minutes walk from town or 1d bus ride. Tenant (keen Socialist but non-smoker, teetotaller and model husband whose boast it is that he has always 1d in pocket and hands the rest over to wife) very satisfied. Those on further parts of estate said to be less satisfied because of expense of getting to town.
Number living in this house, 9 (parents and 7 children.) Two of the children are working, the father out of work.
Rent 10/7 inclusive, recently reduced from 11/10.
Gas runs on penny in slot meter. Tenant estimates that about 3d a day is spent on gas. Coal is at 1/4 a cwt.

(NB. that there appears to be great difference in expense at any rate with electricity between penny in slot and "rateable"—in the latter case the meter etc. has to be installed at the tenant's own expense and costs about £4. With a penny in slot meter it is said that one woman spent 32/6 in 6 weeks–ie. over 5/– a week on lighting alone. With "rateable" electricity cost said to be about 4½d a week. Figures presumably exaggerated but there is no doubt it costs much more with penny in slot meter. Cf. the people in Thomas Street.)

<u>Manor Estate.</u>
3 up 2 down plus bathroom and WC.
<u>Downstairs:</u> Living room about 16 by 14. Kitchen smaller. Bathroom.
<u>Upstairs:</u> 3 bedrooms all fair size. Largest only has fireplace. Walls good. Hot water supply good.
Electric lighting (rateable.) Penny in slot for gas. Electricity bill estimated at 12/– or 14/– a quarter. (about 1/– a week.)
Rent 12/4 inclusive.
Garden small and poor soil.
These are considered superior type of Corporation houses and are rather more ornate than most. Tenant is postman. No one is allowed into these houses whose income is less than £3 a week. People on dole not allowed in but not turned out if they become out of work after coming here.
Tenant very satisfied.
Car ride into town 1 1/2d.

NB. that the drastic rehousing going on in Sheffield, and presumably in some other towns, causes great injustice with regard to shops. In the first place comparatively few shops and practically no pubs are allowed in the housing estates. When a complete area is condemned, as in various parts of the centre of Sheffield, it means that a small shopkeeper's whole clientele is taken away from him and dumped down at the other end of the town. Probably his own premises are condemned too, but in any case he gets no compensation for loss of business. Difficulties are put in the way of his going and setting up in the estate to which his clientele has moved, because, as mentioned above, the number of shops is strictly limited, secondly there are regulations as to what the shops are allowed to sell, thirdly rents are higher, which affects both the shopkeeper himself and his customers, who have less money to spend with him. It is also inconvenient for the householders in Corporation estates, who have less shops to choose from unless they spend money on bus fare[s] into town. It is also alleged that the Corporation gives special facilities to chain stores to set up branches in housing estates. See attached cutting.

351. Statistical Information Provided by Medical Officer of Health, Sheffield

Orwell has evidently underlined 'Not known' twice and added the two exclamation points.

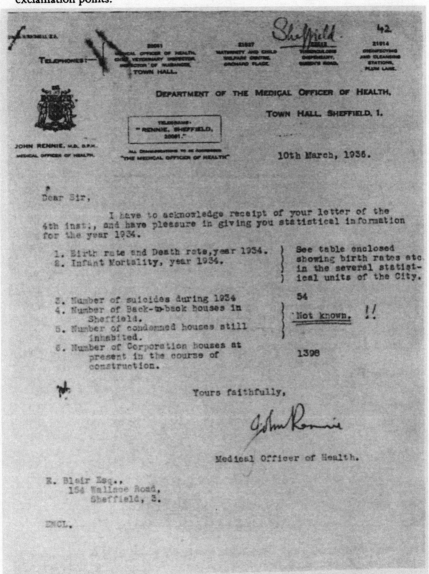

CITY OF SHEFFIELD.
STATISTICAL INFORMATION—YEAR 1934.

Registration Sub-Districts and Sections.	Birth Rates.	Death Rates.	Infant Mortality Rates.
North A.	13.07	14.49	36
B.	18.05	14.21	87
C.	15.24	13.98	90
South A.	15.52	11.69	76
B.	12.32	13.48	57
C.	11.67	11.83	66
Park A.	16.02	10.64	79
B.	17.94	10.78	50
Brightside West A.	18.32	12.31	48
B.	11.46	11.14	70
Brightside East A.	15.89	13.14	87
B.	18.06	12.47	50
Attercliffe A.	19.25	12.61	68
B.	16.86	11.42	26
Darnall	16.34	11.09	46
Handsworth	17.14	10.50	53
Tinsley (part of S.E. Rotherham)	13.31	10.48	38
Hillsborough	12.72	8.85	36
Ecclesfield (part of Wortley)	19.90	8.08	45
Ecclesall North A.	15.17	12.51	95
B.	13.28	12.70	100
Ecclesall West Central	11.09	10.97	39
Ecclesall South (excluding Norton)	9.98	10.85	63
Broomhall A.	16.03	14.04	50
B.	11.22	12.79	60
Sharrow	10.43	13.13	31
Norton	12.38	10.83	38
Dore	11.27	7.01	37
CITY	14.52	11.35	55

CITY OF SHEFFIELD.
HEALTH STATISTICS—1935.

The death-rates and birth-rates for 1935, given in this statement, are provisional only, being subject to alteration for transfers to and from other districts, also for revised population estimate of the Registrar General.

Population.   The last estimate of the Registrar General was for mid-year 1934, 520,950. This is the figure on which the following calculations are based.

Births.   The total number of births registered was 8,025, equivalent to 15.40 per 1,000 persons living per annum. The birth-rate for the year 1934 was 14.5.

Deaths.   The total number of deaths registered was 6,455, equivalent to 12.4 per 1,000 persons living per annum. The death rate for the year 1934 was 11.4.

Infant Mortality.   The infant mortality rate was 51 per 1,000 live births. This represents a new record low rate. The previous lowest infant mortality rate was 55 in 1934.

Maternal Mortality.   The maternal mortality rate per 1,000 live births may be stated as 4.5 for 1935, 1934 rate was 6.1. The figure for 1935 is approximate only, and has been obtained by eliminating deaths of women brought into Sheffield for treatment and assuming also that the number of births to be transferred-out will be the same as for 1934.

Death-rates from certain causes per 1,000 living per annum.

	1935.	1934.	1933.	1932.	1931.
Small Pox	—	—	—	—	—
Measles	0.02	0.05	0.004	0.0	0.01
Scarlet Fever	0.02	0.01	0.01	0.002	0.01
Diphtheria	0.15	0.08	0.04	0.01	0.01
Whooping Cough	0.02	0.07	0.04	0.11	0.06
Enteric Fever	0.00	0.01	—	—	0.01
Diarrhoea and Enteritis (under 2 years)	0.06	0.05	0.10	0.07	0.09
Puerperal Fever	0.07	0.05	0.06	0.03	0.05
Influenza	0.15	0.10	0.58	0.30	0.34
Pneumonia	0.78	0.72	0.83	0.86	0.84
Bronchitis	0.28	0.27	0.40	0.42	0.46
Respiratory Tuberculosis	0.69	0.64	0.69	0.69	0.67
Tuberculosis of Other Organs	0.12	0.12	0.15	0.13	0.15
Cancer	1.65	1.52	1.58	1.32	1.43

2.

CASES OF SICKNESS FROM NOTIFIABLE INFECTIOUS DISEASES REPORTED DURING 1935 AND PREVIOUS FOUR YEARS.

	1935.	1934.	1933.	1932.	1931
Small Pox	—	—	—	—	53
Cerebro-Spinal Fever	14	46	104	74	52
Acute Poliomyelitis	16	8	10	40	45
Scarlet Fever	4210	2374	1454	843	974
Diphtheria	1753	1424	965	407	419
Enteric Fever	6	5	2	14	15
Encephalitis Lethargica	4	1	—	1	7
Erysipolas	388	333	334	278	231
Puerperal Fever	48	76	50	54	66
Puerperal Pyrexia	134	115	99	96	121
Ophthalmia Neonatorum	33	26	36	34	41
*Measles	60	262	2	158	29
Pneumonia	1698	1684	2378	2338	2175
Dysentery	13	4	18	14	2
Malaria	1	2	1	—	—
Continued Fever	—	—	—	—	1
Polioencephalitis	1	—	—	1	—
Tuberculosis of Lung	1211	1274	1385	1540	1515
Other Forms of Tuberculosis.	189	211	199	198	207

*Measles not compulsorily notifiable.

JOHN RENNIE, M.D.,
Medical Officer of Health.

352. COPY OF REPORT OF CITY OF SHEFFIELD BY W. ASBURY (COUNCILLOR.) OUT-DOOR RELIEF

Comparison of weeks ended June 18th 1932 & June 15th 1935.

Week ended.	ORDINARY.		
	Cases	Persons	Amount.
June 18th 1932	8,150	16,493	£5327-8-6
	11,964	23,822	£8695-2-6
June 15th 1935	UNEMPLOYED		
	10,548	33,690	£4924-8-9
June 18th 1932	4,799	11,664	£4792-8-9
June 15th 1935	TOTAL EXPENDITURE.		
	18,698	50,183	£10,251-17-3.
June 18th 1932	16,763	35,486	£13,487-11-5.
June 15th 1935			

EXPLANATORY NOTE: It will be observed that the figures relating to unemployment relief show that the number of cases has been reduced by more than half. Approximately 6,000 cases received supplementary relief during the time the cuts were in operation, and they relinquished relief when the cuts were restored in July 1934. The small saving under that head of £132 per week is explained by the fact that the supplementary relief payments in no case exceeded 2/9 per week, and this has been more than offset by the numbers in receipt of full-scale relief.

(Signed) W. Asbury.
June 25th, 1935.

353. Unemployment Assistance Board Award Form

The verso of this form, which records no additions or deductions, is not reproduced. A second form, for 10 January 1935, is also amongst Orwell's papers.

354. Re Coal-Mining.[1] Figures Taken From *The Coal Scuttle* by Joseph Jones (1936)

At the foot of the second page of these typed notes and on the verso of both sheets are a series of calculations in Orwell's hand. These are reproduced below; they relate to *The Road to Wigan Pier* (see *CW*, V, 38–39) and to the figures he added in manuscript to his notes from the *Colliery Year Book & Coal Trades Directory, 1935*.

Figures etc. taken from Joseph Jones' (ex-miner, Mayor of Barnsley) book "The Coal Scuttle."

————————

Average number of wage-earners on Colliery Books throughout Great Britain:

1924	1929	1934	Decrease 1924–1934
1,191,984	931,670	774,297	417, 687.

Greatest decreases are in South Wales and Monmouthshire, Durham, Lanarkshire and Lancs and Cheshire (in that order.) Only increase is in Kent.

(page 12.)

Number of mineworkers throughout Great Britain insured under the Unemployment Insurance Acts recorded as "unemployed:"

1929	1930	1931	1932	1933	1934
177,248	219,229	297,624	355,325	337,930	281,029.

(page 13.)

Average earnings per (mineworking) person per year in year ended December 1934:

	£ – s–d
Scotland	133– 2–8
Northumberland	109–14–7
Durham	104–19–2
South Wales	119– 7–0
Yorks	114– 9–8
N. Derby & Notts	112–16–3
S. Derby, Leics., Cannock & Warwick	110– 8–7
Lancs. & North Staffs	114–11–1
Cumberland, N. Wales, S. Staffs., Salop, Bristol, Forest of Dean, Somerset & Kent	120–10–4
Great Britain	115–11–6

"These figures cover the earnings of youths as well as adults and of the higher as well as the lower-paid grades. . . . (any particularly high earnings) . . . . would be included in these figures, as would the earnings of certain officials and other higher-paid men as well as the higher amounts paid for overtime work. ·

"Nevertheless, the figures show that the earnings in every district averaged little more than £2 per person per week, and if the value of all allowances in kind were added, little difference would be made, for the average value of all allowances in kind for the country as a whole is only 4d per day. *The figures being averages, fail in fact to reveal the position of thousands of adult workers whose earnings were substantially below the average and who received only 30s to 40s or less per week.*"

(Pp. 15–16. J.J's italics.)

Tonnage of coal raised yearly per person employed in mining:

Year	Tonnage raised per person employed
1914	253 tons
1931	253 "
1932	255 "
1933	262 "
1934	280 "

"The effect of short working is not disclosed by these figures, and as this was substantially greater in the post-war years than in 1914, the actual increase is greater than the figures show."

(Pages 17–18.)

Rate of accidents:

	Men employed	Fatal accidents	Fatal accidents per 1000
Mines	807,848	907	1.11 (*about 1 in 900*)[2]
Shipping	179,200	138	.77
Docks	93,406	63	.68
Quarries	70,401	50	.71
Constructional work.	202,278	71	.35
Railways	444,721	202	.45
Factories	4,785,548	540	.11

(NB. these figures refer to 1932.)

"The rate for mining covers all workers in the industry; for underground workers only it is much higher. . . . . . . For non-fatal accidents the rate in the mining industry is about eight times as high as in shipping; twice as high as at the docks, and about five times as high as any of the other industries. More than 130,000[3] men are injured in the mines every year; many of them very seriously. More men are killed and injured in our mines every year than the whole of the casualties sustained by the Gallipoli Expeditionary Force." (Page 23. NB. that the last sentence is misleading, as in the case of the Gallipoli Expedition an enormously higher proportion of the casualties would be serious.)[4]

It is stated (Page 22) that "over 90 per cent (of accidents) are caused by falls of roof, road and shaft accidents, and other dangers which are incidental to the normal work of the miner in the pit." (ie. explosions are only a minor cause.)

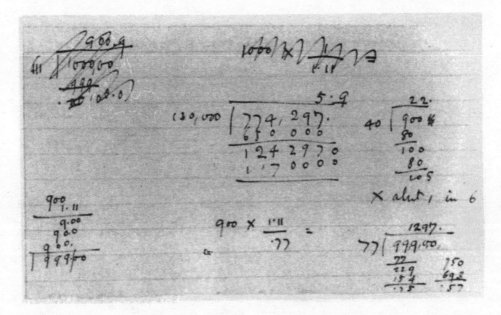

Orwell's calculations on recto of first sheet of details from *The Coal Scuttle*: see *354 headnote*.

1. Title is in Orwell's handwriting.
2. (about 1 in 900)] *handwritten addition*
3. Orwell asterisked '130,000,' referring it to his handwritten calculation illustrated above.
4. The Gallipoli campaign lasted less than a year—289 days. Alan Moorehead, in *Gallipoli* (1956, 361), gives British casualties as 205,000—50% of those engaged. H. W. Nevinson, in *The Dardanelles Campaign* (1918, 406), gives British killed as 28,200 of total British casualties of 214,232 (which included sick and missing, many of whom died). He estimates total British deaths at 36,000. Not only are deaths very much higher but, contrary to Joseph Jones, so are total casualties.

Verso of first sheet of details from *The Coal Scuttle*
The figures relate to *The Road to Wigan Pier*, CW, V, 38–39.

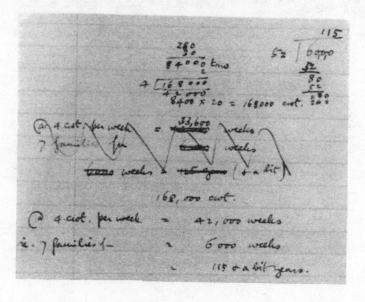

Verso of second sheet of details from *The Coal Scuttle*

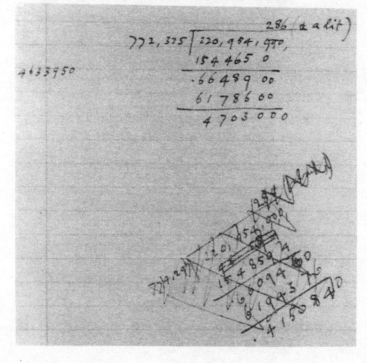

355. Figures Taken from the *Colliery Year Book & Coal Trades Directory, 1935.*

"Output (of coal) increased by nearly 14 million tons during 1934, or equal to the product of at least 50,000 men. The increase in the number of wage-earners last year (1934) was under 2000. Those in employment secured the best part of an extra fortnight's work—and even so, fell short of the average prior to the depression by about a fortnight. . . . . . .

. . . . . . Output rose from a little more than 207 million tons in 1933 to nearly 221 million tons in 1934, the highest recorded since 1930, as will be seen below:

I

Year	Output	Annual change (tons)
1930	243,882,000	. . . .
1931	219,459,000	minus 24,423,000
1932	208,733,000	minus 10,726,000
1933	207,112,000	minus 1,621,000
1934	220,954,000	plus 13,842,000.

(about 285 tons per man. J. J. gives 280)[1]

In all districts output in 1934 was higher than in 1933, the position in each district being as follows:

District	Output in 1934 (million tons)	Comparison with 1933 (million tons)
Durham	30.77	plus 3.16
Yorks	39.71	plus 2.45
Scotland	31.31	plus 2.07
Staffs., Salop, Worcs. & War'k.	18.57	plus 1.56
Northum'd	13.87	plus 1.40
Derby, Notts. & Leics.	29.12	plus 1.32
S. Wales & Mon.	35.34	plus 0.98
Lancs. Cheshire & N. Wales	16.57	plus 0.51
Other districts	5.69	plus 0.39

. . . . . . This welcome improvement in the condition of the industry was partly the effect of a moderate expansion in exports, but more especially owing to a marked increase in industrial activity at home, the result of the imposition of import duties on foreign goods.

II The average selling value at the pit of all coal disposed of commercially continues to decline slowly as it has done since 1930:

Year	Per ton	Year	per ton
	s d		s d
1930	14. 1	1933	13. 6½
1931	14. 0¼	1934	13. 4½
1932	13.10		

(Figure for 1934 provisional.)

. . . . . . For the country as a whole the average value of the coal sold at the pits fell 7½d per ton between 1930 and 1934 . . . . . .

. . . . . . It is significant of the present day tendency that while the production of coal increased by nearly 7 per cent, as compared with 1933, there was little improvement in the number of coal miners employed, namely, from an average of 772,400 in 1933 to 774,300 in 1934. On the other hand, work at the pits was more regular.

III The number of wage-earners on Colliery Books varied as shown below:

End of	Number on books	Change as comp. with 1933	
March	788,300	minus	2,300
June	768,000	plus	3,000
September	763,700	plus	6,900
December	769,300	minus	11,100.

$$4 \underline{/\ 3089,300\ /\ 772,325^2}$$

Greater regularity of work at the pits is indicated by the diminishing amount of time lost through want of trade, which has been as follows since 1921:

Annual average	Days lost	Year	Days lost
1921–1925	24	1931	49 & a third
1926–1930	41¾	1932	63¼
		1933	58¼
		1934	47

. . . . . . The proportion of insured persons in the coal-mining industry who were unemployed fell from 32.9% in 1933 to 28.1% in 1934. Conditions amongst insured coal-miners in the various districts, however, were by no means uniform, as will be seen below:

District	Percentage unemployed in 1934	
	Total number	Wholly unemployed.
Kent	5.6	4.5
Warwick	8.8	7.5
Northum'd	18.0	16.9
Staffs., Worcs., Salop	19.5	10.8
Derbyshire	20.1	10.9
Notts. & Leics.	22.3	14.3
Scotland	25.2	22.5
Durham	26.4	23.6

Lancs. & Cheshire	29.1	19.3
Glos. & Somerset	30.4	11.6
Yorks.	33.6	14.8
Cum'd and West'd.	35.3	33.0
Wales & Mon.	36.8	27.2

IV . . . . . . The average cash earnings per shift *for all workers of all ages and both sexes* since 1930 were as follows:

Year	Earnings per shift	Year	Earnings etc.
1930	9/3½	1933	9/1½
1931	9/2¼	1934	9/1¾
1932	9/2		

(Here stated that cost of living declined by 11% between 1930 & 1934.)

. . . . . . A notable reduction was effected in the costs of production in 1933 and again in 1934. In 1933, this was chiefly attributable to a reduction in wages costs resulting from an increase in the rate of production per unit of labour, and in 1934 partly to a further reduction in wages costs and to the greater regularity of work, the effect of which is chiefly seen in the diminished overhead costs. For the period 1930-1934 the costs of production were as follows:

Year	Total (net) costs.	Wages Cost	
		Amount	% of total
1930	13/8¾	9/3¾	67.8
1931	13/8¾	9/2¾	67.2
1932	13/8	9/0¾	66.3
1933	13/3¾	8/9½	66.0

(Wages cost "amount" given as "per ton of coal commercially disposible.°'")
(Here stated that some 500 pits have been closed during the 3 years ended October 1934.)

NB. From III it emerges that average number of workers on Colliery Books throughout 1934 was 771,328.5. But colliery books would carry those working short time and "temporarily stopped." Number actually employed at any given moment might therefore (at a guess) be round about 750,000. Not clear whether this included *all* those employed in the mines. eg. it would presumably include those working "on top," but not certain whether it would include those working on colliery railways and barges removing the coal, nor whether it includes the higher-grade employees such as engineers etc. The importance of this is that it affects IV. From IV one gathers the impression that the average wage per shift of 7½ hours has been round about 9/- for some years past for *all* workers including women and boys. Many boys at any rate are getting £1 a week and less for full time; therefore according to this the actual "coal-getter" should be getting a good deal more, eg. 10/- or 12/- a shift or £3 to £3-12-0 (gross wages) a week for full time. So far as I know none or very few get as much as this. The coal-getter's wages always seem to be round about £2-10-0 a week (gross wages.) So presumably the figures in IV include salaries of engineers and perhaps managers.

Taking 750,000 as the average number actually employed at any given moment and the output for 1934 (see I) as 220,954,000 tons, the average output of each person employed in the industry would be 294.6[3] tons per annum. From this and the amounts paid for piece-work I gather that for the actual coal-getter 2000 tons a year would not be an exceptional output.

1. (about . . . 280)] *handwritten addition.* 'J. J.' is Joseph Jones, author of *The Coal Scuttle.*
2. '4 / 3089,300 / 772,325] *handwritten addition.* 772,325 replaces 741,325.7, which is crossed out.
3. about 280] *handwritten footnote.*

INDEX

Volume X

This is an index of names of people, places, and institutions, and of titles of books, periodicals and articles; it is not a topical index. It indexes all titles of books and articles in the text, headnotes and afternotes; only passing references to people are unindexed. Numbered footnotes are more selectively indexed; thus books listed by an author in a footnote are not indexed unless they are significant to Orwell. Orwell's book titles are printed in CAPITALS; his poems, essays, articles, broadcasts, etc., are printed in upper and lower case roman within single quotation marks. Book titles by authors other than Orwell are in italic; if Orwell reviewed the book (in this volume), this is noted by 'Rev:', followed by the pagination, which is placed first and followed by a semi-colon; other references follow. Both books and authors are individually listed. If Orwell does not give an author's name, when known this is added in parentheses after the title. Articles etc., by authors other than Orwell are placed within double quotation marks. Page references are in roman except for those to numbered footnotes, which are in italic. The order of roman and italic is related to the order of references on the page. Editorial notes are printed in roman upper and lower without quotation marks. If an editorial note follows a title it is abbreviated to 'ed. note:' and the pagination follows. First and last page numbers are given of articles and these are placed before general references and followed by a semi-colon; specific page references are given for reviews of books reviewed as a group. The initial page number is given for letters. Punctuation is placed outside quotation marks to help separate information. Items in two languages are indexed only in English.

Letters by Orwell are given under the addressees name and the first letter is preceded by 'L:', which stands for letters, letter-cards, and postcards; telegrams are distinguished by 'T:' to draw attention to their urgency. Letters from someone to Orwell follow the name of the sender and are indicated by 'L. to O:'. References to letters are given before general references and are separated by a semi-colon.

Items are listed alphabetically by the word or words up to the first comma, except that Mc and M' are regarded as Mac and precede words starting with 'M'. St and Sainte are regarded as Saint.

Three cautions. First, many names are known only by a surname and occasionally it cannot be certain that surnames appearing at different locations, even with the same initials, refer to the same person. Secondly, the use of quotation marks in the index differs from that in the text in order to make Orwell's work listed here readily apparent. Thirdly, a few titles and names are silently corrected.   P. D.; S. D.

Index

Index

Index

Index

Index

Index

Index

Index